Access 2002 VBA Handbook

ACCESS 2002 VBA HANDBOOK

Susann Novalis and Dana Jones

SYBEX®

San Francisco • Paris • Düsseldorf • Soest • London

Associate Publisher: Richard Mills
Acquisitions and Developmental Editor: Christine McGeever
Editor: Susan Berge
Production Editor: Patricia Oman, Publication Services, Inc.
Technical Editor: Matt Riggsby
Book Designer: Robin Kibby
Graphic Illustrator: Don Waller, Publication Services, Inc.
Electronic Publishing Specialists: David Eynon and T.C. Moore,
    Publication Services, Inc.
Proofreaders: Phil Hamer and Jennifer Putman, Publication
    Services, Inc.
Indexer: Ted Laux
CD Coordinator: Christine Harris
CD Technician: Kevin Ly
Cover Designer: Design Site
Cover Photographer: Pierre-Yves Goavec

To my readers—you make it all worthwhile.
—Susann Novalis

For Adam, who brought me out of myself.
—Dana Jones

ACKNOWLEDGMENTS

Thanks to James Kelley, Dean of San Francisco State University's College of Science and Engineering, and Marci Manderscheid, Executive Director, Downtown Center at San Francisco State University, for their continued support of my work with software applications.

Thanks to everyone at Sybex who worked on this book.

Special thanks to Dana Jones, whose global responsibility for the revision of this book included detailed attention to the new aspects of Access and a real insight into the needs of the readers.

And lastly, thanks to my parents, my sons, and especially Rich, for understanding my absence while the passion to create this book overtook me.

—Susann Novalis

Thanks to Christine McGeever for her support and encouragement, for listening to my suggestions and concerns, and for addressing them. I am grateful also to Matt Riggsby for his invaluable efforts as technical editor, again. Heartfelt thanks to Molly Redenbaugh for her encouragement and enthusiasm for getting this book done.

I have great luck with editors. Particular thanks to Susan Berge, editor, for reading this book almost as many times as I did. I appreciate her responsiveness, professionalism, and impeccable attention to detail. This book is much enhanced by her having worked on it.

Thanks to Ken Getz, Paul Litwin, and Mike Gunderloy, authors of *Access 2002 Desktop Developer's Handbook* (Sybex, 2001), for giving permission to include the Event Logger application on the book's CD-ROM.

Deepest thanks to Mike Gunderloy. He never fails to impress me with his technical knowledge and humility. I am grateful for the help he gave in the writing of this book, but I am more grateful for his unfailing belief that I could do it. To all our tomorrows.

Despite the impressive efforts of the many editors and colleagues who reviewed this book during its production, any errors that remain in the manuscript are my own.

—Dana Jones

CONTENTS AT A GLANCE

CONTENTS

Chapter 6   Understanding the ADO Object Model   241

INTRODUCTION

Microsoft Access is the leading relational database management system for creating database applications on the desktop. Why is Access number one? Two reasons are that Access is easy to learn and fun to use. Microsoft has achieved great success in providing a graphical interface environment that makes it as easy as possible for you to learn to use the enormous power available in Access.

If we think of using Access interactively as walking, then learning how to write the programs that automate Access is running, and learning how to put it all together into a custom application is flying. Several excellent introductory books exist to help you learn all about walking with Access. A particularly helpful book is *Mastering Access 2002 Premium Edition* by Alan Simpson and Celeste Robinson (Sybex, 2001). Far fewer flying manuals are available; one of the best is *Access 2002 Desktop Developer's Handbook* by Ken Getz, Paul Litwin, and Mike Gunderloy (Sybex, 2001). The book you are reading now is the running manual that bridges the gap.

About VBA in Access 2002

Microsoft provides Visual Basic for Applications (VBA) in Access 2002 as a powerful development tool for automating your database. Microsoft incorporated VBA in this product to make Access 2002 a versatile, powerful database management system for today's computer developers and users.

Developers need the additional power and the ability to deal with errors that VBA provides. VBA allows developers to control the user interface and manipulate events to create a database solution that is functional, effective, and user-friendly.

In this book, you'll learn the essentials of Access VBA programming. You'll learn how to create procedures for the three basic database operation categories: navigating through the application, maintaining data, and selecting groups of records for specific purposes.

Who Should Read This Book

This is an intermediate-level book about Microsoft Access. You should be familiar with the basic concepts and techniques of interactive Access, including creating a simple Access database complete with related tables, queries, forms, reports, and data access pages. This book builds on that knowledge and shows you how to automate database operations using Access VBA programming. You do not need any prior experience with programming. Although this book is an intermediate-level Access book, it is a beginning-level programming book.

How This Book Is Organized

This book consists of 15 chapters, a glossary, and a DAO appendix. As an introduction to the concepts involved in building automated applications, the first chapter explains how to use the Access wizards and helpers to automate a database. Chapters 2 and 3 cover fundamental elements of VBA programming—objects and events—and provide an introduction to the Access object model. Because forms play a key role in Access applications, Chapter 4 explores several advanced topics in form design.

Chapters 5 and 6 provide in-depth coverage of the object models used in VBA programming. Chapter 5 revisits the Access object model, focusing on the features available only in VBA. Chapter 6 describes the ActiveX Data Objects (ADO) model, which is used by the database engines.

The next three chapters cover the mechanics of writing procedures for VBA programming. Chapter 7 introduces the basics of writing procedures, Chapter 8 describes how to use variables, and Chapter 9 explains how to control the execution of program statements.

The remaining chapters deal with the techniques for using VBA programming to automate database tasks. In Chapter 10, you will learn how to deal with errors in VBA. Chapters 11, 12, and 13 cover the important tasks of database navigation, data maintenance, and manipulation of records. Chapter 14 describes how to create and modify database objects using VBA procedures. Finally, Chapter 15 introduces some advanced techniques for expanding the functionality of Access, including the use of dynamic-link libraries and ActiveX technologies.

The glossary at the back of the book provides an alphabetical list of the terms used in this book and their definitions.

Organizing Your Work

Access 2002 VBA Handbook is both a reference and a hands-on tutorial. In most chapters, you'll either create a new database from scratch or create a copy of the Northwind sample database. To organize your work,

1. Create a new folder named VBAHandbook in which to store your example databases.

2. Locate the Samples folder. In a default installation of Microsoft Office 2002, the path is `C:\Program Files\Microsoft Office\Office10\Samples`.

3. Drag copies of all the files in the Samples folder to your VBAHandbook folder. Many of the files you copy from the Samples folder are image and other files that the Northwind database uses. These related files must be in the same folder as your working copies of the Northwind database. The files you'll need in the chapters are now readily available in your work folder.

What's on the CD-ROM

The book's CD-ROM contains sample databases for the book's chapters, an application called Event Logger, and tables of additional reference material. To use the CD-ROM, you must have Windows 95, Windows 98, or Windows NT Workstation 4 or later and Microsoft Access 2002 installed on your computer.

The folder named Solutions contains the answer databases for the book's chapters. You can run the answer databases directly from the CD-ROM, or you can copy them to your VBA-Handbook folder. The solutions folder contains the following databases:

Expenses.mdb	A semi-automated database that the Database Wizard creates and that we modify using the other built-in Access tools in Chapter 1. Chapters 2, 3, and 4 also refer to this database.
Northwind_Ch4.mdb	A copy of the Northwind database used in Chapter 4.
Northwind_Ch5,6.mdb	A copy of the Northwind database used in Chapters 5 and 6.
Ch7_Examples.mdb	A solutions file you create from scratch in Chapter 7.
Northwind_Ch8.mdb	A copy of the Northwind database used in Chapter 8.
Northwind_Ch9.mdb	A copy of the Northwind database used in Chapter 9.
Northwind_Ch11.mdb	A copy of the Northwind database used in Chapter 11.
NorthwindCS_Ch11.adp	A copy of the Northwind project used in Chapter 11.
Northwind_Ch12.mdb	A copy of the Northwind database used in Chapter 12.
Northwind_Ch13.mdb	A copy of the Northwind database used in Chapter 13.
Northwind_Ch14.mdb	A copy of the Northwind database used in Chapter 14.
Northwind_Ch15.mdb	A copy of the Northwind database used in Chapter 15.

The Tables folder contains several comprehensive reference tables. You can view the tables using the Adobe Acrobat Reader, which is also included on the CD-ROM.

The Event Logger folder contains the file Eventlogger.mdb. This is the Event Logger database application used in Chapter 2 for hands-on experience with events. This application was created by the authors of *Access 2002 Desktop Developer's Handbook*, who have kindly given permission to include this excellent tutorial database in this book.

New Access 2002 Features

Access 2002 provides several features that were not included in Access 2000. The new features, many of which are covered in this book, include features to make information easy to find and use, Web-enabled features for sharing information, analysis tools for managing information, and additional programming enhancements.

Information Features

The following features have been added or embellished in Access 2002 to make information easier to find and use:

Access taskpane A new toolbar that appears at startup makes it easier to launch saved databases or create new ones. This type of feature has been extended throughout the Office suite.

XML support Enhanced integration with XML (Extensible Markup Language) makes interapplication data sharing easier.

Improved SQL Server integration Extended support for SQL database properties means that Access is more fully functional with existing SQL Server databases than ever before.

Multiple-version file sharing You can open and modify Access 2000 databases in Access 2002 without altering the file type. If you have several people accessing the same database, this is a real benefit.

Multiple Undo and Redo When working with objects in Design view, you can now Undo and Redo multiple actions.

Web-Enabled Features

Offline data access pages have been embellished in Access 2002 to allow a greater degree of information sharing. When working with an Access project, you can alter the project's data access pages and have your changes automatically uploaded to the SQL Server data source the next time you reconnect.

Analysis Tools

The following features have been added or enhanced in Access 2002 to provide better analysis capabilities:

PivotChart and PivotTable views   You can view PivotCharts and PivotTables based on your forms, stored procedures, views, queries, tables, and functions, and can save these views as data access pages.

Conversion error logging   Access 2002 will create a table of any errors that occur when you convert a database from Access 95, 97, or 2000 to Access 2002.

Password changes in projects   If you're using a SQL Server 6.5 or later data source, you can change your logon password from within Access's interface.

Linked table wizard   New wizard lets you link to a SQL Server database from within an Access project.

Conventions Used in This Book

This book uses the following conventions:

- Key combinations that you press are indicated by joining the keys with a plus sign. For example, Shift+F2 indicates that you hold down the Shift key while you press the F2 function key.

- Sequences of menu commands are indicated by the symbol ➤. For example, File ➤ Close indicates the Close command on the File menu.

- Words, phrases, and names that you must type or enter are shown in **bold type**.

- `Monospace` type is used for examples of programming code. Keywords of SQL statements are shown in uppercase (for example, `DISTINCTROW`).

You'll find the following types of special notes throughout the book.

NOTE   Notes give you additional information about the topic.

TIP   Tips usually point out a more efficient way to accomplish a task.

WARNING   Warnings alert you to problems you may encounter.

Sidebars

These boxed sections provide explanations of special topics that are related to the surrounding discussion. For example, Chapter 5, on VBA basics, includes a sidebar about encapsulation; and Chapter 15, on expanding Access, includes a sidebar about obtaining ActiveX controls.

Endnotes

Thank you for selecting this book to help you learn about Access VBA programming. Writing this book has been a wonderful opportunity for us to learn more about programming and to share our insights with you. We hope you enjoy learning from this book. Please send your comments, suggestions, and corrections to Dana Jones at dana@larkfarm.com.

CHAPTER 1

Automating a Database without Programming

- Using the Task Pane

- Using the Database Wizard

- Automating operations with the Command Button Wizard

- Navigating with hyperlinks

- Using the Combo Box Wizard

- Creating a navigation control center with the Switchboard Manager

- Using the Microsoft Exchange/Outlook Wizard

- Using the Link Spreadsheet and Link Text Wizards

- Controlling the user interface

- Creating custom menus and toolbars

A *database* is a collection of records and files. To create a database, you need a system that will help you to store, retrieve, and sort your data, as well as analyze and convert it into useful information. If the database is large or complex, you'll probably want to use a commercial computer database application such as Microsoft Access.

Access has a terrific set of tools and wizards to help you create a database, including *tables* to store data, *database diagrams* to manipulate tables and create associations between fields in those tables, *queries* to retrieve and manipulate data, *forms* to enter and view data, *data access pages* to view and work with data from the Internet or an intranet, and *reports* to print information. But if you stop at this point, you'll have taken advantage of only a fraction of the power that Access offers, having left *macros* and *modules* untouched.

Without macros and modules, a database is *interactive*. In an interactive database, the user initiates each individual action the computer carries out by choosing a menu command or by clicking a toolbar button. The user is the one who supplies the connections between the forms and reports in the database. To perform tasks, the user needs to know which menu commands to use and which sequence to use them in, as well as how the forms and reports are related. In an interactive database, the user has complete control. A knowledgeable user has the power to use the interactive database in productive ways. A less sophisticated user has the power to corrupt the data and damage the database by selecting the wrong command at the wrong time.

In this book, you'll learn how to transform your interactive database into an *automated database application*. A well-designed, fully automated database application can be used by any user. The user doesn't need to know the sequence of steps for a task or the Access commands. The user needs only to click a single button to execute a complicated task.

When you create a fully automated application, you create a custom user interface. The *user interface* is what users see on the screen and how they use the keyboard and mouse to communicate with the computer. In the custom application's user interface, the user clicks command buttons to move between tasks, perform data-entry operations, find records, and print reports. The custom user interface is where the user lives in your database application. From the user's perspective, the custom user interface *is* your database application.

When creating the new interface, you should supply the tools to open forms, perform data entry, locate specific records or groups of records, import data, archive old records, and print reports. You should also provide a choice of paths for navigating through your database, making sure that users always know where they are and how to backtrack along the path.

Access provides a set of wizards and helpers to assist you with some of the automation. This chapter introduces you to the Database Wizard for creating the first draft of a complete application, the Command Button Wizard and Combo Box Wizard for creating automated command buttons and combo boxes, the Microsoft Exchange/Outlook Wizard for importing data from Outlook, the Link Spreadsheet and Link Text Wizards for importing data from other programs, and the Switchboard Manager for creating road maps to the forms and reports in the application.

This chapter also shows you how to use hyperlink techniques from Internet technology to navigate between database objects. You'll learn how to use hyperlinks to navigate directly from a form in your application to any document in your computer's file system or in any other computer that is connected to the Internet.

At each stage of user interface construction, your goals are to build in ease of use, intuitive understanding, and protection of the application. This chapter shows you how to create custom menus and toolbars so your application provides only the tools and commands that a user needs. You'll learn how to protect your application with a password and how to set startup conditions so a user who survives the password test is greeted by your application's startup form and its custom menus and toolbars. This chapter ends with a preview of VBA (Visual Basic for Applications), the powerful programming language used in Access, and gives you a glimpse of the additional power you'll have when you learn to use it.

Using the Task Pane

With Access 2002, Microsoft has instituted a new toolbar to make it easier to open existing files and create new ones. It duplicates many of the options in the File menu and uses hyperlink technology to execute commands (see Figure 1.1).

Most of the functions of this window are fairly straightforward, but some merit further discussion. If you have never opened an Access database or project before, the Open section will have only the "More Files…" option, which opens a Browse window that you can use to open existing databases. Otherwise, you can see recently opened databases and projects here as well. Under New you have four options: Blank Database, Blank Data Access Page, Project (Existing Data), and Project (New Data). Blank Database and Project (New Data) are the same as choosing to create a new database or a new project in Access 2000's startup window. Blank Data Access Page allows you to connect to an existing data source and create a data access page based on that data (data access pages exist separately from a database or project). Project (Existing Data) allows you to create a project based on data that already resides on a SQL server once you connect to that server.

New From Existing File makes a copy of a database that already exists and allows you to manipulate the copy. New From Template has two options—General Templates and Templates On Microsoft.com. General Templates are those you install on your computer when you install Microsoft Access. Choosing to create a new database from a General Template will launch the Database Wizard. The second option allows you to use additional templates

FIGURE 1.1:

The Access Task Pane

you can get from Microsoft's Web site on the Internet. If you click this option, you must already have an active connection to the Internet. You will see that the templates listed on the Web site are not all for Access—there are templates for all of the products in the Microsoft Office Suite. As new templates are created and published to this site, they increase the usefulness of the Access program.

Once you've opened a database or project, the Task Pane disappears. You can reopen it by clicking View ➢ Toolbars ➢ Task Pane.

Using the Database Wizard

The Database Wizard can help you create database applications for several different business and personal scenarios. Some of these are as follows:

Asset Tracking	Ledger
Contact Management	Order Entry
Event Management	Resource Scheduling
Expenses	Service Call Management
Inventory Control	Time and Billing

Once you identify the scenario that is closest to the application you want to create, the wizard displays a series of screens telling you about the application and soliciting your input. After collecting your choices, the wizard uses the template you selected to create and customize the necessary tables, queries, forms, reports, database diagrams, data access pages, and modules.

The Database Wizard can create both simple and complex databases. Depending on the scenario you choose, the wizard may create several groups of tables. The wizard creates simple data-entry forms for each table and may even create a form/subform combination to display a one-to-many relationship. The wizard creates summary reports appropriate to the scenario you choose.

Creating Navigation Paths with Switchboards

After creating the individual data-entry forms and summary reports, the wizard automatically creates forms called *switchboards*, which provide navigation paths between groups of forms and reports. The wizard creates a Main Switchboard to serve as the control center for the application. The Main Switchboard has command buttons for each of the basic database tasks. Clicking a button on the Main Switchboard takes you to a form that you use to perform a database task, such as entering data into one of the tables. Clicking a button on the Main Switchboard may also take you to another switchboard with buttons that take you to other forms, reports, or other switchboards. Figure 1.2 illustrates switchboard navigation paths.

The buttons react when you click them because the wizard has created an individual set of instructions for each button. The wizard writes instructions and stores them in one of two places:

- In *standard modules* that are listed as separate objects in the Modules pane of the Database window

- In *form modules* and *report modules* that are built into the forms and reports (as part of the form or report definition), stored as part of the form listed in the Forms pane or the report listed in the Reports pane of the Database window

To observe the Database Wizard at work, we'll create an application for tracking employees' expenses.

1. Start Access and click General Templates. Click the Databases tab in the New dialog and choose Expenses as the template to use to create your new database (see Figure 1.3).

2. In the next dialog, enter **Expenses** as the name and save the database to the VBAHandbook folder (see Figure 1.4). (If you haven't created this folder, see this book's introduction for instructions on setting it up.) Click the Create button to start the Database Wizard. The wizard's first screen explains the kinds of information the database will manage (see Figure 1.5).

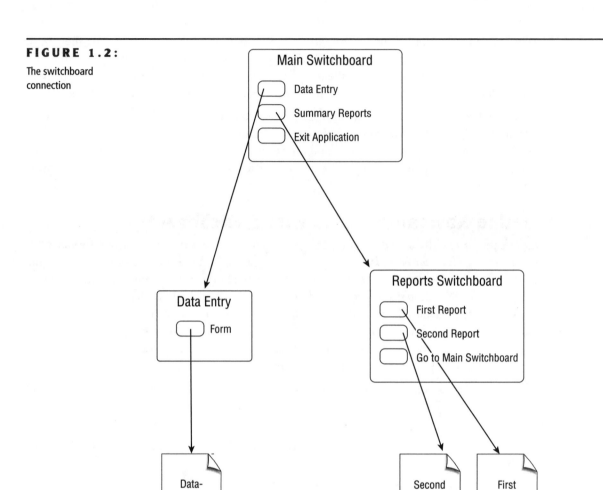

3. The next screen gives you the opportunity to make minor changes in the database (see Figure 1.6). The list box on the left displays the tables to be created. When you click a table, the list box on the right changes to display the fields for the selected table. You can't add new tables or delete tables from the list, but you can add the fields shown in italics, or remove those that are selected. For each table, check the fields you want to include.

4. Specify styles for the forms (see Figure 1.7a) and reports (see Figure 1.7b) in the next two screens.

FIGURE 1.3:

Select a template for the new database.

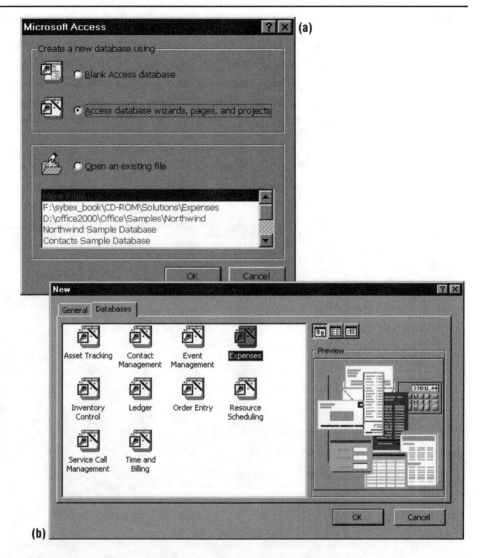

5. You can use the next screen to enter a title for the database and include a bitmap picture (see Figure 1.8a). If you add a picture, it will appear on reports that the wizard creates. In the final screen (see Figure 1.8b), you can select to start the database immediately after it is created and to display help. Clicking the Finish button puts the wizard to work. While the wizard toils, a dialog displays one progress meter showing the overall progress and another progress meter showing the progress in creating a specific object.

FIGURE 1.4:

Name and save your database.

FIGURE 1.5:

The Database Wizard explains the kinds of information the database will manage.

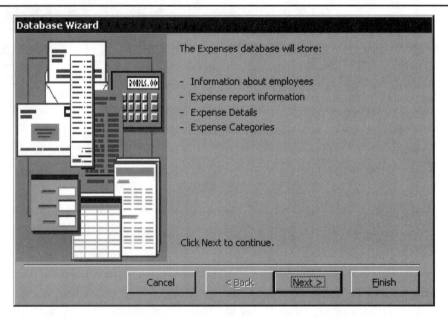

The wizard creates the tables and relationships, a form named Switchboard, and the forms and reports. The last text that flashes above the lower progress meter states that the wizard is setting database properties. When the job is finished, the Main Switchboard is displayed (see Figure 1.9), and the Database window is minimized.

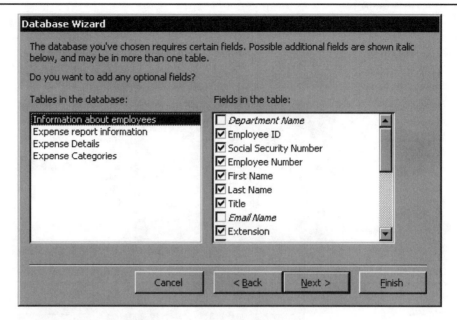

FIGURE 1.6:

You can choose whether to include fields in a table using the Database Wizard.

Exploring the Application

The Main Switchboard is the first stop in navigating through the application. (You'll learn how to use the Main Switchboard as a startup form later in this chapter.) The Main Switchboard gives an immediate sense of the main tasks that the application manages. The command buttons direct you to forms for carrying out database tasks or to other switchboards that may branch to still more forms and switchboards. The last two buttons appear on every Main Switchboard that the Database Wizard creates. We'll explore the Change Switchboard Items button later in the chapter. Clicking the Exit This Database button closes the database without exiting Access.

Take a few minutes to travel to other forms by clicking buttons. The buttons on the switchboards and forms provide navigational paths through the application to the various tasks. The overall organization emerges as shown in the task flow diagram in Figure 1.10. The directional arrows in the task flow diagram indicate whether a form has a command button that takes you back to a previous form.

The first button on the Main Switchboard takes you to the Expense Reports By Employee form (enter your own information as the employee), which has a button that opens the Expense Reports form (enter imaginary data for the Expense Report fields). Clicking the Preview Report button on the Expense Reports form opens a preview of the Expense Report report. Clicking this sequence of buttons takes you along a one-way path from the Main

FIGURE 1.7:

You can specify styles for forms (a) and reports (b).

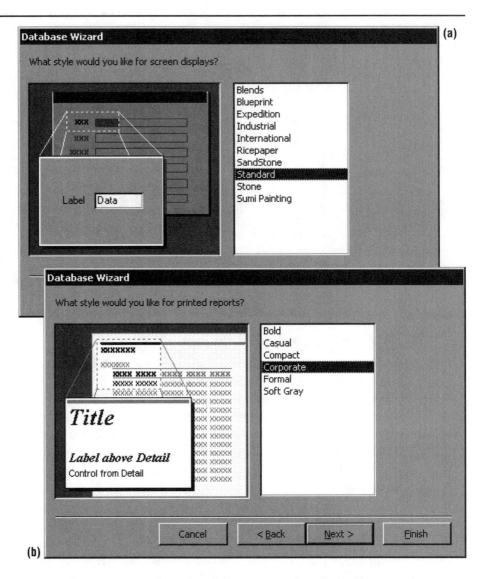

Switchboard to the Expense Report report (see Figure 1.11). The path is one way because there are no command buttons to take you back to the Main Switchboard. (Of course, you can use a form's default Close button in its upper-right corner or choose the Close command from the File menu to close the form and return to the previous form.) Later, we'll make the navigation back to the previous form easier by adding command buttons to the forms.

FIGURE 1.8:

You enter a name for your new database, and you have the option of adding a bitmap picture (a). After you click Finish in the final screen (b), the wizard starts to work.

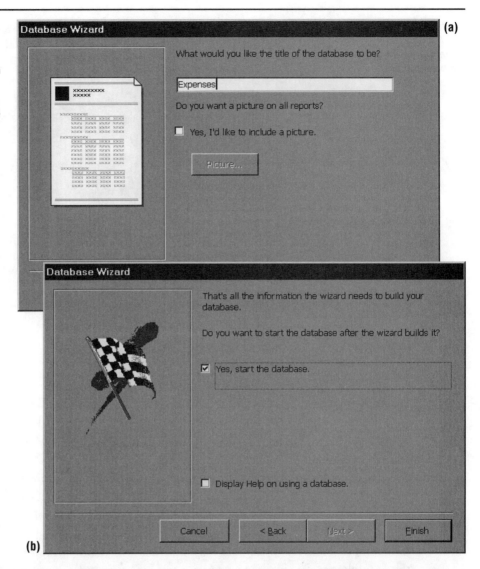

Note that when you select an employee in the Expense Reports By Employee form and click the button on the form, the Expense Reports form opens with information for the same employee; that is, the opened form is *synchronized* with the form that opened it. If you click into the first form, move to a different employee, and then click back into the second form, you'll see that the two forms remain synchronized. Similarly, when you click the Preview

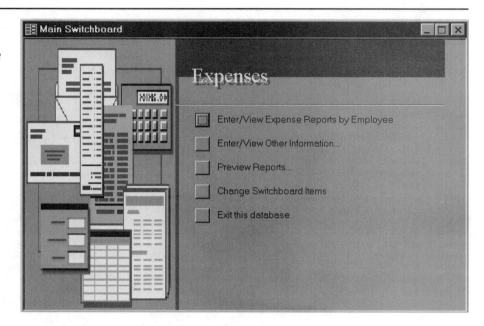

FIGURE 1.9:

The Main Switchboard is
the central dispatch for the
database application.

Report button on the Expense Reports form, the report that opens is synchronized with the
form that opened it.

The second button on the Main Switchboard takes you to another switchboard, called the
Forms Switchboard, where you have the choice of displaying the Expense Categories data-
entry form or returning to the Main Switchboard (see Figure 1.12).

The third button branches to a third switchboard, called the Reports Switchboard, where
you can click either of two summary reports or return to the Main Switchboard. Clicking
either of the summary report buttons opens a custom dialog form, where you enter the
beginning and ending dates for a report (see Figure 1.13). Clicking the Preview button after
entering dates takes you to a preview of a summary report for the specified interval.

The Database Wizard has done more than simply provide navigational paths between
forms and reports. The wizard also has built a custom dialog form for collecting input. In
this example, the date interval is the criterion for a parameter query that selects the appropriate records for the summary report (a parameter query that gets its information from a form
is using a technique called *Query By Form*, which you'll learn about in Chapter 13, "Working
with Groups of Records Using Access VBA").

FIGURE 1.10:

The task flow diagram for the Expenses application displays the underlying sequence, or flow, of the tasks.

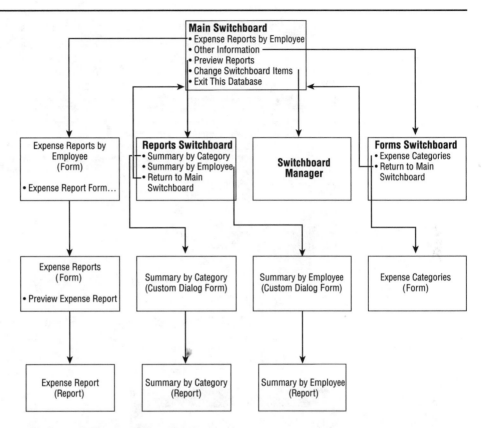

Examining the Wizard's Work

Let's look behind the scenes to explore how the wizard accomplishes some of its tasks. The Database Wizard uses several elementary and advanced techniques, some of which you'll be learning to use in your database applications.

Restore the Database window (by maximizing the Expenses window) and note the following:

- Only one form is called Switchboard, yet we have seen three switchboards in the Expenses example: the Main Switchboard, the Forms Switchboard, and the Reports Switchboard. If you open the Switchboard form in Design view, you see a form with eight command buttons and eight blank labels (see Figure 1.14). The Database Wizard uses this form for all of the switchboards. Each switchboard is created on-the-fly as a different version of the same form when you click a command button. Clicking the second button on the Main Switchboard converts the form into the Forms Switchboard, and clicking the third button converts the form into the Reports Switchboard. The

FIGURE 1.11:

The one-way path from the Main Switchboard to the Expense Reports form to the Expense Report report

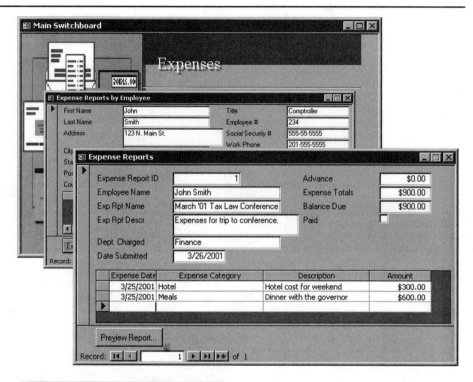

FIGURE 1.12:

The path from the Main Switchboard to the Expense Categories form

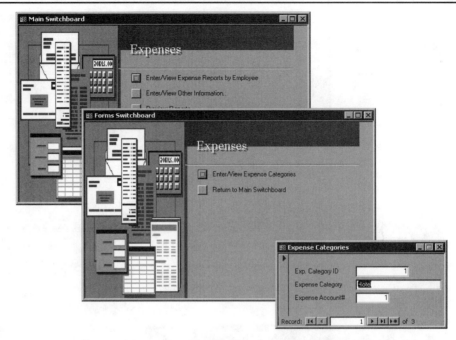

wizard has created instructions for converting the form, including changing the caption, displaying the correct number of buttons and labels, and empowering the command buttons displayed by each version of the form to carry out their specific tasks.

TIP   To open an object in Design view, click the object in the Objects pane of the Database window, then click the Design button.

- In addition to the four data tables is a Switchboard Items table. One of the fields in this table, the ItemText field, holds the labels for the buttons on the various switchboards. The other fields store information for creating the switchboards and making the buttons work. Note that this table is the record source for the Switchboard form (record sources will be discussed in Chapter 6, "Understanding the ADO Object Model").

- Although the wizard has used the Query By Form technique to select records based on your input in a dialog form, no queries are listed in the Queries pane. In fact, no queries are stored as *saved queries* in the Expenses application. If you've studied the way the Form Wizard and Report Wizard create their objects, you know that these wizards use SQL statements instead of saved queries as the record sources for the forms and reports. Most of the applications that the Database Wizard can create have no stored queries and use only SQL statements directly for record and row sources.

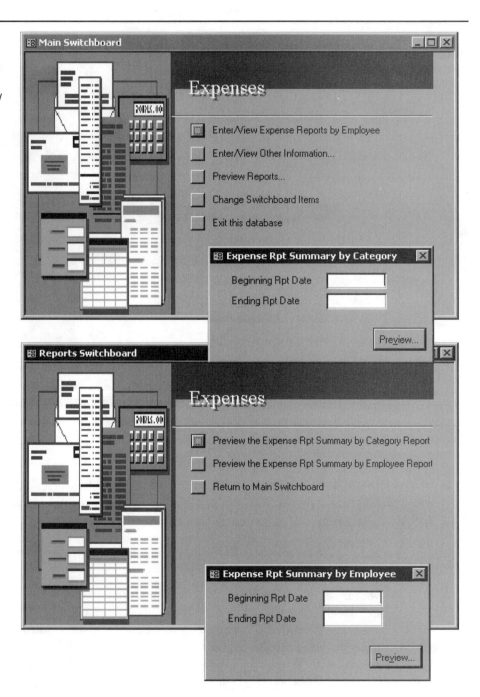

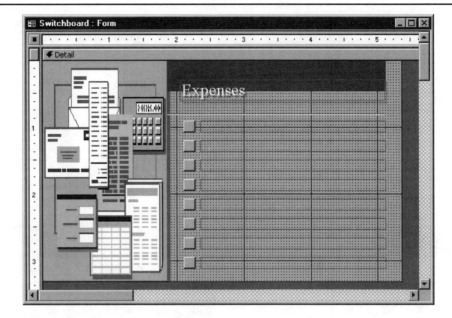

- The wizard uses a single Report Date Range form for both of the custom dialog forms. The wizard has created instructions to change the caption depending on the button you click in the Reports Switchboard.

- A single standard module named Global Code is listed in the Modules pane of the Database window. No macros are listed in the Macros pane.

Exploring the Standard Module

Let's explore the standard module. Double-click the Global Code module in the Modules pane of the Database window to display the Module window. What is displayed in the window depends on the Module window option settings on your computer. Most likely, the window opens to the module's first pane (see Figure 1.15a), called the Declarations section. In this pane, you store directions to Access and "declare" the names of constants, variables, and certain functions that you intend to use in the module. The Declarations section stores a statement for option settings. If you see additional text, then you are displaying Full Module view (see Figure 1.15b); click the button in the extreme lower-left corner of the window to display Procedure view. You use subsequent module panes to store the sets of instructions.

FIGURE 1.15:

The first pane of the Global Code module, the Declarations section, in Procedure View (a) and Full Module View (b)

(a)

```
Expenses - Global Code (Code)
(General)                              (Declarations)

Option Compare Database

Function IsLoaded(ByVal strFormName As String) As Integer
  ' Returns True if the specified form is open in Form view or Datasheet view.

    Const conObjStateClosed = 0
    Const conDesignView = 0

    If SysCmd(acSysCmdGetObjectState, acForm, strFormName) <> conObjStateClos
        If Forms(strFormName).CurrentView <> conDesignView Then
            IsLoaded = True
        End If
    End If

End Function
```

(b)

NOTE   You can change the defult view of the Module window by choosing Tools ➤ Options ➤ Editor tab and checking or clearing the Default To Full Module View check box. For this chapter, clear the check box to display the declarations and the procedures in separate panes.

A module stores instructions written in the VBA programming language. In VBA, you write sets of instructions in units called *procedures*. To see the procedures stored in the Global Code module, click the down arrow of the combo box on the right. The combo box list indicates the module has only one procedure, called IsLoaded (see Figure 1.16).

FIGURE 1.16:

The IsLoaded procedure

```
Expenses - Global Code (Code)
(General)                                      IsLoaded

    Function IsLoaded(ByVal strFormName As String) As Integer
    | ' Returns True if the specified form is open in Form view or Datasheet view.

        Const conObjStateClosed = 0
        Const conDesignView = 0

        If SysCmd(acSysCmdGetObjectState, acForm, strFormName) <> conObjStateClosed Then
            If Forms(strFormName).CurrentView <> conDesignView Then
                IsLoaded = True
            End If
        End If

    End Function
```

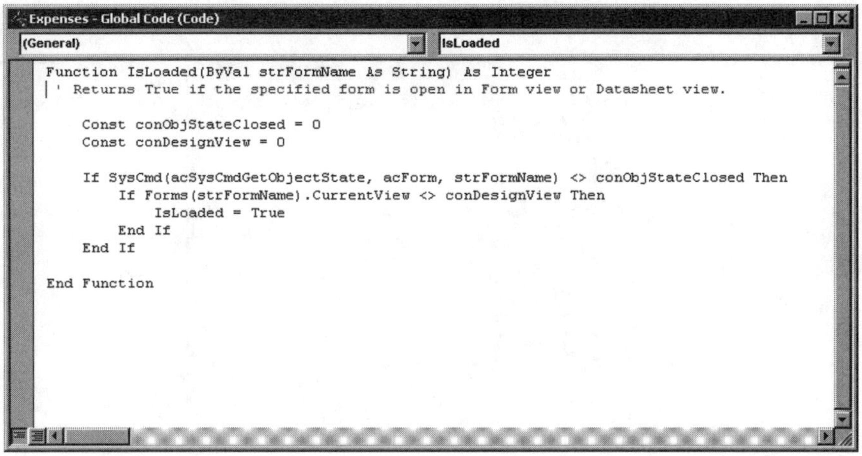

Even though we haven't talked about the VBA language, this procedure is obviously far too simple to be responsible for opening forms or reports, not to mention synchronizing them. As you'll learn later in the book, the Expenses application uses the IsLoaded procedure to determine whether a specified form is open.

Exploring the Procedure for a Command Button

Additional procedures for the command buttons must exist, so let's explore a button. Open the Expense Reports By Employee form in Design view. Then select the Expense Report Form button and, if necessary, open its property sheet by clicking the Properties button in the toolbar.

An object's property sheet lists the properties you can set at design time. In addition, most objects have properties that aren't listed in the property sheet. (You'll learn about the unlisted properties in later chapters.) The full set of an object's properties describes the object at a particular moment and is called the object's *state*.

NOTE   You are in design mode, called *design time*, whenever the active window is the Design view of one of the Database window objects.

Whenever you change a property, you change the object's state. For example, when you click a command button, you change its state from unclicked to clicked. In Access, many of an object's changes in state are given special treatment. Such changes in state are called *events*. When you click a command button, it recognizes the Click event. For each of its events, the object has a corresponding *event property* listed in the Event tab of the object's property sheet. Figure 1.17 shows the 12 event properties for the command button.

FIGURE 1.17:

The event properties for a command button

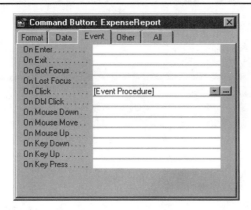

In most cases, the name of the event property is the word "On" followed by the event's name. For example, the OnClick event property corresponds to the Click event. The name of an event property suggests the action that causes the object's state to change. For example, OnMouseDown suggests that when you press a mouse button while the pointer is over the button, the command button recognizes an event called MouseDown. While you can make similar deductions about other event properties and be correct most of the time, it's best to invest some time using online help to learn the precise definition of each event property. Click Help ➤ What's This?, position the pointer over a property, and click. In most cases, doing so opens Microsoft Access Help to the event you selected (see Figure 1.18). If Help is not opened to the event, click the Index tab and type the event's name (without the "On") into the Type Keywords field and press Enter. You'll learn more about specific events and the order of events in Chapter 2, "Getting Started with Objects and Events."

Events are important because they are programming opportunities. You can create a list of instructions—a *program*—and tell Access to execute the program when an object recognizes one of its events. This programming technique is called *event-driven programming*.

Figure 1.17 shows [Event Procedure] as the setting for the OnClick property. This means that a VBA procedure has been created and assigned to the button's Click event. Access runs the procedure when you click the button. A VBA procedure that runs when an object recognizes an

▼ Show All

MouseDown Event

The MouseDown event occurs when the user presses a mouse button.

Remarks

- The MouseDown event applies only to forms, form sections, and controls on a form, not controls on a report.

- This event does not apply to a label attached to another control, such as the label for a text box. It applies only to "freestanding" labels. Pressing and releasing a mouse button in an attached label has the same effect as pressing and releasing the button in the associated control. The normal events for the control occur; no separate events occur for the attached label.

To run a macro or event procedure when these events occur, set the **OnMouseDown** property to the name of the macro or to [Event Procedure].

You can use a MouseDown event to specify what happens when a particular mouse button is pressed or released. Unlike the Click and DblClick events, the MouseDown event enables you to distinguish between the left, right, and middle mouse buttons. You can also write code for mouse-keyboard combinations that use the SHIFT, CTRL, and ALT keys.

To cause a MouseDown event for a form to occur, press the mouse button in a blank area or record selector on the form. To cause a MouseDown event for a form section to occur, press the mouse button in a blank area of the form section.

The following apply to MouseDown events:

- If a mouse button is pressed while the pointer is over a form or control, that object receives all mouse events up to and including the last MouseUp event.

- If mouse buttons are pressed in succession, the object that receives the mouse event after the first press receives all mouse events until all buttons are released.

To respond to an event caused by moving the mouse, you use a MouseMove event.

event is an *event procedure*. When you click the Build button at the right of an event property, the Module window opens, showing the event procedure (see Figure 1.19).

You'll learn how to create VBA event procedures later in this book. For now, note that the Module window's title bar displays the caption Form_Expense Reports By Employee, which means we are looking at the form module for the Expense Reports By Employee form. Access automatically names a form module for a form using the word "Form" and the form's name, separated with an underscore; the general pattern, or syntax, is Form_*formname*. Similarly, Access automatically names a report module using the syntax Report_*reportname*.

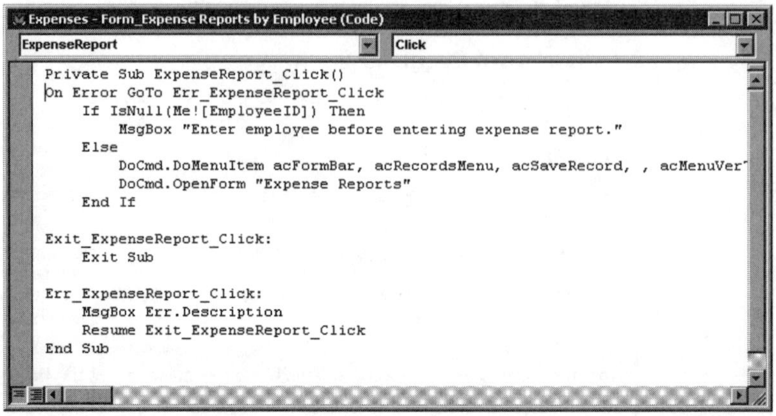

FIGURE 1.19:

The event procedure for the
OnClick property of
the command button

```
Expenses - Form_Expense Reports by Employee (Code)                    _ □ ×
ExpenseReport                    ▼   Click                             ▼
    Private Sub ExpenseReport_Click()
    On Error GoTo Err_ExpenseReport_Click
        If IsNull(Me![EmployeeID]) Then
            MsgBox "Enter employee before entering expense report."
        Else
            DoCmd.DoMenuItem acFormBar, acRecordsMenu, acSaveRecord, , acMenuVer
            DoCmd.OpenForm "Expense Reports"
        End If

    Exit_ExpenseReport_Click:
        Exit Sub

    Err_ExpenseReport_Click:
        MsgBox Err.Description
        Resume Exit_ExpenseReport_Click
    End Sub
```

The Database Wizard creates event procedures for each of the command buttons. Some procedures simply open other forms or reports; other procedures also synchronize the form or report to display the matching record.

The Database Wizard provides a well-designed first draft for the application. Users who know Access can navigate through its tasks easily. However, for the Expenses application to be described as *fully automated*, it must be further developed so that a user who doesn't know Access can use it without detailed instructions. Let's explore some of the other Access helpers you can call on to add features that make the application easier to use.

Using the Command Button Wizard

The Command Button Wizard automatically creates command buttons and VBA event procedures for the buttons' Click events. This powerful wizard can create procedures for many common database operations. Table 1.1 shows the 33 actions you can automate with the Command Button Wizard.

The task flow diagram shown in Figure 1.10 shows that the Database Wizard has created a one-way path from the Main Switchboard to the Expense Reports By Employee form. To make a two-way path between the form and the Main Switchboard, we'll create a command button to close the Expense Reports By Employee form and return to the Main Switchboard.

1. Open the Expense Reports By Employee form in Design view. If the Control Wizards toolbox button is not pressed, click the button now to activate the Control Wizards.

TABLE 1.1: Operations Automated with the Command Button Wizard

Category	Task
Record Navigation	Find Next, Find Record, Go to First, Last, Next, Previous Record
Record Operations	Add New Record, Delete Record, Duplicate Record, Print Record, Save, Undo Record
Form Operations	Apply Form Filter, Close Form, Edit Form Filter, Open Form, Open Page, Print a Form, Print Current Form, Refresh Form Data
Report Operations	Mail Report, Preview Report, Print Report, Send Report to File
Application	Quit Application, Run Application, Run MS Excel, Run MS Word, Run Notepad
Miscellaneous	Auto Dialer, Print Table, Run Macro, Run Query

2. Click the Command Button tool and then click in the form next to the Expense Report Form button. The wizard's first screen shows a list of six categories of tasks and a list of the actions for each category.

3. Select the Form Operations category and the Close Form action (see Figure 1.20). Click the Next button.

FIGURE 1.20:

The Command Button Wizard can automate common database operations.

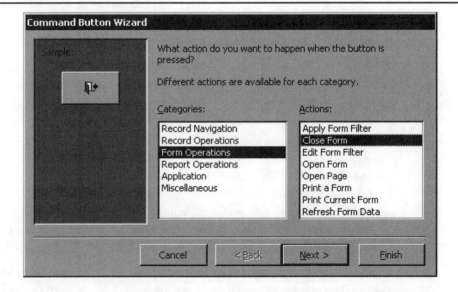

4. In the next screen, you design the button's appearance. For a consistent look, enter **Return** as a text caption instead of using a picture (see Figure 1.21a). Click the Next button.

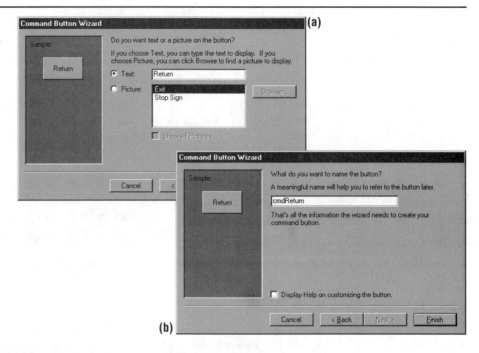

FIGURE 1.21:

You can design the button's appearance (a) and give the button a name (b).

5. The final screen gives you the opportunity to name the button. Enter **cmdReturn** (see Figure 1.21b).

6. Click the Finish button in the last wizard screen. The wizard creates the command button and attaches a VBA procedure to carry out the action you specified. Let's review the procedure.

7. Make sure the Expense Reports By Employee form is open in Design view. With the newly created Return button selected, click the Properties button. Click in the OnClick event property and click the Build button to the right of the property box. The event procedure appears in the Module window (see Figure 1.22). The combo box on the left displays the button's name, and the combo box on the right displays the name of the event. In later chapters, you'll learn about the purpose of each line in the procedure; for now, just note that the DoCmd.Close line is the instruction that closes the form.

8. Save the form, switch back to Form view, and click the new Return button. The form closes, and you are returned to either the Main Switchboard or the Database window, depending on which you used to open the Expense Reports By Employee form.

FIGURE 1.22:

The event procedure to close a form

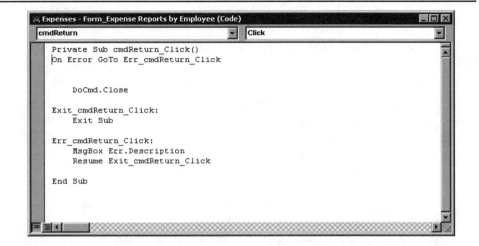

```
Expenses - Form_Expense Reports by Employee (Code)

cmdReturn                              Click

    Private Sub cmdReturn_Click()
    On Error GoTo Err_cmdReturn_Click


        DoCmd.Close

    Exit_cmdReturn_Click:
        Exit Sub

    Err_cmdReturn_Click:
        MsgBox Err.Description
        Resume Exit_cmdReturn_Click

    End Sub
```

NOTE   Choose object names with care. One reason for selecting the name carefully is that it's very inconvenient to change an object's name later. A more important reason is that this is your opportunity to make your work as an application developer much easier by using meaningful names. For example, by choosing the name cmdReturn instead of accepting the default (such as Command7), we document that the object is a command button by using the *cmd* prefix (called a *tag* in naming-standard vocabulary), and we document that clicking the button returns to the previous form by including the word *Return* as the descriptive part (called the *base name*). Chapter 2 discusses naming standards.

Using Hyperlinks to Navigate

A *hyperlink* is a piece of text, an image, a toolbar button, a menu command, or a command button that you click to jump to another location. In Access, you can use hyperlinks to open and jump to the following:

- Another object in your database

- Any available file stored in your computer's file system (on your computer or on another computer in your local area network)

- A specified sublocation within any Microsoft Office file, including a bookmark in a Word document, a range in an Excel spreadsheet, a slide in a PowerPoint presentation, or an object in another Access database

- Any available file in your company's private intranet or in the public Internet—if the file is an HTML document, you can jump to a specified sublocation within the document

- A blank e-mail form preaddressed to the e-mail address you specify

For a hyperlink to work, you must use the correct format to identify the location you want to jump to. For example, to identify a file on an intranet or on the Internet, you use an Internet address, called a *Uniform Resource Locator (URL)*. For example, `http://www.microsoft.com/` identifies the home page for the Microsoft Web site on the World Wide Web; `ftp://ftp.microsoft.com` identifies the Microsoft ftp site. To identify a file in your computer's file system, you use a standard format for specifying the path to the file called the *universal naming convention (UNC)* path. For example, C:\Program Files\Microsoft Office\Office10\ Samples\Sales.htm identifies an HTML document you may have installed as part of Access, and C:\Program Files\Microsoft Office\Office10\Samples\Northwind.mdb identifies the Northwind sample database for Access. The Internet or path address of the file is called the *hyperlink address*. You can specify the location within the Microsoft Office file or an HTML document, called the *hyperlink subaddress*, using the syntax shown in Table 1.2.

TABLE 1.2: Hyperlink Subaddress Syntax

Type of File	Syntax for a Location within the File
Microsoft Access	The name of a Database window object. If several objects have the same name, Access looks up objects in the following order: forms, reports, queries, tables, data access pages, macros, modules, views, schemas, stored procedures, SQL linked tables, linked tables, and triggers. You can also use *object type object name*; for example, to specify a report named Suppliers, use the syntax Report Suppliers.
Microsoft Word	The name of a bookmark. You must define the bookmark in Word before you can jump to it.
Microsoft Excel	The name of a range. Use the syntax *sheet!range*. For example, to specify the target as the L8 cell in the worksheet named Source, use the syntax Source!L8.
Microsoft PowerPoint	The number of a slide. For example, to specify the tenth slide, use the syntax 10.
HTML document	The Name tag.

When the target of the hyperlink is another object in the current Access database, you don't need to specify the hyperlink address; you specify only the hyperlink subaddress. For example, if you are working in the Expenses database and want to create a hyperlink with the Expense Categories form as the target, you need only specify the subaddress as Expense Categories or as Form Expense Categories.

If the target of the hyperlink is another object in the Access database you are currently working with, clicking the hyperlink in Access opens the object. A table or query opens in Datasheet view, a form opens in Form view, a report opens in Print Preview, a data access page opens in Page view, and macros and modules open in Design view. If the target is an object in another Access database, the current Access window minimizes, and a second instance of Access opens and displays the target object. If the target is a file in another Microsoft Office application, the current Access window minimizes, and the application opens and displays the target. If the target is a file or document on an intranet or the Internet, the Access window minimizes and your browser opens to display the document (your network or Internet connection must be open when you click the hyperlink).

Access provides three ways to use hyperlinks for navigation:

- You can store hyperlink addresses in tables and display the hyperlinks in a datasheet or in a form control bound to the hyperlink field.

- You can create a hyperlink in an unbound control on a form using a label, a command button, or an image.

- You can convert a menu command into a hyperlink.

Storing Hyperlinks as Data in a Table

Access 2002 provides a Hyperlink data type for storing hyperlink addresses. For example, in an order-entry database application, you can store the Internet addresses for your suppliers, just as you store their other contact information, and display the addresses in a Suppliers form. When you move the mouse pointer over the text box that displays the hyperlink address, the pointer icon changes to a pointing finger and the status bar displays the hyperlink address. Clicking the hyperlink takes you to the hyperlink target.

The Hyperlink data type lets you store information in three parts: the first part, *displaytext*, is the text that you want to display in the field; the second part, *address*, is the hyperlink address; and the third part, *subaddress*, is the hyperlink subaddress. The first part is optional. The parts are separated by the pound sign, as in *displaytext#address#subaddress#*. If you enter display text in the Hyperlink field, Access shows only the *displaytext* in the cell and does not display the rest of the address; if you omit *displaytext*, Access shows only the hyperlink address.

The easiest way to enter a hyperlink target is to use the Insert Hyperlink toolbar button. As an example, we'll add a hyperlink field to the Employees table. This field will store the URL for each employee's personal home page.

1. Open the Employees table in Design view. Click in a blank Field Name cell and enter **HomePage**. Choose Hyperlink from the Data Type combo box.

2. Save the table and switch to Datasheet view.

3. Click the HomePage cell for the first employee and type the text that you want to display. For example, type **John's Page** and click the Insert Hyperlink button in the toolbar. You can specify a file to link to or a Web page name from among the following options: Existing File Or Web Page, Object In This Database, Create New Page, or E-mail Address (see Figure 1.23). By default, if you entered display text, the file or Web page name in the Address text box appears as the protocol http:// followed by the display text. You'll need to clear the text box before entering the hyperlink address.

FIGURE 1.23:

Using the Edit Hyperlink dialog to enter an address and subaddress

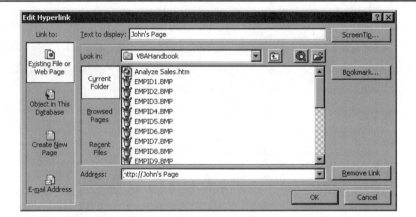

4. Delete the text in the Address text box and type in **http://www.microsoft.com/ employees/jsmith.htm** as the fictitious URL for the home page for the first employee. Click OK. Access displays the hyperlink text in the standard way: The text is shown underlined and blue.

5. When you move the pointer over the cell, the pointer icon changes to a hand with a pointing finger. If we had entered a real URL, clicking the cell would open your browser and display the document.

6. To edit the hyperlink, right-click the cell and choose Hyperlink from the shortcut menu. Click in the Display Text box in the fly-out menu. Select the text (*John's Page*), press Delete to delete the display text, and then press Enter. The cell now shows the hyperlink address. Note that you can change the address or subaddress of the hyperlink by choosing Edit Hyperlink from the fly-out menu to display the Edit Hyperlink dialog.

7. Open the Expense Reports By Employee form in Design view. Display the Field list and drag the HomePage field to the form just below the Work Phone text box. Save the form and switch to Form view. The hyperlink for the employee's home page is displayed in the HomePage text box (see Figure 1.24).

FIGURE 1.24:

Displaying a bound hyperlink in a form

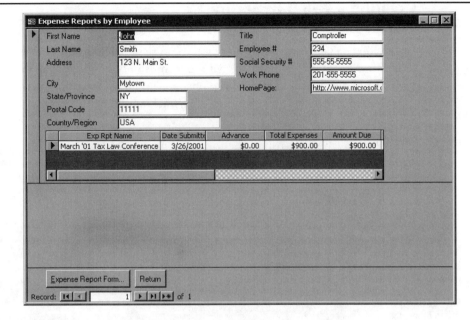

Using a Hyperlink as an Unbound Form Control

When you don't want the hyperlink to change with each record, you can use a label, a command button, or an image to create a hyperlink on a form. For example, when you want to use a hyperlink to navigate from a form to another form or to a report, you create the hyperlink directly on the form. To create an unbound hyperlink, place a label, a command button, or an image on the form. You can use the Caption property of the label or the command button to describe the hyperlink. To create the hyperlink, set the control's HyperlinkAddress and HyperlinkSubAddress properties. To create a hyperlink to another object in the current Access database, leave the HyperlinkAddress property blank.

To explore unbound hyperlinks, we'll create three types:

- A hyperlink for a label that opens and displays another object in the same database

- A clickable image hyperlink that opens and displays an object in another Access database

- A command button hyperlink that opens a browser and displays a Web page on the World Wide Web

TIP   When you refer to an object as "unbound," you mean that it is not connected to a table or automatically computed by a formula. In other words, it does not derive data from an outside source.

Creating a Label Hyperlink

To create a hyperlink as a label control, follow these steps:

1. Create a new form in Design view. Be sure to leave the combo box at the bottom of the New Form dialog blank so that the form is unbound. Save the form and name it frmHyperlinks. Open the form's properties by clicking the square block in the upper-left corner of the form window, then clicking the Properties button. Set the Caption property to Hyperlinks.

2. Place a label control on the form and type **Categories** directly into the label. Press Enter. Click in the Hyperlink SubAddress property in the label's property sheet. Click the Build button at the right of the property box to display the Insert Hyperlink dialog.

3. Click the Object In This Database button. The Insert Hyperlink dialog displays the objects in the current database listed in tree format by type (see Figure 1.25).

FIGURE 1.25:

Use the Insert Hyperlink dialog to choose the database object.

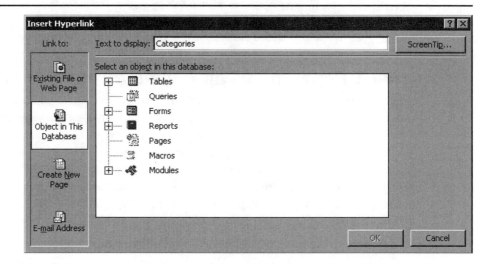

4. Choose the Expense Categories form and click OK. Access sets the Hyperlink Sub-Address property to Form Expense Categories, creates the hyperlink, and displays the label caption in blue, underlined text.

5. Save the form, switch to Form view, and click the label. The Expense Categories form opens.

Creating a Clickable Image

Here are the steps to create a clickable image:

1. Open the Hyperlinks form in Design view and choose Insert ➢ Picture. Select an image in the Insert Picture dialog. We'll use the NA00523_.wmf file in the Microsoft Office\Clipart\Pub60Cor folder. To resize the image, set the SizeMode property to Stretch, click a corner of the image-selection rectangle, and drag to the desired size. We'll use this image to create a hyperlink to a form in another Access database.

NOTE   You may not have the Pub60Cor folder if you didn't install Clipart as part of your Microsoft Office installation. You can use any clipart image for this example.

2. Click the Build button next to the Hyperlink SubAddress property to display the Insert Hyperlink dialog. Click the Existing File Or Web Page button. Then choose the VBAHandbook folder from the Look In combo box.

3. Click the Northwind.mdb file and click Bookmark. This displays the objects in the Northwind database in tree format. Select the Customers form and click OK.

4. The Address field now shows Northwind.mbd#Form Customers (see Figure 1.26). In this instance, Northwind.mdb is the Hyperlink Address, and Form Customers is the Hyperlink SubAddress. Click OK. Access sets the Hyperlink Address property to Northwind.mdb and the Hyperlink SubAddress property to Form Customers.

FIGURE 1.26:

Use the Edit Hyperlink dialog to choose an object from another database.

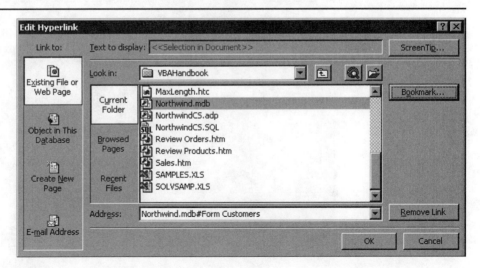

5. Save the form, switch to Form view, and click the image. A second instance of Access 2002 launches. The Northwind database opens, and the Customers form is displayed.

Creating a Command Button Hyperlink

The following steps create a command button as a hyperlink:

1. Switch to Design view. If necessary, click the Control Wizards button to deselect the wizard (the Control Wizards are activated when the button is pressed), then click the Command Button tool and draw a command button on the form. We'll use this button to create a hyperlink to a Web page on the World Wide Web.

2. Set the Caption property to Microsoft Home Page. Set the Name property to cmdMicrosoft.

3. Click the Hyperlink Address property in the command button's property sheet and enter the URL to the Microsoft home page: **http://www.microsoft.com/**. When you press Enter, Access creates the hyperlink, changes the button's font color to blue, and underlines the text to indicate a hyperlink.

4. Save the form and switch to Form view (see Figure 1.27). Click the command button. If your Internet connection is open and you have Internet Explorer installed, a new instance of Internet Explorer starts and the browser locates and displays the Microsoft home page.

FIGURE 1.27:

The Hyperlinks form with hyperlinks for a label, an image, and a command button

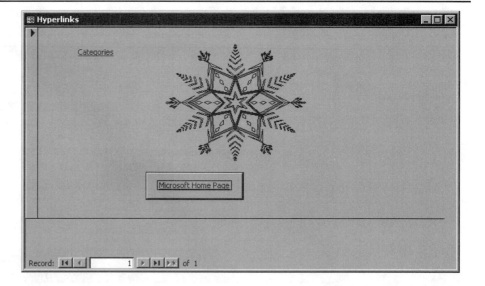

Changing the Hyperlink Control Type

After creating a hyperlink control as one of the three types, you can change the control type for the hyperlink. In Form Design view, select the control and choose Format ➤ Change To. The fly-out menu displays commands for the other two control types as active commands. Click the type you want to change to.

If you change from a label or command button to an image, the Picture property of the image control displays the word "none," because you haven't selected an image. To insert an image, click the Build button to the right of the Picture property and choose a bitmap image to display.

If you change from an image to a label or command button, Access sets the Caption property of the changed control to the value of the Hyperlink Address property. If the Hyperlink Address property is blank, it changes the Caption property to the value of the Hyperlink SubAddress property.

WARNING You can also change a label to a text box. However, the text box will not retain the hyperlink you designated, as text boxes have no Hyperlink Address or Hyperlink SubAddress properties.

Using the Web Toolbar

When you click hyperlinks to jump to other objects, Access 2002 maintains an internal history list of the hyperlink targets you've visited. Access provides a Web toolbar for navigation (see Figure 1.28). You use the Back button to return to the previous hyperlink target and the Forward button to go to the next hyperlink target on the history list (the Forward button can only take you to a target that you have already visited). If you change your mind after activating a hyperlink, you can click the Stop button on the Web toolbar to stop following the link.

FIGURE 1.28:
Use the Web toolbar to navigate between hyperlinks.

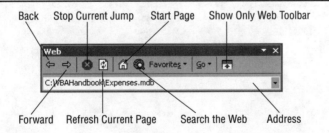

Using images, labels, and command buttons as hyperlinks is an easy way to open and display another object. When you create the hyperlink by setting the HyperlinkAddress and HyperlinkSubAddress properties, you are limited to opening an object and moving to a location within the object; you can't specify additional actions. However, when you click the control to activate the hyperlink, the control recognizes the Click event. If you want to take any other action, such as hiding the form that contains the hyperlink or synchronizing an opened form or report, you can write a program and request that Access run the program when you click the control. We'll discuss programming Click events later in the book.

Using the Combo Box Wizard

The Expense Reports By Employee form in the Expenses database displays a record for each employee. Our database so far contains only one employee as sample data. With very few employees, finding the record for a specific employee is a simple matter of browsing the records using the navigation buttons at the bottom of the form. With more employees, you need a more efficient way to find a specific employee. The Combo Box Wizard provides the solution. You can use the Combo Box Wizard to create a lookup combo box. With a lookup combo box, you select a value from the list, and Access automatically locates and displays the corresponding record.

In our example, we'll use the wizard to create a combo box that lists each employee's name in alphabetical order and a procedure that runs when you select a name. The procedure finds and displays the record for the employee that you selected.

1. Open the Expense Reports By Employee form in Design view. If necessary, click the Control Wizards button to activate the wizards. Click the Combo Box tool in the toolbox and then click in the form next to the Return button. The first screen asks for the source of the values you want in the combo list.

2. Choose the third option to create a lookup combo box (see Figure 1.29).

FIGURE 1.29:

You can use the Combo Box Wizard to create a lookup combo box.

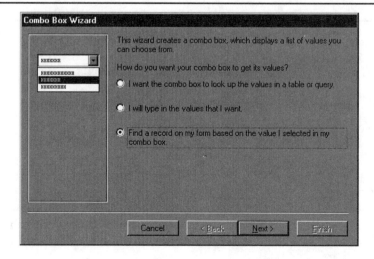

3. The next screen displays a list of the fields in the form's underlying record source (see Figure 1.30). We'll display only the employees' names in the list, but we'll also select the EmployeeID field because it is the primary key for the Employee table. Select the EmployeeID, LastName, and FirstName fields. Then click Next. The wizard creates a VBA procedure that uses the EmployeeID key to find the unique record corresponding to the employee's name you choose.

FIGURE 1.30:

The Available Fields are the fields in the form's underlying record source.

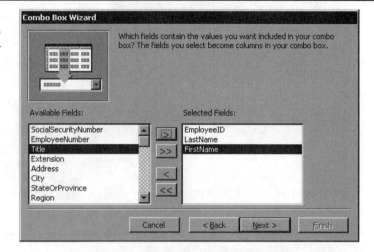

4. You can modify the list's appearance in the next screen (see Figure 1.31a). Be sure to leave the Hide key column check box checked. Click the Next button. The final screen gives the opportunity to customize the label (see Figure 1.31b). Type **Lookup employee** in the text box.

5. Click the Finish button. The wizard creates the lookup combo box and attaches the VBA procedure to find the record.

Note that the property sheet indicates that an event procedure now exists for the AfterUpdate event (see Figure 1.32a). The property sheet also shows that the wizard has assigned a default name using the syntax Combo*nn*, where *nn* is a sequentially assigned number controlled by Access 2002, which doesn't help at all in identifying the purpose of this combo box. (It would have been more helpful if the Combo Box Wizard had allowed you to name the control cbo-Employee instead.) We'll explain how the BeforeUpdate and AfterUpdate events work in Chapter 2. For now, note that the combo box recognizes the AfterUpdate event the instant you select an employee's name. Click the Build button to the right of the AfterUpdate property box to view the VBA procedure (see Figure 1.32b). This procedure *synchronizes* the form to the value displayed in the combo box by finding and displaying the record that matches the combo box.

FIGURE 1.31:

Modify the combo box list (a) and customize the label (b).

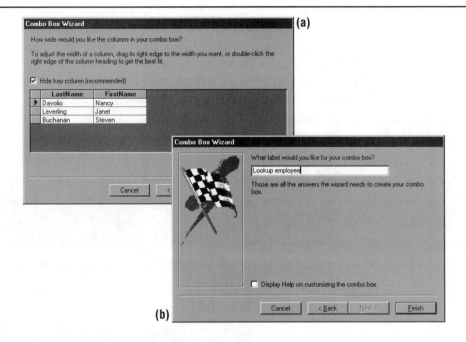

FIGURE 1.32:

The Combo Box Wizard creates an event procedure for the AfterUpdate event (a). The event pro-cedure (b) synchronizes the form's recordset to the combo box value.

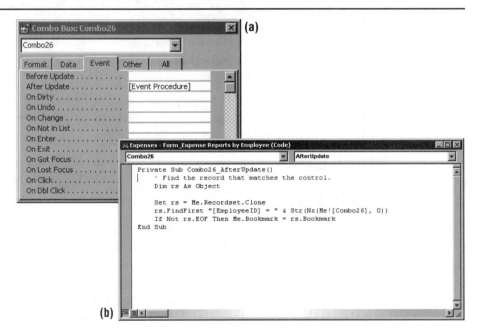

To test the wizard's work, you save the form, switch back to Form view, and enter two more test employees. Select an employee's name from the list (see Figure 1.33). The form automatically displays the synchronized record.

FIGURE 1.33:

The customized Expense Reports By Employee form provides a return path and a lookup.

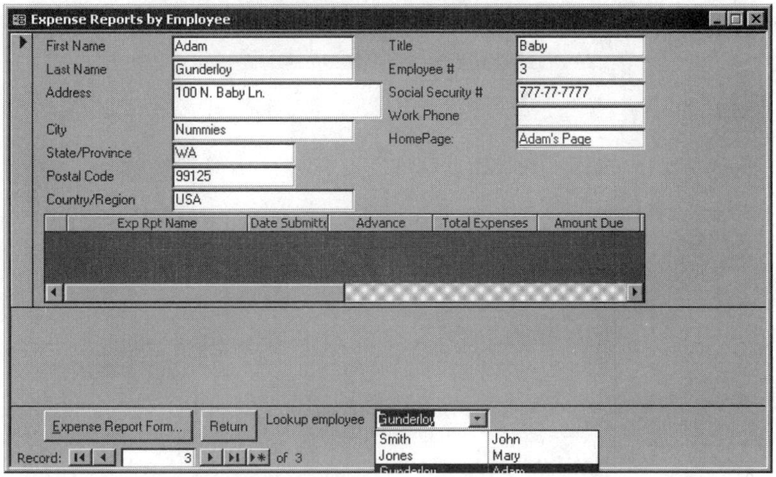

Using the Switchboard Manager

After the Database Wizard creates a basic application, you can customize it by adding forms and reports. When you add a new form or report, you can provide a path to it by adding a command button that runs a program or by adding a hyperlink to the appropriate form or to one of the switchboards. To add a button to a switchboard, click the Change Switchboard Items button on the Main Switchboard. Your click summons another Access helper, the Switchboard Manager. Alternatively, you can launch the Switchboard Manager by clicking Tools ➤ Database Utilities ➤ Switchboard Manager.

NOTE   In Access, you can't place buttons on tables or queries, so tables and queries are not usually displayed in a custom user interface. Instead, you build the new user interface entirely out of forms, pages, and reports. The form, data access page, and report objects have been designed to respond to a user clicking a button, selecting a value from a list, or entering a value in a text box.

The purpose of the Switchboard Manager is to help you modify the Switchboard form created by the Database Wizard. You also can use the Switchboard Manager to create a new Switchboard form if you started from scratch rather than using the Database Wizard to create the database. The Switchboard Manager shown in Figure 1.34 lists the three switchboard pages in the Expenses application. The Main Switchboard is shown as the default; the default page is the one displayed when you first open the Switchboard form.

FIGURE 1.34:

The Switchboard Manager

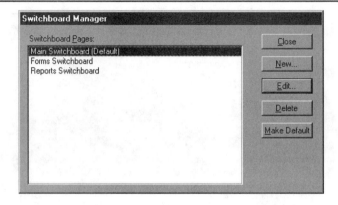

The Switchboard Manager buttons work as follows:

- The New button creates a new switchboard page. Click the New button to name the new switchboard page (see Figure 1.35a).

FIGURE 1.35:

Add a new switchboard page (a) or edit an existing page (b).

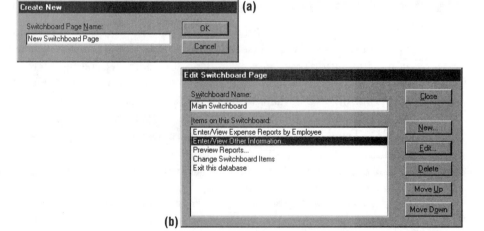

- The Edit button modifies the buttons on the selected switchboard page. Click the Edit button to display the Edit Switchboard Page dialog (see Figure 1.35b). For the selected page, this dialog displays the labels for the buttons on the page. You can add a new button, change the label of an existing button, delete a button, and move a button up or down in the list.

- The Delete button deletes the selected switchboard page.
- The Make Default button changes the default to the selected switchboard page.

As an example of using the Switchboard Manager, we'll change the label for the second button on the Main Switchboard to the slightly more informative label of Enter/View Expense Information.

1. With the Main Switchboard selected in the Switchboard Manager dialog, click the Edit button and select the second item in the list. Click the Edit button on the Edit Switchboard Page dialog to display the Edit Switchboard Item dialog (see Figure 1.36a).

2. Change the label's text in the first box to Enter/View Expense Information. You can change the button's action by selecting any of the eight actions in the Command combo list (see Figure 1.36b). After you select an action, the third box changes to display appropriate choices. In our case, the command Go To Switchboard takes you to another switchboard page, and the third combo box displays the name of the switchboard page (Forms Switchboard).

FIGURE 1.36:

The Switchboard Manager lets you change the button's label (a) and its action (b).

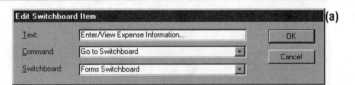
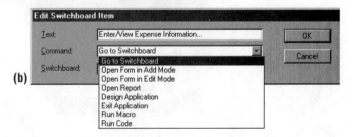

3. Click OK to close the Edit Switchboard Item dialog, click Close to close the Edit Switch-board Page dialog, and click Close to close the Switchboard Manager. The Main Switchboard displays the changed label for the second button.

Using the Microsoft Exchange/Outlook Wizard

One way to increase the usefulness of Microsoft Access is to use its wizards to import and manipulate data that already exists in other programs. The Exchange/Outlook Wizard is a prime example. It allows you to import data already stored in a Microsoft Exchange database or in Microsoft Outlook into an Access table.

Suppose you wanted to add the information from your Contacts in Outlook to your Expenses database. You would have three options for doing this. First, you could create the table, adding the fields you wanted included, then manually add each contact. This method, however, is very time-consuming and inefficient. Second, you could use the Exchange/Outlook Wizard to import the data into a table that already exists. This is useful if you have similar data already in a table in your database. The third method would be to let the wizard create the table and import the data, as shown in the following steps.

NOTE   To complete the following example, you should have Microsoft Outlook installed on the same computer as Microsoft Access and at least three contacts in your Contacts folder.

1. Click File ➢ Get External Data ➢ Import. The Import dialog window opens (see Figure 1.37). You don't need to bother navigating to the Office folder on your computer; the wizard will automatically locate the appropriate files and folders for you.

FIGURE 1.37:

The Import dialog box

2. In the Files Of Type combo box, select Outlook. This launches the Exchange/Outlook Wizard.

3. The first window prompts you to select the appropriate folder or address book (see Figure 1.38). To import your Contacts, choose Personal Folders ➢ Contacts. Click Next.

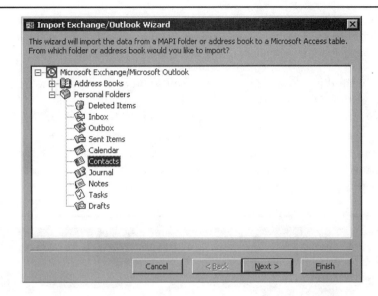

The Exchange/Outlook
Wizard

4. The next window of the wizard allows you to choose whether you'd like to import the data into an existing table or have it create a new table (see Figure 1.39). Choose In A New Table and click Next.

FIGURE 1.39:

The Exchange/Outlook
Wizard allows you to
import data into an existing
table or create a new one.

NOTE   The Exchange/Outlook Wizard will preview your data in the second window of the wizard. If you don't see any Contacts listed here, you need to close the wizard and add some Contacts into Outlook before continuing.

5. The third window of the wizard permits you to customize the fields you will be importing into your new table (see Figure 1.40). If you click the field in the Preview pane, the options are displayed for that field. There are four Field options. The first sets the name that will be used for that field in the new Access table. By default, the same name is used in the table that was used in Outlook. The second option is called Data Type, which controls what type of information can be entered in the specified field. For an explanation of each data type, see Table 7.1.

FIGURE 1.40:

Rename, remove, and change data types of fields in the new table using the wizard.

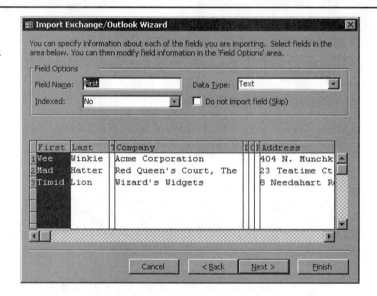

The third option, Indexed, allows you to control the way records are returned and to specify whether the field can have duplicates. After importing the data, you may wish to create a report listing your Contacts in order of last name. If so, you would need to designate "Last" as a Yes (Duplicates OK) index. If you knew that you would only have one person in your table for each e-mail address, you might designate Email Address as a Yes (No Duplicates) index. You will learn more about indexing in Chapter 6.

The final Field option is a check box—select this box if you do not wish to import a field from your Contacts in Outlook to your new table in Access. Click Next.

6. The next window (see Figure 1.41) gives you the option to let Access add a primary key for your new table, choose a primary key from the fields you are importing, or have no primary key. You will learn about primary keys in Chapter 6. For now, select Let Access Add Primary Key. Click Next.

FIGURE 1.41:

Choosing a primary key for your new Access table

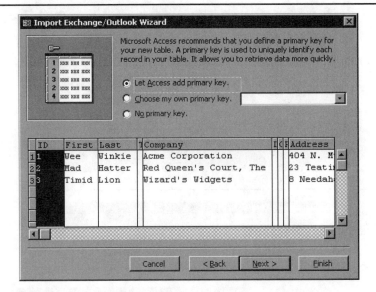

7. The wizard allows you to name the new table (see Figure 1.42). By default, the assigned name is the same as the Folder or Address Book you imported—Contacts, in this case. You can also select the option to have a wizard analyze your new table, or to Display Help. Select the wizard analyzer option and click Finish.

8. Access displays a dialog box (see Figure 1.43a) alerting you that the import was successful. Click OK.

9. The next dialog box asks if you wish to analyze the data in your new table (see Figure 1.43b). Click Yes.

10. The Table Analyzer Wizard is launched (see Figure 1.44a). The Table Analyzer Wizard is a function of the Import Wizard and will analyze your new table's data for common mistakes. This wizard can help improve the efficiency of your new table and your database as a whole. Click Next.

11. The next window explains how the Analyzer Wizard works and what to expect (see Figure 1.44b). Click Next.

FIGURE 1.42:

Naming your new Access table

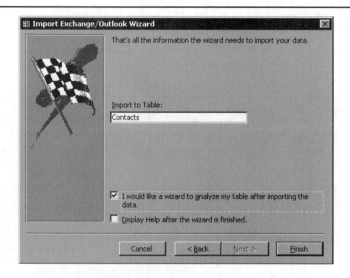

FIGURE 1.43:

Successful import of data from Outlook to Access (a), and launch of the Table Analyzer Wizard (b)

12. The Analyzer Wizard now asks if you want it to automatically make changes in your data, or for you to decide whether to carry out a change (see Figure 1.44c). Choose the second option, and click Next.

13. The next window that is displayed is a schema of how your table looks in diagram form. If you wanted to, you could create additional tables here, move fields from one table to another, and set relationships for the various tables. You could also make many other edits to the tables. For this example, create a new table by dragging and dropping the State field from the existing table to the blank space next to it. The Table Analyzer Wizard then prompts you to name the new table. Name it State (see Figure 1.45) and click OK.

14. Drag and drop the City field from the main table into the blank space next to the State table. Name it City and click OK.

FIGURE 1.44:

The Table Analyzer can improve the performance of your new table.

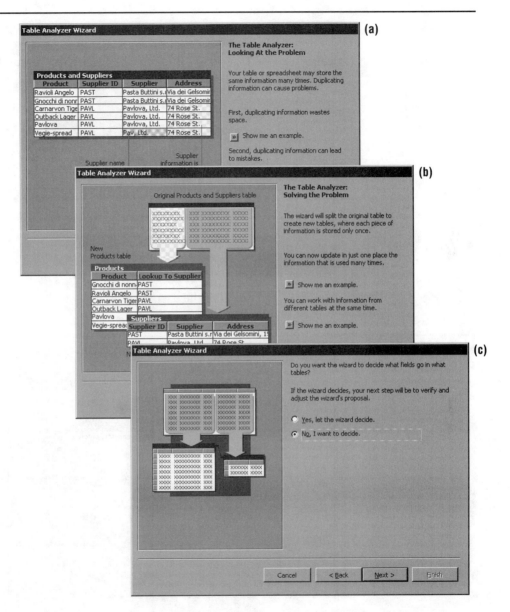

FIGURE 1.44:

The Table Analyzer can improve the performance of your new table.

FIGURE 1.45:

Creating a new table using Table Analyzer Wizard

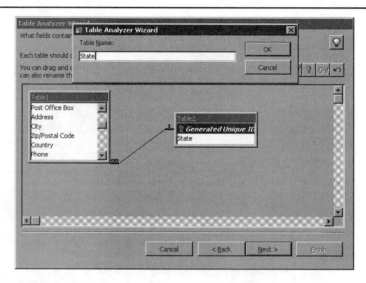

15. You now have three tables. All of the data except the city and state is kept in the first table (see Figure 1.46). Click Next.

FIGURE 1.46:

Moving fields between tables using the Table Analyzer Wizard

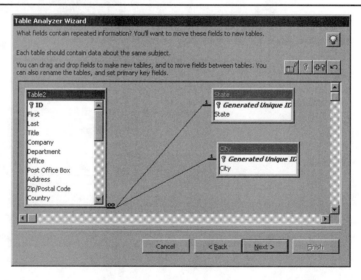

16. The wizard asks if you'd like it to create a query that can generate a table such as the original one you imported, recombining the City, State, and other fields (see Figure 1.47). You can also select the option to display Help after Access creates the query. Click Yes, Create The Query, and deselect the Help option. Click Finish.

FIGURE 1.47:

Access can create a query to combine the fields of the tables you created.

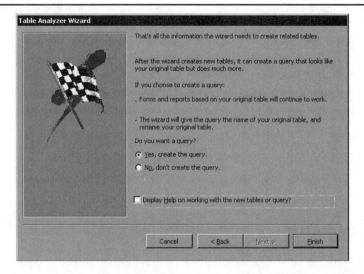

17. Access creates and displays the query, along with a message box telling you that what is displayed is the new query (see Figure 1.48). Click OK.

FIGURE 1.48:

The new query created by Access's Table Analyzer Wizard

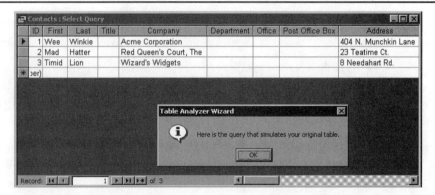

18. If you tab through this query, you see that all of the fields are displayed. The two fields that are in separate tables—City and State—have been renamed Lookup To City and Lookup To State.

19. Close the query and look at the Database Window. Click Tables. You will see three new tables—City, State, and Table1. These are the tables you created with the Lookup Table Wizard.

That's it! You now have your entire Contacts folder from Outlook at your disposal in your Access database.

Using the Link Spreadsheet and Link Text Wizards

Two additional wizards that can enhance the power of Access 2002 are the Link Spreadsheet Wizard and the Link Text Wizard. The difference between linking to a data source and importing it is that linked data is not part of the Access database; it resides in the original data source, independent of your database. Imported data actually becomes part of the Access database file and exists in a table or tables. Changes to the data in the database are not replicated in the original source of imported data, and vice versa. With linked data, a change in one application is replicated in the other. For example, if you link to a Microsoft Excel spreadsheet, Access creates a table and displays the data from the spreadsheet in that table. If you alter a record in the spreadsheet, you will see the change reflected in the table. If you change a record in Access, you can see the change in the spreadsheet as well.

To illustrate this point, we'll import some sample Employee data into the Expenses database.

1. Create a new Microsoft Excel spreadsheet called EmployeeInfo. In the first row, type the field headers **Employee Name**, **Social Security Number**, and **Driver's License Number**.

2. In the next three rows, input three imaginary employees and information for those fields. Save the spreadsheet.

3. In Access, click File ➢ Get External Data ➢ Link Tables. In the Files Of Type combo box, select Microsoft Excel. Locate your EmployeeInfo file and select it, then click Link.

4. This launches the Link Spreadsheet Wizard (see Figure 1.49). You can choose to show either worksheets in the linked spreadsheet or specified ranges. Clicking the name of the worksheet in the upper pane displays that worksheet's fields in the lower pane. Select Worksheet 1 and click Next.

5. The wizard asks if the first row of data in the worksheet should be considered column headings (see Figure 1.50). Select the First Row Contains Column Headings option and click Next.

6. The final window in the wizard enables you to name the linked Table and launch Help if you like. Name the table EmployeeInfo and leave the Help option unchecked (see Figure 1.51). Click Finish.

7. Access displays a confirmation that the spreadsheet has been successfully linked. Click OK to close this window.

8. You can now see the linked spreadsheet in your Access database (see Figure 1.52). As you can see, the icon for linked spreadsheets is the Excel icon with an arrow to the left of it. Double-click the linked spreadsheet to open it (make sure the spreadsheet is still

FIGURE 1.49:

The Link Spreadsheet Wizard

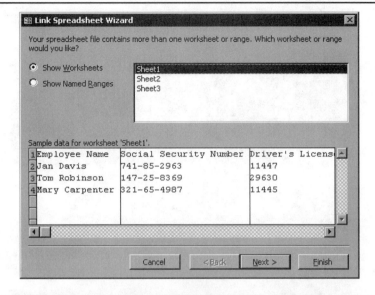

FIGURE 1.50:

The wizard gives you the option to treat the first row as column headings.

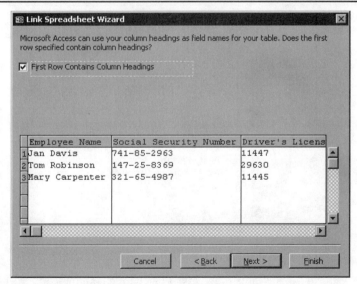

open in Excel). Change the Driver's License field for the first record in Access and press Enter.

9. Look at the Excel spreadsheet; the change should be replicated there. In Excel, change the Social Security Number for the second record and press Enter.

FIGURE 1.51:

Naming the linked table

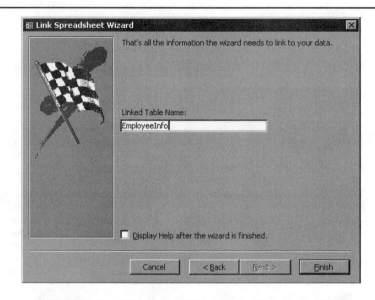

FIGURE 1.52:

Linked spreadsheets are listed with tables in Access.

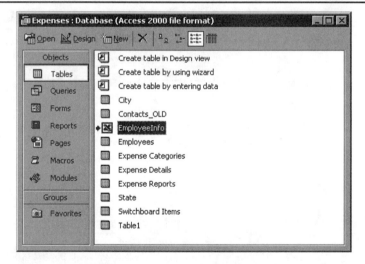

10. Look at the Linked table in Access. The change you made in Excel should be replicated in your table. Exit from Excel, saving your changes, and close the Linked table in Access.

11. The Link Text Wizard has elements of both the Link Spreadsheet Wizard and the Import Exchange/Outlook Wizard. It works best with text entered in columns and rows. Open Notepad and type four rows of three letters each. Save the file as Text-Document.txt, and exit Notepad.

12. In Access 2002, click File ➤ Get External Data ➤ Link Tables. Change the Files Of Type combo box to Text Files and locate your TextDocument file. Select it and click Link. This launches the Link Text Wizard (see Figure 1.53).

FIGURE 1.53:

The Link Text Wizard can link data in text format as an Access table.

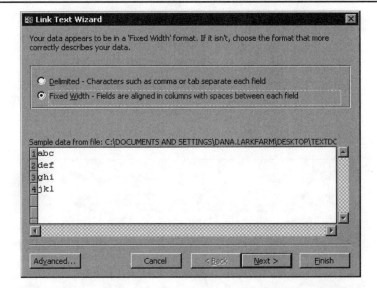

13. In the upper portion of the first window, the wizard presents two options for the data you are importing. Data in text format is considered either Delimited, in which fields in the data are separated by a particular keystroke, or Fixed Width, in which the data is already arranged in columns and rows. Our TextDocument is in Fixed Width format, so leave this radio button selected. Your sample data (the characters you entered) should appear in the lower portion of the window. Click Next.

14. The second window allows you to break the data up into columns (we already entered it into rows) using break lines. If we leave it as is, all of the data is considered one field. Instead, let's have Access consider each column of letters as a separate field, thus resembling a table. To do this, we will insert two break lines. Click the ruler at the line between the first and second characters (see Figure 1.54). This inserts a break line between the first and second characters. Create another break line between the second and third characters. Click Next.

The next window looks and operates exactly like the field-naming window we saw in the Exchange/Outlook Wizard (see Figure 1.55). Name the three fields we created FirstLetter, SecondLetter, and ThirdLetter. The Data Type for all three should be Text. Click Next. The last window is the table-naming window (see Figure 1.56). Name the linked table

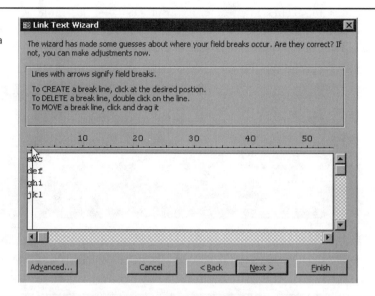

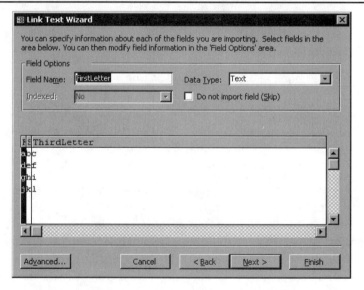

TextDocument and click Finish. Access displays a confirmation box to tell you that the data was successfully linked.

The new linked text document appears in the Tables pane of the Database Window, along with the existing tables and the linked spreadsheet (see Figure 1.57). The icon for the linked text document is the same as for Notepad, with an arrow to the left of it.

FIGURE 1.56:

Naming the new linked table

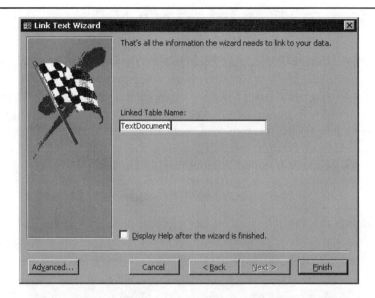

FIGURE 1.57:

Linked text files appear in the Database window with the tables.

An important difference between linked spreadsheets and linked text documents is that the latter cannot be dynamically changed between Access and Notepad. If you change the source document in Notepad, the change will be reflected in Access (although you cannot make any changes if the linked document is open in Access), but you cannot make any changes to the linked document in Access at all.

Controlling the User Interface

After you use the Control Wizards, Switchboard Manager, Import Exchange/Outlook Wizard, Link Spreadsheet Wizard, and Link Text Wizard, your customized application should be easier for you to use, but you still don't want to turn it over to a novice. At this stage, you have designed navigation paths but have not restricted the user to those paths. The complete built-in command environment is exposed, because all of the menu commands, shortcut menu commands, toolbar buttons, and keyboard shortcuts that are built into Access are available for switching to Design view and changing the design of the application. The Database window is also displayed, though it's minimized. The novice user has immediate access to the objects that make up your application.

Before turning the application over to a novice, you should protect the application by hiding any commands that could be used to change the application's design and by hiding the Database window. Access 2002 provides tools for controlling the user interface and protecting your application. In this section, you learn about three of the tools that don't require programming:

- You can control many features of the Access environment by setting startup properties; for example, you can specify whether the Database window is displayed when you start up the application, and you can disable the keyboard shortcuts that display the Database window (the F11 or Alt+F1 key combinations). However, without programming, you cannot prevent users from pressing the Shift key to bypass your startup property settings when opening a database.

- You can prevent unauthorized entry into a database by defining a password. Simple password security restricts entry into your database but offers no protection after a user who knows the password has opened the database.

- You can replace the built-in menu bars, menus, and toolbars with custom versions that include only the commands required for using your application. Without programming, you can include built-in commands and commands for opening database objects. However, you must use macro programming to create custom commands for running a set of instructions and to customize the keyboard.

Setting Startup Properties

Startup properties dictate how a database application looks when it starts up. Choose Tools ➤ Startup to display the Startup dialog and click the Advanced button to display the options (see Figure 1.58).

You use the Startup dialog to set the properties shown in Table 1.3. The application title and icon settings take effect as soon as you close the Startup dialog. The other settings take effect the next time you open the database.

You can set most of the startup properties for a database using the Startup dialog.

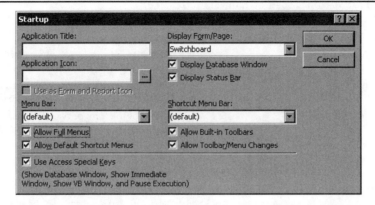

The simplest way to control the commands available to the user is to set startup properties as follows:

- Hide the Database window and prevent the user from displaying the window after starting the database.

- Hide all toolbars and shortcut menus.

- Replace the built-in menus with an alternate reduced set of built-in menus.

The reduced set includes only the commands that are useful when a user is working with a custom database application in views other than Design view and eliminates the menu commands for changing the design of a database object as well as several other menu commands. Figure 1.59 shows the reduced menu bar for Form view. This menu bar doesn't include the View menu or Tools menu and eliminates some menu commands on the remaining menus.

We'll use the Startup dialog to customize the title bar and protect the application.

1. Click Tools ➤ Startup.

2. Set the Application Title property to Expenses.

3. Clear all of the check boxes except the one to display the status bar (see Figure 1.60).

4. Click OK. Notice that the application title bar changes to Expenses immediately. In building the Expenses database, the Database Wizard creates a procedure that runs when the Switchboard form first opens and includes statements that redisplay and minimize the Database window. The procedure runs after Access starts the database according to the startup settings and, therefore, overrides the startup setting to hide the Database window. In the next few steps, we'll modify the procedure to eliminate the statements so that the Database window remains hidden.

TABLE 1.3: Startup Properties in the Startup Dialog

Startup Property	Description
Application Title	Specifies the text that appears in the application's title bar. When this property isn't set, the words "Microsoft Access" appear by default.
Application Icon	Specifies the icon that appears in the application's title bar. When this property isn't set, the Access key icon appears by default.
Display Form/Page	Specifies the name of the form or page to display on startup. When you create an application with the Database Wizard, this property is set to the Switchboard form by default.
Display Database Window	Specifies whether the Database window is displayed when you start up the application.
Display Status Bar	Specifies whether the status bar is displayed when you start up the application. Normally, you want to keep the default to display the status bar because you use it to display on-screen help.
Menu Bar	Displays a custom menu bar that replaces the built-in menu bar in all windows of your application except where you have created a custom menu bar for a specific form or report.
Shortcut Menu Bar	Displays a custom shortcut menu bar that replaces the built-in shortcut menu bar in all windows of your application except where you have created a custom shortcut menu bar for a specific form, report, or form control.
Allow Full Menus	Specifies whether Access should display the full set of built-in menus and menu commands or only the reduced set of built-in menus. The reduced set doesn't include commands that allow you to modify the application.
Allow Default Shortcut Menus	Specifies whether Access should display the built-in shortcut menus.
Allow Built-in Toolbars	Specifies whether Access should display the built-in toolbars. You can clear the check box to hide all of the built-in toolbars but still display custom toolbars.
Allow Toolbar/Menu Changes	Specifies whether Access should allow users to change toolbars and menu bars. If you clear the check box, you disable the right mouse button, the Close button on the toolbars, and the Toolbars command on the View menu. You can still move, size, and dock the toolbars and menu bar and hide or unhide toolbars.
Use Access Special Keys	Specifies whether Access should enable the special built-in key combinations: F11 (displays, unhides, and restores the Database window), Ctrl+G or Alt+F11 (displays the Immediate window in the VB Editor, and launches the VB Editor if it is not already running), Ctrl+F11 (toggles between the built-in menu bar and the custom menu bar), and Ctrl+Break (in a database or a project, suspends execution of a VBA procedure; in a project, also stops Access from retrieving records from the server).

FIGURE 1.59:

The reduced Form view built-in menu bar

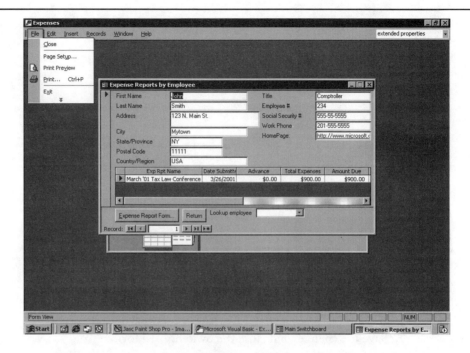

FIGURE 1.60:

Using the Startup settings to hide the Database window and restrict the available menu, toolbar, and keyboard commands

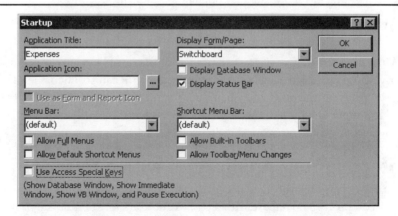

5. Open the Switchboard form in Design view. Open the property sheet by pressing F4. Click the OnOpen property and then click the Build button to the right of the property box. The Module window displays the event procedure that runs when the form opens (see Figure 1.61). The two lines that follow the comment `Minimize the database window` are the instructions that display and minimize the Database window.

The instructions to display and minimize the Database window

```
Expenses - Form_Switchboard (Code)
Form                                        Open
    Private Sub Form_Open(Cancel As Integer)
    ' Minimize the database window and initialize the form.

    On Error GoTo Form_Open_Err

        ' Minimize the database window.
        DoCmd.SelectObject acForm, "Switchboard", True
        DoCmd.Minimize

        ' Move to the switchboard page that is marked as the default.
        Me.Filter = "[ItemNumber] = 0 AND [Argument] = 'Default' "
        Me.FilterOn = True

    Form_Open_Exit:
        Exit Sub

    Form_Open_Err:
        MsgBox Err.Description
        Resume Form_Open_Exit

    End Sub
```

6. Click to the left of the line Minimize the database window, drag to select the three lines, and then press Delete.

7. Save the changes and close the Switchboard form.

8. Click File ➢ Close. Reopen the database by choosing Expenses.mdb in the list of recently opened databases in the File menu. The Expenses application opens with the reduced menus, no toolbars, and no shortcut menus.

With these settings, you won't be able to display the Database window by pressing F11 after you start the database. Note, however, that you can still bypass the startup property settings by pressing the Shift key when you first open the database. (In Chapter 14, "Creating and Modifying Database Objects Using Access VBA," you'll learn how to disable the Shift key bypass as well.)

Protecting Your Application with a Password

You can prevent unauthorized people from opening your application by defining a password. When you protect a database with a password, users must enter the password before they can import its objects into another database or compact the database.

Before you can set a password, you need to establish exclusive access to the database. A database must be closed before you can specify exclusive mode. When you open a database in exclusive mode, you prevent anyone else from opening the database.

We'll define a password for the Expenses database.

1. Close the database by clicking the Exit This Database button in the Main Switchboard.

2. Choose File ➢ Open, select Expenses.mdb, and click Open Exclusive in the Open drop-down list while pressing the Shift key (see Figure 1.62).

FIGURE 1.62:

Open a database in exclusive mode before setting a password.

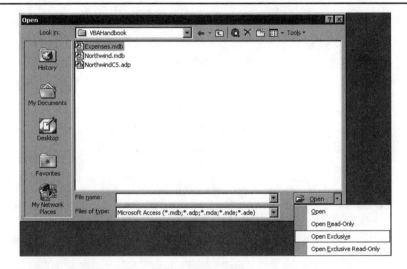
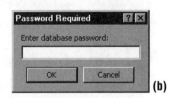

3. Choose Tools ➢ Security ➢ Set Database Password. Use the Set Database Password dialog to set a password (see Figure 1.63a).

FIGURE 1.63:

Use the Set Database Password dialog (a) to set a password and the Password Required dialog (b) to gain entry to the password-protected database.

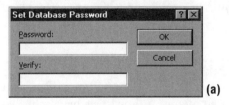

4. In the Password text box, type **expenses**. In Access, passwords are case sensitive. Type **expenses** again in the Verify text box, then click OK. Click File ➢ Close.

5. Choose Expenses from the list of recently opened databases in the File menu. Enter **expenses** in the Password Required dialog (see Figure 1.63b) and click OK. The database opens with the reduced set of menus.

6. For the next section we need access to the full menus, so we'll restart the database. Click the Exit This Database button. Press the Shift key and choose Expenses from the

list of recently opened databases in the File menu. Enter the password and press the Shift key while clicking OK. The database opens with the full set of menus.

WARNING Make sure you record your password somewhere. If you forget or lose your password, you can't open the database.

Although adding a password to a database is an easy way to restrict entry to the database, password protection is limited:

- Anyone with a disk editor or similar utility program can read your data without opening the database. You can prevent this by encrypting the database. To encrypt a database, close the database and choose Tools ➤ Security ➤ Encrypt/Decrypt Database. Select the database in the Encrypt/Decrypt Database dialog and click OK. You will be prompted to supply a name for the encrypted database before the actual encryption occurs. If the database is password protected, you will need to enter the password before naming the encrypted database.

- To remove password protection, you simply choose Tools ➤ Security ➤ Unset Database Password. Enter the password in the Unset Database Password dialog and click OK. This means that anyone who knows the password and has access to the Unset Database Password command can change or clear the password.

TIP A better way to protect your database is to use the user-level security that Access provides. With user-level security, you can define users and groups of users and specify different levels of access to data and the database objects. For more information about user-level security, see *Access 2002 Desktop Developer's Handbook* by Paul Litwin, Ken Getz, and Mike Gunderloy (Sybex, 2001).

Creating Custom Menus and Toolbars

We've used the Startup dialog to display a reduced set of menu bars and menu commands and to hide all toolbars and shortcut menus. Although we have achieved some degree of protection for our database, we still haven't made the command environment as helpful as it could be. Menu bars hide their commands; the new user must search through the drop-down menus to learn what commands are available and then remember where the commands are. In addition, the reduced menu bars may not provide the set of commands the user wants. Toolbars are a better way to display the available commands. With toolbar buttons visible at all times and ScreenTips displayed as the user browses through the buttons, your application is easier to learn and use. Shortcut menus are also helpful; most users are familiar with using the right mouse button to display a shortcut menu.

In Access 2002, you can edit built-in menu bars, shortcut menus, and toolbars, as well as create custom menu bars and toolbars using the Customize dialog. Access 2002 calls these three objects *command bars* and provides common ways to customize them. For example, you can design menu bars that display menus with command buttons and combo boxes, and toolbars that display menu names with drop-down menus. You have enormous flexibility in how you design menu bars, shortcut menus, and toolbars in Access 2002, but you should probably stick to the standard Windows designs to avoid confusing your users.

To display the Customize dialog, right-click in the toolbar and choose Customize from the shortcut menu. The Toolbars tab lists both the built-in toolbars and new toolbars that you create (see Figure 1.64a). A check in front of an item means that the item is currently displayed. You can display any toolbar by clicking its check box. In addition to the toolbars, the list includes Menu Bar as a checked item that represents the menu bar currently displayed. Since the menu bar for every view has a View menu with a Toolbars command, you can display the menu bar you want to work with before opening the Customize dialog.

NOTE Before you can customize the toolbar, you may need to ensure that this option is set in the Startup menu. To do this, select Tools ➢ Startup and make sure a check is in the Allow Toolbar/Menu Changes check box.

The Commands tab displays command categories in the list box on the left (see Figure 1.64b). When you select a category, the list box on the right changes to display the commands in the selected category. The Categories list also includes categories for each of the types of database objects except modules. If you select one of these categories, the list box on the right displays all of the objects of that type. For example, selecting the ActiveX Controls displays the list of ActiveX controls currently installed and registered on your computer in the list box on the right. When you select the New Menu item in the Categories list, the Commands list displays the New Menu command that you use to create a new menu. The Options tab lets you specify additional command-bar options (see Figure 1.64c). For example, you can choose whether to display ScreenTips on toolbars.

The list in the Toolbars tab of the Customize dialog includes the Shortcut Menus item, which represents the shortcut menus. Click the Shortcut Menus item to display a menu bar with menu items for each of the main categories of shortcut menus (see Figure 1.65a). You can click a menu item to display a drop-down menu that lists all the shortcut menus available in that category. Click the Form category to display the shortcut menus available when a form is the active window (see Figure 1.65b). Note that shortcut menus exist for each of the form views. Finally, you can select Form View Record from the list to view the shortcut menu for that view (see Figure 1.65c).

FIGURE 1.64:

Use the Customize dialog to modify existing menu bars, shortcut menus, and toolbars and to create new ones. The dialog has tabs to list the toolbars (a), display most of the built-in commands (b), and display options (c).

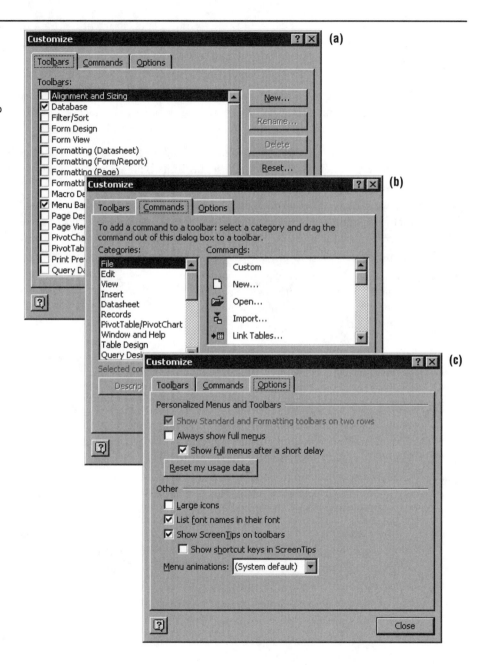

FIGURE 1.65:

The menu bar representing the shortcut menus (a), the shortcut menus when a form is active (b), and the Form Record View shortcut menu (c)

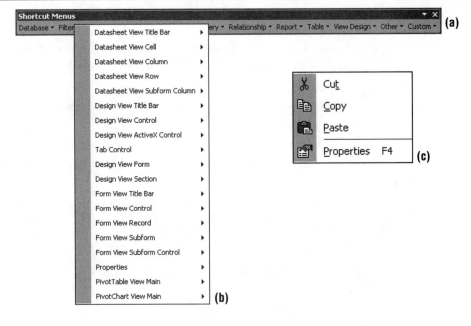

Customizing a Built-in Command Bar

To customize a built-in command bar, you must display the command bar when the Customize dialog is open. As explained earlier, you can display any toolbar or any shortcut menu by checking the item in the Toolbars list, but you can only customize the menu bar that is displayed before you open the Customize dialog.

You can customize the displayed built-in command bar as follows:

- To remove a command from any command bar, click the command or command button and drag it off the command bar and into the work area.

- To move a command to a new location on a command bar or to move a command from one command bar to another command bar, click the command you want to move and drag it to its new location.

- To copy a command from one displayed command bar to another displayed command bar, hold down the Ctrl key as you drag the command to its new location.

- To add a built-in command to a command bar, you can copy the command from another command bar or select the command in the Commands list and drag the command to its new location on a command bar.

- To add a command to open a table, query, form, or report, choose the type in the Categories list, select the object in the Commands list, and drag the object to its new location on a command bar. To add a command that runs a program you have created as a macro, choose All Macros from the Categories list, select the macro you want to run, and drag the macro to its new location on a command bar.

- To undo the changes to a command bar, select the command bar in the Toolbars list in the Customize dialog and click the Reset button. Access displays a message asking you to confirm the reset.

To modify a toolbar button's or menu's name, appearance, or properties, right-click the item to display the shortcut menu (see Figure 1.66a). You can make selections for the following customizations:

- Undo changes to the command, delete the command, or change its name.

- Copy, paste, or modify the button image.

- Specify the command as text, an image, both text and image, or the default style.

- Add a horizontal bar to a menu or a vertical bar to a toolbar to separate commands into groups.

- Assign a hyperlink to the button or menu.

FIGURE 1.66:

Right-click the command with the Customize dialog open to display the shortcut menu (a). Click the Properties command to edit the properties (b).

To display the properties for the button or menu, click the Properties command. This displays the Control Properties dialog for the selected item. For example, Figure 1.66b shows the properties for the Print toolbar button. To run a VBA procedure that you have created as a function procedure (you'll learn about the different kinds of procedures in later chapters), you enter the name of the function procedure in the On Action box using the syntax =*functionname*().

Creating and Displaying Custom Menu Bars

You can create a new custom menu bar that includes built-in menu commands, commands to open any Database window object, and your own custom commands. You can display a custom menu bar in two ways:

- Create an individual custom menu bar and attach it to a specific form or report. The menu bar is displayed whenever the form or report is the active object.

- Create a global menu bar that is displayed in all windows except for those forms and reports that have their own individual custom menu bars.

As an example, we'll create and display a new global menu bar. There are several ways to build the menu bar and menus. We'll look at a few techniques in these steps.

1. Choose View ➢ Toolbars ➢ Customize or right-click the menu bar and select Customize from the shortcut menu. Click the Toolbars tab.

2. Click the New button and type **ExpenseGlobal** in the New Toolbar dialog as the name of the new global menu bar. Click OK. Access creates a small blank command bar and adds the ExpenseGlobal item to the list of toolbars (see Figure 1.67).

FIGURE 1.67:

Creating a new global menu bar

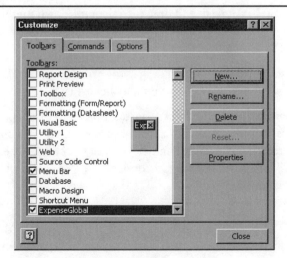

3. Click the Properties button to display the Toolbar Properties dialog. You use this dialog to specify whether the command bar is a menu bar, toolbar, or shortcut menu (choose Popup for a shortcut menu). Choose Menu Bar in the Type combo box and click Close.

4. Hold down the Ctrl key and select the File menu name in the menu bar you are displaying, drag to the blank command bar, and release. When you drag a menu name, you also drag the pull-down menu.

5. Click the File menu on the new menu bar to display the pull-down menu. One by one, select commands and drag them off the menu; leave only the Close, Save As, Page Setup, Print Preview, Print, and Exit commands.

6. Hold down the Ctrl key and select the Edit menu name in the displayed menu bar, drag to the right of the File menu in the blank command bar, and release. Click the Edit menu on the new menu bar to display the pull-down menu. One by one, select commands and drag them off the menu; leave only the Undo, Cut, Copy, and Paste commands. (Undo might be displayed as Can't Undo.)

7. Select New Menu from the Categories list in the Commands tab of the Customize dialog. Click the New Menu command in the Commands list and drag it to the right of the Edit menu on the new menu bar. Right-click in the menu name (New Menu by default) and change the name to Forms. Click the new menu name to display the small, blank pull-down menu.

8. Choose the All Forms category in the Commands tab of the Customize dialog, select Expense Reports By Employee, and drag it to the pull-down menu for the Forms menu. Select Expense Categories and drag it to the pull-down menu below the Expense Reports By Employee form.

9. Click the ExpenseGlobal toolbar and drag it toward the top of the window to dock the new toolbar below the other toolbars you may be displaying.

10. Select the Toolbars tab and click the Properties button to display the Toolbar Properties dialog. You can use this dialog to allow or prevent menu bar changes. Choose ExpenseGlobal from the combo list and clear all of the check boxes to prevent changing or moving. Click Close, and the Customize dialog appears. Click Close again. The global menu bar is finished.

11. You can display the global menu bar by setting one of the startup properties. Click Tools ➢ Startup. Select the ExpenseGlobal menu bar from the Menu Bar combo box and click OK. The new menu bar will be displayed the next time you start up the application.

You use the same technique to create an individual menu bar for a form or a report. The only difference between an individual menu bar and a global menu bar is how you arrange for the menu bar to be displayed. While you specify a global menu bar as a startup property, you specify an individual menu bar for a form or report by setting the form's or report's MenuBar property to the name of the menu bar. When you display a form or report that has its own custom menu bar, Access displays the custom menu bar instead of the custom global menu bar (or the default built-in menu bar if your application doesn't have a global menu bar).

Creating and Displaying a Custom Shortcut Menu

You can create custom shortcut menus for forms, reports, and controls on forms. You can create an individual shortcut menu for each form or report and a global shortcut menu that is displayed whenever the active form or report doesn't have an individual shortcut menu.

As an example, we'll create a simple custom shortcut menu bar that we'll use as a global shortcut menu.

1. Right-click the menu bar and select Customize from the shortcut menu.

2. Click the Toolbars tab. Click the New button and name the new command bar ExpenseShortcut. Click OK. Click the Properties button in the Customize dialog, select Popup from the Type list box, click OK, and click the Close button. The small command bar disappears. To build a shortcut menu, you must display the Shortcut Menus menu bar.

3. Click in the Shortcut Menus item in the Toolbars list. Click the Custom menu at the right end of the Shortcut Menus menu bar to display a drop-down list containing the Expense-Shortcut menu (see Figure 1.68a). Click the ExpenseShortcut menu item to display a small, blank fly-out menu where you can build the new shortcut menu.

4. Click the Form menu on the Shortcut Menu menu bar, then click the Form View Sub-form item to display the shortcut menu. Hold down the Ctrl key and then, one by one, select the Filter By Form, Apply Filter/Sort, and Remove Filter/Sort commands and drag them to the ExpenseShortcut custom menu (see Figure 1.68b). (You drag to the small black arrows to display the menus.)

FIGURE 1.68:

Creating a custom shortcut menu

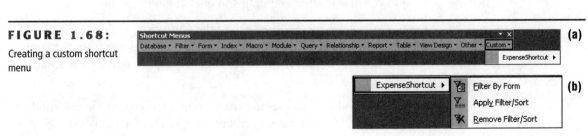

5. Click the Close button to close the Shortcut Menu menu bar and the Customize dialog.

6. Choose Tools ➤ Startup, select ExpenseShortcut from the Shortcut Menu Bar combo box, and click OK. The next time you start up the application, the custom shortcut menu is displayed when you right-click a form.

You use the same technique to create an individual shortcut menu for a form, form control, or report. The only difference between an individual shortcut menu and a global shortcut menu is how you arrange for the shortcut menu to be displayed. You specify a global shortcut menu as a startup property. You specify an individual shortcut menu for a form, form control, or report by setting the form's, control's, or report's ShortcutMenuBar property to the name of the shortcut menu bar. When you display a form or report that has its own custom shortcut menu, Access displays the custom shortcut menu instead of the custom global shortcut menu (or the default built-in menu if your application doesn't have a global shortcut menu).

Creating and Displaying a Custom Toolbar

Although you can display only one menu bar and one shortcut menu at a time, you can display any number of built-in and custom toolbars. One simple strategy for providing custom toolbars for your application is to hide all of the built-in toolbars (by clearing the Allow Built-in Toolbars check box in the Startup dialog), display a custom global menu toolbar, and display custom individual toolbars for forms and reports. You can carry out this simple strategy without programming.

As an example, we'll create a simple custom toolbar.

1. Right-click the menu bar and select Customize from the shortcut menu. Click the Toolbars tab.

2. Click the New button, name the new toolbar ToolbarExpense (see Figure 1.69a), and click OK. Access adds the new toolbar to the list in the Toolbars tab.

3. From the Edit category in the Commands tab of the Customize dialog, select and drag the Undo, Cut, Copy, and Paste commands into the new blank toolbar. From the Records category, drag the Sort Ascending and Filter By Form commands.

4. Click the title bar of the new toolbar and drag and dock it below the menu bar.

5. Click the Properties button on the Toolbars tab of the Customize dialog to display the Toolbar Properties dialog (see Figure 1.69b). Choose ToolbarExpense from the combo list and clear the check boxes to prevent customizing, resizing, or moving the toolbar. Click Close.

6. Make sure that Menu Bar and ToolbarExpense are the only checked items in the Toolbars list in the Customize dialog. (You will need to edit the properties of the ExpenseGlobal

menu you created and recheck Allow Showing/Hiding.) Click the Close button. Figure 1.69c shows the built-in Database window menu bar and the new toolbar.

7. Click File ➤ Close.

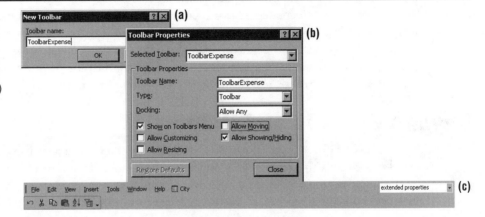

Reviewing Our Automated Access Application

This chapter has introduced you to many of the tools you can use to automate a database, restrict the menu and toolbar commands, and protect your application without programming. We've explored the tools by creating the Expenses application. Let's look at the Expenses application and review its current state.

1. Open the Expenses database. Access displays the Password Required dialog.

2. Type **expenses** in the text box and click OK. The Database window is hidden, and the global menu bar and custom toolbar are displayed.

3. Click Enter/View Expense Reports By Employee. Right-click in the form to display the custom global shortcut menu.

4. Click the Return button and then click the Exit This Database button on the Main Switchboard.

Because the Expenses database has some protection from design changes, you can comfortably turn it over to someone who doesn't know Access. Keep in mind, though, that these protection measures can still be disabled if a user presses Shift when entering the password.

You can continue to use the techniques described in this chapter to improve the application. For example, by using the Command Button Wizard, you can make it easy to navigate on two-way paths to all of the application's forms and reports, and you can add the other automated tasks in Table 1.1. In addition, you can add more lookup combo boxes using the Combo Box Wizard. You can also add forms and reports, and use the Switchboard Manager to include the new objects on switchboards. Also, you can import and link additional data using the Exchange/Outlook Import Wizard, the Link Spreadsheet Wizard, and the Link Text Wizard. You can create additional custom menu bars, shortcut menus, and toolbars to make your application easier to use. Working with only the Access helpers and the various property dialogs such as the Startup dialog and the Customize dialog, you have the power to create fully automated database applications without going any further in this book. Do you need to read any further? Yes. Read the next section to find out why.

Beyond Wizards and Helpers

The Database Wizard is very powerful, but it can create only databases based on the few templates that come with Access. If your application does not fall into one of those categories, you'll need to build the database from scratch and then use the other wizards and helpers to automate it. And although it is possible to create a fully automated application with the Access wizards, the applications you can create are still limited in the kinds of operations they can carry out.

For example, an application created with the wizards limits data validation to the kinds of data-validation rules you can enter in table field properties and form control properties. This means that you can use only a single validation rule to validate a record, even though in some cases you might want to carry out a sequence of validation tests. Also, if the data entered doesn't satisfy the validation rule, you can display only a single message, even though you might want to display different messages depending on the value that was entered.

The validation tests are performed according to default timing rules. For example, Access tests the validation rules for a control on a form when you try to tab out of the control and tests the validation rules for a record, such as uniqueness of the primary key value (entity integrity), when you try to save the record. Often, you'll want to change the timing of the validation tests. For example, you may want to test for uniqueness when you tab out of the primary key control instead of waiting until the other data for the record has been entered.

Another example of a database operation you can't set up with the wizards is *transaction processing*. A *transaction* is a set of operations that you handle as a single unit; either you carry out all of the operations in the set or you don't carry out any of them. If you begin the transaction and one operation fails, you roll back the previous operations by returning the data to the state it was in before you started the transaction. A good candidate for transaction processing is the archive process, in which you append records to historical tables and then delete them from the current data tables. Either both operations should occur or neither. Access doesn't provide a transaction processing helper.

The rest of this book takes you beyond the helpers. You'll create your own programs to automate a database from scratch using the Access VBA programming language. In VBA programming, you create procedures stored either in standard modules listed in the Modules pane of the Database window or in form or report modules that are built into forms and reports. Access 2002 also offers an independent class module.

The part of Microsoft Access that you interact with to create and display the database objects is called the *application,* and the part that manages the data in a database is called the *database engine.* In an Access database, the database engine is called *Jet.* In an Access project, the database engine is known as the Microsoft SQL Server 2000 Desktop Engine, formerly MSDE. The two parts of Access communicate with each other using *data-access languages.*

Data-access languages are not stand-alone programming languages; instead, they are special-purpose languages that you use along with a programming language to specify the data you want to retrieve from or add to the tables.

You've been using one of the data-access languages from the beginning of your work with Access, perhaps without being aware of it. Structured Query Language, or SQL (sometimes pronounced "sequel"), is the language that Access uses every time you create a query in Design view. SQL is also the language that the Form, Report, Combo Box, and List Box Wizards often use to specify record sources and row sources. VBA programming uses SQL for working with tables and queries.

Another data-access language is called Microsoft ActiveX Data Objects, or ADO. The ADO language uses OLE DB providers to manipulate data in a database server. You use ADO to write instructions for creating and manipulating the objects that are managed by the database engine. These objects include the tables and queries in your database, but also the objects that the database engine uses to restrict access to the data and manage the database. There are two basic roles for ADO:

- To give an alternative method for specifying data
- To provide the ability to create and modify database objects as part of VBA procedures

Before the introduction of ADO, Data Access Objects (DAO) was the data access language widely used in VBA to manipulate data. DAO technology is no longer being developed and has been replaced by ADO as the standard for VBA programming. Many older databases still use DAO technology. For your convenience, information about the DAO language is included on the CD for this book.

Most of the time, you create all of the tables and queries in an application using their Design windows. However, there are times when you prefer to create tables and queries programmatically. For example, you use ADO when you write a VBA procedure that creates a new temporary table as part of an automated data-import process.

Summary

This chapter has introduced you to the tools that you can use to automate a database without doing any programming yourself. The tools rely on setting properties in dialogs and property sheets and on using the wizards and helpers to write programs for you. The wizards demonstrate the concept of writing a program as either a macro or a VBA procedure and then arranging for Access to run the program automatically when the user takes an action. The programming environment in Access is event driven. Certain user actions cause controls, forms, and reports to recognize changes called events. Access runs programs when events occur.

Following is a summary of the helpers we've explored:

- The Database Wizard creates partially automated applications, complete with switchboards for navigation, command buttons to open and synchronize forms and reports, and custom dialog boxes that collect user input before selecting records for summary reports.

- The Command Button Wizard creates command buttons with scripts for automating a wide variety of simple database tasks.

- The Combo Box Wizard creates lookup combo boxes that can automatically look up and display a record that matches the value in the combo box.

- The Switchboard Manager creates and modifies a Switchboard form for providing navigation paths to forms, reports, and other switchboards.

- The Exchange/Outlook Import Wizard allows data to be imported into Access from a Microsoft Exchange server or from Microsoft Outlook.

- The Link Spreadsheet and Link Text Wizards allow you to access data in applications outside Microsoft Access.

- The Startup dialog lets you control how your application starts up and lets you protect your application's design.

- The Customize dialog lets you create custom menu bars, shortcut menus, and toolbars.

You are ready to use programming to provide the automatic connections between the objects in your database—not only the familiar Database window objects, but also additional objects that will be new to you. The next chapter starts you thinking about how objects are designed in Access and how you can control them with your programs.

CHAPTER 2

Getting Started with Objects and Events

- Choosing names to document objects

- Describing an object by setting properties

- Setting startup, database and security properties, and environmental options

- Manipulating objects

- Understanding the Access event model

- Canceling default behavior

This chapter introduces two concepts fundamental in VBA programming: objects and events. The first part of the chapter discusses the familiar Database window objects and the not-so-familiar data access objects supplied by the ADO library. The data access objects are used by the database engine, which manages the data and controls who can use each of the Database window objects. When you work interactively with Access, you don't work explicitly with the data access objects; the database engine works in the background, creating and managing the data access objects automatically. For example, when you create a new Database window object such as a table, the database engine creates a corresponding data access object, called a Table object, for the table and another data access object, called an AccessObject object, that stores administrative information about the new table. Also, when you set database and security properties, you are actually working with the data access objects. This chapter explores using properties to describe the characteristics of objects and teaches you how to read, set, and change different categories of properties.

The second part of the chapter introduces *events*, which are triggered by actions. As soon as you interact with an object, you change the object. For example, when you open a form or move the mouse cursor to a text box, your action changes at least one property. Some of the changes that an object experiences are made available as programming opportunities; these special changes are the object's events. Programming in Access consists of writing programs and arranging to have Access run them automatically when events occur. This chapter describes the events that objects recognize. Knowing the precise conditions that trigger events is crucial to VBA programming.

Naming Objects

Even the simplest Access database has hundreds of items: tables, fields, indexes, relationships, queries, forms, controls, reports, properties, and so on. Each of the items that you create, or that Access creates for you, is an *object*, a concept that we'll return to at different times in the book. You can think of an object as an onion with several layers. At the outside layer, an object is just a "thing" that you can use or change by setting properties in a property sheet or dialog or by running a VBA procedure. We'll peel away the layers as we go along.

The hundreds of objects in a database need to be organized so that you can make sense out of them. The Database window helps out by displaying the main objects, called the Database window objects, in separate sections for tables, queries, forms, reports, data access pages, macros, and modules. In an Access project, the available objects are tables, views, stored procedures, database diagrams, forms, pages, macros, and modules. You can introduce another level of organization by using an object's name to provide information about the object's type and purpose.

Self-Documenting Names

Naming an object is your first opportunity to uniquely identify it. The name you choose can provide no information at all, or it can richly document the object. For example, when you name the controls on a form, you are free to name them numerically, as in Control1, Control2, and so on. Alternatively, you can include descriptive information within the name, as in txtLastName. From the name txtLastName, you can easily deduce both the control's type and its purpose—the name implies that the control is a text box control holding someone's last name.

A name packed with such information is *self-documenting*. When you use self-documenting names, you don't need to set up a separate dictionary to define the type and purpose of your objects. You can make up your own naming codes, or you can adopt a naming scheme created by others. It's important that you use some sort of naming standard and take the time to apply it consistently. Most professional Access developers follow a naming standard based on a style for naming objects called the Hungarian style after the native country of its inventor, Charles Simonyi.

In the Hungarian naming style, an object's name has four parts:

[*prefix*][*tag*][*BaseName*][*Suffix*]

The name parts have the following meanings:

- The prefix modifies the tag and is usually a single lowercase letter. A tag may have one or more prefixes to provide additional information about the object's type.

- The tag refers to the type of the object and is usually three or four lowercase letters.

- The base name is the name you would probably use if you weren't following a naming convention. The base name is typically one or two words that describe the object's purpose. Capitalize the first letter of each word and don't use spaces. It is preferable to spell out words entirely, but abbreviations are okay if they are long enough to be memorable (or better still, recognizable by someone else trying to understand your work).

- The suffix modifies the base name. A suffix is usually a single word with the first letter capitalized. A name may have one or more suffixes to provide additional information about how the object is used.

When you name an object, you decide on the base name and the suffix or suffixes. Tags and prefixes, however, are normally selected from standardized lists that you create or adopt.

The following are some common tags for Database window objects and controls on forms and reports:

Object	Tag
Table	tbl
Query	qry
Form	frm
Report	rpt
Data Access Page	dap
Macro	mcr
Module	bas
Check box	chk
Combo box	cbo
Command button	cmd
Custom control	ocx
Image	img
Label	lbl
Line	lin
List box	lst
Option button	opt
Option group (frame)	fra
Page break	brk
Section	sec
Text box	txt
Toggle button	tgl
Subform	sfr
Subreport	srp

NOTE   Two special macros without tags, called AutoExec and AutoKeys, must have exactly these names to be recognized by Access. Also, we use *bas* as the module tag instead of the mnemonic *mod* to maintain consistency with Visual Basic.

Unfortunately, the wizards don't follow the Hungarian naming style. The Northwind sample application that we'll be using throughout this book doesn't follow the Hungarian naming style either, so this book does not practice the consistency rule that it preaches. We decided to use the Northwind database so that you would be working with the same, familiar database used in the Access documentation rather than needing to learn a new database. As a result, we'll be using both the given names for existing objects and the Hungarian-style names for the new objects we create.

Here are a few examples of how some of the objects in the Northwind database could be renamed using tags:

Object	Tagged Name
Customers table	tblCustomers
Customers form	frmCustomers
Orders form	frmOrders
Orders Subform form	sfrOrders
Customers macro	mcrCustomers
CustomerID combo box	cboCustomerID
PrintInvoice command button	cmdPrintInvoice

NOTE See *Access 2002 Desktop Developer's Handbook* by Paul Litwin, Ken Getz, and Mike Gunderloy (Sybex, 2001) for a complete list of commonly used tags.

Names in VBA Programming

A significant feature in VBA programming is its ability to deal with variable information. Suppose you want to keep a count of the number of times you run an operation. To keep track, you define a Counter variable to store the number representing how many times you run the operation and to increase the count by one each time you run the operation. In VBA programming, you define, or *declare*, a variable using a declaration statement in a module. When you declare a variable, VBA sets aside a location in memory to hold the current value. By definition, a *variable* is a temporary storage location in memory that you name and use to hold a value or refer to an object. Here are some common prefixes for VBA variable data types:

Variable Type	Prefix
Array	a
Yes/No (Boolean)	bool
Currency	cur
Date/Time	date
Double	dbl
Integer	int
Long	lng
Memo	mem
OLE	ole

Continued on next page

Variable Type	Prefix
Single	sng
Text (string)	str
Variant	var
Object	obj

Chapter 8, "Using Variables," deals with VBA variables and explains storing different types of data, limiting which procedures can "see" a variable (called the variable's *scope*), and limiting the variable's lifetime. For now, note that the following prefixes are commonly used for VBA variable scope and lifetime:

- A local variable, procedure-level lifetime has no prefix.
- A local variable, object-level lifetime (static variable) has the prefix s.
- A private (module) variable, object-level lifetime has the prefix m.
- A public (global) variable, object-level lifetime has the prefix g.

You can also define variables to refer to objects such as forms, reports, or controls. These special variables are called *object variables*. The following are some common tags for VBA object variables:

Object Type	Tag
Application	app
Control	ctl
Controls	ctls
Form	frm
Report	rpt

In VBA programming, you can work directly with the SQL database engine using its own data access objects. The following are some common tags for ADO objects:

Object Type	Tag
Command	cmd
Connection	cnn
Error	err
Errors	errs

Continued on next page

Object Type	Tag
Field	fld
Fields	flds
Parameter	prm
Parameters	prms
Properties	prps
Property	prp
Recordset	rst

In addition to the ADO objects, you can use objects from the ADOX library to control design and security elements of the database. Common tags for some ADOX objects are as follows:

Object Type	Tag
Column	clm
Index	idx
Procedure	prc
Table	tbl
View	vw

What the User Sees

When you create a custom database application using the techniques in this book, the users see only forms, pages, and reports. Users see the form, page, or report caption in the window's title bar, not the coded name you use when you create the application. Make the captions informative, include spaces as appropriate, and avoid using jargon. Here are some examples:

Object Name	Caption
rptMailLabelCust	Mailing Labels: Customers
cboCustomerID	Lookup Customer
frmCustomers	Customers

Name Changes

With older versions of Access, there was no way to propagate name changes. Whenever you wanted to change the name of a table, field, control, form, query, and so on, you needed to go through all of your tables, queries, forms, reports, data access pages, macros, and modules and make all of the changes manually. One of the new features of Access 2000 was Name AutoCorrect. While Name AutoCorrect can't fix all of the problems associated with renaming objects, it certainly makes renaming easier. As long as Name AutoCorrect is on, it can correct problems that occur when you rename forms, reports, tables, queries, or controls on forms and reports. When you open or change an object in Microsoft Access, and you have Name AutoCorrect enabled, Name AutoCorrect looks for all objects that the object you open depends on to see if any discrepancies exist in the names of the relative objects. For example, if your database contains a form with fields bound to a table, and you change the names of fields in the table, Access will perpetuate those name changes to the form. If you make object name changes with Name AutoCorrect turned off, you will need to manually make the changes Name AutoCorrect would normally make for you.

Name AutoCorrect cannot fix several things, including the following:

Projects Name AutoCorrect only works with Access databases, not with projects.

SQL code Access can't make changes in an invalid SQL statement.

VB Name AutoCorrect cannot correct references in Visual Basic. For VBA modules, the job is made easier with a replace command.

Linked tables Changes made to the names of fields in linked tables will not be propagated by Access.

Replicated databases If you replicate a database, Access turns Name AutoCorrect off. You can't turn it on in a replicated database.

Toolbar and menu macros Macros used for toolbar and menu objects cannot be fixed with Name AutoCorrect.

Name AutoCorrect is a very simple tool to use. To activate it, click Tools ➤ Options and select the General tab. You will see three options under Name AutoCorrect:

Track Name AutoCorrect Info Allows Access to maintain the information it needs to make changes. Use this option alone if you want Access to store information about name changes but not make any corrections to object references.

Perform Name AutoCorrect Use this option along with the previous option to have Access propagate changes to object references as objects are renamed.

Log Name AutoCorrect Changes Not needed for Access to run Name AutoCorrect, but may be useful. Select this option to have Access create a Name AutoCorrect Log table to save a log of changes. Each change is shown as an individual record.

In light of the limitations of name-changing tools, a basic Access guideline is "Don't make any name changes!" However, even with careful planning, you may need to change names. For example, when you use the Combo Box Wizard to create a lookup combo box, you don't have the opportunity to name the control; the wizard uses the default name Combo*n*, where *n* is a number. Because the default name doesn't identify the purpose of the object, it is preferable to change the name to one that follows a naming standard and includes information about both the object's type and its purpose.

Describing an Object's Properties

Objects have properties that describe their characteristics. In a sense, an object is the sum of its properties. At any instant, each form, control, field, relation, and so on is uniquely defined by the current values of its properties. The set of current values is stored in memory as the object's *state*.

Objects have two kinds of properties that you can set:

- Design-time properties are properties you can set when you are working in Design view. They are listed in the object's property sheet.

- Run-time properties are properties you can set or read only at run time. They are not listed in the object's property sheet.

NOTE In this book, we'll use the terms *design time* to refer to the time when you are working in the Design view of an object; the term *run mode* to refer to the time when you are viewing an object in Datasheet view, Form view, Page view, or Print Preview; and the term *run time* to refer to when you are running a VBA procedure.

Design-Time Properties

Each Database window object has one or more property sheets listing the properties that you can set at design time. For example, Figure 2.1 shows the Field, Table, and Index property sheets available when you create a table.

You set the design-time properties for a field in a table by selecting the field in the upper pane of the Design window and entering property values in the lower pane. A field's design-time properties fall into two tabbed categories: General and Lookup.

FIGURE 2.1:

Field, Table, and Index property sheets in table Design view

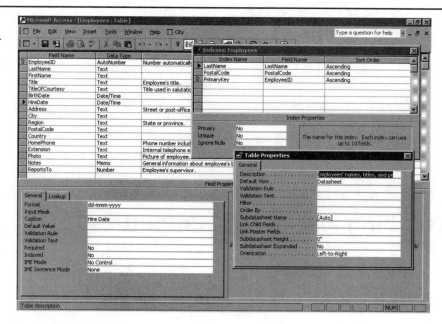

General properties include data properties such as FieldSize, format properties such as InputMask, and data-validation properties such as ValidationRule and Required. You can use the Lookup tab to specify properties for a lookup field. A lookup field makes data entry easier by displaying a list of values in a combo box or list box when you click the field in Datasheet view or click a form control bound to the lookup field. The Lookup properties include data properties such as RowSource and control design properties such as ListRows.

In addition to setting design-time properties using the property sheets, you can change the settings at run time when a VBA procedure is running. Usually, when you change one of these settings at run time, the change is in effect only during run time. For example, you can use a VBA procedure to change the Caption property of a form, but when you open the form in design time, you can observe that the stored value of the Caption property has not changed.

You can specify the way data is displayed in controls on a form or report by using Conditional Formatting, shown in Figure 2.2. With the form or report in Design view and the control selected, click Format ➢ Conditional Formatting. Access assigns a default formatting style for the control. To change it, simply enter the information in the Condition 1 section. With Conditional Formatting, you can set multiple criteria for the data entered in that control. For example, you can specify in Condition 1 that if an employee's hire date is earlier than 02/01/01, it will be highlighted in yellow, and in Condition 2 that if the hire date is later than 02/02/01, it will be highlighted in green. You use the Enabled button to toggle a condition to active and inactive states.

FIGURE 2.2:

The Conditional Formatting window

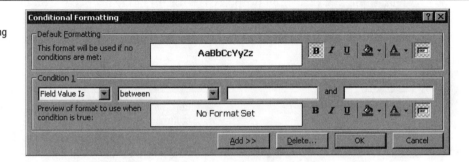

Run-Time Properties in VBA Programming

In addition to the design-time properties listed in their property sheets, most objects have run-time properties that you can set or read only when a VBA procedure is running. Run-time properties are not listed in an object's property sheet. Here are a few examples:

Property	Applies To	Description
Value	Controls	Determines or specifies the text contained in a text box control or the text box portion of a combo box control. The Value property can also determine or specify whether a control is selected or which value or option within the control is selected.
Painting	Forms and reports	Specifies whether a form or report is repainted. (`Repaint` completes any pending screen updates and redraws the screen.)
Text	Text box and combo box controls	Sets or returns the text in a text box control or the text box portion of a combo box control.
Bookmark	Forms	Sets or returns a bookmark that uniquely identifies a particular record in the form's underlying recordset.
Selected	List boxes	Selects an item or determines if an item is selected in a list box.

Earlier in the chapter, you learned that the data access objects that you use to work directly with the database engine are available only in VBA procedures. No Design windows or property sheets exist for these objects. You set, read, and change their properties by writing statements in VBA procedures.

Read-Only Properties

Some objects have *read-only* properties, which are properties that you can't set or change. An example of a read-only property is a form's Dirty property. You use the Dirty property to determine if the current record has been modified since it was last saved. Read-only properties are not listed in an object's property sheet. Here are a few more examples of read-only properties:

Property	Applies To	Description
Form	Forms	Refers to the form itself or to the form associated with a subform control.
ActiveControl	Forms, Reports, Screen	Refers to the control that has the focus.
Count	Open forms, pages, and reports	Determines the number of open forms, open reports, or controls on an open form or report.
CurrentObjectName	Application	Determines the name of the active database object.
CurrentRecord	Forms and reports	Identifies the current record being viewed in a form or report.
HasData	Reports	Determines if a report is bound to an empty recordset.

Other Property Sheets

The Database/Project window objects and the objects they contain have property sheets where you can set their design-time properties as described in the previous section. Access also provides property sheets in the form of dialogs for setting properties of the database you are currently working with, for setting options of the Access environment itself, and for setting security permissions. The following sections describe the dialogs you can use to set these properties and options. In most cases, you can also set them in VBA procedures.

Startup Properties

Most of the startup properties are in the Startup dialog, which is displayed when you choose Tools ➤ Startup. As explained in Chapter 1, "Automating a Database without Programming," when you set startup options in the Startup dialog, you are setting properties of the database itself (see the "Setting Startup Properties" section in Chapter 1). While it is easiest to set startup properties in the Startup dialog, you can also set them using VBA, as explained in later chapters.

NOTE   An important startup property that is not displayed in the Startup dialog is the Allow BypassKey property. This property enables and disables the Shift key used to bypass startup property settings, as explained in Chapter 14, "Creating and Modifying Database Objects Using Access VBA."

Database Properties

You set administrative properties for a database in the Database Properties dialog. To display this dialog, choose File ➢ Database Properties or right-click the Database window title bar and select Database Properties from the shortcut menu. The administrative properties of the database are actually properties of several Document objects managed by the database engine. There are five tabbed categories of administrative information:

- The General tab displays the same information that is displayed when you right-click the database's filename in the Windows Explorer and choose the Properties command. This information is read-only.

- The Summary tab (see Figure 2.3a) displays text boxes in which you can enter summary information that allows you to identify and locate a database more easily.

- The Statistics tab displays read-only administrative information about the date and time the current database was created and the date and time the database was last modified, accessed, and printed. May also contain additional information about who last edited the database, the total editing time, and the revision number.

- The Contents tab displays a list of names of the Database window objects contained in the database (also read-only).

- The Custom tab (see Figure 2.3b) provides the opportunity for you to create custom database properties.

Although it is easiest to set the Summary properties and create the Custom properties in the Database Properties dialog, you'll also learn how to set or create them using VBA.

Environmental Options

You can shorten development time by customizing your Access working environment. You set Access environmental options in the Options dialog (see Figure 2.4), displayed by clicking Tools ➢ Options. There are 11 tabbed categories with options you can set.

FIGURE 2.3:

The Summary tab (a) and
the Custom tab (b) of the
Database Properties dialog
display properties that you
can change.

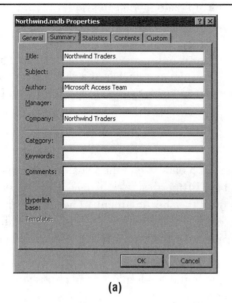

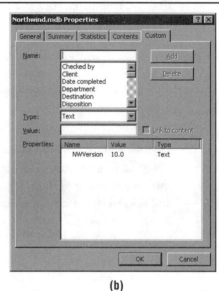

(a)

(b)

FIGURE 2.4:

Use the Options dialog to
set environmental options.

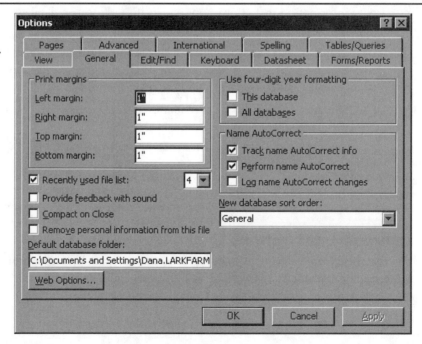

In addition to general options, such as whether items in the Database window are opened by being clicked or double-clicked, you can set options for some of the Access objects. For instance, you can change the default field sizes for various data types used in creating Access tables.

Security Properties

You secure an application to protect its data and the application itself. You protect the application's structure (its tables, queries, forms, data access pages, and reports) and the programming (macros and modules) from inadvertent changes that could break the application. Security in Access databases is the responsibility of the Jet database engine. Jet has two security models: database password security and workgroup security. Security in Access projects is the responsibility of the Microsoft SQL Server 2000 Desktop Engine, and utilizes only workgroup security.

There are two parts to the workgroup security model: users and permissions. Users have usernames and passwords to identify themselves to the database engine as valid users. Each Database window object has a set of permissions, such as ReadData and ModifyDesign. In the workgroup security model, you assign a set of permissions for each object in the database to each user or to each group of users. The two kinds of security information are stored in different locations. The permissions information is stored with the individual database. In a database, the users information is stored in the workgroup information file. The Setup program for Access installs a default workgroup information file named System.mdw, but you can create a new workgroup information file for each workgroup. (An Access *workgroup* is a group of users who share data in a multiuser environment.) In a project, the users information is stored either in the SQL server system tables or in the operating system.

> **TIP** For more information on Access SQL Server security, see *Access 2002 Desktop Developer's Handbook* by Paul Litwin, Ken Getz, and Mike Gunderloy (Sybex, 2001).

When working with a database, you can store information about users, groups, and their passwords in the User And Group Accounts dialog (see Figure 2.5). To open this dialog, choose Tools ➢ Security ➢ User and Group Accounts. When you use this dialog, you are creating data access objects called the User and Group objects.

You can specify permissions for each database object in your database in the User And Group Permissions dialog (see Figure 2.6). To access this dialog, choose Tools ➢ Security ➢ User and Group Permissions.

Each Database window object that you create has a corresponding data access object called a Document object. Jet uses the Document object to keep track of any permissions

FIGURE 2.5:

The User And Group Accounts dialog creates users, groups, and their passwords.

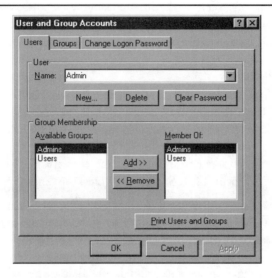

FIGURE 2.6

Use the User And Group Permissions dialog to assign permissions for each object to users and groups.

you have set in the User And Group Permissions dialog, as well as to keep track of other administrative information, such as when you created the object and who created it. Each category of Database window objects, such as forms or macros, has a corresponding data access object called a Container object. Jet uses the Container object to keep track of permissions you have set, as well as to keep track of administrative information for the category such as its name. (As a special case, two categories of Database window objects, tables and queries, have a single Container object named Tables.) The permissions you set are properties of the Document and Container data access objects.

Manipulating Objects

When you start up an Access database, the database's objects just sit waiting for you to do something. When you take some action by clicking a mouse button, entering keystrokes, or choosing a menu command, your computer executes programs that manipulate objects. In essence, there are two kinds of programs: the built-in programs that are part of Access and the programs you write yourself. In either case, programs are instructions passed to the computer to do something to your objects or to Access. The built-in programs include programs that run when you choose a built-in menu command or toolbar button; these are the internal programs that make Access work. The programs that you write yourself are the ones that run when you choose a custom menu or toolbar button, click a custom command button, or open a form.

The purpose of programs is to manipulate objects. Programs open and close forms, run queries to select or modify groups of records, print reports, and save changes in data to the database file. Programs start up and close a database, and programs set startup conditions and quit Access.

Another way to separate programs is by where they are stored:

- Programs that are stored as internal components of the objects are called *methods*. You can ask an object to run one of its methods. Objects have built-in methods, and you can also create your own custom methods.

- Programs that are stored as external components separate from the objects are called *macros* and *procedures*. You ask Access to run a macro or a procedure to take actions on an object.

NOTE The procedures that you store in a form's or report's module don't fall neatly into one of these categories. The procedures in a form or report module that you designate as *private* can be considered as methods of the form or report; other procedures that you designate as *public* can be considered as external components (even though they are stored with the form or report). See Chapter 7, "Writing Procedures," for more information about procedures.

When you work interactively with Access or when you use macro programming to automate a database, you don't work directly with the data access objects. However, you can write VBA programs to control the objects that the database engine manages.

The Lifetime of Objects

An object exists for a time interval called its *lifetime*. When you create a Database window object and save your work, the object is saved to either an MDB or ADP file; this means that the Database window objects are permanent, or *persistent*, objects. A Database window object's lifetime begins when you first create it and ends when you delete it from the MDB or ADP file.

NOTE   Access databases have a file type of MDB. Projects have a file type of ADP.

By contrast, the objects managed by the database engine are all temporary, or *nonpersistent*, objects and are not saved in the database file. Some temporary objects are created automatically each time the database file is opened; you create other temporary objects in VBA procedures. Temporary objects exist only in memory. The lifetime of a temporary object may be as long as the database is open or may be a shorter time interval. For example, you can create a Recordset object in a VBA procedure; the object you create lives in memory until you set its value to Nothing or close the database. When the VBA procedure terminates, the Recordset object ceases to exist.

Using Macros

In macro programming, you manipulate objects using individual instructions called *macro actions*. There are more than 50 macro actions in Access. The macro actions have been individually optimized for performance. Many of the macro actions are equivalent to menu commands, others mimic manual user interactions, and others provide capabilities not available in the user interface.

Most of the macro actions are used to manipulate the Database window objects and the objects they contain, such as fields, sections, and controls. You use these macro actions to manipulate the objects; for example, macro actions open, close, move, import, export, and delete objects. You use one of the macro actions, the SetValue macro action, to change the values of an object's properties. You also use the SetValue action to change the values of fields and controls. Figure 2.7 depicts the way that you use macro actions to manipulate objects.

FIGURE 2.7:

Manipulating an object using a macro action. The macro action is stored separately from the object.

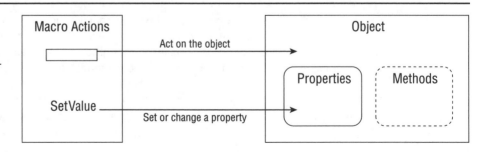

There is no way to create your own custom macro actions. To run more than one macro action at a time, you create a macro. A *macro* is a list of macro actions that runs as a unit.

One reason macro programming is easy to learn is that the instructions you create using macro actions simulate the instructions you give when you work interactively. In fact, the best way to get started writing macros is to work through the interactive steps of an operation and then translate each step into a macro action. When you work interactively, one of the steps you must take is to select the object before you can perform any action on it. You select an open window by clicking it, you select a control by tabbing to it or clicking it, you select a record by clicking its record selector or by choosing one of the Go To commands in the Edit menu, and so on. Macro programming is *selection-centric* because a macro must establish which object is selected. In macro programming, there are two ways to identify the selected object. One of these two ways must take place before any action can be performed on the object:

- You can use a macro action, such as OpenForm, SelectObject, and GoToControl, that selects an object.

- If the object has already been selected, you can use object properties, such as ActiveForm and ActiveControl, that refer to the active object properties.

When you use a macro to manipulate an object, there is no way to ask the object to run one of its methods. When you use only macro programming, methods simply are not part of the programming environment. Figure 2.7 shows the methods in a dotted rectangle inside the object to indicate that the methods exist but are not available.

Object selection involves some understanding of an object's focus. An object has the *focus* when it has the ability to receive the result of your mouse or keyboard action. Only one control at a time can have focus. The control that has the focus is called the *active control*. When a control has the focus, there is usually some visible indication. For example, the command button that has the focus is enclosed in a dotted rectangle. Some controls, such as labels, lines, rectangles, images, and page breaks, cannot receive the focus. Controls that are capable of receiving the focus have both an Enabled and a Visible property; you must set both of these properties to allow a particular control to receive the focus.

When you click a form, it becomes the active form, and the color of its title bar changes to indicate the form's active status. The first control in the form's tab order that can receive the focus becomes the active control. If the form doesn't contain any controls that can receive the focus, the form itself receives the focus.

NOTE   For more information about macros, see *Mastering Access 2002 Premium Edition* by Alan Simpson and Celeste Robinson (Sybex, 2001).

Using VBA Procedures

In Access VBA programming, there are basically two ways to manipulate objects. The first way to take action on the object you want to manipulate is by running a program that is external to the object. In Access VBA, the external programs are defined as methods of a special Access VBA object called the DoCmd object. The DoCmd methods are analogous to running a macro action in macro programming. Figure 2.8 depicts using DoCmd methods to manipulate an object.

FIGURE 2.8:

Using a DoCmd method to manipulate an object in VBA is analogous to using a macro action in macro programming.

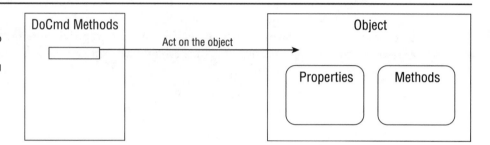

Access VBA provides a second way to manipulate an object, referred to as the *object-enabled approach*, that lets you work directly with the object and its internal programs. You can use an assignment statement to set or change a property of an object, or you can ask the object to run its own methods. The methods are a set of more than 100 predetermined actions built into Access as internal components of objects. In VBA programming, your view of an object includes both the set of its properties that define what the object *is* and the set of its methods that define what the object can *do* to itself. Figure 2.9 depicts the object-enabled approach to manipulating an object.

FIGURE 2.9:

You can manipulate an object directly in VBA by changing one of its properties with an assignment statement or by running one of its methods.

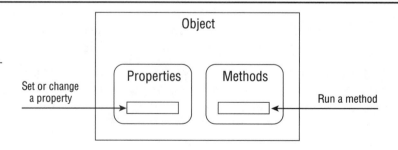

You can write VBA procedures that are selection-centric. Selection-centric procedures must either select the object or recognize that the object is the active object. The selection can be established using various methods and properties:

- Methods of the DoCmd object—such as OpenForm, SelectObject, or GoToControl—and the SetFocus method of the control or form you want to select

- Object properties such as ActiveForm or ActiveControl when the object has already been selected

- The Me object when you want to refer to the form or report in which the procedure is running

You can also write VBA procedures that manipulate objects directly without first selecting them. It is more difficult to learn how to write such *object-centric* procedures because they don't mimic the familiar interactive steps; however, your time and effort are rewarded by procedures that run faster because Access doesn't need to take the time to select the object. In later chapters, you'll work with examples of both selection-centric and object-centric programming techniques.

Access Events

The state of an object is the sum of its characteristics at an instant. An object's state is recorded in memory. When any of the characteristics changes, the state changes. Some of the changes in an object's state are opportunities for you to interrupt the processing that normally follows the change; these changes in state are called events. When you open a form, you change the form's state from unopened to opened; this change in state is defined as an event for the form, called the Open event.

NOTE   Not all changes in state are events. If you change the color of a form's background, you change the form's state, but this change in state is not defined as an event. You cannot create custom events.

For each event defined for a form, form control, or report, a corresponding event property exists. An object's event properties are listed in the Event category in the object's property sheet. For example, Figure 2.10 shows the event properties of a form.

FIGURE 2.10:

The event properties
for a form

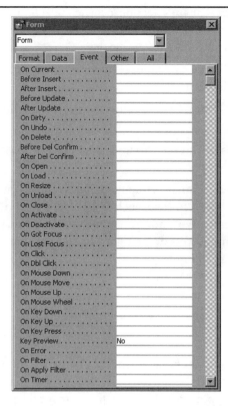

The Access Programming Model

The Access programming model is an event-driven programming model. You create a VBA procedure that you want Access to run when an object recognizes an event, and you assign the program to the object's event property. When the event occurs, it *triggers* the program, which means that Access runs the assigned VBA procedure. The program that is executed when an event occurs is called an *event procedure*.

NOTE   In VBA, there are two kinds of procedures: function procedures and sub procedures. A sub procedure used as an event handler is commonly referred to as an event procedure; a function procedure used as an event handler is an event function procedure.

When you assign a program to an event property, you are *trapping* the event. When you set an event trap by assigning a program to an event property, you interrupt the default processing that

Access would normally carry out following the occurrence of the event. After the program is executed, Access returns to normal processing. For example, you can trap the AfterUpdate event of a lookup combo box by assigning a program for Access to find the record corresponding to the value in the combo box before continuing its normal processing, which, in this case, is to stop and wait for your next action. For some events, your program not only interrupts the default processing that would normally follow the event, but it can also terminate the default processing.

Access defines events for forms and reports, for sections on forms and reports, and for controls on forms. No events are defined for tables and queries, and no events are defined for data access pages.

NOTE Seventy events are defined in Access. Two tables on the CD that accompanies this book (under Tables\Chapter2.pdf) show different ways to organize events. One way to organize events is according to what caused the event (see the "Access Events Grouped by Cause" table). Because an event is a special change in the state of an object, you can also organize events according to object (see the "Access Events Recognized by Forms, Reports, and Controls" table).

Sequences of Events

When a user, a VBA procedure, or the computer does something, typically a sequence of events is recognized by one or more objects. Let's look at some examples.

Clicking a Mouse Button

When you click the left mouse button while the mouse pointer is over a control, the control recognizes a sequence of three events:

- MouseDown when you press a mouse button
- MouseUp when you release a mouse button
- Click after you press and release the left mouse button

The control recognizes the MouseDown and MouseUp events regardless of which mouse button you clicked; however, the control recognizes the Click event only if you click the left mouse button.

Clicking a Command Button

When the control can receive the focus, additional events are recognized. For example, the simple click of the left mouse button when the mouse pointer is over a command button triggers a sequence of five events recognized by the command button:

- Enter before the command button actually receives the focus from another control on the same form, or is the first control on the form to receive the focus when the form first opens

- GotFocus after the command receives the focus
- MouseDown when you press a mouse button
- MouseUp when you release a mouse button
- Click when you press and then release the left mouse button

A similar sequence of events is recognized by other controls such as text boxes, option buttons, list boxes, and check boxes.

Changing Text in a Text Box or Combo Box

You can change text in a text box or in the text box part of a combo box by pressing a key. Not all keystrokes result in sending characters; for example, pressing the Tab or Enter key does not result in sending a character. Windows uses the ANSI character set to relate the keys on the keyboard to characters displayed on the screen. Pressing an ANSI character set key results in sending a character to the text box. If the keystroke changes the text, the text box recognizes the sequence of five events:

- KeyDown when you press any key
- KeyPress when you press a key that sends an ANSI character
- Dirty when the data in a text box or the text portion of a combo box is changed for the first time
- Change when Access recognizes that the contents of a text box or text box portion of a combo box have changed
- KeyUp when you release any key

If the keystroke doesn't change the text, the Change event doesn't occur. If you do change the text and then try to update the control by pressing Enter or by moving to another control or record, what happens next depends on whether the control is a text box or a combo box.

Text Box Events When your keystroke has changed the text in a text box and you take some action to update the control by moving to another control on the form, the text box recognizes two additional events:

- BeforeUpdate when Access recognizes the changed value of the text box and just before updating the changed data to the record buffer
- AfterUpdate when Access recognizes the changed value of the text box and just after updating the changed data to the record buffer

Combo Box Events When you change the text in the text box part of a combo box by sending keystrokes and then try to update the control by pressing Enter or by moving to another control or record, Access compares the value to the values in the combo box list. If the value is not on the list, the combo box recognizes the NotInList event. What happens next depends on the setting of the LimitToList property:

- If the LimitToList property is set to Yes, Access cannot accept the change, and the combo box recognizes the Error event. The full sequence is as follows:

  KeyDown ➤ KeyPress ➤ Dirty ➤ Change ➤ KeyUp ➤ NotInList ➤ Error

- If the LimitToList property is set to No, Access updates the combo box control. The sequence of events recognized by the combo box is as follows:

  KeyDown ➤ KeyPress ➤ Dirty ➤ Change ➤ KeyUp ➤ NotInList ➤ BeforeUpdate ➤ AfterUpdate

If you make changes to a text box and then undo the changes by either clicking the Undo Field/Record button on the command bar, clicking the Undo button, or pressing the Escape key, the Undo event occurs. The sequence is as follows:

Key Down ➤ KeyPress ➤ Dirty ➤ Change ➤ KeyUp ➤ Undo

The Undo event does not occur if you press Ctrl+Z to undo a change or if you undo changes to an unbound control.

You can also send keystrokes programmatically using the SendKeys macro action or the SendKeys VBA statement. Sending keystrokes programmatically triggers the same sequence of events as if you had pressed the keys.

Changing the Value of an Option Group

When you change the value of an option group by clicking an option button, a toggle button, or a check box that is in the option group, the option group recognizes the following sequence:

- BeforeUpdate when Access recognizes the changed value of the option group and just before updating the changed data to the record buffer

- AfterUpdate when Access recognizes the changed value of the option group and just after updating the changed data to the record buffer

- Click immediately after the AfterUpdate event

The Update Process

Access uses a two-buffer system to track changes in data:

- When a record is first displayed, Access places a copy of the data contained in its controls into a temporary storage location called a *record buffer*.

- When you type a character into a control, Access places a copy of the data you typed into another temporary storage location called a *control buffer*.

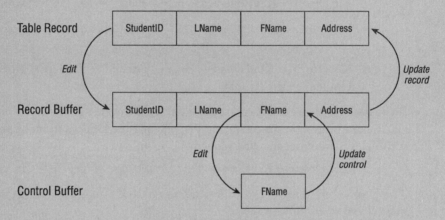

When you try to move out of the control, Access compares the data in the two buffers to determine if you have made any changes. If you have made a change, the following sequence occurs:

- The control recognizes the BeforeUpdate event.

- Access *updates the control* by copying the changed data from the control buffer to the record buffer.

- The control recognizes the AfterUpdate event. If you haven't changed the data in the control, the control update process doesn't occur.

When you attempt to save the record, Access compares the data in the record buffer with the data stored in the table. If you have made changes to at least one control, the following sequence occurs:

- The form recognizes the BeforeUpdate event.

- Access *updates the record* by copying the changed data from the record buffer to the table fields.

- The form recognizes the AfterUpdate event. If you haven't changed the data, the record update process doesn't occur.

Tabbing from One Control to Another Control

When you tab out of one control into a second control on the same form without making any changes, the two controls recognize the following sequence of events:

- The first control recognizes the Exit event when you leave the control but before it loses the focus.

- The first control recognizes the LostFocus event after the control loses the focus.

- The second control recognizes the Enter event when you go to the control but before it receives the focus.

- The second control recognizes the GotFocus event when the control receives the focus.

If you changed the data in the first control before tabbing out, then the first control recognizes the following two events before the sequence listed:

- The first control recognizes the BeforeUpdate event before the changed data is updated to the record buffer.

- The first control recognizes the AfterUpdate event after the changed data is updated to the record buffer.

Opening a Form

When you open a form, the form recognizes the following sequence of events:

- Open when you first open the form but before the first record is displayed

- Load after the records are loaded from memory and are displayed

- Resize when the form is first displayed

- Activate when the form receives the focus and becomes the active window (except this event is not recognized if the form receives the focus from another form whose PopUp property is set to Yes or from a window in another application)

- GotFocus when the form has received the focus, but only if all controls on the form are disabled or hidden

- Current before the first record becomes the current record

When the form has at least one control that is visible and is enabled, the form doesn't recognize the GotFocus event. Instead, the first visible, enabled control recognizes the following sequence immediately after the form's event sequence:

- Enter just before the control receives the focus

- GotFocus when the control receives the focus

Timing Is Everything

In the event-driven programming model, you must decide the correct event to trigger a program. When a sequence of events is recognized by one or more objects, you need to select an event that is appropriate for your program. Sometimes, you have a choice and selecting any of several events will cause the action to be carried out as you intended. More often, only one event gives the result you want, and your task as the programmer is to determine that single correct event. A good place to start is to search in online help for the topic "Order of events for database objects."

NOTE   Seven tables on the CD that accompanies this book (under Tables\Chapter2.pdf) show the events for controls on forms ("Focus and Data Events for Controls on Forms" and "Mouse and Keyboard Events for Controls on Forms"), for forms and form sections ("Window and Focus Events for Forms," "Data and Filter Events for Forms," and "Error and Timer Events for Forms"), and for reports and report sections ("Events for Reports" and "Print Events for Report Sections").

Events for Controls on Forms   A control on a form recognizes events when the control gains or loses the focus and when you change the data and the control is updated.

Events for Forms and Form Sections   A form recognizes window and focus events when you open, close, or resize the form or when the form gains or loses the focus. A form recognizes events when a record gains or loses the focus, when you change the data and the record is updated, when you create a new record or delete an existing record, when you leave a record, and when you apply or remove a filter. A form recognizes an event when Access detects an error in the interface or the database engine and the form has the focus. Finally, a form recognizes an event when a specified time interval has elapsed.

Events for Reports and Report Sections   A report recognizes events when you open or close the report, when the report gains or loses the focus, or when Access detects an error and the report has the focus. Additionally, report sections recognize events related to formatting and printing.

Canceling Default Behavior

After an object recognizes an event, Access carries out the default behavior. Sometimes, the default behavior is to stop and wait for the next user action. For example, when a command button recognizes the Click event, Access looks to see if you have written VBA code for the OnClick event property. If you have, then Access runs the VBA code; if you haven't, Access stops and waits for your next action. Other times, Access goes through a series of default operations either before or after running the VBA code assigned to the event. For example, when you change the data in a control and then tab to the next control, the changed control recognizes the BeforeUpdate event. In response, the following default behavior occurs:

- Access updates the control to the record buffer.
- The changed control recognizes the AfterUpdate event.
- The changed control recognizes the Exit event.
- The changed control recognizes the LostFocus event.
- The next control recognizes the Enter event.
- The next control recognizes the GotFocus event.

For some events, including the BeforeUpdate event, Access runs the assigned VBA procedure before the default behavior takes place. For these events, you can include a step in the procedure to cancel the subsequent default behavior. The events with default behavior that can be canceled are listed in Table 2.1. For the events not listed in the table, Access runs the VBA procedure *after* carrying out the default behavior so the default behavior can't be canceled.

TABLE 2.1: Events for Which You Can Cancel Subsequent Default Behavior

Event	Result of Canceling Default Behavior
ApplyFilter	Cancels applying the filter.
BeforeDelConfirm	Cancels the display of the delete confirm dialog box and cancels the deletion of the records. Note that the AfterDelConfirm event still occurs.
BeforeInsert	Cancels the insertion of a new record. You can't cancel the behavior following the AfterInsert event.
BeforeRender	Cancels the rendering of a PivotChart view.
BeforeUpdate	Cancels the updating of the control or the record. You can't cancel the behavior following the AfterUpdate event.
CommandBeforeExecute	Cancels the specified command.
DblClick	When you double-click a command button, the following events occur: Click, DblClick, Click. You can cancel the second Click.
Delete	Cancels the deletion of the record.
Dirty	Rolls back the changes to the current record.
Exit	Cancels the exit from the control. You can't cancel the Enter event.
Filter	Cancels the opening of the filter window.
Format	Cancels formatting the section.

Continued on next page

TABLE 2.1 CONTINUED: Events For Which You Can Cancel Subsequent Default Behavior

Event	Result of Canceling Default Behavior
NoData	Cancels the printing of the report.
Open	Cancels the opening of the form or report. You can't cancel the behavior following the Close event.
Print	Cancels printing the section.
Undo	Cancels the Undo operation.
Unload	Cancels the unloading of the form. You can't cancel the behavior following the Load event.

Getting Hands-On Experience with Events

The examples of event sequences demonstrate how careful you must be in selecting an event to trigger your programs. Selecting the correct event becomes particularly delicate when you are working with interacting event sequences for two different objects, such as two forms. You don't have to be an event expert to get started with macro and VBA programming; but as your applications become more complex, you'll need to study the event model.

You can get hands-on experience and see events as they occur by working with the Event Logger application included on the book's CD. The Event Logger application was created by the authors of *Access 2002 Desktop Developer's Handbook* (Sybex, 2001). (The authors—Paul Litwin, Ken Getz, and Mike Gunderloy—have kindly given permission to include the Event Logger in this book.)

The application is an excellent way to understand the complex and subtle event sequences. You can use the application by itself as described below. Additionally, you can incorporate the application into your databases. The *Access 2002 Developer's Handbook* describes how to use the Event Logger application to view events in your own forms and explains the VBA procedures that make the application work.

1. Copy EventLogger.mdb to the VBAHandbook folder on your hard disk. Open the database and open frmLog in Form view (see Figure 2.11). This form logs events as they occur in the form's list box. After logging a group of events, you can clear the list box by clicking the Clear button. The events are grouped into eight types as shown on the next page. Check the event types you want to study and clear the check boxes for the other types.

FIGURE 2.11:

The Event Logger form

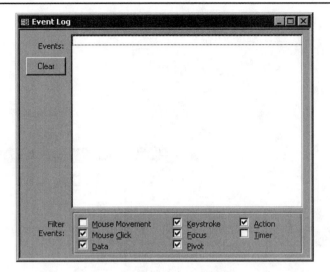

Event Type	Event
Mouse Movement	MouseMove
Mouse Click	Click, DblClick, MouseDown, MouseUp, MouseWheel
Data	AfterDelConfirm, AfterInsert, AfterUpdate, BeforeDelConfirm, Before Insert, BeforeUpdate, Change, Current, Delete, Dirty, Undo
Keystroke	KeyDown, KeyPress, KeyUp
Focus	Activate, Deactivate, Enter, Exit, GotFocus, LostFocus
Pivot	DataChange, ViewChange, BeforeQuery, CommandEnabled, Command-Checked
Action	Close, Error, Load, Open, Resize
Timer	Timer

2. Check the Mouse Click, Data, Focus, and Action check boxes.

3. Open the frmEventTest form in Form view. Figure 2.12a shows the Event Test Form as it appears when you first open the form. The form includes a variety of test controls for studying the events associated with a form, a subform, and form controls. Figure 2.12b lists all the events of the selected types that occurred when you opened the form with the first event at the top of the list. Notice that the subform opens, loads its records, resizes, and recognizes its current event and then the text box on the subform receives the focus. After the subform events occur, the main form recognizes its events as the form opens, loads its records, resizes, and recognizes the Activate, Current, Enter, and

FIGURE 2.12:

Opening the Event Test Form (a) triggers the set of events shown in the Event Log (b).

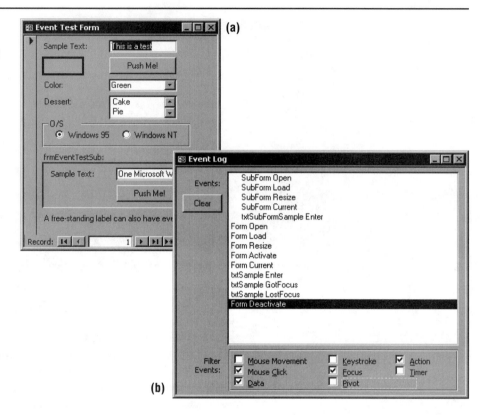

GotFocus events. Finally, the first control on the main form's tab order that can receive the focus, the txtSample text box, recognizes the Enter and GotFocus events.

4. Click the Clear button on the Event Log form and then click the main form's Push Me! command button. Figure 2.13 shows that the Event Test Form recognizes the Activate event and the focus moves first to the main form's text box. When you click the command button, the text box recognizes the Exit event followed by the LostFocus event. The command button recognizes the sequence of events shown in the figure.

5. Click the Clear button on the Event Log form and then click the subform's Push Me! command button. Figure 2.14 shows that the main form recognizes the Activate event, then the focus moves to the control that last had the focus, the Push Me! command button. The main form's Push Me! command button recognizes its loss of focus. The subform control recognizes the Enter event, the text box on the subform recognizes the Exit event, and then the Push Me! command button on the subform recognizes its sequence of events.

FIGURE 2.13:

Clearing the Event Log and then clicking the Push Me! button on the main form of the Event Test Form triggers events recognized by the form, the first control that can receive the focus, and then the command button.

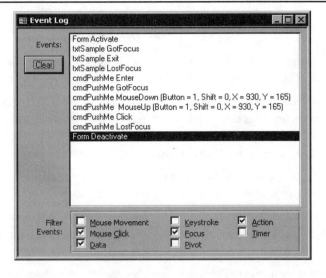

FIGURE 2.14:

Clearing the Event Log and then clicking the Push Me! button on the subform of the Event Test Form triggers events recognized by the main form and the last control that had the focus on the main form and then by the subform and controls on the subform.

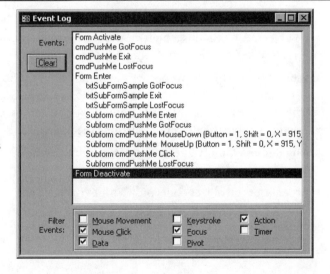

6. Explore the events recognized by the other controls on the Event Test Form. For example, click the Windows NT option button to observe the events recognized by the option buttons and the option group, click the down arrow for the combo box and select another item, edit the text in the text boxes in the main form and the subform, and so on.

Summary

This chapter has introduced the concept of objects. Here are the important points:

- Adopting a naming convention such as the Hungarian style makes your objects self-documenting by providing information on the object's type and purpose.

- Objects have properties that describe their characteristics. Most Access objects have design-time properties that you can set in property sheets. Access, the Microsoft SQL Server 2000 Desktop Engine, and Jet objects have run-time properties that you can set or read only when a procedure is running. Some run-time properties are read-only.

- While some properties are available in both macro and VBA programming, there are many properties that you can use only in VBA programming.

- The database itself has properties that you can set using dialog boxes available by choosing menu commands. You can set startup, general database information, and security properties.

- You can set environmental options. Settings are stored in a separate workgroup information database file.

- One important attribute of the VBA programming model is that it has access to the methods of an object. A method is a built-in program stored internally with the object that you can run to take an action on the object.

- The settings for all of an object's properties define its state at an instant. User, macro, procedure, or computer action can result in changing the state. Some changes in state are called events and are available as programming opportunities. Only form controls, forms, form sections, reports, and report sections recognize events.

- Typically, a single user action triggers a sequence of events. Selecting an appropriate event for a procedure is an important skill.

Now that you know about the object concept, it's time to learn about the specifics of the Access object model. The next chapter focuses on the objects and properties that are available in VBA programming.

CHAPTER 3

Introducing the Access Object Model

- Relating objects to each other

- Introducing the object hierarchies

- Understanding the Access Application object model

- Referring to objects and properties by name

- Using the Expression Builder to create references

When you automate a database operation, you create instructions that run when an object recognizes an event. You must understand which objects you can write instructions for, the events that an object recognizes, and how to write the instructions. The last chapter introduced you to the concept of an object as a thing you can use or change by running a VBA procedure. This chapter focuses on the specific objects—which objects are available, which properties can be changed, how the objects are related to each other, and how you identify an object when you write a program.

The Access object model is large and complex. The purpose of this chapter is to get you started with the model by introducing you to those objects and properties that are available in VBA programming.

Relating Objects to Each Other

You are familiar with the Database window objects of interactive Access: the tables, queries, forms, data access pages, and reports. We'll continue to use the word *object* informally and add a few more objects to our list: table fields, query fields, form controls, and report controls. When you work interactively with Access, you don't need to be concerned with how objects are related to each other; the Access user interface takes care of the relationships for you. However, to create programs that manipulate the objects, you need to understand how objects are related so you can use these relationships to refer to an object in a program.

Understanding groups of objects means understanding how they are tied together in relationships. Two kinds of relationships are obvious: some objects are *similar* to other objects, and some objects *contain* other objects.

Similar Objects

It is natural to group together objects with similar properties and behaviors. For example, it is natural to group the forms in a database, to group command buttons, or to group text boxes. A group of similar objects is called a *collection*.

Object Collections

In Access, most of the objects are in collections. For example, a database has a single collection of tables that contains all of the tables in the database; each table has a collection of fields that contains all of the fields you have defined for the table; a database has a single collection of open forms; and each open form has a collection of controls that contains all of the controls you have placed on the form. Access begins the name of each type of object with a capital letter, such as Form, Report, Control, and Field objects. Access names a collection by adding the letter *s* to the name of the object type in the collection; for example, the Controls collection of a specific form contains the Control objects placed on the form. Access treats the collection itself as an object; for example, a Controls collection is an object that contains the Control objects for a specific form or report.

Another example of collections involves the distinction between a form that is open and one that is closed. An open form is a Form object, and the collection of open forms is the Forms collection. By contrast, a closed form is not a Form object and is not a member of the Forms collection—a closed form is just a closed form. Figure 3.1 depicts the Forms collection for the Expenses application when the Switchboard and the Expense Reports By Employee forms are the only open forms.

FIGURE 3.1:

The Forms collection contains the open forms. Each open form has its own Controls collection containing the controls on the form.

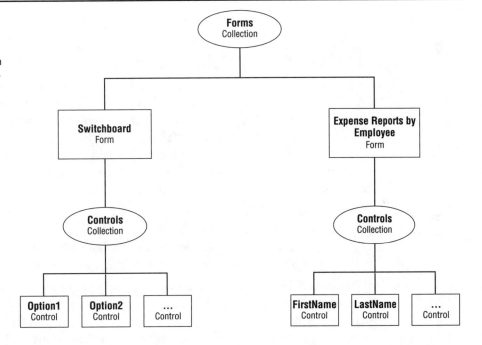

Objects that are not in collections are *singular objects*. For example, the object named Application represents the Access application; the object named Screen represents the form, report, or control that currently has the focus. Each of these is a singular object, because Access has only one Application object and the one Screen object, as only one object has the focus at a time. A collection object is also a singular object; for example, there is only one Forms collection object in the application, and each Form object in the collection has only one Controls collection. Whether an object is a singular object or is in a collection becomes important when you refer to the object.

Classes and Instances

Another way to look at groups of similar objects is to separate the definition of a group from the objects in the group. When you think of a group of objects with similar properties and behaviors, there are really two parts: the definition of the group, which is the class, and the objects themselves, which are the instances.

We use the word *class* to refer to the definition of a group: the class of forms or the class of text boxes, for example. A class is a blueprint for its objects. As a simple example, you can think of table Design view as representing the class of tables. When you create a specific table by defining table fields and setting table properties, you are creating an *instance* of the class.

As another example, the Text Box tool in the toolbox represents the text box class. When you use the Text Box tool to create a text box with a specific set of properties, you are creating an instance.

Objects Containing Other Objects

The second important relationship among objects is that of objects containing other objects. For example, a form contains its controls, and a table contains its fields. A table also contains its indexes, and each index contains its fields. In general, objects contain objects, which may contain other objects, and so on. The container relationship is a parent and child relationship; an object is the *parent* of the objects it contains, and an object is the *child* of the object that contains it. For example, a form is the parent of the controls it contains, and a control on a form is the form's child.

The different levels of container relationships can be shown as tiers in a hierarchy. For example, let's look at the hierarchy of container relationships for tables. In Access, a table object that you define in table Design view is called a Table object and is one of the data access objects managed by the database engine. A table contains four collections:

- A Table object in ADO has a Columns collection containing Column objects. Each Column object has a Properties collection containing a number of Property objects, such as field size, input mask, and default value. In the table's Design view, you will see Columns referred to as Fields, as shown in Figure 3.2a. Many of the Property objects appear as properties listed in the lower pane of Design view, but a Table object has other properties that are available only in code.

- If an index is set on an ADO table, the Table object has an Indexes collection, which contains Index objects. Each Index object in the collection has both a Properties collection, which contains Property objects, and a Columns collection, which contains Column objects. In turn, each of these Column objects has a Properties collection that contains Property objects for that column. In design view, the Indexes collection is represented by the Indexes dialog (see Figure 3.2b).

- A Table object in ADO has a Keys collection containing Key objects. There are three types of keys: foreign, unique, and primary. Foreign keys are those columns in a table that are related to rows in other tables. If a column in a table is assigned as a unique key, each record in the database must have a different entry for that column. Each table can have at most one primary key. Primary keys are the database's way of differentiating one record from another, so they must also be unique. In the Access interface, Key objects are represented within the Indexes dialog (primary keys have a key icon to the left; unique keys are displayed as indexes with the Unique property set to Yes). To see Foreign keys for a database, click Tools ➢ Relationships (see Figure 3.2c).

- An ADO Table object has a Properties collection containing Property objects, as listed in the Table Properties dialog (see Figure 3.2d).

FIGURE 3.2:

The Column objects (shown as Fields in Design view) for a table and the Property objects for a table field (a), the Property objects and the Column objects for a table index (b), foreign keys displayed as Relationships (c), and the Property objects for a table (d)

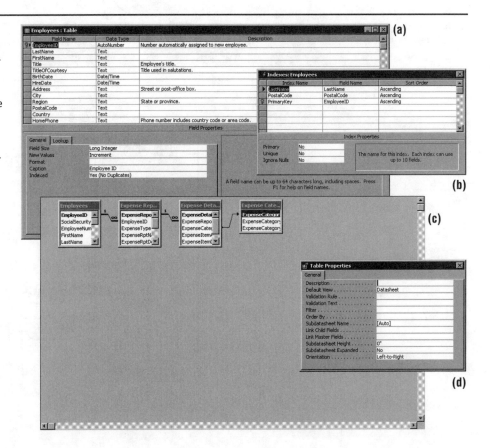

Figure 3.3 shows a partially expanded view of the Tables collection for the Expenses database. In this figure, the Employees table is expanded to show its four collections, which are expanded to show some of their members. In each case, one of the collection members is expanded to show its collections, which are expanded to show their members, and so on. The expanded views of container relationships quickly become large and overwhelming; the important concept here is the structure of the hierarchy.

You need to know the container relationships for all of the objects in Access, because when you write programs to manipulate the properties and behaviors of an object, you may need to refer to all of the objects that lie along a hierarchical path to the object.

FIGURE 3.3:

A partially expanded view of the Tables collection for the Expenses database

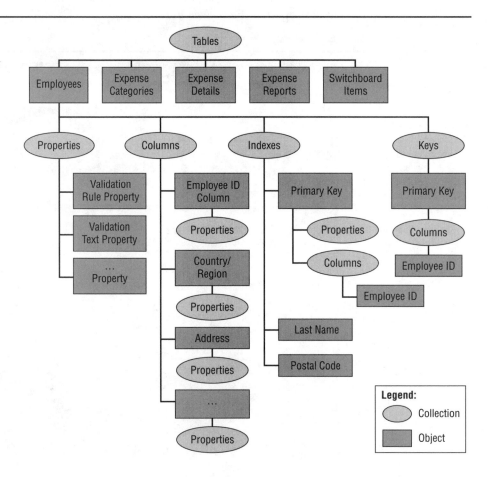

TIP   When working with ADOX library objects, you will encounter exceptions to the container relationships concept. Notably, some objects have properties that are not part of the Properties collection for those objects. For our purposes, we will refer to these properties as "intrinsic" properties, as they are part of the definition of the object. You will learn more about ADOX in Chapter 6, "Understanding the ADO Object Model."

Introducing the Architecture of Access

When you install Access, you actually install two major components: the Access Application layer and the Jet database engine. To work with Access projects on Microsoft SQL Server, you will also need to install the Microsoft SQL Server 2000 Desktop Engine.

The Application Layer

The Application layer consists of all the files necessary to control the user interface and all the files needed for writing and running VBA procedures. The Application layer contains the menu bars, toolbars, and windows for creating and viewing Database window objects.

When you create a database interactively, you work directly in the Application layer using the Design windows to create the individual tables, queries, forms, data access pages, and reports, as well as the macros and modules that fuse the objects into an application. Although you use the Application layer's interface to create all seven Database window objects, only data access pages, forms, reports, and modules are defined as Application objects. The tables and queries you create in the Access interface are data access objects.

When you create an Access project, you are essentially creating a client/server application that works with a database, such as Microsoft SQL Server. Instead of the Jet database engine, a project uses the Microsoft SQL Server 2000 Desktop Engine. Projects use 10 objects: tables, views, stored procedures, database diagrams, forms, reports, pages, data access pages, macros, and modules. A major difference between a project and a database is in the location of the actual data stored in tables. In a project, tables are stored on a server; in a database, tables are stored locally within Access itself. Once you connect to the server database, you can view, create, modify, and delete data, so working with an Access project is very similar to working with an Access database.

NOTE   You must install the MS SQL Server 2000 Desktop Engine using a different setup file. Insert the Access installation CD and double-click SETUP.EXE in the MSDE2000 folder to install the engine.

Beginning with Access 2000, new databases are created using the ADO data access object model. You were introduced to ADO in Chapter 2, "Getting Started with Objects and Events," and the concept will be explained in more depth in Chapter 6. For now, what's important to understand is that ADO uses OLE DB "interpreters" (technically known as "providers") to communicate with programs and databases. OLE DB providers exist for a wide range of database/application combinations. There is an Access-Jet OLE DB provider, which enables communication between Microsoft Access 2002 and the Jet database engine. There is also a Microsoft SQL Server OLE DB provider, which enables communication between Microsoft Access 2002 (or any other OLE DB client program) and SQL Server database engines, including the Microsoft SQL Server 2000 Desktop Engine.

The Jet Database Engine

When working with an Access database, the Jet database engine consists of the files necessary to manage data, to control access to the data in the database file, and to store objects that belong to the Application layer. Jet includes the internal programs for six basic database management functions:

Data definition and integrity   With Jet, you can create and modify the objects that hold the data. You can use both the interface and VBA programming to create and modify databases, tables, fields, indexes, relationships, and queries. Jet enforces the entity and referential integrity rules that you specify when you design tables and create relationships.

Data storage   Jet uses a method called the Indexed Sequential Access Method (ISAM) to store data in the file system. With ISAM, data is stored in pages 2KB in size containing one or more records; records have variable length and can be ordered using an index.

Data retrieval   Jet provides two ways to retrieve data. One way is to use Jet's powerful query engine, which uses SQL to retrieve data. The second way is to access the data programmatically using the data access objects in VBA procedures.

Data manipulation   With Jet, you can add new data and modify or delete existing data. You can manipulate data using either the Jet query engine with SQL action queries or the data access objects in VBA procedures.

Security   Jet has two security models, including a database password model for simple password security to the entire database and a workgroup security model in which individual users and groups have permissions to individual database objects.

Data sharing   Jet enables multiple users to access and modify data in the same database. Jet locks the data on a given page when a record is being modified by a user. It does so as soon as one user starts editing (*pessimistic locking*) and unlocks the page when the editing is completed, or it allows multiple users to edit a record and locks the page only when a user tries to save or commit the changes (*optimistic locking*). Because a page contains 2KB of data, locking an entire page may lock multiple records—Access 2002 includes a single-record-locking mode that solves this problem. You can select this mode from the Advanced tab of the Tools ➤ Options dialog box.

WARNING   Don't confuse data access pages with table pages. Data access pages are part of the object model and can be used to show report-type data using the Internet or an intranet. Table pages are the 2KB sections of data used by tables for storage. Data access pages are often referred to simply as *pages*.

The Microsoft SQL Server 2000 Desktop Engine

When working with an Access project, the Microsoft SQL Server 2000 Desktop Engine allows the Application layer to connect to a variety of servers and manage data. A project is so named because it does not contain any data or data definition objects; it does not have tables, views, database diagrams, or stored procedures. These database objects are stored in the server database, but they are affected by a project's other objects: forms, reports, data access pages, macros, and modules.

The advantage of the MS SQL Server 2000 Desktop Engine is that it provides local data storage that is compatible with the host server, or it serves as a remote data-storage solution. It performs the same functions (data storage, data retrieval, data manipulation, security, and data sharing) by using the functions of the host server, such as Microsoft SQL Server Design Tools. The Design Tools are conveniently integrated into Microsoft Access and are called into service whenever you create a new table, view, database diagram, or stored procedure in an Access project.

Object Hierarchies

You create VBA procedures to manipulate objects. The objects available for manipulation are the built-in objects that the developers of Access have defined. These built-in objects are grouped into their own collections and arranged into separate hierarchies. In each case, the top of the hierarchy is occupied by a singular object: the Application object heads the Access Application hierarchy and the Connection object heads the ADO object hierarchy. The upper portion of Figure 3.4 shows the Application hierarchy that you use for programming in VBA. (The figure includes the DBEngine object, which is used in DAO programming, a topic discussed in Appendix B, "The Data Access Object (DAO) Model," on this book's CD.)

Figure 3.5 shows the data access objects in the ADO object hierarchy. ADO allows for manipulation of data using VBA programming. You'll learn more about ADO in Chapter 6.

FIGURE 3.4:

The Access Application hierarchy

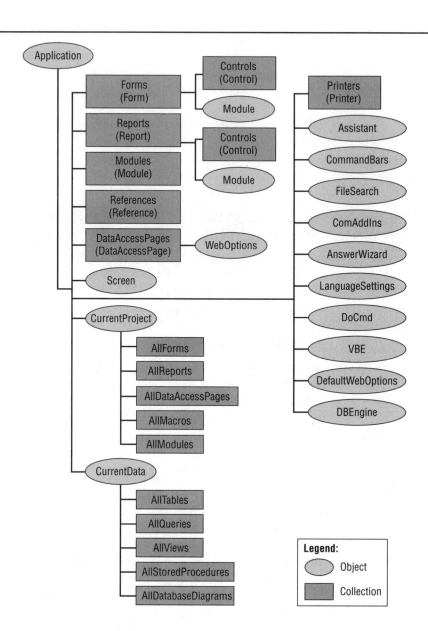

FIGURE 3.5:

The ADO object hierarchy

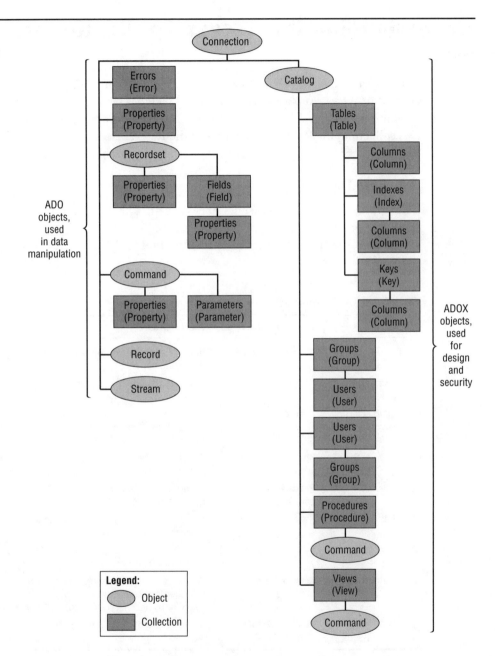

Understanding the Access Application Object Model

Let's take a quick tour of the Access Application object model, starting at the top of the hierarchy. The Access Application object model includes several objects that are available only in VBA programming. These objects include the DoCmd object, the Module object, the Modules collection, the Reference object, and the References collection. You'll learn more about these objects in Chapter 5, "VBA Programming Essentials."

The Application Object

The Application object represents Access itself. The Application object also represents the environment in which VBA procedures and macros run. The Application object properties affect the entire Access environment. Table 3.1 lists some of the Application object properties.

TABLE 3.1: Application Object Properties

Property	Access/Data Type	Description
Build	Read-only/Long	Represents the build number of the currently installed build of Access.
BrokenReference	Read-only/Boolean	Indicates whether the current database has broken references to other databases or type libraries.
CurrentObjectName	Read-only/String	Access sets this to a string expression containing the name of the active object. Use to determine the name of the Database window object that has the focus.
CurrentObjectType	Read-only/Enum constant	Access sets this to one of the intrinsic constants in VBA. Use to determine the type of the active Database window object.
FeatureInstall	Read-write/Enum constant	Determines what action to take if a user tries to run a feature that isn't yet installed.
MenuBar	Read-write/String	Set in VBA. Set the menu bar name to display a custom menu bar throughout your application.
ShortcutMenuBar	Read-write/String	Set in VBA. Use to display a global custom shortcut menu bar when a form, report, or control is right-clicked.
UserControl	Read-only/Boolean	Access sets this property to True/False in VBA. Use to determine whether the current Access application was started by the user (True) or by another application using automation (False).
Version	Read-only/String	Represents the version number of the currently installed version of Access.

Any custom menu bar or shortcut menu bar you set for a form or control will override a custom menu bar or shortcut menu bar you set through the Application object's properties. If you have set a form or report's MenuBar property to a different menu bar, when that form or report has the focus, its custom menu bar is displayed instead of the menu bar set as the Application object's MenuBar property. If you have set a form control, form, or report's ShortcutMenuBar property to a different menu bar and the mouse pointer is over the object when you right-click the object, its custom shortcut menu is displayed instead of the one you set for the Application object.

NOTE When you set the Menu Bar and the Shortcut Menu Bar options in the Startup dialog, you are setting the Database object's StartupMenuBar and StartupShortcutMenuBar properties, not the Application's MenuBar and ShortcutMenuBar properties. The difference is that Access uses the properties you set in the Startup dialog when starting up the database. You can set the corresponding Application properties in a VBA procedure that runs after the database starts up and overrides the Startup dialog settings.

The Forms, Reports, DataAccessPages, and Controls Collection Objects

When you first open a database, Access creates three collections: Forms is the collection of all open forms, Reports is the collection of all open reports, and DataAccessPages is the collection of all open data access pages. Access updates each collection as you open and close individual forms, reports, and pages. Each form and each report has a Controls collection object that contains all of the controls on the form or report. Each page has a WebOptions object that contains attributes used by Access when you save a data access page as a Web page or open a Web page. The Forms, Reports, DataAccessPages, and Controls collections have the properties shown in Table 3.2.

TABLE 3.2: Forms, Reports, DataAccessPages, and Controls Collection Object Properties

Property	Access/Data Type	Description
Application	Read-only/Object	Use to access the active Application object.
Count	Read-only/Long	Use to determine the number of open forms, open reports, open pages or controls on a form or report.
Item	Read-only/Object	Use to return a specific member of a collection.
Parent	Read-only/Object	Refers to the parent of a control or section.

The Form, Report, and DataAccessPage Objects

The Form object refers to a specific open form. Form objects are members of the Forms collection. You can't add or delete a Form object from the Forms collection (except by opening or closing a form). There are almost 200 Form object properties that describe a form's appearance and behavior; you can set about 100 of the properties in the form's property sheet. The property sheet includes more than 50 event properties that a form recognizes.

The Report object refers to a specific open report. Report objects are members of the Reports collection. You can't add or delete a Report object from the Reports collection (except by opening or closing a report). More than 100 Report object properties describe a report's appearance and behavior; you can set more than 40 of the properties in the report's property sheet. The list includes the seven event properties that a report recognizes.

The DataAccessPage object refers to a specific open data access page. DataAccessPage objects are members of the DataAccessPages collection. You can't add or delete a Data-AccessPage object from the DataAccessPages collection (except by opening or closing a page). Fourteen object properties describe a page's appearance and behavior; you can set three of them (ConnectionString, RemovePersonalInformation, and Visible). Because a data access page has no module, it does not recognize any events.

Table 3.3 lists some of the Form, Report, and DataAccessPage object properties that are particularly useful in VBA programming; many of these properties are available only in VBA programming and are not listed in the property sheet of the form, report, or data access page.

TABLE 3.3: Selected Form, Report, and DataAccessPage Object Properties

Property	Access/Data Type	Available In	Description
ActiveControl	Read-only/Object	VBA, macro	Use to determine the active control on an open form or report.
Application	Read-only/Object	VBA	Use to access the active Application object.
Count	Read-write/Integer	VBA, macro	Use to determine the number of items in a specified collection.
CurrentRecord	Read-write/Long	VBA, macro	Use to identify the current record.
CurrentView	Read-write/Integer	VBA, macro	For forms and data access pages only, use to determine how a form or page is currently displayed. The property has the value 0 for Design view, 1 for Form view (called Page view when referring to a data access page), and 2 for Datasheet view.
Cycle	Read-write/Byte	VBA, macro, property sheet	For forms only, use to specify what happens when you tab out of the last control on a form. Set to All Records, Current Record, or Current Page.

Continued on next page

TABLE 3.3 CONTINUED: Selected Form, Report, and DataAccessPage Object Properties

Property	Access/Data Type	Available In	Description
Dirty	Read-write/Boolean	VBA, macro	For forms and reports only, use to determine whether the current record has been modified since it was last saved (True) or not (False).
Filter	Read-write/String	VBA, macro, property sheet	Use to specify a subset of records to be displayed when the filter is applied to the form or report. This property is a WHERE clause of a SQL statement without the WHERE keyword. A new form or report inherits the Filter property of the data source it was created from. Filters are saved with the form or report but aren't automatically applied when the form is opened.
FilterOn	Read-write/Boolean	VBA, macro	Use to determine or specify whether the Filter property of the form or report is applied (True) or not (False).
Form	Read-only/Object	VBA, macro	For forms only, use to refer to the Form object or to the active form.
HasData	Read-write/Long	VBA, macro	Use to determine if a report is bound to an empty recordset. Value is −1 if the object has data, 0 if there is no data, or 1 if the report or form is unbound.
HasModule	Read-write/Boolean	VBA, macro, property sheet	By default, this property is set to No until the first time you view the form's or report's module. A form or report without a module is called a *lightweight* form or report. You can set the property only in form or report Design view.
Hnd	Read-write/Long	VBA, macro	For forms or reports only, use to determine the unique Long Integer (called the window's handle) that Windows assigned to the current window.
KeyPreview	Read-write/Boolean	VBA, macro, property sheet	For forms only, use to specify whether the form receives keyboard events before the active control receives them (True) or not (False).
MenuBar	Read-write/String	VBA, macro, property sheet	Set the MenuBar property to the name of the menu bar you want to display. To display the built-in menu bar using a macro or VBA, set this property to the zero-length string (" "). To display a form without a menu bar, set the property to a value that is not the name of an existing menu bar or menu bar macro.
Modal	Read-write/Boolean	VBA, macro, property sheet	For forms and reports only, set the Modal property to True to specify that all other Access windows are disabled when you open the form/report in Form/Report view from the Database window, a macro, or VBA or by switching from Design view.
NewRecord	Read-only/Integer	VBA, macro	For forms only, use to determine whether the current record is a new record.

Continued on next page

TABLE 3.3 CONTINUED: Selected Form, Report, and DataAccessPage Object Properties

Property	Access/Data Type	Available In	Description
OrderBy	Read-write/String	VBA, macro, property sheet	Use to specify how you want the records sorted in a form or report. Separate fields with a comma; to sort a field in descending order, type **DESC** after the string.
OrderByOn	Read-write/Boolean	VBA, macro	Use to specify whether the OrderBy property is applied (True) or not (False).
Painting	Read-write/Boolean	VBA, macro	Use to specify whether a form or report is repainted (True) or not (False).
Picture	Read-write/String	VBA, macro, property sheet	Use to specify the path of a bitmap to be displayed as a background picture on a form or report. Can also be used to display a bitmap on a command button, image control, toggle button, or tab control.
PopUp	Read-write/Boolean	VBA, macro, property sheet	Set this property to True to specify that the window remains on top of other Access windows when you open the form or report in Form or Report view from the Database window, a macro, or VBA or by switching from Design view.
RecordsetClone	Read-only/Object	VBA, macro	For forms only, use to gain access to some properties of the form's recordset as specified by the RecordSource property, such as RecordCount.
RecordSource	Read-write/String	VBA, macro, property sheet	Use to specify the data source for a form or report. The data source may be a table, query, or SQL statement.
Report	Read-only/Object	VBA, macro	For reports only, use to refer to the Report object.
Section	Read-only/Object	VBA, macro	Use to identify a section or controls in a section of a form or report and provide access to the properties of the section.
ShortcutMenuBar	Read-write/String	VBA, macro, property sheet	Set to the name of the shortcut menu that is displayed when a form, form control, or report is right-clicked. To display the built-in shortcut menu, set to the zero-length string (" ").
Tag	Read-write/String	VBA, macro, property sheet	Use to hold any additional information you want to store about forms, reports, or sections.
Toolbar	Read-write/String	VBA, macro, property sheet	Set to the name of the toolbar you want to display on a form or report. To display the built-in toolbar, leave the Toolbar property setting blank.
Visible	Read-write/Boolean	VBA, macro	Use to show or hide a form, report, section, data access page, or control.

NOTE With the Modal property set to Yes, the form is called a *modal* form. The Access menus and toolbars continue to be active on a modal form, and you can still activate a window in another application. To disable the Access menus and toolbars and the windows of other applications, set both the Modal and PopUp properties to Yes. With the PopUp property set to Yes, the form is called a *popup* form, and the form's toolbar is not active.

The Control Object

The Control object represents a control on a form or report. The controls on a form or report belong to the Controls collection for that form or report. You are familiar with the built-in controls that appear in the toolbox (see Figure 3.6). You can also use custom controls, called ActiveX controls, to provide your application with additional features (see Chapter 15, "Expanding Access," for more information about custom controls). The Control object represents both built-in and custom controls.

FIGURE 3.6:

The built-in controls in the toolbox

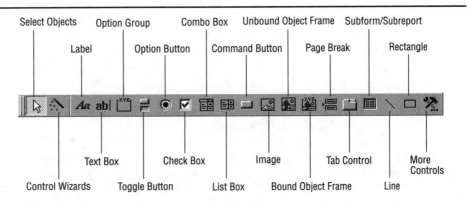

Each type of control has its own set of properties, including event properties for the events that the control recognizes. For some types of controls, there is a special property, called the *default property,* which is the most commonly used property for that type of control. The default property is the property that Access assumes when you refer to a control without specifying a property name. For example, when you refer to a text box, Access assumes you are referring to the Value property.

Data controls are controls that can hold data and can be bound to table fields. A data control has a ControlSource property to indicate the source of the data. The seven built-in data controls include text boxes, combo boxes, list boxes, check boxes, option buttons, toggle buttons, and option groups. Other controls may be associated with another object, such as a form or report; such controls have a SourceObject property to indicate the object or a SourceDoc property to indicate the source of an embedded or linked file. As an example, the subform control has a SourceObject property that you use to specify the form that you want to display in the control. Controls that can display a picture have a Picture property to indicate the source of the image: command buttons and toggle buttons may display images, for example. Table 3.4 lists the built-in controls, their default properties, and whether each control is associated with data, another object or file, or an image.

TABLE 3.4: Built-in Controls

Control	Default Property	Associated With
Bound object frame	Value	SourceDoc
Check box	Value	ControlSource
Combo box	Value	ControlSource
Command button		Picture
Image		Picture
Label		
Line		
List box	Value	ControlSource
Option button	Value	ControlSource
Option group	Value	ControlSource
Page break		
Rectangle		
Subform	Controls	SourceObject
Tab control	Value	
Text box	Value	ControlSource
Toggle button	Value	ControlSource, Picture
Object frame		SourceObject, SourceDoc

Each individual type of control has its own set of properties, but all control types share a set of core properties. Table 3.5 lists the core Control object properties.

The Parent property returns a control object if the parent is a control and returns an AccessObject object if the parent is a Microsoft Access object. An AccessObject is a particular Access object within the following collections: AllForms, AllReports, AllMacros, AllModules, AllDataAccessPages, AllTables, AllQueries, AllViews, AllStoredProcedures, and AllDatabaseDiagrams. The Parent property of a label control returns the control that the label is linked to. The Parent property of an option button, check box, or toggle button in an option group returns the option group control.

Most controls have numerous additional properties; at the extreme, the Combo Box control has more than 90 properties. Table 3.6 lists some of the properties for controls that are particularly important when you create programs to automate an application.

TABLE 3.5: Core Control Object Properties

Property	Access/Data Type	Available In	Description
Application	Read-only/Object	VBA	Use to access the active Access Application object.
EventProcPrefix	Read-write/String	VBA, macro	Use to determine the prefix part of an event procedure name.
InSelection	Read-write/Boolean	VBA, macro	Use to determine or specify whether a control on a form in Design view is selected (True) or not (False).
Left	Read-write/Integer	VBA, macro, property sheet	Use to specify the control's location on a form or report. The value of this property is the distance from the control's left border to the left edge of the section containing the control.
Name	Read-write/String	VBA, macro, property sheet	Use to specify a string expression that identifies the name of the control.
Parent	Read-only/Object	VBA, macro	Use to refer to the parent of the control or section.
Section	Read-write/Integer	VBA, macro	Use to identify the section of the form or report where the control appears. This property is an integer corresponding to a particular section.
Tag	Read-write/String	VBA, macro, property sheet	Use to store additional information about the control. You can use this property to create your own user-defined properties.
Top	Read-write/Integer	VBA, macro, property sheet	Use to specify the control's location on a form or report. The value of this property is the distance from the control's top border to the top edge of the section containing the control.
Visible	Read-write/Boolean	VBA, macro, property sheet	Use to show or hide a control. (This property for the Page-Break control cannot be set through the property sheet.) When you set a control's Visible property to No, the effect is to disable the control.

A few of the control properties listed in Table 3.6 are worth a bit more explanation. The ControlSource property specifies the source of the data in a control. There are three possibilities:

- Leave the property blank. The control is *unbound* and you can set its value in a macro or VBA, or by having the user type in a value.

- Enter an expression. The control is called a *calculated control*. It is unbound, and the data in the control cannot be changed.

- Specify the name of a field in the form's underlying recordset. The control is called a *bound control*. When you edit the data in the control and save the changes, you change the value stored in the field.

TABLE 3.6: Selected Additional Properties of Control Objects

Property	Control	Access/Data Type	Available In	Description
BackColor	Label, text box, combo box, list box, image, option group, rectangle, section	Read-write/Long Integer	VBA, macro, property sheet	Use to specify the color for the interior of a control or section. To use the BackColor property, the BackStyle property must be set to Normal (if available).
BackStyle	Label, text box, combo box, image, option group, rectangle	Read-write/Byte	VBA, macro, property sheet	Use to specify whether a control will be transparent. Set to 1 in VBA (or Normal in the property sheet) to indicate the interior color is set by the BackColor property, or set to 0 (or Transparent in the property sheet) to indicate the control is transparent.
Column	Combo box, list box	Read-only/Variant	VBA, macro	Use to refer to a specific column or column/row combination, in a multi-column box: 0 refers to the first column or row, 1 to the second column or row, and so on; e.g., Column(0,2) refers to the first column and the third row.
ControlSource	Text box, combo box, list box, check box, toggle button, option button, option group	Read-write/String	VBA, macro, property sheet	Use to specify the source of the data in a control. The ControlSource property doesn't apply to check box, option button, or toggle button controls in an option group; it applies only to the option group itself.
Form	Subform control	Read-only/Object	VBA, macro	Use to refer to the form associated with a subform control.
Height	Form section, report section, check box, combo box, command button, image, label, line, list box, option button, option group, rectangle, text box, toggle button	Read-write/Integer	VBA, macro, property sheet	Use to size an object to a specific height.

Continued on next page

TABLE 3.6 CONTINUED: Selected Additional Properties of Control Objects

Property	Control	Access/Data Type	Available In	Description
HyperlinkAddress	Command button, image, label	Read-write/String	VBA, macro, property sheet	Use to specify or determine the path to an object, document, e-mail address, or Web page that is the target of a hyperlink.
HyperlinkSubAddress	Command button, image, label	Read-write/String	VBA, macro, property sheet	Use to specify or determine a location within the target file specified in the HyperlinkAddress property. To specify an object in the current database, leave the HyperlinkAddress property blank and specify the HyperlinkSubAddress using the syntax *objecttype objectname*.
LimitToList	Combo box	Read-write/Boolean	VBA, macro, property sheet	Use to limit the value of a combo box to the listed values (True) or not (False).
ListRows	Combo box	Read-write/Integer	VBA, macro, property sheet	Use to set the maximum number of rows to display in the list box portion of the combo box.
MultiSelect	List box	Read-write/Byte	VBA, macro, property sheet	Use to specify whether a user can make multiple selections in a list box.
OldValue	Text box, combo box, list box, check box, toggle button, option button, option group, image	Read-only/Same data type as the field to which the control is bound	VBA, macro	Use to determine the unedited value in a bound control. (When you save the change, the current value and the OldValue are the same.)
Report	Subreport	Read-only/Object	VBA, macro	Use to refer to the report associated with a subreport control.
RowSource	Combo box, list box	Read-write/String	VBA, macro, property sheet	Use to specify the source of the data for the control. Used in conjunction with the RowSourceType property.
RowSourceType	Combo box, list box	Read-write/String	VBA, macro, property sheet	Use to specify the type of data that fills the list.

Continued on next page

TABLE 3.6 CONTINUED: Selected Additional Properties of Control Objects

Property	Control	Access/Data Type	Available In	Description
SpecialEffect	Label, text box, option button, check box, combo box, list box, image, line, option group, rectangle subform	Read-write/Byte	VBA, macro, property sheet, Special Effects button	Use to specify whether special formatting will apply to a section or control. SpecialEffect options are Flat, Raised, Sunken, Etched, Shadowed, or Chiseled. In VBA, these are set to 0, 1, 2, 3, 4, and 5, respectively.
Text	Text box, combo box	Read-write/String	VBA, macro	Use to determine or specify the data displayed in the control when the control has the focus.
Transparent	Command button	Read-write/Boolean	VBA, macro, property sheet	Use to specify whether a command button is transparent (True) or not (False). With this property, the button is not displayed, but it is still enabled. Use this property to create a control or bitmap section that responds to clicking.
Value	Check box, combo box, list box, option button, option group, text box, toggle button	Read-write/Variant	VBA, macro	Use to determine or specify the saved value of the control.
Width	Form section, report section, check box, combo box, command button, image, label, line, list box, option button option group, rectangle, text box, toggle button	Read-write/Integer	VBA, macro, property sheet	Use to size an object to a specific width.

The Text property is available for setting or reading only when the control has the focus. The value of the Text property is the data currently displayed in the control when the control has the focus. The Text property may be different from the control's Value property, which is the last saved data for the control. When you move to another control, the control's Value property is set to the current data. If you save the record without moving to another control, the Text property and the Value property settings are the same. For a combo box, the value can be either a selected list item or a string that you type in. You use the Text property to return or set the text.

The Value property has different settings depending on the type of control:

- For a check box, option button, or toggle button, use the Value property to determine or specify if the control is selected. The setting is True/False.

- For a text box, use the Value property to determine the saved value of the control and to set the value to the control's Text property. The data is a string.

- For a combo box, list box, or option group, use the Value property to determine which value or option is selected. You use the Value property to set a combo box to the control's Text property, a list box to the value in the bound column for the selected list item, and an option group to the OptionValue setting for the selected control within the group.

The Screen Object

The Screen object refers to the particular form, report, data access page, or control that currently has the focus. By using the Screen object in a VBA procedure, you can refer to the active object without knowing the object's name. Referring to the Screen object does not, however, make the form, report, data access page, or control the active object. Table 3.7 lists the properties of the Screen object; all except MousePointer are read-only and return a reference to the object.

Chapter 2 explains the selection-centric approach to programming, which requires that a VBA procedure establish a connection with an object before performing an action on it. You can use the properties of the Screen object to make the connection to the active object.

The Access Visual Basic Object Model

The Access Visual Basic model provides three objects: the Debug, Err, and Collection objects. Only the Debug object is used in VBA programming.

TABLE 3.7: Screen Object Properties

Property	Description
ActiveControl	Use to refer to the control that currently has the focus.
ActiveDataAccessPage	Use to refer to the data access page that has the focus.
ActiveDatasheet	Use to refer to the datasheet that has the focus.
ActiveForm	Use to refer to the form that has the focus. If a subform has the focus, this property refers to the main form.
ActiveReport	Use to refer to the report that has the focus.
Application	Use to refer to Access.
MousePointer	Use to specify or determine the type of mouse pointer currently displayed.
Parent	Use to refer to the current object's parent object.
PreviousControl	Use to refer to the control that previously had the focus.

You use the Debug object to send a command to a special window called the Immediate window. You can display the Immediate window when any Access window is active by pressing Ctrl+G (see Figure 3.7). You can use the Immediate window like a scratch pad to evaluate expressions, view and set the values of properties, and run procedures.

The Debug object has no properties. However, it has two methods. The `Assert` method pauses execution at the current line. The `Print` method prints text in the Immediate window. Here is the syntax:

```
Debug.Print outputlist
```

where *outputlist* is a numeric or string expression or a list of numeric or string expressions separated by either spaces or semicolons. If you omit the *outputlist* argument, a blank line is printed. When you are working in the Immediate window, you don't need to refer to the Debug object explicitly. You can use the following syntax:

```
Print outputlist
```

Alternatively, you can use the question mark (?) as the shortcut abbreviation for `Print`, as follows:

```
? outputlist
```

We'll use the Immediate window to test some of the object and property references discussed in the next section.

FIGURE 3.7:

The Immediate window

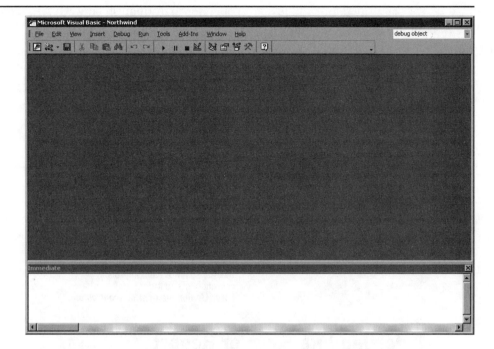

Referring to Objects and Properties by Name

Before manipulating an object in a VBA procedure, you must identify the object using the Access rules for referring to objects. Although you may use a naming standard to identify and document the objects you create, Access has its own rules for referring to objects that you must follow when you write programs.

NOTE   We'll be using the Immediate window to test and evaluate some of the references, so you'll want to be at your computer to work through this section using the Expenses application we created in Chapter 1, "Automating a Database without Programming." If you didn't work through Chapter 1, follow the steps in that chapter to create the Expenses database now. Remember to press the Shift key as you open the Expenses database so you have access to the full menus and shortcut keys.

Referring to an Object by Name

One way to refer to an object is to start with the top object in the hierarchy and traverse along the hierarchical path to the object, recording the names of the specific objects and collection objects you encounter as you move along the path. You use the exclamation point (!), or bang, operator and the dot (.) operator to distinguish between steps and between objects and collections, as follows:

- Use the bang operator when you are stepping from a collection to one of its members, in the format *collectionname!objectname*.

- Use the dot operator when you are stepping from an object to one of its collections, in the format *objectname.collectionname*.

Figure 3.8 illustrates how the bang and dot operators work.

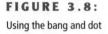

FIGURE 3.8:

Using the bang and dot operators

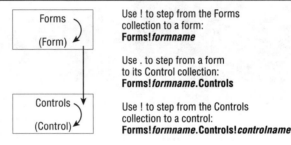

Use ! to step from the Forms collection to a form:
Forms!*formname*

Use . to step from a form to its Control collection:
Forms!*formname*.Controls

Use ! to step from the Controls collection to a control:
Forms!*formname*.Controls!*controlname*

Referring to a Form or Report

To refer to an open form, say the Switchboard form in the Expenses application, start with the Application object and traverse to the Forms collection and then to the Switchboard form in the collection, as follows:

```
Application.Forms!Switchboard
```

To refer to an open report, say the Expense Report report, start with the Application object and traverse to the Reports collection and then to the Expense Report report in the following collection, as shown:

```
Application.Reports![Expense Report]
```

When an object's name contains spaces, you must enclose the name in square brackets; otherwise, you can omit the square brackets. (Access may enter the square brackets for you.)

You can decrease the length of a reference by using defaults. For example, Access assumes that you are in Access when you refer to objects; this means you don't need to refer explicitly to the Application object, and the references become

```
Forms!Switchboard
Reports![Expense Report]
```

These references are still full-path references that refer to the specific form or report by name.

Referring to Form and Report Properties

You use the dot operator to separate an object from a property of the object, in the form *objectname.propertyname*. For example, to refer to the RecordSource property of the Expense Categories form, use this reference:

```
Forms![Expense Categories].RecordSource
```

NOTE   When the name of a property contains more than one word, the property sheet displays spaces between the words; for example, the property sheet for a form displays the label for the RecordSource property as Record Source. You must omit the spaces when you create a reference to a property.

Using the Immediate Window to Evaluate an Object Property

You can use the Immediate window to determine the setting of an object property. Simply press Ctrl+G to open the Immediate window. With the form or report open, type **Print** or **?**, followed by the property reference you want to evaluate, and then press Enter. Access evaluates the property reference immediately and displays the value of the property setting in the next line of the Immediate window.

The Immediate window executes a single line each time you press Enter. You can use many of the familiar text-editing commands in the Immediate window, including the Cut, Copy, Paste, Delete, and Select All commands in the Edit menu. You can edit a line that you have already executed and then press Enter to execute the edited line (Access inserts a new line below the edited line and displays the result of the execution).

Figure 3.9 shows two examples for the Expenses application. Note that when the value is a Yes/No value, such as the value for the NavigationButtons property, Access converts Yes to True and No to False. Also, if no value has been set for the property, Access displays a blank line.

If the property is one that you can set in Design view (a design-time property), then the form or report can be open in any view when you evaluate the property. If the property has a value that is determined only when the form or report is in run mode, such as the Dirty property, then the form or report must be in its run mode; otherwise, Access displays an error message.

The Immediate window can display only text values. If you type a reference to an open form, such as `?Forms![Expense Reports by Employee]`, and then press Enter, Access displays an error message (see Figure 3.10). If the form or report is closed when you try to evaluate a

FIGURE 3.9:

Using the Immediate window to evaluate the setting of a property

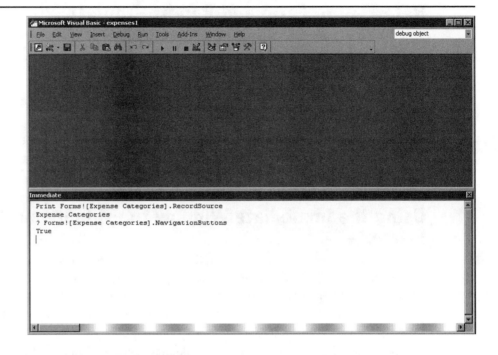

FIGURE 3.10:

The error message generated when you try to evaluate a reference to an object

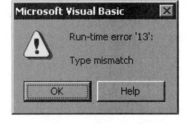

property, such as ?Forms![Expense Categories].RecordSource, Access displays a different error message (see Figure 3.11).

Referring to a Control

To refer to a control on an open form, you start at the top of the hierarchy with the Application object, traverse to the Forms collection, step to the specific form, traverse to the Controls collection, and finally, step to the control, as follows:

```
Forms!formname.Controls!controlname
```

FIGURE 3.11:

The error message
generated when you try to
evaluate a reference to a
property of a closed form or
report

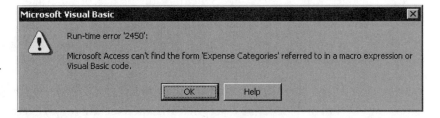

For example, to refer to the command button named Option1 on the Switchboard, step along the path first to the Controls collection and then to the specific control as follows:

```
Forms!Switchboard.Controls!Option1
```

However, you can shorten the reference by using defaults. An object can have a *default collection* that Access assumes when you specify a member of a default collection without specifying the collection. The Form and Report objects have the Controls collection as the default collection, so you can omit the reference to Controls along with the dot, and the reference becomes

```
Forms!Switchboard!Option1
```

Referring to a Control's Properties

To refer to a property of a control, append a dot and the property name to the end of the control reference, as follows:

```
Forms!formname!controlname.propertyname
```

For example, to refer to the saved data in the ExpenseCategory text box control on the Expense Categories form, use the Value property, as follows:

```
Forms![Expense Categories]!ExpenseCategory.Value
```

An object may have a *default property* that Access assumes when you don't explicitly specify a property name. The default property for a text box control is the Value property. Using the defaults, the reference to the saved data in the text box is as follows:

```
Forms![Expense Categories]!ExpenseCategory
```

The Value and Text properties of Control objects were discussed earlier in the chapter. To explore the Value and Text properties,

1. Open the Expense Categories form in Form view.

2. Enter **Meals** in the Expense Category field and save the Record.

3. Change the Expense Category field for the first record to Meal. Press Ctrl+G to bring up the Immediate window.

4. Without saving the record, type each of the following lines and press Enter to evaluate the expression (see Figure 3.12).

?Forms![Expense Categories]!ExpenseCategory

?Forms![Expense Categories]!ExpenseCategory.Text

?Forms![Expense Categories]!ExpenseCategory.Value

FIGURE 3.12:

Exploring the Text and Value properties for a text box control

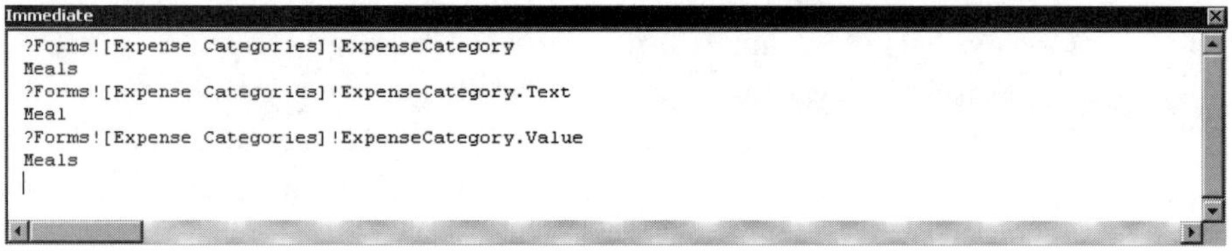

```
Immediate
?Forms![Expense Categories]!ExpenseCategory
Meals
?Forms![Expense Categories]!ExpenseCategory.Text
Meal
?Forms![Expense Categories]!ExpenseCategory.Value
Meals
```

Properties That Represent Other Objects

Most properties have a text value as their setting. You can display this value in the Immediate window. Some objects have special properties that you can use to refer to another object. For example, a control's Parent property refers to the control's parent object. A label's Parent property refers to the control the label is linked to, and a text box's Parent property refers to the form that contains the text box. Table 3.8 lists some of the objects that have properties that refer to other objects.

Because these properties refer to an object and not a value, you can't test these references in the Immediate window. For example, you can use the Parent property of a text box to refer to the form itself, but if you type the expression

```
?Forms![Expense Categories]!ExpenseCategory.Parent
```

and press Enter, Access displays an error message.

Referring to a Subform

A common way to display data from two tables is to create forms based on each of the tables, place a subform control on one of the forms, and display the second form within the subform control. In this arrangement, the form containing the subform control is called the *main form* and the form displayed within the subform control is called the *subform*.

TABLE 3.8: Object Properties That Refer to Other Objects

Object	Object Property	Refers To
Screen	ActiveForm	The form that contains the control that has the focus or the form that has the focus
Screen	ActiveDataAccessPage	The data access page that has the focus
Screen	ActiveDatasheet	The datasheet that has the focus
Screen	ActiveReport	The report that has the focus
Screen	ActiveControl	The control that has the focus
Screen	Parent	The parent object of the current object
Screen	PreviousControl	The control that had the focus just before the control on the same form that currently has the focus
Control	Parent	The object that is the parent of the specified control
Subform control	Form	The form displayed within the subform control
Subreport control	Report	The report displayed within the subreport control
Form	ActiveControl	The control within the form that has the focus
Form	DefaultControl	The default properties for a particular type of control
Form	Form	The form itself
Form	Me	The form itself
Form	Module	The form's module
Form	Printer	A printer available on the system
Form	Recordset	The record source for the form
Form	RecordsetClone	The recordset underlying the form, as specified by the RecordSource property
Form	Section	A section of the form
Report	ActiveControl	The control within the report that has the focus
Report	DefaultControl	The default properties for a particular type of control
Report	Me	The report itself
Report	Module	The report's module
Report	Printer	A printer available on the system
Report	Recordset	The record source for the report
Report	Report	The report itself
Report	Section	A section of the report

To explore the references for a subform, do the following:

1. Open the Expense Reports By Employee form in Form view. The Name property of the subform control is Employees Subform, so you can refer to the subform control using the reference `Forms![Expense Reports by Employee]![Employees Subform]`.

2. You can evaluate properties of the subform control in the Immediate window. As an example, we'll use the SourceObject property to determine the name of the form displayed in the subform control. Type **?Forms![Expense Reports by Employee]![Employees Subform].SourceObject** and press Enter.

3. You can refer to the form displayed within the subform control using the Form property of the subform control as follows: `Forms![Expense Reports by Employee]![Employees Subform].Form`. You can evaluate properties of this form in the Immediate window. We'll evaluate the DefaultView property. Type **?Forms![Expense Reports by Employee]![Employees Subform].Form .DefaultView** and press Enter. Access displays the integer 2, which represents Datasheet view.

4. You can refer to a control on a form displayed in a subform control by first referring to the form then traversing to the Controls collection and stepping to the specific control. We'll refer to the value in the Total Expenses control on the subform. Type **?Forms![Expense Reports by Employee]![Employees Subform].Form .Controls![Total Expenses]** and press Enter.

5. Fortunately, you can use defaults to simplify the reference to a control on a subform. The default collection for the subform is the Controls collection, so the first simplification is to omit the reference to the Controls collection. Type **?Forms![Expense Reports by Employee]![Employees Subform].Form![Total Expenses]** and press Enter.

6. In addition, Access treats the Form property as the default property for the subform control when you are referring to a control on the subform, so you can omit the reference to the Form property. Type **?Forms![Expense Reports by Employee]![Employees Subform]![Total Expenses]** and press Enter.

The general syntax for referring to a control on a subform is as follows:

```
Forms!formname!subformcontrolname!controlname
```

Figure 3.13 shows the results of testing these references in the Immediate window.

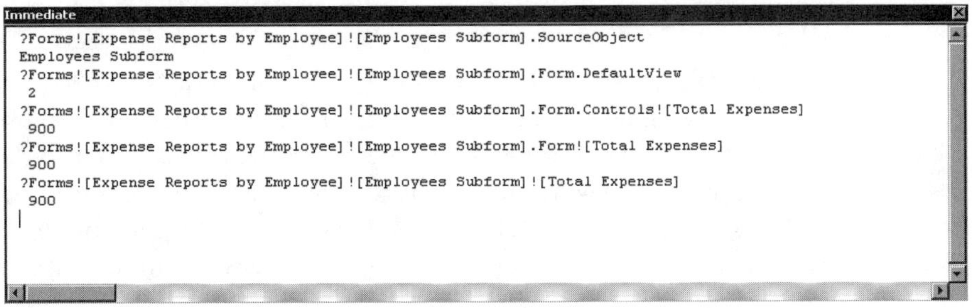

FIGURE 3.13:

Testing references to a
subform control and to the
form displayed in the subform
control in the Immediate
window

```
Immediate                                                                        ×
?Forms![Expense Reports by Employee]![Employees Subform].SourceObject
Employees Subform
?Forms![Expense Reports by Employee]![Employees Subform].Form.DefaultView
  2
?Forms![Expense Reports by Employee]![Employees Subform].Form.Controls![Total Expenses]
  900
?Forms![Expense Reports by Employee]![Employees Subform].Form![Total Expenses]
  900
?Forms![Expense Reports by Employee]![Employees Subform]![Total Expenses]
  900
|
```

Referring to Controls on the Active Form or Report

The references, or *identifiers*, we've been exploring are full-path references obtained by starting at the top of the object hierarchy and traversing the path to the object. We've shortened the references by referring to the Application object implicitly and using default collections and default properties. You can also shorten the reference when you want to refer to a control on the active form or the active report. Because Access knows which form is the active form, you can reference the active form implicitly; in other words, you can omit the reference to the active form or report. For example, if Expense Reports By Employee is the active form, you can identify the FirstName text box control using simply FirstName; you can identify the Total Expenses control displayed in the Employees Subform control using [Employees Subform]![Total Expenses].

An identifier that refers to the active form or report implicitly is called the *short syntax* or *unqualified reference*. An identifier that includes the full hierarchical path (and uses defaults and an implicit reference to the Application object) is called the *fully qualified reference*. Normally, you can use the fully qualified reference without problems, but there are exceptions when you must use the short syntax instead. These are discussed in detail in later chapters.

You can't test identifiers that refer to the active object when you are working in the Immediate window because the Immediate window is the active window. If you try to test an unqualified reference in the Immediate window, Access displays a "Compile error: External name not defined" message.

Using the Screen Object to Refer to the Active Object

Access has a way to uniquely identify the active form, report, or control without using the specific names you've given the object. Avoiding specific names is necessary when you create objects that you want to reuse in your application. You can use the properties of the Screen object to identify the active object. For example, to refer to the RecordSource property of the active form, use the reference Screen.ActiveForm.RecordSource. To refer to the Locked property of a control named LastName on the active form, use the reference `Screen` `.ActiveForm!LastName.Locked`.

Additionally, you can refer to the active control on the active form using the Screen object. For example, to refer to the name of the active control, you use the reference `Screen.ActiveControl.Name`. As another example, you can refer to the TabIndex property of the control on the active form that previously had the focus using the reference `Screen.PreviousControl.TabIndex`. You can use the Screen object in calculated controls on forms and in VBA procedures to refer to an object without naming it explicitly.

Referring to a Field

Often, you need to refer to a field in a table or query. The syntax for the reference depends on whether the table or query is in the underlying record source of an open form.

Referring to a Field in the Form's Record Source

You can refer to a field in the table or the query that is the record source for the form, whether the field is bound to a control on the form, using the following reference:

`Forms!formname!fieldname`

As an example, add a DateHired field to the Employees table and enter sample hire dates for each employee. (Do not add a control to the Expense Reports By Employee form.) Open the Expense Reports By Employee form in Form view. Then type **?Forms![Expense Reports by Employee]!DateHired** and press Enter. The Immediate window displays the sample hire date for the employee.

NOTE   By default, when you create a form using a form wizard, the Name property of each control created is the same as the name of the field the control is bound to. When you add a control to a form by dragging a field from the field list, the control inherits the field name. However, the control name and the field name need not be the same.

Referring to a Field in a Table or Query

When you are designing a query or a SQL statement, you often need to refer to a column or field in a table or query. The Column object belongs to the Columns collection of the table. The Columns collection is the default collection for tables, so you can use either of the following syntax forms for a table field:

`tablename.Columns!columnname`
`tablename!columnname`

If you wish to refer to a field in a query (a Command in the ADO model), you have to first have a query return its results to a recordset. The Field object belongs to the Fields collection of the Recordset object. The Fields collection is the default collection for the recordset, so you can use either of the following syntax forms:

```
recordsetname.Fields!fieldname
recordsetname!fieldname
```

However, tables and commands are managed by the database engine. The engine uses either the dot operator or the bang operator when you step from a collection to one of its members. For example, you can use either `Employees!LastName` or `Employees.LastName` to refer to the LastName column in the Employees table.

You can't test table and query references directly in the Immediate window. When you work in the Immediate window, you can use the `DLookup()` function to test a reference to a column or field in a table or a query. For example, to look up the first value in the LastName field in the Employees table, type **?DLookup("LastName", "Employees")** in the Immediate window and press Enter. Access displays Smith (or whatever name you used for your first employee). See Chapter 4, "Communicating with Forms," for more information about the `DLookup()` function. In Chapter 6, you'll learn how to use the data access objects to retrieve data from tables and queries.

Using the Expression Builder to Create References

The expressions for referring to properties and controls on forms and subforms can be very complex. Fortunately, Access provides the Expression Builder to help you create expressions of any kind, including expressions for query criteria and property settings, as well as references for VBA programming. Unfortunately, the Expression Builder is not available in the Immediate window.

You can start the Expression Builder in several ways:

- Right-click the location where you want the expression, choose the Build command from the shortcut menu, and then click Expression Builder.

- Click the location where you want the expression, then click the Build button in the toolbar.

- When you are creating an expression in a property edit box or in an argument edit box, you can summon the Expression Builder by clicking the Build button that appears to the right of the edit box.

In the Expression Builder dialog, the list box on the left contains folders for all of the tables, queries, forms, and reports in your database, as well as folders for built-in functions, constants, operators, common expressions, and custom Visual Basic functions (see Figure 3.14a). The Expression Builder is context-sensitive. The set of folders that appears in the first list box depends on where you started the builder. In Figure 3.14, the builder was started from the property sheet of the Expense Categories form. Folders that contain other folders have a plus sign. When you click to expand the folder, the plus sign changes to a minus sign.

The Forms and Reports folders contain folders for each of your forms and reports and separate folders for the open forms (in the Loaded Forms subfolder) and for the open reports (in the Loaded Reports subfolder). If a form with a subform is open when you start the Expression Builder, Access recognizes the relationship between the form and the sub-form and shows a folder for the subform within the folder for the form. In Figure 3.14b, the Forms folder is fully expanded. The figure shows that the Expense Categories form is the only open form.

FIGURE 3.14:

Use the Expression Builder to create object references (a). Click the plus sign to expand the Forms folder (b).

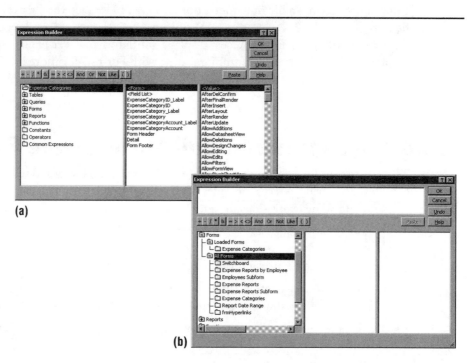

(a)

(b)

When you select a specific object in the list box on the left, the list box in the center changes to show the objects contained in the selected object. If you select a form, the first item in the center list is <Form>, representing the form itself; the second item is <Field List>, representing the field list for the table or query that underlies the form; and the remaining items are the controls and sections on the form. When you select an item in the center list box, the list box on the right changes to display the properties of the item you selected. Figure 3.15 shows the choices for the Total Expenses text box on the Employees Subform form.

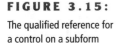

FIGURE 3.15:

The qualified reference for a control on a subform

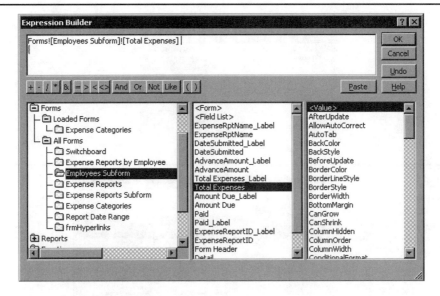

After you have made your choices, click the Paste button. The Expression Builder creates the reference based on your choices and the context where you started the builder and pastes the reference in the edit box at the top of the dialog. Figure 3.15 shows the qualified reference for the Total Expenses text box (note that the Expression Builder includes the default Forms reference). You can edit the reference in the edit box by using the keyboard and the operator buttons in the Builder dialog. In this example, you can edit the reference to delete the Forms reference, or you can shorten the reference to the unqualified reference.

To show how the starting location affects the Expression Builder, let's start the builder with the Expense Reports By Employee form as the active object:

1. With the Expense Reports By Employee form in Design view, select the form and click the Build button in the toolbar. Access displays the Choose Builder dialog (see Figure 3.16).

2. Choose the Expression Builder and click OK. The Expression Builder displays a folder for the form as the first folder in the list box on the left and fills the list box in the center with the controls on the form (see Figure 3.17a).

3. Expand the Expense Reports By Employees folder and choose the Employees Subform. Select Total Expenses in the center list box and <Value> in the right list box. Then click the Paste button. The Expression Builder pastes the short reference for the control (see Figure 3.17b).

FIGURE 3.16:

The Choose Builder dialog

FIGURE 3.17:

Opening the Expression Builder with a form as the active object (a) allows the Expression Builder to create an unqualified reference (b).

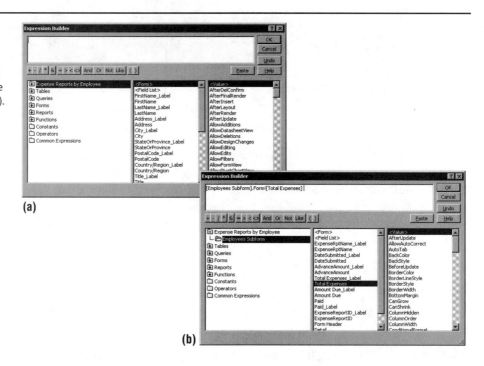

You can also use the Expression Builder to create expressions involving custom functions. Double-click the Functions folder in the list box on the left to display folders for the built-in functions and for the current database. When you select the current database, the list box in the center displays the standard modules in the current database. When you select a standard module, the list box on the right displays the custom functions stored in the module. When you select a custom function and click the Paste button, the syntax for the function is displayed in the edit box. Figure 3.18 shows the syntax for the IsLoaded function in the Global-Code standard module in the Expenses database.

FIGURE 3.18:

Using the Expression
Builder to display the
syntax for a custom
function

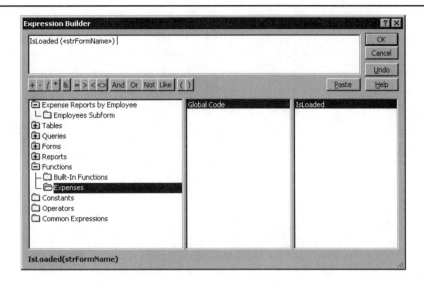

Summary

This chapter has taken you on an introductory tour of the Access object model that focuses on the objects and properties that are common to VBA programming. The important points are as follows:

- Access has two major components, each with its own object hierarchy: the Access Application and ADO.

- In general, to refer to an object in a VBA procedure, you must use a fully qualified reference. To obtain the fully qualified reference, you start at the top of the object hierarchy and traverse down to the object, recording the names of all the collections and objects you step through on the way. In the Access object hierarchy, you use the dot operator to indicate stepping from an object to one of its children and the exclamation point (or bang) operator to indicate stepping from a collection to one of its members.

- You can use default collections and properties to shorten references.

- To refer to a property of an object, you include the reference to the object and the name of the property, separating the two with the dot operator.

- The properties of the Screen object let you refer to an active object without using its name.

- You can refer to a field in the form's underlying record source even if there is no control on the form that is bound to the field.

- You can use the Expression Builder to create both fully qualified and unqualified references.

CHAPTER 4

Communicating with Forms

- Relating controls to data

- Understanding how controls communicate with each other

- Using an unbound control as a variable

- Using a combo box to look up information

- Synchronizing two forms

Forms play a key role in most Access applications. When you create a fully automated application for others to use, you normally create a custom interface composed entirely of forms and reports. All data entry and data review take place in forms. Normally, you use the events on forms to trigger the VBA procedures that automate the application. This chapter is devoted to two fundamental form topics: the relationship between a form and the data stored in the database tables and the communication between controls on one or more forms.

Data access pages allow for user interaction with data in tables that are accessed over the Internet. The way that Access handles data access pages is similar to the way that it handles forms. Therefore, most of the discussion in this chapter pertains to data access pages as well as to forms.

This chapter covers several of the more advanced topics in form design:

- Using AutoLookup queries to display information from two or more tables and look up information from one of the tables automatically

- Using subdatasheets to view and edit related or joined data in a table, query, form datasheet, or subform

- Using calculated query fields

- Using calculated form controls to look up information in other controls on the same form or on another form and to look up information in table and query fields using the DLookup domain aggregate function

- Using unbound form controls to hold temporary values

- Using combo boxes to display records from a table or query as the rows of a mini-datasheet

- Synchronizing two forms by using the built-in form/subform technique

- Synchronizing two forms displayed in separate windows by creating procedures with the Form Wizard

The theme of this chapter is how information is communicated from one element to another element. We'll consider the situations in which Access updates the display automatically and the situations in which you'll need to either update the display interactively or write programs to update the display.

Relating Forms and Controls to Data

The primary reason for using a relational database to manage information is to minimize the duplication of stored information by storing facts about different subjects in separate tables. If you design a relational database correctly, the only fields that must have duplicated information are the fields that you use to join the tables; the data in all other fields needs to appear only once. If you change data (such as an address or the spelling of a name), you can make the change in just one place, and the changed data is automatically reflected in your queries, data access pages, forms, and reports.

By contrast, in a flat-file database, the same data may appear in fields in many records. For example, each order may duplicate the customer's name and address. In a flat-file database, changing the data in one record doesn't trigger an automatic change in the other fields with the same data.

Figure 4.1 shows the tables and the relationships in the Northwind database that comes with Access (we'll be using this sample database throughout the rest of the book). Having data stored in separate tables gives a relational system its power but makes it more difficult when you want to see and use information from different tables simultaneously. Access provides several ways to retrieve data stored in multiple tables.

FIGURE 4.1:

The tables and relationships in the Northwind database

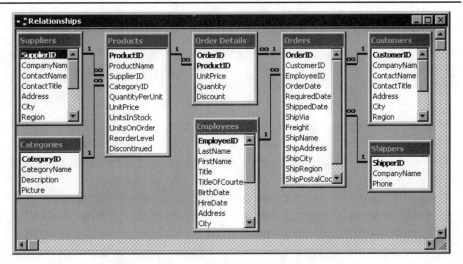

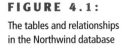

NOTE   The examples in this chapter use the Northwind sample database. To follow along, create a fresh copy of Northwind.mdb and save it to the VBAHandbook folder as Northwind_Ch4.mdb. (See this book's introduction for instructions on setting up this folder.)

Retrieving a Recordset

When you open a table, run a stored query, or run a SQL statement, the result is a *recordset* that is created in memory by the database engine. A recordset is the set of records in a table or the set of records produced by running a query or a SQL statement. (Not all queries and SQL statements produce records; recall that action queries do not produce records when you run them.)

Sometimes, the data you want to retrieve is stored in a single table. For example, if you want to review employee addresses, you work with the Employees table. More frequently, the data is stored in several different tables. Suppose you wanted to review the addresses only for the employees who handled orders shipped to Ireland. The shipping information is stored in the Orders tables, so you need to work with fields from both the Employees and the Orders tables. An essential role of the query is to join the data stored in two or more tables. We'll quickly step through creating a new query and review some of the important Access query basics. You can open your copy of Northwind_Ch4.mdb and follow the example.

Graphical query design   When you create a query in query Design view (see Figure 4.2a), you add tables with the data you want to retrieve to the upper pane and you drag fields from the tables to columns in the design grid. Create a new query in Design view. Add the Orders and Employees tables. Drag ShipCountry from the Orders table and the name and address fields from the Employees table.

FIGURE 4.2:

The Design view (a) and the SQL view (b) for the qryEmployeeShipCountry query

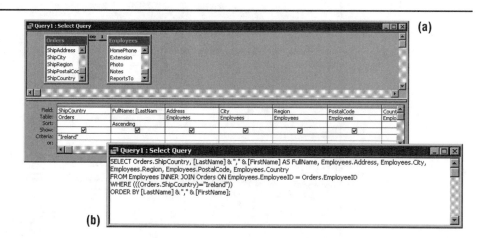

Relating the tables   The table relationships you create in the Relationships window are maintained when you add the tables to a query. You can also create new temporary query relationships by modifying the join lines of existing relationships or creating new join

lines. Access uses the join lines between fields to match records in the tables and constructs a query row for each set of matching records. The Employees and Orders tables have a one-to-many relationship. The bold join line with the 1 and ∞ symbols at either end indicate that the option to enforce referential integrity has been checked in the Relationships layout.

Doing calculations When creating a query, you can include fields from tables, and you can also create new calculated fields by entering expressions in vacant Field cells in the query design grid. The value in a calculated field is the result of the expression you entered in the Field cell. The value in a calculated field is not saved anywhere in the database and is recalculated each time the query is run. The value in a calculated field is read-only. Replace the LastName and FirstName fields with a calculated field named FullName that concatenates the data in the two fields.

Limiting and sorting the rows You can limit the rows in the query result by entering expressions in the Criteria and Or cells in the query design grid. You can sort the rows by entering sort instructions in the Sort cells. Limit the rows by entering **Ireland** in the Criteria cell below the ShipCountry field. Sort the FullName calculated field in ascending order.

Equivalent SQL statements When you create a query in query Design view, Access automatically creates a corresponding SQL statement that you can observe by changing to SQL view (see Figure 4.2b). You can also create queries directly as SQL statements in SQL view. *SQL-specific queries* can be created only in SQL view and can't be viewed in query Design view. An example of a SQL-specific query is the Customers and Suppliers union query in the Northwind database.

Storing the query Whether a query is created in Design view or SQL view, there are two ways to store the query:

- You can save the query as a query object in the database. The saved query is displayed in the Queries pane of the Database window. When you save a query, the database engine analyzes the query and creates an optimized plan for running the query; when you run a saved query, the optimized plan is used.

- You can store the SQL statement as a property setting of another object. For example, if a form is based on a query, you can store the SQL statement as the form's RecordSource property. Each time you open the form, the database engine analyzes the SQL statement, creates an optimized plan on-the-fly, and runs the query.

Save the query you created as a query object, with the name qryEmployeeShipCountry.

NOTE Queries cannot be used by an Access project. Instead, projects afford the database developer two additional objects that can be used for the same purposes as queries: stored procedures and views. A *stored procedure* is a precompiled collection of SQL statements stored under a name and processed as a unit. The stored procedure can be run by being called from an application. *Views* are virtual tables generated by a query whose definition is stored in the database. Views help optimize the use of Access with a SQL server by limiting the amount of data downloaded from the server to only those items the user is interested in.

When you open a table or run a stored query or a SQL statement, Access displays a datasheet as a visual representation of the recordset for your convenience (see Figure 4.3). The recordset itself exists as an object residing in memory. When you close the datasheet, the recordset ceases to exist and the memory it occupied is released.

You can open a table or query directly and display its data in the grid of Datasheet view. When you open a form or report based on a table or query, Access sends a request to the database engine to open a recordset in memory and then displays the data from the recordset in the controls of the form or report. When you close the form or report, the recordset is cleared automatically. Access handles the arrangements with the database engine and manages the connection between the data and the form or report for you. When you work interactively, you don't need to know the details of the connection. However, when you automate a database, you often need to write programs that change the data displayed in a form or report, so it is important that you understand the recordset-to-form or recordset-to-report connection.

FIGURE 4.3:

Datasheet view is a visual representation on the screen of a recordset in memory.

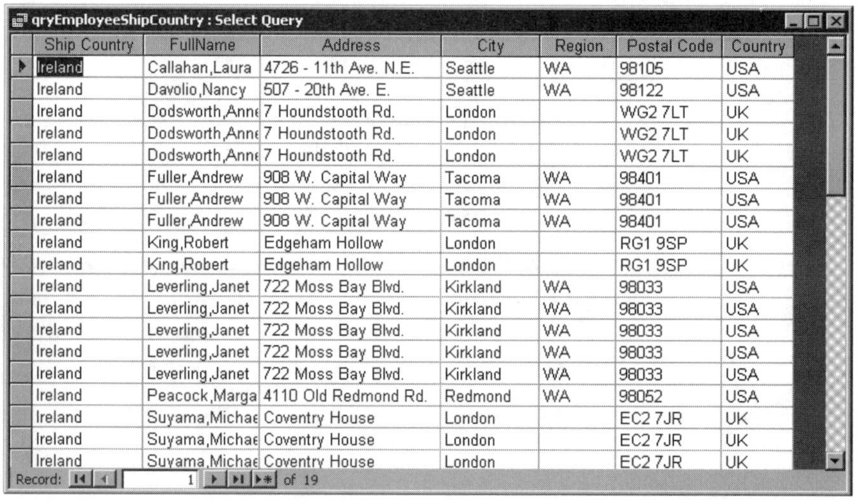

Ship Country	FullName	Address	City	Region	Postal Code	Country
Ireland	Callahan,Laura	4726 - 11th Ave. N.E.	Seattle	WA	98105	USA
Ireland	Davolio,Nancy	507 - 20th Ave. E.	Seattle	WA	98122	USA
Ireland	Dodsworth,Anne	7 Houndstooth Rd.	London		WG2 7LT	UK
Ireland	Dodsworth,Anne	7 Houndstooth Rd.	London		WG2 7LT	UK
Ireland	Dodsworth,Anne	7 Houndstooth Rd.	London		WG2 7LT	UK
Ireland	Fuller,Andrew	908 W. Capital Way	Tacoma	WA	98401	USA
Ireland	Fuller,Andrew	908 W. Capital Way	Tacoma	WA	98401	USA
Ireland	Fuller,Andrew	908 W. Capital Way	Tacoma	WA	98401	USA
Ireland	King,Robert	Edgeham Hollow	London		RG1 9SP	UK
Ireland	King,Robert	Edgeham Hollow	London		RG1 9SP	UK
Ireland	Leverling,Janet	722 Moss Bay Blvd.	Kirkland	WA	98033	USA
Ireland	Leverling,Janet	722 Moss Bay Blvd.	Kirkland	WA	98033	USA
Ireland	Leverling,Janet	722 Moss Bay Blvd.	Kirkland	WA	98033	USA
Ireland	Leverling,Janet	722 Moss Bay Blvd.	Kirkland	WA	98033	USA
Ireland	Leverling,Janet	722 Moss Bay Blvd.	Kirkland	WA	98033	USA
Ireland	Peacock,Marga	4110 Old Redmond Rd.	Redmond	WA	98052	USA
Ireland	Suyama,Michae	Coventry House	London		EC2 7JR	UK
Ireland	Suyama,Michae	Coventry House	London		EC2 7JR	UK
Ireland	Suyama,Michae	Coventry House	London		EC2 7JR	UK

qryEmployeeShipCountry : Select Query

Record: 1 of 19

The Record Source for a Form or Report

There are two kinds of forms and reports: unbound and bound. When you create a form or report, you use the RecordSource property to specify the source of the data for the form or report. If you leave the RecordSource property blank, the form or report is *unbound;* that is, the form or report has no connection to a recordset.

You can specify the RecordSource property as the name of a table, the name of a saved query, the name of a view, or the name of a SQL statement that produces records. In this case, the form or report is *bound* to the specified table, query, view, or SQL statement, which is called the *data source* of the form or report. The controls on a bound form or report act like windows into the fields of the recordset. When you open a bound form or report, the database engine creates in its memory the recordset corresponding to the specified RecordSource property setting.

Figure 4.4 shows the Customers form based on the Customers table. When you open the Customers form, the database engine creates a recordset based on the Customers table, and the controls on the form display the data in the fields of the first row of the recordset. When you click a navigation button, Access moves to another record, and the controls display the data from the corresponding row of the recordset. When you close the form, the recordset is cleared.

NOTE   Data access pages do not have RecordSource properties. They are composed of sections (caption section, group header, group footer, and record navigation section) that contain controls. These sections have a RecordSource property that can be set to bind the section to a table, query, view, or SQL statement. You can then bind controls within the section using the ControlSource property (discussed in the next section).

FIGURE 4.4:

When you open the Customers form, the database engine opens a recordset in memory based on the Customers table, and the form controls display data from fields of the recordset.

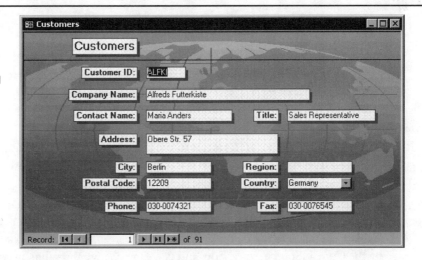

The Control Source for a Control

When you create a data control on a form, report, or data access page section, you use the ControlSource property to specify the source of the control's data. You can place two kinds of data controls on a form, report, or section: bound and unbound.

Bound Controls

If the page section, form, or report is bound to a data source, then you can *bind* a control on the section, form, or report to a field in the section's, form's, or report's data source by entering the name of the field in the ControlSource property. The bound control acts like a window into the specified field. Figure 4.5 illustrates binding the CompanyName control to the CompanyName field in the form's data source.

FIGURE 4.5:

Setting the ControlSource property binds the control to a field in the form's data source.

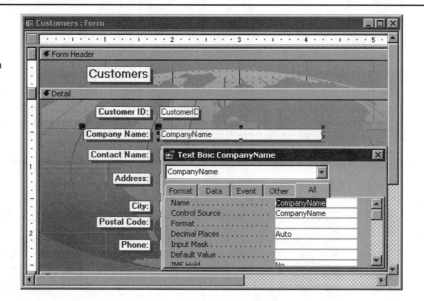

Unbound Controls

If the ControlSource property is not set to the name of a field in the section's, form's, or report's data source, the data control is unbound. Two kinds of unbound controls exist:

- When you enter an expression in the ControlSource property, the control is called a *calculated control*. When you open a form, page, or report with a calculated control, Access automatically uses the expression in the ControlSource property to generate a value and displays the value in the control. The value displayed in a calculated control is determined by the ControlSource expression, and you can't change the value by typing in the control.

- When you leave the ControlSource property setting blank, the unbound control has no editing restrictions. You can enter and edit the value in this type of unbound control.

Whether the ControlSource property is set to an expression or is left blank, the value displayed in an unbound control exists only while the form, page, or report is open; it ceases to exist when you close the form, page, or report.

Controls with Two Sources of Data

The combo box and list box are interesting controls because they can be associated with two different sources of data. A combo box or list box control has a ControlSource property that you can use to specify the source of the control's data. You can bind a combo box or list box to a field in the data access page section's, report's, or form's data source or leave the control unbound, just as you can for a text box. These controls also have RowSource and RowSourceType properties that you use to specify the source of the data displayed in the rows of the list. The source of the data for the rows in the list can be one of four types:

- A table, query, or SQL statement that produces records
- A list of values that you specify
- A list of the field names in a table, query, or SQL statement
- A list of values that you specify using a custom function

When you open a form, page, or report with a list box or drop down a combo box's list, Access creates the list you specify. If you specify a table, query, or SQL statement, the database engine creates a recordset for the list, and Access displays fields from the recordset in the rows. This means that a form, page section, or report with a list box or a combo box can be associated with two recordsets: the form's, section's, or report's recordset (specified in the RecordSource property) and the control's row recordset (specified in the control's RowSource and RowSourceType properties). For example, in the Orders form shown in Figure 4.6, the subform is associated with two recordsets: the subform's recordset is based on the Order Details Extended query and the Product combo box's row recordset is based on the Products table.

Controls without a ControlSource Property

There are two kinds of controls without a ControlSource property: controls that aren't associated with data in any way and controls that are associated with data in some way but don't display a specific value. For example, when you place a check box, option button, or toggle button directly on a form, the control has a ControlSource property that you can use to specify the data source for the control. However, when you place one of these controls inside an

FIGURE 4.6:

The combo box control has a dual nature: it can be bound to a field in the form's recordset, and it displays rows from its own row recordset.

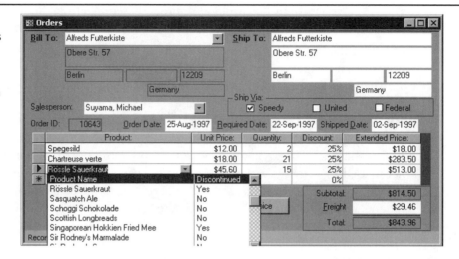

option group, the control becomes a *subcontrol* and loses its independence. The ControlSource property of each subcontrol is replaced with an OptionValue property, and only the option group control itself has a ControlSource property that you can use to specify the data source for the option group. When you select a check box, a toggle button, or an option button in an option group, the value of the option group control equals the OptionValue of the subcontrol you selected (see Figure 4.7).

FIGURE 4.7:

The option button inside an option group passes the value of its OptionValue property to the option group.

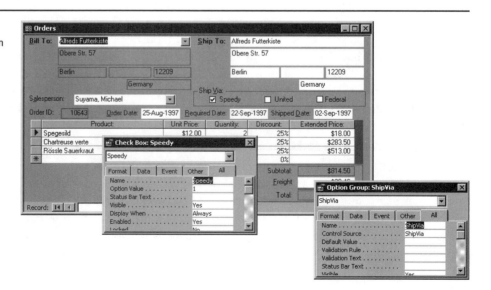

Another control without a ControlSource property is the subform/subreport control. In this case, the control doesn't display a value; instead, the subform/subreport control displays another form or report. Because the source of the control is another form or report instead of a field, you use the SourceObject property to specify the name of the form or report that the control displays.

The One Form–One Record Source Model

Access uses the one form–one record source model: a page section, form, or report can have only a single source of data. Through the use of a query or a SQL statement, the section, form, or report can display data from several tables, but only a single table, query, view, or SQL statement can be entered as the RecordSource property. When the form must be based on data from two tables that are related to each other, you can create a query, view, or SQL statement for the record source. For example, to display contact information for employees who have customers in Ireland, you can base the form on the qryEmployeeShipCountry query we created earlier.

Depending on the relationship between the tables and how you build the query, the form can appear to be based on two recordsets instead of one. As an example, suppose you are creating a form for entering new orders in the Northwind database. The form needs to display customer address information as well as the order information. You can create a query based on the Customers table and the Orders table and then base the form on the query. Because most of your customers are regular customers, you would like to set up the form so that the customer's address information is entered automatically. You can design the query as an AutoLookup query, so as soon as you enter a CustomerID, the query looks up and displays the customer information automatically. Then you can enter order information into the remaining controls. Because Access fills in the customer information controls automatically and you type the information in the order-entry controls yourself, it seems as though the form is based on two data sources: a data source for customer information and a second data source for order information.

AutoLookup Queries

An AutoLookup query is a query based on two tables in a one-to-many relationship. This type of query automatically fills in field values from the one table when you enter a value in a join field for a new record. A query is an AutoLookup query when the following four conditions are met:

- Two tables in the query have a one-to-many relationship. The relationship can be a temporary relationship created in the query or can be a permanent relationship created in the Relationships window. (Referential integrity doesn't need to be enforced.)

- The join field on the one side of the relationship has a unique index. This means that the Indexed property for the field is set to Yes (No Duplicates). (The join field does not need to be a primary key.)

- The join field that you add to the query must be from the many side of the relationship. For an AutoLookup query based on the Customers and Orders tables, this means you must include the CustomerID field from the Orders table and not from the Customers table.

- The value you enter in the join field of a query row must already exist in the join field on the one side. In the example, this means you must enter the CustomerID value for an existing customer; that is, you can enter only the CustomerID value for a record already saved in the Customers table.

If these conditions are satisfied, when you enter a value in the join field, Access automatically looks up the associated values from the table on the one side.

Here are the steps for creating an AutoLookup query:

1. Create a new query based on Customers and Orders.

2. Drag some fields from Customers to the grid, but do not include CustomerID.

3. Drag some fields from Orders, including CustomerID.

4. Switch to Datasheet view and select a customer from the CustomerID combo list. The fields you dragged from the Customers table are filled in automatically.

The Orders form in Northwind uses an AutoLookup query as the record source for the main form. Figure 4.8 shows the automatic lookup of customer information that occurs when you enter a new order. When you select a customer in the Bill To combo box, the customer address information is automatically entered in the Bill To section of the main form. Notice that information is also entered automatically in the Ship To section of the form; the Ship To information is not the result of automatic lookup, however. We'll return to the technique used for the Ship To controls later in this chapter.

AutoLookup is a valuable technique when you are designing a form for data entry into a table and you want to automatically look up information from another table.

Subdatasheets

Subdatasheets give you the ability to view and edit related or joined data. Any time there is a one-to-one relationship to a table, Access automatically creates a subdatasheet. Access will also create a subdatasheet in instances of a one-to-many relationship, when the Subdatasheet property of the table is set to Auto. Subdatasheets are somewhat more restrictive in terms of referential integrity; a relationship must include a primary key of one table and a foreign key in the other table. You can add a subdatasheet to any table, query, form, datasheet, or subdatasheet and

FIGURE 4.8:

When you select a customer, the AutoLookup query of the main form automatically displays the customer's address in the Bill To section of the form.

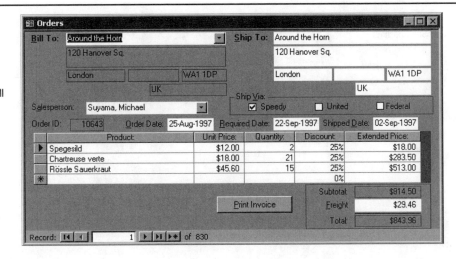

can specify either tables or queries as its source objects. You can have a maximum of eight levels of nested datasheets. Each datasheet or subdatasheet can have only one nested subdatasheet.

Let's create a sample subdatasheet that shows combined data from the Orders and Employees tables:

1. Open the Northwind database. Open the Orders table in Datasheet view.

2. Select Insert ➤ Subdatasheet. This opens the Insert Subdatasheet dialog. This dialog allows you to select which kind of object you want to use as the record source for the subdatasheet. Click the Tables tab (see Figure 4.9).

3. Click the Employees table in the list box.

4. The Link Child Fields drop-down list is used to indicate the foreign key, or matching field for the subdatasheet. Choose EmployeeID.

5. The Link Master Fields drop-down list is used to indicate the primary key, or matching field for the datasheet opened. Choose EmployeeID. Click OK.

6. Click the + next to a row in the Orders table. This expands the newly created subdatasheet and shows details for the employee who entered the order (see Figure 4.10).

NOTE   You cannot use subdatasheets in Access projects; they are available only in Access databases.

FIGURE 4.9:

The Insert Subdatasheet dialog for the Northwind database

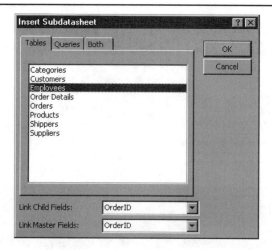

FIGURE 4.10:

The Employees subdatasheet of the Orders table

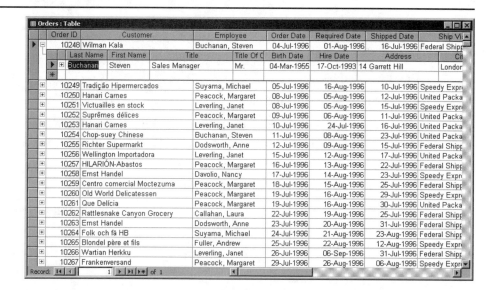

Communicating between Controls and Fields

When you use an AutoLookup query as the record source for a form, the control that is bound to the join field plays a special role. When you change the value in this control, Access automatically changes the values displayed in the controls bound to the lookup fields. The join control and the lookup controls do communicate with one another. However, when the form is not based on an AutoLookup query and all of the controls on a form are bound to table fields from the form's recordset, no communication occurs among the controls. For example, each control in the Employees form in Northwind is bound to a field in the Employees table. If you change the value in any one control, such as the FirstName control, no other control is affected.

Binding a control to a table field creates a two-way communication path between the control and the field. When you first display a record in a form, each bound control displays the data stored in its table field. When you enter or change data in a form control, the new or changed data is placed in a control buffer in memory. The control displays the edited value in the buffer, but the table field continues to store the unedited data. When you move to another control of the same record, Access updates the control buffer, placing the edited data in a record buffer in memory. While you are editing a record, the form controls display the edits, while the table continues to store the original record. Only when you save the record does Access update the record buffer and save the new or changed data to the table record. After saving the record, the data displayed in the form controls and stored in the table fields is identical. The table field sends the stored value to the form control, and in the other direction, the form control sends the edited value back to the table field when you save the record. This process is illustrated in Figure 4.11.

When a control is bound to a table field, you can enter new data or change existing data by typing a value into the control. Each control that is bound to a table field is independent of the other controls on the form.

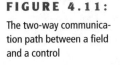

FIGURE 4.11:

The two-way communication path between a field and a control

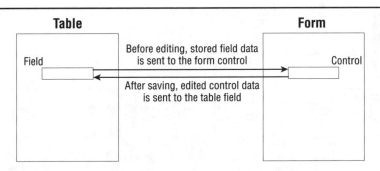

There are two ways you can arrange for the controls on a form to pass information to each other: by using calculated fields in the form's record source or by using a calculated control on the form.

Using Calculated Query Fields

A *calculated field* is a query field that displays the result of a calculation instead of displaying a data value stored in a database table. You can create a calculated field by typing an expression in an empty Field cell in the query design grid. You name the calculated field by typing in a name followed by a colon and the expression. (If you don't name the field, Access uses the default name Expr*N* where *N* is an integer that Access increments for each calculated field in the query.) The expression can include operators, functions, references to other fields in the query, and references to values that can be returned by other objects, such as values in controls on open forms. For example, suppose you wanted to display the full name of an employee in a single control in a form based on the Employees table. Here are the steps:

1. Create a query based on the Employees table and include the EmployeeID, FirstName, and LastName fields in the query.

2. Add a calculated query field by entering the following expression in a new Field cell in the query design grid (see Figure 4.12a):

   ```
   FullName: LastName & ", " & FirstName
   ```

3. Save the query as qryEmployeeField.

4. Use the AutoForm Wizard to create a new form based on the query (see Figure 4.12b).

5. Confirm that you can't change the value in the FullName control.

6. Change the value in the LastName control and tab to the next control. When you tab out of the changed control, the change is communicated to the FullName control automatically.

7. Close the form and save it as frmEmployeeField.

FIGURE 4.12:

Using a calculated field in a query (a) to concatenate two field values. The control bound to the calculated field updates automatically when the field values are changed (b).

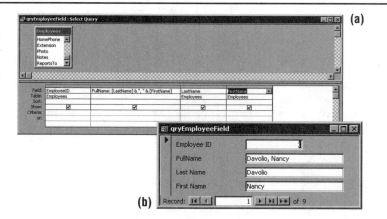

Using Calculated Form Controls

As an alternative to using a calculated query field, you can use a calculated form control. A calculated control is a control that displays the result of an expression. You enter the expression preceded by an equal sign (=) in the control's ControlSource property. The expression can include operators, functions, references to other controls on the form, references to fields in the form's data source, and references to values that can be returned by other objects, such as values in controls on other open forms. You set the control's Name property to a name that is different from the name of any other control on the form.

Instead of using a calculated query field to display the full name of an employee in a single control, as demonstrated in the previous section, you can use a calculated control, as follows:

1. Using the AutoForm Wizard, create a new form based on the Employees table.

2. Place an unbound text box on the form named FullName and set the ControlSource property to this expression:

    ```
    =LastName & ", " & FirstName
    ```

3. Confirm that you cannot change the value in the calculated control.

4. Change the value in the FirstName control and tab to the next control. When you tab out of the changed control, the FullName control shows the changed value automatically.

5. Close the form and save it as frmEmployeesControl.

An unbound, calculated control has a one-way communication path to the data in its ControlSource expression (see Figure 4.13). You set the ControlSource property to an expression that "pulls" data into the control. You can use the ControlSource expression to pull in data from three sources: the same form, another open form, or another data source, by using the DLookup() function (see Figure 4.14). The path is one way because changes you make in the data source are communicated to the calculated control, but you can't make changes directly to the calculated control (so the calculated control can't send any changes back to the data source).

FIGURE 4.13:

The one-way path between a data source and a calculated control

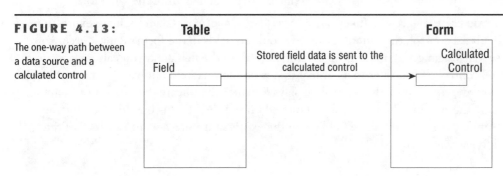

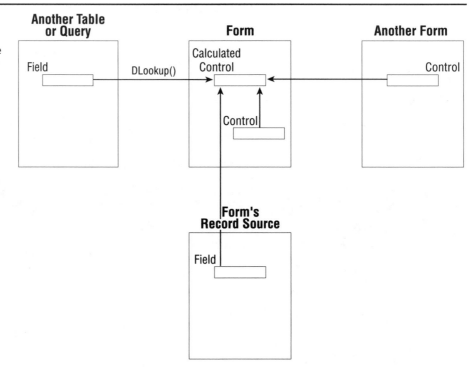

FIGURE 4.14:

A calculated control can get data from another table or query, the same form, or another data source.

Pulling Data from the Same Form

You can pull data into an unbound control from other controls on the same form or from fields in the form's data source, by setting the control's ControlSource property to an expression that refers to these controls or fields. You use the short syntax (the unqualified reference) when you refer to a field or control. When you use the short syntax and refer to a field or control by its name, Access assumes a field in the form's data source or a control on the same form. Table 4.1 lists examples of expressions for calculated controls that pull data from the same form.

When you use an aggregate function, such as Sum(), Avg(), or Count(), in an expression for a calculated control, the function can refer only to fields in the form's data source. You must use a field name and not a control name to refer to the field, and you cannot refer to a calculated control. If you refer to a control that is bound to a field but has a name that is different from the field name, the control displays #Name? to indicate the error. For example, to calculate the sum of values in a control named GrandTotal that is bound to a table field named Amount, refer to the table field using the expression =Sum(Amount) instead of the expression =Sum(GrandTotal).

TABLE 4.1: Some ControlSource Expressions for Calculated Controls That Get Data from the Same Form

ControlSource Expression	Description
=FirstName & " " & LastName	Displays the values in the FirstName and LastName controls separated by a space.
=Left(CompanyName,4)	Displays the first four characters of the value of the CompanyName control.
=Sum(Quantity*Price)	Displays the sum of the product of the values of the Quantity and Price fields for all the records displayed by the form.
=IIf(IsNull(Sum(Quantity*Price), 0,Sum(Quantity*Price))	Displays a zero if the sum is Null; otherwise, displays the sum.
=Count(EmployeeID)	Displays the number of records displayed by the form that have a non-Null value in the EmployeeID field.
=Count(*)	Displays the number of records displayed by the form. Use the asterisk (*) to count all of the records.

You can use the properties of the Screen object in the ControlSource expression of an unbound control. For example, you can display the number of the current record in an unbound control by setting the control's ControlSource property to =Screen.ActiveForm.CurrentRecord. When you navigate to a different record, Access automatically recalculates the new values in the unbound controls on the form. Explore the Screen object as follows:

1. Place two unbound text boxes on the frmEmployeeField form. Name one control txt-Previous and give it the ControlSource property =Screen.PreviousControl. Name the other control txtActive and give it the ControlSource property =Screen.ActiveControl.

2. When you switch to Form view, the txtActive control displays the EmployeeID value (1) in the active control. The txtPrevious control displays #Error because no control previously had the focus when you first opened the form (see Figure 4.15a).

3. Tab to the next control without making any changes. Neither txtActive nor txtPrevious updates automatically.

4. Force the unbound controls to update by selecting Records ➢ Refresh or by pressing the F9 function key (see Figure 4.15b).

5. Edit the LastName control and then tab to the next control. The FullName, txtActive, and txtPrevious calculated controls update automatically.

FIGURE 4.15:

Using properties of the
Screen object in calculated
controls to pull data from
the same form. When you
first display the form, there
is no "previous control" (a).
When you tab to another
control, you must force the
update of the calculated
controls (b).

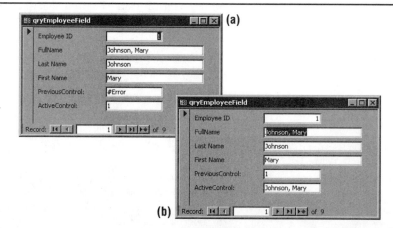

Displaying Current Data

In our example, the unbound controls don't update automatically unless you edit a control on the form. If you are working interactively, you can force the update of calculated controls by pressing the F9 function key. It takes programming to achieve consistent automatic update behavior. Specifically, you can write a program to refresh the record when you move to a second control whether or not you edited the first control.

The trick to creating an updating program is deciding which event should trigger the program. When you move to a different control on the same form, the control you move out of recognizes the Exit and LostFocus events, and the control you move to recognizes the Enter and GotFocus events. You can use any of these events to trigger the program, as long as you are moving among controls on the same form. If you are moving back and forth between controls on two separate forms or on a main form and a subform, the choice of an event is subtler because the controls may not recognize all of these events. (See Chapter 2, "Getting Started with Objects and Events," for information about when these events are triggered.)

The data displayed in the active window may not be current for several reasons. Here are a few examples:

- When you have two windows open or when you are viewing data in a multiuser environment, changes made in one window may not be reflected automatically in the other window.

- The values in calculated controls on a form may not be recalculated automatically until you move to a different record.

- Data in the list box or combo box of a lookup field from another table is not updated automatically when changes are made to the other table.

Continued on next page

There are three ways to update the display:

- Refresh updates data in the existing record. To refresh the active window, choose Records ➢ Refresh or press F9. Refresh does not reorder the records, display added records, remove deleted records (a deleted record is indicated with the value #Deleted in each field of the record), or remove records that no longer satisfy specified filter or query criteria. For these updates, you must requery the form.

- You can recalculate calculated controls by pressing F9.

- Requery reruns the query on which the object is based, or if the object is based on a table, requery "reruns" the table and displays only the current table records. You can requery the form interactively by pressing Shift+F9.

You can automate the refresh, requery, and recalculate operations with VBA procedures.

Note that if the form contains a combo box or a list box that displays rows from a data source other than the form's data source, requerying the data source of the form doesn't requery the data source of the combo box or list box control. You can observe this behavior with the Products and Categories forms in Northwind. The data source of the Products form is the Products table, and the data source of the form's Category combo box is a SQL statement based on the Categories table. Open both forms in Form view, add a new category in the Categories form, and save the new record. When you display the Category combo list in Products, the new category is not displayed. Pressing Shift+F9 requeries the data source of the form, but does not requery the data source of the combo box. Pressing F9 refreshes the form and requeries the combo box but does not requery the form. Updating the Products form interactively is a two-step process: press F9 and then press Shift+F9. Another interactive method for requerying both the form and its combo box and list box controls is to close and reopen the form.

Pulling Data from Another Open Form or an Open Report

You can pull data into an unbound control from controls on another open form or from fields in another form's data source by setting the control's ControlSource property to an expression that refers to these controls or fields. In this case, you use the fully qualified reference because you are referring to controls or fields on another open form. For example, with the Orders and Employees forms in Northwind both open, you can display the employee's full name on the Orders form by placing an unbound control on the Orders form and setting the ControlSource property as follows:

```
=Forms!Employees!LastName & ", " & Forms!Employees!FirstName
```

Table 4.2 lists examples of ControlSource expressions that pull data from another open form. In these examples, the unbound control is on the Orders form or its subform and refers to controls on the Customer Orders form in Northwind.

TABLE 4.2: Some ControlSource Expressions for Referring to Another Open Form

ControlSource Expression	Description
=Forms![Customer Orders]!CustomerID	Displays the value of the CustomerID field in the data source of the Customer Orders form.
=Forms![Customer Orders]![Customer Orders Subform1]!OrderDate	Displays the value of the OrderDate control of the current record in the Customer Orders Subform1 subform of the Customer Orders form.
=[Orders Subform]!UnitPrice	Displays the value of the UnitPrice control of the current record in the Orders Subform of the active form. The calculated control is located on the main form.
=Parent!OrderID	Displays the value of the OrderID control on the parent form of the current subform. The calculated control is located on the subform.

You can combine references to two open forms in an expression. For example, with the Customers and Employees forms open,

1. Place an unbound text box named txtBoth on the Customers form that displays the current record numbers of the two open forms by setting the ControlSource property as follows:

```
="The Customers current record is " & Screen.ActiveForm. _
CurrentRecord & " and the Employees current record is " & _
Forms!Employees.CurrentRecord
```

2. Browse through the records on the Customers form. Note that the control updates automatically to display the record number of the current form (see Figure 4.16a).

3. Browse through the records on the Employees form and then click back into the Customers form. Note that the txtBoth control does not update automatically (see Figure 4.16b).

4. Force the recalculation of the controls on the Customers form by moving to another record, by choosing Records ➢ Refresh, or by pressing F9.

With programming, you can automate the update. You can create a VBA procedure to update the Customers form when you click into it. When you click a form, it recognizes the Activate event, so you could use the Activate event to trigger the program.

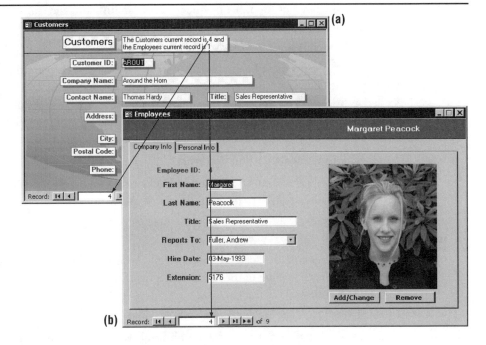

FIGURE 4.16:

The calculated control updates automatically when you browse the records of the Customers form (a), but not when you browse the records of the Employees form (b).

Using *DLookup()* and Other Aggregate Functions

Sometimes, you want a form to look up information that is stored in a table or query that is not the form's underlying record source. In this case, you can use the DLookup() function in the ControlSource property of a calculated control to display data from the other table or query. For example, when you enter a new product in the Products form, you may want the form to look up and display the category description from the Categories table. You can create an unbound control on the Products form and set the control's ControlSource property to a DLookup() function that looks up the description directly from the Categories table. You can use the DLookup() function as follows:

In a query   In a calculated field expression in a Field cell, to specify criteria in a Criteria cell, or in an expression in the Update To cell in an update query.

In a VBA procedure   In a condition or method argument.

In a form or report   In a calculated control.

The DLookup() function takes three arguments. In the simplest case, the first argument is the name of the field in the table or query that holds the data you want to look up, the second argument is the name of the table or query (the domain), and the third argument is the search condition you are using to select the record. The syntax is as follows:

```
DLookup("fieldname", "tablename" or "queryname", " searchcondition")
```

All three arguments must be expressed as strings. If the search condition returns more than one record, the DLookup() function returns the value of the field in the first record that satisfies the condition. If you don't specify a search condition at all, the DLookup() function returns the field value from a random record in the domain. If no record matches the search condition, or if the table or query have no records, the DLookup() function returns a Null value.

To see how the DLookup() function works,

1. Place an unbound text box named txtDescription on the Products form and set the ControlSource property to the following expression:

   ```
   =DLookup("Description","Categories","CategoryID = _
   Forms!Products!CategoryID")
   ```

   In this expression, the search condition tells Access to select the record whose CategoryID field matches the value in the form's CategoryID control. The syntax for the search condition is as follows:

   ```
   fieldname = Forms!formname!controlname
   ```

   where the left side of the search condition is the name of the field in the table or query you are searching, and the right side is the fully qualified reference to the form control with the value you are searching for.

2. Browse through the records in the Products form. Note that the Category Description text box updates automatically (see Figure 4.17).

3. Select a different category from the Category combo box. Note that the unbound control does not update automatically.

4. Update the control interactively by pressing F9.

The DLookup() function is an example of a *domain aggregate function*—a built-in Access function that you can use to perform calculations based on the values in a field of a table or query. You can specify criteria to select the set of records in the table or query that you want to use for the calculation. The selection criteria are optional; if you don't specify additional criteria, then all of the records in the table or query are used. The table or query is called the *domain*. You must also specify the field that you want the function to work with (instead of specifying a field, you can specify an expression that performs a calculation on values in a field). Once the domain and criteria are specified and the particular field is selected, the function performs a calculation on the values in the field and returns the result of the calculation. The domain aggregate functions are listed in Table 4.3.

The Category Description control uses the DLookup() function to look up the description in the Categories table.

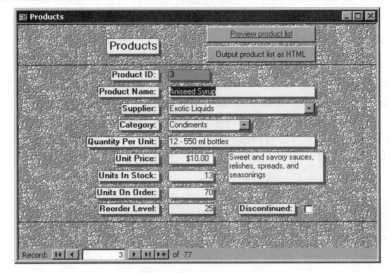

You can use any of the domain aggregate functions in the ControlSource expression. All of the domain aggregate functions use the same syntax. In the most general case, the first argument can be either a field name for one of the fields in the domain or an expression based on at least one of the fields. The second argument is the set of records in the table or query (the domain). The third argument is the search condition that restricts the set to a smaller group (the restricted domain). The third argument is optional; if you don't specify a search condition, the function uses the larger set of records (the domain). If no record satisfies the search condition, or if the domain contains no records, the domain aggregate function returns a Null. The syntax is as follows:

```
DFunction("fieldname" or "expression", "tablename" or "queryname",
  "searchcondition")
```

TABLE 4.3: Domain Aggregate Functions

Function	Description
DLookup()	Returns the value in the specified field
DMin(), DMax()	Return the minimum or maximum value in the specified field
DFirst(), DLast()	Return the value in the specified field from the first or last physical record
DAvg()	Returns the arithmetical average of the values in the specified field
DSum()	Returns the sum of the values in the specified field
DStDev(), DStDevP()	Return the standard deviation or population standard deviation for the specified field
DVar(), DVarP()	Return the variance or population variance for the specified field
DCount()	Returns the number of records with non-Null values in the specified field

When there is no search condition to restrict the domain, the syntax is as follows:

```
DFunction("fieldname" or "expression", "tablename" or "queryname")
```

For example, you can use the DSum() function to return the sum of a set of values. The ControlSource expression,

```
=DSum("Freight", "Orders", "CustomerID=Forms!Customers!CustomerID")
```

displays the sum total of the values of the Freight field in the Orders table for all of the orders for the customer currently displayed in the Customers form. The expression,

```
=DSum("Quantity*UnitPrice", "Order Details", "ProductID = " & [ProductID])
```

displays the sum total of the product of the Quantity and UnitPrice fields in the Order Details table for the product currently displayed in the Products form. The calculated control is on the Products form.

NOTE The domain aggregate functions are actually SQL statements in a different format. You can think of a domain aggregate function as a query that returns a single value. The search condition is equivalent to a SQL WHERE clause without the word WHERE. Every time you use one of these functions, you run a query as a SQL statement. Before running a SQL statement, the database engine must analyze the statement to determine the optimal way to execute it. As a result, the domain aggregate functions may be slower than other alternatives for looking up information.

There are also SQL aggregate functions, which operate similarly to domain aggregate functions. However, unlike domain aggregate functions, SQL aggregate functions cannot be called directly from Visual Basic. Because they use SQL statements instead of Visual Basic, SQL aggregate functions are usually more efficient than domain aggregate functions. The SQL aggregate functions are listed in Table 4.4.

TABLE 4.4: SQL Aggregate Functions

Function	Description
Avg	Returns the average of a set of values in a field or query
Count	Returns the number of records returned by a query
First, Last	Return a field value from the first or last record in the results of a query
Min, Max	Return the minimum or maximum of a field's or query's value set
StDev, StDevP	Return estimates of standard deviation from a sample
Sum	Returns the sum of a set
Var, VarP	Return estimates of variance (the square of the standard deviation)

Using an Unbound Control as a Variable

In programming terminology, a *variable* is a named temporary storage location in memory that is used to hold a value. You can think of an unbound form control as a type of variable. The value displayed in an unbound control is not stored anywhere in the database and exists only as long as the form is open. This means that the lifetime of the unbound control variable is the time interval when the form is open. An unbound control is a *global variable* because its value is available to all other queries, forms, and reports in the database. (In later chapters, you'll learn ways to create variables without using form controls as temporary storage containers.)

Pulling and Pushing Data into an Unbound Control

There are two ways to set a value in an unbound control. We've seen that you can use the ControlSource property of an unbound control to "pull" data into the control. You can pull data from controls on other forms or reports, from fields in the form's underlying record source, and from fields in another table or query (using DLookup() or another domain aggregate function).

You can also place an unbound control with a blank ControlSource on a form. To set a value in such a control, you must perform an action. The action you perform "pushes" data into the unbound control. You can push a value into an unbound control with a blank ControlSource property by typing the value directly from the keyboard, or you can push the value with a VBA procedure. These methods are illustrated in Figure 4.18.

FIGURE 4.18:

Pushing data into an unbound control

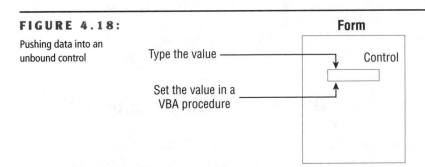

For example, the lookup combo box we placed on the Expense Reports By Employee form in Chapter l, "Automating a Database without Programming," is an unbound control with a blank ControlSource property. This variable holds the value of the EmployeeID for the customer we want to look up. Choosing a value from the combo list pushes the value into the control. After you choose the value, a VBA procedure synchronizes the form to the value in the combo box variable.

Using a Global Variables Form

Depending on what you are trying to do, you can place unbound controls as variables directly on the task forms in your application or you can create a separate global variables form to hold some of your global variables. If you need some of the values to be available the next time you start up the application, create a table to store the values that you want to be permanent, or *persistent*. In general, a global variables form may have both unbound controls for transient variables and bound controls for persistent variables. The form must be open whenever the application is open so that the values will be available to other forms and queries. If the user needs to type values directly into some of the controls, the form must be visible. However, if the values are pulled into calculated controls or query expressions or are pushed into the controls with VBA procedures, the form can be hidden.

Saving a Calculated Result to the Database

Sometimes, you use an expression to perform a calculation on a form and you want to save the result to the database. For example, suppose you calculate the total revenue for all orders for each customer and you want to save the total in the Customers table.

NOTE   One of the guidelines of database design is that you don't store calculated values but that you recalculate them each time you need them. However, for summary values it is often convenient and faster to bend this rule and store the values.

When you use a calculated control for the calculation, you use the ControlSource property to hold the expression, so you can't also use the ControlSource property to bind the control to a table field. The solution to the problem is to do the calculation in a VBA procedure, instead of using the ControlSource property, and then push the result of the calculation into a bound control using another VBA procedure. We'll see how to push values into bound and unbound controls in later chapters.

Using a Combo Box or List Box to Look Up Information

In Access 2002, a form can have only one table, query, view, or SQL statement as its record source. As explained in the previous sections, you can get around the limitation of one data source per form by looking up values in another open form or report or by using the DLookup() function to look up values in any table or query. The result of these techniques is a single value that you can either pull into an unbound control using the ControlSource property or push into either a bound control or an unbound control that has a blank ControlSource property. These techniques are useful when you want to display a single value based on another data source but are less helpful when you want to display several values at the same time. The combo box and list box controls provide an efficient way to look up and display entire rows of values from a second data source.

A combo box or a list box has RowSource and RowSourceType properties, which you can use to specify a data source for the control that can be different from the data source of the form. This means that you can display records from the table, query, view, or SQL statement in the RowSource property as rows of a *mini-datasheet*. The RowSource property pulls entire rows of data from a data source into the combo box list. When you display the combo list, you display the mini-datasheet of the second data source. The combo box also has a ControlSource property and a BoundColumn property. You can use the BoundColumn property of the combo box or list box to specify which column in the mini-datasheet to use for the value of the control. Finally, you can use the ControlSource property to bind the control to a field in the form's data source.

To explore these concepts, we'll modify the SupplierID combo box on the Products form to display additional fields from the Suppliers table.

1. Open the Products form in Design view and click the SupplierID combo box. Figure 4.19a shows the properties of the combo box. The ControlSource property setting indicates that the combo box is bound to the SupplierID field in the Products

FIGURE 4.19:

The properties of the SupplierID combo box indicate that the first column is held in the control and the second column is displayed in the combo box list (a). Add the ContactName and Phone columns to the combo box row source (b).

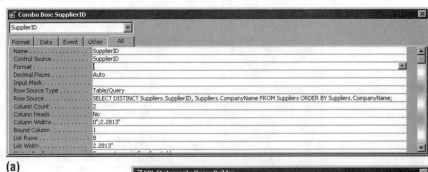

table. The RowSource property setting is a SQL statement that retrieves rows with SupplierID and CompanyName from the Suppliers table and alphabetizes them by CompanyName. The BoundColumn property setting indicates that the value in the first column of the selected row is held in the combo box. The ColumnWidths property indicates that the SupplierID is hidden and the CompanyName values are displayed in the combo list.

2. Click the Build button at the right of the RowSource property box to display the Query Builder. Drag the ContactName and Phone fields to the design grid (see Figure 4.19b). Close the Query Builder and save the changes.

3. Change the combo box properties to display the additional fields as rows of a mini-datasheet as shown below.

ColumnCount   4
ColumnWidths   0", 1.2", 1", 0.5"
ListWidth   3.2"

4. Save the form, switch to Form view, and drop the Supplier combo list (see Figure 4.20). The combo list displays three columns from the Suppliers table as a mini-datasheet.

FIGURE 4.20:

The Products form is based on the Products table, and the Suppliers combo box list displays a mini-datasheet based on the Suppliers table.

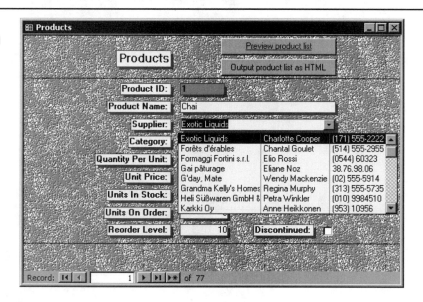

You can display the value from any column of a combo box (or list box) in another control on a form in one of two ways: you can pull the value in a calculated control using the ControlSource property, or you can push the value into a bound or unbound control using a VBA procedure to set the value of the control. In either case, you use the Column property of the combo box or list box to refer to a specific column or to a specific column and row.

Pulling Data from a Combo Box List into an Unbound Control

To demonstrate the pulling technique, we'll pull the contact name and phone information into unbound controls on the Products form using the ControlSource property.

1. Open the Products form in Design view. Place two unbound text box controls on the Products form. Name one txtContactName and give it the ControlSource property =SupplierID.Column(2). Name the other txtPhone and give it the ControlSource property =SupplierID.Column(3). (When you enter the ControlSource expressions, Access encloses each word in square brackets.) The Column property is zero-based; this means that Column(0) refers to the first column, Column(1) refers to the second column, and so on. Save the form and switch to Form view.

2. Browse through the records. The unbound controls automatically update to display the information passed using the combo box (see Figure 4.21). Any time the value in the combo box changes, the unbound controls on the form that refer to the columns in the combo box pull their values from the combo box. As always, calculated controls are read-only, so you can't modify the pulled values.

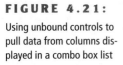

FIGURE 4.21:

Using unbound controls to pull data from columns displayed in a combo box list

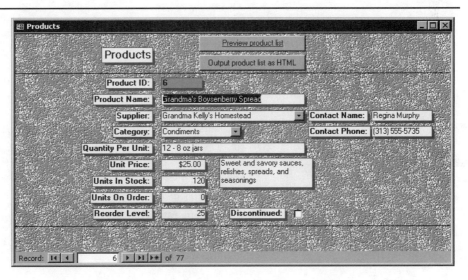

You can also refer to the values in one or more columns in an expression. For example, you can concatenate the information in two columns of the mini-datasheet and display the result in a single unbound text box by setting its ControlSource property.

3. Switch back to Design view. Delete the txtContactName and txtPhone text boxes and place a single unbound text box on the form. Name it txtContactInf and give it the following ControlSource property:

```
=SupplierID.Column(2) & ": " & SupplierID.Column(3)
```

4. Switch to Form view and browse the records.

By default, the values you display in the columns of a combo box have the Text data type. Before you can use a value in calculations, you may need to convert the data type from Text to another data type, using one of the conversion functions in Table 4.5.

TABLE 4.5: Data-Conversion Functions

Function	Converts String or Numeric Expression to
CBool	Boolean. If the expression is zero, False is returned; otherwise, True is returned.
CByte	Byte.
CCur	Currency.
CDate	Date.
CDbl	Double.
CDec	Decimal.
CInt	Integer.
CLng	Long.
CSng	Single.
CStr	String.
CVar	Variant.
CVDate	Variant of subtype Date.
CVErr	Variant of subtype Error.
Fix	Returns the integer portion of a number; rounds negative numbers up.
Hex	Variant (hexadecimal).
Int	Returns the integer portion of a number; rounds negative numbers down.
Oct	Variant (octal).
Str	Variant (string).
Val	Converts a string of number characters into a number of appropriate type.

TIP   The Val conversion property has some unique features. In converting a string of characters into a number type, it skips over spaces, tabs, and linefeed characters. When it encounters a non-number character, it stops the conversion. Thus, "123 45A23" is converted to "12345"—an integer type.

Pushing Data from a Combo Box List into a Bound Control

Because it is the expression in a control's ControlSource property that pulls the value from a combo box column into the control, the pull method works only for unbound controls. A bound control necessarily has its ControlSource property set to the field it is bound to, so the Control-Source property is not available for pulling values. When you want to fill a bound control with a value from a column in the mini-datasheet of a combo box or list box, you must create a VBA procedure to *push* the data into the control. For example, the Bill To combo box on the Orders form in Northwind uses a VBA procedure to push the CustomerName selected in the combo box into the ShipName text box and the address data into the shipping address controls. In later chapters, you'll learn how to push data from a combo box list column into a control.

Synchronizing Forms

This section focuses on the communication between the controls on two open forms. When two forms with different data sources are open, the forms are related if there is a relationship between their underlying tables, views, or queries. For example, the Customers form and the Orders form are related because their underlying tables, the Customers table and Orders table, have a one-to-many relationship.

When you open the two related forms, each form displays the first record in its own recordset, and the forms are not synchronized. Synchronizing two related forms means displaying related records in both forms.

Either form can regulate the synchronization. For example, if the Customers form regulates the synchronization, then synchronizing the forms means filtering the Orders form to display only the orders corresponding to the customer currently displayed in the Customers form. Keeping the forms synchronized means keeping the filter updated so that when you browse to another customer in the Customers form, the Orders form changes automatically to display only the corresponding records. On the other hand, if the Orders form regulates the synchronization, then synchronizing the forms means looking up the customer record corresponding to the order displayed in the Orders form. Keeping the forms synchronized means updating the customer lookup procedure so that when you browse to a different order, the Customers form always displays the related customer.

When two forms are displayed in separate windows, synchronizing the forms and keeping them synchronized is best handled with programming. In later chapters, you'll learn synchronization techniques in VBA programming. For now, we'll use the powerful Form Wizard to synchronize two forms.

The Form Wizard uses two different techniques for synchronizing related forms, depending on whether the forms are displayed in separate windows or in a single window. When you want to display the forms in two separate windows, the Form Wizard uses VBA procedures to synchronize and resynchronize two related forms. When you display the forms in a separate window as a main form/subform combination, Access handles the synchronization internally, and all you (or the wizard) need to do is set linking properties.

Using the Form Wizard to Synchronize Two Forms

You can use the Form Wizard to create separate forms for two related data sources and to write the procedures that keep the forms synchronized. To see how the wizard works, we'll use it to create synchronized forms for the Customers table and the Orders table in the Northwind_Ch4 database.

1. Start the Form Wizard by clicking the Forms button in the Database window and double-clicking Create Form By Using Wizard.

2. In the first screen, you select the fields from the tables or queries that you want on the two forms (see Figure 4.22a). Select a few fields from the Customers table and then select a few fields from the Orders table.

3. The next screen gives you the opportunity to specify which form regulates the synchronization and to specify whether the result is a form with a subform or linked forms in separate windows (see Figure 4.22b). Select the second option, Linked Forms.

4. The next screen provides a choice of styles for the forms. Select the Standard style.

5. You use the final screen to specify titles for the linked forms. Enter **CustomersLinked** and **OrdersLinked** for the titles and then click the Finish button.

The Form Wizard creates the forms and displays the CustomersLinked form (see Figure 4.23a). The CustomersLinked form regulates the synchronization. When you click the toggle button on the controlling form, the OrdersLinked form opens, displaying the corresponding records; the lower left of the form indicates that a filter is being used to select the records (see Figure 4.23b). When you browse to another record on the CustomersLinked form, the filter in the OrdersLinked form is automatically changed and reapplied to keep the records synchronized.

FIGURE 4.22:

Use the Form Wizard to create and synchronize related forms.

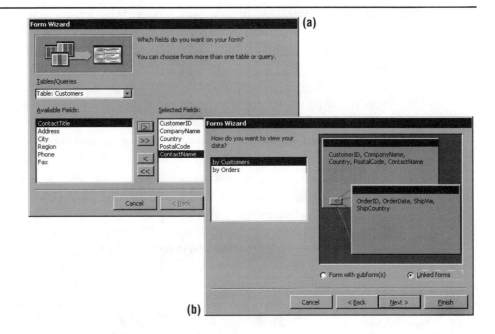

(a)

(b)

FIGURE 4.23:

The Form Wizard creates a toggle button on the form that regulates the synchronization (a). Clicking the button opens the second form and filters its records (b).

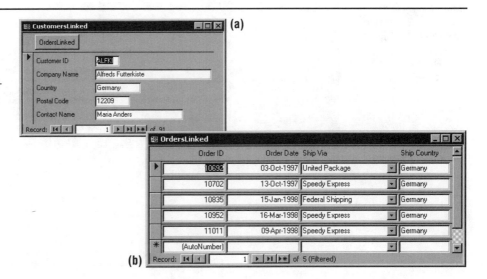

(a)

(b)

As long as the OrdersLinked form is open, the toggle button on the CustomersLinked form remains pushed in. When you click the pushed-in toggle button, the OrdersLinked form closes and the toggle button returns to an unpushed state. The wizard uses at least two events to trigger each program:

- It uses the Click event of the toggle button (see Figure 4.24a). When the toggle button is clicked, the OrdersLinked form is either opened or closed depending on the form's state when you click the button. If the OrdersLinked form is already open, clicking the button closes it; if the OrdersLinked form is closed, clicking the button opens it and also creates and applies a filter to select the related records.

- It uses the Current event of the CustomersLinked form (see Figure 4.24b). When you browse to another customer, the form recognizes the Current event. (A form recognizes the Current event after the focus leaves one record and before the focus moves to another; a form also recognizes the Current event when the form is first opened but before the first record is displayed and whenever you requery the form.) If the OrdersLinked form is closed, nothing happens; but if the OrdersLinked form is open, a new filter is created and applied to the OrdersLinked form to select the correct records.

FIGURE 4.24:

The Form Wizard creates event procedures for the toggle button's Click event (a) and the controlling form's Current event (b).

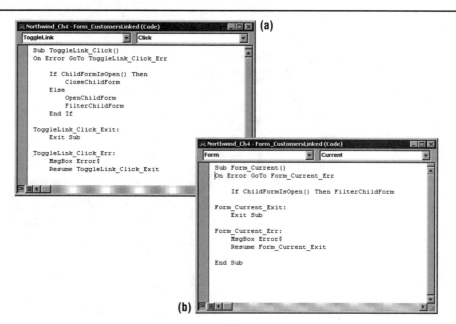

FIGURE 4.25:

The Form Wizard creates four support procedures that are used by the two event procedures.

```
Northwind_Ch4 - Form_CustomersLinked (Code)                              _ □ ×
(General)                                    ▼  (Declarations)                  ▼
    End Sub
    Private Sub FilterChildForm()

        If Me.NewRecord Then
            Forms![OrdersLinked].DataEntry = True
        Else
            Forms![OrdersLinked].Filter = "[CustomerID] = " & """" & Me.[CustomerID] & """"
            Forms![OrdersLinked].FilterOn = True
        End If

    End Sub
    Private Sub OpenChildForm()

        DoCmd.OpenForm "OrdersLinked"
        If Not Me.[ToggleLink] Then Me![ToggleLink] = True

    End Sub
    Private Sub CloseChildForm()

        DoCmd.Close acForm, "OrdersLinked"
        If Me![ToggleLink] Then Me![ToggleLink] = False

    End Sub
    Private Function ChildFormIsOpen()

        ChildFormIsOpen = (SysCmd(acSysCmdGetObjectState, acForm, "OrdersLinked") And acObjStateOpen)

    End Function
```

After you work with the two forms, you realize that additional events are triggering programs. Because the two forms are separate, you can open and close each form independently of the other. You can open the OrdersLinked form by clicking the toggle button on the CustomersLinked form, or you can open it directly from the Database window. Once open, the OrdersLinked form can be closed by clicking the toggle button on the CustomersLinked form, or it can be closed by clicking its default Close button. Whatever the sequence, notice that the toggle button automatically changes in its appearance to reflect the state of the OrdersLinked form. Suppose the CustomersLinked form is open. No matter how you open the OrdersLinked form, the toggle button is pushed in. No matter how you close the OrdersLinked form, the toggle button is pushed out. The behavior of the toggle button means that the wizard must be using events to trigger programs that change the state of the toggle button. The two additional events are the Load and Unload events recognized by the OrdersLinked form. Figure 4.26 shows the event procedures for each of these events, and Figure 4.27 shows the support procedure they use. In later chapters, you'll learn how to write programs like these.

Using the Form/Subform Technique to Synchronize Forms

You can use the built-in form/subform technique to display two forms in a single window. When you use this technique to display information in related forms, Access handles the synchronization and resynchronization for you.

FIGURE 4.26:

The Form Wizard creates event procedures for the Load event (a) and the Unload event (b).

FIGURE 4.27:

The Form Wizard creates a support procedure used by both event procedures that keep the toggle button in sync.

Properties of the Subform Control

Access provides the subform/subreport control as a way to synchronize two forms (or two reports, or a report and a form) and keep their records synchronized. One of the forms becomes the main form when you place a subform control on it. The three crucial properties of the subform control are SourceObject, LinkChildFields, and LinkMasterFields. You connect the second form to the first when you set the SourceObject property of the subform control to the name of the second form; the second form then becomes a subform. When you open the main form in Form view, the subform control displays the second form. If you leave blank the two record-linking properties, LinkChildFields and LinkMasterFields, the forms are connected but their records aren't linked and you can browse their records independently. In fact, the underlying tables or queries for the two forms do not need to be related in order to display the forms in the single window of the form/subform arrangement.

If the data sources of the two forms are related, you can link the records by setting the subform control's two record-linking properties to the matching fields. If the forms are related on multiple fields, enter the field names separated by semicolons into the property boxes; make sure you enter matching fields in corresponding order. You can use the Subform/Subreport Linker to help set the record-linking properties. To start the Linker, open the main form in Design view, display the property sheet for the subform control, and then click the Build button to the right of either of the record-linking properties. Figure 4.28 shows the Subform Field Linker dialog where you specify the linking fields. The record-linking fields do not need to be included as controls on either the main form or the subform. After you set the two record-linking properties, the records are linked (synchronized) and remain synchronized. As you browse through the records of the main form, Access displays the synchronized records in the second form.

FIGURE 4.28:

Use the Subform/Subreport Linker to set record-linking properties.

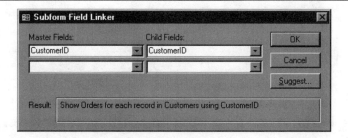

In the form/subform technique, all you need to do is set the subform control properties, and Access automatically keeps the forms synchronized. Under certain conditions, Access even sets the subform control properties for you. If you create the subform or subreport by dragging a form or report from the Database window onto another form or report, Access automatically displays the dragged object within a subform/subreport control and sets the record-linking properties, if the following two conditions are met:

- The main form or report is based on a table with a primary key. Access sets the LinkMasterFields property to the primary key field(s).

- The subform or subreport is based on a query or a table that contains a field (or fields) with the same name and the same or a compatible data type as the primary key of the table underlying the main form. Access sets the LinkChildFields property to the identically named fields from the subform's or subreport's data source.

You can use the form/subform technique to display a one-to-many relationship by basing the main form on the one side and the subform on the many side. For example, the Customers and Orders tables have a one-to-many relationship. With the main form based on the Customers table and a subform based on the Orders table, the form/subform displays all of the orders for a customer. Figure 4.29 shows the CustomerswithOrders form/subform that the Form Wizard creates.

FIGURE 4.29:

You can use the form/ subform technique to display a one-to-many relationship.

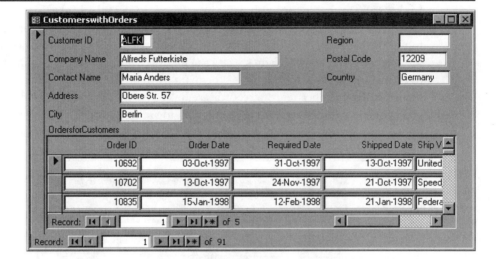

Using the Form Wizard to Synchronize Two Subforms

The Form Wizard is capable of creating both a simple form/subform combination (such as the form shown in Figure 4.29) and a complex combination of a main form with a synchronized subform and a second subform synchronized to the first subform. The Customer Orders form in Northwind demonstrates the wizard's power. Figure 4.30 shows the Customer Orders form with two synchronized subforms; the arrangement is called a one-to-many-to-many form.

The main form displays a customer record, and the first subform displays the orders for the customer. This much is ordinary and uses the record-linking properties of the subform control to synchronize the records in the Customers table and the Orders table. Things get interesting when we look at the second subform, which displays the details of an order. The second subform is based on the Order Details Extended query. Each record in this query corresponds to a product purchased in an order. The second subform is linked to the first subform using OrderID as the matching field in both recordsets. Figure 4.31 shows the linking property settings set in the subform control for the second subform; these settings match the OrderID value in the second subform to the OrderID value in the first subform.

FIGURE 4.30:

The one-to-many-to-many form

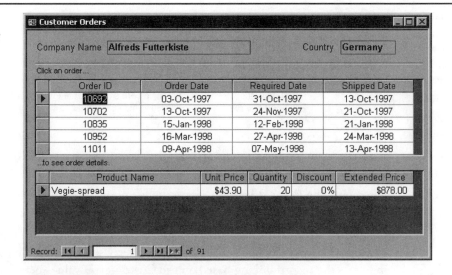

FIGURE 4.31:

The linking properties in the second subform control synchronize the second subform to the first subform.

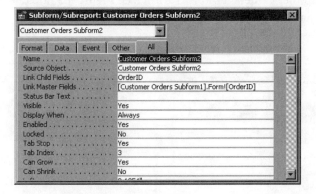

Note that the identifier for the LinkMasterFields property uses the Form property of the subform control to refer to the form displayed inside the subform control. (The OrderID field in the second subform is not displayed in a control, but you can still use the values in the field for linking.) When you select an order in the first subform, the second subform is synchronized to display the products purchased in the order. Figure 4.32 illustrates these relationships.

If you tried to create this form without using the Form Wizard, you would find that the second subform doesn't update automatically. When you select a different order, the second subform continues to display the records for the previous order. You can update the second subform interactively by selecting an order in the second subform, clicking into a

FIGURE 4.32:

The LinkMasterFields property references the OrderID field.

The Form property refers to the form displayed in the subform control

[Customer Orders Subform1].Form![OrderID]

Refers to the subform control

A field in the record source of the form displayed in the subform control

control on the main form, and then pressing F9. Note that selecting Records ➤ Refresh does not force the update of the second subform.

When you use the Form Wizard to create the form, the wizard handles updating for you. To observe how the wizard automates the synchronization, follow these steps:

1. Open the Customer Orders form in Design view. The main form regulates the synchronization with the first subform. The property sheet for the first subform control indicates the record linking based on the CustomerID values between the main form and the Customer Orders Subform1 form (see Figure 4.33a). The property sheet for the second subform control (see Figure 4.33b) indicates the record linking between the two subforms based on the OrderID values.

FIGURE 4.33:

The record-linking properties for the linking between the main form and the first subform (a), and between the first and the second subforms (b)

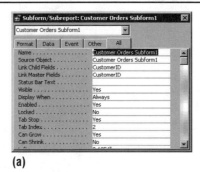

(a)

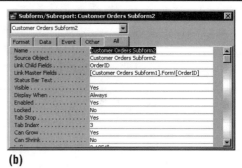

(b)

2. Open the first subform in Design view. The property sheet for this form indicates that the Form Wizard has created an event procedure that is triggered by the form's Current event.

3. To view the VBA procedure, click the Build button at the right of the On Current property box. Note the line that includes `Requery` is the instruction to requery the second subform (see Figure 4.34). Whenever you click a different record in the first subform, this procedure runs and requeries the second subform.

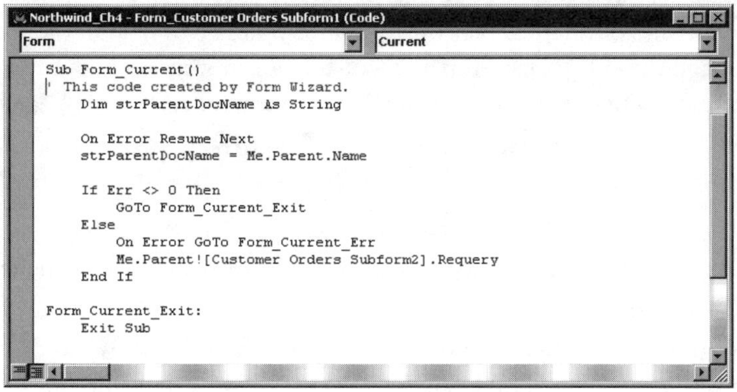

FIGURE 4.34:

The Form Wizard creates an event procedure for the Current event of the second subform that keeps the second subform in sync with the first subform.

```
Northwind_Ch4 - Form_Customer Orders Subform1 (Code)
Form                              Current
    Sub Form_Current()
    ' This code created by Form Wizard.
        Dim strParentDocName As String

        On Error Resume Next
        strParentDocName = Me.Parent.Name

        If Err <> 0 Then
            GoTo Form_Current_Exit
        Else
            On Error GoTo Form_Current_Err
            Me.Parent![Customer Orders Subform2].Requery
        End If

    Form_Current_Exit:
        Exit Sub
```

Summary

In most automated Access applications, the interface consists entirely of pages, forms, and reports. In automating a database, you write VBA procedures that depend on understanding the connection between forms and pages and data in tables, as well as how forms and pages can communicate information to each other.

- The setting of the RecordSource property of a form, data access page section, or report indicates whether the form or report is connected to a table, view, query, or SQL statement. If the RecordSource property is blank, the form, section, or report is unbound. If the setting is the name of a table, the name of a view, the name of a stored query, or a SQL statement, the form, section, or report is bound to the underlying data source.

- If the form has an AutoLookup query based on two tables in a one-to-many relationship as its record source, you can use the form to automatically look up information from the "one" table when you enter a value in a join field.

- A form, section, or report has a single record source, but the form can obtain information from other data sources in several ways:

Calculated controls You use calculated controls to look up information in another open form or report. You can use the DLookup() function in a ControlSource expression of a calculated control to look up information in any table or query. ControlSource property expressions pull data into the control.

Programming You use programming to look up or calculate a value and then push the value into an unbound control (if the control has a blank ControlSource property) or a bound control.

Combo box or list box control A combo box or list box control can be connected to two different tables or queries: the control can be bound to a field in the form's underlying record source, and the control can display records from another data source. You can use these controls to pass values from another table, view, query, or SQL statement into the form.

- When the form doesn't update automatically to display the most current data, programming is necessary to automate updating.

- When forms are based on related tables or queries, you can use the built-in linking properties of the subform control to keep the forms synchronized in a main form/subform arrangement.

- Programming is required to synchronize related forms when the forms are displayed in separate windows. The Form Wizard uses VBA programming for the synchronization.

This chapter completes the preliminary topics essential for VBA programming. You are now ready to learn how to write the programs you have been observing in these chapters.

CHAPTER 5

VBA Programming Essentials

- Using assignment statements to set and get property values

- Calling methods

- Using VBA-only features of forms and reports

- Creating a second current record pointer

- Referring to objects in VBA

- Exploring VBA-only object properties and methods

- Using the Object Browser

This chapter describes the fundamentals of VBA programming. We begin by reviewing some basic programming concepts. Then you'll learn how to get and set object properties, call object methods, and refer to objects in VBA programs. The chapter next covers the VBA-only features of forms and reports.

A good portion of this chapter is devoted to the Access Application object model. We continue the discussion of the model we began in Chapter 3, "Introducing the Access Object Model," focusing on the VBA-only aspects and methods of the objects. Finally, you'll learn how to use the Object Browser to explore objects.

Basic Programming Concepts

This chapter revisits the basic concepts of the Access programming model that were introduced in earlier chapters:

- Access defines a set of entities that you can manipulate and calls them *objects*.

- Access defines a set of changes in state that an object recognizes and calls them *events*.

- You manipulate an object by writing a program and telling Access to run the program when an object recognizes an event.

As we move on to VBA programming, we need to examine some other concepts:

Variables In VBA programming, a *variable* is a temporary storage location in memory that you name and use to hold a value or to refer to an object. In VBA programming, a variable resides in memory without a physical representation in the user interface.

Objects The word *object* has been used freely and informally to refer to physical entities in the Database window that have properties and events. Now, we'll use the word *entity* to describe those things, and we'll formalize the definition of object as a fundamentally different concept.

Recordsets We'll look at how a form is related to the records it displays. In VBA programming, there is a fundamentally new way to work with forms in which you can manipulate a copy of a form's *recordset* in memory without affecting the records displayed by the form.

NOTE   The examples in this chapter and in Chapter 6, "Understanding the ADO Object Model," use the Northwind sample application. Make a fresh copy of Northwind.mdb named Northwind_Ch5,6.

Objects, Properties, and Methods

VBA programming views the Access world as objects that have three characteristics:

- Properties that describe an object's characteristics

- Methods that describe the operations an object can perform on itself

- Events that you can use to run programs (procedures)

A VBA object is a programmed element that knows how to perform operations. You can think of a *method* as a small program or a script for one of the operations the element can perform on itself. Here are some examples of methods: Delete, Close, Edit, Quit, Move, Requery, Save, Update, and Undo. Methods are prewritten, built-in scripts for actions, and they are an integral part of objects.

In VBA programming, we perceive the object as a package of its properties and methods. You read and change properties directly (using an assignment statement), and you ask an object to use one of its methods to manipulate itself. Figure 5.1 depicts the object in VBA programming.

FIGURE 5.1:

In a VBA procedure, you set or read a property, or you ask the object to use one of its methods to manipulate itself.

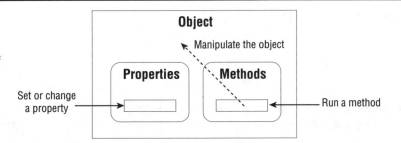

Events are associated with changes in an object's state. These offer programming opportunities, because you can interrupt the processing that normally follows the change. Events were discussed in detail in Chapter 2, "Getting Started with Objects and Events." The following sections describe getting and setting properties and using object methods.

Encapsulation

The packaging together of properties and methods with the object is called *encapsulation*. Encapsulation is one of the basic elements of the object-oriented model. We can't say that VBA is an object-oriented programming language, because it lacks one of the other basic elements (called inheritance). We can say, however, that VBA is *object-enabled* and that Access is an object-enabled database management system, because VBA does use the model of properties and methods stored together as a unit inside the capsule. In this model, the capsule is a barrier to the outside world; anyone who wants to manipulate the object calls one of the object's methods to do the work.

Although we *perceive* an object as a package of its properties and methods, in reality, it doesn't work quite this way. Actually storing the scripts for each object's methods together with the object would lead to enormous redundancy. True encapsulation would mean, for example, that each form in the database would have its own copy of the scripts for each of the Form object methods. In reality, an object's methods are stored only once with the object's class. Nevertheless, it is useful to think of an object as a *virtual* package of its properties and methods.

Setting Properties

When you work with properties in VBA, you can take two actions:

- You can change the value of a property; that is, *set* a property.

- You can read the value of a property; that is, *get* a property setting.

In either case, you refer to the object's property by using the dot operator to separate the reference to the object from the name of the property. When you *set* a property, you assign a value to the property. To set a property, you use the equal (=) sign as an *assignment operator*, as follows:

```
object.propertyname = value
```

object is a reference to the object, *propertyname* is the name of the property you want to set, and *value* is what you are changing the property setting to. For example, this statement changes the Caption property of the Employees form to Hi there!:

```
Forms!Employees.Caption = "Hi there!"
```

Because the Caption property value is a string, you must enclose the text in quotation marks. You can think of the assignment operator as a left-pointing arrow that takes whatever is on the right side of the equal sign, sends it to the left side, and stores it in whatever is on the left side:

```
object.propertyname ← value
```

NOTE To read or change the value of a property, the form or report containing the property must be open.

The Immediate window was introduced in Chapter 3. You can use the Immediate window to set property values. Use the full identifier reference for the object. As an example, we'll change the Caption property of a form. Follow these steps:

1. Open the Employees form in Form view.

2. Press Ctrl+G to open the Immediate window. Type the expression **Forms!Employees .Caption = "Hi there!"** and press Enter. The form's title bar displays Hi there! (see Figure 5.2). The changed property setting exists as long as the form is open; when you close the form, the changed value is discarded.

FIGURE 5.2:

If the form is in Form view when you set the Caption property in the Immediate window, the property setting lasts until you close the form.

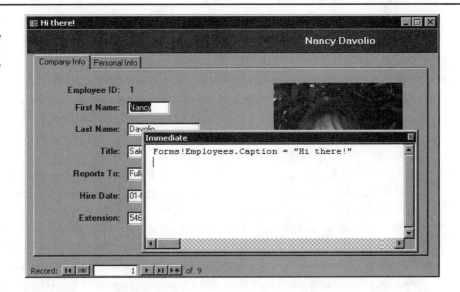

3. Click in the form, switch to Design view, and click the Properties button. The form's Caption property is not changed in the property sheet.

4. Click in the Immediate window, place the insertion point anywhere in the line you entered in step 2, and press Enter. Click in the form. VBA executes the line again and changes the Caption property in the property sheet. You can save or discard the change.

5. Close the Employees form without saving the changes.

NOTE   If a form is in Form view when you set a property value programmatically (in a VBA procedure), the setting is temporary and is discarded when you close the form. If you want to change a property such as the Caption property permanently, change the setting in Design view (either interactively or programmatically) and save the change. In Chapter 8, "Using Variables," we examine the lifetime of settings.

Getting Properties

When you get a property setting, you are reading the current setting of the property, and you need to hold the result somewhere. You usually use a variable for this purpose. When a property setting is a text value, you can hold the result by assigning the value to a variable using the equal sign as an assignment operator, as follows:

```
Let variable = object.propertyname
```

The Let keyword indicates that the value on the right of the equal sign is assigned to the variable on the left. The Let keyword is optional, and you'll find that most programmers prefer the simpler assignment statement:

```
variable = object.propertyname
```

For example, if strSource is the name of a string variable (using the str tag of the Hungarian naming style, discussed in Chapter 2), then this statement assigns the value of the RecordSource property of the Employees form to the strSource variable:

```
strSource = Forms!Employees.RecordSource
```

Once you assign the value to a variable in a VBA procedure, you can use the variable when you want to work with the property; for example, you can use strSource in the procedure instead of typing the reference Forms!Employees.RecordSource each time you need to refer to the property. A mundane, but practical, reason for using variables in VBA programming is to reduce the number of characters you need to type by using short names.

In VBA programming, you can also work with properties that represent objects; for example, the ActiveForm property of the Screen object represents the active form. When a property setting refers to an object, you assign the result to an *object variable* using this statement:

```
Set variable = object.propertyname
```

The Set keyword indicates that the object on the right is assigned to the object variable on the left. For example, this statement assigns the active form to the frm object variable:

```
Set frm = Screen.ActiveForm
```

The Set keyword is not optional.

Implicit Declaration versus Explicit Declaration

Creating a new variable by just using it is called *implicit declaration*. Although we'll use implicit declaration of variables for the explorative work we are doing in this chapter and Chapter 6, we'll use *explicit declaration* when we start writing VBA procedures in Chapter 7, "Writing Procedures." When you allow variables to be created just by using them, you can't protect your work from typos. For example, if you create a variable by typing **varname** and later want to refer to this variable but mistakenly type **vername**, VBA sets up a new variable for vername and doesn't recognize that you have made a typing error; VBA is unable to associate vername with varname.

When you use explicit declaration, you specify the names that you will be using for variables. Later, when you enter text that you intend as a variable name, VBA compares the entry with the list of declared variables and displays an error message if the entry isn't found on the list.

When a property setting is a text value, you can display the value in the Immediate window by entering a question mark (?) followed by the reference to the property. The Immediate window can only print text; if the property setting refers to an object, using the syntax ? object.property causes a compile error, "Invalid use of property."

To explore getting a text property, follow these steps:

1. Open the Employees form in Form view. Press Ctrl+G to open the Immediate window, and type **?Forms!Employees.RecordSource**. Press Enter. "Employees" is displayed on the next line, indicating that the Employees table is the RecordSource for the Employees form. You can create a variable to hold a text value and assign a value to the variable in the Immediate window. One way to create a variable in the Immediate window is to simply type the name.

2. Type **strVar = Forms!Employees.RecordSource** and press Enter. VBA creates the strVar variable and assigns the value to it.

3. Type **? strVar** and press Enter (see Figure 5.3).

FIGURE 5.3:

You can use the Immediate window to set and get properties.

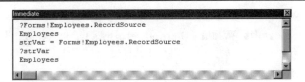

```
?Forms!Employees.RecordSource
Employees
strVar = Forms!Employees.RecordSource
?strVar
Employees
```

Calling Methods

When you want to ask an object to run one of its methods, you *call* the method by using a reference for the object and the name of the method, separating the two with the dot operator. The syntax for calling a method is as follows:

```
object.method
```

For example, the Form object has a Requery method. The Requery method updates the data in a form's data source. To ask a form to requery itself, you call its Requery method, as follows:

```
Forms!formname.Requery
```

Passing Arguments to Methods

Most methods have additional information, called *arguments*, that you use to specify how the method is carried out. Specifying arguments is called *passing* arguments to the method. The syntax for arguments depends on whether the method returns a result.

Methods that don't return results When a method doesn't return a result, you pass arguments to it by listing the arguments immediately after the name of the method, separating multiple arguments with commas, as follows:

```
object.methodname argument1, argument2, ..., [argumentN]
```

Arguments that are shown in square brackets are optional. In the expression above, the last argument is optional. Arguments that are not enclosed in square brackets are required.

For example, the GoToPage method of the Form object moves the focus to the first control on a specified page in the active form and does not return a result. The GoToPage method takes three arguments. Its syntax is as follows:

```
form.GoToPage pagenumber[,right, down]
```

form is a reference to the form, *pagenumber* is a numeric expression that is a valid page number for the active form, and *right* and *down* are numeric expressions for horizontal and vertical offsets from the upper-left corner of the window. For example, if Employees is the active form, the following statement moves the focus to the first control on the second page:

```
Forms!Employees.GoToPage 2
```

Methods that return results When a method returns a value, you enclose the argument list in parentheses, as follows:

```
object.methodname (argument1, argument2, ..., [argumentN])
```

An example of a method that returns a result is the GetOption method of the Application object, which returns the current value of an option in the Options dialog (choose Tools ➤ Options to display this dialog). If you want to find out if the status bar is displayed, use the statement

```
Application.GetOption ("Show Status Bar")
```

If the Status Bar check box is checked, the GetOption method returns True; otherwise, the GetOption method returns False.

NOTE   To test a method that returns a value in the Immediate window, you must precede the statement with a Print command. For example, to test the GetOption method, type **?Application.GetOption ("Show Status Bar")**. This returns a –1 if the condition is True or a 0 if the condition is False. When writing VBA procedures, you can use True and –1 and False and 0 interchangeably.

Passing arguments by order and by name   You can pass arguments to a method in two ways:

By order   When you pass arguments by order, you list the values of the arguments in the order specified in the method's syntax. You can leave an optional argument blank in the middle of the argument list, but you must include the argument's comma. If you leave one or more trailing arguments blank, don't use a comma following the last argument that you do specify.

By name   When you pass arguments by name, you specify the name of the argument followed by the colon equal (:=) assignment operator, followed by the value for the argument. You can list named arguments in any order, and the need for placeholders for omitted arguments is eliminated.

For example, to move the focus to the second page with a vertical offset of 600 twips, you can pass the arguments by order:

```
Forms![Employees (page break)].GoToPage 2, ,600
```

The second comma is a placeholder for the blank right argument. To leave both trailing arguments blank, you can use this:

```
Forms![Employees (page break)].GoToPage 2
```

You can pass named arguments in any order, as follows:

```
Forms!Employees.GoToPage 2, ,600
Forms!Employees.GoToPage down:=600, pagenumber:=2
Forms!Employees.GoToPage  pagenumber:2, down:=600
```

Assigning the Result of a Method

Most methods do not return a result, but there are methods that return text values and other methods that return objects. When the method returns something, you can assign the result to a variable. If the method returns a text value, you can use a `Let` assignment statement to assign the value to a variable, as follows:

```
Let variable = object.method
```

Alternatively, since the `Let` keyword is optional, you can use this:

```
variable = object.method
```

For example, when you determine if the status bar is displayed, you can assign the result using the following:

```
blnStatus = Application.GetOption ("Show Status Bar")
```

When the method returns an object, you use the `Set` assignment statement to assign the result to an object variable:

```
Set variable = object.method
```

Calling Methods in the Immediate Window

You can call a method in the Immediate window by entering the reference to the object and the method name, separating the two with the dot operator. Enter the list of arguments following the method name and enclose the arguments with parentheses if the method returns a result. You can pass arguments to the methods either by order or by name. When the method returns a value, you can display the value in the Immediate window or assign the value to a variable. When the method returns an object, you can assign the object to an object variable. Here are some examples:

1. Open the Employees form in Form view. In the Immediate window, type **Forms!Employees.Move 0,0** and press Enter. The Move method moves the form to the location you specify—in this case, 0 twips from the top and 0 twips from the left of the program space.

2. Type **?Application.GetOption ("Show Status Bar")** and press Enter. As you type, the Immediate window offers assistance. After you type the dot, the Immediate window displays a list of the properties and methods of the Application object (see Figure 5.4a). When you type the first parenthesis, the Immediate window displays the syntax for the `GetOption` method as a guide (see Figure 5.4b). If the status bar is turned on, –1 (True) is returned; otherwise, 0 (False) is returned.

3. Type **blnStatus = Application.GetOption ("Show Status Bar")** and press Enter. The `blnStatus` variable is created in memory, and the value of the property is assigned to it. To test the value of the variable, type **?blnStatus** and press Enter.

FIGURE 5.4:

The Immediate window may display a list of the properties and methods of the object (a) and the syntax for the selected method (b).

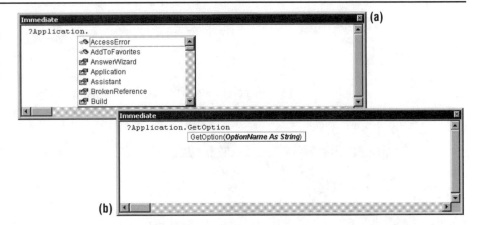

> **NOTE** Calling one of an object's methods is one way to manipulate an object. For the Access Application objects, you can operate on objects in two additional ways: using the methods of the DoCmd object and using built-in functions and statements. The DoCmd object methods are discussed later in this chapter, in the section "The DoCmd Object." You can use a few special built-in functions and statements to carry out operations. For example, to create new Form, Report, or Control objects, you use `Create` functions. To delete a control, you use a `DeleteControl` statement. These functions and statements are discussed in Chapter 14, "Creating and Modifying Database Objects Using Access VBA."

VBA-Only Form and Report Features

In this section, we look at some features of forms and reports that are available only in VBA programming.

Understanding Record Sources and Recordsets

When you open a table or view, or when you run a query or SQL statement, a set of records is returned and displayed in a datasheet. You can think of the set of returned records as an object: The Recordset object represents the set of records in a table or view, or returned by a query or SQL statement.

When you specify the RecordSource property of a form, you are assigning a specific Recordset object to the form. When you open the form, the database engine automatically creates the form's Recordset object, and Access displays the records in the form. Two forms may have the same RecordSource property, but each form has its own Recordset object that Access creates in memory.

Record Locking

When the forms have the same current record, the record-locking procedure in effect determines the access. By default, the records are not locked, and you can edit the data in the same record with both forms at the same time. If you save edits made in one form and then try to save the edits made in the second form, a message is displayed, giving you the option to overwrite the changes made in the first form, copy the record in the second form to the Clipboard, or discard the changes in the second form.

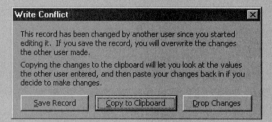

You can change the record-locking options in the Advanced page of the Options dialog (choose Tools ➤ Options to display this dialog).

When you first open two forms with the same RecordSource property, they may display the same record; however, because each form has its own recordset, you can navigate among the records in each form independently. To see an example, create a copy of the Customers form named frmMyCustomers in Northwind_Ch5,6. Figure 5.5 shows the Customers form with record number 1 as its current record and frmMyCustomers with record number 5 as its current record. As long as the forms have different current records, you can edit records in each form independently.

Creating a Second Current Record Pointer

When you open a form that is bound to a table, view, or query, the database engine creates a Recordset object in memory. The form may display one or several records, depending on whether you are in Single Form, Continuous Forms, or Datasheet view, but the record selector points to a single record called the *current record*.

As you browse to another record using the form's default navigation buttons, the record selector points to the record to which you moved. In VBA, you can create another, separate current record pointer that you can use to browse through the records in memory independent of the records displayed by the form. You create the new pointer using the form's

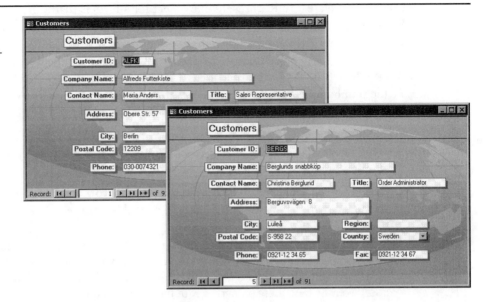

RecordsetClone property. Figure 5.6 depicts a form, the form's recordset, and the independent current record pointer that you create using the RecordsetClone property.

The form's RecordsetClone property is one of the properties that refers to another object.
The RecordsetClone property refers to the form's recordset but with a separate current
record pointer; this object is called the Recordsetclone. For example, you can create a
Recordsetclone object for the Customers form using this syntax:

```
Set clone = Forms!Customers.RecordsetClone
```

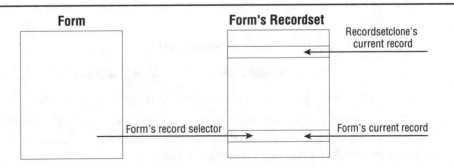

One reason to create a Recordsetclone object for a form is that using a Recordsetclone object gives you access to most of the properties and methods of the Recordset object. For example, suppose you want to determine programmatically the number of records displayed by a form. The Form object has no properties for determining the number, but the Recordset object does. The Recordset object has a RecordCount property that you can use to determine the number of records in a recordset. You can also determine the value in a particular field of the current record.

- Open the Customers form in Form view. Press Ctrl+G to open the Immediate window. Type **?Forms!Customers.RecordsetClone.RecordCount** and press Enter. The number of records in the recordset is returned.

- Type **?Forms!Customers.RecordsetClone!CustomerID** and press Enter. The value in the CustomerID field for the current record is returned.

NOTE When you create a clone of the form's recordset using the RecordsetClone property, you can't use all the properties and methods of the Recordset object. For example, although the Recordset object has Sort and Filter properties that you can use to sort or select the records in the recordset, you can't use these properties with the clone because the clone doesn't have a Filter or Sort property.

The main purpose of the recordsetclone concept is to provide a way to let you navigate or manipulate records without affecting the records displayed in the form; you navigate and manipulate records using the clone's independent current record pointer. You can navigate in the form's recordset without affecting the recordsetclone using the navigation buttons on the form. You can also navigate through the recordsetclone without affecting the form and use the Move methods of the Recordset object to move the clone's current record pointer from one record to another in the recordset. Let's use the Immediate window to observe the two current record pointers:

1. Open the Customers form in Form view and test the following references in the Immediate window:

   ?Forms!Customers!CustomerID

   ?Forms!Customers.RecordsetClone!CustomerID

   Both return the CustomerID of the first record.

2. Browse to a different record in the Customers form and test the references again; the form's recordset points to the new current record, and the recordsetclone continues to point to the first record (see Figure 5.7a).

FIGURE 5.7:

You can navigate in the form's recordset without affecting the recordset clone (a). You can use the Move methods to navigate in the clone without affecting the form's recordset (b).

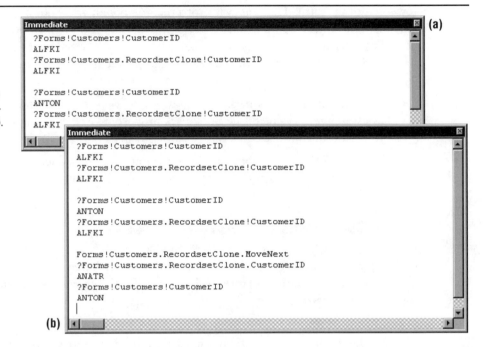

3. Call the MoveNext method for the clone in the Immediate window by typing **Forms!Customers.RecordsetClone.MoveNext** and pressing Enter.

4. Type **?Forms!Customers.RecordsetClone.CustomerID** and press Enter. The clone now points to the second record and the form is not affected (see Figure 5.7b).

In Chapter 6, you'll learn more about the properties and methods of the Recordset object, including the Move methods.

You can use the RecordsetClone property whenever you want to work with two current record pointers for a form's recordset. In Chapter 1, "Automating a Database without Programming," we used the Combo Box Wizard to create a lookup combo box. The wizard wrote a VBA procedure that uses the RecordsetClone property to find a record. In Chapter 11, "Navigating with Access VBA," we'll use this technique for finding a specific record.

Using Bookmarks

To track records in a recordset, Access creates bookmarks. A *bookmark* is a unique binary string that Access creates for each record in a form's recordset each time you open a form. The value of a record's bookmark is not the same as the record number displayed in the lower left of the form. The exact value of a record's bookmark is not important; you can't display the value or use the value in any way. Nevertheless, you can refer to the value of a record's bookmark using the form's Bookmark property. The value of the form's Bookmark property is the value of the bookmark of the current record. You can perform two operations with bookmarks:

- You can store the bookmark. You can store the value of the current record's bookmark by assigning the value of the Bookmark property to a string variable. In other words, you can save your place in a recordset by storing a bookmark.

- You can set the form's bookmark to a previously stored value. You can set the value of the form's Bookmark property to the value of the variable. The result is that the form displays the original record.

Using Bookmarks to Return to Records

Bookmarks provide the fastest way to return to a record. If you know that you want to return to the current record, store the current record's bookmark in a string variable. For example, if strMark is a string variable, store the bookmark for the current record in the Customers form using this statement:

```
strMark = Forms!Customers.Bookmark
```

To quickly return to the original record after you have moved to a different record, set the form's Bookmark property to the value of that variable. For example, you can return to the record that was current when you set the bookmark using this statement:

```
Forms!Customers.Bookmark = strMark
```

You can try out bookmarks in the Immediate window as follows:

1. With the Customers form open, type the assignment statement **strMark = Forms!Customers.Bookmark** into the Immediate window and press Enter. This statement implicitly creates the strMark variable and sets the variable to the bookmark for the current record in the Customers form. Note the record number.

2. Navigate to a different record. You can return to the original record by setting the bookmark to the value stored in the variable.

3. Type the assignment statement **Forms!Customers.Bookmark = strMark** and press Enter. The form displays the original record.

You can save bookmarks for other records in the recordset by assigning other variables to additional forms' bookmarks.

Bookmarks are not saved with the records; when you close the form, the recordset and the bookmarks cease to exist. Access creates a new unique set of bookmarks every time you open the form.

Storing Bookmarks for the RecordsetClone

As a general rule, bookmarks from different recordsets can't be used interchangeably, because each recordset has its own set of bookmarks. When you create a recordsetclone, however, you are creating an independent current record pointer to the form's recordset. You can, therefore, store a bookmark for a record in the clone as follows:

```
strMark = Forms!formname.RecordsetClone.Bookmark
```

You can then display the record in the form by setting the form's Bookmark property to the stored value as follows:

```
Forms!formname.Bookmark = strMark
```

You can see how this works by using the Immediate window. Open the frmMyCustomers form. We'll move the current record pointer in the recordsetclone and save our place with a bookmark. We'll then move the form's current record pointer to the place we saved in the recordsetclone. Here are the steps:

1. Type **Forms!frmMyCustomers.RecordsetClone.Move 10** and press Enter. This statement creates the clone, moves 10 records forward, and makes the record you moved to the current record in the clone. Confirm by testing the value of **?Forms!frmMyCustomers.RecordsetClone!CustomerID**.

2. Type **strMark = Forms!frmMyCustomers.RecordsetClone.Bookmark** and press Enter.

3. Move the form to the saved place by typing **Forms!frmMyCustomers.Bookmark = strMark** and pressing Enter. Confirm by clicking the form and noting that the CustomerID matches the value of the clone.

Using Me to Refer to a Form or Report

Another VBA-only object property that returns an object is the Me property. Me is a property of both the Form and the Report objects. You use the Me property to refer to the form or report in a VBA procedure that is stored in the form's or report's module.

For example, in procedures stored in the form module of the frmEmployees form, you can set the form's Caption property with this statement:

```
Me.Caption = "Hi there!"
```

You can get the form's RecordSource property and store it in the `strDataSource` variable using this statement:

```
strDataSource = Me.RecordSource
```

You can update the form's data source by calling its `Requery` method as follows:

```
Me.Requery
```

NOTE   You can't use test statements that include the Me property in the Immediate window. You can use the Me property only in a procedure stored in a form or a report module.

Often, when you are running a procedure stored in a form or a report module, the form or report is also the active object. In this case, you could use either the Me property or the ActiveForm or ActiveReport property of the Screen object to refer to the form or report. However, the form or report in which the procedure is running may not be the active object. Because the Me property always refers to the form or report housing the procedure, you should use the Me property instead of the ActiveForm or ActiveReport property when you need to refer to the form or report with the VBA code.

Both the Screen object and Me property are useful in referring to a form or report without using its name. The differences between the Screen object properties and the Me properties are the following:

- Me has to do with where you are when you are referring to a form or report. Me can be used only in a procedure that is stored in the form's or report's module, and Me only refers to the form or report with which the module is stored. Me has nothing to do with whether the form or report has the focus.

- The Screen object has to do with whether the object you are referring to has the focus. You can be anywhere when you use the Screen object to refer to the active form or report—in a procedure, in a ControlSource property expression for an unbound control, or in an expression for a query.

References to Objects in Collections

When you want to manipulate an object in a program, you must first refer to it. In Chapter 3, we focused on referring to an object explicitly by its name; we used the exclamation point (bang) operator syntax for referring to an object in a collection. For example, `Forms!Employees!LastName` refers to the LastName control in the Controls collection of the Employees form in the Forms collection. You use the exclamation point syntax whenever you need to refer to an object explicitly by its name; this syntax is required in query expressions and SQL statements, in macro conditions and arguments, and in ControlSource expressions for unbound controls.

Access VBA provides three additional ways to refer to objects in collections. Each uses a syntax with parentheses to point to, or *index*, the object. In VBA programming, you can use parenthetical syntax to refer to an object explicitly by its name, by the variable you are using to refer to the object, and by a number. Table 5.1 lists the four types of references.

TABLE 5.1: Four Ways to Refer to an Object in a Collection

Syntax	Description
collectionname!objectname	Use the exclamation point reference to refer to an object in a collection explicitly by its name.
collectionname("*objectname*")	Use the index by name reference to refer to an object in a collection explicitly by its name.
collectionname(*index*)	Use the index by number reference to refer to an object in a collection by the index number assigned to it.
collectionname(*objectvariable*)	Use the index by variable reference to refer to an object in a collection by using a string variable to refer to the object.

Each syntax has advantages. We'll look at some examples using the Immediate window.

Using Index by Name

You can use the index by name reference to refer to the object using a string expression that evaluates to the object's name. Open the Customers form. In the Immediate window, type **?Forms("Customers").Caption** and press Enter. The Customers form's Caption property setting is displayed.

Using Index by Variable

Often in a VBA procedure, you create a variable to represent a value. In the Immediate window, type **strName = "Customers"** and press Enter to create strName as a variable and assign the string expression to it. You can use the index by variable reference to refer to the object using the variable. In the Immediate window, type **?Forms(strName).RecordSource** and press Enter. The form's RecordSource property setting is displayed.

Using Index by Position

When you know the position number of an object in its collection, you can refer to the object using just the number. If Customers is the first form you opened, you can refer to it using Forms(0) (an index number of zero corresponds to the first open form). In the Immediate window, type ?**Forms(0).Caption** and press Enter. The Caption property of the first form in your Forms collection is displayed.

Using Index by Number

Access organizes the objects in a collection in a list and automatically assigns each member an index number. Both VBA and the database engine assign index numbers beginning with zero instead of one, so their collection indexes are called *zero-based*. Members can be added to or deleted from collections, and the positions of individual members can change when the collection changes.

A new set of index numbers is assigned to the objects the first time you refer to the collection. When an object is added to or removed from the collection, the positions of the other objects in the list may be affected because Access automatically updates the index numbers when the collection changes. For example, for the Forms collection, Access assigns index numbers according to the order in which forms are loaded and changes the index numbers when forms are unloaded. If Employees is the first open form, its index number is 0, and Forms(0) refers to it. If you open Customers next, its index number is 1, and Forms(1) refers to Customers. If you close Employees, the index number of Customers changes to 0, and Forms(0) refers to it.

As another example, the second control in the Detail section of the Customers form is the CustomerID control (the first control is the label control). You can use any of the following references for the CustomerID control:

```
Forms!Customers!CustomerID
Forms!Customers("CustomerID")
Forms!Customers(1)
```

You can use the Immediate window to test these references. If a VBA procedure is stored in the Customers form module, you can use the following references to the CustomerID control in the procedure:

```
Me!CustomerID
Me("CustomerID")
Me(1)
```

When you want to operate on each member of a collection—for example, to change the locked property of all the controls on a form—it is most efficient to refer to the controls by index number and loop through the collection. You will learn how to loop through a collection in Chapter 9, "Controlling Execution."

The Access Application Object Hierarchy

In Chapter 3, we looked at the Access Application objects and those properties that are particularly useful in VBA programming. Here, we'll examine the additional objects and properties that are useful for automating tasks. In addition, we'll look at the methods for the Access Application objects.

NOTE   Chapter 3 describes many of the properties available in VBA programming, and the following sections list additional properties, as well as many of the available methods. This gives you a good idea of the range of possibilities for your own programs. However, before using a property or a method in your code, you should search online help for information about using the property, for the method's syntax, and for code examples.

The Application Object

Some of the additional Application object properties available in VBA are listed in Table 5.2. Table 5.3 lists the methods of the Application object.

The Collection Objects

The Forms, Reports, Modules, and Controls collection objects have four properties: Application, Count, Item, and Parent (see Table 3.2 in Chapter 3).

The Forms, Reports, Modules, and Controls collection objects have no methods. Access manages these collections for you. For example, when you open a form or create a new form using the CreateForm function in a VBA procedure, Access automatically adds the form to the Forms collection and assigns it the next consecutive index number. When you close a form, Access automatically removes it from the Forms collection and adjusts the index numbers of the other open forms.

TABLE 5.2: Additional Properties of the Application Object

Property	Access	ReturnValue	Description
BrokenReference	Read-only	Boolean	Checks to see if the project contains any broken references to databases or type libraries.
CodeContextObject	Read-only	Object	Determines the object in which a VBA procedure is running.
CurrentObjectName	Read-only	String	Use to determine which database object has the focus, or in which object is running code or has the focus.
CurrentObjectType	Read-only	Integer	Returns the object type of the object that currently has the focus.
FeatureInstall	Read/write	Enum constant	Determines how to handle situations in which calls are made to methods and properties that require features not yet installed.
IsCompiled	Read-only	Boolean	Determines whether all the modules in the project are in a compiled state. Returns True if all the modules are in a compiled state.
VBE	Read-only	VBE object	Represents the VBA editor and can be used to return a reference to the VBA editor object and its related properties.
Visible	Read/write	Boolean	Shows or hides the Access application. If the Visible property is True, the application is visible; otherwise, the application isn't visible. When the user starts Access, the Visible property is True and can't be changed. When another application using Automation starts Access, the Visible property is False by default. You can set this property in a VBA procedure only when the application is started by another application using Automation (and when the UserControl property value is False).

TABLE 5.3: Methods of the Application Object

Method	Description
AccessError	Returns the descriptive string for an Access error or an ADO error. Adds the name or the current database to the Favorites folder.
Addto Favorites	Adds the name of current database to the Favorites folder.

Continued on next page

TABLE 5.3 CONTINUED: Methods of the Application Object

Method	Description
BuildCriteria	Returns a parsed criteria string as it would appear in a Criteria cell in query design grid or as a Filter property setting. Use this method to construct criteria for a query of filter based on user input.
CloseCurrentDatabase	Closes the current database or project (the one that is open in the Access window) from another application that is controlling Access through Automation. After you close the database that is open in the current instance of Access, you can create a new database or open another existing database in the same instance of Access.
CodeDb	Returns the name of the database in which the code is running.
CompactRepair	Compacts and repairs the database or project.
ConvertAccessProject	Converts a database from one version of Access to another.
CreateAccessProject	Creates a new project from within Access, or from within another application using OLE Automation.
CreateControl	Creates a control on an open form.
CreateForm	Creates a new form in minimized, Design view.
CreateGroupLevel	Specifies groupings within a form or report.
CreateNewWorkgroupFile	Creates a new workgroup file for a specified user.
CreateReport	Creates a new report in minimized, Design view.
CreateReportControl	Creates a control on an open report.
CurrentDb	Refers to the database currently open in Access.
DAvg	Calculates the average of a set of values.
DCount	Gives the number of records in a specified recordset.
DDEExecute	Sends a command from client to server via a DDE channel.
DDEInitiate	Opens a DDE channel between a server and client.
DDEPoke	Transmits text from client to server via a DDE channel.
DDERequest	Requests information of a server by a client via a DDE channel.
DDETerminate	Closes a DDE channel between a server and client.
DDETerminateAll	Closes all DDE channels active on the computer running the code.
DefaultWorkspaceClone	Creates a new Workspace object without requiring the user to log in again. This method creates a clone of the default Workspace object.
DFirst	Returns a record from a table or query. If the records are sorted ascending or descending, returns the data from the first record.
DLast	Returns a record from a table or query. If the records are sorted ascending or descending, returns the data from the last record.
DLookup	Returns the value of a particular field from a domain.
DMax	Determines the maximum value in a domain.
DMin	Determines the minimum value in a domain.

Continued on next page

TABLE 5.3 CONTINUED: Methods of the Application Object

Method	Description
DStDev	Estimates the standard deviation across a sample of values in a domain.
DstDevP	Estimates the standard deviation of all values in a domain.
DSum	Calculates the sum of a set of values.
DVar	Estimates the variance across a sample of values in a domain.
DVarP	Estimates the variance across all values in a domain.
Echo	Turns screen painting off. If you turn screen painting off in a VBA procedure, you must turn it back on or it will remain off, even if you press Ctrl+Break or if the procedure encounters a breakpoint.
EuroConvert	Converts to or from the euro.
Eval	Evaluates a text-string or numeric-value expression.
ExportXML	Exports data for the specified Access object as XML files.
FollowHyperlink	Opens the document or Web page specified in the hyperlink address that you supply as an argument. Use this method to follow a hyperlink supplied by you or by the user.
GetHiddenAttribute	Returns the value (Boolean) of a hidden attribute of an object.
GetOption	Returns the current value of an option in the Options dialog.
GUIDFromString	Converts a string to a GUID.
hWndAccessApp	Determines the handle assigned by Microsoft Windows to the Access window.
HyperlinkPart	Returns information about data stored as a hyperlink.
ImportXML	Imports data about a specified Access object from XML files.
LoadPicture	Loads a graphic into an ActiveX control.
NewAccessProject	Creates and opens a new Access project.
NewCurrentDatabase	Creates a new Database object in the Access window from another application that is controlling Access through Automation. This method adds the database to the Databases collection automatically. After you create an instance of Access from the other application, you must either create a new database or open an existing database.
Nz	Returns a zero or a zero-length string when a variant's value is Null.
OpenAccessProject	Opens an existing Access project.
OpenCurrentDatabase	Opens an existing Database object as the current database in the Access window from another application that is controlling Access through Automation.
Quit	Quits Access. This method has the same effect as selecting File ➢ Exit. Use this method's option argument to specify the treatment for any unsaved objects.

Continued on next page

TABLE 5.3 CONTINUED: Methods of the Application Object

Method	Description
RefreshDatabaseWindow	Updates the Database window after a Database window object has been added, deleted, or renamed.
RefreshTitleBar	Updates the Access title bar after you set the AppTitle or AppIcon startup properties in VBA.
Run	Runs a procedure you have defined in an Access database from another application through Automation or from another Access database.
RunCommand	Runs a built-in menu or toolbar command.
SetDefaultWorkgroupFile	Sets a specified workgroup file as the default.
SetHiddenAttribute	Sets an object's hidden attribute.
SetOption	Sets the current value of an option in the Options dialog. Use SetOption together with GetOption to observe and change the environmental options in VBA. You can get and set any option in the Options dialog. Changes you make are permanent; if you want to restore the original values when you close a database, hold them in public variables.
StringFromGUID	Converts a GUID to a string.
SysCmd	Displays text or a progress meter in the status bar. Also returns information about Access and associated program files, or returns the state of a specified database object.

The Form Object

The Form object refers to a specific open form. Form objects are members of the Forms collection. You can't add or delete a Form object from the Forms collection (except by opening or closing a form). There are about 150 Form object properties for changing a form's appearance and its behavior. You can set most of the properties in the form's property sheet. The property sheet also includes the 52 event properties that a form recognizes. Table 5.4 lists some of the properties of the Form object, and Table 5.5 lists its methods.

The Report Object

Table 5.6 lists some of the properties of the Report object. Table 5.7 lists the methods of the Report object.

The Module Object

The Module object refers to a specific open module. The two kinds of Module objects are standard and class.

TABLE 5.4: Additional Properties of the Form Object

Property	Access	Return Value	Description
AllowDesignChanges	Read/write	Boolean	Specifies whether changes can be made to a form in all views or only in Design view.
Bookmark	Read/write	Variant	Stores the value of the current record's bookmark as a unique binary string expression created by Access for each record each time you open the form. Available only for the form's current record.
DefaultControl	Read-only	Control	Sets the default properties for a particular type of control on a form.
Me	Read-only	Form object	Refers to the form itself when used in the Me property in a VBA procedure stored in a form's module.
Module	Read-only	Object	Refers to a form's module. If you refer to the Module property of a form with the HasModule property set to False, an error occurs.
OpenArgs	Read/write	Variant	Determines the string expression specified as the `OpenArgs` argument of the `OpenForm` method.
UniqueTable	Read/write	String	Specifies or determines a table to be updateable when a form is bound to a multiple table view or stored procedure in an Access project.

A standard module is listed in the Modules pane of the Database window. You use it to store procedures that you want to make available to other procedures and to store function procedures that you want to use as event handlers in one or more forms or reports.

A class module contains the definition of new objects; you create the object by creating a new instance of the class defined by the module. The two kinds of class modules are form and report modules and independent class modules. Form and report modules are stored as part of forms and reports, and independent class modules are stored as separate objects in the Modules pane of the Database window. When you open a form or report interactively or by using the OpenForm or OpenReport macro action or method, you are creating the form or report as the default instance of the form or report module. You use VBA procedures to create non-default instances of form and report modules and to create all instances of independent class modules (see Chapter 14 for more information about creating non-default instances of a class module).

Normally, you create modules interactively by typing in the Module window. However, at times you might want to create or change a module programmatically. The purpose of defining a Module object is to allow you to create and modify modules directly from other VBA

TABLE 5.5: Methods of the Form Object

Method	Description
GoToPage	Moves the focus to the first control on a specified page of the active form.
Move	Relocates a form to the location you specify, in twips from the upper and left edges of the program space.
Recalc	Updates all calculated controls on a form. This method has the same effect as pressing the F9 function key when the form has the focus. Use **Recalc** to update calculated controls that have ControlSource expressions based on other controls or fields in the form's data source. When the ControlSource property setting includes domain or SQL aggregate functions, use the **Requery** method instead.
Refresh	Updates the records in the current set with changes to the existing data made by you or by others in a multiuser environment. This method does not change the recordset to include records that were added or exclude records that were deleted since the current set was last requeried and does not exclude changed records that may no longer satisfy the query or filter criteria that are specified for the form's data source.
Repaint	Updates the screen and completes any pending recalculations of the form's controls. Use **Repaint** to update the screen when repainting has been delayed while Access carries out other tasks.
Requery	Updates the data source of the specified form. The syntax is *object*.Requery, where *object* refers to the form; if you omit *object*, the method requeries the source of the active form.
SetFocus	Moves the focus to the control that last had the focus on the specified form. If the specified form has no enabled controls, this method moves the focus to the form itself. You can move the focus only to a visible form.
Undo	Resets a form that has changed. All changes to the form are discarded. This method is the equivalent of pressing the Escape key.

TABLE 5.6: Additional Properties of the Report Object

Property	Access	Return Value	Description
DefaultControl	Read-only	Control	Sets the default properties for a particular type of control on a report.
Me	Read-only	Report object	Refers to the report itself in a VBA procedure stored in a report's module.
Module	Read-only	Object	Refers to a report's module. If you refer to the Module property of a report with the HasModule property set to False, an error occurs.
PrintCount	Read/write	Integer	Returns or sets the number of times the OnPrint property has been evaluated for the current section of a report.

TABLE 5.7: Methods of the Report Object

Method	Description
Circle	Draws a circle, an ellipse, or an arc on a report when the Print event occurs
Line	Draws lines and rectangles on a report when the Print event occurs
Move	Relocates a report to the location you specify, in twips from the upper and left edges of the program space
Print	Prints the text on a report
PSet	Sets a point on a report to a specified color when the Print event occurs
Scale	Defines the coordinate system for a Report object
TextHeight	Returns the height of a text string as it would be printed in the current font
TextWidth	Returns the width of a text string as it would be printed in the current font

procedures. You use the properties and methods of the Module object to create new procedures in standard and class modules; to create new event procedures in form and report modules; and to insert, replace, and delete lines of code in a module.

Independent class modules allow you to define new objects that are not associated with a form or report. Access itself uses independent classes for defining its objects. For example, a built-in class defines each control in the toolbox; when you place a control on a form or a report, you are creating a new instance of the control's class.

You can use an independent class module to define your own objects. For example, you can create an Orders class with the properties typically stored in an Orders table and with methods for calculating sales tax, for checking inventory levels, and for printing an invoice. Each order is an instance of the class. By creating an Orders class module, you package (encapsulate) all the information for the class into a single module and make it easier to modify the class later. Ease of modification is one reason for using class modules, but the main reason is that you can create class modules that are reusable in other Access databases and even in non-Access applications. With a set of reusable objects on hand, development time can be reduced. The use of independent class modules gives Access VBA the object-oriented features necessary for creating the reusable objects required for efficient database development.

A class module recognizes the Initialize event when you create a new instance of the class module in a VBA procedure, and it recognizes the Terminate event when the instance is removed from memory.

Table 5.8 lists the properties of the Module object, and Table 5.9 lists the methods of the Module object.

TABLE 5.8: Properties of the Module Object

Property	Access	Return Value	Description
Application	Read-only	Object	Accesses the active Application object.
CountOfDeclarationLines	Read-only	Long integer	Returns the number of lines of code in the Declarations section of a module. The value equals the line number of the first line following the Declarations section.
CountOfLines	Read-only	Long integer	Returns the number of lines of code in a module.
Lines	Read-only	String	Returns a string containing the contents of a specified line or lines. Specify the number of the first line and the number of lines you want to return.
Name	Read/write	String	Specifies or returns the name of the module.
Parent	Read-only	Object	Refers to the parent of the module. If the module is a form or report module, its parent is the form or report in which it runs.
ProcBodyLine	Read-only	Long integer	Returns a number that identifies the line on which a specified procedure begins in a module. Specify the type of the procedure and a string expression that evaluates to the name of the procedure.
ProcCountLines	Read-only	Long integer	Returns the number of lines in a specified procedure. Specify the type of procedure and a string expression that evaluates to the name of the procedure.
ProcOfLine	Read-only	String	Returns the name of the procedure that contains a specified line. Specify the line number and the type of procedure.
ProcStartLine	Read-only	Long integer	Returns the number of the line on which a specified procedure begins. Specify the type of procedure and the name of the procedure (as a string expression).
Type	Read-only	Enum constant	Determines whether a module is a standard module or a class module.

TABLE 5.9: Methods of the Module Object

Method	Description
AddFromFile	Adds the contents of a text file to an open module. This method places the contents immediately after the Declarations section and before the first procedure.
AddFromString	Adds a string to an open module. This method places the contents of the string immediately after the Declarations section and before the first procedure.
CreateEventProc	Creates the code template for an event procedure. Returns a long integer indicating the line number of the first line. After creating the template, you can add lines of code using a method such as InsertLines.
DeleteLines	Deletes lines in a module. Specify the number of the first line and the number of lines you want to delete.
Find	Finds specified text in a module. Specify the string expression you want to find, the search parameters—including whether to search for the whole word, match case, or include wildcards—and the beginning and end of the search. Returns True if the string is found and False otherwise.
InsertLines	Inserts a line or a group of lines in a module. Specify the text to be inserted and the number of the line to begin inserting.
InsertText	Inserts a specified string into a module. The inserted text is placed at the end of the module.
ReplaceLine	Replaces one line with another line.

Control Objects

Chapter 3 lists many of the properties of controls that are available in VBA programming. Here, we describe other VBA properties and methods of the Control objects, including the Hyperlink object and the Page object and Pages collection associated with the Tab control. Tables 5.10 and 5.11 describe a few properties and methods shared by general categories of controls.

You can use the Immediate window to test these methods. For example, with the Customers form open in Form view, follow these steps:

1.   Type **Forms!Customers!Country.SetFocus** and press Enter. The Country control has the focus; confirm by clicking in the Customers form and observing that Country is the active control.

2.   Type **Forms!Customers!Country.Requery** and press Enter. The Country control is updated by requerying the SQL statement that is the row source for the combo box.

3.   Type **Forms!Customers.Requery** and press Enter. The record source of the Customers form is requeried.

TABLE 5.10: VBA-Only Properties of Controls

Property	Access	Return Value	Description
ControlType	Read/write	Byte	Determines or changes the type of control on a form. This property is set in form Design view.
Hyperlink	Read-only	Hyperlink object	Accesses the properties and methods of a Hyperlink object associated with a command button, label, or image.

Requery Methods

You use the **Requery** methods to ensure that a form or a control displays the most recent data. In VBA, there are two **Requery** methods: the **Requery** method for a Form or Control object and the **Requery** method for the DoCmd object. The DoCmd **Requery** method is the equivalent of the **Requery** macro action; both update only the active object. The DoCmd **Requery** method and the **Requery** method of a form or report vary in two key ways:

- You can use the **Requery** method of a form or control to update data when the form is not the active object. The DoCmd Requery method updates data only on the active object.

- When you use the DoCmd **Requery** method, Access closes the query or table and reloads it from the database. When you use the **Requery** method of a form or control, Access reruns the query or table without closing and reloading it. As a result, the **Requery** method of a form or control is faster.

The **Requery** method of a form or control does one of the following:

- Reruns the query or SQL statement that is the data source for the form or control

- Updates a table data source for a form or control by displaying new or changed records and removing deleted records

- Updates records displayed in a form based on changes to the form's Filter property

When the control is based on a table or query—which is often the case when the control is a list box, a combo box, a subform control, or an ActiveX control or when the control is a calculated control with a ControlSource expression based on an aggregate function—the **Requery** method requeries the data source; otherwise, the **Requery** method refreshes the control's data. If you don't specify which object you want requeried, the **Requery** method requeries the data source for the form that has the focus.

TABLE 5.11: Methods of Control Objects

Method	Applies To	Description
Move	Controls that are visible	Relocates a control to the location you specify, in twips from the upper and left edges of the program space.
Requery	Data controls	Updates a control on a form. The syntax is *object*.Requery where *object* refers to the control. If you omit *object*, the method requeries the source of the active control on the active form.
SetFocus	Controls that can receive the focus	Moves the focus to the specified control on the active form. You can move the focus only to a visible, enabled control. Some control properties can be set only when a control doesn't have the focus, such as the control's Visible, Locked, or Enabled properties.
SizeToFit	Controls that have a size	Sizes a control to fit the text or the image it contains.
Undo	Controls that have a value	Resets a control when its value has changed. Has the same effect as pressing the Escape key.

Combo Box and List Box Controls

Combo boxes and list boxes have several properties and methods that are particularly useful in VBA programming. Table 5.12 lists examples of these properties, and Table 5.13 lists the methods.

TABLE 5.12: Properties of Combo Box and List Box Controls

Property	Access	Return Value	Description
ItemData	Read-only	Variant	Returns the bound column for the specified row in a combo box or list box.
ListCount	Read/write	Long integer	Determines the number of rows in a list box or in the list box portion of a combo box.
ListIndex	Read/write	Long integer	Determines which item is selected in a list box or in the list box portion of a combo box.
Selected	Read/write	Long integer	Selects an item or determines if an item is selected in a list box. (Only for list boxes.)

TABLE 5.13: Methods of Combo Box and List Box Controls

Method	Description
AddItem	Adds a new item to the list displayed by the combo box or list box.
Dropdown	Forces a combo box to drop down. (Only for combo boxes.)
RemoveItem	Removes an item from the list displayed by the combo box or list box.

You can use the Immediate window to test these properties and methods. For example, with the Customers form open in Form view, follow these steps:

1. Type **Set cbo = Forms!Customers!Country** and press Enter. This statement creates cbo as an object variable to represent the combo box. We'll use the variable as an abbreviation for the full reference.

2. Type **?cbo.ListCount** and press Enter. The list contains 21 countries.

3. Type **?cbo.ListIndex** and press Enter. The index number for the country in the current row is displayed.

4. Type **?cbo.ItemData(3)** and press Enter. The Immediate window displays the data in the fourth row. Although you use the ItemData method to return the data in a specific column (the bound column), you can use the Column property to display the data in any column. The Column property has two arguments that you use to specify the index for the column and row. Both index numbers are zero-based; the first argument is the column that contains the data, and the second argument is the row. If you omit the second argument, the data for the current row is returned.

5. Type **?cbo.Column(0)** and press Enter. The Immediate window displays the data in the first column of the current row. To display the data in any row, use the second parameter of the Column property. For example, type **?cbo.Column(0,2)** and press Enter to display the data in the third row.

The ItemsSelected Collection

The standard list box allows you to select a single item from the list; however, you can use the MultiSelect property to choose more than one item. A dotted rectangle encloses the current row in a list box. The MultiSelect property has the following values:

None For a single selection. You select an item by clicking the row or by using the arrow keys to move the current record pointer up or down a row and select the new current record. When you select a new record, the previous record is deselected automatically. After you select a row, the only way to deselect it is to select another row.

Simple To select multiple items by choosing each item separately. You select an item by clicking the row. After you select a row, you can deselect it by clicking it a second time.

Extended To extend the selection of multiple items. After you select an item, you can extend the selection in three ways:

- You can hold down the left mouse button and drag to another row.
- You can press the Shift key and click another row.
- You can press the Shift key and then press an arrow key.

In each case, you extend the selection from the previously selected item to the current item. After you have made an extended selection, you can select or deselect any item by pressing the Ctrl key and then clicking the item.

When you select multiple items in the list, Access creates a collection called the ItemsSelected collection. Each member of the ItemsSelected collection is an integer that refers to a selected row in the list box or combo box. Even though the members of the ItemsSelected collection are integers, their data type is Variant by default. The ItemsSelected collection has no methods and has the single Count property that returns the number of items selected. See Chapter 13, "Working with Groups of Records Using Access VBA," for more information about the multi-select list box.

The Hyperlink Object

Access VBA provides a Hyperlink object that is associated with the command button, image control, and label control. You use the Hyperlink object to manipulate the hyperlink in VBA procedures. The command button, image control, and label control have a Hyperlink property that refers to the Hyperlink object and gives you access to the properties and methods of the Hyperlink object.

Although you can set the HyperlinkAddress and HyperlinkSubAddress properties in the control's property sheet, you can also specify the address in VBA using the Address and Sub-Address properties of the Hyperlink object. The Hyperlink object also has the methods shown in Table 5.14. The syntax for these methods is as follows:

```
object.Hyperlink.methodname
```

object is a reference to the control object that contains the hyperlink. Search for the method name in online help for the syntax of the method's arguments and code examples.

The TabControl Object

A tab control has one or more pages, each with its own tab. You can place other form controls on each page. When the user clicks a tab, the corresponding page becomes active.

TABLE 5.14: Methods of the Hyperlink Object

Method	Description
AddToFavorites	Adds the hyperlink address contained in the control to the Favorites folder.
CreateNewDocument	Creates a new document when you click the hyperlink.
Follow	Opens the document or Web page specified by a hyperlink address associated with a control. When the hyperlink address is not associated with a control, use the Application's FollowHyperlink method instead.

Tab controls enable you to make information much more easily accessible and yet not have forms appear cluttered or busy. You can group similar information within each tabbed page and have several of these pages included in the same single window. Northwind's Employees form uses a tab control (see Figure 5.8).

FIGURE 5.8:

You can display several pages in a single form by using the tab control.

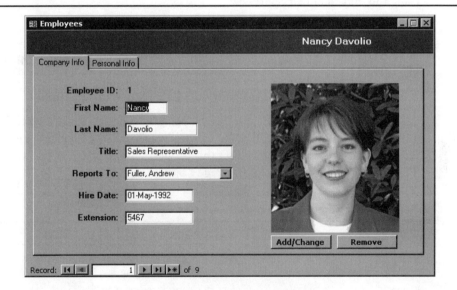

The Page Object and the Pages Collection

Normally, you create the tab control and its pages in form Design view; however, you can also create, move, or delete pages programmatically using VBA. A page is represented by a Page object, and the tab control has a Pages collection containing all the Page objects. The Pages collection is zero-based and has a Count property that you can use to determine the number of pages in the tab control. Table 5.15 lists the methods of the Pages collection.

TABLE 5.15: Methods of the Pages Collection

Method	Description
Add	Adds a new page to the tab control
Remove	Deletes a page from the tab control

WARNING Members of the Pages collection are not to be confused with data access pages, which are members of the DataAccessPages collection. Pages in this context are used as a type of tab index, whereas data access pages are a data access object unto themselves.

Each page has a unique name and is represented by a Page object. You can refer to a specific page using any of the syntax types listed in Table 5.1. For example, in the Employees form, the name of the tab control is Tabctl0, and you can refer to the Company Info page using the fully qualified reference:

```
Forms!Customers!Tabctl0.Pages!CompanyInfo
```

You can refer to a control on the page by referring to the page's Controls collection and then to the control; for example, to refer to the LastName control on the CompanyInfo page, use this reference:

```
Forms!Customers!Tabctl0.Pages!CompanyInfo.Controls!LastName
```

The Page object has the PageIndex property, which specifies or determines the position of a Page object in the Pages collection of a tab control. PageIndex has read/write access and returns an integer value. You can set this property in the property sheet, a macro, or in VBA. Table 5.16 lists the methods of the Page object.

TABLE 5.16: Methods of the Page Object

Method	Description
Move	Relocates a page to the location you specify, in twips from the upper and left edges of the program space.
Requery	Updates the controls on the page.
SetFocus	Moves the focus to the control that last had the focus on the specified page; if the specified page has no enabled controls, the method moves the focus to the page itself.

The Screen Object

As explained earlier, the Screen object refers to the particular form, report, or control that currently has the focus or to the control that previously had the focus. By using the Screen object in a VBA procedure, you can refer to the active object without knowing the object's name. Referring to the Screen object does not make the form, report, or control the active object, however.

Chapter 3 described the properties of the Screen object. An additional VBA-only property of the Screen object is MousePointer, which specifies or determines the type of mouse pointer currently displayed. This property has read/write access and returns an integer, as follows:

0	Default pointer
1	Normal (Arrow)
3	Text Select (I-beam)
7	Vertical Resize (Size N,S)
9	Horizontal Resize (Size E,W)
11	Busy (Hourglass)

All of the Screen object's properties return objects. When you use the Screen object in a VBA procedure, you normally create an object variable to refer to the returned object:

```
Set frmvar = Screen.ActiveForm
```

The Screen object has no methods.

In VBA, the role of the Screen object is often taken over by the Me object. For example, when you want to refer to a form in a VBA procedure that is stored in the form's module, it is preferable to use the Me object to avoid errors if, for some unexpected reason, an object other than the form is active.

The DoCmd Object

The DoCmd object is an extraordinary object available only in VBA. The DoCmd object doesn't represent a physical entity with properties and behaviors. Instead, it represents an important connection between macro and VBA programming. Most of the operations you can take on the Application objects duplicate the steps you take when working interactively in Access. These operations are defined as macro actions. Most macro actions are available in VBA as methods of the DoCmd object.

The DoCmd Object and Automation

When Microsoft designed the DAO object model theory, they evolved VBA as the common language for the Office applications and settled on Automation (called OLE Automation in previous versions) as the way for one application to work with the objects in another application. For external applications, such as Excel or the stand-alone Visual Basic application, to be able to use Automation to work fully with Access, there had to be a way for these external applications to execute macro actions. In the Automation model, an application such as Access makes its objects available to other applications. Through programming, the external application can ask an Access object to use its methods. To make a macro action available to an external application in Automation, the macro action had to be the method of some object. The simple solution was to create an artificial object that could have the macro actions as its methods; thus, the DoCmd object was born.

The external application can execute a macro action through Automation, by asking the DoCmd object to use the method that corresponds to the macro action. Most of the macro actions are available in VBA as methods of the DoCmd object.

With the requirements of Automation taken care of, Microsoft had to decide how Access VBA should deal with the operations that macro actions carry out. Many of these macro actions could have been defined as methods for each of the other Access objects to which they apply. For example, the Beep macro action that you can use to sound a beep when a user enters the wrong kind of data into a control might have been defined as a method of the Control object instead of as a method of the DoCmd object. Decisions regarding the macro actions are not consistent: Although the macro actions have corresponding methods for the DoCmd object, several of the macro actions have also been defined as methods of specific objects. For example, Move is defined as a method of the Form object, which carries out the same behavior as the MoveSize method of the DoCmd object; Repaint is defined as a method of the Form object, and RepaintObject is a method of the DoCmd object. On the other hand, Close is only a method of the DoCmd object and is not also defined as a method of the object that is closed.

DoCmd and Macro Actions

You can use the DoCmd object to run 49 of the 56 macro actions as corresponding VBA methods. Table 5.17 lists the seven macro actions that do not have corresponding DoCmd methods and describes how these operations are handled in Access VBA.

> **NOTE** For more information about macros, see *Mastering Access 2002 Premium Edition* by Alan Simpson and Celeste Robinson (Sybex, 2001).

TABLE 5.17: Macro Actions without Corresponding VBA Equivalents

Macro Action	Access VBA Equivalent
MsgBox	Use the MsgBox() function.
RunApp	Use the Shell() function.
RunCode	A VBA procedure calls another procedure using a Call statement; the Call keyword is optional.
SendKeys	Use the SendKeys statement.
SetValue	Use the assignment statement with the equal (=) sign as an assignment operator.
StopAllMacros	There is no way to stop all running macros from within a VBA procedure. Use a Stop statement to suspend execution of a procedure or an End statement to terminate execution.
StopMacro	There is no way to stop a macro from within a VBA procedure. Use Exit Sub, Exit Function, or Exit Procedure to exit a VBA procedure.

Methods of the DoCmd Object

For the 49 macro actions that do have corresponding DoCmd methods, typically the method carries out the equivalent of the corresponding macro action with the action arguments listed as method arguments in the same order as the action arguments appear in the macro Design window.

NOTE   Some DoCmd object methods differ from the corresponding macro action. These are listed in the "Differences between DoCmd Methods and the Corresponding Macro Actions" table on the CD. In some cases, even though a DoCmd method may correspond to a macro action, there may be a preferred way to carry out the operation. The "DoCmd Methods and Preferred Techniques" table on the CD lists those methods. Both tables can be found under Tables\Chapter5.pdf.

The methods of the DoCmd object do not return values or objects, so the syntax for a method is as follows:

```
DoCmd.method argument1, argument2, ..., argumentN
```

For example, the GoToControl macro action with the control name argument has an exact equivalent GoToControl method with this syntax:

```
DoCmd.GoToControl controlname
```

where *controlname* is a string expression that is the name of a control on the active form or datasheet.

Method arguments use intrinsic constants in place of the built-in macro action argument lists. For example, the intrinsic constants acTable, acQuery, acForm, acReport, acDataAccessPage, acMacro, and acModule are used in place of a list of the Database objects. In addition, method arguments use the Boolean values, True (–1) and False (0), in place of the macro action argument Yes and No values.

A fundamental difference between a macro action and its corresponding method is that whenever an argument for a macro action specifies the name of an object, the argument for the method is a string expression that is the name of the object. For example, the *FormName* argument of the OpenForm macro action must be the name of a specific form, but the *formname* argument of the OpenForm method is an expression. The expression can be a variable.

There are two types of DoCmd methods for working on an Access Application object. In one type, you must specify the object as an argument for the method. In the second type, the DoCmd method applies to the active object, so you don't specify the object as an argument. In the first two examples below, the OpenReport and OpenForm methods open objects that you must specify as arguments; in the last three examples, the methods operate on the active object.

Statement	Description
DoCmd.OpenReport "Customer Labels", acPreview	When you use the OpenReport method, you specify the report as an argument of the method.
strName = "Customers" DoCmd.OpenForm strName	The first statement creates strName as a variable and assigns the value "Customers". The second statement opens the Customers form.
DoCmd.GoToRecord , , acNext	This statement moves the focus to the next record in the active form or datasheet.
DoCmd.GoToControl "Country"	This statement moves the focus to the control named Country on the active form.
DoCmd.Close	This statement closes the active window.

NOTE When an argument of a method is a string expression that is the name of an object and the name contains spaces, do not enclose the name in square brackets. For example, using "[Customer Labels]" as the *reportname* argument generates an error; use "Customer Labels" instead.

The Properties Collection

Every Access Application object contains a Properties collection with a set of built-in Property objects that we normally just call *properties*. In Chapter 14, you will learn how to create custom properties for forms and reports. The custom properties you create for forms and reports are not added to the Properties collection, which is reserved for built-in properties only.

The Properties collection has the same two properties as the Forms, Reports, Modules, and Controls collections: Application and Count. To see how the Count property works with this collection, open the Customers form in Form view and try these examples:

- Type **? Forms!Customers.Properties.Count** in the Immediate window and press Enter. The number of built-in form properties, 161, is displayed in the Immediate window.

- Type **? Forms!Customers!Country.Properties.Count** and press Enter. The number of built-in properties for the combo box control, 91, is displayed in the Immediate window.

The Property Object

Each built-in property of an Access object has a corresponding Property object. For example, the Visible property of a control has a corresponding Property object. A Property object has properties of its own, including the properties listed in Table 5.18.

To see how the Value property works, try these examples with the Customers form open:

- Type **? Forms!Customers!Country.Properties!Visible.Value** in the Immediate window and press Enter. The Immediate window displays True.

- Type **? Forms!Customers!Country.Visible** and press Enter. The result is the same because Properties is the default collection for a control and Value is the default property.

TABLE 5.18: Properties of the Property Object

Property	Description
Name	A string that uniquely specifies the property
Value	A variant that contains the property setting

The References Collection

When you create an Access application that uses VBA to manipulate objects in other Access databases or in other applications such as Microsoft Excel or Word, you provide information about the objects in the other application by creating a reference to the other application's type library. Normally, you create and remove references interactively using the References dialog (choose Tools ➢ References) when a Module window is the active window (see Figure 5.9). You can also add and remove references programmatically using VBA.

Use the References dialog to create a reference to the type library of another Access database or to another application.

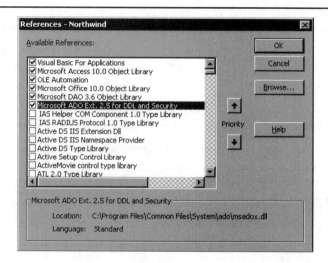

Each reference is represented by a Reference object, and the References collection of the Application object contains the Reference objects currently set for the database. The References collection has a Count property that you can use to determine the number of references currently set, and it has the methods listed in Table 5.19. When you add a reference programmatically, the References collection recognizes the ItemAdded event. When you remove a reference programmatically, the References collection recognizes the ItemRemoved event.

TABLE 5.19: Methods of the References Collection

Method	Description
AddFromFile	Sets a reference to a type library using the path to the file.
AddFromGuid	Sets a reference to a type library using the file's replication ID (GUID).
Item	Returns a specified member of the collection. Item is the default member of the References collection.
Remove	Removes a reference from the References collection.

The Reference Object

The Reference object represents a specific reference currently set to the type library of another application or another Access database. You can refer to a Reference object using the normal syntax for a member of a collection. For example, to refer to the Access type library, use the syntax References!Access. The Reference object has the properties listed in Table 5.20, all of which are read-only. The Reference object has no methods.

TABLE 5.20: VBA-Only Properties of the Reference Object

Property	Return Value	Description
BuiltIn	Boolean	Determines whether a Reference object represents a default reference that cannot be removed if Access is to function properly.
Collection	Object	Refers to the References collection.
FullPath	String	Determines the path and name of the type library.
Guid	String	Determines the unique replication ID (GUID) for the type library.
IsBroken	Boolean	Determines whether the Reference object points to a valid reference in the Registry. Use this property to determine if the type library file has been moved or deleted.
Kind	Enum constant	Determines whether the Reference object represents another Access database or a type library.
Major	Long integer	Determines the major version number of an application represented by the Reference object.
Minor	Long integer	Determines the minor version number of an application represented by the Reference object.
Name	String	Determines the string expression that identifies the Reference object.

The Access VBA Objects

Access VBA has three objects: Err, Debug, and Collection.

The Err Object

The Err object holds information about an error in a VBA procedure that occurs while the procedure is running (called a *VBA run-time error*). The properties of the Err object are filled by the generator of the error with information that uniquely identifies the error. (A VBA run-time error can be generated by an object, by VBA, or by you as the VBA programmer.) Because there is only one Err object, you work with a single VBA run-time error at a time. The Err object's properties are cleared (reset to zero or the zero-length string) automatically after any Resume, On Error, Exit Sub, Exit Function, or Exit Property statement. Table 5.21 lists the properties for the Err object, and Table 5.22 lists the methods for the Err object.

TABLE 5.21: Properties of the Err Object

Property	Access	Data Type	Description
Description	Read/write	String	A message that corresponds to the specific error
HelpContext	Read/write	Long integer	The Visual Basic Help file context ID identifying a topic within HelpFile that provides help for the specific error
HelpFile	Read/write	String	The fully qualified path of the Visual Basic Help file in which help on the specified error can be found
LastDLLError	Read-only	Long integer	The error code for the last call to a DLL
Number	Read/write	Long integer	A Long integer that corresponds to a specific error in the list of valid VBA run-time error codes
Source	Read/write	String	The name of the object or application that originally generated the error

TABLE 5.22: Methods of the Err Object

Method	Description
Clear	Explicitly clears all property settings of the Err object. Use this method when you defer error handling using the **On Error Resume Next** statement.
Raise	Generates a VBA run-time error. Use this method to simulate any VBA run-time error by specifying the method's **Number** argument as a valid VBA run-time error code. In addition, you can generate custom user-defined errors by specifying the method's **Number** argument as a Long integer that doesn't correspond to a valid VBA run-time error code.

The Debug Object

The Debug object has no properties and has a single method, Print, which prints text in the Immediate window. The syntax is Debug.Print [outputlist]. When you are working in the Immediate window, you can use the question mark as an abbreviation (? [outputlist]), but when you want to print to the Immediate window from a VBA procedure, you must use the full syntax to refer to the Debug object.

The Collection Object

The Collection object refers to a set of items of the same kind. The purpose of the Collection object is to allow you to create your own collections. (You'll use the Collection object in Chapter 14 when you create multiple form objects; that is, multiple instances of a form module.)

When you add members to the Collection object, they are automatically indexed. Note that the index for a user-defined collection begins with one and not with zero. The Collection object has the same Application and Count (to determine the number of members of the collection) properties as the various collections objects and the methods listed in Table 5.23.

TABLE 5.23: Methods of the Collection Object

Method	Description
Add	Adds a member to the Collection object
Item	Returns a specific member of a Collection object
Remove	Removes a member from the Collection object

TIP   Microsoft Office 2002 uses a set of shared features, including command bars for customizing menu bars, shortcut menus, and toolbars; the Office Assistant for providing a new type of online help; and FileSearch for providing enhanced file-search capabilities. Normally, you work with these features interactively; however, Office 2002 provides object models so that you can control and customize these features programmatically with VBA.

Using the Object Browser

Using the Object Browser is a good way to learn more about the Access Application objects as well as the data access objects and the objects that other applications make available through Automation. The Object Browser displays information in the application's type library, which is the file that includes information about the application's objects, properties, and methods, as well as the intrinsic constants that the application uses.

To explore the Object Browser, press Alt+F11 to open the Visual Basic Editor. Select View ➤ Object Browser. Figure 5.10 shows the Object Browser window.

The Project/Library selection combo box at the top of the window contains a list of the type libraries that the current database knows about. The default choice <All Libraries> indicates that items from all these type libraries are included. Select the type library you want to work with.

FIGURE 5.10:

The Object Browser

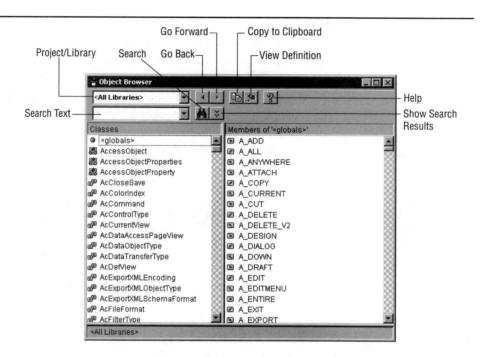

You use the Search Text combo box to search in the selected library for an item; enter the text string you want to search for and click the Search button. Figure 5.11 shows the result of a search for the text string "line." Click the Show Search Results button with the double-arrow to hide or display the results of the search.

The Classes list box on the left contains a list of the contents of the selected library, including constants and objects. The <globals> item is the top-level item for the selected type library. The list box is called Classes because the definition of each type of object is called its class; when you create a new object such as a form, you use the form class module as the definition or blueprint to create the form as an *instance* of the class.

When you select an item in the Classes list box, the Members list box on the right changes to display the information for the item, such as constants, properties, methods, and events. When you select an item in the Members list box, the bottom of the Object Browser window displays information such as the syntax for a selected method. Click the Help button or press F1 to display online help for the selected item. Use the Go Back and Go Forward buttons to browse between selected items.

If the item you selected in the Classes list box is a standard or class module, click the View Definition button to open and display the module. If you select a procedure in the module

FIGURE 5.11:

You can search for a text string in a selected type library.

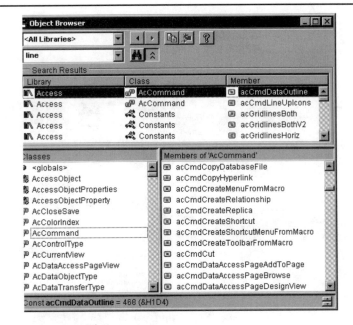

and then click the View Definition button, the module opens with the insertion point in the selected procedure. To paste code into a module, choose an item in the Members list box, click the Copy To Clipboard button, click in the module where you want to paste the item, and press Ctrl+V to paste the selection.

You can use the Object Browser to explore the Access type library and an Access project, as follows:

1. Select Access from the combo list. The Classes list box on the left includes a list of the Access Application objects and categories of intrinsic constants.

2. Select the Form object class in the Classes list box, and select GoToPage in the Members list box. The Members list box displays the properties, methods, and events for the Form object class using different icons for each kind of member. The lower part of the Object Browser window displays the syntax for the method (see Figure 5.12a).

3. Click the Object Browser's Help button to display online help for the selected member. Go back to the Object Browser.

4. Click the Copy To Clipboard button in the Object Browser to copy the member's code template. You can switch to the Module window and paste the code template into the module.

FIGURE 5.12:

The Object Browser uses different icons for the members of the Form class, including the properties, methods, and events, and displays the syntax for the selected member (a). Choose Constants to display the Access application and VBA constants (b).

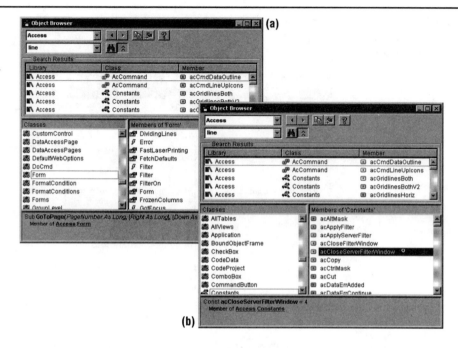

5. Select Constants in the Classes list box. The Members list box displays the intrinsic constants that Access and VBA provide. When you select a constant, the numeric value of the constant is displayed at the bottom of the window (see Figure 5.12b).

6. In the Project/Libraries combo box, choose the Northwind project. By default, the project name doesn't change when you create a new copy of a database, so the current database is listed by its project name. When you select an Access project, the Classes list box lists in bold font all the standard and class modules you have created. When you select a module in the Classes list box, the Members list box on the right changes to display information relevant to that module.

7. Select the Form_Main Switchboard form module in the Classes list box. The Members list box includes the form's built-in properties, events, and methods and displays in bold the names of procedures stored in the module using different icons for each type of member (see Figure 5.13a).

8. Choose the Startup standard module. When you choose a standard or an independent class module, the Members list box displays in bold the names of the procedures stored in the module (see Figure 5.13b).

FIGURE 5.13:

Use the Object Browser to explore an Access project. You can view the class module for a form or a report (a) or the procedures in a standard or independent class module (b).

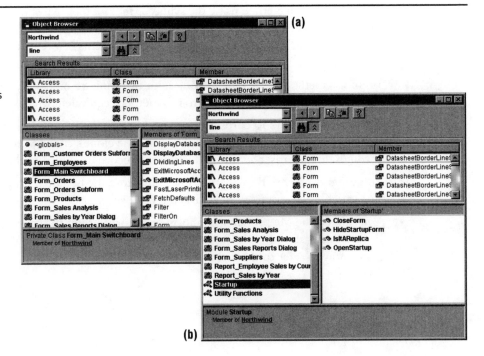

Summary

This chapter has expanded the tour of the Access Application object model to cover the most important features in VBA programming. The important points are as follows:

- An object is an element with an identity described with a set of properties that define the object's characteristics and with a set of methods that define the actions an object can take on itself. The objects in the Access Application model have properties and methods that are available only in VBA programming. Some objects in the Access Application model are available only in VBA programming, including the Module object and Modules collection and the Reference object and References collection.

- You can set a property to a text value using an assignment statement as follows: `object.propertyname = value`. You can read, or get, a text value for a property and assign the value to a variable using an assignment statement as follows: `variable = object.propertyname`. If the property returns an object, you get the reference to the object and assign the reference to an object variable using an assignment statement as follows: `Set objectvariable = object.propertyname`.

- You run, or call, a method using the syntax *object.method*. Most methods return nothing, but a method can return either a text value or an object. Most methods have additional information that you must specify as method arguments before you run the method.

- You manipulate an object by setting a property, by running one of the object's methods, by running a method of the DoCmd object, or by running a built-in Access function or statement. You use the DoCmd object to run methods equivalent to most of the macro actions.

- You can use a form's RecordsetClone property to create an independent current record pointer in the form's recordset. You can use the clone's current record pointer to walk through the recordset without affecting the record displayed in the form.

- You can use a form's Bookmark property to store the bookmark for the current record in a variable and return to the marked record later.

- You can use the Me property of a form or report to refer to the form or report in a procedure that is stored in the form's or report's module. Using the Me reference is the fastest way to refer to the form or report.

CHAPTER 6

Understanding the ADO Object Model

- Understanding the ADO hierarchy

- Referring to data access objects

- Creating new data access objects

- Navigating in a recordset

- Adding, editing, and deleting records

- Using clones and recordsetclones

This chapter introduces the database engine component of Microsoft Access, as well as those objects that your VBA programs will manipulate. With VBA, you can control when and how the application interacts with the engine, because the engine gives you access to the objects you need to specify the interaction. The objects that the engine makes available are the data access objects, which are part of the ADO (ActiveX Data Objects) model. Each data access object has its own properties and methods. In this chapter, you'll get some hands-on experience with those data access objects, properties, and methods that you'll need as you learn to use VBA to automate an Access database.

Access Database Management Services

The database engine is the database management system for Access databases. Depending on which type of database you're working with, you may be using Access's Jet database engine or the Microsoft SQL Server 2000 Desktop Engine. Both of these are components of the Access application. Microsoft Access communicates with these database engines through an interpreter language—either DAO or ADO. You can imagine DAO and ADO as mediators between the Access Application layer and the database engine layer. DAO and ADO each contain their own objects, methods, properties, and events that you can use to automate your database.

Earlier versions of Access relied on DAO as their sole mediator. Beginning with Access 2000, however, Microsoft introduced ADO—a much simpler, more versatile interpreter language. ADO enables communication between a wide range of applications (such as Access) and database engines (see Figure 6.1). It does so through drivers known as OLE DB providers, which are each written for specific database engines. For example, the Microsoft.Jet.OLEDB.4.0 provider

FIGURE 6.1:

ADO uses OLE DB providers to act as the interpreter between the application and the database.

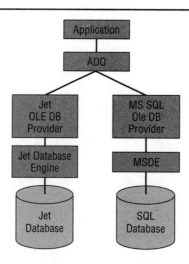

enables ADO to communicate with Jet database engines, such as the one installed as part of Access. And SQLOLEDB is the provider ADO uses to communicate with Microsoft SQL database engines, such as the Microsoft SQL Server 2000 Desktop Engine included with Access.

Since ADO was first released, it has largely replaced DAO as the developer's interpreter language of choice. For that reason, examples and explanations in this book employ the ADO object model. You can find information about DAO on the CD that accompanies this book, in the DAO directory.

Some of the functionality that used to be incorporated into DAO is now housed in a separate object library known as ADO Extensions for DDL and Security, or ADOX. Generally speaking, ADO manages data retrieval and manipulation tasks, while ADOX handles design and security tasks. Microsoft split the functionality this way so that you can install only those components of the object model that you need, thus decreasing as much as possible the amount of space your database will take up.

When you work interactively with Access or when you create macros to automate your database, you don't need to be aware of the functions and capabilities of the two major components of Access: the Application layer and the database engine. The Access interface takes care of all the negotiations with the database engine for you because Microsoft Access has all the necessary ADO and ADOX instructions built into its internal code. Here are some examples of the database management services available in Access:

- When you design a table or a query in a database, the Application layer uses its built-in, hard-coded routines to arrange for the database engine to create and store the object you designed in Design view.

- When you select referential integrity options in the Relationships window (opened by choosing Tools ➢ Relationships), the engine enforces those options.

- When you link to an external table (by choosing File ➢ Get External Data), the interface arranges for the database engine to create and manage the connection.

- When you run a query in a database or a view or stored procedure in a project, the interface sends the equivalent SQL statement to the database engine for processing; the engine creates the appropriate recordset and passes it back for Access to display in some interface object.

- When you set up security for an Access database using one of the Security dialogs (opened by choosing Tools ➢ Security), the interface arranges for the database engine to create and store the security information.

- When two or more users attempt to edit the same record or when one user attempts to work with two versions of the same record, the Access application arranges with the database engine to handle the conflicts.

An advantage of VBA programming is that you can create procedures for these database services. Within your VBA application, you can write procedures to create new tables and queries and even create your own custom objects. You can modify built-in objects by creating custom properties and methods for them. You can create procedures that link the database to external tables and that update the links automatically when a table is moved. You can create procedures to enforce referential integrity, monitor security, and modify record locking.

NOTE   With most Microsoft Access databases, data may be stored locally, as part of the MDB file. Conversely, ADP (project) files contain no data objects. They contain only interface objects (such as forms and reports) and programming objects (macros and modules). The actual data is stored in a database file (for example, a DAT file for SQL Server) on a host server. ADO contains events and methods capable of quickly retrieving data from a variety of source database types.

The ActiveX Data Objects (ADO) Hierarchy

The ADO object model hierarchy exists separately from the Access application hierarchy. Table 6.1 lists the 13 data access objects, and Figure 6.2 shows the hierarchy of the objects.

TABLE 6.1: The Data Access Objects of the ADO Model

Object	Description
Connection	Represents the connection between an application and a data source
Command	Represents a request that you are sending to the data source for it to take some action
Parameter	Represents a parameter of, or additional information about, the Command object
Parameters	The collection of parameters associated with a Command
Recordset	A collection of records retrieved from a data source
Field	A column in a Recordset object
Fields	The collection of all the Field objects in a Recordset object
Record	Represents a file or directory within a file system
Stream	Represents the data within a Record object
Error	Represents a data access error that occurs during the processing of a single operation
Errors	The collection of Error objects created because of a single data access failure
Property	Represents one of the dynamic properties of an ADO object
Properties	The collection of all the Property objects for a particular object

At the top of the hierarchy is the Connection object, which you use to refer to the connection between the client application (in this case, Microsoft Access) and the data server, whether a SQL database, a Jet database, or some other data source. In addition to the dynamic, application-assigned Property objects within the Properties collections shown in Figure 6.2, each object has several intrinsic, or constant, properties.

FIGURE 6.2:

The ADO object hierarchy. In addition to the objects shown, each object has both intrinsic and dynamic properties. The dynamic properties are represented as Property objects within the Properties collection.

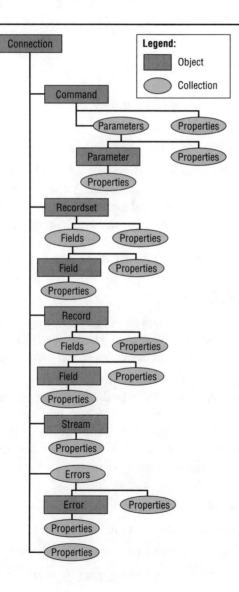

The ADO Extensions for DDL and Security (ADOX) Hierarchy

The ADO library alone cannot easily complete several tasks essential to creating an automated database. Changes to security or schema usually involve the ADOX library. These changes include the following:

- Creating a new table in a data source
- Creating queries
- Adding fields to existing tables
- Changing security settings for a particular user or group
- Adding new users or groups
- Setting indexes on tables

Figure 6.3 shows the ADOX object hierarchy, and Table 6.2 lists the objects in the hierarchy. In addition to the objects shown in Figure 6.3, the Table, Index, and Column objects have both a dynamic Properties collection and intrinsic properties. The other objects have dynamic properties and intrinsic properties, but the dynamic properties are not part of a collection. The Connection object, shown at the top of the figure, is not really part of the ADOX library; it is the object in the ADO library that ties the two libraries together.

ADO Object References

In a VBA procedure, you work with the data access objects using two fundamental operations: you read and change properties, and you ask an object to use one of its methods to manipulate itself. Before you can carry out either operation, you must refer to the object.

When you open an existing database, ADO creates in memory a Connection object to represent the connection between Access and the database you opened, and a Recordset object to represent the records in the database. You can refer to children of a collection by traversing along the hierarchical path to the object, recording references to the objects and collection objects that you encounter along the way. You use the dot operator (.) when stepping from an object to one of its collections. When you are stepping from a collection to one of its members, you can use any of the four references:

- Use the exclamation point (!) operator to refer to a member explicitly by name.
- Use the parenthetical syntax to refer to a member by name.
- Use the parenthetical syntax to refer to a member by its position in the collection.
- Use the parenthetical syntax to refer to a member by a variable.

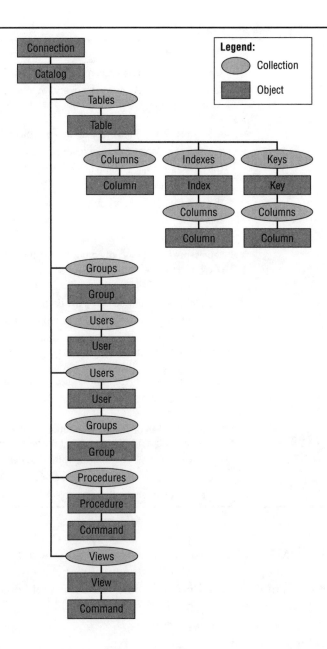

FIGURE 6.3:
FIGURE 6.3:

ADOX object hierarchy

TABLE 6.2: The Objects in the ADOX Model

Object	Description
Catalog	Represents a database's schema and security settings.
Table	Represents a table, a view, or a query without parameters in a database. A Table object defines the table but does not represent the data stored in the table.
Tables	The collection of all Table objects in a database.
Column	Represents a single column in a table, index, or key.
Columns	The collection of all Column objects within the parent object.
Index	Represents an index on a table.
Indexes	The collection of all Index objects within a table.
Key	Represents a foreign, primary, or unique key on a table.
Keys	The collection of all Key objects within a table.
Group	Represents a single security group within the database or a group to which a particular user belongs.
Groups	The collection of all Group objects related to the parent object.
User	Represents a single user within the database or a user in a Group.
Users	The collection of all User objects related to the parent object.
Procedure	Represents a query or a stored procedure. A Procedure object defines the query or stored procedure but does not represent the data stored in the query or procedure.
Procedures	The collection of all Procedure objects within the database.
Command	Represents a request that you are sending to the data source for it to take some action.
View	Represents a view or a query without parameters. A View object defines the view or query but does not represent the data stored in the view or query.
Views	The collection of all View objects within a database.
Property	Represents one of the dynamic properties of an ADO object.
Properties	The collection of all the Property objects for a particular object.

The collections in ADO are all zero-based. Normally, you use a mixture of syntax types. For example, when you open a form, ADO automatically opens a Recordset object that represents the records in the form's RecordSource, as well as Field objects to represent each column in the Recordset. You can refer to the third field in the Recordset by name, or you can refer to it by position, using `Fields(2)`:

```
Recordset.Fields(2)
```

Suppose you want to refer to the ValidationRule property of the CustomerID field in the Customers table in the current database. You continue traversing the path as follows:

```
Recordset.Fields(2).Properties!ValidationRule
```

Using Default Collections

Fortunately, two data access objects have default collections, so you can abbreviate some references by omitting the names of the default collections. The Fields collection is the default collection for the Recordset object, and the Parameters collection is the default collection for the Command object.

You separate an object reference and a built-in property with the dot operator: *object.property*. Taking advantage of these default collections, you can abbreviate the reference to the third field in the Recordset as `Recordset(2)`, and use the following syntax for the reference to the ValidationRule property:

```
Recordset(2).Properties!ValidationRule
```

Using the CurrentProject Property

The Application object in Access contains a special property called CurrentProject. This property returns the CurrentProject object, which represents the database in which you're currently working. Because ADO requires that there be a Connection object established to make changes to or receive data from a data source, CurrentProject is most useful in implicitly creating a Connection object to the open database that is sure not to fail.

The CurrentProject object contains five collections that represent the Access application objects in the database: AllForms, AllReports, AllMacros, AllModules, and AllDataAccessPages. The AllForms collection contains all of the forms in the database, whether or not they are open. CurrentProject doesn't contain any of the ADO data access objects but is useful in programmatically automating your Access application.

When you use the CurrentProject property to refer to the database object, the three references to an object in a collection look like this:

Index by name	`CurrentProject.AllReports("Invoice")`
Index using a variable	`strName = "Invoice"`
	`CurrentProject.AllReports(strName)`
Index by number	`CurrentProject.AllReports(9)`

NOTE When working through the examples in this book, it is important that you have references in the Object Browser for Access, ADO, and ADOX. To make sure that these are selected, open the Northwind_Ch5,6.mdb file you created in Chapter 5, "VBA Programming Essentials," and press F11. Then press F2 to open the Object Browser. Click Tools ➢ References to open the References dialog. Make sure that Microsoft Access 10.0 Object Library, Microsoft ActiveX Data Objects 2.5 Library, and Microsoft ADO Ext. 2.5 for DDL and Security are all selected.

You can use the Immediate window to show information about the open database using the CurrentProject property. Press Ctrl+G to open the Immediate window.

- Type **?Application.CurrentProject.Name** and press Enter. The name of the open database is returned.

- Type **?CurrentProject.Name** and press Enter. Because Application is the default object in the Access Object Library, you can omit the explicit reference to it and the Immediate window will still return the name of the open database.

- Type **?CurrentProject.AllForms("Customers").Name** and press Enter. The Immediate window displays the value of the Name property of the Customers Form.

- Type **strName="Customers"** and press Enter. This creates the string strName in memory and stores Customers as its value. Now type **?CurrentProject .AllForms(strName).Name** and press Enter. Customers is returned.

- Type **?CurrentProject.AllForms(0).Name** and press Enter. Because the collections of the CurrentProject object are all zero-based, this command returns the name of the first form in the collection.

- Type **?CurrentProject.Connection.ConnectionString** and press Enter. The Immediate window returns the value of the Connection object's ConnectionString property for the current database. You will learn more about the Connection object and the ConnectionString property later in this chapter.

Two Recordsets Opened Simultaneously

When you work interactively or use only macro programming, you can open only one database at a time. When you work with VBA programming, you can open multiple databases simultaneously by opening multiple Recordset objects.

You can use the Open method of the Recordset object to open a recordset from a specified database. Opening a second recordset, however, is not like opening a second workbook in Excel or a second document in Word, because you can't see the second database. Access opens the second recordset in memory; there is no visual representation. With VBA programming, however, you can work with the second invisible recordset almost as though it were visible in the Access interface.

The Open method returns the opened recordset as a Recordset object. When you use a method that returns something, you can assign the result to a variable. Because the Open method returns an object, you assign the result to an *object variable*. The assignment statement for an object variable is as follows:

```
Set objectvariable = object
```

The Set keyword indicates the assignment of the object to an object variable. Chapter 8, "Using Variables," gives a detailed treatment of object variables.

The syntax for the Open method is

```
Set objectvariable = New ADODB.Recordset
objectvariable.Open Source, ActiveConnection, CursorType, LockType, Options
```

where

- *Objectvariable* is a variable that represents the Recordset object that will be returned.

- *Source* is an optional variant expression that is the name of a valid Command object, SQL statement, table, stored procedure, URL, or file or Stream object that contains a persistently stored Recordset.

- *ActiveConnection* is an optional argument that represents a valid Connection object. It must either contain the information to make a valid connection or be set to a string variable that represents a valid Connection.

- *CursorType* is another optional argument. It can be set to a limited number of values that determine the type of recordset to be returned.

- *LockType* is an optional string expression for specifying the type of record locking to be placed on the Recordset that is returned.

- *Options* is an optional Long value that tells the source which type of object is being called in the *Source* argument.

All of the arguments are considered optional because you can set them before you call the Recordset object's Open method. For example, if you wanted to omit the ActiveConnection argument, you could insert a line such as *recordset*.ActiveConnection = *strConn* before the recordset.Open line. In this case, strConn would be a string expression that evaluated to a valid Connection object. If you set ActiveConnection as a property of the Recordset object rather than as an argument of the Recordset's Open method, you must do the same with the Source. The other arguments can be set either as properties or as arguments, regardless of whether Source and ActiveConnection were set as arguments or properties. In fact, you don't have to set them at all. If you leave them blank, they default to adOpenForwardOnly, adLockReadOnly, and adOptionUnspecified, respectively.

When you call the Open method, Access opens the recordset in memory and creates the Recordset and Field objects. It also adds the Field objects to the Fields collection.

As an example, we'll open a recordset based on the database we created in Chapter 1, "Automating a Database without Programming," Expenses.mdb. With Northwind_Ch5,6.mdb open in the Access window, follow these steps in the Immediate window:

1. Type **Set rst = New ADODB.Recordset** and press Enter. This creates a variable, rst, in memory and declares it as being of the ADO Recordset type.

2. Type **Set cnn = New ADODB.Connection** and press Enter. This statement creates a variable named cnn in memory and assigns it the ADO Connection type.

3. Type **cnn.ConnectionString="Provider=Microsoft.Jet.OLEDB.4.0; Data Source=c:\VBAHandbook\Expenses.mdb; Jet OLEDB:Database Password=expenses"** and press Enter. (This is the path to the Expenses.mdb file used in Chapter 1. If you saved this database in another directory or used a different password, you may need to alter the ConnectionString.) This tells the Connection object all it needs to know to open the data source. You will learn more about Connection-Strings later in this chapter.

4. Type **cnn.Open** and press Enter. This establishes the connection between the Northwind_Ch5,6.mdb client application and the Expenses.mdb data source. Type **rst.Open "Employees", cnn** and press Enter. This opens a Recordset object using the existing Connection object and the Employees table in the Expenses database. Access opens the Recordset immediately; the rst variable refers to, or *points to*, the data in the Employees table. You can confirm that the database is open by retrieving the value of the State property for the recordset—that is, by retrieving rst.State.

5. Type **?rst.State** and press Enter. The Immediate window displays a 1. If an ADO object is open, it returns a value of 1 for its State property. If it is closed, it returns a 0. Having confirmed that the second recordset is open, close it using the Close method of the Recordset object. When you use the Close method, the data is removed from the Recordset object, but the object itself still exists in memory.

6. Type **rst.Close** and press Enter. Access closes the recordset based on the Expenses.mdb database. To confirm the closure, take the next step.

7. Type **?rst.State** and press Enter. The Immediate window displays a 0 to indicate that there are no records in the Recordset, but that the Recordset object itself still exists in memory.

New Data Access Objects

If a data access object doesn't exist when you want to refer to it in a VBA procedure, you'll need to create it. In general, creating a new data access object is a three-step process:

- Create a variable to represent the new object and declare its type (this is called *instantiating* the object).

- Define the new object's characteristics by setting its properties. Many of an object's properties can be set only when you create the new object, and they become read-only after the object is saved to the database. In some cases, you also must create child objects for the new object; for example, when you create a new table, you must also create at least one field before you can save the table.

- Append the object to its collection using the Append method of the collection.

In general, the object that is created in memory is saved to the database only when you append it to its collection. There are three exceptions: Catalog, View, and Procedure objects. To create a new Catalog object, you simply instantiate the Catalog then call its Create method. This method works only with the Jet OLE DB provider, however, so it cannot be used to create new databases using the Microsoft SQL Server 2000 Desktop Engine, for example. To create a new View or Procedure, you create a Command object, set the Command's properties so that it carries out the query represented by the View or Procedure, then append it to the Views or Procedures collection.

Creating Databases

The syntax for the Catalog's Create method is as follows:

```
Set cat = New ADOX.Catalog
cat.Create ConnectionString
```

where

- *Cat* is a reference to the new database you are creating.

- *ConnectionString* is a valid connection string or a reference to an existing Connection object.

As an example, we'll create a new empty database using the `Create` method of the Catalog object and using `newdb` as the object variable. Create a new form called frmADO_ADOX in the Northwind_Ch5,6.mdb database. Add a command button to the form called cmdNewCatalog. Click the Build button next to the OnClick event property and select Code Builder from the Choose Builder dialog box. Type the following between the `Private Sub cmdNewCatalog_Click()` and `End Sub` lines:

```
Dim newdb As ADOX.Catalog
Set newdb = New ADOX.Catalog
newdb.Create "Provider=Microsoft.Jet.OLEDB.4.0;" & _
  "Data Source=c:\VBAHandbook\MyNewDB.mdb"
```

Save the module and save the frmADO_ADOX form. Switch to Form view and click the command button. A new empty database is created and saved on disk. To check this, choose File ➢ Open and select MyNewDB.mdb. The new empty database opens.

WARNING   Remember, by default the ADOX object library is not installed, so you need to add it in the Tools ➢ References dialog. You also should make sure you are using the latest reference library for ADO objects, as an older version may be installed by default.

Creating Tables

Often, the object you want to create has required child objects; for example, you can't create a table without at least one field. Another example is the Index object, which requires at least one child Field object. In these cases, creating the parent requires additional steps. As an example, here are the steps for creating a new Table named tblShipping with a single field named colShipperID:

1. Create a new form in the MyNewDB database you created and name the form frmCreator.

2. Place a command button on the frmCreator form and name it cmdNewTable. Click the Build button next to the button's OnClick property and choose Code Builder.

3. Type the following as the event's procedure:

```
Dim tbl As New ADOX.Table
Dim col As New ADOX.Column
Dim cat As New ADOX.Catalog

' Create a new ADOX table
Set tbl = New ADOX.Table
tbl.Name = "tblShipping"

' Create the ShipperID column in the new table
Set col = New ADOX.Column
```

```
col.Name = "ShipperID"
col.Type = adInteger

' Associate the Table with the current database
Set cat = New ADOX.Catalog
Set cat.ActiveConnection = CurrentProject.Connection
Set col.ParentCatalog = cat

' Append the Column to the Table
tbl.Columns.Append col

' Append the Table to the Catalog
cat.Tables.Append tbl
```

4. Save the changes to the form and switch to Form view. Click the command button.

If you open the Database window and click the Tables button, you will see a new tblShipping table. Open this table, and you will see a single field named ShipperID.

TIP   In VBA code, anything preceded by a single apostrophe (') is considered a comment and is not read by the program running the code. It is useful for helping explain what your code is intended to do.

Creating Indexes

It is often very helpful to create an index in a database to speed searching. Index objects, like Tables, have a collection of Column objects. For this reason, creating an Index is similar to creating a Table. In the following example, we will set our new SupplierID field to be a Primary index.

1. Open the frmCreator form in Design view.

2. Place a command button on the frmCreator form and name it cmdNewIndex. Click the Build button next to the button's OnClick property and choose Code Builder.

3. Type the following as the event's procedure:

```
Dim idx As New ADOX.Index
Dim col As New ADOX.Column
```

```
Dim tbl As New ADOX.Table
Dim cat As New ADOX.Catalog

' Create a new ADOX index and set its properties
Set idx = New ADOX.Index
idx.Name = "PrimaryIndex"
idx.PrimaryKey = True

' Declare the column for the new index
idx.Columns.Append "ShipperID"

' Associate the Table with the current database
Set cat = New ADOX.Catalog
cat.ActiveConnection = CurrentProject.Connection
Set tbl = cat.Tables!tblShipping

' Append the Index to the Table
tbl.Indexes.Append idx
```

If you open the tblShipping table in Design view and click View ➤ Indexes, you will see a
new PrimaryKey (see Figure 6.4).

FIGURE 6.4:

You can use VBA to create
Indexes for tables.

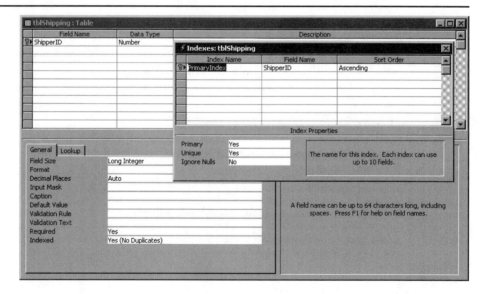

Creating Queries

Frequently, you need to create new queries in a VBA procedure. You create a new query as a View object if the query has parameters and as a Procedure if it does not. Views and Procedures both use the ADO Command object to retrieve data from the data source when creating the query results. Creating new queries in VBA requires that you know how to write SQL statements. In truth, if you don't know SQL, you can avoid learning it a little longer by creating a sample of the new query in query Design view, switching to SQL view, and pasting the equivalent SQL statement into the *sqltext* argument. As an example, we'll create a new query that displays the records in the Employees table and sorts the records by LastName. We will be using the Northwind_Ch5,6.mdb database for this example. Here are the steps:

1. In query Design view, create a new query based on the Employees table. Use the asterisk (*) method to include all the fields. Drag the LastName field to the grid, deselect the Show check box to hide the field, and enter Ascending in the Sort cell.

2. Switch to SQL view and copy the following SQL statement to the Clipboard:

    ```
    SELECT Employees.*
    FROM Employees
    ORDER BY Employees.LastName;
    ```

3. Create a new module named basNewQuery. Type the following into the VB window:

    ```
    PublicSub NewQuery()

        Dim cnn As ADODB.Connection
        Dim cat As ADOX.Catalog
        Dim cmd As ADODB.Command

        ' Establish that you are using the open connection and database
        Set cnn = CurrentProject.Connection
        Set cat = New ADOX.Catalog
        Set cat.ActiveConnection = cnn

        ' Create a new Command object representing a view
        Set cmd = New ADODB.Command
        cmd.CommandText = "SELECT Employees.* FROM Employees " & _
          "ORDER BY Employees.LastName;"

        ' Append the Command to the Views collection
        cat.Views.Append "vwEmployeesbyLastName", cmd

    End Sub
    ```

WARNING Make sure you have added a reference to both the ADO and ADOX object libraries, or running the module will result in an error.

4. Save the basNewQuery module. In the Immediate window, type **NewQuery** and press Enter.

5. Open the Database window and click the Queries tab. You can see the new query, vwEmployeesbyLastName. Open it, and you can see that the Employees' names are listed and are sorted by last name in Ascending order.

NOTE If the query you want to create is a SQL-specific query that can't be created in query Design view, you'll need to create the SQL statement directly. See the *Access 2002 Developer's Handbook* by Paul Litwin, Ken Getz, and Mike Gunderloy (Sybex, 2001) for guidance on creating SQL statements.

Creating Recordsets

The most common type of data access object you create in VBA procedures is the Recordset. You'll notice in Table 6.2 that neither the Table, the View, nor the Procedure objects represent the data stored in the database tables. The data values are available only as the Value property setting of the Field object of the Recordset object. Thus, if you are going to manipulate data in VBA using the data access objects, you'll be working with Recordset objects.

In Chapter 4, "Communicating with Forms," we worked with recordsets as data sources for forms. By definition, a recordset is the set of records in a table, or the set of records produced by running a query or a SQL statement that produces records. The Recordset data access object represents a recordset. The Recordset object has 25 properties and more than 25 methods for working with data. All the power to sort, search, update, add, and delete data resides in the Recordset object.

Types of Recordsets

Four types of Recordset objects, or cursors, are available in the ADO model. The four types differ in significant ways and are used for different purposes. Each offers advantages and disadvantages. The following sections explain the features of the recordset types.

Dynamic Cursor

This type of Recordset object is the most flexible, yet runs the slowest. With a dynamic cursor recordset, you can view changes, additions, and deletions made to a recordset by other users who have access to it. You can move through the records in any direction that is supported by the data source, and you can use bookmarks if the data source supports them.

Keyset Cursor
The keyset cursor type is identical to the dynamic cursor, except that you can't see additions or deletions by other users. You can still see changes to records that have not been deleted.

Static Cursor
The static cursor type is a static copy of a set of records based on a table, query, or SQL SELECT statement. You can use this type to retrieve data or generate reports. In a static cursor recordset, the object consists of a copy of the entire record. It allows movement in any direction, including bookmarks. Because a static cursor is only a copy of the data and you are not working with the actual data source, it is faster than a dynamic or keyset cursor type, but you will not see changes, additions, or deletions made to the source data.

Forward-Only Cursor
The forward-only cursor type is the same as the static cursor except that you can only scroll forward through the records. This type provides better performance than the static cursor recordset, but is very limiting in the type of movement allowed. This is the default type of Recordset object returned by ADO, which is important to keep in mind if you prefer to use bookmarks or reverse navigation in your recordset.

Creating a Recordset Object
You can manipulate data in a VBA procedure in two ways:

- You can open a form that is bound to the data and use the Application objects to manipulate the data.

- You can create a Recordset object in memory to represent the data and use the data access objects to manipulate the data.

Using the Application objects involves writing less code because the application does so much of the work for you (see Chapter 12, "Maintaining Data with Access VBA," for examples of procedures for both approaches). Using the data access objects means writing more code, but it gives you more opportunity to specify how and when you want the database engine to carry out each step of an operation. This chapter focuses on using data access objects.

Earlier in this chapter, you learned the process for opening a recordset using the Open method of the Recordset object. As you recall, the syntax is as follows:

```
Set objectvariable = New ADODB.Recordset
objectvariable.Open Source, ActiveConnection, CursorType, LockType, Options
```

where

- *Objectvariable* is a variable that represents the Recordset object that will be returned.

- *Source* is an optional variant expression that is the name of a valid Command object, SQL statement, table, stored procedure, URL, or file or Stream object that contains a persistently stored Recordset.

- *ActiveConnection* is an optional argument that represents a valid Connection object. It must either contain the information to make a valid connection or be set to a string variable that represents a valid Connection.

- *CursorType* is another optional argument. It can be set to a limited number of values that determine the type of recordset to be returned:

adOpenDynamic	Creates a dynamic cursor.
adOpenForwardOnly	ADO's default setting. Creates a forward-only cursor.
adOpenKeyset	Creates a keyset cursor.
adOpenStatic	Creates a static cursor.
adOpenUnspecified	Doesn't specify a cursor type.

- *LockType* is an optional string expression for specifying the type of record locking to be placed on the Recordset that is returned. If set, must be to one of the following values:

adLockBatchOptimistic	Optimistic batch update mode. This mode is required if you will be doing batch updates.
adLockOptimistic	This designates the recordset as using optimistic locking, meaning it only locks records when you call the Recordset object's Update method.
adLockPessimistic	Evokes pessimistic locking on the recordset, so that records are locked when editing on them begins rather than when you execute an update.
adLockReadOnly	The recordset is designated read-only. Changes cannot be made to the data. This is ADO's default setting.
adLockUnspecified	No type of record locking is specified for the recordset.

- *Options* is an optional Long value that tells the source which type of object is being called in the *Source* argument. It can be set to one or more of the following values:

adCmdText	Tells the provider that the Source argument is a textual file, such as a SQL statement.

adCmdTable	Tells the provider that the Source argument is the name of a table generated by a SQL query.
adCmdStoredProcedure	Tells the provider that the Source argument is the name of a stored procedure.
adCmdUnknown	This is ADO's default. Tells the provider that the type of source specified in the Source argument is not known.
adCmdFile	Tells the provider that the Source argument is the name of a persistently stored recordset file.
adCmdTableDirect	Tells the provider that the Source argument is the name of a table, all of whose columns are returned.
adAsynchExecute	Specifies that the command in the Source argument should execute asynchronously.
adAsynchFetch	When used with the CacheSize property, tells the provider which rows should be retrieved asynchronously.
adAsynchFetchNonBlocking	Tells the provider which rows to retrieve asynchronously without blocking the main thread of execution.
adExecuteNoRecords	Indicates that the Source argument is one that does not return rows.

WARNING If you open a recordset using ADO and don't specify a type, it creates a read-only, forward-only cursor recordset. If you plan to make changes to the data, or if you wish to use any type of data navigation other than moving forward through the records, be sure to set appropriate arguments when you call the Recordset's Open method.

Closing a Recordset

Every Recordset object that you create in a VBA procedure exists until you explicitly close it or until the Connection object that the recordset used is closed. If you need to close a Recordset object during a procedure, use the Close method. Using the Close method closes an open Recordset object but does not remove it from memory. If you need to remove the Recordset from memory, you set the Recordset object's variable to Nothing. For example, to close rstSales, you would type **rstSales.Close** in your procedure. To remove it from memory, you would type **rstSales = Nothing**.

NOTE It isn't necessary to explicitly close Recordset objects before the procedure ends. However, you make your code easier to understand if you explicitly close the Recordset objects.

ADO Recordset Object Manipulation

When you create a Recordset object, you are placing rows of data in a memory buffer; the rows are not displayed on the screen. You are pointing to one row at a time; the row you are pointing to is called the *current record*. The current record is the only record that you can modify or retrieve data from. When you refer to fields in a Recordset object, you get values from the current record. Only one record in the recordset can be the current record at any one time. When you first create a Recordset object using the Open method, the first record is the current record if there are any records. At times, a Recordset object doesn't have a current record. For example, if the recordset has no records, the Recordset object doesn't have a current record.

With only a single record available at one time, you'll need ways to navigate from one record to another record, making the record you navigate to the current record so that you can work with it. The two basic kinds of navigation among records are *physical navigation* and *logical navigation*. In interactive Access, you are using physical navigation when you click the navigation buttons in the lower-left corner of a form or datasheet to move from one record to another according to their physical location within the recordset. When you use the Find dialog (choose Edit ➢ Find) and enter search criteria in the Find What text box, you are using logical navigation to move directly to the first record that matches the criteria. The Recordset object has methods and properties for both kinds of navigation.

Using Physical Navigation

You can move from one record to another according to physical location in two ways. You can use the Move... methods to duplicate the effect of the navigation buttons of interactive Access, or you can save your place in a recordset by setting a bookmark and then returning later to the same record.

Using the *Move...* Methods

You can move from one record to another record according to the record's physical location in the recordset using the Move... methods of a Recordset object. The MoveFirst, MoveLast, MoveNext, and MovePrevious methods move the current record position to the first, last, next, or previous record of a specified Recordset object, respectively. The syntax of the Move... methods is as follows:

```
rst.{MoveFirst | MoveLast | MoveNext | MovePrevious}
```

rst refers to an open Recordset object. In a forward-only cursor recordset, you can use only the MoveNext and MoveFirst methods, because you can only move the current record pointer forward toward the last record of the recordset or to the beginning of a recordset. If you use the MoveFirst method on a forward-only cursor recordset, it may cause the data provider to retrieve the entire Recordset object again rather than just moving the pointer to the first record in the existing recordset.

You can use the Immediate window to test the Move... methods as follows:

1. Type **Set rst = New ADODB.Recordset** and press Enter.

2. Type **Set cnn = New ADODB.Connection** and press Enter.

3. Type **Set cnn = CurrentProject.Connection** and press Enter.

4. Type **rst.Open "Employees", cnn** and press Enter. This opens a Recordset object using the existing Connection object and the Employees table in the current database.

5. Type **?rst!EmployeeID** and press Enter. The number 1 is displayed. Now let's move to the next record.

6. Type **rst.MoveNext** and press Enter. Then type **?rst!EmployeeID** and press Enter. The number 2 is displayed. Let's move to the last record and see what happens if we try to use the MoveNext method.

7. Type **rst.MoveLast** and press Enter. The VB Editor generates an error message (see Figure 6.5). Since we didn't specify a cursor type when we created the Recordset object, ADO assigned it the default, forward-only. The MoveLast method is invalid for forward-only recordsets.

FIGURE 6.5:

The error generated when you attempt the Move-Last method on a forward-only cursor recordset

8. Type **rst.MoveFirst** and press Enter. You are now back at the first record in the recordset. Type **?rst!EmployeeID** and press Enter. The number 1 is again displayed. Type **rst.Close**.

Using the BOF and EOF Properties

You use the BOF (Beginning of File) and EOF (End of File) properties of the Recordset object to determine whether you've gone beyond the limits of the recordset. Both properties have the value False as long as you are pointing to a record in the recordset—that is, as long as there is a current record. If you move after the last record, there is no current record, and the EOF property is set to True; if you move before the first record, there is no current record, and the BOF property is set to True. If the recordset has no records at all, both the BOF and EOF properties are True.

A standard VBA procedure for working with a set of records is to create a Recordset object and use the MoveNext method to loop through the records one by one. To determine when you are finished, you test the value of the EOF property at the beginning of each pass through the loop. As long as EOF is False, you take another pass, but as soon as EOF is True, you have moved beyond the last record of the recordset, and the loop is finished. Chapter 9, "Controlling Execution," describes how to create procedures for looping through a recordset.

Setting Bookmarks

In Chapter 5, you learned that Access tracks records in a form's recordset by creating a bookmark as a unique binary string for each record as soon as you open the form. The database engine also creates bookmarks. When you create a Recordset object, the engine automatically assigns a set of unique bookmarks. If you are pointing to a record that you want to return to later, you can save your place by saving the record's bookmark to a variable; to return to the record later, you set the Bookmark property to the saved value. Test the technique in the Immediate window as follows:

1. Type **Set rst = New ADODB.Recordset** and press Enter. Type **Set cnn = New ADODB.Connection** and press Enter.

2. Type **Set cnn = CurrentProject.Connection** and press Enter.

3. Type **rst.Open "Employees", cnn, adOpenStatic** and press Enter. The recordset is now open and the first record is the current one. To verify this, type **?rst!EmployeeID** and press Enter. The number 1 is returned.

Tip   The Jet OLE DB provider does not support using bookmarks with the dynamic or keyset cursor recordsets. To use bookmarks with a Jet database, you have to create a static cursor recordset.

4. Type **rst.MoveNext** and press Enter. The current record is the second record (EmployeeID = 2). You save your place in the next step.

5. Type **strMark = rst.Bookmark** and press Enter. The strMark variable stores the bookmark.

6. Use a Move... method to move to some other record.

7. Type **rst.Bookmark = strMark** and press Enter to return to the saved place. Confirm by entering **?rst!EmployeeID** and pressing Enter. You have returned to the bookmarked record.

Using the *Move* Method

You can use the Move method to move the current record position forward (toward the last record) or backward (toward the first row) a specified number of rows. You can even specify that you want to start moving from a particular record. The syntax of the Move method is as follows:

```
rst.Move NumRecords, Start
```

where

- *rst* is the reference to the Recordset object.
- *NumRecords* is a signed Long integer indicating the number of rows. If *rows* is positive, you move forward; otherwise, you move backward. For a forward-only-type Recordset object, *rows* must be a positive integer.
- *Start* is an optional string variable that identifies a bookmark.

You can test the Move method in the Immediate window. Type **rst!Move 4** and press Enter. Confirm that you are now at the record with EmployeeID = 6.

Using Logical Navigation

When you want to locate a record that satisfies a search condition, the technique you use depends on the type of Recordset you've created. The Seek method works only with server-side cursor recordsets that were opened with the adCmdTableDirect option set. If you are working with other recordsets, indexes are not appropriate, and you use the Find method instead. If either search technique succeeds in finding a record that matches the search condition, the found record becomes the current record. If no record is located, the pointer moves to the space just after the last record. To determine if the search is successful, you check the EOF property of the Recordset object. If the search is successful, a match has been found, and EOF is False; if the search fails, there is no match, and the EOF property is True.

Using the *Seek* Method

The Seek method uses indexes to locate records in the fastest way possible. You can use the Seek method only for a Recordset retrieved using adCmdTableDirect because the search condition is based on values in an index. Before you can use the Seek method, the table you are working with must have at least one index, and you must set the Index property of the Recordset object to the particular index you want to use in the search. For example, the Customers table has the indexes shown in Figure 6.6.

FIGURE 6.6:

The indexes defined for the Customers table

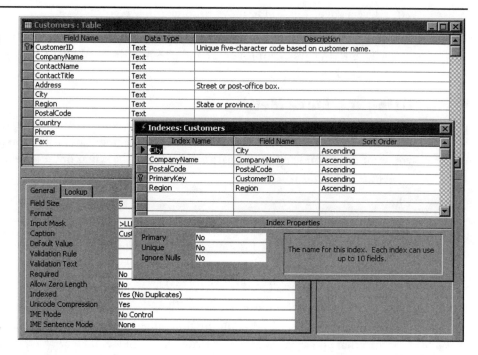

You can use any of the existing indexes, or you can create a new Index object. The value of the Index property is called the *current index*.

The syntax for the Seek method is as follows:

```
recordset.Seek KeyValues, SeekOption
```

where

- *recordset* is a reference to the existing Recordset object that has a current index specified by the Recordset object's Index property.

- *KeyValues* is an array of Variant values that the database engine uses to compare against the values in the columns of the Index.

- *SeekOption* specifies the type of Seek to make:

adSeekFirstEQ	Find the first key equal to the KeyValues.
adSeekLastEQ	Find the last key equal to the KeyValues.
adSeekAfterEQ	Find the key equal to the KeyValues or just after where a match would have occurred.

adSeekAfter	Find the key just after the first match with the KeyValues.
adSeekBeforeEQ	Find the key equal to the KeyValues or just before where a match would have occurred.
adSeekBefore	Find the key just before the first match with the KeyValues.

For example, to search for customers from a particular city, follow these steps:

1. Close the Customers table if it is open. In the Immediate window, type the following:

```
Set rst = New ADODB.Recordset
Set cnn = New ADODB.Connection
Set cnn = CurrentProject.Connection
Set idx = New ADOX.Index
```

2. To open the recordset, type **rst.Open "Customers", cnn, adOpenStatic, adLockOptimistic, adCmdTableDirect** and press Enter.

3. To set the current index to City, type **rst.Index = "City"** and press Enter.

4. To locate the first customer from London, type **rst.Seek "London", adSeekFirstEQ** and press Enter.

5. To determine if the search was successful, type **?rst.EOF** and press Enter. The search is successful, and False is returned.

6. Type **?rst!CompanyName** and press Enter. The name of the first customer is returned as Around The Horn.

Using the *Find* Method

The Seek method works only with server-side direct-access table Recordsets. When your Recordset object is of a different type, you use the Find method instead.

You can duplicate the effect of the Find command of interactive Access with the Find method of the Recordset object. The Find method locates the first record that satisfies specified criteria and makes that record the current record. The syntax for the Find method is as follows:

```
rst.Find Criteria, SkipRows, SearchDirection, Start
```

where

- *rst* is a reference to an existing Recordset.

- *Criteria* is a string expression for locating the record, specifying the column name, comparison operator, and search value.

- *SkipRows* is an optional argument that specifies the number of rows to skip from the current row or the bookmark specified in the Start argument. The default for this argument is 0 and the search begins with the current row.

- *SearchDirection* is an optional argument and can be either adSearchForward or adSearchBackward to specify the direction in which the search should be conducted. The default is to search forward.

- *Start* is an optional Variant argument specifying a bookmark from which to begin a search.

For example, find the first customer from Berlin as follows:

1. Type **rst.MoveFirst** and press Enter. This ensures that you will not miss searching on any records that are before the location of the current record pointer.

2. Type **rst.Find "City = 'Berlin'"** in the Immediate window and press Enter.

3. To determine the name of the customer, type **?rst!CompanyName** and press Enter. Alfreds Futterkiste is displayed.

Adding, Editing, and Deleting Records

What experienced programmers find so satisfying about the data access objects is that they *are able* to control every operation; what inexperienced programmers find so overwhelming is that they *must* control every operation. To understand which methods you must include in procedures that modify data using the data access objects, you need to be aware that the database engine does not automatically carry out the steps that are automatically carried out when you write procedures to modify data with a form using the Application object.

Editing and Updating Records

When you want to modify the data in a record, you must first make that record the current record. You can use the Move... methods or the Find or Seek methods to move the current record pointer to the record you want to change. The crux of editing data is that the changes are not made directly to the record; instead, the record is copied into a location in memory called the *copy buffer* that the database engine creates for editing. Your VBA code must deal with moving content in and out of the copy buffer. To copy the contents of the copy buffer back to the Recordset object, you must either use the Update method or move the record pointer to a different record. If you move the record pointer, ADO will automatically call the Update method to copy any changes you made in the current record back to the Recordset. If you perform any operation that closes the Recordset object without first using the Update method (either explicitly or implicitly), your changes are not saved, and the contents of the copy buffer are discarded without warning. If you opened the recordset in batch update mode, you must call the Recordset object's BatchUpdate method before closing the recordset so that changes are copied back to the data source.

You can work in the Immediate window to change the data in the rst Recordset object. Follow these steps:

1. To assign the new values to the field you want to change, type **rst!CompanyName = "Around the Cape"** and press Enter. The new value is now in the copy buffer.

2. To save the changes to the current record using the Update method, type **rst.Update** and press Enter.

3. To confirm that the change was saved, type **?rst!CompanyName** and press Enter. The Immediate window displays the new value.

4. Change the name of the customer again by typing **?rst!CompanyName = "Around the Block"** and pressing Enter.

5. Type **rst.MoveNext** and press Enter to move the record pointer forward one record. Moving to a new record implicitly evokes the Recordset's Update method.

6. Type **rst.MovePrevious** and press Enter, then type **?rst!CompanyName** and press Enter. The new value is displayed.

Editing a record provides an example of the fundamental differences between modifying data using the Access interface and using the data access objects: When you work interactively, you locate the record you want to change in a form and type your changes into a control. The moment you type the first character, the edit pencil in the record selector indicates that you are entering the new values into the copy buffer. When you are finished making changes, you can save the changes in a variety of ways, such as clicking into another record, pressing Shift+Enter, or closing the form (effectively, the application calls the Update method for you).

If you decide not to save the changes to the record, use the CancelUpdate method to flush out the copy buffer.

Adding and Updating Records

As with record changes, new records are not added directly to the recordset; instead, the new record is added to the copy buffer in memory. Your VBA code uses the AddNew method to add the contents of the copy buffer to the recordset.

When you add the new record, the database engine creates a bookmark for it (if the recordset supports bookmarks) and the new record you created becomes the current record. Depending on what type of cursor recordset you created when you created the Recordset object, you may need to evoke the Recordset object's Requery method to access the new record.

The syntax for the AddNew method is as follows:

```
rst.AddNew FieldList, Values
```

where

- *rst* is a reference to an existing Recordset.
- *FieldList* is a name or an array of names of the fields for which you wish to enter values.
- *Values* is a single value or an array of values for the FieldList fields you declared. You must insert a value for each field you declared, or ADO generates an error.

You can use the Immediate window to add a new record to the rst Recordset object. Follow these steps:

1. To create a new record in the buffer using the AddNew method of the Recordset object, type **rst.AddNew** and press Enter.

2. To assign new values to fields in the buffer, type the following assignment statements in the Immediate window and press Enter after each:

> **rst.Fields("CustomerID") = "ROUND"**
>
> **rst.Fields("CompanyName") = "Round the Bend"**
>
> **rst.Fields("City") = "London"**

3. To add the contents to the recordset, type **rst.Update** and press Enter. The current record is now the record you just added.

4. To confirm, type **?rst!CompanyName** and press Enter.

If you decide not to add the new record, you can use the CancelUpdate method to flush out the buffer.

Deleting Records

When you delete a record, the record is placed in a location in memory, which we'll call the *delete buffer*, that ADO creates for deletions. Interestingly, the record continues to be the current record even though you can't edit or use it; referring to the deleted record produces a run-time error. Note that there is no CancelDelete method to undo the operation; effectively, the record is simply gone without warning.

TIP If you want to display a delete confirmation message, you can create a set of statements called a *transaction* to undo the deletion if the user decides not to delete the record. See Chapter 13, "Working with Groups of Records Using Access VBA," for information about creating transactions.

You can use the Immediate window to delete the record that you just added to the `rst` Recordset object. Follow these steps:

1. To place the record in the delete buffer using the `Delete` method, type **rst.Delete** and press Enter. Confirm by typing **?rst!CompanyName**. An error message indicates the record is unavailable.

2. Move to another record to make it the current record. Type **rst.MovePrevious** and press Enter. Confirm by typing **?rst!CompanyName** and pressing Enter.

3. Type **?rst.Close** and press Enter.

Cloning Recordsets

In later chapters, you learn that at times it is convenient to have more than one current record pointer for a Recordset object. You use the `Clone` method to create a new Recordset object that duplicates an existing Recordset object. The syntax is as follows:

```
Set rstclone = original.Clone LockType
```

where

- *rstclone* is the new object variable for the cloned Recordset object.

- *original* is the reference to the original Recordset object.

- *LockType* is an optional value to specify the lock type for the original Recordset object.

When you create a clone, the clone object and the original Recordset object each have their own current records, and you can navigate in the Recordset object independently. You can only create a clone of a recordset that supports use of bookmarks. An important feature of the `Clone` method is that the duplicate Recordset has the same bookmarks as the original Recordset object; thus, you can set a bookmark with the clone and retrieve the bookmark with the original and vice versa. The original and the clone are not exactly identical, however. For example, when you create a clone of an existing record, the clone's current record is the first one, regardless of which is the current record in the original recordset.

Because both the original and the clone recordsets refer to the same stored table or query, you can modify data, add new records, or delete records using either the original or the duplicate. You can use the `Close` method for either the original or the clone object without closing the other object. The original and the clone will stay in synch until you execute the `Requery` method on the original.

Chapter 5 introduced the RecordsetClone property of the Form object. When you open a bound form, the database engine creates a Recordset object based on the table, query, or SQL statement specified in the form's RecordSource property. When you use the form's Recordset-Clone property, you are creating a new current record pointer for the form's Recordset object but you are not creating a new Recordset object. The benefit of using the RecordsetClone property in your VBA code is that it is faster and more efficient than creating a new recordset. With the RecordsetClone property, you create a reference to a data access object without needing to instantiate a new recordset, establish a valid connection, or declare a source. Having created the RecordsetClone, you can use the methods of the Recordset object for the clone.

NOTE   Don't be confused by the similar terminology. The RecordsetClone property only creates an independent current record pointer for the form's recordset and does not create a separate Recordset object. In contrast, the `Clone` method creates a separate Recordset object that is the duplicate of the original Recordset object and has the same bookmarks as the original.

The ADO Object Model

The next portion of this chapter is a reference to the data access objects. For each object, a description of the important features is followed by tables of the object's documented properties, methods, and events. Before using a property, method, or event for the first time, refer to the complete description available in online help in Access.

The Connection Object

The Connection object represents the environment required for exchanging data between a data source and the Access application. A *transaction* is the series of data access operations that occur across a connection. Operations in a transaction are "all or nothing," which means that if any operation is unsuccessful, no changes to the data source are made. Thus, if you cancel a transaction at any point, it is as if none of the operations were performed. The transaction's operations are embodied in the Connection object's methods, which are listed in Table 6.3.

ADO can connect to and access data from any OLE DB provider. The Connection object is used to specify the OLE DB provider, as well as to specify any parameters necessary to connect to the provider, including the user ID and password.

The Connection object has several properties that define its functionality. Table 6.4 lists these properties. In addition to these built-in properties, you can specify additional, provider-specific properties. For example, earlier in the chapter in the section on opening two recordsets simultaneously, we supplied the `Jet OLEDB: Database Password` argument so that we could pass the database password to the provider.

TABLE 6.3: Methods of the Connection Object

Method	Description
BeginTrans	Begins a new transaction.
Cancel	Cancels the Execute method's call.
Close	Closes the connection to the data source.
CommitTrans	Saves changes and ends the current transaction. Can also start a new transaction.
Execute	Executes the specified query, SQL statement, stored procedure, or provider-specific text.
Open	Opens a connection to a data source.
OpenSchema	Obtains database schema information from the provider.
RollbackTrans	Cancels changes made during the current transaction; ends the transaction.

TABLE 6.4: Properties of the Connection Object

Property	Access	Data Type	Description
Attributes	Read/write	Long integer	A read/write value that specifies certain attributes of the transaction.
CommandTimeout	Read/write	Long integer	Indicates how long to attempt to carry out a command before timing out and generating an error.
ConnectionString	Read/write	String	Contains all the information needed to make the connection to the data source. This is the Connection object's default property.
ConnectionTimeout	Read/write	Long integer	Indicates how long to wait for the connection to the data source to be made before timing out and generating an error.
CursorLocation	Read/write	Enum constant	Indicates whether to use a client-side or server-side cursor.
DefaultDatabase	Read/write	String	Indicates the default database to be used when making a connection.
Errors	Read-only	Object	Returns the Connection object's Errors collection.
IsolationLevel	Read/write	Enum constant	Indicates the isolation level of the transaction.
Mode	Read/write	Enum constant	Indicates the permission level for modifying data.
Properties	Read-only	Object	Returns the Connection object's Properties collection.
Provider	Read/write	String	Indicates the OLE DB provider for the Connection object.
State	Read-only	Long integer	Can be used to determine whether the connection is open or closed.
Version	Read-only	String	Returns the version number of ADO.

Several events are associated with the Connection object. These events are programming opportunities, as you can write VBA modules that run when one of these events occurs. The events associated with the Connection object are listed in Table 6.5.

TABLE 6.5: Events of the Connection Object

Event	Description
BeginTransComplete	Occurs after the `BeginTrans` method has run.
CommitTransComplete	Occurs after the `CommitTrans` method has run.
ConnectComplete	Occurs after a connection has begun.
Disconnect	Occurs after a connection has ended.
ExecuteComplete	Occurs after a command has been executed.
InfoMessage	Occurs when a warning message is generated during a connection.
RollbackTransComplete	Occurs after the `RollbackTrans` method has run.
WillConnect	Occurs just before a connection begins.
WillExecute	Occurs just before a command is executed.

The Command Object

A Command object represents a command you wish to run on a data source. Most often, Command objects you will encounter will be in the form of SQL statements. You use Commands to retrieve, change, or delete data, or to make changes to the schema of a database.

The Command object has nine properties that define many of its characteristics. These are listed in Table 6.6.

The Command object also has three methods that it can perform on itself. Those are listed in Table 6.7. The Command object has no events.

The Parameter Object

A Parameter is a child of the Command object. It represents a parameter or argument of the parent Command for a parameterized query or stored procedure. The Parameter object has the properties listed in Table 6.8

A Parameter has a single method, AppendChunk, which can be used to manipulate large values in chunks rather than in their entirety. Parameters have no events.

TABLE 6.6: Properties of the Command Object

Property	Access	Data Type	Description
ActiveConnection	Read/write	Object	Represents the Command's parent Connection object.
CommandText	Read/write	String	Contains the executable part of the Command; for example, the SQL statement.
CommandTimeout	Read/write	Long integer	Indicates how long to attempt to carry out a command before timing out and generating an error.
CommandType	Read/write	Enum constant	Tells the provider which type of command the Command object represents.
Name	Read/write	String	Indicates the name of the Command.
Parameters	Read-only	Object	Returns the Command object's Parameters collection. This is the Command object's default property.
Prepared	Read/write	Boolean	Indicates whether to compile a command before executing it.
Properties	Read-only	Object	Returns the Command object's Properties collection.
State	Read-only	Long integer	Can be used to determine whether the command is open or closed.

TABLE 6.7: Methods of the Command Object

Method	Description
Cancel	Cancels execution of a Command object.
CreateParameter	Used to create a member of the Command's Parameters collection.
Execute	Runs the Command object.

The Recordset Object

The Recordset object represents the set of records in a table in the database or the set of records that result from running a query or SQL statement. In a Recordset object that has at least one record, you point to one record at a time as the current record. The Fields collection of the Recordset object contains Field objects that represent the fields in the current record; in particular, the Value property setting of each of the Field objects is the value of the data stored in the field in the table.

TABLE 6.8: Properties of the Parameter Object

Property	Access	Data Type	Description
Attributes	Read/write	Long integer	Indicates whether the Parameter is signed or accepts null or long values.
Direction	Read/write	Enum constant	Indicates whether the Parameter is input, output, input/output, or the return value from a stored procedure.
Name	Read/write	String	Indicates the name of the Parameter.
NumericScale	Read/write	Byte	Indicates the number of digits to the right of the decimal that will be resolved if the Parameter is a numeric value.
Precision	Read/write	Byte	Indicates the maximum number of digits used to represent the Parameter if it is a numeric value.
Properties	Read-only	Object	Returns the Parameter object's Properties collection.
Size	Read/write	Long integer	Indicates the maximum size, in bytes or characters, of the Parameter object if it is a numeric value.
Type	Read/write	Enum constant	Indicates what type of parameter is represented by the Parameter object, such as a Boolean or Currency type.
Value	Read/write	Variant	Indicates a Parameter's value. This is the Parameter object's default property.

Earlier sections of the chapter describe techniques for navigating through a recordset and for manipulating data and the types of Recordset objects: dynamic cursor, keyset cursor, static cursor, and forward-only cursor. Tables 6.9 and 6.10 list the properties and methods of the Recordset object.

TABLE 6.9: Properties of the Recordset Object

Property	Access	Data Type	Description
AbsolutePage	Read/write	Enum constant	Indicates which page the current record resides on.
AbsolutePosition	Read/write	Enum constant	Positions the current record pointer to a specific record based on its ordinal position; 1-based.
ActiveCommand	Read-only	Object	Refers to the Command object that created the Recordset.
ActiveConnection	Read/write	Variant	Refers to the Recordset's parent Connection object.
BOF, EOF	Read-only	Boolean	Determines whether a **Seek** or **Find** method was successful, or whether you have moved beyond the limits of the Recordset object.
Bookmark	Read/write	Variant	Saves your place in a Recordset object.
CacheSize	Read/write	Long integer	Specifies the number of records in Recordset object containing data that can be locally cached.

Continued on next page

TABLE 6.9 CONTINUED: Properties of the Recordset Object

Property	Access	Data Type	Description
CursorLocation	Read/write	Enum constant	Indicates whether the Recordset uses a server-side or client-side cursor.
CursorType	Read/write	Enum constant	Indicates whether the Recordset uses a dynamic, keyset, static, or forward-only cursor.
DataMember	Read/write	String	Not applicable to Access.
DataSource	Read/write	Unknown	Not applicable to Access.
EditMode	Read-only	Enum constant	Indicates whether changes are pending in the record buffer or whether a new record has been added.
Fields	Read-only	Object	Returns the Recordset object's Fields collection. This is the Recordset object's default property.
Filter	Read/write	Variant	Indicates whether a data filter has been set for the Recordset.
Index	Read/write	String	Determines or specifies the name of an existing Index object as the current index for the Recordset object.
LockType	Read/write	Enum constant	Determines the type of locking that is in effect during editing.
MarshalOptions	Read/write	Enum constant	Determines which records are to be marshaled back to the server if you are working with a client-side cursor.
MaxRecords	Read/write	Long integer	Sets a limit on the number of records to include in a recordset that is the result of a query.
PageCount	Read-only	Long integer	Indicates how many pages of data the recordset contains.
PageSize	Read/write	Long integer	Indicates how many records are on each page in the recordset.
Properties	Read-only	Object	Returns the Recordset object's Properties collection.
RecordCount	Read-only	Long integer	Indicates the total number of records in a recordset.
Sort	Read/write	String	Indicates the column(s) on which to sort the data, and whether to sort in ascending or descending order.
Source	Read/write	Variant	Specifies the data source for a recordset.
State	Read-only	Long integer	Can be used to determine whether the recordset is open or closed.
Status	Read-only	Long integer	Indicates the status of a batch update.
StayInSync	Read/write	Boolean	When used with hierarchical recordsets, determines whether the child recordset stays in sync with the parent recordset when changes are made to the parent.

TABLE 6.10: Methods of the Recordset Object

Method	Description
AddNew	Creates a new record in the copy buffer of the Recordset object. The new record becomes the current one.
Cancel	Cancels execution of an asynchronous method call.
CancelBatch	Cancels execution of a batch update.
CancelUpdate	Cancels any pending updates due to an **Update** or **AddNew** operation.
Clone	Creates a duplicate Recordset object that refers to the original. The clone's first record is the current one.
Close	Closes the open Recordset object (does not affect a clone).
CompareBookmarks	Compares two bookmarks and returns their relative association.
Delete	Removes the current record.
Find	Locates the next record in the recordset that satisfies the specified criteria and makes that record the current record.
GetRows	Copies one or more entire records from a recordset to a two-dimensional array and moves the current record pointer to the next unread row.
GetString	Returns the recordset as a string object.
Move	Moves a specified number of rows to another record and makes that record the current record.
MoveFirst, MoveLast, MoveNext, MovePrevious	Moves to the first, last, next, or previous record in a Recordset object and makes that record the current record. (In forward-only cursors, only **MoveNext** and **MoveFirst** are available.)
NextRecordset	Clears the current Recordset object and retrieves a new recordset.
Open	Opens a Recordset object.
Requery	Updates the data in a recordset by reexecuting the query on which the object is based. When you use this method, the first record becomes the current record.
Resync	Resynchronizes a Recordset with the underlying data source.
Save	Saves the recordset to a persistent file or Stream object.
Seek	Locates the record in an indexed Recordset object satisfying specified criteria for the current index; makes the found record the current record. The Index property must be set to an existing Index object before using this method.
Supports	Specifies whether the Recordset object supports a certain type of functionality.
Update	Saves the contents of the copy buffer to the recordset. Changes to a record are lost if you don't use the **Update** method, either explicitly or implicitly.
UpdateBatch	Makes pending updates to disk when working with a batch update mode recordset.

In addition to properties and methods, the Recordset object has several events for which you can write VBA procedures. These are listed in Table 6.11.

TABLE 6.11: Events of the Recordset Object

Event	Description
EndofRecordset	Occurs when you attempt to move past the end of a Recordset.
FetchComplete	Occurs after all the events in an asynchronous operation have completed and all records are returned to the Recordset object.
FetchProgress	Occurs periodically during a long asynchronous operation, and returns the number of rows that have been retrieved since the event last occurred.
FieldChangeComplete	Occurs just after the Value property of one of the Recordset object's Field objects has been changed.
MoveComplete	Occurs just after the current record pointer in a recordset has changed.
RecordChangeComplete	Occurs just after a record in the recordset has been changed.
RecordsetChangeComplete	Occurs just after the recordset has been changed.
WillChangeField	Occurs just before the Value property of one of the Recordset object's Field objects will be changed.
WillChangeRecord	Occurs just before a record in the recordset will be changed.
WillChangeRecordset	Occurs just before the recordset will be changed.
WillMove	Occurs just before the current record pointer in a recordset will change.

The Field Object

The Field object represents a column of data that has a common set of properties and a common data type. The Record and Recordset objects both have Fields collections containing Field objects. The Field object has a Value property that reflects the data stored in the Field. You can use the Immediate window to evaluate the Field properties:

1. Type the following to open a new recordset:

    ```
    Set cnn = New ADODB.Connection
    Set rst = New ADODB.Recordset
    Set cnn = CurrentProject.Connection
    rst.Open "Customers", cnn, adOpenStatic, adLockOptimistic
    ```

2. Type **?rst!CustomerID.DefinedSize** and press Enter to view the property setting.

3. Type **?rst!CustomerID.Value** and press Enter. Access displays the data contained in the CustomerID field of the current record.

You use the Field objects in a Recordset object to inspect or change the data in the current record. The Value property of a Field object returns the value of the data in a field in the current record.

Table 6.12 lists the properties of the Field object.

TABLE 6.12: Properties of the Field Object

Property	Access	Data Type	Description
ActualSize	Read-only	Long integer	Indicates the length of the data in a Field object.
Attributes	Read/write	Long integer	Specifies certain attributes about the Field object.
DataFormat	Read/write	Unknown	Represents the DataFormat object that controls formatting for a bound field.
DefinedSize	Read/write	Long integer	A field's maximum size in bytes.
Name	Read-only	String	Indicates the name of the Field.
NumericScale	Read/write	Byte	Indicates the number of digits to the right of the decimal that will be resolved if the field is a numeric value.
OriginalValue	Read-only	Variant	The value that existed in a field before it was changed.
Precision	Read/write	Byte	Indicates the maximum number of digits used to represent the field if it is a numeric value.
Properties	Read-only	Object	Returns the Field object's Properties collection.
Status	Read-only	Long integer	Indicates the status of a Field object. For the field of a Recordset object, always returns adFieldOK, which indicates that the field was successfully added or deleted.
Type	Read/write	Enum constant	Indicates what type of data is represented by the Field object, such as a Boolean or Currency.
UnderlyingValue	Read-only	Variant	Indicates the current value in a database for a Field object.
Value	Read/write	Variant	Indicates a field's value. This is the default property for the Field object.

Table 6.13 lists the methods of the Field object. The Field object has no events.

TABLE 6.13: Methods of the Field Object

Method	Description
AppendChunk	Appends data to a field in smaller portions rather than in its entirety.
GetChunk	Returns all or a portion of the contents of a Field object.

The Error Object

The Error object represents a single data access error involving the OLE DB provider, and the Errors collection contains all the Error objects that occur because of a single data access operation. Each time a new operation generates an error, the Errors collection is cleared and the new Error objects are placed in the collection. To see the details of a specific error, you access the error's properties. The Error object properties are listed in Table 6.14. The Error object has no methods or events.

TABLE 6.14: Properties of the Error Object

Property	Access	Data Type	Description
Description	Read-only	String	The Error object's default property. Describes an error. The string comes either from the OLE DB provider or from ADO.
HelpContext	Read-only	Long integer	If the HelpFile specifies a help topic, HelpContext automatically displays it.
HelpFile	Read-only	String	Indicates the appropriate help topic for the error.
NativeError	Read-only	Long integer	Returns the code given to an error by the OLE DB provider.
Number	Read-only	Long integer	Returns the number that uniquely identifies the error.
Source	Read-only	String	Returns the name of the object or application that generated the error.
SQLState	Read-only	String	Returns the five-character error code that the OLE DB provider returns when processing a SQL statement generates a code.

The Property Object

The Property object represents a dynamic property of a data access object. Every data access object has a Properties collection containing Property objects. Table 6.15 lists the properties of the Property object. The Property object has no methods or events.

TABLE 6.15: Properties of the Property Object

Property	Access	Data Type	Description
Attributes	Read/write	Long integer	Specifies certain attributes about the Property object.
Name	Read-only	String	Indicates the name of the Property.
Type	Read-only	Enum constant	Indicates what type of data is represented by the Property object, such as a Boolean or Currency.
Value	Read/write	Variant	Indicates a property's value. This is the default property for the Property object.

The Record Object

The Record object represents a row in a hierarchical recordset, or a file or directory in a file system. You will not use the Record object in your programming for Microsoft Access. It is included here for the sake of completeness.

The Stream Object

The Stream object represents a stream of binary data or text, or a persistently stored record-set. Use of the Stream object is beyond the scope of this book, so it is listed here only for the sake of completeness. For more information about the Record or Stream objects, see the *Access 2002 Developer's Handbook* by Paul Litwin, Ken Getz, and Mike Gunderloy (Sybex, 2001).

The ADOX Object Model

The last section of this chapter is a reference to the objects in the ADOX object model. For each object, a description of the important features is followed by tables of the object's documented properties and methods. ADOX objects have no events. Before using a property or method for the first time, refer to the complete description available in online help in Access.

The Catalog Object

The Catalog object represents the entire database—its schema (tables, queries, stored procedures, indexes, and keys) and its security settings (users and groups). The Catalog object's properties are listed in Table 6.16, and its methods are listed in Table 6.17. The Catalog object has no events.

TABLE 6.16: Properties of the Catalog Object

Property	Access	Data Type	Description
ActiveConnection	Read/write	Variant	Represents the Connection object that hooks the Catalog object to the data.
Groups	Read-only	Object	Returns the Catalog object's Groups collection.
Procedures	Read-only	Object	Returns the Catalog object's Procedures collection.
Tables	Read-only	Object	Returns the Catalog object's Tables collection. This is the default property for the Catalog object.
Users	Read-only	Object	Returns the Catalog object's Users collection.
Views	Read-only	Object	Returns the Catalog object's Views collection.

TABLE 6.17: Methods of the Catalog Object

Method	Description
Create	Creates a new catalog
GetObjectOwner	Returns the owner of a child object of the Catalog object
SetObjectOwner	Sets the owner of a child object of the Catalog object

The Table Object

A Table object represents a table in a database and includes the table's columns, indexes, and keys. If your database includes a query without parameters, it will be listed as a Table object. Table 6.18 lists the properties of the Table object. Tables have no methods.

TABLE 6.18: Properties of the Table Object

Property	Access	Data Type	Description
Columns	Read-only	Object	Returns the Table object's Columns collection. This is the default property for the Table object.
DateCreated	Read-only	Variant	Identifies the date the table was created.
DateModified	Read-only	Variant	Identifies the date the table was last modified.
Indexes	Read-only	Object	Returns the Table object's Indexes collection.
Keys	Read-only	Object	Returns the Table object's Keys collection.
Name	Read/write	String	Indicates the name of the table.
ParentCatalog	Read/write	Object	Specifies the Table object's parent Catalog object.
Properties	Read-only	Object	Returns the Table object's Properties collection.
Type	Read-only	String	Indicates what type of table the Table object is.

The Column Object

Tables are made up of columns and rows. A row in a table represents a record, and a column represents a field. These fields are Column objects in the ADOX model. Table 6.19 lists the properties of the Column object. Columns have no methods.

The Index Object

An index on a table is represented by an ADOX Index object. Table 6.20 lists its properties. Indexes have no methods.

TABLE 6.19: Properties of the Column Object

Property	Access	Data Type	Description
Attributes	Read/write	Enum constant	Describes certain characteristics of the Column object.
DefinedSize	Read/write	Long integer	Indicates the maximum number of characters long data in a column can be.
Name	Read/write	String	Indicates the name of the Column. This is the Column object's default property.
NumericScale	Read/write	Byte	Indicates the number of digits to the right of a decimal for a numeric value in the column.
ParentCatalog	Read/write	Object	Specifies the Column object's parent Catalog object.
Precision	Read/write	Long integer	Indicates the maximum number of digits used to represent numeric data.
Properties	Read-only	Object	Returns the Column object's Properties collection.
RelatedColumn	Read/write	String	Indicates the name of the related key column in a Table.
SortOrder	Read/write	Enum constant	For indexed columns, indicates whether to sort values in ascending (the default) or descending order.
Type	Read/write	Enum constant	Indicates what type of data is stored in the Column object, such as a Boolean or Currency.

TABLE 6.20: Properties of the Index Object

Property	Access	Data Type	Description
Clustered	Read/write	Boolean	Specifies whether the index is clustered.
Columns	Read-only	Object	Returns the Index object's Columns collection.
IndexNulls	Read/write	Enum constant	Indicates whether records can have a Null value for the Indexed field.
Name	Read/write	String	Indicates the name of the index. This is the Index object's default property.
PrimaryKey	Read/write	Boolean	Specifies whether the Index is a primary key.
Properties	Read-only	Object	Returns the Index object's Properties collection.
Unique	Read/write	Boolean	Specifies whether the index keys must be unique.

The Key Object

A Key object represents a primary, foreign, or unique key. Its properties (it has no methods) are listed in Table 6.21.

TABLE 6.21: Properties of the Key Object

Property	Access	Data Type	Description
Columns	Read-only	Object	Returns the Index object's Columns collection.
DeleteRule	Read/write	Enum constant	Indicates what happens when a primary key is deleted.
Name	Read/write	String	Indicates the name of the key. This is the Key object's default property.
RelatedTable	Read/write	String	Specifies the name of the related table.
Type	Read/write	Enum constant	Specifies the type of key (whether primary, foreign, or unique).
UpdateRule	Read/write	Enum constant	Indicates what happens when a primary key is updated.

The Group Object

A Group object represents a set of user accounts for which you have set common access permissions. Table 6.22 lists the properties of the Group object, and Table 6.23 lists its methods.

TABLE 6.22: Properties of the Group Object

Property	Access	Data Type	Description
Name	Read/write	String	Indicates the name of the Group. This is the Group object's default property.
ParentCatalog	Read/write	Object	Specifies the Group object's parent Catalog object.
Properties	Read-only	Object	Returns the Group object's Properties collection.
Users	Read-only	Object	Returns the Group object's Users collection.

TABLE 6.23: Methods of the Group Object

Method	Description
GetPermissions	Returns the permission settings for the Group object.
SetPermissions	Declares the permission settings for the Group object.

The User Object

A User object represents a specific user that has been given permission to use the objects in the database when security has been implemented for the workspace. You identify a *user account* with a username and a personal identifier. When security has been implemented, each user logs on using a username and password and has the access privileges that you have set up as permissions for specific users and groups. Table 6.24 lists the properties of the User object, and Table 6.25 lists its methods.

TABLE 6.24: Properties of the User Object

Property	Access	Data Type	Description
Groups	Read-only	Object	Returns the User object's Groups collection.
Name	Read/write	String	Indicates the name of the User. This is the User object's default property.
ParentCatalog	Read/write	Object	Specifies the User object's parent Catalog object.
Properties	Read-only	Object	Returns the User object's Properties collection.

TABLE 6.25: Methods of the Group Object

Method	Description
ChangePassword	Changes the user's password.
GetPermissions	Returns the permission settings for the user.
SetPermissions	Declares the permission settings for the user.

WARNING You must know the current password before you can change it. If you lose your password, you cannot open the database again unless a member of the Admins group changes your password for you.

The Procedure Object

A stored procedure is represented in ADOX as a Procedure object. The Jet database engine also considers a query with parameters to be a Procedure object. The Procedure object's properties are listed in Table 6.26. Procedures have no methods.

TABLE 6.26: Properties of the Procedure Object

Property	Access	Data Type	Description
Command	Read/write	Variant	Specifies an ADO command object that can be used to create or execute the procedure.
DateCreated	Read-only	Variant	Indicates the date the Procedure object was created.
DateModified	Read-only	Variant	Indicates the date the Procedure object was last modified.
Name	Read-only	String	Specifies the name of the Procedure object.

The Command Object

The Command object is not part of the ADOX model, but two of the ADOX objects use it—the Procedure object and the View object. For information about the Command object's methods and properties, see the section on the ADO hierarchy earlier in this chapter.

The View Object

The ADOX View object represents a view or a query without parameters. The View object's properties (it has no methods) are listed in Table 6.27.

TABLE 6.27: Properties of the Procedure Object

Property	Access	Data Type	Description
Command	Read/write	Variant	Specifies an ADO command object that can be used to create or execute the view.
DateCreated	Read-only	Variant	Indicates the date the View object was created.
DateModified	Read-only	Variant	Indicates the date the View object was last modified.
Name	Read-only	String	Specifies the name of the View object.

Summary

This chapter has introduced you to the ADO and ADOX data access objects that you can manipulate in VBA procedures. The important points are listed here:

- When you are referring to an ADO object in a VBA procedure, you first set a variable for the Recordset object, then name all other objects after that variable, with a bang (!) or dot (.) separator.

- A data object has both intrinsic (built-in) and dynamic (provider-supplied) properties. Each dynamic property is represented by a Property object contained in the object's Properties collection.

- You can create new data access objects. Each object has specific creation and destruction rules: some objects require that child objects be created before saving, some objects must be appended to their collection before saving, and some objects are created anew and destroyed automatically when the procedure ends or when the database closes.

- You use the Recordset object to work with the data in the database. There are four types of ADO Recordset objects: dynamic cursor, keyset cursor, static cursor, and forward-only cursor.

- When you create a new recordset, you can work with only one record (called the current record) at a time.

- You can navigate among the records of a recordset using the Move... methods. You can use the EOF and BOF properties to determine if you have moved beyond the limits of the recordset.

- You can locate a specific record satisfying search criteria using the Seek and Find methods. You can use the EOF property to determine if the search was successful.

- You can use the data access objects in VBA procedures to add new records, modify existing records, and delete records.

- You can use the Clone method to duplicate a Recordset object. The duplicate Recordset object has the same bookmarks as the original.

This chapter and Chapter 5 have provided you with tours of the object models that contain the objects you can manipulate in VBA programs. As you learn to write programs in the remainder of the book, you'll be returning to these chapters as a reference to determine whether an object has a property or method that your program needs. Before using a property or method for the first time, search the item in the Object Browser or online help to understand the item's capabilities and limitations.

CHAPTER 7

Writing Procedures

- Understanding the Access VBA data types

- Understanding procedures and modules

- The Access VBA programming environment

- Running function procedures

- Running sub procedures

This is the first of three chapters that describe all of the basic features of the VBA programming language as it is used in Access. In this chapter, you learn the basics of writing procedures. The chapter begins with a review of the statements you've learned so far, and continues with a discussion of the data types in Access VBA. Then it introduces the mechanics of writing procedures—the kinds of procedures you can write, where you store them in the database file, and how to run them. In Chapter 8, "Using Variables," you will learn about using variables and constants in procedures. In Chapter 9, "Controlling Execution," you will learn about controlling execution and about many of the useful statements and functions that are built into Access.

VBA Statements and Procedures

A *statement* is a combination of keywords, constants, variables, operator symbols, objects, properties, and methods that expresses a single definition, declaration, or operation. These elements must be combined correctly according to the syntax rules of the Access VBA interpreter before the statement can be executed. In the Immediate window, you use a single line for each statement. Here is an inventory of the statements you learned in Chapters 5, "VBA Programming Essentials," and 6, "Understanding the ADO Object Model":

Description	Syntax
Printing a value	`? value` or `Debug.Print value` or `Print value`
Assigning a value to a property	`object.property = value`
Assigning a property value to a variable	`Let var = object.property` or `var = object.property`
Assigning an object returned by a property to an object variable	`Set obj = object.property`
Calling a method with nothing returned	`object.method argumentlist`
Calling a method with a value returned	`Let var = object.method (argumentlist)` or `var = object.method (argumentlist)`
Calling a method with an object returned	`Set obj = object.method (argumentlist)`

The Immediate window is a terrific tool for running individual VBA statements. VBA programming involves packaging one or more statements together into a unit called a *procedure* and asking the computer to run the procedure.

Data Types

The types of values that variables can hold are referred to as *data types*. When you work interactively with Access, you specify data types when you create table fields, but otherwise you don't need to pay too much attention to them. In VBA programming, data type is an important concept. When you create a variable to hold a value or refer to an object, you can let VBA handle the data type for you. VBA has an all-purpose data type, called the *Variant* data type, that it uses unless you specify another one. The problems with this approach are that variables with the Variant data type take a lot of memory and VBA procedures that use them run slower. So, to create programs that use less memory and run as fast as possible, you'll need to learn something about data types.

NOTE   The topic of data types is complicated by the fact that you'll be dealing with four systems of data types: the field data types you specify when you create tables interactively, the VBA and ADO data types you'll learn about in this chapter, and the SQL data types.

Fundamental Data Types

You are already familiar with the field data types you assign to table fields when you create Access tables. Access VBA has its own set of VBA data types, most of which match the familiar field data types. Table 7.1 lists the VBA data types, the commonly used name tags, the compatible field data types, and a brief description of each data type. Two VBA data types have no counterpart in the field data types: Variant and Object. You'll learn about these data types in the next sections.

Literals

When you assign literal values to a variable with one of the fundamental data types, you must follow these rules:

String Enclose a literal string in double quotation marks; for example, strName = "Adam Gunderloy". If you want the string to appear with the quotation marks in the graphical interface, you can either enclose it in single quotes, as with '"Adam Gunderloy"', or in triple quotes, as with """Adam Gunderloy""".

Date Enclose a literal date in number signs or single quotes; for example, dtmOrderDate = #5/10/2001# or '5/10/2001'.

Currency Omit the dollar sign and commas; for example, curAmount = 3200.

TABLE 7.1: The Fundamental Data Types in VBA

VBA Data Type	Name Tag	Corresponding Field Data Type	Storage Size	Description
Boolean	bln	Yes/No	2 bytes	Stored as 2 byte numbers but have the values True or False. The default value is False. When converted to other data types, False becomes 0 and True becomes −1.
Byte	byt	Number (Byte)	1 byte	Binary, 0 to 255 (no fractions).
Currency	cur	Currency	8 bytes	Scaled integer, fixed-point. Uses up to 4 digits to the right of the decimal and 15 to the left; accurate fixed-point data type.
Date	dtm	Date	8 bytes	Date/time, Jan. 1, 100, to Dec. 31, 9999.
Decimal		Number (Double)	12 bytes	Unsigned integer scaled by a power of 10 indicating the number of digits to the right of the decimal point. Decimal precision up to 28.
Double	dbl	Number (Double)	8 bytes	Double-precision, floating-point. Subject to small rounding errors.
Integer	int	Number (Integer)	2 bytes	Integer, −32,768 to 32,767 (no fractions). Arithmetic operations are faster with integers.
Long	lng	Number (Long Integer) and AutoNumber	4 bytes	Integer, −2,147,483,648 to 2,147,483,647 (no fractions).
N/A		Lookup Wizard	Same size as the primary key field	Holds the values used to look up values in another table or list.
Object	obj		4 bytes	Holds the address for any type of object.

Continued on next page

TABLE 7.1 CONTINUED: The Fundamental Data Types in VBA

VBA Data Type	Name Tag	Corresponding	Storage Field Data Type	Description Size
Single	sng	Number (Single)	4 bytes	Single-precision, floating-point. Subject to small rounding errors.
String		OLE Object	Up to 1 gigabyte	An object such as a Word document, image, or sound file embedded or linked in a table.
String		Hyperlink	Up to 2048 characters for each of the three address parts	Text, or a combination of text and numbers stored as text, used as a hyperlink address.
String (fixed length)	str		String length	1 to approximately 65,400 characters. In form or report modules, fixed-length strings must be declared as Private.
String (variable length)	str	Text and Memo	10 bytes + string length	String, 0 to 2 billion characters. By default, a string variable is a variable-length string.
Variant (with characters)	var		22 bytes + string length	String, 0 to 2 billion characters.
Variant (with numbers)	var		16 bytes	Holds different types of data. Any numeric value up to the range of Double.

TIP   You don't need to use number signs or single quotes around a literal date if the field's data type is set to Date/Time.

The Variant Data Type

The Variant data type is a chameleon data type: it can store any other fundamental data type except the fixed-length String data type. The purpose of the Variant data type is to let you manipulate values with different data types without needing to convert their data types yourself. The Variant data type is the default data type in Access VBA, so if you don't explicitly specify the data type for a variable, VBA assigns the Variant data type. When you work in the

Immediate window, you can't explicitly specify a data type using the data-type-declaration statements that you'll learn about in the next chapter. You can specify a variable's data type in the Immediate window using the type-declaration characters for those data types that have them (as listed in the previous section). If you don't use type-declaration characters, the variables that you create in the Immediate window have the Variant data type.

• The main advantage of using Variant variables is that it is easier to create code because you don't need to know about data types and you don't need to worry about whether the data types of your variables are compatible.

The main disadvantages of using the Variant variables include the following:

• They take the most memory—the more memory tied up in storing variables, the less is available to run your application.

• Procedures that use Variant variables are slower. Each time code refers to a Variant variable, VBA must take the time to convert the data type and, for an object variable, to determine if the properties and methods referred to in your code are appropriate to the object.

Data-Type Conversion

VBA automatically attempts to convert between data types when necessary for a calculation. Of course, the conversion isn't always possible and there are restrictions on the operations that you can perform with Variant data types. For example, to perform arithmetic calculations on Variant variables, the variables must contain valid numbers; otherwise, a run-time error is generated. You can use the built-in `IsNumeric` function to determine if the value of a Variant variable is a valid number before doing the arithmetic calculation. Similarly, performing date arithmetic on Variant variables requires that the variables contain valid date/time values. You can use the built-in `IsDate` function to determine if a Variant variable contains a value that can be converted to a date before doing date arithmetic.

The result of using the + operator with two Variant variables depends on the values of the Variant variables. If both Variant variables contain strings, the + operator concatenates the strings. If both Variant variables contain numbers, the + operator adds the numbers. If one of the values is a number and the other is a string, VBA attempts to convert the string to a number; if the conversion is successful, VBA adds the two numbers; otherwise, VBA generates an error. You can avoid ambiguity by using the ampersand operator (&) when you want to concatenate two strings; leave a space between the variable names and the & operator.

To explore these concepts, open the Immediate window and enter each of the following expressions:

1. Type **varone = 4** and press Enter. The Variant variable named varone is created and holds the integer 4.

2. Type **? IsNumeric(varone)** and press Enter. The value True is displayed.

3. Type **vartwo = "3"** and press Enter. The Variant variable named vartwo is created and holds the string `"3"`.

4. Type **? IsNumeric(vartwo)** and press Enter. The value True is displayed.

5. Type **?varone+vartwo** and press Enter. The value 7 is displayed.

6. Type **?varone & vartwo** and press Enter. The value 43 is displayed as the result because VBA converts varone to a string and concatenates the two results.

Access provides a set of data-type-conversion functions that you can use to force, or coerce, a string or numeric expression to a specific data type. Some of these functions are listed in Table 7.2.

TABLE 7.2: Selected Data-Type-Conversion Functions

Function	Description
Abs(*number*)	Converts a numeric expression to the absolute value of the number. Abs(-4) and Abs(4) both return 4.
Asc(*string*)	Returns the ANSI character code (Integer) for the first letter in a string.
AscB(*string*)	Returns the first byte corresponding to the first character in a string.
AscW(*string*)	Returns the Unicode character corresponding to the first character in a string.
CBool(*expression*)	Returns False if the expression is zero, or if the expression is an evaluative expression that is incorrect, and True otherwise. CBool(3<5) returns True, CBool(5<3) returns False.
CByte(*expression*)	Converts an expression to a Byte. CByte(12.345) returns 12.
CCur(*expression*)	Converts an expression to Currency. CCur(12.345678) returns 12.3457.
CDate(*expression*)	Converts date and time literals and some numbers to a Date. CDate(#8/14/2000#) returns 8/14/2000.
CDbl(*expression*)	Converts an expression to a Double. Use to require double-precision arithmetic.
CDec(*expression*)	Converts an expression to a Decimal. CDec(3/4) returns 0.75.
CInt(*expression*)	Converts an expression to an Integer. Use to force integer arithmetic. CInt(12.2345) returns 12.
CLng(*expression*)	Converts an expression to a Long. Use to force integer arithmetic. CLng(31234.65) returns 31235.

Continued on next page

TABLE 7.2 CONTINUED: Selected Data-Type-Conversion Functions

Function	Description
CSng(*expression*)	Converts an expression to a Single. Use to force single-precision arithmetic. CSng(12.3422356) returns 12.34224.
CStr(*expression*)	Converts an expression to a String. The data in the expression determines what is returned. CStr(12.3422) returns "12.3422".
CVar(*expression*)	Converts an expression to a Variant. CVar(1234 & "5678") returns the string 12345678.
CVDate(*expression*)	Converts date and time literals to a Variant with a Date subtype.
CVErr(*expression*)	Converts an error number to a Variant.
Fix(*number*)	Removes the fractional part of a number and returns the integer portion. If the number is negative, returns the first integer larger than the number.
Int(*number*)	Removes the fractional part of a number and returns the integer portion. If the number is negative, returns the first integer less than the number.

The Null Value

The Variant data type has two special values: Null and Empty. The purpose of the Null value is to indicate missing, unknown, or inapplicable data. The special Null value is not a real value like "Peacock" or $12.45 but is an indicator that data is missing, unknown, or doesn't apply. The data in a table or query field or in a form or report control has the Variant data type by default. When you leave a field or control blank, Null is stored automatically. You are familiar with ways to determine if a field or control contains a Null value. As examples, you can use a query to search for records with a Null value in a field by setting the criteria cell for the field to Is Null, and you can determine if a control contains a Null value using the IsNull function.

The Null value requires special handling for the following reasons:

- If any part of an expression evaluates to the Null value, the entire expression also has the Null value. This is called *propagation of Null values*. In addition, if an argument of a built-in or custom function evaluates to Null, the function usually returns a Null value. For example, if you use a SQL or domain aggregate function to calculate a summary value of a field for a group of records, records with Null values in the field won't be included.

- When you join tables in a query, records with Null values in the join field are not included in the query result. For example, if you create a query based on the Orders and Employees tables in Northwind, only records for employees who handled orders and records for orders handled by specific employees are included; the query result does not contain records for employees who didn't handle orders or for orders not assigned to an employee.

- When you create a relationship and enforce referential integrity, you can still create orphan records in the child table by leaving the join field blank in the child table. In the Northwind database, you can add new orphan orders just by leaving the EmployeeID or the CustomerID fields blank.

You can determine if a variable contains the Null value using the `IsNull` function. You can set a variable to the Null value using an assignment statement as follows:

```
variable = Null
```

To explore Null values, open the Northwind database and enter each of the following expressions in the Immediate window:

1. Type **varone = 4** and press Enter. The Variant variable holds the integer 4.

2. Type **vartwo = null** and press Enter. The Variant variable holds the Null value.

3. Type **?varone + vartwo** and press Enter. Null is displayed as the result because the Null value in vartwo has been propagated to the sum.

4. Type **?DCount("Fax", "Suppliers")** and press Enter. The value 13 is displayed as the number of suppliers with a value entered as a fax number.

The Empty Value

The purpose of the Empty value is to be a placeholder when you have not assigned a value to a variable. When you first create a variable, it has the Empty value until it is assigned a value. You can use the `IsEmpty` function to determine if a variable has the Empty value. After assigning a value to a variable, you can set the variable back to the Empty value using the following assignment statement:

```
variable = Empty
```

The Empty value is not the same as zero, the zero-length string (" "), or the Null value. However, because VBA automatically converts Variant variables to the data type needed in a manipulation, when you use a Variant variable with the Empty value in expressions, VBA automatically converts the value to a zero if the expression requires a numeric value or to the zero-length string (" ") if the expression requires a string value.

To get hands-on experience with these concepts, enter the following in the Immediate window:

1. Type **varthree = "test"** and press Enter. The Variant variable varthree is created and assigned the string value test.

2. Type **?IsEmpty(varthree)** and press Enter. The value False is displayed because the variable holds a value.

3. Type **varthree = Empty** and press Enter. The variable now holds the Empty value.

4. Type **?IsEmpty(varthree)** and press Enter. The value True is displayed because the variable holds the Empty value.

5. Type **varthree = Null** and press Enter. The variable now holds the Null value.

6. Type **?IsNull(varthree)** and press Enter. The value True is displayed because the variable holds the Null value.

7. Type **?IsEmpty(varthree)** and press Enter. The value False is displayed because the variable holds the Null (not Empty) value.

Using the *VarType* Function

Since a Variant variable can hold different data types and the data type can change each time you assign a value to the variable, you need a way to determine what type of data the variable is currently holding. You can use the VarType function for this purpose. The VarType function returns an integer value corresponding to the current data type of the variable. Table 7.3 shows some of the integer values and corresponding intrinsic constants that the VarType function returns.

TABLE 7.3: Values Returned by the VarType Function

Variant Variable Contents	Return Value	Constant
Empty	0	vbEmpty
Null	1	vbNull
Integer	2	vbInteger
Long integer	3	vbLong
Single-precision, floating-point number	4	vbSingle
Double-precision, floating-point number	5	vbDouble
Currency	6	vbCurrency
Date	7	vbDate
String	8	vbString
Object	9	vbObject
Boolean	11	vbBoolean
Byte	17	vbByte

You can test the VarType function in the Immediate window by entering the following expressions:

1. Type **varone = Empty** and press Enter. The Variant variable now holds the Empty value.

2. Type **?VarType(varone)** and press Enter. The result is 0.

3. Type **varone = "test"** and press Enter. The Variant variable now holds a string value.

4. Type **?VarType(varone)** and press Enter. The result is 8.

5. Type **varone = #5/9/2001#** and press Enter. The Variant variable now holds a date value.

6. Type **?VarType(varone)** and press Enter. The result is 7.

7. Type **varone = False** and press Enter. The Variant variable now holds a Boolean value.

8. Type **?VarType(varone)** and press Enter. The result is 11.

The Object Data Type

You use an object variable to refer, or point, to an object. You can use the Object data type as the data type for the pointer to an object. (The pointer, or reference, is the 4-byte memory address of the object.) The Object data type listed in Table 7.1 is generic and can be used for any object; however, you can use specific *object data types* instead. Table 7.4 lists examples of object data types, name tags commonly used in VBA code, and corresponding database objects. Using specific object data types results in faster execution because VBA knows which properties and methods are appropriate to an object with a specified object data type and doesn't have to take time during execution to determine whether a property or method used in your code is appropriate.

You can use the IsObject function to determine whether a variable refers to an object. The IsObject function returns True if the variable refers to an object and False otherwise.

The Nothing Value

The Object data type has a special value called the Nothing value. The purpose of the Nothing value is to act as a placeholder when you have not assigned an object to a variable with the Object data type. The Nothing value is analogous to the Empty value for the Variant data type. When you first create an object variable, it has the Nothing value until you assign an object to it. After assigning an object to an Object variable, you can set the variable back to Nothing so that it no longer refers to the object using an assignment statement:

```
Set object = Nothing
```

You can explore these concepts in the Immediate window. When you work with objects in the Immediate window, a variable you create to refer to an object has the Variant data type

TABLE 7.4: Examples of Object Data Types

Object Data Type	Name Tag	Corresponding Database Object
Catalog	cat	An open database
Table	tbl	A table in a database
Procedure	sp	A stored procedure in a database
Connection	con	An ADO connection object
Command	cmd	An ADO command object
Parameter	par	A parameter of a command
Recordset	rst	The representation in memory of a set of records in a table or records that result from running a query or a SQL statement
Field	fld	A field in a table, query, recordset, index, or key
Index	idx	An index for a table
Form	frm	A form or subform
Report	rpt	A report or subreport
Control	ctl	A generic control on a form or report
TextBox	txt	A text box control
ComboBox	cbo	A combo box control
CommandButton	cmd	A command button control

with the object subtype. Open the Employees form in Form view and type the following in the Immediate window:

1. Type **Set frm = Forms!Employees** and press Enter. The Variant variable named frm is created and points to the Employees form.

2. Type **?VarType(frm)** and press Enter. The value 9 is displayed because the variable points to an object.

3. Type **?IsObject(frm)** and press Enter. The value True is displayed because the variable points to an object.

4. Type **Set frm = Nothing** and press Enter. The variable no longer points to any object.

5. Type **?IsObject(frm)** and press Enter. The value True is displayed because the variable once referred to an object.

6. Type **Set frm = Empty** and press Enter. A type mismatch error is generated because you can't set an object variable to Empty.

7. Type **Set frm = Null** and press Enter. A type mismatch error is generated because you can't set an object variable to Null.

Procedures and Modules

A procedure is a sequence of statements that is executed as a unit. Procedures are the basic building blocks of VBA. A procedure performs a specific task; the task may be a single operation such as opening a form or running a query to select and display a group of records, or a complex set of multiple operations such as importing and manipulating data. A procedure can accept additional information as *arguments* that determine how the procedure operates.

Types of Procedures

There are three kinds of procedures in VBA: *function*, *sub*, and *property* procedures. Each has a different purpose and its own pair of special statements to indicate its beginning and end.

Function Procedures

A function procedure performs a task and may return a single value. The returned value is computed in the procedure and assigned to the function name as one of the procedure's statements. You use function procedures to create your own custom functions and use them in expressions in the same way you use the built-in functions. You begin a function procedure with a Function statement and end it with an End Function statement. The basic syntax for a function procedure is as follows:

```
Function functionname [(argumentlist)]
    [statements]
    [functionname = expression]
End Function
```

Figure 7.1 shows the IsLoaded function procedure in Northwind. The IsLoaded function takes the name of a form as an argument, determines if the form is open, and sets the function name to True if the form is open.

FIGURE 7.1:

The IsLoaded function determines whether a form is open in Form or Datasheet view.

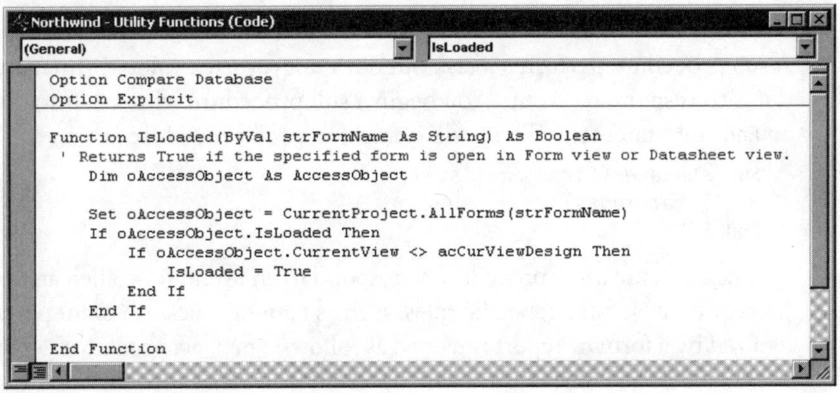

```
Northwind - Utility Functions (Code)

(General)                                          IsLoaded

Option Compare Database
Option Explicit

Function IsLoaded(ByVal strFormName As String) As Boolean
    ' Returns True if the specified form is open in Form view or Datasheet view.
    Dim oAccessObject As AccessObject

    Set oAccessObject = CurrentProject.AllForms(strFormName)
    If oAccessObject.IsLoaded Then
        If oAccessObject.CurrentView <> acCurViewDesign Then
            IsLoaded = True
        End If
    End If

End Function
```

You can also use a function procedure to respond to an event. Access runs the procedure automatically when the event occurs and discards the function's returned value if there is one. Figure 7.2 shows the OpenForms function used to open a specified form by clicking a command button on the Main Switchboard form in Northwind. The OpenForms function takes the name of a form as an argument, opens the form, and ends without returning a value.

FIGURE 7.2:

The OpenForms function procedure is assigned to the Click event of the Categories command button on the Main Switchboard.

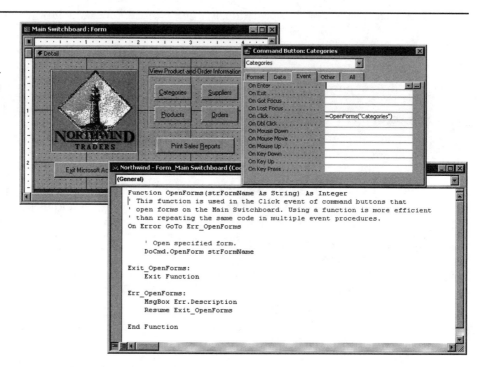

```
Function OpenForms(strFormName As String) As Integer
' This function is used in the Click event of command buttons that
' open forms on the Main Switchboard. Using a function is more efficient
' than repeating the same code in multiple event procedures.
On Error GoTo Err_OpenForms

    ' Open specified form.
    DoCmd.OpenForm strFormName

Exit_OpenForms:
    Exit Function

Err_OpenForms:
    MsgBox Err.Description
    Resume Exit_OpenForms

End Function
```

Sub Procedures

A sub procedure performs a task but does not return a value. Primarily, you use sub procedures to respond to events. You begin a sub procedure with a Sub statement and end it with an End Sub statement. The basic syntax for a sub procedure is

```
Sub subname [(argumentlist)]
    [statements]
End Sub
```

When you use a sub procedure to respond to an event, it is called an *event procedure*. An event procedure must follow specific rules, such as naming rules. An event procedure for an event recognized by a form or report is named as follows: Form_*eventname* or Report_*eventname*, where eventname is the name of the event. An event procedure recognized by a section or a control on a form or report is named as follows: *sectionname_eventname* or *controlname_eventname*. In addition, for each event, the argument list for an event procedure is predefined; for example, an event procedure for the Click event has no arguments. Figure 7.3 shows the DisplayDatabaseWindow_Click event procedure. This event procedure closes the Main Switchboard form, displays the Database window, and ends.

FIGURE 7.3:

The DisplayDatabase-Window_Click sub procedure (a) is assigned to the Click event of the DisplayDatabaseWindow command button (b) in the Main Switchboard form (c).

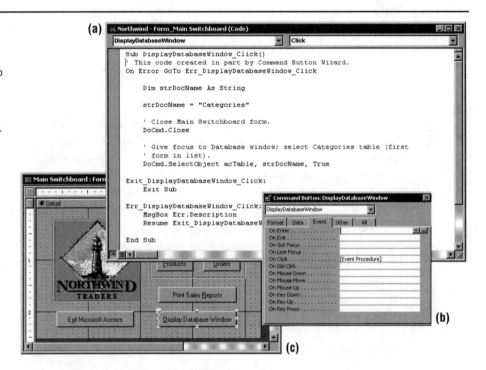

Property Procedures

A property procedure performs the task of creating a custom property for an object. Normally, you create a custom property with a pair of property procedures using one kind to set the property and another to return the setting. You begin a property procedure to set the property with either a Property Let statement when you are assigning a value or a Property Set statement when you are assigning a reference to an object. Property Let and Set procedures do not return values. You begin a property procedure to return the setting with a Property Get statement. You end a property procedure with an End Property statement. We'll discuss property procedures in Chapter 14, "Creating and Modifying Database Objects Using Access VBA."

Procedure Calls

When you request that Access execute a procedure, you are *calling* the procedure. You can classify procedures according to how you call them as follows:

In expressions and as property settings Because function procedures return values, you can call them directly in expressions and property settings in the same way you call the built-in functions. You can use function procedures as settings in the property sheets of tables, queries, forms, and reports; in the condition cells and argument settings in macros; and in the field and criteria cells in queries.

As event-handling procedures You can use both sub and function procedures to respond to events. A procedure that you assign to an event is called an *event-handling procedure*. Microsoft reserves the term *event procedure* for a sub procedure that is assigned to an event.

As support or general procedures You call a procedure indirectly when you include it in a statement of another procedure. A procedure that you call from another procedure is referred to as a *support procedure* or *general procedure*. You use support procedures to divide a complicated task with several operations into a set of simpler procedures and to create general-purpose procedures that can be called from several other procedures. You can use both function and sub procedures as support procedures; use a function procedure when you need to pass a value from one procedure to another and a sub procedure otherwise. For example, the event procedures for the Print Preview and Print buttons on the Sales Reports Dialog form in Northwind call the PrintReports sub procedure (see Figure 7.4). When a procedure calls a support procedure, Access interrupts execution of the calling procedure, executes the support procedure, and then returns to continue executing the calling procedure.

Modules

A *module* is the object you use to create and store procedures. A module is a code listing of one or more procedures, declarations, and statements that you store together as a unit. There are two kinds of modules that you use to organize your procedures: *class modules* and *standard modules*.

Class Modules

A class module contains the procedures that you can use to create the definition for a new object. The procedures in the module include the properties and methods for the new object. There are two kinds of class modules: those associated with forms and reports, and those that exist independently of forms and reports. (Independent class modules are an advanced topic not covered in depth in this book.)

FIGURE 7.4:

The Preview_Click and Print_Click event procedures call the PrintReports sub procedure.

You create a form or report module by opening the form or report in Design view and choosing View ➢ Code or clicking the Code button in the toolbar. The Module window opens and displays a module that will be stored as part of the form or report when you save the form or report. Access automatically sets the form's or report's HasModule property to Yes and names the built-in form or report module using the form's or report's name as follows: Form_*formname* or Report_*reportname*. These built-in modules are stored with the form or report and are not listed separately in the Database window.

The primary purpose of a form or report module is to store all of the event procedures for the events recognized by the form or report and its controls and sections; however, the form or report module can also store general function and sub procedures. Form and report modules are convenient ways to store the procedures associated with a form or report; if you copy the form or report, you also copy the form or report module. When you delete a form or report, you delete the form or report module also. You can delete the form or report module without deleting the form or report by setting the form's or report's HasModule property to No.

Standard Modules

Each standard module is listed as a separate object in the Modules pane of the Database window. Naming rules for a standard module are the same as the rules for any Database window object. Usually, you use standard modules to hold the custom functions and support procedures that you want to call from anywhere in the application.

The Layout of a Module

All modules have the same layout. A module begins with a Declarations section that contains option settings and declarations that apply to every procedure in the module. You use the Declarations section to define custom data types and to declare those constants and variables that you want to share among the procedures in the module and among procedures in other modules and even in other databases. In addition, if you are using procedures that are stored externally in a separate file called a dynamic link library (DLL), you provide information about the name of the procedure and the library in the Declarations section. Code that you enter in the Declarations section is called *module-level code*.

Following the Declarations section is the Procedures section, where you store the module's procedures. Procedures in a module must have unique names; however, procedures in different modules can have the same name.

Procedure References

The syntax for referring to a procedure in a module is as follows:

```
modulename.procedurename
```

This syntax is the *fully qualified reference* for the procedure. For example, the following refer to procedures in Northwind:

```
[Utility Function].IsLoaded
[Form_Main Switchboard].OpenForms
```

In both examples, the module names must be enclosed in square brackets because the module names contain spaces. Often, you can omit the module name and just refer to a procedure by its name. The basic rules are as follows:

- When you are referring to a procedure from within the same module, you can usually omit the reference to the module name because VBA assumes you are referring to the same module when you omit the module name. As an exception, if the procedure has the same name as the module, you must include the module name.

- When you are on a form or report, you can usually refer to a procedure in the form's or report's module just by its name because VBA assumes you are referring to the form's module when you omit the module name. As an exception, if the form or report has a control with the same name as the procedure, you must include the module name.

- When you are referring to a procedure in a form or report module from outside the module, you must include the module name.

- When you are referring to a procedure that has the same name in two or more other modules, you must include the module name in the reference so that VBA knows which procedure you are referring to.

Names in Visual Basic

The names of modules, procedures, variables, and constants must begin with a letter, cannot contain embedded periods or type-declaration characters, and cannot be restricted keywords that VBA uses as part of its language. Examples of restricted keywords are `If`, `Then`, `End`, `While`, `Loop`, and `Sub`.

The name of a module must not conflict with the naming convention that Access uses for form and report modules; don't preface a module name with `Form_` or `Report_`.

A procedure can have the same name as a module. In this case, you must use the fully qualified reference to the procedure.

Public versus Private Procedures

When you create a procedure, you can specify whether the procedure is *public* or *private*. A public procedure can be run by procedures in other modules; a private procedure can be run only by procedures in the same module.

You can use the `Public` and `Private` keywords to specify the procedure's availability to other procedures, called its *visibility* or *scope*. By default, procedures with neither keyword in their declaration statements are public and can be called by any procedure in the application. You don't need to use the `Public` keyword, but your code is easier to understand if you use the `Public` keyword in a public procedure's declaration statement. For example, `Public Function FirstFunction` explicitly specifies the `FirstFunction` procedure as public.

When you use the built-in code-building tools for an event procedure, Access includes the `Private` keyword in the code template by default because, normally, event procedures are used only in the form or report in which they are stored. However, you can delete the `Private` keyword to make an event procedure public.

TIP   Make it a rule to use either the `Public` or `Private` keyword when creating procedures. You'll learn more quickly about scope, which is one of the subtler and more difficult VBA programming concepts.

The public procedures stored in standard modules are also available to other databases by default. You can restrict the public procedures in a standard module for use in the current database only by including `Option Private` with the other option settings in the module's Declarations section. By contrast, the public procedures stored in form and report modules are available only to the current database.

You can refer to a public procedure in a form module of a subform when the form is open in Form view as a method of the form displayed in the subform control. Use the reference `Forms!formname!subformcontrolname.Form.procedurename`. To use the public procedures in a standard module that is stored in another database, you must first add a reference to the other database. See Chapter 15, "Expanding Access," for information about adding a reference.

Simple Examples of Procedures

Let's begin our exploration of procedures by creating and calling a few simple sub and function procedures. The procedures that we create now do little more than display custom messages using the `MsgBox` function to indicate that they are being executed. After we introduce the mechanics (in this chapter and the next two chapters), we'll talk about the more complicated procedures necessary to automate a database. Also, in the next section of this chapter, we'll do a thorough study of the module Design window, so don't worry about the details for now.

Creating an Event Procedure

Because event procedures are so common in an Access application, Access provides special event procedure code-building tools. To create an event procedure using the built-in tools, in Design view, select the object that recognizes the event and click in the event property in the property sheet. Then click the Build button at the right of the property box, select Code Builder, and click OK.

The Module window for the built-in form or report module is displayed. VBA automatically displays two lines of code, called a *code template* (or *stub*), and places the insertion point between them ready for you to enter the code for the procedure. The first line of the code template signals the beginning of the event procedure and depends on the event you selected. Access automatically names event procedures and specifies the arguments. If you selected an event recognized by the form or report, the first line is one of the following:

```
Private Sub Form_eventname(eventargumentlist)
Private Sub Report_eventname(eventargumentlist)
```

If you selected an event recognized by a control or section, the first line is as follows:

```
Private Sub objectname_eventname(eventargumentlist)
```

The second line, `End Sub`, signals the end of the procedure and is the same for all sub procedures.

We'll create the first procedure as an event procedure that runs when a command button is clicked:

1. Create a new database and name it Ch7_Examples.mdb.

2. Create a new form named frm1. Place a command button on the form and set the Name property to cmdButton1 and the Caption property to Call an Event Procedure.

3. Click in the button's OnClick event property, click the Build button at the right of the property box, select Code Builder in the Choose Builder dialog (see Figure 7.5a), and click OK. The Module window for the built-in form module opens (see Figure 7.5b).

FIGURE 7.5:

Clicking the Build button for an event property displays the Choose Builder dialog (a). Choosing the Code Builder displays the form's module with the event procedure for the event (b).

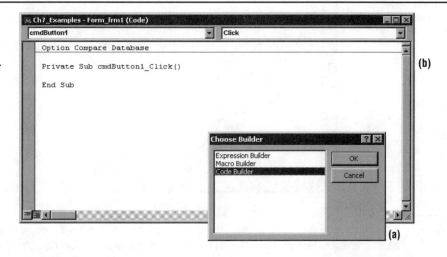

The module begins with the Declarations section. The Declarations section displays the option statement that VBA includes by default: `Option Compare Database`. You use the `Option Compare Database` statement to specify that you want Access to compare string expressions according to the database sort order that has been set for the database. The line below the `Option` statement, called a procedure separator, separates the Declarations section from the first procedure. Following the Declarations section are the two lines of the code template, with the insertion point between them.

4. Create the event procedure by typing the two lines of code between the code template lines as shown below. The first line uses an assignment statement to set the form's Caption property to the current date using the built-in Date function. The second line uses the built-in MsgBox function to display a custom message box. As you type, VBA checks your entries and makes suggestions and corrections. For example, after you type MsgBox, VBA displays a box with the syntax for the function as a guide to its required and optional arguments and returned value (see Figure 7.6).

```
Private Sub cmdButton1_Click()
    Forms!frm1.Caption = "Today is " & Date
    MsgBox "This is cmdButton1_Click in module Form_frm1"
End Sub
```

FIGURE 7.6:

When you type a built-in function, VBA displays a syntax box as a guide to the function's arguments and returned value.

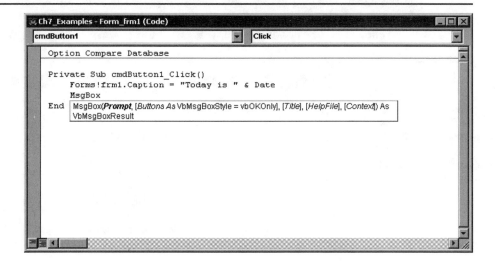

NOTE If you enter the parentheses after the Date function, Date(), VBA automatically removes the parentheses. When you use the Date function in a property setting, query expression, or macro, you must include parentheses after the function; however, the parentheses are not used in VBA programming, and VBA removes them.

5. Click in the form. The OnClick property for the command button displays the setting [Event Procedure] to indicate that an event procedure has been assigned automatically to the button's Click event.

6. Switch to Form view and click the command button. The procedure sets the form's caption to the current date and displays the message box (see Figure 7.7). Click OK to close the message box. Save the form.

The event procedure changes the form's caption and displays a message box.

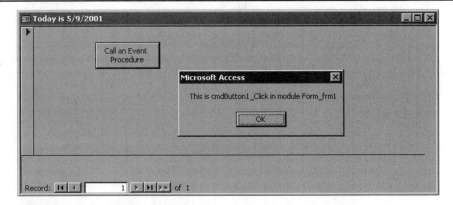

Creating a Function Procedure

Next, we'll create a function procedure and call the function in an expression for the Control-Source property of a calculated control. We'll display the value returned by the function in a text box on the form.

1. Switch to Design view and click the Code button or choose View ➤ Code. Choose Insert ➤ Procedure, enter **Function1** in the Name text box of the Add Procedure dialog, select Function in the Type option group, click Private in the Scope option group (see Figure 7.8), and click OK. VBA inserts a procedure separator line below the previous procedure and displays the code template for the function.

You use the Add Procedure dialog to name the new procedure and to specify its type and scope.

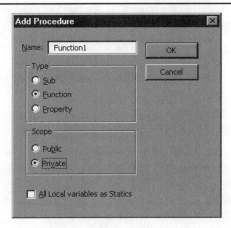

String Comparisons

By default, the first statement in the Declarations section of a module is the `Option Compare Database` statement, which indicates that VBA is using the same sort order for comparing string expressions in the module that Access is using to compare string expressions in the database. You can change the alphabet that is used for string comparisons in the General tab of the Options dialog. The combo box list for the New Database Sort Order displays the available sort orders.

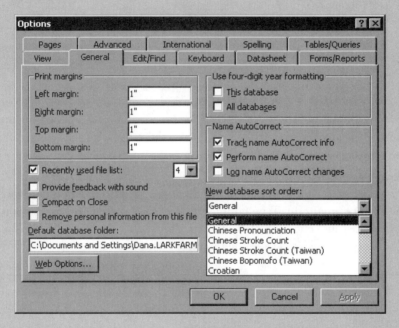

The default General value represents a case-insensitive sort order based on the English alphabet. If you change the setting, the sort order is changed only for new databases; existing databases, including the current database, are not affected.

The syntax for the `Option Compare` statement is as follows:

```
Option Compare {Binary| Text| Database}
```

Using `Binary` results in string comparisons made according to a case-sensitive sort order that is based on the ASCII code for the characters. Using `Text` results in case-insensitive string comparisons based on the ASCII code. Normally, you use the default; if you don't include an `Option Compare` statement, VBA uses `Option Compare Binary`.

2. Enter the Function1 procedure below. This function procedure has an argument named A, which must be supplied when you run the procedure. The first line of code adds one to the argument and assigns the sum as the function's return value. The second line displays a message.

```
Private Function Function1(A)
    Function1 = A + 1
    MsgBox "This is Function1 in module Form_frm1"
End Function
```

3. Place a text box on the form. Set the Name property to txtCalculated and type the following expression in the ControlSource property:

```
= "The value calculated by Function1 in module Form_frm1 is " & _
    Function1(2)
```

4. Switch to Form view and click OK when the message box is displayed. The text box displays the result (see Figure 7.9). Save the form.

FIGURE 7.9:

The expression for the ControlSource property includes the custom function.

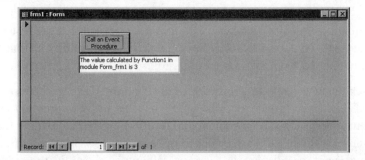

When you display the form in Form view, VBA evaluates the ControlSource expression as follows: the function procedure runs with its argument set to 2, the function returns the value 3, then VBA uses the returned value in the ControlSource expression and displays the result in the text box.

Running Another Procedure in the Module

In VBA, you can call a procedure from another procedure. This means that you can divide a complicated programming task into a set of simpler tasks and create separate procedures for each task. You get two important benefits from this division of labor:

- Shorter procedures for simple tasks are easier to write and debug.

- When there is a task you need to use again in another part of your application or in another application, you can often write a procedure so that you can reuse it without modification.

The second reason is so important that you should adopt it as a fundamental programming guideline: Create reusable procedures whenever possible.

We'll create a command button that calls the Function1 procedure.

1. Switch to Design view, place a command button on the form, and set its Name property to cmdButton2 and its Caption property to "Call a procedure in the form's module."

2. Click the button's OnClick event property, click the Build button at the right of the property box, select Code Builder in the Choose Builder dialog, and click OK. The Module window opens and displays the code template for the new event procedure.

3. Type the event procedure below. The first line of code calls the Function1 procedure with the argument 3. The procedure that is called is referred to as a *called procedure* or a *nested procedure*. The second line displays a message.

```
Private Sub cmdButton2_Click ()
    Call Function1(3)
    MsgBox "This is cmdButton2_Click in module Form_frm1"
End Sub
```

4. Switch to Form view. The expression in the text box's ControlSource property calls Function1 with argument 2 as before. Click the OK button so that VBA can continue evaluating the ControlSource expression.

5. Click the new command button with the caption "Call a procedure in the form's module." The event procedure calls Function1 with 3 as the argument. The Function1 procedure adds one to the argument and returns 4 as the value of the function. However, when you use the Call statement to call a function, VBA ignores the function's returned value. Function1 displays its message. When you click OK, the cmdButton2_Click event procedure displays its message. Save the form.

Running a Procedure in Another Module

You can also run a procedure that is stored in another module. In most databases, you create one or more standard modules and use them to store general procedures that you use in several forms or reports. We'll create a standard module and use it to store a new function procedure that we'll run from a third button on the form.

1. Click the New Object drop-down button in the toolbar and choose Module. The Module window opens, displaying the Declarations section of the standard module. The Declarations section displays the default option statement. Save the new module as **bas1**.

2. Create a new function procedure by typing **Public Function Function1(A)** on a new line. You use the Public keyword to make the procedure available to procedures in other modules. When you press Enter, VBA automatically enters a procedure separator

and displays the code template. Enter the procedure shown below. (We are deliberately using the same name for the new function.)

```
Public Function Function1(A)
    Function1 = A + 2
    MsgBox "This is Function1 in module bas1"
End Function
```

3. Click in the form and switch to Design view. Create a new command button and set its Name property to cmdButton3 and its Caption property to "Call a procedure in another module." Create the event procedure below for the button's Click event. Because there are two Function1 procedures, VBA will need to make a choice.

```
Private Sub cmdButton3_Click()
    Call Function1(3)
    MsgBox "This is cmdButton3_Click in module Form_frm1"
End Sub
```

4. Switch to Form view. As before, the expression in the text box's ControlSource property calls Function1 with argument 2. Click the OK button.

5. Click the new button. The message box indicates the choice VBA makes: VBA runs the Function1 procedure in the form module. When a procedure calls a second procedure, VBA looks for the called procedure in the same module first; if the called procedure isn't in the module, VBA looks for the called procedure in other modules. In this case, VBA found a Function1 procedure in the form module and ran it. To call the Function1 procedure in the standard module, you must include a reference to the module name (the fully qualified reference for the procedure).

6. Click in the form module and modify the event procedure as shown below.

```
Private Sub cmdButton3_Click()
    Call bas1.Function1(3)
    MsgBox "This is cmdButton3_Click in module Form_frm1"
End Sub
```

7. Click the new button. This time, VBA runs the Function1 procedure in the standard module. Save the form.

Hiding a Procedure

When you use the built-in event procedure code-building tools, the code template for the event procedure includes the Private keyword. In VBA, you can decide which procedures in your application can use a specified procedure. You can make a procedure available only to other procedures stored in the same module and hide the procedure from procedures stored in other modules by using the `Private` keyword in the first line of the procedure's declaration statement.

1. Click in the `Function1` procedure of the bas1 module and change `Public` to `Private` in the first line of the `Function1` declaration statement. With this declaration, the procedure is available only to other procedures in the bas1 module.

2. Click in the form and then click the new button. Access is unable to run the procedure and displays the error message shown in Figure 7.10a. When you use the `Private` keyword to hide a procedure, the procedure is not visible to procedures in other modules. From the viewpoint of a procedure in the form module, the `Function1` procedure in bas1 doesn't exist, so a run-time error is generated.

3. Click OK. The Module window displays clues to the problem. VBA highlights the name of the procedure that failed, displays an arrow in the margin at the left, and changes the background color for the code statement that failed (see Figure 7.10b).

FIGURE 7.10:

The run-time error when you call a Private procedure from a procedure in a different module (a). When a procedure fails, VBA highlights the name of the procedure and changes the background color for the statement that failed (b).

(a)

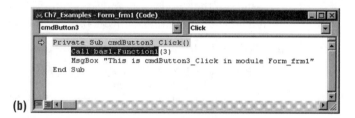
(b)

4. Click the Close box of the Module window. Click the Reset button to reset the code and stop running the procedure.

The examples we've worked through so far are especially simple because they don't use variables (except for the argument of the function procedure). The rest of this chapter explains more fully the mechanics of creating and running procedures.

The Access VBA Programming Environment

We begin our study of the Access VBA programming environment with an investigation of the Module view and the mechanics of creating and editing code.

Displaying a Module in Module View

You create code in a Module window in the Module view. You can open a standard, form, report, or independent class module as explained in the following sections. In each case, the Module window opens, displaying the Declarations section with the default option; the window's title bar indicates the name and type of the module (see Figure 7.11).

FIGURE 7.11:

The Module window for a standard module (a), a form module (b), and an independent class module (c). The title bar displays the module's name and type.

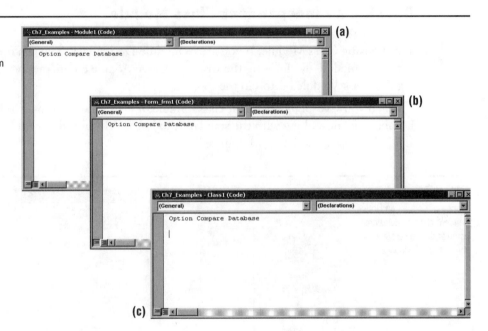

Opening a Standard Module

You open a new standard module by clicking the New button in the Modules pane of the Database window or by clicking the New Object button in the toolbar and choosing Module. If you are in Module view, you can open a new standard module by choosing Insert ➤ Module or by clicking the Insert Module button in the toolbar.

You open an existing standard module by selecting the module in the Database window and double-clicking or by clicking the Design button.

Opening a Form or Report Module

You open a form or report module by opening the form or report in Design view and choosing View ➤ Code from the menu or clicking the Code button in the toolbar. You can open a form or report and its module simultaneously by selecting the form or report in the Database window and clicking the Code button in the toolbar. By default, a new form or report doesn't have a module and the form or report is called *lightweight*. Access creates the form's or report's module the first time you try to open the module.

A form or report module is saved along with the form or report and is not listed in the Modules pane of the Database window.

Opening an Independent Class Module

You open a new independent class module by clicking the New Object button in the toolbar and choosing Class Module. If you are in module Design view, you can open a new independent class module by choosing the Insert ➤ Class Module command in the menu or by clicking the Class Module button in the toolbar.

When you save an independent class module, it is listed within the Modules tab of the Database window along with the standard modules. VBA uses different icons for standard and independent modules (see Figure 7.12).

FIGURE 7.12:

Standard modules and independent class modules are listed with different icons in the Database window.

You open an existing independent class module by selecting the module in the Database window and double-clicking or clicking the Design button.

Determining a Module's Contents

You use the two combo boxes below the Module window title bar to determine the contents of the module.

For a standard module, the combo box on the left displays (General) as its only item. The (General) item represents the module itself. The combo box on the right displays (Declarations) as the first item followed by the names of the general procedures in the module. Figure 7.13 displays the IsLoaded procedure stored in the UtilityFunctions standard module in the Northwind.mdb sample application. The (Declarations) item represents the Declarations section of the module. When you select a procedure name from the list, the code for the procedure is displayed.

FIGURE 7.13:

The IsLoaded procedure of the UtilityFunctions module in the Northwind.mdb database

```
Northwind - Utility Functions (Code)
(General)                              IsLoaded

    Option Compare Database
    Option Explicit

    Function IsLoaded(ByVal strFormName As String) As Boolean
        ' Returns True if the specified form is open in Form view or Datasheet view.
        Dim oAccessObject As AccessObject

        Set oAccessObject = CurrentProject.AllForms(strFormName)
        If oAccessObject.IsLoaded Then
            If oAccessObject.CurrentView <> acCurViewDesign Then
                IsLoaded = True
            End If
        End If

    End Function
```

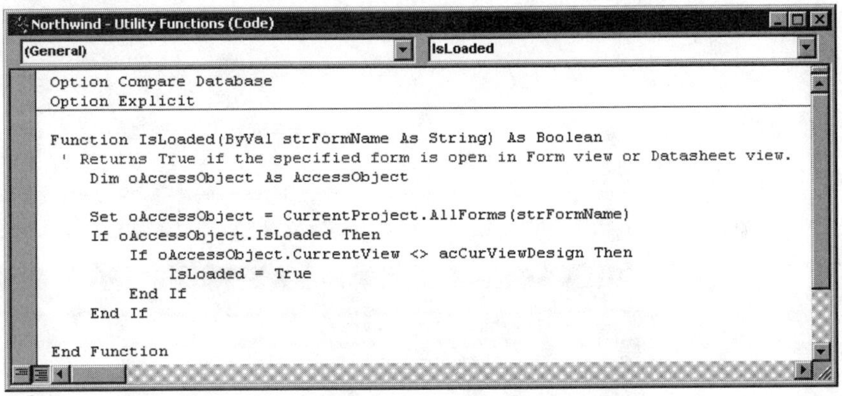

For a form or report module, the combo box on the left lists (General) followed by a list of objects associated with the form or report, including the name of each control that recognizes events, the name of each section displayed, and the form or report itself indicated by Form or Report. Figure 7.14a shows the list of objects in the Orders form in the Northwind.mdb database. When you select the (General) item, the combo box on the right displays (Declarations) as the first item, followed by the names of the general procedures in the module. When you select a general procedure name from the list, the Module window displays the code for the procedure. When you select an object from the combo box on the left, the combo box on the right displays a list of the events that the object recognizes.

When the module contains an event procedure for an object's event, that event is shown in bold. When you select an event shown in bold, the corresponding event procedure is displayed. For example, Figure 7.14b shows the Form_AfterUpdate event procedure for the Employees form. When you select an event that is not listed in bold, VBA creates and displays a code template for the event procedure. Once the code template for an event has been created, the list displays the event in bold even if you don't enter any code between the lines of the template. After you delete an event procedure or the code template for an event, the list displays the event in regular font.

TIP   You can navigate through all the procedures in a module using shortcut keys: pressing Ctrl+Up Arrow or Ctrl+Down Arrow displays the previous or next procedure, respectively.

FIGURE 7.14:

The combo boxes for a form or report module provide an inventory of the module. The Object combo box lists the objects in the form or report (a) and the Procedures combo box lists the events recognized by a selected object (b).

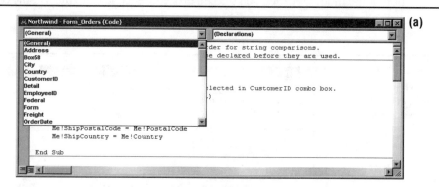

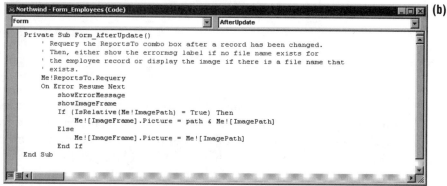

Viewing an Event Procedure Directly

Another way to view a particular event procedure is to click in the event property in the object's property sheet. If an event procedure exists for an event, the event's property setting is [Event Procedure]; clicking the Build button at the right of the property box opens the form or report module and displays the event procedure.

You can create a new event procedure for an event by clicking the Build button to the right of the event's property box and choosing Code Builder in the Choose Builder dialog. When you click OK, the form or report module opens, displaying the code template for the event procedure. The next section describes a faster way to display an event procedure.

Working in Module View

The Module view toolbar, shown below, includes buttons for most of the commands.

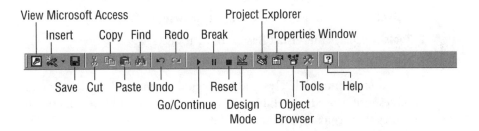

The following list describes the buttons, from left to right, and includes their keyboard shortcuts:

View Microsoft Access Toggles between the Visual Basic Editor and Microsoft Access (Alt+F11).

Insert Click the arrow to display the choices. Module creates a new standard module, Class Module creates a new independent class module, and Procedure opens the Insert Procedure dialog and inserts a code template for the specified procedure in the active module.

Save Saves changes to the current procedure (Ctrl+S).

Cut Removes the selected text and places a copy on the Clipboard (Ctrl+X).

Copy Places a copy of the selected text on the Clipboard (Ctrl+C).

Paste Pastes the contents of the Clipboard at the insertion point and removes the current selection (Ctrl+V).

Find Finds selected text in the module (Ctrl+F).

Undo Undoes the most recent reversible keyboard or mouse action (Ctrl+Z).

Redo Restores whatever you undid with the Undo button.

Go/Continue Continues execution of code after you have paused execution, unless the suspension prevents the code from executing (F5).

Break Pauses execution of procedures in the module (Ctrl+Break).

Reset Terminates execution of procedures in the module and reinitializes both public and private variables (Alt+F5).

Design Mode Toggles a procedure in and out of design mode.

Project Explorer Displays a tree-format list of all current databases and projects with modules, as well as forms and reports containing modules (Ctrl+R).

Properties Window Shows any alterable properties in a module (F4).

Object Browser Displays the Object Browser (F2).

Tools Displays the Visual Basic Editor tools.

Help Displays the Visual Basic Help window (F1).

The menus in module Design view contain commands to help you create, edit, run, and troubleshoot procedures. Table 7.5 lists most of the additional menu commands specific to modules that aren't represented by default toolbar buttons.

TABLE 7.5: Selected Menu Commands and Keyboard Shortcuts

Command and Shortcut	Description
Edit ➤ Clear (Delete)	Removes the selected text from the Module window without placing a copy on the Clipboard.
Edit ➤ Select All (Ctrl+A)	Selects all text in the Module window.
Edit ➤ Find (Ctrl+F)	Displays the Find dialog for designing a search and searches for the specified expression in the current procedure, module, or all modules as specified in the Find dialog.
Edit ➤ Find Next (F3)	Finds the next occurrence of the search string in the current procedure, module, or all modules as specified in the Find dialog.
Edit ➤ Replace (Ctrl+H)	Displays the Replace dialog for designing a search and specifying search and replacement expressions.
Edit ➤ Indent (Tab)	Indents the selected lines of code or the line of code at the insertion point by four spaces (or the number of spaces set as the Tab Width in the Options dialog).
Edit ➤ Outdent (Shift+Tab)	Shifts the selected lines of code or the line of code at the insertion point to the left by four spaces (or the number of spaces set as the Tab Width in the Options dialog).

Continued on next page

TABLE 7.5 CONTINUED: Selected Menu Commands and Keyboard Shortcuts

Command and Shortcut	Description
Edit ➤ List Properties/Methods (Ctrl+J)	Lists properties and methods for the code element or statement containing the insertion point.
Edit ➤ List Constants (Ctrl+Shift+J)	Displays constants for the statement containing the insertion point.
Edit ➤ Quick Info (Ctrl+I)	Displays the syntax information for the variable, constant, or procedure containing the insertion point.
Edit ➤ Parameter Info (Ctrl+Shift+I)	Displays all parameters for the statement containing the insertion point.
Edit ➤ Complete Word (Ctrl+Alt+A)	Completes typing the built-in property, method, or constant word fragment at the insertion point, displaying a list of choices when more than one word begins with the same letters.
Edit ➤ Bookmarks	Displays a fly-out menu with commands for setting, removing, and navigating among bookmarks.
View ➤ Definition (Shift+F2)	Displays the procedure code for the procedure name at the insertion point.
View ➤ Last Position (Ctrl+Shift+F2)	Returns to the line position you were viewing in the previous procedure.
Debug ➤ Compile (*database*)	Compiles all procedures in open modules.
Debug ➤ Add Watch	Displays the Add Watch dialog for specifying an expression to be added to the Watch pane of the Visual Basic Editor.
Debug ➤ Edit Watch	Displays the Edit Watch dialog for editing an expression in the Watch pane of the Visual Basic Editor.
Debug ➤ Quick Watch (Shift+F9)	Allows you to see the value of a variable while a procedure is in break mode.
Debug ➤Toggle Breakpoint (F9)	Toggles the breakpoint on or off from the current line.
Debug ➤ Clear All Breakpoints (Ctrl+Shift+F9)	Removes all breakpoints in all procedures in all modules in the current database.
Debug ➤ Set Next Statement (Ctrl+F9)	Sets the next statement in the same procedure to be executed. Available only in break mode.
Debug ➤ Show Next Statement	Shows the next executable statement.
Tools ➤ References	Displays the References dialog for adding references to other object libraries and to other databases so that you can use their procedures.
Tools ➤ Options	Opens the Options dialog.
Window ➤ Split	Toggles between splitting the Module window in two panes and restoring the window to a single pane.

Useful commands in the Edit menu allow you to display lists of properties, methods, constants, parameters, or syntax information for selected code in the Module window. For example, if you type **IsNull** and choose the Quick Info command, VBA displays a small text box with the syntax for the built-in function (see Figure 7.15a).

You also have the ability to save your place in a procedure by setting a bookmark. To set a bookmark, place the insertion point in the line of code you want to mark, choose Edit ➢ Bookmarks, and then choose Toggle Bookmark from the fly-out menu. VBA displays a blue rectangle in the margin indicator bar to the left of the line of code (see Figure 7.15b). Alternatively, you can right-click next to the line of code and click Toggle ➢ Bookmark. You can set as many bookmarks as you need in a module and browse the bookmarks using the Next Bookmark and Previous Bookmark commands in the Bookmarks fly-out menu. You can remove all bookmarks in the active module by choosing the Clear All Bookmarks command in the fly-out menu.

FIGURE 7.15:

Use menu commands to display the syntax for a variable, constant, or method (a) or set a bookmark to quickly return to a marked line of code (b).

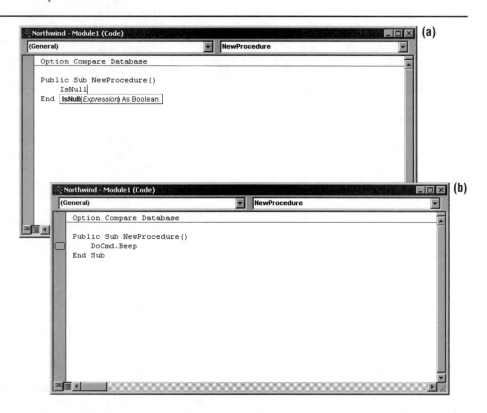

Writing VBA code is similar to writing text. In fact, you can create procedures in any text editor, such as Notepad, and then paste them into VBA modules. The usual text-editing tools are available in Module view. You can cut, copy, and paste text selections using menu commands or the usual keyboard shortcuts Ctrl+X, Ctrl+C, and Ctrl+V (or clear a selection without placing a copy on the Clipboard by choosing Edit ➢ Clear). You can also use the drag-and-drop feature to move selected text to another location.

You can use the familiar Find and Replace commands on the Edit menu to search for a specified text expression or search for a specified text expression and replace it with another expression. You can search for the specified string in the current procedure, the current module, or in all modules of the current database (see Figure 7.16).

FIGURE 7.16:

Use the Find dialog to search in the current procedure, the current module, or all modules in the current database.

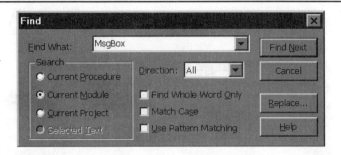

Setting Visual Basic Editor Options

You can set various options to suit your preferences for working with the Visual Basic Editor. To access these options, open the Visual Basic Editor by pressing Alt+F11 and select Tools ➤ Options. Click the Editor tab to see the dialog shown in Figure 7.17.

FIGURE 7.17:

The Editor tab of the Visual Basic Editor Options dialog

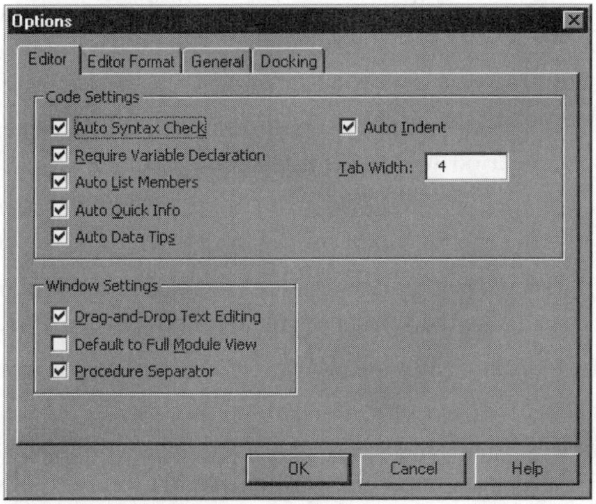

The Editor tab of the Options dialog includes the following options:

Auto Syntax Check Checks for syntax errors as you type in code. Figure 7.18 shows typical syntax error-checking messages. With Auto Syntax Check turned on, VBA may reformat your statement by adding or removing spaces, change the capitalization of keywords and variables to match the capitalization in the variable declaration statement, and correct minor syntax errors such as adding a missing double-quotation mark.

FIGURE 7.18:

Typical syntax error-checking messages: A statement is missing a parenthesis (a), you have misspelled a keyword in a structure (b), you omitted a required part of a structure (c)

(a)

(b)

(c)

Auto Indent Automatically indents a subsequent line of code the same number of tab stops as the current line.

Require Variable Declaration Requires that all variables be explicitly declared. With this option checked, the Option Explicit statement is included in the Declarations statement of all new modules.

Auto List Members Displays a list of valid choices for the code element you just typed when you refer to an object or an object variable. Press Ctrl+Enter or Tab to enter the selected item. Press Escape to close the list.

Auto Quick Info Displays the syntax of a procedure or method when you type the name followed by a space, a period, or an opening parenthesis.

Auto Data Tips Displays the current value of a selected variable when you are in break mode and you pause the mouse cursor over the variable.

Tab Width Sets the number of spaces between tab stops in the Module window. The default is 4. You can change the setting to any number between 1 and 32.

Drag-and-Drop Text Editing Allows you to select text and drag it to another location in the Module or Immediate window.

Default to Full Module View Displays the Declarations section and all procedures in the same pane separated by horizontal lines. (Uncheck this option to display the Declarations section and each procedure in a separate pane.)

Procedure Separator Separates the Declarations section and each procedure with horizontal lines. (Uncheck this option to remove the procedure separator lines.)

Following Good Programming Style

As you write code, consider the following recommendations for making your code easier to read and understand:

Indent Normally, a procedure has several sections. There may be a section for error-handling code, groups of code lines for repetitive operations, alternative groups of statements to be executed under some conditions but not under other conditions. Indenting lines is a useful way to identify code sections. Figure 7.19 shows the IsLoaded function procedure that determines if a particular form is loaded. Even before studying how to write code that makes decisions, you can easily observe the structure of the code because of the levels of indentation.

FIGURE 7.19:

Indenting makes the structure of code easier to understand.

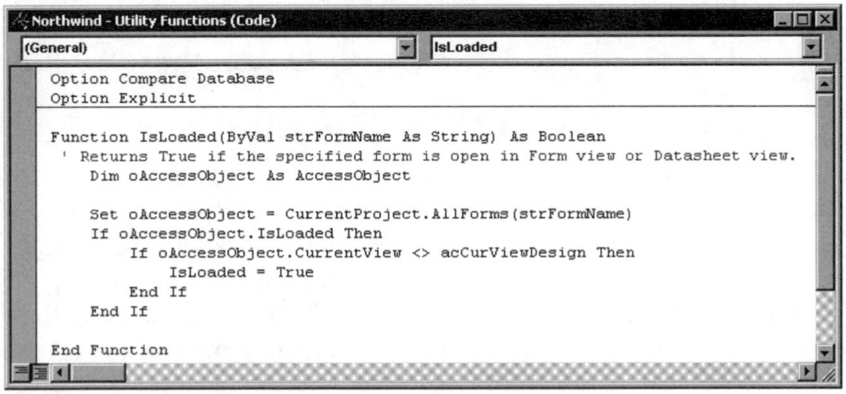

```
Northwind - Utility Functions (Code)

(General)                              IsLoaded

Option Compare Database
Option Explicit

Function IsLoaded(ByVal strFormName As String) As Boolean
  ' Returns True if the specified form is open in Form view or Datasheet view.
    Dim oAccessObject As AccessObject

    Set oAccessObject = CurrentProject.AllForms(strFormName)
    If oAccessObject.IsLoaded Then
        If oAccessObject.CurrentView <> acCurViewDesign Then
            IsLoaded = True
        End If
    End If

End Function
```

Use comments As you are creating code, the purpose and logic of a procedure's statements may seem obvious. Days or weeks later, the logic may be elusive to you and downright opaque to someone else. You can save yourself and others time and effort by commenting your code. You should include comments at the beginning of a procedure to describe the procedure's purpose, the arguments, and the value returned by a function procedure. While it is unnecessary and probably excessive to comment every line of code, you should at least include a comment to explain the logic of each group of statements. Comment lines are preceded with a single apostrophe. By default, the Visual Basic Editor will change comment lines to green.

Use naming conventions Chapter 2, "Getting Started with Objects and Events," discusses the importance of naming conventions for naming the objects you create in your application. With a properly chosen, consistently applied naming convention for procedures, objects, constants, and variables, your VBA code becomes more self-documenting and easier to understand.

Use separate lines for each statement Although you can string together several statements separated by colons (:) on a single line, doing so may make your code difficult to read.

Use the line-continuation character The Module window does not have a word-wrapping feature. If you enter a very long statement, you can "wrap" the statement yourself using the *line-continuation character*. The line-continuation character consists of a space followed by an underscore (_). If you don't break the line with the line-continuation character, you will need to use the horizontal scrollbar to view parts of the statement. You can't use the line-continuation character to wrap a string expression to another line; instead, you can divide the string into smaller pieces and concatenate the pieces (see Chapter 13, "Working with Groups of Records Using Access VBA," for examples).

Declare variables and constants at the beginning of a procedure By grouping all declaration statements at the beginning of a procedure, you can see the constants and variables at a glance and avoid needing to hunt through procedure code to find them.

Using the Access VBA Compiler

The statements that you enter into a module are called *source code*. Access doesn't run the statements as you enter them. Before you can run a procedure, Access must first compile it. Compiling is the process of converting the readable source code that you entered into a format called a *compiled state* that the computer can run. Compilation prepares your code for execution but doesn't execute it. During compiling, Access views the procedure as a whole and checks for errors that may involve more than one statement. Errors that Access detects during compiling are called *compile-time* errors. When Access discovers compile-time errors, an error message is displayed. Figure 7.20 shows typical compile-time errors. Access won't run the procedure until you eliminate the source of the error.

FIGURE 7.20:

Typical compile-time error messages

Saving a Database without Source Code

You can also save a version of a database with VBA code as an *MDE file* that includes only the compiled version and has the source code removed. An MDE file has the following features:

- The forms, reports, and modules cannot be changed.

- Modules cannot be viewed. Your code is fully secured and cannot be read or used by others.

- The MDE file is smaller than the original database file.

- Memory usage is optimized and performance may improve.

- Forms, reports, and modules cannot be imported or exported; however, tables, queries, and macros can be imported or exported to non-MDE databases.

- You cannot change references to object libraries or databases.

- You cannot change the VBA project name for the database.

WARNING   Before you can create an MDE file, you must first successfully compile the VBA modules in the database. Choose Debug ➢ Compile *databasename* to explicitly compile the code.

To create an MDE file, follow these steps:

1. Close the database. If you are in a multiuser environment, all copies of the database must be closed.

2. Even if you created the database using Access 2002, it is saved by default in Access 2000 format. Therefore, you must choose Tools ➢ Database Utilities ➢ Convert Database ➢ To Access 2002 File Format.

3. Select the database in the Database To Convert From dialog box and click Convert (see Figure 7.21a).

4. Choose a name for the converted database in the Convert Database Into dialog box and click Save (see Figure 7.21b). Click OK to close the confirmation dialog box.

5. Click Tools ➢ Database Utilities and then the Make MDE File command in the fly-out menu. Select the converted database in the Database To Save As MDE dialog (see Figure 7.22a) and click the Make MDE button.

6. Specify the name of the new file and select the folder for storing the file in the Save MDE As dialog (see Figure 7.22b). Then click the Save button.

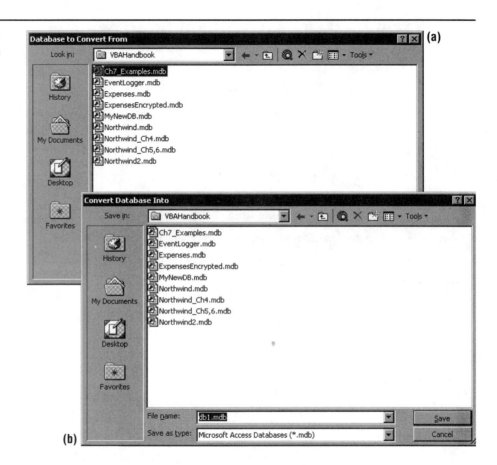

FIGURE 7.21:

Converting a database to Access 2002 file format

WARNING   You should always save the original version of the database that you use to create an MDE file. If you need to change the forms, reports, or modules, you must make the changes to the original database and then create a new MDE file. In addition, you probably won't be able to run or convert an MDE file in future versions of Access, but you will be able to convert the original database file.

There are some restrictions to saving a database as an MDE file. For example, if the database refers to other databases or add-ins—that is, if you have set a reference to another database or an add-in in the References dialog—you must save all of the other databases and add-ins as MDE files. For more information on the restrictions, search for ".mde files" in online help.

FIGURE 7.22:

Creating an MDE file with the VBA source code removed

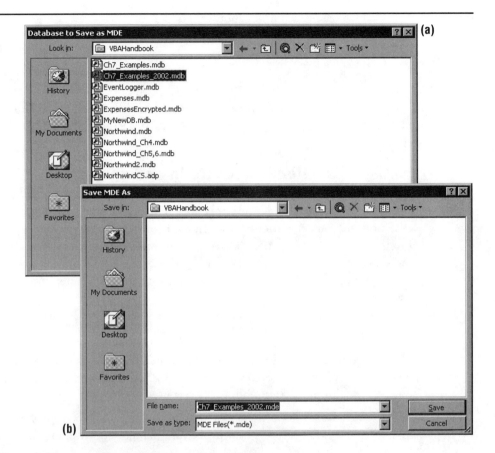

Methods for Running Procedures

This section looks at calling, or running, procedures. (The terms *call* and *run* are used interchangeably.) Because a function procedure can return a value but a sub procedure cannot, you have more flexibility in calling function procedures; for example, you can call a function procedure but not a sub procedure in an expression.

Running Function Procedures

The following is a list of the ways you can call a function procedure:

- Call in an expression
- Run in the Immediate window
- Call from a procedure in the same module

- Call from a procedure in another module
- Trigger by an event
- Call from a macro
- Call from another application

When you call a function procedure in an expression, VBA uses the function's return value in evaluating the expression. In all the other ways of calling a function, VBA discards the return value.

Calling a Function Procedure in an Expression

You can call a function procedure in an expression the same way you call a built-in function: You can include a function procedure in expressions for calculated fields or criteria cells in queries, in expressions for calculated controls on forms and reports, in macro conditions and action arguments, in property settings, and in expressions used in VBA statements and SQL statements. For example, the Concatenate function below is useful for concatenating a person's first and last names into the last name, first name format.

```
Public Function Concatenate (A,B)
    Concatenate = A & ", " & B
    MsgBox "This is the Concatenate procedure in bas2"
End Function
```

The function has the arguments A and B. When you pass values for the arguments, the function concatenates the values with the string ", " between them and returns the string. To see the function in action, follow these steps:

1. Create a new standard module named bas2 in Ch7_Examples. Choose Insert ➤ Procedure and create a new procedure named Concatenate with the Function type and Public scope.

2. Enter the two lines of code for the Concatenate function procedure above, as well as the values (A and B) to be passed to the function in the function template.

3. Import the Employees table from the Northwind database. Create a new query named qryEmployees based on the Employees table and enter the following expression in the first Field cell:

   ```
   FullName: Concatenate(LastName, FirstName)
   ```

4. Run the query.

When you run the query, VBA executes the following sequence for each row in the query result: first, it calculates the return value of the function and holds the value in memory, then it displays the message, and then it creates and displays the calculated field in the query's datasheet (see Figure 7.23).

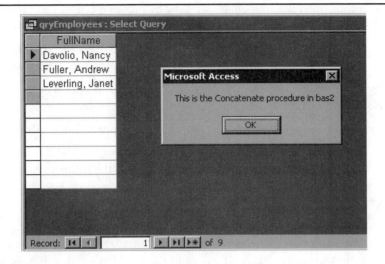

FIGURE 7.23:
The Field cell expression in the query calls the `Concatenate` function for each row in the query result.

NOTE We include the `MsgBox` function in most of the procedures in the chapter as a learning tool or as a troubleshooting tool to observe when a procedure runs. You can comment out, or delete, the statements with the `MsgBox` function when you use the procedures in an application.

Running a Function Procedure in the Immediate Window

The Immediate window is an extremely useful tool for running procedures. Because it is a debugging tool, the Immediate window has the advantage of better eyesight: The Immediate window sees and can run both public and private procedures if you use a fully qualified reference. The syntax you use to run a function procedure depends on whether it is stored in a standard module or a form or report module and whether you want to use the return value.

Running Standard Module Function Procedures

If the function is stored in a standard module, you can print the return value by typing ? *functionname* (*argumentlist*) and pressing Enter. If you want to use the return value in another statement, you can create a variable in the Immediate window to hold the function's return value. If the function returns a value, use the following syntax:

```
var = functionname (argumentlist)
```

If the function returns an object, use the following syntax:

```
Set objvar = functionname (argumentlist)
```

For example, open the Immediate window by pressing Ctrl+G and type the following statements:

- Type **?** **Concatenate("Johnson", "Diane")** and press Enter. The function runs, the message is displayed, and the result is printed in the Immediate window.

- Type **var = Concatenate("Johnson", "Diane")** and press Enter. The message is displayed and the returned value is stored in the variable.

- Type **?var** and press Enter. The stored result is printed in the Immediate window.

If you don't need the return value of a function stored in a standard module, you can run the function in the Immediate window using either of the following:

```
Call functionname (argumentlist)
functionname argumentlist
```

If you use the Call keyword to call a function procedure that requires arguments, you must enclose the argument list in parentheses. If the function doesn't require arguments, you can include or omit the parentheses. If you omit the Call keyword, you must also omit the parentheses enclosing the argument list. When you use either of these statements, VBA throws away the function's return value. For example, type the following statements in the Immediate window:

- Type **Call Concatenate ("Johnson", "Diane")** and press Enter. VBA runs the function, displays the message, and throws away the function's return value; the insertion point just moves to the next line without printing anything.

- Type **Concatenate "Johnson", "Diane"** and press Enter—you get the same result.

- Type **Concatenate ("Johnson", "Diane")** and press Enter. VBA generates an error and displays an error message (see Figure 7.24).

FIGURE 7.24:

The error message when you omit the Call keyword but enclose the arguments in parentheses

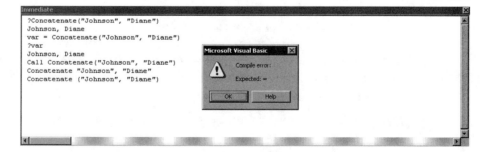

You can run both public and private function procedures in the Immediate window. To run a private function in the Immediate window, you must use the full identifier. Follow the steps below to see how this works:

1. Change `Public` to `Private` as the keyword in the declaration statement of the `Concatenate` function in the bas2 module. Click the Save button in the toolbar.

2. Type **?bas2.Concatenate ("Johnson", "Diane")** and press Enter. VBA runs the `Concatenate` procedure, displays the message, and displays the returned value.

3. Type **?Concatenate ("Johnson", "Diane")** and press Enter. VBA generates a run-time error when you try to run a private function without including the module name in the reference.

4. Change `Private` back to `Public` as the keyword in the declaration statement of the `Concatenate` function and save the module.

Running Form or Report Module Function Procedures

If the function procedure is stored in a form or report module, you must use the full identifier of the function in these expressions. For example, if a function in a form module returns a value, you can print the value in the Immediate window using the following syntax:

```
? Form_formname.functionname (argumentlist)
```

You can run the function and discard its return value using the following syntax:

```
Call Form_formname.functionname (argumentlist)
```

The form or report does not need to be open to run a procedure in its module. In the Immediate window, follow these steps:

1. Type **? Form_frm1.Function1(3)** and press Enter. VBA runs the function, displays the message, and prints 4 (`Function1` adds one to the argument and returns the sum). Make sure the frm1 form is closed when you call the function.

2. Type **?Function1(3)** and press Enter. When you try to run a function in a form or report module in the Immediate window without including the reference to the module, a run-time error occurs ("Sub or Function not defined").

3. Open the bas1 function module and change `Private` to `Public`. Now the procedure is available to other modules besides the bas1 module. Type **?Function1(3)** in the Immediate window. The bas1 module's `Function1` procedure is executed, returning a value of 5.

Calling from a Procedure in the Same Module

When you call a function procedure from another function or sub procedure, the syntax you use depends on whether you want to use the function's return value.

If you want to use the return value, you must use the function procedure in an expression in a VBA statement. For example, follow these steps:

1. Create a new function procedure named GetReturnValue in the bas2 module as shown below. The GetReturnValue function calls the Concatenate function as an argument of the MsgBox function and displays the returned value in a message box.

   ```
   Public Function GetReturnValue()
       MsgBox Concatenate ("Johnson", "Diane")
   End Sub
   ```

2. Run the GetReturnValue function in the Immediate window by typing **Call GetReturnValue()** and pressing Enter. You can also call the function by typing **GetReturnValue** and pressing Enter. Because the GetReturnValue function has no arguments, you can also call the function by typing **Call GetReturnValue** and pressing Enter. Notice that the GetReturnValue function does not have a return value.

If you don't need its return value, you can run the function procedure from another function or sub procedure using either of the following statements:

```
Call functionname (argumentlist)
functionname argumentlist
```

If you use the Call keyword to call a function procedure that requires arguments, you must enclose the argument list in parentheses. If the function doesn't require arguments, you can include or omit the parentheses. If you don't use the Call keyword, you must omit the parentheses around the argument list. In either case, the function's return value is discarded. For example, the DiscardReturn function below runs the Concatenate function discarding the return value. The DiscardReturn function takes no arguments and doesn't return a value.

```
Public Function DiscardReturnValue()
    Call Concatenate ("Johnson", "Diane")
End Sub
```

Follow these steps to test the DiscardReturnValue function:

1. Enter the DiscardReturnValue function in bas2.

2. Run the function in the Immediate window by typing **Call DiscardReturnValue** and pressing Enter. VBA runs the Concatenate function, displays the message, and discards the return value.

3. Modify the procedure by omitting both the Call keyword and the parentheses as follows:

   ```
   Public Function DiscardReturnValue()
       Concatenate "Johnson", "Diane"
   End Sub
   ```

4. Run the function by typing **DiscardReturnValue** and pressing Enter.

Calling from a Procedure in Another Module

You can call a public, but not a private, function procedure from a procedure stored in another module. If you are calling a public function procedure in another module, you may need to include the module name in the reference. For example, the function procedure RunFormFunction shown below runs the public Function1 function in the form module of the frm1 form.

```
Public Function RunPublicFunction()
    MsgBox Form_frm1.Function1(3)
End Function
```

Test public and private procedures as follows:

1. Enter the RunPublicFunction procedure in the bas2 module. Open the Form_frm1 module and change Private to Public in the form's Function1 function.

2. Type **Call RunPublicFunction** in the Immediate window and press Enter. The Function1 procedure runs and displays its message boxes.

3. Enter the RunPrivateFunction procedure in the bas2 module as follows:

```
Public Function RunPrivateFunction()
    MsgBox bas1.Function1(3)
End Function
```

4. Type **Call RunPrivateFunction** in the Immediate window and press Enter. VBA generates a run-time error ("Method or data member not found") because you can't run a private procedure stored in another module. VBA highlights the name of the procedure, displays an arrow in the margin bar, and changes the background color of the statement that failed.

5. Click the Reset button in the toolbar to reset the code.

Triggering a Procedure by an Event

You can use an event to trigger a function. To run a function when an event occurs, use the following syntax in the event's property box:

```
= functionname(argumentlist)
```

The parentheses are required even if the function has no arguments. The function's return value, if there is one, is discarded.

Follow these steps to trigger a function by an event:

1. Select the frm1 form in the Database window and click the Code button in the toolbar. The form and its module open.

2. Click the Insert button in the toolbar and choose Procedure. Name the new procedure **EventFunction** and then choose the Function type and Public scope.

3. Enter the EventFunction below. This function takes no arguments and returns the Boolean value True.

```
Public Function EventFunction()
    EventFunction = True
    MsgBox "This is the EventFunction in the Form_frm1 module"
End Function
```

4. Open the form's property sheet, click the OnClick event property box, and type **= EventFunction()**. Save the form and switch to Form view.

5. When the Function1 function procedure finishes running, click in the form's detail section. VBA runs the EventFunction procedure, displays its message box, and discards the function's return value.

The syntax for the event property setting uses the function name without a qualifying module name; in fact, you cannot use the fully qualified reference for a procedure as the event property setting. This means that you can use an event to trigger a public function stored in a standard module, as long as the function's name is unique and doesn't require the fully qualified reference, but you can't trigger a public function stored in another form or report module because using a function in another form or report module requires the fully qualified reference. Try this example:

1. Switch to Design view, click in the txtCalculate text box, and then click in the OnClick property. We'll use the Click event of the txtCalculate text box to trigger the Concatenate function stored in the bas2 standard module.

2. Type **= Concatenate ("Johnson", "Diane")** in the property box. Save the form and switch to Form view.

3. When the Function1 function finishes running, click the text box. VBA runs the Concatenate function, displays its message, and discards the returned value.

Calling a Procedure from a Macro

To run a function procedure from a macro, use the RunCode macro action. Use the following syntax for the action's function name argument:

functionname (argumentlist)

Include arguments in parentheses and do not use an equal sign. The function's return value is discarded. The syntax for the function name argument requires an unqualified function name. This means that you can use the RunCode action to run a public function stored in a standard module if you don't need to qualify its name. In addition, if the macro action runs in response to an event on a form or report, Access looks for the function first in the form or report module before looking in standard modules, so in this case, you can also run a function stored in a form or report module.

For an example of how to run a function in a standard module, we'll run the Concatenate function:

1. Open a new macrosheet named mcrRunCode. Select the RunCode action in the first action cell and set the function name argument to Concatenate ("Johnson", "Diane"). Figure 7.25 shows the macrosheet.

FIGURE 7.25:

You can run a function procedure from a macro.

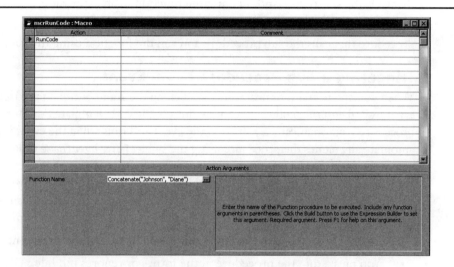

2. Save the macrosheet. Click the Run button in the Macro toolbar. Access runs the macro. The macro runs the Concatenate function, which displays its message, discards the function's return value, and then quits.

Calling a Procedure from Another Application

You can use the Run method to run a function from another application through Automation, using the following syntax:

```
Application.Run functionname[, argument1, argument2, ..., argumentN]
```

Access ignores the function's return value.

Running Sub Procedures

The following is a list of ways to call a sub procedure:

- Trigger by an event
- Run in the Immediate window
- Call from another procedure
- Call from another application

Because a sub procedure doesn't return a value, you can't use a sub procedure in an expression. If you want to run a sub procedure as part of an expression, you can create a function that calls the subroutine and then use the function in an expression.

You also can't call a sub procedure directly from a macro; however, you can create a function procedure that calls the sub procedure and run the function using the RunCode macro action.

Triggering a Sub Procedure by an Event

When you create an event procedure by clicking the Build button at the right of an event property box and entering code between the lines of the code template that Access provides, the sub procedure is automatically assigned to the event and runs when the event is recognized. Access automatically names the procedure using the syntax Form_*eventname* or Report_*eventname* for an event recognized by a form or a report and the syntax *objectname_eventname* for an event recognized by an object. Access also includes the predefined argument list for the event procedure. After naming the procedure, Access sets the event property to [Event Procedure]. If you want to create an event procedure from scratch, you must follow the same rules:

- You must use the same naming convention and the same argument list.
- You must store the procedure in the form's or report's module.
- You must set the event property to [Event Procedure].

As an example, we'll create an event procedure from scratch to close a form:

1. Open the frm1 form in Design view, place a command button on the form, and set the Name property to cmdClose and the Caption property to Close.

2. Click the Code button in the toolbar and place the insertion point in the line following the last statement in the module.

3. Enter the following procedure at the insertion point:

```
Private Sub cmdclose_Click()
    DoCmd.Close
    MsgBox "This is cmdclose_Click in module Form_frm1"
End Sub
```

4. When you enter the first line, VBA automatically inserts a procedure separator and completes the code template. Access matches the event procedure name with the new button and automatically assigns the procedure to the button's Click event. Click in the property sheet of the command button to observe the assignment.

5. Save the form and switch to Form view. The Function1 procedure runs.

6. Click the Close button. Access closes the form and then displays the message for the cmdClose_Click event procedure.

If you change the name of a control after assigning an event procedure to it, VBA won't be able to match the event procedure to the control. VBA moves the event procedure to the General section of the module. You must change the event procedure's name so that it matches the new name of the control. Select (General) from the Object combo box, select the event procedure from the Procedure combo box, change the event procedure's name, and save the form.

NOTE   When you copy and paste a control with event procedures to another form, the event procedure is not copied to the form module of the new form. If you want to be able to copy and paste procedures along with controls, use event-handling function procedures instead of event procedures and store the functions in a standard module.

Running a Sub Procedure in the Immediate Window

You run a sub procedure in the Immediate window using the same syntax that you use to run a function when the return value is discarded. The syntax you use depends on whether the sub procedure is stored in a standard module or a form or report module. When the sub procedure is stored in a standard module, use either syntax below:

```
Call subroutinename (argumentlist)
subroutinename argumentlist
```

If the sub procedure is stored in a form or report module, you must use the fully qualified reference for the function in these expressions; for example,

```
Form_ formname.subroutinename argumentlist
```

You can run both public and private sub procedures in the Immediate window. A form or report must be open to run a sub procedure in its module. By contrast, a form or report does not need to be open to run in the Immediate window a function procedure stored in its module. For example, to call the event procedure for the cmdButton1 button on the frm1 form, open the frm1 form in Design or Form view, type **Call Form_frm1.cmdButton1_Click** in the Immediate window, and press Enter. VBA runs the event procedure and displays its message.

Calling a Sub Procedure from Another Procedure

You run a sub procedure from another procedure using the same syntax that you use to run a function (when the return value is discarded). The syntax you use depends on whether you use the Call keyword. If you use the Call keyword to call a sub procedure that requires arguments, you must enclose the argument list in parentheses. If the sub procedure doesn't require arguments, you can include or omit the parentheses.

```
Call subroutinename (argumentlist)
subroutinename argumentlist
```

Calling a Sub Procedure from Another Application

You can use the Run method to run a sub procedure from another application through Automation. Use this syntax:

```
Application.Run subroutinename[, argument1, argument2, ..., argumentN]
```

Summary

This chapter introduces you to some of the fundamentals of writing Access VBA code. Here are the important points:

- Access VBA has its own set of data types. While it is possible to avoid assigning data types yourself by letting VBA assign the Variant type for all variables, your code runs faster when you assign specific data types.

- Access VBA has an Object data type that you can use for object variables that refer to objects. In addition, subtypes exist for the Access and data access objects.

- There are two kinds of modules. Standard modules store procedures that are not associated with a specific object. Class modules store the definitions for new objects. There are two kinds of class modules. Independent class modules are not associated with a form or a report and are stored as separate objects in the database. Form or report modules are stored as part of a form or report.

- There are two kinds of procedures. Function procedures may return a value. Normally, you use function procedures in expressions, and VBA runs the procedure when the expression is evaluated. When you run a function procedure using any other calling technique, the function's return value is ignored. Sub procedures do not return a value. Normally, you store a sub procedure in a form's or report's module and run the procedure when an object on the form or report recognizes an event.

- The Access VBA programming environment includes a Module window in which you enter code statements and a set of built-in command bars with commands for creating, editing, and troubleshooting code.

- You can save the database as an MDE file in which the Visual Basic source code is removed and only the compiled version remains. The forms, reports, and modules in an MDE file cannot be changed.

- You can run function procedures by calling them in expressions, calling them from other procedures, calling them from a macro or another application (using Automation), triggering them by events, and calling them in the Immediate window.

- You can run sub procedures by calling them from other procedures, calling them from another application (using Automation), triggering them by events, and calling them in the Immediate window.

The next chapter continues with the fundamentals of Access Visual Basic by introducing you to using variables and constants in procedures.

CHAPTER 8

Using Variables

- Declaring variables and constants

- Understanding the lifetime and visibility of a variable

- Passing data to a procedure

- Understanding procedure-level and module-level variables and constants

- Using arrays

- Creating your own data types

In the last chapter, you learned the basics of creating procedures and storing them in modules. This chapter continues to lay the foundation for creating VBA procedures by teaching you how to use variables in procedures. The use of variables is the key to creating reusable code.

The concept of a variable can be stated quite simply: A *variable* is a named location in memory that holds a value or refers to an object. However, the implementation of the concept in Access VBA is rather complicated because of the enormous flexibility that using variables provides. In this chapter, we'll examine how to create a variable, how to share a variable with other procedures, how to pass variables when you call a procedure, and how to destroy a variable when you are finished with it. Because variables are kept in memory, we'll consider the effects that variables have on memory usage and performance. After discussing variables, the chapter covers creating custom constants and using arrays to work with several variables at the same time. In the last section of the chapter, you'll learn how to create your own data types.

Using Variables in Procedures

All of the procedures you created in the last chapter are of the simplest variety:

- The code statements you wrote are trivial, because you were learning only how to create, store, and run procedures (we'll postpone more interesting and practical statements until later chapters).

- The use of variables was extremely limited because the procedures used variables only as arguments. When we ran procedures with arguments, we specified literal values for the arguments such as Concatenate ("Johnson", "Diane") and Function1(3).

- We did not explicitly declare data types, so the arguments, the values we specified, and the function return values are all variants. As explained in the previous chapter, the Variant data type uses more than twice as much memory as any other fundamental data type and causes slower performance than if we had declared a specific data type.

The purpose of this section is to learn how to use variables in procedures. Here are the two most important reasons for using variables:

- To create reusable code. If you can reuse procedures, you end up writing less code!

- To create faster code. Nobody wants slow code.

Two simple examples of how this works should remove any doubts you may have.

NOTE   For hands-on experience with the concepts we'll explore in this chapter, create a copy of the Northwind database named Northwind_Ch8. Make sure that you have selected the Always Use Event Procedures option in the Forms/Reports tab in the Options dialog (displayed by choosing the Tools ➤ Options command).

Using Variables to Create Reusable Code

Suppose you are creating a Switchboard form with command buttons to open other forms and hide the switchboard. The first approach is to place command buttons on the new switchboard and create event procedures to carry out the actions. As an example, we'll go through the steps to open the Customers form in the Northwind application:

1. Create a new form in Northwind_Ch8 named frmSwitchboard.

2. Place a command button on the form and set the Name property to cmdCustomers and the Caption property to Customers.

3. Click in the OnClick property and click the Build button to the right of the property box. Access creates and opens the form module and displays the code template for the event procedure.

4. Enter the event procedure shown below:

```
Private Sub cmdCustomers_Click()
    DoCmd.OpenForm "Customers"
    Forms!frmSwitchboard.Visible = False
End Sub
```

The cmdCustomers_Click procedure runs the OpenForm method of the DoCmd object to open the form. The procedure specifies the form name argument of the OpenForm method as the literal value "Customers". To hide the switchboard, the procedure sets the form's Visible property to False. With no more tasks to carry out, the procedure ends.

5. Save the form, switch to Form view, and click the button. The Customers form opens and the switchboard is hidden.

Now let's improve the procedure.

Using the Me Property for Better Performance

In the cmdCustomers_Click procedure, to run the statement that hides the switchboard, Access must deal with the hierarchical reference for the Visible property:

```
Forms!frmSwitchboard.Visible
```

Each level of the reference requires processing time; that is, each exclamation point and each dot represents execution time required to process the reference. You can avoid the hierarchy in this statement by using the Me property. This property is one of the special optimization tools that Access provides when you are creating procedures in a form or report module. Using the Me property in a procedure in a form's or report's module is the fastest way to refer to the form or report because VBA doesn't need to take time to process a fully qualified reference. In this procedure, the first step toward improved performance is to replace Forms!frmSwitchboard with Me.

Using an Argument Instead of a Literal

A Switchboard form typically has several buttons to open different forms. Instead of creating a separate event procedure for each button, the goal is to create a single procedure that we can reuse. The first step in making an existing procedure reusable is to determine exactly what prevents it from being reusable. In the cmdCustomers_Click procedure, the problem is the presence of the literal "Customers" as an argument of the OpenForm method. We'll move the literal out of the procedure by replacing the literal in the OpenForm argument with a string variable that we'll name strFormName (using the str name tag because we are now concerning ourselves with data types) and then arrange to pass the literal back into the procedure as an argument of the procedure. To declare the data type for an argument, use the following syntax:

```
procedurename (argumentname [As datatype])
```

Using a "typed" argument, the procedure looks like this:

```
Private Sub cmdCustomers_Click(strFormName As String)
    DoCmd.OpenForm strFormName
    Me.Visible = False
End Sub
```

Changing to a Function Procedure

The modified version of our procedure is no longer an event procedure because, by definition, an event procedure for the Click event can't have any arguments. If you try to compile the procedure, VBA generates a compile error. There are two alternatives. One is to change the name of this sub procedure so that it doesn't use the syntax reserved for an event procedure and call the sub procedure from a new event procedure. This isn't a very good solution, however, because we would only be passing the problem of the literal to the new event procedure. If we rename the sub procedure to OpenAForm and call it from an event procedure, the literal is still part of the VBA code:

```
Private Sub cmdCustomers_Click()
    Call OpenAForm("Customers")
End Sub
```

A literal value that is entered in the Module window is called a *hard-coded value* and usually prevents the code from being reusable.

A better solution is to change the procedure to a function procedure named OpenAForm so that the literal can be entered in the property sheet instead of being hard-coded in the module. When you create a function procedure, VBA automatically sets aside a memory location for a return value, whether or not the function actually returns a result; if we don't specify a data type for this location, VBA assumes the Variant data type. To avoid the memory-hungry, performance-degrading Variant data type, we'll type the function's phantom return value as

Integer. You specify the data type for a function procedure's return value in the function dec-laration statement using the following syntax:

```
[Public|Private] Function functionname [(argumentlist)] [As type]
```

The function procedure shown below can now be reused by other command buttons on the same form:

```
Public Function OpenAForm(strFormname As String) As Integer
    DoCmd.OpenForm strFormname
    Me.Visible = False
End Sub
```

You assign the function procedure to the Click event for a command button on the form using this syntax:

```
=OpenAForm("formname")
```

The next step is to make the function procedure reusable on any form. Because a fully reusable function procedure is not associated with a specific form, we'll store the function procedure in a standard module. A price of moving the procedure to a standard module is that you can no longer use the Me reference (you can use Me to refer to a form or report only in a procedure stored in the form's or report's module). To keep the procedure reusable, you can use the Screen object to refer to the form that holds the command button and hide the form before opening the Customers form. (If you don't interchange the order of the statements, the procedure opens and then closes the specified form because the newly opened form becomes the active form.)

1. Create a new standard module named basNavigation and insert a new public function named OpenAForm. Enter the procedure shown here:

    ```
    Public Function OpenAForm(strFormName As String) As Integer
        Screen.ActiveForm.Visible = False
        DoCmd.OpenForm strFormName
    End Function
    ```

2. Open the frmSwitchboard form in Design view. Click in the Customers button's OnClick property and replace the [Event Procedure] with the event function proce-dure with a literal argument by typing **=OpenAForm("Customers")**.

3. Set the form's HasModule property to No. Click Yes in the verification dialog. Save the form and switch to Form view.

4. Click the button. VBA runs the event function procedure to hide the frmSwitch-board form and open the Customers form. You'll copy and paste the button to open another form (see Figure 8.1a).

5. Open the frmSwitchboard form in Design view. Copy and paste the button. Select the pasted button, change the Name property to cmdEmployees, and change the Caption property to Employees. Click in the OnClick property and change the argument of the event function to "Employees" (see Figure 8.1b).

6. Save the form, switch to Form view, and click the Employees button. Access runs the event function procedure (Figure 8.1c shows the procedure in the Module window).

FIGURE 8.1:

The command buttons on the form (a) run the same event function procedure. Assign the function as an expression in the event property setting (b). Clicking the command button passes the name of the form you want to open to the function (c).

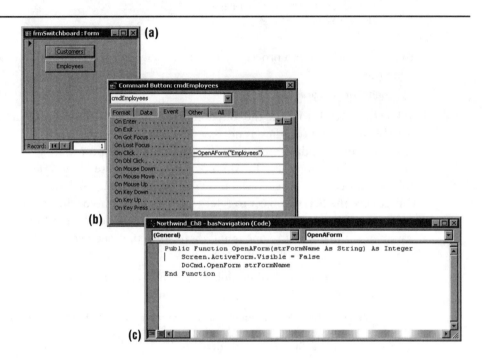

As a final step, the OpenAForm function procedure would be even more reusable if you used the form name as the command button's caption. In this case, the procedure determines the Caption property of the command button and you don't need to pass the form name as an argument. The modified function is as follows:

```
Public Function OpenAForm() As Integer
    Dim strFormName As String
    strFormName = Screen.ActiveControl.Caption
    Screen.ActiveForm.Visible = False
    DoCmd.OpenForm strFormName
End Sub
```

The OnClick property is =OpenAForm().

TIP   An advantage of using an event function procedure is that when the object is copied and pasted, assignments to event function procedures are pasted too (and assignments to event sub procedures are discarded).

Using Variables for Faster Code

Suppose you have a form that you want to use both for review and for data entry. In the typical data-entry mode, the data controls are enabled and unlocked, and they have the standard white background. For review mode, you disable and lock each data control to prevent inadvertent changes to the data, and you change its background color to match the form's background color as a visual cue that the data can't be changed. We'll look at a procedure to change the properties of one control.

1. Create a new form named frmDots. Place a command button with the Name property cmdChange, the Caption property Change, and a text box control named txtChange on the form. Make sure the command button is first in the tab order so that it has the focus when the form opens. The command button should have a Tab Index property of 0 and the text box should have a Tab Index of 1. In the next step, we create a procedure that disables the txtChange text box, and because you can't disable a control that has the focus, the txtChange control cannot have the focus when the procedure runs.

2. In the basNavigation standard module, insert the Change procedure shown below. The Change procedure changes the properties of the txtChange text box:

```
Public Function Change()
    Forms!frmDots!txtChange.Enabled = False
    Forms!frmDots!txtChange.Locked = True
    Forms!frmDots!txtChange.BackColor = 12632256
End Function
```

3. Click in the OnClick property of the command button and type **=Change()**. Save the form and switch to Form view (see Figure 8.2).

4. Click the Change button. The properties of the text box control change.

Let's improve the procedure.

FIGURE 8.2:

Click the Change button in Form view.

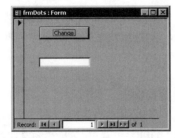

Eliminating Points and Dots

As explained previously, each exclamation point and dot represents execution time spent processing the reference. The Change procedure has nine points and dots. Each point or dot that you eliminate results in faster code. For a single procedure, the number of points and dots may not matter much, but think of the number of points and dots there can be in a fully automated application. So, the name of the game is to count and minimize the dots. How do you get rid of points and dots? With variables!

In the Change procedure, the object referred to is a text box control, so you create a new object variable to represent the text box. To create a variable in a procedure, you can use a statement with this syntax:

```
Dim variablename [As type]
```

This statement is called a *variable declaration statement* and causes Access to set aside a memory location and assign it the name *variablename*. The amount of memory set aside is determined by the As *type* part of the statement; this part is optional and Access will assign the memory-hungry Variant data type unless you specify another data type. In our case, the object is a text box control, so we use the TextBox object data type:

```
Dim ctl As TextBox
```

This statement creates ctl as an object variable of the TextBox type. The memory location is set aside but contains nothing (the Nothing value, that is) until you assign an object with an assignment statement:

```
Set ctl = Screen.ActiveForm.txtChange
```

Here, we use the Screen object to refer to the active form and eliminate the reference to a specific form. We can now replace the hierarchical reference to the control with the variable. The Change procedure is now as follows:

```
Public Function Change()
    Dim ctl As TextBox
    Set ctl = Screen.ActiveForm.txtChange
    ctl.Enabled = False
    ctl.Locked = True
    ctl.BackColor = 12632256
End Sub
```

Count the points and dots—now there are only five! The procedure should run much faster than when there were nine.

Creating a Custom Constant

A final adjustment to the procedure is to deal with the number that Access uses for the color gray, by creating a custom constant. By defining a custom constant, you can avoid needing to type the number ever again. You can create a custom constant in a procedure using the following *constant declaration statement*:

```
Const constantname [As type] = value
```

Like a variable declaration statement, a constant declaration statement sets aside a memory location and names it with the specified name; you use the As *type* part of the statement to specify the constant's data type so that Access knows how much memory to allocate for the constant. A difference between a variable and a constant declaration statement is that you actually use the constant declaration statement to assign the unchanging value.

In our example, the number is an integer but exceeds the limits of the Integer data type, so we declare it as Long, as follows:

```
Const Gray As Long = 12632256
```

The improved procedure is shown below (and in Figure 8.3). In Chapter 9, "Controlling Execution," you'll learn about an additional technique (With…End With) for improving the performance of this procedure.

```
Public Function Change()
    Dim ctl As TextBox
    Const Gray As Long = 12632256

    Set ctl = Screen.ActiveForm.txtChange
    ctl.Enabled = False
    ctl.Locked = True
    ctl.BackColor = Gray
End Function
```

```
Northwind_Ch8 - basNavigation (Code)
(General)                              Change
      Public Function Change()
          Dim ctl As TextBox
          Const Gray As Long = 12632256

          Set ctl = Screen.Active.Form.txtChange
          ctl.Enabled = False
          ctl.Locked = True
          ctl.BackColor = Gray
      End Function
```

How Procedures Use Variables

The two examples of the last section demonstrate some of the ways procedures use variables and constants. A procedure can use variables and constants in these ways:

- It can create variables and constants for its own use. Variables and constants that are created within a procedure are available only to the procedure in which they are created and are not available to any other procedures, even to other procedures in the same module. Variables and constants created within a procedure are called *local* or *procedure-level*.

- It can use variables as arguments. A procedure may require additional information as arguments to specify how the procedure is to be carried out. The additional information in the form of variable arguments can be given to, or *passed to*, the procedure when you call the procedure.

- It can use variables and constants created elsewhere. You can create public variables and constants in the Declarations section of a module and make them available to some or all of the procedures in the database. Variables and constants created in the Declarations section of a module are called *module-level*.

- It can execute statements that can change the values of the variables that the procedure has access to.

- It can return a variable. A function procedure may return a variable.

The next sections describe the different ways to create and destroy variables and how to pass variables from one procedure to another.

Declaring Variables

You can create both constants and variables just by using them in statements. The first time you use the name of a constant or variable, VBA automatically creates a temporary storage location in memory with the name you selected; this is called *implicit declaration*. One problem with implicit declaration is that VBA doesn't recognize your typographical errors and simply creates a new variable if you misspell a name without associating the two names. You avoid this unnecessary error source by adding an `Option Explicit` statement in the Declarations section of every module to require that all variables and constants be explicitly created in declaration statements. Typical declaration statements are the two statements placed at the beginning of the `Change` procedure shown earlier:

```
Dim ctl As TextBox
Const Gray As Long = 12632256
```

NOTE   This chapter assumes that all variables and constants are explicitly declared and that the `Option Explicit` statement is used in the Declarations section of every module. You can have VBA enter the `Option Explicit` statement automatically by checking the Require Variable Declaration check box in the Editor tab of the Visual Basic Editor's Options dialog, available by choosing Tools ➢ Options in the Visual Basic Editor (the option is deselected by default).

You can create a variable in only two places:

- Place a declaration statement within a procedure or in the procedure's argument list to create a *local* or *procedure-level variable*.

- Place a declaration statement in the Declarations section of a module to create a *module-level variable*.

Figure 8.4 shows a procedure-level variable and a module-level variable.

When you create a constant or variable, you specify the following four characteristics:

- The name

- The data type of the constant or regular variable, or the object data type of an object variable

- The *lifetime* of the variable (the lifetime is the execution time between the creation of the constant or variable and when it ceases to exist)

- The *scope* of the constant or variable (the scope defines which procedures can "see" and use the constant or variable—private or public)

FIGURE 8.4:

A procedure-level variable, str, and a module-level variable, strName

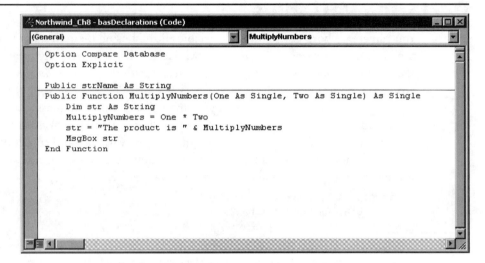

```
Northwind_Ch8 - basDeclarations (Code)
(General)                                    MultiplyNumbers
    Option Compare Database
    Option Explicit

    Public strName As String
    Public Function MultiplyNumbers(One As Single, Two As Single) As Single
        Dim str As String
        MultiplyNumbers = One * Two
        str = "The product is " & MultiplyNumbers
        MsgBox str
    End Function
```

Naming Constants and Variables

You use declaration statements to specify the constant's or variable's name. VBA names are not case sensitive, meaning that VBA does not distinguish between frmcustomers and frm-Customers. However, after you explicitly create a variable, VBA automatically changes subsequent occurrences of the name to match the uppercase and lowercase letters that you specify in the declaration statement.

Names of constants and variables must begin with a letter; contain only letters, numbers, and the underscore character (_); contain no keywords; and contain no more than 255 characters. Chapter 2, "Getting Started with Objects and Events," discusses adopting a naming convention to help make your VBA code more readable and easier to understand.

Specifying a Data Type

You can use the As *type* phrase in the declaration statement to specify the data type for variables. While declaring the data type is optional, if you don't specify a data type, VBA assigns the Variant data type. As Table 7.1 (in Chapter 7, "Writing Procedures") indicates, the Variant data type uses more than twice the memory of any other fundamental data type. Because memory is always limited, the more memory that is tied up in variable storage, the less is available for Access and other applications you are running. With less memory, Access runs slower, so you should avoid using the Variant data type on the basis of memory management alone. However, there are additional performance reasons for avoiding the Variant data type:

- Each time a procedure assigns a value to a variable with the Variant data type, VBA must take execution time to determine what kind of data the value has and then change the data type of the variable to match the data; this process is called *coercing* the variant variable.

- When you use a coerced variant variable in a calculation, VBA may need to take additional execution time to convert the data type to do the calculation. If VBA can't convert the data type, a run-time error is generated.

- To avoid run-time errors, you often need to include statements to check the variable's data type. For example, if you are doing a numeric calculation, you can avoid errors by using the IsNumeric function to determine whether a variable has a numeric data type before doing the calculation. Executing code to check the data type takes additional execution time. If you use a specific data type instead, VBA can check the data-type compatibility for you when you compile your code.

Unless there is a specific reason to use the Variant data type, you should type variables explicitly. For regular variables, this means choosing the data type with the smallest memory requirement from the list of fundamental data types listed in Table 7.1.

Similarly, for object variables, you should avoid using the generic Object data type. Using the Object data type for an object variable is like using the Variant data type for a regular variable, because each time a procedure assigns an object, VBA must take execution time to determine what kind of object has been assigned, and each time the procedure refers to a property or method, VBA must take execution time to determine if the property or method is valid for the object. If you use a specific object data type instead, VBA can check the property and method validity when you compile the code. For an object variable, using a specific object data type is called *hard typing*.

NOTE   For the most efficient memory management and the fastest code, use the most specific data type for regular variables and the most specific object type for object variables.

Understanding the Life Cycle of a Variable

When VBA reads the declaration statement for a variable, such as

```
Dim intX As Integer
Dim txt As TextBox
```

it creates and names the temporary memory location, allocates the amount of storage specified by the data type you specify, and sets the variable to a default value depending on that data type. A variable with any numeric data type is set to zero, a variable with the string data type is set to the zero-length string (" "), a variable with the Variant data type is set to the special Empty value, and an object variable is set to the special Nothing value. The declaration statements shown at the beginning of this section set the variable intX to zero and the object variable txt to Nothing. What happens next depends on whether the variable is a regular variable or an object variable.

The Life Cycle of a Regular Variable

After a regular variable is created, you can manipulate the variable in statements. You start by using an assignment statement to assign a value to the variable name, such as intX = 1. After the variable is assigned, you use the variable name in other statements to change the value, such as the statement intX = intX + 1, which increases the value of intX by one and assigns the result to intX.

You can also use an assignment statement to reinitialize a variable by setting the variable to its default value. For regular variables with a specific data type, initializing the variable simply means setting its value to either zero or the zero-length string. For example, the statement intX = 0 reinitializes the intX variable.

Finally, the variable itself is destroyed. Destroying a variable means destroying its temporary memory location and releasing the memory for reuse. How do you destroy a variable? Let's postpone the answer for a moment.

The Life Cycle of an Object Variable

For an object variable, the story is more complicated because there are two items to keep track of: the object variable and the object itself. After an object variable is declared, you use an assignment statement to point the object variable to an object, such as this:

```
Set txt = Forms!frmDots!txtChange
```

The object that the variable points to may already exist in memory, or the assignment statement may actually create the object in memory. For example, when you open a form interactively, such as when you open frmDots from the Database window, Access creates the Form object in memory. When you declare an object variable, such as Dim frm As Form, and point frm to the form with the assignment statement Set frm = Forms!frmDots, you are pointing the object variable to an object that already exists in memory.

Because there is both an object variable and an object, there are two memory requirements: the memory consumed by the object variable and the memory taken by the object. As Table 7.1 (in Chapter 7) indicates, an object variable takes 4 bytes no matter what it is pointing to (the 4 bytes simply store an address, which is usually a long integer), but the object being pointed to may take up hundreds or thousands of bytes of memory.

After the object variable is assigned, you use the object variable in other statements to change the object. When you change an object variable in a VBA statement, you are actually changing the object. For example, in the Change procedure, the three statements that change the properties of the txt object variable actually change the properties of the txtChange text box that sits on the form.

You can also use an assignment statement to reinitialize an object variable by setting the object variable to its default value. When you set an object variable to Nothing, you are destroying the link between the object variable and the object itself. After you destroy the link, the object variable still exists (and still takes up its 4 bytes of memory), while the object may or may not continue to exist. For example, if frm is the object variable that was pointing to the frmDots form and you set frm = Nothing, the Form object continues to exist in memory as long as the form is open; setting frm to Nothing only severs the link between the object variable and the object. By contrast, if rst is the only object variable pointing to a Recordset object, then setting rst to Nothing severs the link and destroys the object. In this case, the object is destroyed because for an object to remain in existence in memory, it must either be assigned to an object variable or have an implicit reference created by Access.

When you open a form, Access automatically creates an implicit reference to the Form object that continues as long as the form is open. Your code cannot affect the implicit reference to the form as long as the form is open. By contrast, when you open a recordset, there is no implicit reference to the Recordset object. As long as your code has at least one object variable pointing to a Recordset object, the Recordset object continues to exist in memory. When all references to the Recordset object are severed, either by setting object variables to Nothing or by destroying the object variables, the Recordset object itself is destroyed and its memory is released for other purposes.

You can destroy objects in memory by closing them. For example, you can close a form in a procedure using the Close method of the DoCmd object, and you can close a recordset using its own Close method. When you use one of the Close methods on an object, the object variable that pointed to the object is in a state of limbo: the object it pointed to may no longer exist, but the variable itself still exists and can be assigned to another object.

Destroying Variables

Because of the memory that variables take up, you'll want to destroy them as soon as you are finished with them. But, the question we haven't answered yet is how do you destroy a variable? Interestingly, Access does not provide a "destroy" statement, so there is no way you can explicitly destroy a variable. Instead, Access provides two alternatives:

- You can declare a variable within a procedure as a local or procedure-level variable. Access will destroy it automatically, by default, when the procedure finishes.

- You can declare a variable in the Declarations section of a module as a module-level variable. Access will destroy it when you close the database but not before.

We'll see in the next section that there are valid reasons for using module-level variables. However, the general rule is obvious: Because of the memory that variables consume, use local or procedure-level variables instead of module-level variables whenever you can.

TIP   For an "at-a-glance" summary of the declaration statements for procedures and variables and the data typing of variables and function procedure return values, see the "Summary of Declarations" table on the CD under Tables\Chapter8.pdf.

Using Procedure-Level Variables

There are two ways to declare a variable in a procedure: in a separate declaration statement within the procedure and in the argument list of a procedure called by another procedure.

Declaring a Variable within the Procedure

A procedure-level variable can be created by placing a declaration statement within a procedure. The basic syntax is as follows:

```
Dim variablename [As type]
```

Here are a few examples:

```
Dim intCounter As Integer
Dim strLastName As String
Dim frmCustomers As Form
```

You can declare several variables with a single declaration statement, but you need to include the data type for each variable separately. This statement declares frm1 and frm2 as the Form object type:

```
Dim frm1 As Form, frm2 As Form
```

But this statement declares frm2 as the Form object type and frm1 as a Variant:

```
Dim frm1, frm2 As Form
```

The declaration statement creates and names the variable, allocates the memory as specified in the As *type* phrase, and initializes the variable. The declaration statement does not assign a value; you need a separate assignment statement to assign the value. For example, consider the following procedure:

```
Public Sub SomeProcedure()
    Dim cnn As ADODB.Connection
    Set cnn = CurrentProject.Connection
    ...
End Sub
```

This declaration statement creates cnn as an object variable of the ADO Connection object type:

```
Dim cnn As ADODB.Connection
```

The assignment statement points the object variable to the current connection:

```
Set cnn = CurrentProject.Connection
```

NOTE There is another version of the declaration statement that you can use for an object variable. You can use the **New** keyword in declaring an object variable, using the syntax Dim *objvar* As New *objecttype*. When you include the **New** keyword, VBA creates a new instance of the object automatically and for some object types you don't need to use the **Set** statement to assign the object variable. See Chapter 14, "Creating and Modifying Database Objects Using Access VBA," for more information about the **New** keyword.

Declaring a Variable in the Argument List

When you place an argument in a procedure's argument list, you are also creating a procedure-level variable. You can use an As *type* phrase to specify each argument variable's type, as follows:

```
argumentname As type
```

Here is an example:

```
Public Function Concatenate (A As String, B As String)
```

When you declare a variable in an argument list, VBA automatically allocates the memory specified in the variable's type phrase and initializes the variable. However, you don't need a separate assignment statement because VBA automatically assigns a value to the variable in an argument list when you call the procedure. For example, when VBA executes the following statement,

```
MsgBox Concatenate ("Johnson", "Diane")
```

VBA goes to the Concatenate function and automatically assigns the value "Johnson" to the variable A and "Diane" to the variable B.

```
Public Sub CallingProcedure()
    MsgBox Concatenate ("Johnson","Diane")
End Sub

Public Function Concatenate(LName As String, FName As String)
    Concatenate = LName & ", " & FName
End Sub
```

Understanding the Visibility of Procedure-Level Variables

A procedure-level variable created either in a declaration statement or in the argument list is visible only to the procedure in which it is created. Other procedures cannot see or use the variable. The only way another procedure can get access to a procedure-level variable is for the procedure that created the variable to call the other procedure and pass it the variable as an argument. A variable passed as an argument to a called procedure can, in turn, be passed if the called procedure calls yet another procedure. The subsequent chain of called procedures is referred to as the procedure's *call tree*.

Let's look at an example to clarify these ideas:

1. Create a new module named basVariables. Insert a new public sub procedure named LocalVariable as shown below. The LocalVariable procedure declares strLocal as a local or procedure-level string variable.

```
Public Sub LocalVariable()
    Dim strLocal As String
    strLocal = "'Local variable in LocalVariable procedure'"
    MsgBox strLocal
End Sub
```

2. Run the procedure in the Immediate window by typing **Call LocalVariable** and pressing Enter. The only procedures that can use the strLocal variable are the LocalVariable procedure and the procedures that the LocalVariable procedure passes the variable to as an argument.

3. Create the GetLocal procedure below in either the same module (or another module) and run it in the Immediate window.

```
Public Sub GetLocal()
    MsgBox strLocal
End Sub
```

The procedure fails because the GetLocal procedure can't see the strLocal variable in the LocalVariable procedure. As far as the GetLocal procedure is concerned, the strLocal variable has not been defined.

4. Click the Reset button in the toolbar. Insert a Call GetLocal statement after the MsgBox statement in the LocalVariable procedure and then run the LocalVariable procedure in the Immediate window.

The LocalVariable procedure runs, prints the value of strLocal, then fails with a "Variable not defined" error. The procedure fails whether you call it independently or from LocalVariable because the GetLocal procedure cannot see the strLocal variable. Just calling a procedure from a procedure that has a local variable does not make the local variable available to the called procedure. If you want the called procedure to use the variable, you must pass the variable as an argument to the called procedure.

5. Modify both procedures as shown below. With these changes, the LocalVariable procedure calls GetLocal and passes strLocal as an argument, and the GetLocal procedure receives the variable as an argument.

```
Public Sub LocalVariable()
    Dim strLocal As String
    strLocal = "'Local variable in LocalVariable procedure'"
    MsgBox strLocal
    Call GetLocal(strLocal)
End Sub

Public Sub GetLocal(strA As String)
    MsgBox strA & " passed as an argument to GetLocal"
End Sub
```

6. In the Immediate window, type **Call LocalVariable** and press Enter. The LocalVariable procedure defines and displays the local variable in a message box (see Figure 8.5a) and then calls the GetLocal procedure, passing the strLocal variable to it as an argument. The GetLocal procedure can use the passed variable and displays it in a message box (see Figure 8.5b).

FIGURE 8.5:
The procedure displays its local variable (a) and then passes the local variable to another procedure, which displays the passed variable (b).

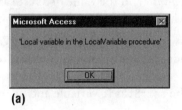

(a)

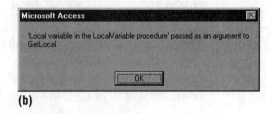

(b)

NOTE   It is good programming practice to place declaration statements for all procedure-level variables at the beginning of the procedure.

Changing the Lifetime of Procedure-Level Variables

After you declare a procedure-level variable and assign it a value in a procedure, other statements may change its value. The variable retains the new value until the value is changed again or until the procedure terminates.

By default, procedure-level variables cease to exist when the procedure ends; Access discards their values and releases their storage locations in memory for reuse. However, you can extend the lifetime of a procedure-level variable beyond the life of the procedure by using the Static keyword instead of the Dim keyword when you create the variable. Using the Static keyword extends the lifetime of a procedure's variable to the entire time VBA code is running in any module. When you create a static variable, VBA preserves its value when the procedure ends and sets the variable to the preserved value the next time the procedure runs.

As an example, we'll create a procedure that uses a static variable. Insert the StaticVariable procedure below in the basVariables module.

```
Public Sub StaticVariable()
    Dim strNonStatic As String
    Static sstrStatic As String
    strNonStatic = strNonStatic & " nonstatic"
    sstrStatic = sstrStatic & " static"
    Debug.Print strNonStatic
    Debug.Print sstrStatic
End Sub
```

The StaticVariable procedure creates the strNonStatic variable as a nonstatic variable and sstrStatic as a static variable. It initializes both variables to the zero-length string. (You use the s prefix to indicate a static variable.) The assignment statements concatenate the value of strNonStatic with the word *nonstatic* and the value of sstrStatic with the word *static*. The concatenated values are then printed in the Immediate window.

Run the procedure in the Immediate window by typing **Call StaticVariable** and pressing Enter. The first time you run the procedure, both variables are initialized to the zero-length string, so Debug prints a single word on each line. When the procedure ends, Access destroys the strNonStatic variable but retains the sstrStatic variable and its value.

Now run the procedure a second time. The second time you run the procedure, the strNonStatic variable is recreated and reinitialized to the zero-length string, but the sstrStatic variable still has its retained value. The assignment statement for strNonStatic produces the word *nonstatic* as before, but the assignment statement for sstrStatic appends the word *static* to the current string. Each time you run the procedure, the nonstatic variable is reinitialized and the assignment statement sets the variable to the word *nonstatic*, but the value of the static variable is retained, and the assignment statement appends the word *static* to the current value. Figure 8.6a shows the Immediate window after running the procedure three times.

You can make all of the local variables in a procedure static by placing the Static keyword in the procedure's declaration statement. Try this example:

1. Select all the statements of the StaticVariable procedure and press Ctrl+C to make a copy. Place the insertion point after the last procedure in the module and press Ctrl+V to paste. (Make sure you are in Full Module view by selecting Default To Full Module View in the Tools ➢ Options dialog.) Change the procedure's declaration statement by inserting the Static keyword and changing the procedure's name as shown below:

```
Public Static Sub StaticProcedure()
    Dim strNonStatic As String
    Static sstrStatic As String
    strNonStatic = strNonStatic & " nonstatic"
    sstrStatic = sstrStatic & " static"
    Debug.Print strNonStatic
    Debug.Print sstrStatic
End Sub
```

2. Click in the Immediate window, choose Edit ➢ Select All, and press Delete.

3. Run the StaticProcedure procedure in the Immediate window three times. Observe that both variables are now static. Using the Static keyword in the procedure definition overrides the declaration using the Dim keyword inside the procedure (see Figure 8.6b).

FIGURE 8.6:

A static variable retains its value between calls to the procedure, and a nonstatic variable is reinitialized each time you call the procedure (a). Using the Static keyword in the procedure's declaration allocates storage space for all of the local variables and preserves their values the entire time the module runs, until you restart or reset the module (b).

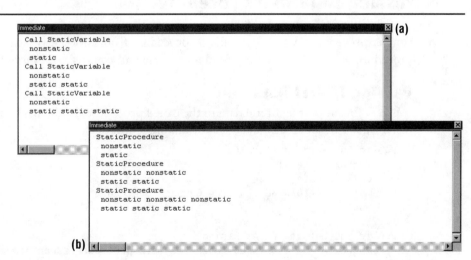

4. Click in the basVariables module and click the Reset button in the toolbar. When you reset the module, you discard all variables declared in the module and release their storage space.

When you insert a new procedure, you can make all of the local variables static by selecting Insert ➤ Procedure and checking the All Local Variables As Statics option in the Add Procedure dialog (see Figure 8.7). With this option checked, VBA inserts the `Static` keyword in the procedure declaration for you.

FIGURE 8.7:

Select the All Local Variables As Statics option in the Add Procedure dialog to preserve the values of all local variables declared in the procedure.

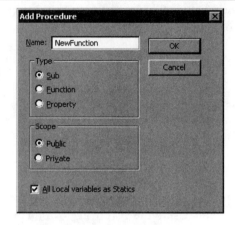

Passing Data to a Procedure

The ability to call one procedure from another allows you to separate your code into smaller, simpler procedures. When you call one procedure from another, you can send data to the procedure being called. You can send literal data and you can send variables.

Passing Literal Data

We look first at passing literal data to the called procedure. In the basVariables module, insert the `PassingLiteral` and `GetData` sub procedures:

```
Public Sub PassingLiteral()
    MsgBox "Literal"
    Call GetData("'Literal'")
    MsgBox "Returning from the GetData procedure"
End Sub

Public Sub GetData (A As String)
    MsgBox A & " is passed to the GetData procedure as an argument."
End Sub
```

The statement `Call GetData("'Literal'")` in the `PassingLiteral` procedure calls the `GetData` procedure and passes the literal value `"Literal"`.

Run the PassingLiteral procedure in the Immediate window. The PassingLiteral procedure displays its message (see Figure 8.8a) and then calls the GetData procedure, passing it the literal value. VBA replaces the letter *A* everywhere it appears in the called procedure with the value passed in. The GetData procedure displays its message (see Figure 8.8b) and quits. VBA returns to the PassingLiteral procedure at the next statement, displays the message (see Figure 8.8c), and quits.

FIGURE 8.8:

The calling procedure displays the literal (a) and passes the literal to the called procedure (b). After the called procedure ends, control returns to the calling procedure (c).

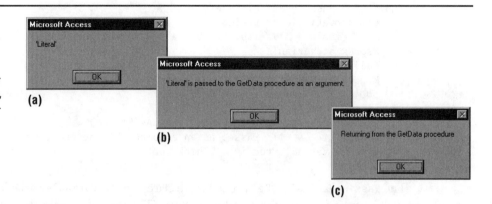

Passing a Variable by Reference or by Value

Access provides two ways of sending variable data: You can send the variable itself, or you can send a copy of the variable's value.

When you send the variable itself, the called procedure can manipulate the variable and change its value. Sending the variable itself is called *passing the variable by reference* and is the default method of sending a variable.

When you send a copy of the variable's value, VBA creates a copy in another temporary storage location in memory and sends the copy. The called procedure can use the copy and may even change its value, but because the called procedure is working with a copy, the variable itself is not affected. Sending a copy of the variable is called *passing the variable by value*.

To specify which method you are using, you precede the argument name, in the argument list of the procedure being called, with either the keyword ByRef to pass the variable itself or ByVal to pass a copy, as follows:

```
[ByRef|ByVal] argumentname [As type]
```

To explore, we'll create a pair of procedures that pass a variable first by reference and then by value. In the basVariables module, create the PassingVariableByRef and GetVariableByRef procedures, as shown below.

```
Public Sub PassingVariableByRef()
    Dim strVariable As String
    strVariable = "'Variable to be passed to another procedure'"
    MsgBox strVariable
    Call GetVariableByRef(strVariable)
    MsgBox strVariable
End Sub

Public Sub GetVariableByRef (ByRef strA As String)
    MsgBox strA & " is passed as an argument of the procedure."
    strA = "Variable received. Thank you"
End Sub
```

The PassingVariableByRef procedure declares the strVariable variable and assigns and then displays the string value (see Figure 8.9a). The procedure calls the GetVariableByRef procedure, passing it the variable. The GetVariableByRef procedure receives the variable itself, displays the variable (see Figure 8.9b), and changes its value. When the GetVariableByRef procedure ends, VBA returns to the next statement of the calling procedure, displays the changed variable (see Figure 8.9c), and ends.

FIGURE 8.9:

When you pass a variable (a) by reference, the called procedure receives the variable itself (b) and can change its value. The calling procedure uses the changed value (c).

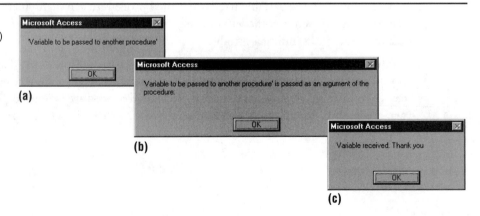

Follow these steps to see how the passed variables work:

1. Run the `PassingVariablesByRef` procedure in the Immediate window.

2. In the Module window, copy all of the code for both procedures to the Clipboard. Place the insertion point below the last procedure and paste the contents of the Clipboard.

3. Select the pasted procedures and choose Edit ➤ Replace. Type **ByRef** in the Find What text box and **ByVal** in the Replace With text box. Make sure the Selected Text option is selected in the Search option group, and click Replace All (see Figure 8.10). Click OK to confirm the four replacements. Select the pasted procedures again. Type **passed** in the Find What text box and **passed by value** in the Replace With text box and click Replace All. Click OK to confirm the two replacements and close the Replace dialog.

FIGURE 8.10:

Using the Replace dialog to modify procedures by replacing values

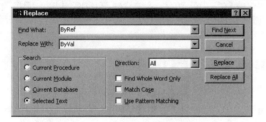

4. Run the `PassingVariableByVal` procedure in the Immediate window.

This time, only a copy of the variable's value is passed to the called procedure. The calling procedure displays the variable (see Figure 8.11a). The called procedure receives a copy of the variable and displays its message (see Figure 8.11b) and then changes the value as before, but only the copy is changed. After finishing the called procedure, VBA returns to the calling procedure and displays the last message box with the value of the unaltered variable (see Figure 8.11c).

FIGURE 8.11:

When you pass a variable by value (a), the called procedure uses a copy of the variable (b). Although the called procedure may change the value of the copy, the original variable retains its value (c).

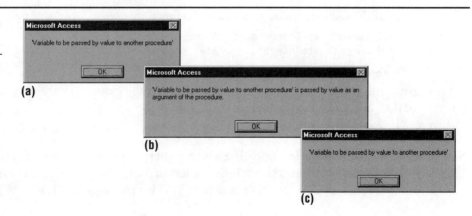

Although the terms are different, the two methods are analogous to the familiar methods of linking and embedding a document. When you pass an argument ByRef, you are "linking" the procedure to the variable so that changes made in the procedure are made to the variable. When you pass an argument ByVal, you are "embedding" a copy of the variable and there is no link to the variable itself, so changes made in the procedure are not made to the variable. Sending a variable by reference is faster because VBA doesn't need to take the time to create a copy of the variable.

NOTE   Passing variables by reference blurs the distinction between a function procedure and a sub procedure. When you pass variables by reference, the function or sub procedure that receives the variables as arguments can change their values or the objects they refer to and then return the changed variables. This means that both function procedures and sub procedures can return values through the arguments that are passed by reference. Only a function procedure has the ability to return an additional value separate from the values returned by its arguments.

Passing Arguments to a Procedure

There are two ways to pass arguments to a procedure: by order and by name.

When you pass arguments by order, you list the values of the arguments in the order specified in the procedure's syntax. If you omit an optional argument, you must include a comma as a placeholder for a missing argument in the argument list.

When you pass arguments by name, you specify the name of the argument followed by the colon-equal (:=) assignment operator, followed by the value for the argument. You can list named arguments in any order, and you can omit optional arguments.

As an example, the Concatenate procedure's declaration specifies its arguments as follows:

```
Public Function Concatenate(A,B)
```

Each of the following statements calls the function:

```
Call Concatenate("Johnson", "Diane")
Call Concatenate(B:="Diane", A:="Johnson")
```

We created the Concatenate function in the previous chapter, so it is stored in another database. You can make the function available in the current database by setting a reference to the Ch7_Examples database.

1. Choose Tools ➤ References and click the Browse button in the References dialog.

2. In the Add Reference dialog, choose Microsoft Access Databases in the Files Of Type combo list, locate the Ch7_Examples database (see Figure 8.12a), and click OK. The reference to the database is added to the list (see Figure 8.12b).

FIGURE 8.12:

Adding a reference to
another database

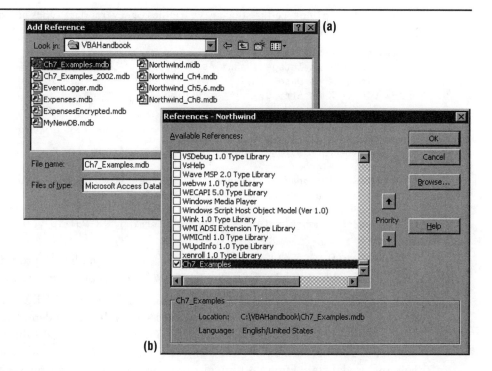

3. In the Immediate window, type each of the following and press Enter.

> **? Concatenate("Johnson", "Diane")**

> **? Concatenate(B:="Diane", A:="Johnson")**

This example shows that when you pass arguments by name, you can list the arguments in any order.

Using Variant Arguments

You can create a procedure that accepts data with more than one data type by using variant arguments. For example, the Multiply function multiplies its arguments and returns the product.

```
Public Function Multiply (X,Y)
    Multiply = X*Y
End Function
```

You can call this function and pass it two values of any data type. If VBA is able to convert the data types to compatible types, the product can be calculated.

The GetMultiply procedure declares variables of several data types and attempts to calculate the product by passing the variables to the Multiply function.

```
Public Sub GetMultiply()
    Dim intX As Integer, sngY As Single
    Dim dtmX As Date
    Dim strX As String, strY As String
    intX = 2
    sngY = 3
    dtmX = #5/11/2001#
    strX = "2"
    strY = "Three"
    MsgBox "Numbers of different data type " & Multiply(intX, sngY)
    MsgBox "Number and date " & Multiply(dtmX, sngY)
    MsgBox "Number and convertible string " & Multiply(strX, sngY)
    MsgBox "Number and non-convertible string " & Multiply(intX, strY)
End Sub
```

Enter the Multiply public function procedure and the public sub procedure GetMultiply in the basVariables module. Then run the GetMultiply procedure in the Immediate window.

When you pass two numbers of different numerical data types, VBA successfully converts the data types (see Figure 8.13a). When you pass a number and a date, VBA converts the date to its numerical equivalent and calculates the product (see Figure 8.13b). When you pass a number as a string, such as "2", VBA converts the string to a numerical data type and calculates the product (see Figure 8.13c). However, when you pass a string, such as "Three", VBA can't convert the data type and displays a "Type mismatch" error message (see Figure 8.13d).

FIGURE 8.13:

The procedure successfully converts numbers of different data types (a), a date (b), and a convertible string (c), but fails when VBA can't convert an unconvertible string to a number (d).

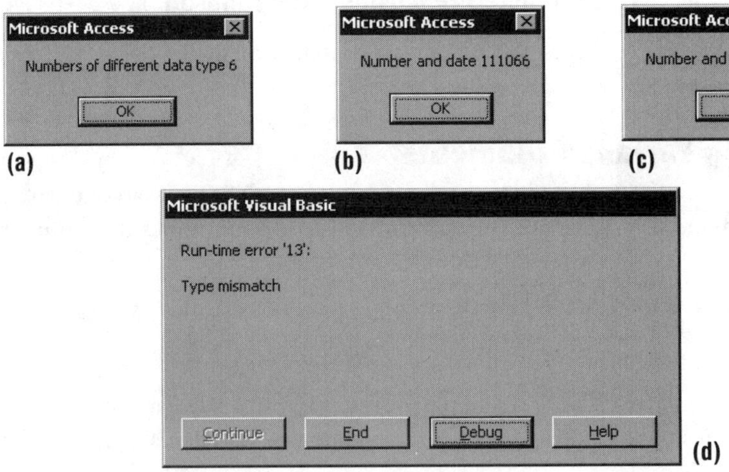

You can avoid run-time errors in procedures that have variant arguments by doing your own data-type checking in the procedure before performing the calculations. You can use the built-in functions shown in Table 8.1 to examine the data. See Chapter 9 for examples of procedures that test data types before doing calculations.

TABLE 8.1: Built-in Functions for Examining Data

Function	Description
IsArray(*varname*)	Returns True if the variable is an array.
IsDate(*expression*)	Returns True if the expression can be converted to a date and False otherwise. The expression can be any date or string expression.
IsEmpty(*expression*)	If the expression is a single variant variable, returns True if the variable has not been assigned a value or has been set to the Empty value and False otherwise.
IsErr(*expression*)	Returns True if a numeric expression has been converted to an error value by the CVErr function, and False if it has not.
IsMissing(*argname*)	Returns True if a function's argument that was to be passed from another function is missing, and False if it is not.
IsNull(*expression*)	Returns True when the expression contains no valid data. The expression can be any numeric or string expression.
IsNumeric(*expression*)	Returns True if the entire expression can be recognized as a number and False otherwise. Returns False if the expression is a date expression. The expression can be any numeric or string expression.
IsObject(*expression*)	Returns True if the expression is a variable of the Variant or Object type and False otherwise.
TypeName(*varname*)	If *varname* is the name of a variable with a fundamental data type, returns a string providing information about the variable.
VarType(*varname*)	If *varname* is the name of a variable with a fundamental data type, returns a value indicating the data type.

Passing Objects as Arguments

You can pass objects as arguments of procedures. As an example, we'll create a function procedure that changes the Caption property of an object. We'll use the Object data type for the argument so that we can pass any type of object that has a Caption property. Then we'll call the function, passing it the object whose caption we want to change.

1. Create a new form named frmCaption. Place a label control on the form, type **Label** as the Caption property, and set the label's Name property to lblCaption.

2. Insert the ChangeCaption function as shown below in the basVariables standard module.

```
Public Function ChangeCaption(objectname As Object)
    objectname.Caption = "My Caption"
End Function
```

3. Place a command button named cmdLabel on the form and set its Caption property to Change Label Caption. Click in the OnClick property and click the Build button at the right of the property box. Enter the code below in the code template:

```
Private Sub cmdLabel_Click()
    Call ChangeCaption(lblCaption)
End Sub
```

This procedure calls the ChangeCaption function and passes the label control as an argument using the short syntax to refer to the control. When you click the button, the label's caption changes to My Caption.

4. Place a command button named cmdForm on the form and set its Caption property to Change Form Caption. Click in the form's module and insert the event procedure below (VBA automatically assigns the procedure to the button's OnClick property):

```
Private Sub cmdForm_Click()
    Call ChangeCaption(Forms!frmCaption)
End Sub
```

This procedure calls the ChangeCaption function and passes the form as an argument using the exclamation point syntax to refer to the form by name. When you click the button, the form's caption changes to My Caption.

5. Save the form and switch to Form view. Click the Change Label Caption button (see Figure 8.14a). Click the Change Form Caption button (see Figure 8.14b).

FIGURE 8.14:

Passing a label control (a) and the Form object (b) as arguments to a procedure

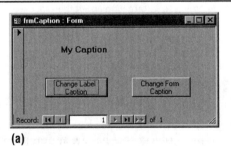
(a)

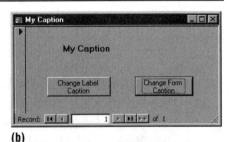
(b)

Passing the Form as an Argument

When you are running a procedure stored in a form's module and you want to call another procedure and pass a reference to the form, you can use the Me property to refer to the form. (When a procedure is running in a form's module, the Me property refers to the form.) For example, click in the frmCaption form and switch to Design view. Click in the form's module and change the `cmdForm_Click()` event procedure as shown below:

```
Private Sub cmdForm_Click()
    Call ChangeCaption(Me)
End Sub
```

Save the form, switch to Form view, and click the Change Form Caption button. The form's caption changes as before.

You can also use the Form property to refer to the form. For example, change the `cmdForm_Click` event procedure as shown below and test the button.

```
Private Sub cmdForm_Click()
    Call ChangeCaption(Form)
End Sub
```

Using the Form property to pass the form as an argument is useful when you are using an event function procedure. For example, you can call the `ChangeCaption` function to change the form's caption when the form opens. To see how this works, switch to Design view and enter **=ChangeCaption (Form)** in the form's OnOpen event property. Save the form and switch to Form view. The function procedure runs and changes the form's caption.

You can't use the Me property to refer to the form in an event property setting. Entering the expression =ChangeCaption(`Me`) in the form's OnOpen event property causes the form to be unable to open in Form view. The form reverts to Design view.

Using an Indefinite Number of Arguments

By default, the arguments in a procedure's argument list are required. A run-time error occurs if you fail to send values for all of the arguments. Sometimes, it is convenient to create a procedure with an indefinite number of arguments. There are three ways to provide this flexibility:

- Specify that arguments are optional.
- Use arguments with user-defined data types.
- Use array arguments.

This section shows you how to specify optional arguments. See the sections "Using Arrays" and "Creating Your Own Data Types" later in this chapter for information about those methods for creating procedures with an indefinite number of arguments.

You can specify that some of the arguments in the argument list are optional by preceding the optional arguments with the `Optional` keyword. Optional arguments can have any data type. The optional arguments must be at the end of the argument list. Once you specify that an argument is optional, all subsequent arguments in the list must be specified as optional also.

To illustrate these concepts, suppose you want to create a function that calculates the product of two or three numbers. The Product function procedure below multiplies three numbers when three variables are passed, but fails when the optional argument is not sent. In the basVariables module, insert the Product procedure.

```
Public Function Product (X, Y, Optional Z)
    Product = X*Y
    Product = Product*Z
End Function
```

In the Immediate window, type **?Product(2,3,4)** and press Enter. Then type **?Product(2,3)** and press Enter. The first product is calculated, but the second entry causes an error.

When the code in a procedure would cause a run-time error if the argument is not passed, you can use the IsMissing function to determine whether an optional argument has been passed. The IsMissing(*argname*) function returns True if no value has been passed for the *argname* argument and False otherwise. In this example, you can modify the Product function to use the IsMissing function as shown below.

```
Public Function Product (X, Y, Optional Z)
    Product = X*Y
    If IsMissing(Z) Then Exit Function
    Product = Product*Z
End Function
```

The modified procedure determines whether the third argument has been passed to the function. If the third argument has not been passed, the procedure exits without executing the Product = Product*Z statement. See Chapter 9 for information about making decisions in a procedure.

Passing Data to an Event Procedure

Access specifies both the names and arguments of sub event procedures automatically. You can't change the argument list in any way (except as noted below). The purpose of the default argument list for an event is to provide a means of communication between your code and Access. As an example, the event procedure for the NotInList event recognized by a combo box has this syntax:

```
Private Sub controlname_NotInList(NewData As String, Response As Integer)
```

NewData is a (read-only) string that Access uses to pass the text that the user entered into the text box part of the combo box; Access passes the text to the event procedure. *Response* is a constant that you use to specify whether to display or suppress the default message and to add the value in *NewData* to the combo box list; the event procedure passes the constant back to Access.

NOTE The one change you can make to the argument list of an event procedure is that you can use the standard prefixes for VBA variables. For example, you can replace the arguments of the NotInList event procedure with **strNewData** and **intResponse**.

Most of the events do not have associated arguments; for example, the Click, Load, Activate, AfterUpdate, Initialize, and Terminate events have no arguments. An event for which you can cancel the default behavior following the event has an argument named Cancel with an Integer data type; for example, the DblClick, Unload, and BeforeUpdate events each have a Cancel As Integer argument. To cancel the default behavior following the event, you set the Cancel argument to True in an assignment statement in the event procedure. You'll see examples of passing arguments to event procedures in the next chapters.

NOTE For a list of the arguments for the event procedures, see the "Arguments for Event Procedures" table, on the CD under Tables\Chapter8.pdf.

Using Module-Level Variables

You create a module-level variable by placing a declaration statement in the Declarations section of a module using this syntax:

```
[Private|Public] variablename As type
```

The keyword you use in the declaration statement determines the scope of the variable—that is, which procedures can see and use the variable. Just as with procedures, module-level variables can be private or public. Use the Private keyword to create private module-level variables, which can be seen only by procedures within the module; use the Public keyword to create public module-level variables, which can be seen by all procedures in all modules in the database or project. A public module-level variable is also called a *global variable*, and you can use the prefix g to indicate a public module-level variable.

To explore module-level variables, follow these steps:

1. Declare the module-level variables in the Declarations section of the basVariables module as shown below.

   ```
   Private strPrivate As String
   Public gstrPublic As String
   ```

2. Insert the PublicScoping and SamePublic procedures shown below in the basVariables module. The PublicScoping procedure assigns the value 'Public' to the

public module-level variable `gstrPublic` and calls the `SamePublic` procedure stored in the same module and the `OtherPublic` procedure stored in another module.

```
Public Sub PublicScoping()
    gstrPublic = "'Public'"
    Call SamePublic
    Call OtherPublic
End Sub

Public Sub SamePublic()
    MsgBox gstrPublic & " from the same module.", , "SamePublic"
End Sub
```

3. Create a new module named basOther and insert the `OtherPublic` procedure as follows:

```
Public Sub OtherPublic()
    MsgBox gstrPublic & " from another module.", , " OtherPublic"
End Sub
```

4. Type **PublicScoping** in the Immediate window and press Enter.

After assigning a value to the public variable, the `PublicScoping` procedure calls another procedure in the same module, which displays the variable (see Figure 8.15a). It then calls another procedure in another module, which displays the variable (see Figure 8.15b). Both called procedures see the public module-level variable.

FIGURE 8.15:

A public module-level variable can be seen by procedures in the same module (a) and by procedures in any other module in the project (b).

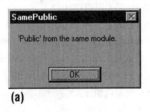
(a)

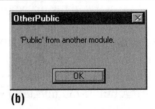
(b)

5. Insert the `PrivateScoping` and `SamePrivate` procedures below in the basVariables module. The `PrivateScoping` procedure assigns the value `'Private'` to the private module-level variable `strPrivate` and calls procedures in the same module and in another module.

```
Public Sub PrivateScoping()
    strPrivate = "'Private'"
    Call SamePrivate
```

```
        Call OtherPrivate
    End Sub

    Public Sub SamePrivate()
        MsgBox strPrivate & " from the same module.", , "SamePrivate"
    End Sub
```

6. Insert the OtherPrivate procedure in the basOther module as follows:

```
    Public Sub OtherPrivate()
        MsgBox strPrivate & " from another module. ", , "OtherPrivate"
    End Sub
```

7. Type **PrivateScoping** in the Immediate window and press Enter.

After assigning a value to the private variable, the PrivateScoping procedure calls another procedure in the same module, which displays the variable (see Figure 8.16a). The Private-Scoping procedure calls another procedure in another module. This time, VBA generates a run-time error (see Figure 8.16b). Because the strPrivate variable is private to the procedures in the basVariables module, it is not visible to the OtherPrivate procedure stored in the basOther module.

FIGURE 8.16:

A private module-level variable can be seen only by procedures in the same module (a) and not by procedures in other modules (b).

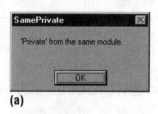

(a)

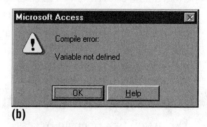

(b)

8. Click the Reset button.

NOTE   To declare a private variable at the module level, you can also use the Dim keyword instead of Private, but using the Private keyword makes your code easier to understand.

Public module-level variables declared in a standard or an independent class module (but not in a form or report module) can also be used in any other databases that reference the database in which the public variables are declared. You can restrict public module-level variables to the current database by including the Option Private Module statement in the Declarations section of the standard or independent class module in which they are declared. Don't be confused by the use of the Private keyword. When used in the Option Private Module statement, the Private keyword means private to the database, but when used in a variable or procedure declaration statement, it means private to the module.

Understanding the Visibility of Module-Level Variables

The visibility (scoping) rules differ between module-level variables created in standard modules and independent class modules and module-level variables created in form and report modules. The basic purpose of a form or report module is to store the constants, variables, and procedures that are needed by the form or report. In keeping with this purpose, the visibility of constants and variables declared in a form or report module is limited. In particular, you cannot create public constants at all, and only some variables can be made public. Here are the specific details for module-level variables in a form or report module:

- You cannot declare a public variable as a fixed-length string.

- You cannot declare a public array.

- Public variables created in form or report modules are available only to other modules in the current database and are not available to other databases.

Procedures that are stored in dynamic link libraries (DLL procedures) and declared in the Declarations section of a module can be public or private. A DLL procedure declared with a `Public Declare` statement can be called by any procedure in any module, and a DLL procedure declared with a `Private Declare` statement can be called only by procedures in the module in which the procedure is defined. For a standard or independent class module, you can declare both public and private DLL procedures (if you don't use either keyword, the DLL procedure is public by default). By contrast, in a form or report module, you can declare only private DLL procedures.

Exploring the Lifetime of Module-Level Variables

When you first open an Access database, Access opens only the modules it needs to get started and then opens modules as the procedures in them are called. For example, if a form has a form module, that module is loaded into memory the first time you open the form. A standard or class module is loaded the first time you call a procedure stored in it. When a module is loaded into memory, VBA allocates storage space for all of the variables and constants declared in the Declarations section.

Once a module is loaded into memory, it is not removed from memory while the application is running. This is true even for form and report modules—closing the form or report does not remove its module from memory. A consequence is that module-level variables (and static procedure-level variables) consume memory and retain their values until you close the database. The obvious performance tip is to use module-level variables only when they are absolutely necessary.

To explore the lifetime of module-level variables, follow these steps:

1. Declare a public module-level variable in the Declarations section of the basVariables module by typing **Public strModule As String**. (The `Public` keyword also makes the variable available in the Immediate window.)

2. Insert the `LifeTimeModule` procedure shown below into the basVariables module:

```
Public Sub LifeTimeModule()
    strModule = "'Module-level variable exists until you close "
        & "the database.'"
    MsgBox strModule, , "LifeTimeModule"
End Sub
```

The `LifeTimeModule` procedure sets the value of the `strModule` variable, displays a message, and ends.

3. Type **LifeTimeModule** in the Immediate window and press Enter. The procedure assigns and displays the value (see Figure 8.17a).

FIGURE 8.17:

The `LifeTimeModule` procedure assigns a value to a public module-level variable (a). The StillThere procedure displays the current value of the variable (b). After resetting the module, the variable is initialized (c).

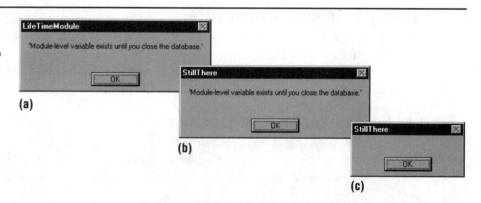

The `strModule` variable retains the value set by this procedure until you change the value or close the database, or until you click the Reset button.

4. Insert the `StillThere` procedure shown below into the basVariables module. The `StillThere` procedure displays the current value of the `strModule` variable.

```
Public Sub StillThere()
    MsgBox strModule, , "StillThere"
End Sub
```

5. Type **StillThere** in the Immediate window and press Enter. The message box displays the current value (see Figure 8.17b).

6. Click the Reset button in the toolbar. VBA clears all public and private variables in the module and releases their storage space.

7. Run the StillThere procedure in the Immediate window. The message box is blank because the variable has been reinitialized to the zero-length string (see Figure 8.17c).

Using Constants

When you find that certain constant values appear over and over again in your code, you can make your code more readable by using *constants*. A constant is a meaningful name that takes the place of a number or string that does not change. Usually, the operating system and the applications you are using supply sets of intrinsic constants, but you can also create your own user-defined constants. Using constants makes your code run faster because VBA writes the value into the compiled version when you compile the code and doesn't need to look up the values during run time.

Using Intrinsic Constants

In Access VBA, you can use system-defined constants, Access intrinsic constants, VBA intrinsic constants, and ADO intrinsic constants. A *system-defined constant* is a constant provided by the operating system. An *intrinsic constant* is a meaningful name provided by an application to replace a number that doesn't change.

Using System-Defined Constants

Access has four system-defined constants that you can use in all database objects except in modules: Yes, No, On, and Off. Access also supplies three additional system-defined constants that you can use in all database objects including modules: True, False, and Null.

Using Access Intrinsic Constants

Access VBA has a set of intrinsic constants that you use to represent the arguments of various Access methods, functions, and properties. These constants have an ac prefix. Examples are acCmdRefresh, acForm, acPrevious, and acPreview. A valuable feature is the grouping of intrinsic constants. When an argument for a method, function, or property requires an intrinsic constant, the set of constants for the argument, called the set of *enumerated constants* for the argument, is given a name. For example, the record argument of the GoToRecord method has a set of intrinsic constants called AcRecord that includes the enumerated constants acFirst, acGoTo, acLast, acNewRec, acNext, and acPrevious.

Using VBA Intrinsic Constants

VBA also has a set of intrinsic constants that you use primarily to specify property settings and arguments of methods in VBA code. These constants have a vb prefix. Examples are vbAbort, vbRetry, and vbCancel, which you can use to specify the arguments for the MsgBox function. VBA groups intrinsic constants into categories including ColorConstants, Constants, KeyCodeConstants, and SystemColorConstants. VBA also groups intrinsic constants into sets of enumerated constants, including the prefix Vb in the group name. For example, VbDayOfWeek is the name of the set of enumerated constants vbFriday, vbMonday, vbSaturday, vbSunday, vbThursday, vbTuesday, vbUseSystemDayOfWeek, and vbWednesday.

Using ADO Intrinsic Constants

The ADO object model has a set of intrinsic constants that you use primarily to specify data access object property settings and method arguments. These constants have an ad prefix. Examples are adEditNone, adEditinProgress, adEditAdd, and adEditDelete, which you use to specify the EditMode property of the Recordset object. ADO also groups intrinsic constants into sets of enumerated constants and names each group using a descriptive name and the suffix Enum. For example, LockTypeEnum is the set of enumerated constants representing the types of record locking available, including adLockBatchOptimistic, adLockOptimistic, adLockPessimistic, and adLockReadOnly.

Viewing Intrinsic Constants

You can use the Object Browser to view the intrinsic constants for an application. To open the Object Browser from Module view, click the Object Browser button in the toolbar, press F2, or choose View ➢ Object Browser.

In the Object Browser dialog, the Project/Library combo list includes the current project and the reference we set earlier to the Ch7_Examples project (see Figure 8.18a). The combo list also includes references to the seven object libraries that are created in the System directory in your Windows folder when you install Access: Access (Microsoft Access 10.0 Object Library), ADODB (Microsoft ActiveX Data Objects 2.6 Library), ADOX (Microsoft ADO Ext. 2.6 for DDL and Security), DAO (Microsoft DAO 3.6 Object Library), Office (Microsoft Office 10.0 Library), stdole (OLE Automation), and VBA (Visual Basic for Applications). These object libraries contain references to the constants provided by these applications in addition to other reference information on objects and commands. Follow these steps to view some intrinsic constants:

1. Select Access as the object library. Select AcFormView in the Classes list box in the lower left of the dialog. The Members list box displays the set of enumerated constants (see Figure 8.18b). AcFormView is the name of the group of enumerated constants for the

FIGURE 8.18:

The Project/Library combo box lists the projects and object libraries for which the current database has references set (a). You can use the Object Browser to learn about the set of enumerated constants for an argument of a method, function, or property in Access (b) or in ADO (c).

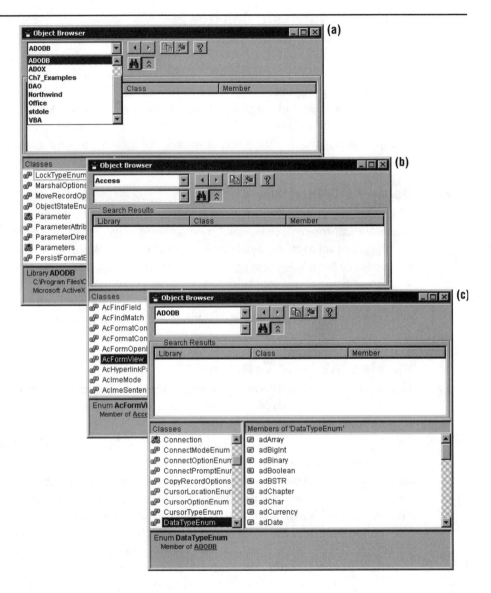

view argument of the OpenForm method. The Classes list box includes the names of all the sets of enumerated constants for the methods, functions, and properties using the prefix Ac to indicate a name. The enumerated constants in each set are displayed in the Members list box and have the prefix ac.

2. Select Constants from the Classes list box in the lower left of the dialog box. The Members list box on the right displays the intrinsic constants. Choose acPrompt in the Members list box. The area below the list boxes displays the number that corresponds to the constant and additional information about the constant. Click the Help button, if it is enabled, to display online help.

3. Select ADODB as the object library. Select DataTypeEnum in the Classes list box. The Members list box displays the set of enumerated constants (see Figure 8.18c). The Classes list box includes the names of the sets of enumerated constants using a syntax that includes a descriptive name with the suffix Enum. For example, DataTypeEnum is the set of intrinsic constants that represent the data types used by ADO.

4. Choose adBoolean in the Members list box to view additional information about the constant.

NOTE   The numerical values represented by intrinsic constants may change in future versions of Access. Because of this, you should always use the intrinsic constants instead of their actual values in your code.

Creating Your Own Constants

You can create your own constants using declaration statements. Creating constants is similar to creating variables: you can create both procedure-level and module-level constants. The difference is that the declaration statement for a constant also includes the assignment of the constant value, as follows:

```
Const constantname As type = constantvalue
```

When VBA reads the declaration statement for a constant, it creates and names a temporary memory location, allocates the amount of storage specified by the data type you specify, and stores the value. The As *type* part is optional; if you don't specify a data type, VBA chooses the most efficient storage type for the value you entered.

Creating Procedure-Level Constants

You create a procedure-level constant and set its value using a declaration statement within a procedure, as follows:

```
Const constantname As type = constantvalue
```

For example, this statement sets the constant intMax to the Integer value 144:

```
Const intMax As Integer = 144
```

A procedure-level constant is not visible outside the procedure.

Creating Module-Level Constants

You create module-level constants by placing the declaration statement in the Declarations section of a module. For a standard module, you can create public and private module-level constants using the following syntax:

```
[Public|Private] Const constantname [As type] = constantvalue
```

If you omit the `Public` or `Private` keyword, the constant is private by default and available only to procedures in the module in which the constant is created. For example, the following lines create `gsngInterestRate` as a public constant that can be seen and used by any procedure in the project and `sngTaxRate` as a constant that can be seen and used only by the procedures in the module and is invisible to procedures in other modules:

```
Public Const gsngInterestRate As Single = 7.75
Private Const sngTaxRate As Single = 32.5
```

For a form or report module, you can create only private constants. This means that entering a statement such as `Public Const intMyConstant As Integer = 2` in the Declarations section of a form or report module leads to an error (see Figure 8.19).

FIGURE 8.19:

The error message displayed when you try to declare a public constant in a form or report module

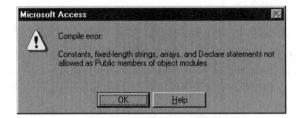

Using Arrays

VBA provides *arrays* as a way to work efficiently with several variables that have the same data type. For example, you can create an array of the text box controls on a form or an array of open forms in the database.

An array is a series of variables that you refer to using the same name and using a number, called the *index*, to tell the variables apart. The variables in an array must have the same data type. However, if the array has the Variant data type, the individual elements of the array can contain different kinds of data, such as numbers, strings, or objects. You can create an array with a fundamental data type, an object data type, or a user-defined data type. The collections of the Application objects and the data access objects discussed in Chapters 5, "VBA Programming Essentials," and 6, "Understanding the ADO Object Model," are object arrays; for example, Forms is an array of the open forms and Tables is an array of the tables in the database.

The main purpose of arrays is to make your code simpler and more efficient. When you want to process a set of items in an array, you can easily loop through each item using the index number to keep track of the repetitions. Chapter 9 explains looping through an array.

You can create an array with a fixed number of elements. (A *fixed-size array* is also called an *ordinary array*.) You can also create an array without specifying the number of elements and then size the array while a procedure is running; an array declared without a specific number of elements is a *dynamic array*. Suppose you need to keep track of the values in the controls on a specific form. Because you know the number of controls on the form, you could use a fixed-size array to hold the values. However, if you want to use the procedure for any form, you could use a dynamic array because the number of controls may be different for each form.

You can create *local arrays* within procedures and *shared arrays* in the Declarations sections of modules. By default, VBA uses zero as the first index number (the *lower bound*) for the array; in this case, the highest index number (the *upper bound*) is one less than the number of elements. Arrays can be multidimensional and can have up to 60 dimensions.

> **NOTE**   The basic memory requirement of an array of any data type is 20 bytes plus 4 bytes for each array dimension plus the number of bytes for the data itself. The memory for the data itself is the product of the number of data elements and the size of each element. A Variant variable containing an array requires 12 bytes in addition to the memory required by the array.

Creating Fixed-Size Arrays

You create a procedure-level fixed-size array using a `Dim` or `Static` statement within the procedure or in the argument list of the procedure. To declare the array, follow the array name with the bounds for the index numbers in parentheses, as in the following examples. (You can use the prefix a in the variable name to indicate an array if you are using the Hungarian-style naming standard.)

The statement

```
Dim astrNames(20) As String
```

declares an array named `astrNames` of 21 elements with the String data type and with index numbers from 0 to 20. When the lower bound of an array is 0, you enclose the upper bound in parentheses in the declaration statement.

The statement

```
Static asngTaxRates(1 To 10) As Single
```

declares a static array named `asngTaxRates` of 10 elements with the Single data type and with index numbers from 1 to 10. When the lower bound of an array is greater than 0, include both bounds and the `To` keyword in parentheses in the declaration statement.

The statement

```
Public Function Addresses(astrNames(20) As String)
```

declares an array named astrNames of 21 elements with the String data type as an argument of the Addresses function.

You can create a module-level, fixed-size array by declaring the array in the Declarations section of the module. Use the Public keyword to share the array among all procedures in all modules in the project, or use the Private keyword to share the array only among the procedures in the module in which the array is created. As an exception, you cannot create a public array in a form or report module. Here are some examples of shared array declarations. The statement

```
Public aintMatrix(9,9) As Integer
```

declares a two-dimensional public array named aintMatrix of 100 elements with the Integer data type, having index number pairs from (0,0) to (9,9).

The statement

```
Private atxtAmounts(1 To 6) As TextBox
```

declares a private array named atxtAmounts of six text box object elements with index numbers from 1 to 6.

Reinitializing Elements in an Array

You can use the Erase statement to reinitialize the elements of a fixed-size array. To explore arrays, create a new module named basArrays to store the procedures we create in this section. Then create the CreateArray procedure shown below.

```
Public Sub CreateArray()
    Dim astrArray(3) As String
    astrArray(0) = "Margaret"
    astrArray(1) = "Peacock"
    astrArray(2) = "Sales Representative"
    MsgBox astrArray(1) & ", " & astrArray(0) & " is a " & astrArray(2)
    Erase astrArray
    MsgBox astrArray(1) & ", " & astrArray(0) & " is a " & astrArray(2)
End Sub
```

Run the procedure in the Immediate window. The procedure creates a fixed-size string array with three elements, assigns the string values, and displays the values in a message box (see Figure 8.20a). After you dismiss the message, the procedure uses the Erase statement to reinitialize the elements to zero-length strings and displays the initialized values in a message box (see Figure 8.20b).

FIGURE 8.20:

Creating a fixed-size array (a) and using the Erase statement to reinitialize the elements of the array (b)

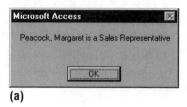

(a)

(b)

NOTE The Erase statement works differently for fixed-size arrays and dynamic arrays. When you use the Erase statement for a dynamic array, the storage space that was used by the dynamic array is reclaimed and available for reuse. However, when you use the Erase statement with a fixed-size array, the elements are reinitialized but the memory is not reclaimed. If you only need to use an array part of the time, you can declare it as a dynamic array and reclaim the memory when you are finished by using the Erase statement.

Creating an Array Based on Values in a List

You can use the Array function to create an array based on values in a list, using the following syntax:

```
Array(arglist)
```

The Array function creates an array using the values in the *arglist* argument list and returns a Variant containing the array. You must separate multiple values by commas; if there are no values in the list, an array of zero size is created.

The LBound and UBound functions return the smallest and largest index for the specified dimension of the array, respectively:

```
LBound(arrayname,dimension)
UBound(arrayname,dimension)
```

The optional *dimension* argument is the whole number indicating which dimension's lower or upper bound you want to return, where 1 is the first dimension, 2 is the second, and so on. If you omit the dimension, the first dimension is assumed.

To explore using these functions, create the ArrayFunction procedure shown below in the basArrays module.

```
Public Sub ArrayFunction()
    Dim varData As Variant
    varData = Array("Margaret", "Peacock", #5/3/2001#)
    MsgBox LBound(varData) & " to " & UBound(varData)
    MsgBox varData(0) & " " & varData(1) & " was hired on " & _
        varData(2)
End Sub
```

Run the procedure in the Immediate window. The procedure creates a variant variable, uses the Array function to create an array of the three values in the list, and assigns the result to the variant variable. (The varData variable must have the Variant data type to store values that have different data types.) A message box displays the lower and upper bounds of the array (see Figure 8.21a) and a second message box displays the values (see Figure 8.21b). In this procedure, the varData variable contains an array.

FIGURE 8.21:
Use the UBound and LBound functions to determine the size of an array created using the Array function (a). The message displays the three values of the array (b).

(a)

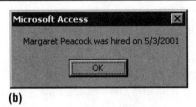

(b)

Creating Dynamic Arrays

You use a dynamic array instead of a fixed-size array when you don't know beforehand how many elements the array has. You create a dynamic array using two statements: one statement to declare the array and a second statement to specify the size. You declare the array using the same syntax as for a fixed-size array without specifying the number of elements (leave a blank between the parentheses) and use the ReDim statement in a procedure to specify the size and allocate the storage space required by the specified data type.

Creating a Procedure-Level Dynamic Array

You can create a procedure-level dynamic array by including a declaration statement within the procedure using the following syntax:

```
(Dim|Static) arrayname() [As type]
```

and then including a ReDim statement in the procedure to specify the size. For example, this statement creates a local dynamic array:

```
Dim astrNames() As String
```

This statement sets the number of elements to 5 with index numbers from 0 to 4:

```
ReDim astrNames(4)
```

Creating a Module-Level Dynamic Array

You can create a module-level dynamic array by placing a declaration statement in the Declarations section of a module using the following syntax:

```
[Public|Private] arrayname() [As type]
```

and then including a ReDim statement in any procedure that refers to the array to specify its size. For example, placing the following statement in the Declarations section of a module creates a module-level dynamic array:

```
Public asngTaxRates() As Single
```

Placing the following statement within a procedure sets the number of elements to 5 with index numbers from 1 to 5:

```
ReDim asngTaxRates(1 To 5)
```

Setting the Bounds of a Dynamic Array

You can set the bounds of a dynamic array using integer variables, as in the following example:

```
ReDim asngTaxRates(intlower To intupper)
```

The ReDim statement specifies the size of the array and initializes its elements according to the array's data type. This means that ReDim initializes each value to zero for a numeric array, to the zero-length string for a string array, to Empty for a Variant array, and to Nothing for an array of objects. You can use the ReDim statement to change the size of an array as often as you want; however, ReDim discards any values currently stored in the array elements when you run the statement unless you include the Preserve keyword.

You can use the Preserve keyword when you want to preserve the values in the array and also change the size of the array at the same time. You can only resize the last array dimension. If you decrease the size of the last array dimension, the data in the eliminated elements is discarded. When you use the Preserve keyword, you cannot change the number of dimensions, only the size of the last array dimension.

To explore these ideas, create the DynamicArray procedure below in the basArrays module:

```
Public Sub DynamicArray()
    Dim avar() As Variant, str As String
    ReDim avar(2)
    avar(0) = 101
    avar(1) = 202
    MsgBox avar(0) & vbCrLf & avar(1), , "Two element array"
    ReDim avar(3,2)
    avar(0,0) = "zero": avar(0,1) = 0
    avar(1,0) = "one": avar(1,1) = 1
    avar(2,0) = "two": avar(2,1) = 2
    str = avar(0,0) & "; " & avar(0,1) & vbCrLf
    str = str & avar(1,0) & "; " & avar(1,1) & vbCrLf
    str = str & avar(2,0) & "; " & avar(2,1)
    MsgBox str, , "Three rows and two columns"
    ReDim Preserve avar(3,1)
```

```
        str = avar(0,0) & vbCrLf & avar(1,0) & vbCrLf & avar(2,0)
        MsgBox str, , "Discard the second column"
    End Sub
```

The procedure creates the avar array as a dynamic array of variants and uses a sequence of ReDim statements to size the array. The first ReDim statement sizes the array as a two-element array. The second ReDim statement discards the values assigned and resizes the array as a two-dimensional array with three rows and two columns. Each of the next three lines includes a pair of assignment statements using a colon to separate the statements. The third ReDim statement includes a Preserve keyword to "save with values" when the last dimension of the array is resized; the array is resized to a three-element array with three rows and one column and discards the data in the second column.

Run the procedure in the Immediate window. The message boxes track the progress through the procedure (see Figure 8.22).

FIGURE 8.22:

The procedure uses a dynamic array and the ReDim statement to represent a two-element array (a) and a two-dimensional array with three rows and two columns (b). The procedure uses the ReDim Preserve statement to discard the second column (c).

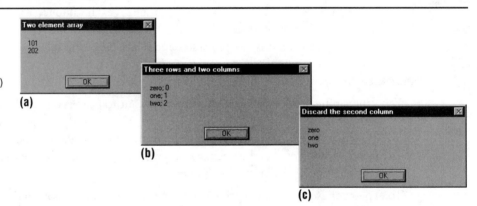

NOTE   The VBA intrinsic constant vbCrLf represents a carriage return followed by a line feed. Use the constant to begin a new line in the message box.

Using Arrays as Arguments

If you don't want to specify the number of arguments that a called procedure can receive, you can use the ParamArray keyword to take an arbitrary number of arguments from the calling procedure and place them in an array of variants. The ParamArray argument must be the last argument in the argument list. For example, if you are creating a generic procedure to calculate the average of a set of numeric values, you can use the ParamArray keyword in the argument as follows:

```
    Public Function Average(ParamArray aArgs())
```

The *aArgs* argument is the name of the array. When you call the Average function, you can send an arbitrary number of arguments, as shown in the following calling statement:

```
Call Average(2,5,46,23,1)
```

When you use the ParamArray keyword, the arguments are the Variant data type by default and you cannot specify another data type. You cannot include the ByRef, ByVal, or Optional keywords together with the ParamArray keyword.

Creating Your Own Data Types

You can also create your own data type based on the fundamental data types listed in Table 7.1 in Chapter 7. You can create a custom data type for a single variable that holds several elements of information with different data types. For example, you can use a single variable to refer to a customer's name (String data type), the date of an order (Date data type), and the amount of the order (Currency data type). You can define a custom data type only in the Declarations section of a module.

You create the custom data type using the Type and End Type statements. After defining a custom data type, you can declare a variable with the custom data type as a procedure-level or module-level variable. Once you have declared a variable with the custom data type, you can refer to an element of the variable using this syntax:

```
variablename.elementname
```

You can assign values to its elements using the normal assignment statements.

To explore these concepts, create the custom data type named OrderInfo shown below in the Declarations section of basVariables and the ViewOrder procedure shown below in the basVariables module:

```
Public Type OrderInfo
Customer As String
OrderDate As Date
Amount As Currency
End Type

Public Sub ViewOrder()
    Dim ord As OrderInfo
    ord.Customer = "Alfreds Futterkiste"
    ord.OrderDate = #5/10/2001#
    ord.Amount = 3124.98
    MsgBox ord.Customer & " placed an order on " & ord.OrderDate & _
        " for $" & ord.Amount
End Sub
```

Run the ViewOrder procedure in the Immediate window. The procedure declares a variable of the new OrderInfo data type and assigns values to each element. The message box displays the elements of the ord variable (see Figure 8.23).

FIGURE 8.23:

A single variable with a custom data type holds the customer's name, order date, and order amount.

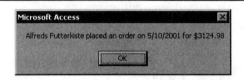

When you use the Public keyword, the custom data type is available (visible) to all procedures in all modules of the project. Use the Private keyword instead to restrict visibility to the module in which the custom data type is defined. When you create a custom data type in a standard module, the custom data type is public by default. When created in a form or report module, a custom data type can be private only and you can't change its visibility with the Public keyword.

User-defined data types can contain objects, fixed-size arrays, and dynamic arrays, as shown in the following examples:

```
Private Type Orders
frmInput As Form
rptOutput As Report
dbOrders As Database
End Type

Public Type CustomerInfo
Customer As String
Address(2) As String
    ' A fixed-size array with two elements
Phone() As String
    ' A dynamic array
FirstOrder As Date
End Type
```

You can use a single custom data type to pass several arguments to a procedure using a single variable. For example, you can pass the four variables of the CustomerInfo data type to the CustomerDataEntry procedure as a single variable as follows:

```
Public Sub CustomerDataEntry(CurrentCustomer As CustomerInfo)
```

Summary

This chapter has introduced you to using variables in procedures. The main reasons for using variables are that your code runs faster when you use variables and specify their data types and that you can create procedures that are reusable because you can use variables to replace the names of specific objects. The important points we covered are these:

- You can control which other procedures can use a variable and how long a variable "lives" by specifying a variable as a procedure-level or a module-level variable and using keywords in the declaration.

- You should declare variables with the most specific data types for faster code.

- You can declare procedure-level variables in two places: in a separate declaration statement within the procedure or in the argument list of a procedure called by another procedure.

- You create a procedure-level variable with a declaration statement placed inside a procedure using the syntax Dim [Static] *variablename* As *type* or as an argument in the procedure's argument list using the syntax *argumentname* As *type*.

- The procedure-level variable is not visible to any other procedure directly. The only way a procedure can make a procedure-level variable available to another procedure is to pass the local variable as an argument to the other procedure.

- When the procedure ends, Access destroys the procedure-level variables and releases their storage space, by default. You can override the default behavior by declaring a procedure-level variable with the Static keyword instead of the Dim keyword or by using the Static keyword in the procedure's declaration to make all of its local variables static. The value of a static variable is preserved until you restart or reset the module. You cannot extend the life of an argument declared in the procedure's argument list.

- You can declare module-level variables in the Declarations section of the module.

- You can pass values and objects to a procedure as arguments in two ways: by reference, so that the procedure receives the variable itself, or by value, so the procedure receives a copy of the variable.

- Event procedures have predefined names and argument lists.

- You can create custom constants to make your code more readable.

- You can use arrays to handle several variables that have the same data type. If the array has the Variant data type, the elements may have different data types.

- You can create a custom data type for a variable that can hold several elements with different data types.

The next chapter completes the introduction to Access VBA by explaining the special statements you can use to control which instructions are executed and how many times a set of instructions is executed.

CHAPTER 9

Controlling Execution

- Making decisions in a procedure

- Using loops to repeat operations

- Using the With...End With statements for faster code

- Using Not to toggle a property

- Understanding the Timer and DoEvents functions

- Understanding the SysCmd function

In this chapter, you'll learn about the different versions of control structures that VBA provides. You'll learn how to apply several standard programming techniques, such as testing the data type of variables before doing calculations, efficient ways to loop through a collection, and looping through a recordset. The second part of the chapter is a brief discussion of useful built-in statements and functions.

Understanding Control Structures

Unless you include specific directions to the contrary, VBA executes a procedure's statements consecutively, beginning with the first statement. VBA executes each statement from left to right and then moves down to the next consecutive statement. When VBA comes to the End... statement, the procedure terminates. This left-to-right, top-to-bottom execution pattern is called *sequential flow*.

VBA provides several statements you can use to change the *flow of execution:* you can change the order in which statements are executed, whether a set of statements is executed at all, and whether a set of statements is repeated. To indicate that you want to change the order of execution for a set of statements, you use a keyword or a control statement to mark the beginning and another keyword or control statement to mark the end of the set. The control statements you use to control the flow are called *control structures*. Most of the power of VBA comes from two kinds of control structures:

- You use *decision structures* to test conditions and perform different sets of statements depending on the outcome of the test.

- You use *loop structures* to execute a set of statements repetitively.

NOTE   For hands-on experience with the control structures described in this chapter, create a new copy of the Northwind database named Northwind_Ch9 and create a new module named basControlStructures. Create the sample procedures in the basControlStructures module or in the form module specified in the example.

Making Decisions with Conditions

You use a decision structure to execute different sets of statements depending on the result of testing a condition. The condition can be any string or numeric expression that evaluates to True or False. The condition is usually a comparison, such as intCount > 0, but it can be any expression that evaluates to a numeric value, such as intCount. If the numeric value is zero, the condition is False; if the numeric value is nonzero, the condition is True.

Using the *If...Then* Structure

Suppose you have a set of statements that you want to execute if a condition is True and that you want to skip otherwise. In this case, you can use the If...Then decision structure. You use the If...Then structure to evaluate a test condition and perform a statement, or a set of statements, if the test condition evaluates to True. The test condition can be any expression that evaluates to True or False. There are two versions of the If...Then structure: single-line syntax and multiple-line syntax.

The single-line syntax is written as follows:

```
If condition Then statements
```

If the test condition evaluates to True, the statements on the line are executed, and VBA moves to the next statement in the procedure. If the test condition evaluates to False, the statements on the line are not executed, and execution flows to the next statement in the procedure.

The multiple-line syntax (also called the *block syntax*) is written as follows:

```
If condition Then
    statements
End If
```

If the test condition evaluates to True, the statements are executed, and VBA moves to the End If statement and exits the control structure. If the test condition evaluates to False, the statements are skipped, and VBA moves to the End If statement and exits the control structure. Figure 9.1 depicts the If...Then decision structure.

FIGURE 9.1:

The If...Then decision structure

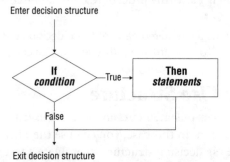

You can use the single-line syntax for multiple statements, but the statements must be on one line and separated by colons (:). The single-line syntax is useful for simple tests; however, the multiple-line syntax is usually easier to read even when there is a single statement.

Let's try some examples of the If...Then structure. In the basControlStructures module of the Northwind_Ch9 database you created for the examples in this chapter, insert the NullToZero procedure shown below.

```
Public Function NullToZero(X)
    If IsNull(X) Then NullToZero = 0
End Function
```

This procedure tests the function's argument. If the argument's value is Null, the procedure sets the function's value to zero; otherwise, the procedure does nothing. In the Immediate window, type **?NullToZero(4)** and press Enter. The condition is False, so the procedure ends without returning a value. Now, type **?NullToZero(Null)** and press Enter. The condition is True, and the value of the function is set to zero. The Immediate window displays the returned value.

Open the Customers form in Design view, click in the form's OnUnload event property, and click the Build button. Enter the Form_Unload event procedure shown below.

```
Private Sub Form_Unload (Cancel As Integer)
    If MsgBox ("Close form?", vbYesNo) = vbNo Then
        Cancel = True
    End If
End Sub
```

Save the form, switch to Form view, and click the form's Close box. The procedure displays a Yes/No message box. If you click the No button, the condition is True, and the procedure sets the Cancel argument to True (which informs Access to cancel the closing of the form). If you click the Yes button, the condition is False, the procedure ends, and Access closes the form.

> **NOTE** The If, Then, and End If keywords are required parts of these decision control structures. If you omit a required keyword in any control structure, VBA generates a compile error.

Using the *If...Then...Else* Structure

Suppose you have two alternative sets of statements and want to execute only one set depending on the value of a condition. In this case, you can use the If...Then...Else decision structure. You use the If...Then...Else decision structure to evaluate a test condition and execute one set of statements if the test condition evaluates to True and another set of statements if the test condition evaluates to False. As with the If...Then structure, there are single-line and multiple-line syntax versions of the If...Then...Else structure.

The single-line syntax is written as follows:

```
If condition Then statements [Else elsestatements]
```

VBA evaluates the condition. If the condition evaluates to True, VBA executes the statements following Then; otherwise, VBA executes the statements following Else. After executing either set of statements, VBA moves to the next statement in the procedure. You can use the single-line syntax for multiple statements, but the statements must be on one line and separated by colons (:). Normally, to make your code easier to read, you use the single-line syntax only when there is a single statement for each alternative.

The multiple-line syntax can be used when there is one test condition and a pair of alternative sets of statements:

```
If condition Then
    statements
[Else
    elsestatements]
End If
```

This syntax also can be used when there is more than one test condition and several blocks of statements as possible blocks to be executed.

You can use the If...Then...Else structure to determine which one of the several blocks of statements to perform, as follows:

```
If condition1 Then
    block1statements
[ElseIf condition2 Then
    block2 statements]
...
[Else
    blockN statements]
End If
```

VBA evaluates the first condition. If the first condition evaluates to True, VBA executes the first block of statements and then jumps out of the decision structure to the next statement following the End If statement, skipping the remaining statements in between. If the first condition evaluates to False, VBA tests the next condition in the ElseIf statement. If that condition is True, VBA carries out its statement block and jumps out of the decision structure. If that condition is False, VBA moves to testing the next condition. When it finds a True condition, VBA executes its statement block and jumps out. If none of the conditions evaluates to True, VBA can execute the optional Else statement block and then leave the decision structure. You can have any number of ElseIf clauses or none. The only required lines of the syntax are the If...Then and End If statements. Figure 9.2 depicts the If...Then...Else decision structure in the case of a single condition.

FIGURE 9.2:

The If...Then...Else decision structure

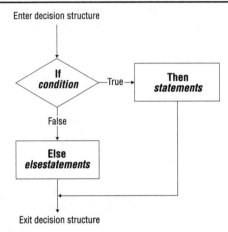

As an example of the If...Then...Else structure, enter the Multiply3 function shown below in the basControlStructures module.

```
Public Function Multiply3(X,Y,Optional Z)
    If IsMissing(Z) Then Multiply3 = X*Y Else Multiply3 = X*Y*Z
End Function
```

The Multiply3 function determines if the optional argument has been passed and uses different formulas depending on the result. In the Immediate window, type **? Multiply3(2,3)** and press Enter. The condition is True, so Access multiplies the two numbers and displays their product. Now, type **? Multiply3(2,3,4)** and press Enter. In this case, the condition is False, so Access multiplies the three numbers and displays their product.

Next, enter the MultiplyTest function shown below in the basControlStructures module.

```
Public Function MultiplyTest(X,Y)
    If IsNumeric(X) and IsNumeric(Y) Then
        MultiplyTest = X*Y
    Else
        MsgBox "Non-numeric arguments"
    End If
End Function
```

The MultiplyTest function determines if the arguments have a numeric data type before calculating the product. In the Immediate window, type **? MultiplyTest(2,3)** and press Enter. The condition is True, so the numbers are multiplied and the product is displayed. Now, type **? MultiplyTest("two",3)** and press Enter. The condition is False, so the message is printed.

Using *TypeOf...Is* to Determine an Object Type

Often, when you are working with controls on forms, you need to be able to determine the control's type. For example, suppose you want to use a form for both reviewing and editing; you need to toggle the controls' Locked property (and possibly the Enabled property) between the review and edit modes. The problem is that not all control types have a Locked property, so you need a way to determine if an arbitrary control has a specific control type before setting the property. You can use the expression TypeOf *objectname* Is *objecttype* as the test condition to determine whether an object has the specified object data type.

The PreviousControlType procedure shown below determines if a control is a text box and displays a message if it is. This procedure is set up as a generic procedure that works with any form by using the PreviousControl property of the Screen object to refer to the control that previously had the focus.

```
Public Function PreviousControlType()
    If TypeOf Screen.PreviousControl Is TextBox Then
        MsgBox "This is a text box", , "Text Box Tester"
    End If
End Function
```

If you want to test this function, enter it in the basControlStructures module. Then open the Customers form in Design view and add a command button named cmdControlType with the caption Control Type. Click the button's OnClick property and set the property to =PreviousControlType(). By using an event-handling function stored in a standard module instead of an event procedure, you can paste the button to any form.

To test a control, switch to Form view, click the control and then click the button. If you click a text box, the message box is displayed; otherwise, there is no response. If you click a label, the focus moves to the text box control associated with the label and clicking the button displays the message.

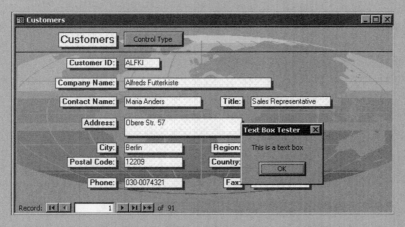

Using the *Select Case* Structure

Suppose you have several sets of alternatives and you want to execute one set depending on the value of an expression. In this case, you can use the Select Case...End Select decision structure as an alternative to the If...Then...Else structure. In the Select Case decision structure, you evaluate a test expression and consider possible cases by comparing the value of the test expression to the values appropriate to each case.

The Select Case decision structure has the following syntax:

```
Select Case testexpression
    Case expressionlist1
        [block1 statements]
    Case expressionlist2
        [block2 statements]
    ...
    [Case Else
        blockN statements]
End Select
```

Each *expressionlist* is a list of one or more values appropriate to the case. The corresponding statement block contains zero or more statements that are executed if the value of the test expression satisfies the *expressionlist*. An item in *expressionlist* can have any of the following three forms:

expression	An example is Case 2, 4, 5, 7.
expression To *expression*	The expression that precedes To must be smaller than the expression that follows To. An example is Case 2 To 5.
Is *operator expression*	The operator can be any comparison operator except Is or Like. An example is Case Is >10.

After evaluating the test expression in the Select Case statement, VBA tests the values in *expressionlist1*; if any value in *expressionlist1* matches the value of the test expression, VBA executes the block1 statements and then jumps out of the decision structure to the next statement following the End Select statement, skipping any blocks in between. If no value in *expressionlist1* matches the value of the test expression, VBA moves to the next Case statement and tests the values in its *expressionlist*. If there is a match, VBA carries out its statement block and jumps out; if there isn't a match, it moves to the next Case statement. If there are no matching values in any *expressionlist*, VBA can execute the statements in the optional Case Else clause and then jump out of the decision structure. When the value of the test expression matches a value in more than one Case, VBA executes the statements for the first matching Case clause. Figure 9.3 illustrates the Select Case decision structure.

FIGURE 9.3:

The Select Case deci-sion structure

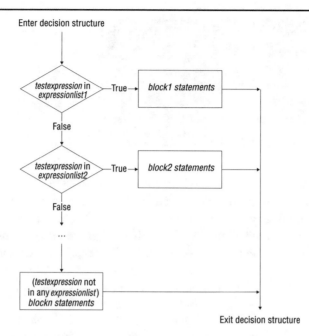

You can't use the TypeOf *objectname* Is *objecttype* clause in the Select Case control structure.

As an example, enter the NumberGame procedure shown below in the basControlStructures module.

```
Public Sub NumberGame()
    Dim intNumber as Integer
    intNumber = InputBox("Enter an integer from 1 to 20", "Number Game")
    Select Case intNumber
        Case 2, 4, 6, 8
            MsgBox "The number is even and less than 9"
        Case 9 To 20
            MsgBox "The number is from 9 to 20"
        Case Else
            MsgBox "The number is odd and less than 9"
    End Select
End Sub
```

The procedure uses the InputBox function to collect an integer from the game player (see Figure 9.4); the number you enter is assigned to the intNumber variable. The Select Case decision structure tests the value of the number against the expressions in each Case and displays a message box for the matching Case.

FIGURE 9.4:

The value you enter in the input box is assigned to a variable, which is tested using the Select Case decision structure.

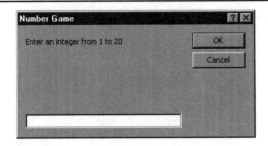

Run the NumberGame procedure in the Immediate window. When you enter an integer between 1 and 20 in the input box, the procedure displays the correct message box, depending on whether the number you entered is in the first case (2, 4, 6, or 8), the second case (9 to 20), or the else case (odd and less than 9). Note that the procedure does not test to determine if the value you entered in the input box is actually an integer between 1 and 20.

NOTE   Another way to perform multiple branching is to use the On...GoSub and On...GoTo statements. These statements are a carryover from older versions of Basic in which line number and line labels are used to identify lines of code. The Select Case structure provides a more flexible way to do multiple branching and is the only method this book recommends.

Using Loops for Repetitive Operations

There are times when you need to cycle through every element of an array or every member of a collection. For example, suppose you want to change a form from a data-entry form to a review form. To protect the data controls on the form, you need to cycle through the controls on the form and lock each control that holds data. One approach is to write a separate statement for each specific control on the form that tests to determine if the control holds data and locks the control if it does. A more efficient solution is to write a single statement that tests and locks an arbitrary data control and then uses control statements to instruct VBA to loop through the controls on the form and execute the statement for each control. VBA provides several styles of loop structures that you can use to execute the same set of statements repeatedly a specified number of times or until a condition is satisfied.

Using the *For...Next* Structure

When you know how many times you want to execute the statements in the loop, you can use the For...Next structure. You use a *counter* variable to keep track of the repetitions and specify the counter's *start* and *end* values. The start, end, and increment arguments can be numeric values or expressions. The syntax for the For...Next loop structure is as follows:

```
For counter = start To end [Step increment]
    statements
Next [counter]
```

Figure 9.5 illustrates the For...Next loop structure.

 FIGURE 9.5:

The For...Next loop structure

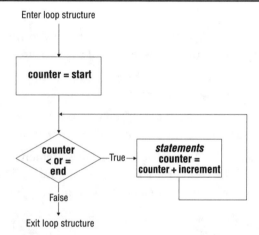

Enter loop structure

counter = start

counter < or = end —True→ *statements* counter = counter + increment

False

Exit loop structure

To understand how the loop works, let's assume the increment is positive or zero. When the loop begins, VBA sets the counter to the start value, tests the value of the counter, and takes one of the two alternatives:

- If the counter is greater than the end value, VBA jumps out of the loop and executes the next statement following the Next statement.

- If the counter is less than or equal to the end value, VBA executes the statements in the loop and increases the counter by the value of the increment argument. If you omit the Step clause, VBA increments the counter by one.

After executing the statements, VBA goes back to the For statement and repeats the process. The loop repeats until the counter is greater than the end value. When the increment is positive, the end value must be greater than the start value; otherwise, the loop repeats endlessly.

Here is an example of a positive increment:

```
For Count = 2 To 10 Step 2
    statements
Next Count
```

In the structure, VBA begins the loop by setting Count to 2 and begins the first pass through the loop. VBA executes the statements, increases Count by 2, and returns to the For statement to compare the value of Count to 10. As long as the value of Count is less than or equal to 10, VBA takes another pass through the loop.

NOTE While it is possible to set the increment to zero and change the value of the counter in the statements of the loop, you should avoid this practice because your code will be harder to debug than if you use a nonzero increment.

If the increment is a negative number, VBA begins as before by setting the counter to the start value, tests the value of the counter, and takes one of the two alternatives:

- If the counter is less than the end value, VBA jumps out of the loop and executes the next statement following the Next statement.

- If the counter is greater than or equal to the end value, VBA executes the statements in the loop and decreases the counter by the value of the increment argument.

After executing the statements, VBA goes back to the For statement and repeats the process. The loop repeats until the counter is less than the end value. The end value must be less than the start value. Here is an example of a negative step:

```
For Count = 7 to 3 Step -1
    statements
Next Count
```

NOTE You can omit the counter in the Next statement, but your code is easier to read if you include the counter.

To explore the For...Next loop structure, insert the Counting procedure shown below in the basControlStructures module.

```
Public Sub Counting()
    Dim intCount As Integer
    For intCount = 1 To 10 Step 2
        Debug.Print intCount
    Next intCount
End Sub
```

The procedure defines intCount as the counter. The loop begins by setting the intCount variable to 1 and printing the value in the Immediate window. VBA increments the counter by 2 and runs the loop again. VBA continues to increment the counter and runs the loop five times. When the counter has the value 11, VBA exits the loop.

To test the procedure, in the Immediate window, type **Counting** and press Enter. VBA prints the odd integers from 1 through 9 in the Immediate window.

You can use the For…Next structure to loop through the elements of a collection. Every collection is an array and has a Count property that returns the number of elements in the array; use the syntax *collectionname*.Count to determine the number of elements in the collection. You can refer to an item in a collection by its position in the collection using its index number. Because object collections are zero-based in Access, the index number begins with 0 and ends with Count - 1. For example, Forms.Count is the number of forms that are currently open in a database, Forms(0) is the first open form, and Forms.Count - 1 is the form you last opened. To use the For…Next structure to loop through the items in a collection, you can use the index number as the loop counter, starting the counter at 0 and ending at *collectionname*.Count - 1.

As an example of using For…Next with a collection, insert the NameForms procedure shown below in the basControlStructures module.

```
Public Sub NameForms()
    Dim intCount As Integer
    For intCount = 0 To Forms.Count - 1
        Debug.Print Forms(intCount).Name
    Next intCount
End Sub
```

The NameForms procedure uses a For…Next loop structure with the collection's index number as the loop counter to list the names of the forms that are currently open. Open a few forms in either Form or Design view and then type **NameForms** in the Immediate window and press Enter. VBA lists the name of each open form.

Using the *For Each…Next* Structure

The For Each…Next loop is similar to the For…Next loop, but instead of repeating the statements a specified number of times, the For Each…Next loop repeats the statements once for each element of an array or each object in a collection. The For Each…Next loop is extremely powerful because it lets you loop through the array or collection without needing to know how many elements there are. The syntax is as follows:

```
For Each element In group
    statements
Next [element]
```

Group is the name of a collection of objects or the name of an array. For a collection of objects, `element` is the variable representing an object in the collection and must have either the Variant data type or an Object data type; for an array, `element` must have the Variant data type.

You can use the `For Each…Next` structure to work with collections of Application objects and data objects. When you work with collections of data objects, you must use the full reference for the collection. If the collection contains Access objects and is in the current database, you can use the `CurrentProject` object to refer to the current database. For example, `CurrentProject.AllForms` refers to the collection of forms in the current database. You can use the `For Each…Next` loop structure to process each member of a collection.

Using the `For Each…Next` structure to loop through a collection is faster than using the `For…Next` structure. The reason is that when you use the `For…Next` structure, VBA looks up the item using its index number. VBA must test the entire list until the matching item is found. By contrast, when you use the `For Each…Next` structure, VBA remembers its position in the list and simply moves forward by one item for each repetition of the loop. The only time you should use the `For…Next` structure for a collection is when you are using the loop to remove items from the collection. When you remove an item from the collection, the positions of the remaining items are affected, and VBA may lose its place with unpredictable results if you use the `For Each…Next` structure.

The following examples show how to use the `For Each…Next` structure to get or set the values of properties and to execute methods. The first example is the `NameEachForm` procedure shown below, which you can insert in the basControlStructures module.

```
Public Sub NameEachForm()
    Dim obj As Object
    For Each obj in CurrentProject.AllForms
        Debug.Print obj.Name
    Next obj
End Sub
```

This procedure uses the `For Each…Next` structure to print the name of each form in the database; that is, it prints the name of each AccessObject form in the AllForms collection. While it is true that the AllForms collection contains the forms in the database, ADO does not assign the Form object type to the members. Instead, it assigns an object type—the AccessObject type.

After you enter the procedure, type **NameEachForm** in the Immediate window and press Enter. VBA prints the name of each form in the database, including those that are not open (see Figure 9.6).

FIGURE 9.6:

The NameEachForm procedure uses a For Each...Next loop structure to print the names of the forms in the Northwind database.

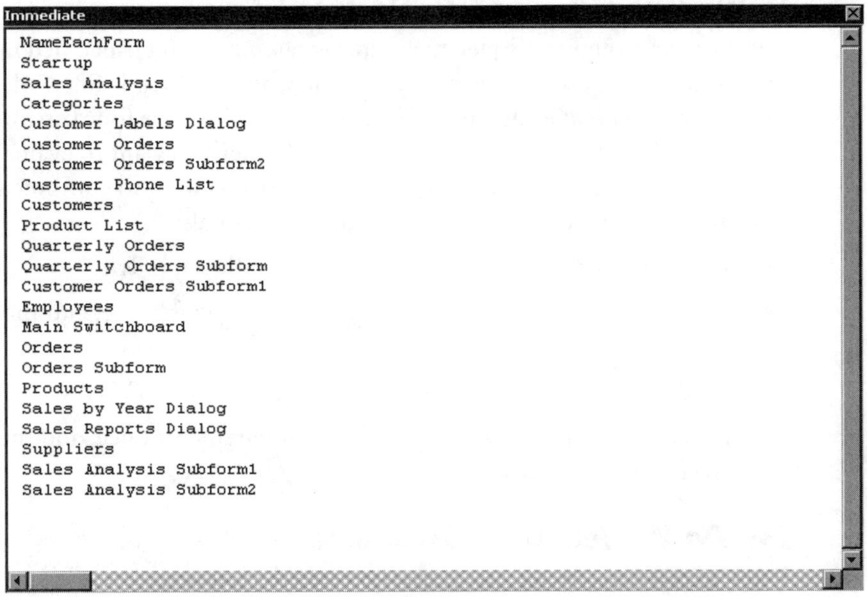

```
Immediate
    NameEachForm
    Startup
    Sales Analysis
    Categories
    Customer Labels Dialog
    Customer Orders
    Customer Orders Subform2
    Customer Phone List
    Customers
    Product List
    Quarterly Orders
    Quarterly Orders Subform
    Customer Orders Subform1
    Employees
    Main Switchboard
    Orders
    Orders Subform
    Products
    Sales by Year Dialog
    Sales Reports Dialog
    Suppliers
    Sales Analysis Subform1
    Sales Analysis Subform2
```

Next, enter the FontToRed function procedure shown below in the basControlStructures module.

```
Public Function FontToRed()
    Const Red As Integer = 255
    Dim ctl As Control
    For Each ctl in Screen.ActiveForm!Controls
        ctl.ForeColor = Red
    Next ctl
End Function
```

The FontToRed procedure changes the font color of all the controls on a form to red. This procedure is designed as a generic function procedure that works with any form in which all controls have a ForeColor property. To allow the procedure to be reusable, the procedure uses the ActiveForm property of the Screen object to refer to the form and refers to the Controls collection as Screen.ActiveForm!Controls. (Because Controls is the default collection of the Form object, you can also refer to the collection as Screen.ActiveForm instead of Screen.ActiveForm!Controls.)

After you've entered the procedure, open the Customers form in Design view. Add a command button named cmdRed with the caption Change Font Color to Red. Click the button's OnClick property and set the property to =FontToRed(). Save the form, switch to Form view, and click the button. The font color of all of the controls changes to red.

Using the *Do...Loop* Structure

The Do...Loop structure also lets you repeat statements an unspecified number of times. The Do...Loop structure uses a condition to decide when the loop is finished. The condition must be an expression that evaluates to True or False. There are four versions of the Do...Loop structure. The version you use depends on whether you want to evaluate the condition at the beginning or at the end of the loop and whether you want to continue the loop as long as the condition is True or as long as the condition is False.

- Do While...Loop continues as long as the condition is True.

- Do...Loop While always executes the loop statements once, and then continues as long as the condition is True.

- Do Until...Loop continues as long as the condition is False.

- Do...Loop Until always executes the loop statements once, and then continues as long as the condition is False.

The *Do While...Loop* Structure

The syntax for the Do While...Loop structure is as follows:

```
Do While condition
    statements
Loop
```

VBA begins execution of the loop by testing the condition. If the condition evaluates to False, VBA immediately jumps out of the loop, skipping all of the loop statements, and executes the statement following the Loop statement. The loop statements are never executed if the condition is initially False. If the condition evaluates to True, VBA executes the statements and then returns to the Do While statement and tests the condition. The loop continues as long as the condition evaluates to True. Figure 9.7 illustrates the Do While...Loop structure.

FIGURE 9.7:

The Do While...Loop structure

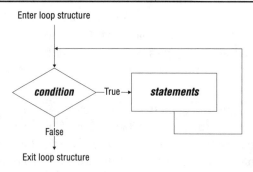

The `DoWhile` procedure shown below uses the `Do While...Loop` structure. Add this procedure to the basControlStructures module.

```
Public Sub DoWhile()
    Dim intCounter As Integer
    intCounter = 0
    Do While intCounter < 3
        Debug.Print intCounter
        intCounter = intCounter + 1
    Loop
End Sub
```

Run the `DoWhile` procedure in the Immediate window. The loop runs three times.

The *Do...Loop While* Structure

When you place the `While` condition clause at the end of the structure, VBA is guaranteed to execute the statements within the loop at least once.

```
Do
    statements
Loop While condition
```

VBA executes the Do...Loop While structure by executing the loop statements first. After executing the statements, VBA moves to the `Loop While` statement and tests the condition. If the condition evaluates to False, VBA exits the loop and executes the next statement following the `Loop While` statement. If it evaluates to True, VBA goes to the beginning and executes the loop statements again. Figure 9.8 illustrates the Do...Loop While structure.

FIGURE 9.8:

The Do...Loop While loop structure

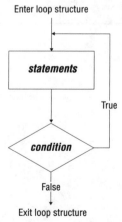

The DoLoopWhile procedure shown below uses the Do...Loop While structure. Add this procedure to the basControlStructures module.

```
Public Sub DoLoopWhile()
    Dim intCounter As Integer
    intCounter = 0
    Do
        Debug.Print intCounter
        intCounter = intCounter + 1
    Loop While intCounter < 3
End Sub
```

Run the DoLoopWhile procedure in the Immediate window. The loop runs three times.

The *Do Until...Loop* and *Do...Loop Until* Structures

When you replace the While keyword with the Until keyword, VBA continues repeated execution of the loop statements *until* the condition evaluates to True (which is the same as repeated execution *while* the condition evaluates to False).

The Do Until...Loop structure has this syntax:

```
Do Until condition
    statements
Loop
```

If the condition is False, VBA executes the loop statements and returns to the Do statement. If the condition evaluates to True, VBA exits the loop and executes the next statement following the Loop statement. If the condition evaluates to True initially, the statements of the Do Until...Loop structure are not executed at all. Figure 9.9 illustrates the Do Until...Loop structure.

FIGURE 9.9:

The Do Until...Loop structure

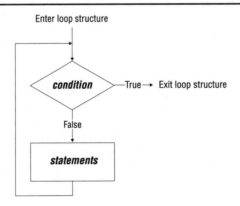

The Do...Loop Until structure has the following syntax:

```
Do
    statements
Loop Until condition
```

VBA executes the statements and tests the condition. If the condition is False, VBA returns to the Do statement. If the condition is True, VBA exits the loop and continues with the next statement. If the condition evaluates to True initially, the statements of the Do...Loop Until structure are executed once. Figure 9.10 illustrates the Do...Loop Until structure.

FIGURE 9.10:

The Do...Loop Until loop structure

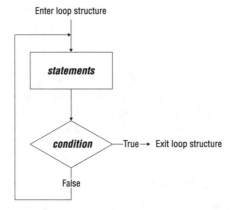

WARNING   You must be sure that at least one of the statements in the **Do...Loop** changes the value of the condition, so that sooner or later the condition evaluates to False. Without such a statement, the structure is an *endless loop*. You can stop execution of most endless loops by pressing Ctrl+Break. It is possible, however, to create an endless loop called a *tight loop* that locks up the computer so that the only way to end the loop is to press Ctrl+Alt+Delete and exit from Access.

The DoUntil procedure shown below uses the Do Until...Loop structure. Add this procedure to the basControlStructures module.

```
Public Sub DoUntil()
    Dim intCounter As Integer
    intCounter = 0
    Do Until intCounter < 3
        Debug.Print intCounter
        intCounter = intCounter + 1
    Loop
End Sub
```

Run the DoUntil procedure in the Immediate window. The loop is not executed at all because the condition is True initially.

The `DoLoopUntil` procedure shown below uses the `Do...Loop Until` structure. Add this procedure to the basControlStructures module.

```
Public Sub DoLoopUntil()
    Dim intCounter As Integer
    intCounter = 0
    Do
        Debug.Print intCounter
        intCounter = intCounter + 1
    Loop Until intCounter < 3
End Sub
```

Run the `DoLoopUntil` procedure in the Immediate window. The loop runs once. At the end of the first loop, the condition evaluates to True, so VBA exits the loop.

NOTE Another way to perform looping is with the `While...Wend` structure. With the `While...Wend` structure, you can specify the test condition only at the beginning of the loop, and you can specify that the loop continues to execute until the test condition becomes True. The `Do...Loop` is more flexible because you can specify the test condition at the beginning or at the end of the loop and can specify whether the loop continues to execute until the test condition is True or until the test condition is False.

Looping through a Recordset

A common operation in Access VBA is "walking a recordset." You can use a `Do` loop to walk through every record of a recordset from beginning to end. Each pass through the loop points to a record (the current record) in the recordset, takes some action on the current record, and uses the `MoveNext` method to move the current record pointer to the next record. You use the recordset's EOF property to determine when the loop is finished. The EOF property is False as long as you are pointing to a record in the recordset and True if you move past the last record. When you are on the last record in the recordset, the `MoveNext` method moves the current record pointer beyond the recordset limits, the EOF property becomes True, and the loop terminates.

Normally, you want the loop statements to execute only if a recordset actually has records, so you usually use a `Do Until...Loop` to walk the records; if the recordset has no records, the EOF property is True, so the loop never executes. The structure for "walking a recordset" is as follows:

```
Do Until rst.EOF
    statements acting on the current record
    rst.MoveNext
Loop
```

In this structure, `rst` is an object variable representing a Recordset object.

As an example, we'll use a `Do Until...Loop` to walk through the records of the Employees table. Enter the `LoopRecordset` procedure shown below in the basControlStructures module.

```
Public Sub LoopRecordset()
    Dim rst As New ADODB.Recordset
    Dim cnn As New ADODB.Connection
    Set cnn = CurrentProject.Connection
    rst.Open "Employees", cnn
    Do Until rst.EOF
        Debug.Print rst!LastName
        rst.MoveNext
    Loop
End Sub
```

This procedure declares object variables to point to the open connection and the recordset and uses the reference `CurrentProject.Connection` to assign the open connection to the object variable. The procedure uses the `Open` method of the Recordset object to open a recordset on the Employees table.

Run the `LoopRecordset` procedure in the Immediate window. Each pass through the `Do Until` loop prints the value in the LastName field of the current record and moves the current record pointer to the next record (see Figure 9.11). When the current record pointer has moved past the last record in the recordset, the EOF property is True and the loop ends.

FIGURE 9.11:

Walking a recordset using
`Do Until...Loop`

Nesting Control Structures

You can place control structures within other control structures. A control structure that is placed within another control structure is *nested*. As an example, suppose you want to lock all of the text boxes on a form. You can use a `For Each...Next` structure to loop through all of the controls on the form. For each control, you can use an `If TypeOf...Then...Else` structure to determine whether the control is a text box and lock it if it is.

The LockControls procedure shown below nests control structures to lock text boxes. The If…Then decision structure is nested within the For Each…Next loop structure. The procedure uses Screen.ActiveForm.Controls to refer to the Controls collection of the active form. Enter the procedure in the basControlStructures module.

```
Public Function LockControls()
    Dim ctl As Control
    For Each ctl In Screen.ActiveForm.Controls
        If TypeOf ctl Is TextBox Then ctl.Locked = True
    Next ctl
End Function
```

Open the Customers form in Design view. On the form, place a command button named cmdLockControls with the caption Lock the Text Boxes. Set the button's OnClick property to =LockControls(). Save the form, switch to Form view, and run the LockControls procedure by clicking the button. VBA locks all of the text box controls. You can test this by trying to change the data in any of the fields.

Abbreviating Object References

Sometimes you may need to take several actions on an object. For example, suppose you want to disable the text boxes that are locked by the LockControls procedure shown in the previous section. In addition, you want to provide visual cues to indicate that the form is in review mode instead of data-entry mode. You can provide a visual cue by changing the background color of the text boxes. One solution for setting several properties for an object is to use a separate statement for each property: *object.property = value*. For each statement, VBA must look up the object. If the reference to the object includes traversing other objects in the hierarchy, looking up the object for each statement takes execution time. An alternative is to use the With…End With structure.

The With…End With block allows you to perform a set of statements on the same object without needing to look up the object for each statement; instead, you use an abbreviated reference, as follows:

```
With object
    [statements]
End With
```

Each statement may be one of the following simple types that sets a property or runs a method:

```
.property = value
.method
```

A statement may also contain an expression that refers to a property or a method.

When *object* is a simple object variable, using the With structure may not save execution time, but it will save programming time because you need to enter the object variable only once. When the object is an expression that returns an object, such as Screen.ActiveControl, using the With structure saves execution time because VBA evaluates the expression just once. VBA evaluates the expression and assigns a reference to the object internally. VBA then places this hidden object variable in front of the dots in the statements inside the With structure.

As an example, the ReviewMode function procedure shown below uses the With...End With structure to set the Locked, Enabled, and ForeColor properties for a control.

```
Public Function ReviewMode()
    Const Red As Integer = 255
    Dim ctl As Control
    For Each ctl in Screen.ActiveForm
        If TypeOf ctl Is TextBox Then
            With ctl
                .Locked = True
                .Enabled = False
                .ForeColor = Red
            End With
        End If
    Next
End Function
```

The procedure uses three levels of nested control structures to change any form from edit mode to review mode:

- The function procedure uses a For Each...Next structure to loop through the controls on the active form.

- For each control, the procedure nests an If TypeOf structure to determine if the control is a text box.

- If the control is a text box, the procedure uses a nested With...End With structure to change the control's properties.

The procedure walks through the controls on the active form. Controls is the default collection, so the procedure uses Screen.ActiveForm to refer to the collection. For each control, the procedure determines if the control is a text box and, if so, changes the control's properties; otherwise, it moves to the next control.

Insert the ReviewMode procedure in the basControlStructures module. Open the Customers form in Design view and add a command button named cmdReviewMode, with the caption Change to Review Mode. Set the button's OnClick property to =ReviewMode(). Save the form, switch to Form view, and click the button to run the procedure. The procedure locks and disables the text boxes and sets their font color to red.

Introducing Some Useful Statements and Functions

VBA provides an extensive set of built-in statements and functions that are useful in writing procedures. This section includes brief descriptions of a few of them.

Using Toggle Statements

Many object properties have the value True or False. A toggle statement reverses the current value from True to False or from False to True. You can use an If...Then...Else structure as a toggle statement, as follows:

```
If object.property Then object.property = False Else object. _
    property = True
```

VBA tests the *object.property* expression. If the expression evaluates to True, then VBA changes the value to False; otherwise, VBA changes the value to True.

A shorter toggle statement uses the Not operator, as follows:

```
object.property = Not object.property
```

The Not operator reverses the expression on which it operates, so this statement assigns the value of *object.property* to its opposite value. For example, if a control is named ctl, the statement ctl.Locked = Not ctl.Locked toggles the control's Locked property.

As an example, the ToggleMode procedure shown below toggles any form between review mode (with data controls locked and disabled) and edit mode (with data controls unlocked and enabled). The procedure toggles only the text box controls, but you can modify the procedure to test and toggle other types of controls. Insert the ToggleMode procedure in the basControlStructures module.

```
Public Function ToggleMode()
    Dim ctl As Control
    For Each ctl in Screen.ActiveForm
        If TypeOf ctl Is TextBox Then
            With ctl
                .Locked = Not .Locked
                .Enabled = Not .Enabled
            End With
        End If
    Next ctl
End Function
```

Open the Customers form in Design view. Add a command button named cmdToggleMode with the caption Toggle the Mode. Set the button's OnClick property to =ToggleMode(). Save the form, switch to Form view, and click the button a few times to run the ToggleMode procedure. The mode toggles back and forth between review and data-entry mode (for the text box controls only).

Using *Exit* Statements

VBA provides a set of Exit statements that you can use to exit a function procedure, sub procedure, property procedure, or repetitive block of statements in a Do...Loop, For ...Next, or For Each...Next structure.

The Exit statements work as follows:

- Exit Function, Exit Sub, and Exit Property immediately exit the function, sub, or property procedure in which the corresponding Exit... statement appears. Execution continues with the statement following the statement that called the procedure.

- Exit Do can be used only in a Do...Loop and immediately transfers control to the statement following the Loop statement.

- Exit For can be used only in a For...Next or For Each...Next loop and immediately transfers control to the statement following the Next statement.

Using the Timer Function

You can use the built-in Timer function to time an operation in a procedure. The Timer function returns the number of seconds since midnight and provides the easiest way to approximate how long an operation takes. To use the Timer function as a timer, place the Timer function immediately before and after the operation you want to time and then calculate the difference.

As an example, the QueryRunTime procedure shown below tells you the number of seconds it takes to run a query.

```
Public Function QueryRunTime(strQueryName As String) As Single
    Dim sngBegin As Single, sngEnd As Single
    sngBegin = Timer
    DoCmd.OpenQuery strQueryName
    sngEnd = Timer
    QueryRunTime = sngEnd - sngBegin
    MsgBox strQueryName & " run time is " & QueryRunTime
End Function
```

This procedure has the name of the query you want to time as a string argument. The procedure declares variables of the Single data type to hold the values of the Timer function at the beginning and at the end of the query execution.

Insert the QueryRunTime function procedure in basControlStructures. In the Immediate window, type **QueryRunTime("Invoices")** and press Enter. The procedure runs the query, displays its datasheet, and displays the message box (see Figure 9.12).

FIGURE 9.12:

Using the Timer function to time the execution of the Invoices query

Using the *DoEvents* Function

There are two kinds of processes in Access:

- Processes that send and receive Windows messages to and from the Access objects

- Processes that do not send and receive Windows messages

For example, Access sends keyboard input and mouse clicks to Windows as messages, but VBA code that manipulates database objects does not send messages. When VBA is running a procedure, it uses processor time, and Windows may not be able to process the messages it receives in a timely fashion. The unprocessed messages line up in a queue waiting to be processed. In addition, keystrokes line up in a SendKeys queue.

One solution to the problem of unprocessed messages and keys is to use the DoEvents function to pass control to Windows so that the waiting messages and keys can be processed. When you use the DoEvents function, control is not returned to Access until Windows has finished processing the messages in the queue. Normally, you include a DoEvents function in a loop that takes a long time and use the function to yield control only occasionally.

To illustrate the DoEvents function, the DoEventsLoop procedure shown below puts the computer to work calculating the square root of the loop index for values from 1 to 1 million.

```
Public Sub DoEventsLoop()
    Dim sngBegin As Single, sngEnd As Single, sngElapsed As Single
    Dim lngCounter As Long, dblRoot As Double
    sngBegin = Timer
    For lngCounter = 1 To 1000000
        dblRoot = Sqr(lngCounter)
    Next
    sngEnd = Timer
    sngElapsed = sngEnd - sngBegin
    MsgBox "Run time is " & sngElapsed
End Sub
```

Insert the `DoEventsLoop` procedure in the basControlStructures module and run the procedure in the Immediate window. (The million loops took 0.3476563 seconds on my computer.) Next, modify the `DoEventsLoop` procedure so that it passes control to Windows once every 100,000 loops, as follows.

```
Public Sub DoEventsLoop()
 Dim sngBegin As Single, sngEnd As Single, sngElapsed As Single
 Dim lngCounter As Long, dblRoot As Double
 sngBegin = Timer
 For lngCounter = 1 To 1000000
        dblRoot = Sqr(lngCounter)
        If lngCounter Mod 100000 = 0 Then DoEvents
 Next
 sngEnd = Timer
 sngElapsed = sngEnd - sngBegin
 MsgBox "Run time is " & sngElapsed
End Sub
```

In the modified loop, the `DoEvents` function runs whenever the counter is a multiple of 100,000. This version uses the `Mod` operator to determine when control passes. The `Mod` operator has the following syntax:

```
result = number1 Mod number2
```

Result is the remainder after dividing the first number by the second number (for example, `1 = 7 Mod 3`).

Run the modified procedure. (The million loops took 0.5898438 seconds on my computer.)

Using the *MsgBox* and *InputBox* Functions

You use the `MsgBox` and `InputBox` functions to allow the user to communicate directly with your application. Most of the examples in this book use the `MsgBox` function to display a message to the user. When you use the `MsgBox` function, the user communicates by choosing from a set of buttons in a dialog box. When you use the `InputBox` function, the user communicates by entering text in a text box in a dialog box.

You can create your own custom dialog boxes for direct communication that duplicate or improve on these two functions; nevertheless, the `MsgBox` and `InputBox` functions provide fast and simple ways to display default dialog boxes and collect a choice or text input from the user.

The `InputBox` function has the syntax

```
InputBox (prompt, title, default, xpos, ypos, helpfile, context)
```
where

- *Prompt* is the required string expression that is displayed as the message.

- *Title* is the optional string expression displayed as the title of the dialog.

- *Default* is the optional string expression displayed in the text box as the default response.

- *Xpos* and *ypos* are optional numerical expressions that specify the distance in twips from the upper-left corner of the dialog to the upper-left corner of the screen.

- *Helpfile* is the optional string expression identifying the Help file you want to use.

- *Context* is the optional numeric expression that is the Help context number for the Help file. (If you include the *helpfile* argument, you must also include *context*, and vice versa.)

The dialog created by the InputBox function has a single text box for collecting a response and OK and Cancel buttons. When the user clicks one of the buttons or presses Enter, the value in the text box is returned to Access. Normally, you store the returned value in a variable.

You can explore the InputBox function in the Immediate window. Type **var = InputBox ("Enter your name now.")** and press Enter. VBA displays the input dialog box and waits for your response (see Figure 9.13). Enter your name and click OK. VBA stores your input in the var variable. Type **? var** and press Enter to print the value of the variable.

FIGURE 9.13:

Using the InputBox
to collect a value

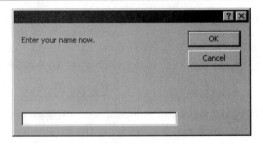

Using the *SysCmd* Function

The SysCmd function is actually three functions in one. You can use it as follows:

- To return the state of a Database window object

- To return Access system information

- To display a progress meter

Returning the State of a Database Window Object

A common use of the SysCmd function is to determine the state of a database object—whether the object is open, whether the object is new, or whether the design of the object has been changed but not saved. The syntax for this version of the function is as follows:

```
returnvalue = SysCmd(acSysCmdGetObjectState, objecttype, objectname)
```

Objecttype is one of the enumerated constants for specifying one of the Database window objects: acTable, acQuery, acForm, acReport, acMacro, acModule, acDataAccessPage, acDefault, acDiagram, acServerView, acFunction, or acStoredProcedure. *Objectname* is a string expression that is the valid name you have specified for the object. The function returns an integer that is a combination of the following values:

Value	Enumerated Constant	Object State
0		Not open or does not exist
1	AcObjStateOpen	Open
2	AcObjStateDirty	Changed but not saved
4	AcObjStateNew	New

You can explore this version of the SysCmd function in the Immediate window. With the Customers form closed, type **? SysCmd(acSysCmdGetObjectState, acForm, "Customers")** and press Enter. The Immediate window prints 0 to indicate that the form is not open (we know it exists). Next, open the Customers form in Design view and change the RecordSelectors property to Yes. Type **? SysCmd(acSysCmdGetObjectState, acForm, "Customers")** and press Enter. The Immediate window prints the combined flag 3 to indicate that the form is both open (1) and that the form has been changed but the change has not been saved (2).

Returning Access System Information

You can use the SysCmd function to return information about Access, such as the version number, whether the version is a run-time version, the location of the Access file, and the location of the workgroup file (System.mdw). In this case, the syntax is as follows:

```
returnvalue = SysCmd(action)
```

The return value is the information, usually returned as a string.

You can explore this version of the SysCmd function in the Immediate window:

- Type **?SysCmd(acSysCmdAccessVer)** and press Enter. The Immediate window prints the version number of Access.

- Type **?SysCmd(acSysCmdGetWorkgroupFile)** and press Enter. The Immediate window prints the path to the workgroup file.

- Type **?SysCmd(acSysCmdRuntime)** and press Enter. The Immediate window prints True or False depending on whether you are running a run-time version of Access (the Access Developer's Toolkit allows you to create run-time versions of Access).

- Type **?SysCmd(acSysCmdAccessDir)** and press Enter. The Immediate window prints the name of the directory that contains Msaccess.exe.

- Type **?SysCmd(acSysCmdProfile)** and press Enter. The Immediate window prints the /profile setting specified when starting Access from the command line.

Displaying a Progress Meter

You can use the SysCmd function to display a progress meter with text or to display a text message in the status bar to indicate the progress of an operation. In this version of the function, the syntax is

```
returnvalue = SysCmd(action[,text][,value])
```

where

- *Action* is an enumerated constant that you use to specify the action to take, including initializing, updating, or removing the progress meter and setting or resetting the status bar text.

- *Text* is the optional argument to identify the text that you want to display.

- *Value* is the optional argument to specify the maximum value of the progress meter when you use the function to initialize the meter and to specify the relative value of the meter when you use the function to update the meter.

To display a progress meter, you must first use the function to display an initial meter specifying the action as the enumerated constant acSysCmdInitMeter, the text you want to display, and the value as the maximum value of the meter. To show the progress of an operation, use the function specifying the action as the enumerated constant acSysCmdUpdateMeter and the value as the measure of progress. The SysCmd function calculates the percentage of progress to the maximum value and updates the meter.

To explore this version of the SysCmd function, insert the Meter procedure shown below in the basControlStructures module.

```
Public Function Meter()
    Dim varReturn As Variant, str As String, lngCounter As Long
    Dim dblRoot As Double
    str = "Calculating square roots…"
    varReturn = SysCmd(acSysCmdInitMeter, str, 1000000)
    For lngCounter = 1 To 1000000
        dblRoot = Sqr(lngCounter)
        If lngCounter Mod 100000 = 0 Then
            varReturn = SysCmd(acSysCmdUpdateMeter, lngCounter)
        End If
    Next lngCounter
    varReturn = SysCmd(acSysCmdRemoveMeter)
End Function
```

This procedure uses a For…Next loop to calculate the square roots of the numbers between 1 and 1,000,000. Before starting the loop, the procedure displays the initial progress meter, setting the maximum value to 1,000,000. Once every 100,000 loops, the procedure updates the progress meter using the value of the Counter variable. When the loop is finished, the procedure removes the progress meter.

Open the Customers form in Design view and add a new command button named cmdSquareRoot with the Caption property Calculate Square Roots. Click in the OnClick property and type **= Meter()**. Save the form and switch to Form view. Click the new button. The progress meter displays the progress of the operation (see Figure 9.14).

Summary

This chapter has introduced you to the keywords and statements that VBA provides for controlling the order in which statements are executed, whether statements are executed at all, and the number of times a set of statements is repeated. The following are the important points.

- To control execution of a set of statements, use control statements at the beginning and end of the set to create a control structure.

- To make a decision, create one or more test conditions and use a decision control structure to test the conditions and execute different sets of statements depending on the value of the conditions. The decision control structures are If…Then, If…Then…Else, and Select Case.

- The control structures that you can use to repeat a set of statements are For…Next, For Each…Next, and Do…Loop.

FIGURE 9.14:

Use the SysCmd function to display an initial progress meter, update the meter, and then remove the meter.

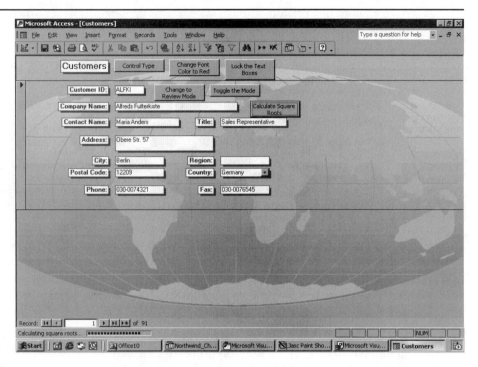

- You can nest a control structure inside another control structure to create more complicated execution flow patterns.

- You can use the With...End With structure when you are setting several properties for the same object.

- Access provides many built-in statements and functions that make your programs more useful, efficient, and powerful. Examples are the Timer function for timing execution; the DoEvents function to interrupt execution of a procedure and allow Windows to respond to messages; the MsgBox and InputBox functions for communicating with the user; and the SysCmd function for determining the state of a Database window object, gathering system information, or displaying a progress meter.

This chapter completes the introduction to Access VBA. You now know the concepts and techniques that are required to automate a database. However, before automating specific database operations, you should study the error-handling capabilities of Access VBA in the next chapter. The ability to handle errors is a fundamental component in Access VBA. Error handling is typically a major reason for including VBA procedures in a database.

CHAPTER 10

Dealing with Errors in VBA

- Understanding the kinds of errors

- Using the compiler to detect errors

- Using the VBA troubleshooting tools to analyze errors

- Handling database engine and interface errors

- Handling VBA errors

In the broadest terms, an error is any deviation from correctness. An error occurs any time something happens that you didn't intend to happen. Depending on the type of error, any of the following may occur:

- You may not be able to run a part of your application.

- The application may start to run, but when the error occurs, Access uses its default error handling by displaying a default error message and, in some cases, by "crashing" your application and suspending further execution.

- The application runs but fails to carry out the operation you intended, even though Access gives no sign of a problem.

VBA provides help by detecting some of the errors that can occur. VBA also provides a set of troubleshooting tools that you can use to analyze an error. Once you understand why an error occurred, you can take the necessary steps to correct the problem. Sometimes, you can correct the problem so that the error won't occur again. Other times the error is not one that you can eliminate, and you must deal with the fact that it may occur again. Correcting this type of problem means writing a VBA procedure to provide instructions on how you want to handle the error the next time it occurs.

As you create custom applications, you *are* going to experience errors. The first step in dealing with errors is understanding how and why they occur. This chapter describes the different kinds of errors, how you can use the built-in syntax checking and the compiler to avoid some of them, how to use the troubleshooting tools to analyze an error, and how to replace the default error handling with your own error-handling code.

Avoidable and Unavoidable Errors

You will be faced with two fundamentally different kinds of errors: those you can avoid and those you can't.

Avoidable Errors

Avoidable errors are the result of your own mistakes. Everyone makes mistakes! As your programming experience increases and if you are very careful, you'll make fewer mistakes, but you'll still make mistakes. Knowing the kinds of errors that can occur and knowing how to predict them is the best way to learn how to avoid them as you write your code. There are three kinds of avoidable errors:

- *Compile-time errors* occur when you violate the rules of VBA syntax, such as when you misspell a word or forget the `End If` statement in an `If…Then` decision structure. You can eliminate these errors with VBA's built-in syntax checking and compiling. (Enable the built-in syntax checking by checking the Auto Syntax Check option in the Visual Basic Editor's Options dialog.)

- *Run-time errors* occur when Access can't run a VBA statement because you made a mistake, such as when you specify the wrong data type or try to run the wrong method.

- *Logic errors* occur when your VBA procedures execute without failing but you don't get the result you intended. For example, a logic error occurs when you assign an event procedure to the wrong event and two procedures run in the wrong order as a result. (Logic errors are commonly called *bugs*, although *bug* is also used to refer to any error.)

You deal with avoidable errors by eliminating the source of the error (for example, correcting a typing error), using only valid properties and methods for an object, or triggering event procedures with the appropriate event. You can prevent many errors by writing your VBA procedure to test the value of a precondition first and then execute a statement only if the precondition evaluates to True. For example, a statement to select a form fails if the form is not open, but you can avoid the error by using the `IsLoaded` function to determine if the form is open and running the statement to select the form only if the form is open. If the `IsLoaded` function evaluates to False, you can precede the statement to select the form with the `OpenForm` method. This can be accomplished with a simple `If…Then` decision.

Unavoidable Errors

Unavoidable errors are those that continue to occur even after you have eliminated all of your mistakes through careful design, testing, and troubleshooting. Here are some situations in which unavoidable errors occur:

- The user tries to save a new record without a primary key.
- The user enters a value in a combo box that isn't in the combo list.
- The power fails or the disk is full.
- The network disconnects unexpectedly.
- The user inserts the wrong floppy disk.

You can think of unavoidable errors as somebody else's fault—the user or the computer has done something that you have no control over. Nevertheless, it's your project, so your code still needs to deal with unavoidable errors.

Fatal and Nonfatal Errors

Unavoidable errors come in two varieties: those that cause your procedure to fail (fatal errors) and those that don't cause failure (nonfatal errors).

When a nonfatal error occurs, the default error handling is that Access displays a default error message and the VBA procedure continues to run. For example, if a procedure runs the ApplyFilter method with the name of a nonexistent query as the filtername argument, the procedure continues to run without displaying a run-time error message, because the built-in method is designed so that a VBA run-time error is not generated.

Unfortunately, most errors are fatal! Fatal errors occur when a VBA statement can't execute and no built-in measures prevent a VBA run-time error from being generated. When a fatal error occurs, the default error handling is that VBA may display a default error message, Access displays the run-time error dialog box for the procedure, and Access suspends execution. For example, suppose you place a command button on a form and create an event procedure that runs the built-in Save Record command to save the record, as follows:

```
Private Sub cmdSave_Click()
    DoCmd.RunCommand acCmdSaveRecord
End Sub
```

When you enter a new record but leave the primary key blank and try to save the record, the database engine won't be able to save the record, and Access displays the run-time error message shown in Figure 10.1 and suspends execution of the procedure at the DoCmd statement.

FIGURE 10.1:

The run-time error message
for a fatal error

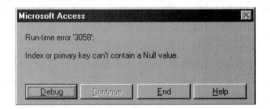

Error Trapping

You deal with unavoidable errors by writing VBA code to replace the default error handling with your own custom error-handling code. Intercepting the default error handling when an error occurs is called *trapping the error*. You can write your own error handler that replaces the default error message with a custom message and that includes additional instructions for dealing with the error. Occasionally, the instructions may require ending the procedure without accomplishing the intended task, but at least you can do so gracefully without displaying the failed procedure dialog. Not trapping the error puts the procedure into the limbo state of suspended execution and the novice user into the panic state of suspended understanding.

As an illustration of custom error handling, the cmdSave_Click procedure for saving a record, shown below, intercepts the default error handling that Access would carry out when the fatal error occurs because the primary key value is missing. The procedure includes statements to trap the error, replace the default message shown in Figure 10.1 with a custom message, and move the focus to the CustomerID control.

```
Private Sub cmdSave_Click()
    On Error GoTo Err_cmdSave_Click
        DoCmd.RunCommand acCmdSaveRecord
Exit_cmdSave_Click:
Exit Sub
Err_cmdSave_Click:
    MsgBox "You must enter a unique Customer ID before saving " _
        & "the record."
    DoCmd.GoToControl "CustomerID"
        Resume Exit_cmdSave_Click
End Sub
```

Error handling is discussed in more detail later in this chapter.

The VBA Compiler

VBA does not use a true compiler. A true compiler translates the code that you write in a programming language such as C++, Basic, or Pascal, called the *source code*, and generates a machine-language version of the code called the *object code*. The advantages of using a true compiler are that the object code can run on a computer that doesn't have the compiler installed and that the object code runs much faster than noncompiled source code.

The VBA compiler translates the code into a state that is somewhere between source code and object code called *pseudocode*. You can't view or read the pseudocode, but it runs faster than source code (although not as fast as equivalent code that is compiled by a true compiler). Your computer must have Access installed to run the pseudocode.

NOTE   In spite of the misnomers, this book follows the common practice of referring to the pseudocode generated by the VBA compiler as the *compiled state* and refers to the process of translating the source code into pseudocode as *compiling*.

Errors that Access detects during compiling are called compile-time errors. Typical compile errors occur under the following conditions:

- When you use a variable that has not been declared or misspell a variable name without having set the module's Declarations section to include the Option Explicit statement
- When you omit a required argument for a function or a method (see Figure 10.2a)

- If you omit a required statement in a set, such as the End If statement in an If…Then control structure (see Figure 10.2b)

- If your procedure calls another procedure that doesn't exist (see Figure 10.2c)

FIGURE 10.2:

Typical compile-time error messages

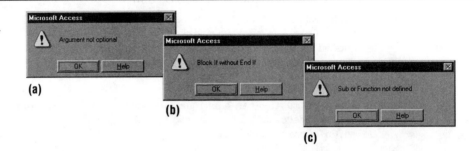

(a)

(b)

(c)

Automatic Compiling

The first time you try to run a new or changed procedure, Access compiles the procedure automatically. By default, Access compiles only the code it must compile to run the procedure. Access compiles the procedure you want to run and also compiles any procedures that the current procedure calls, any procedures that the called procedures may call, and so on. The set of procedures that the current procedure may call forms the *current execution path* for the current procedure. The *call tree* of the procedure is the set of all modules that contain procedures that might be called by any procedure stored in the procedure's module.

In addition to compiling the current procedure and the procedures in its call tree, Access checks these procedures for errors in referring to variables to ensure that all the variables referred to are correctly declared (but only if the Option Explicit statement is included in the Declarations sections of all modules). In compiling a procedure, Access checks all references to the called procedures and also checks the variables that the procedure uses that are declared elsewhere (for example, in the Declarations section of a module).

During compilation, Access loads the modules containing all procedures in the current execution path and the modules declaring variables referred to in these procedures. If no compilation errors occur, Access compiles the procedures in the current execution path and creates a compiled version of the code. After compiling, when you call the procedure, Access runs the compiled version. Access also keeps track of the compilation state of a procedure. After compiling a procedure, Access doesn't compile the procedure again unless you make a change that causes the procedure to become decompiled.

NOTE   The editable version of a procedure displayed in the Module window is called *source code*. After compiling a procedure, Access creates the compiled version. You cannot view or edit the compiled version. You can save your application in an MDE file that has the source code removed. In an MDE file, your programming efforts are completely secure: No one can see or change your code. When you create an MDE file, be sure to keep a copy of the original database so that you'll be able to view and change your own code. See Chapter 7, "Writing Procedures," for information about saving a database as an MDE file.

You can set two levels of automatic compiling, available through the Visual Basic Editor's Options dialog. Display the dialog by choosing Tools ➢ Options and clicking the General tab (see Figure 10.3). Here, you can enable or disable the Compile On Demand option.

FIGURE 10.3:

With the Compile On Demand option checked, Access compiles only the procedures in the current execution path of the procedure you are running.

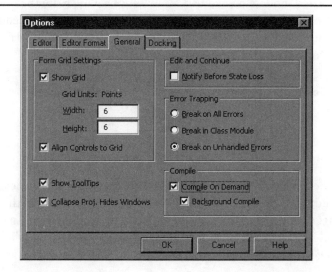

With the Compile On Demand option checked (the default), Access compiles only the procedures in the call tree of the procedure you are running. Although the Compile On Demand option makes writing and testing individual procedures faster, it doesn't find errors that may exist in your modules. When you uncheck this option, Access compiles all of the procedures in the call tree (whether they are called by the current procedure or not) and also compiles modules that declare variables referred to in the current and call tree procedures.

To explore the Compile On Demand option, follow these steps:

1. Create a new database named Ch10_Examples.mdb. Make sure the Compile On Demand option is checked in the General tab of the Visual Basic Editor's Options dialog.

2. Create a module named basCompileNumber and insert the following procedures:

```
Public Sub TestOne()
    Call TestA
End Sub

Public Sub TestTwo()
    Call TestB
End Sub
```

3. Create a second module named basCompileAlpha and create the next two procedures. The TestC procedure has a compile error because the TestD procedure does not exist. Note also that the TestTwo procedure in the basCompileNumber module has a similar compile error because the TestB procedure does not exist.

```
Public Sub TestA()
    MsgBox "This is TestA"
End Sub

Public Sub TestC()
    Call TestD
End Sub
```

4. In the Immediate window, type **Call TestOne** and press Enter. Access compiles TestOne and TestA and displays the message box. Access records the compilation state of the TestOne and TestA procedures and will not compile them again unless you make a change. Because the Compile On Demand option is checked, VBA does not compile the TestTwo or TestC procedures.

5. Choose Tools ➢ Options, select the General tab, and clear the Compile On Demand check box.

6. Change the TestOne procedure by adding a comment as shown below to force VBA to recompile the TestOne procedure. Run the procedure in the Immediate window. This time, VBA tries to compile all of the procedures in the basCompileNumber module and detects the compile error in the TestTwo procedure. VBA displays the compile

error message box (Figure 10.4a) and highlights the problem statement in the `TestTwo` procedure (Figure 10.4b).

```
Sub TestOne()
    'call another procedure
    Call TestA
End Sub
```

FIGURE 10.4:

When you uncheck the Compile On Demand option, VBA attempts to compile all procedures in a module, whether or not the procedures are called by the current procedure.

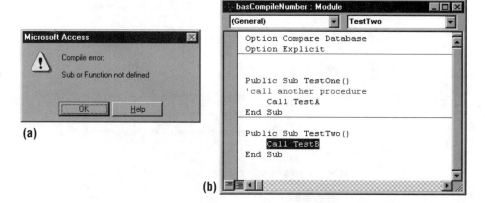

(a)

(b)

7. Change the highlighted statement to Call TestA and then run the `TestOne` procedure in the Immediate window. This time the basCompileNumber module compiles successfully, but when Access tries to compile the basCompileAlpha module, a compile error is detected in the `TestC` procedure in the basCompileAlpha module, even though this procedure isn't called by the current procedure or by any of the procedures in the basCompileNumber module.

8. Choose Tools ➤ Options, select the General tab, and check the Compile On Demand option.

Explicit Compiling

To compile a single procedure, you can just run it. You can also instruct Access to compile all the procedures in modules that are in the database.

To compile all procedures in all modules in the database, choose Debug ➤ Compile (*database*). After running this command, your database is in a compiled state with all procedures in all modules compiled and ready to run. Because compiling takes time, you should make sure that your database is in a compiled state after you finish making changes and that you are ready to run the completed database application.

Decompiling

Any changes to code in a module decompiles the module. Changes to objects that have code assigned to them, such as forms, reports, and controls, also cause modules to become decompiled. Access stores the name of the database as part of the compilation state, so if you perform an operation that changes the name of the database, such as compacting the database to a new name, the database becomes decompiled.

TIP   You can avoid decompiling your application when you compact it by compacting the database to the same name.

Troubleshooting Tools

VBA has tools that help you analyze both run-time errors that occur when VBA is unable to execute a statement while the code is running and logic errors that occur when VBA can execute your code but doesn't produce the result you expected. VBA has two kinds of troubleshooting tools:

- Tools that let you observe what happens to data as code is running
- Tools that suspend execution of your code at a statement and let you use the Immediate window to test and view data

Modules have *three* states (also called *modes* or *times*): design time when you enter and edit code, run time when the code is running, and break mode when the code is running but is suspended between executing statements. Most of the troubleshooting tools require the code to be in break mode. In break mode, the Module window displays the code that is running, and the variables and properties retain the values they had at the moment execution was suspended.

Entering and Leaving Break Mode

VBA enters break mode at a line of code in the following circumstances:

- A statement on a line generates a run-time error and no error trapping is in effect when the error occurs.
- You have set a breakpoint on a line. If you close a database and reopen it, all the breakpoints are cleared.
- A Stop statement occurs on the line. Stop temporarily halts execution, but you can continue running code by choosing Run ➤ Continue.
- You press Ctrl+Break, select Run ➤ Break, or click the toolbar's Break button when code is executing.

Using a breakpoint or Stop statement is useful when you know which statement caused the error or the general area of code in which the error occurred.

NOTE   The difference between the Stop and End statements in a procedure is that the End statement terminates all execution and resets module-level variables and all static variables in all modules; the Stop statement temporarily halts execution, leaving the current values of all variables intact.

The procedure that is running when the execution is suspended and enters break mode is called the *current procedure*. VBA displays a yellow arrow in the margin bar to the left of the statement at which execution is paused and displays the text with a yellow background (see Figure 10.5). The marked statement is called the *current statement* and is the statement that will run next.

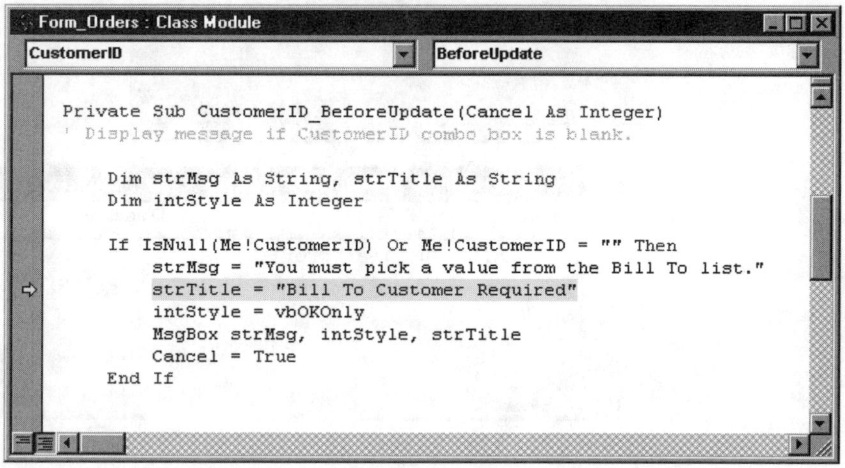

FIGURE 10.5:

When a procedure is in break mode, VBA marks the current statement with an arrow and a colored background.

```
Form_Orders : Class Module                              _ □ ×

CustomerID                          ▼    BeforeUpdate                    ▼

  Private Sub CustomerID_BeforeUpdate(Cancel As Integer)
  ' Display message if CustomerID combo box is blank.

      Dim strMsg As String, strTitle As String
      Dim intStyle As Integer

      If IsNull(Me!CustomerID) Or Me!CustomerID = "" Then
          strMsg = "You must pick a value from the Bill To list."
⇨         strTitle = "Bill To Customer Required"
          intStyle = vbOKOnly
          MsgBox strMsg, intStyle, strTitle
          Cancel = True
      End If
```

To leave break mode and reenter run time, you can either choose Run ➢ Go/Continue or click the Continue button in the toolbar. To end code execution and reset all variables, click the Reset button in the toolbar.

When VBA enters break mode by generating an error and custom error handling is not in effect, Access displays a run-time error message. For example, if you try to change the Caption property of the Customers form using the assignment statement,

```
Forms!Customers.Caption = "Customer Information"
```

but the Customers form isn't open when you run the statement, a run-time error is generated (see Figure 10.6a).

Clicking the Debug button in the procedure error message dialog displays the current procedure in the Module window with the current statement marked by the arrow and a colored background (see Figure 10.6b). Sometimes you can fix the error immediately by changing the code. In this example, you can fix the error by including code to test whether the Customers form is open before running the statement. Clicking the End button in the run-time error message box ends code execution; when you click this button, module-level variables retain their values. If you want to reset the variables after clicking End, click the Reset button in the toolbar.

FIGURE 10.6:

Clicking the Debug button in the error message (a) displays the current procedure with the current line marked by an arrow and a colored background (b).

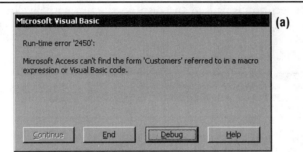

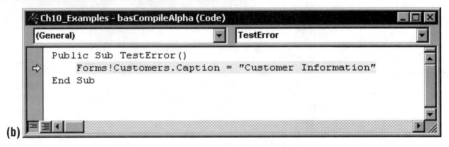

Testing in Break Mode

With execution suspended, you can examine what happened before the code halted by using the following techniques:

- Switching to other windows and inspecting their state
- Inspecting values of variables, controls, and properties to see if some statement set their values incorrectly
- Making changes to your code and then continuing execution by choosing Run ➤ Continue

Reinitializing Code

Some changes require code to be reinitialized. VBA displays a message when this is the case. You can reinitialize code when the program is running or is in break mode.

Reinitializing sets all variables, including static and public variables, to their default initial values: numeric variables are set to zero, variable-length string variables are set to the zero-length string, fixed-length string variables are set to ANSI zero, variant variables are set to Empty, and object variables are set to Nothing. To reinitialize all variables, choose Run ➢ Reset or click the Reset button in the toolbar.

Setting and Removing Breakpoints

You set a breakpoint by clicking in the margin bar to the left of an executable statement, by placing the insertion point in an executable statement and pressing F9, or by choosing Debug ➢ Toggle Breakpoint. (Each of these actions is a *toggle;* by taking the action when the insertion point is in a breakpoint statement, you remove the breakpoint.)

When you set a breakpoint, VBA displays a red circle in the margin bar and displays the line with white text on a red background by default. You can set more than one breakpoint in a procedure, and you can set breakpoints in multiple procedures.

You can remove all breakpoints in all modules by choosing Debug ➢ Clear All Breakpoints or by pressing Ctrl+Shift+F9. You can customize the Visual Basic Editor toolbar by adding a Clear All Breakpoints button. Figure 10.7 shows the Debug category of toolbar buttons, including the Clear All Breakpoints button and buttons for several other menu commands.

FIGURE 10.7:

You can customize the Visual Basic Editor toolbar by adding a Clear All Breakpoints button.

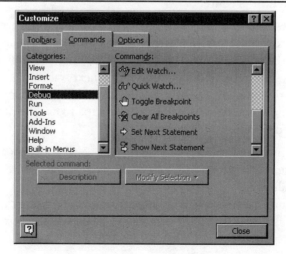

When you run a procedure with a breakpoint, VBA executes the statements before the breakpoint and then enters break mode by pausing before executing the breakpoint statement. With the procedure in break mode, you can single-step through your code, or you can leave break mode and return to normal execution mode by clicking the Go/Continue button in the toolbar, pressing F5, or choosing Run ➢ Continue.

You can use breakpoints to help locate a bug. Set a breakpoint at the statement you suspect is causing the problem and then run the procedure. When the breakpoint is reached and the procedure is paused, you can determine whether the error occurred before reaching the breakpoint. If the error has already occurred (in which case, execution may terminate before you reach the breakpoint), you'll know that an earlier statement caused the error. You can examine the preceding statements and set an earlier breakpoint for further exploration. If the procedure reaches the breakpoint and the error has not occurred yet, you can step through the procedure statements line by line until the error occurs.

Stepping through Code

VBA has three different ways to let you step through statements one at a time. (Stepping through statements is also called *tracing* statements.)

Step Into If you press F8 or choose Debug ➢ Step Into, VBA switches into run time, executes the current statement, and then switches back to break mode. The F8 key is one of the most useful keys for troubleshooting a procedure. When a line has two or more statements (separated by a colon), you can step one statement at a time. If the current statement is a call to another procedure, VBA proceeds to step into the statements of the called procedure one step at a time; when the called procedure finishes, VBA returns to the next statement in the current procedure.

Step Over Sometimes you need to step through the statements in a procedure, but you don't need to step through the statements in a called procedure. When you use the Step Over command and the current statement is a call to another procedure, VBA executes the called procedure as a single step and then steps to the next statement of the current procedure. When you use the Step Over command, the Module window continues to display the current procedure while the called procedure is running. To use the Step Over command, choose Debug ➢ Step Over or press Shift+F8.

Step Out When you use the Step Out command and the current procedure has been called by another procedure, VBA executes the rest of the current procedures and any nested procedures that it calls as a single step and then returns to the calling procedure and stops. If the current procedure was not called by another procedure, using the Step Out command is identical to using the Continue command. To use the Step Out command, choose Debug ➢ Step Out or press Ctrl+Shift+F8.

You can alternate between the three types of stepping. When you want to stop running the procedure one statement at a time, press F5 to continue execution without interruption. It is often useful to set multiple breakpoints in a procedure when testing code. Doing so allows you to run chunks of code, rather than having to either run the entire procedure or step through the procedure line by line.

Setting the Next Statement

If you are in break mode, you can skip lines or go back and repeat code by selecting the next statement that you want to execute. Use one of the following techniques:

- Move the insertion point to any line of code in the same procedure, right-click in the line, and choose the Set Next Statement command in the shortcut menu.

- Move the insertion point to a line of code and select Debug ➤ Set Next Statement.

- Press Ctrl+F9 with the cursor positioned on the line at which you wish to resume execution.

VBA marks the selected statement as the current statement with the yellow arrow in the margin and the yellow background. After specifying the next statement to be executed, you can click the Go/Continue button in the toolbar or the Step Into or Step Over commands in the Debug menu.

The Debug ➤ Show Next Statement command lets you see the next statement that will execute in the procedure.

TIP   You can add toolbar buttons to the toolbar for the Set Next Statement, Show Next Statement, Step Into, Step Over, and Step Out commands.

Executing a Group of Statements

When a procedure is in break mode, you can use the Run To Cursor command to run the program until the line you selected is run. Move the insertion point to any line of code in the same procedure, then right-click and choose the Run To Cursor command in the shortcut menu; choose Debug ➤ Run To Cursor; or press Ctrl+F8. VBA runs code beginning with the current statement to the line with the insertion point and then reenters break mode. Using Run To Cursor lets you avoid stepping through every statement in a procedure.

Viewing Current Values in the Module Window

Access provides a feature that lets you view the current value of a variable or constant referred to in a procedure when the procedure is in break mode. Move the mouse pointer to the variable or constant that you want to inspect. VBA displays the current value as a Data

Tip directly below the item (see Figure 10.8). You can turn off this feature by clearing the Auto Data Tips check box in the Editor tab of the Visual Basic Editor's Options dialog.

FIGURE 10.8:

You can inspect the current value of a variable or constant referred to in a procedure that is in break mode.

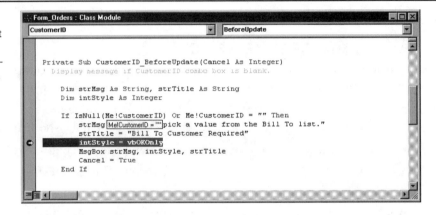

```
Form_Orders : Class Module
CustomerID                                    BeforeUpdate

Private Sub CustomerID_BeforeUpdate(Cancel As Integer)
' Display message if CustomerID combo box is blank.

    Dim strMsg As String, strTitle As String
    Dim intStyle As Integer

    If IsNull(Me!CustomerID) Or Me!CustomerID = "" Then
        strMsg  Me!CustomerID = ""  pick a value from the Bill To list."
        strTitle = "Bill To Customer Required"
        intStyle = vbOKOnly
        MsgBox strMsg, intStyle, strTitle
        Cancel = True
    End If
```

NOTE   As you've learned in previous chapters, you can also use the Immediate window to print current values. The Immediate window is available whether or not a module is in break mode.

Using the Locals Window in Break Mode

The Locals window is a valuable tool in debugging VBA modules. To open the Locals window, choose View ➤ Locals Window. The Locals window lists the variables and constants referred to in the current procedure in the Expression column and their data types in the Type column. The Value column displays the values of the variables and constants just before the current statement executes. As you step through statements, the Locals window updates to display the current values. You can also assign new values to variables in the Locals window. To change a value, click the value in the Value column, type a new value, and press Enter.

When VBA is in break mode, the Module window displays the currently running procedure with the current statement marked by a yellow arrow and background. Figure 10.9a shows the Locals window when a procedure is in break mode at the statement shown in Figure 10.9b.

The Locals window also displays information about objects. When the current procedure is an event procedure stored in a form or report module, the Locals window includes information about the objects in the corresponding form or report. The form or report is referred to as Me. Click the plus sign to the left of an object in the Locals window to expand the object and display all of its members.

FIGURE 10.9:

The Locals window (a) when a procedure is in break mode (b)

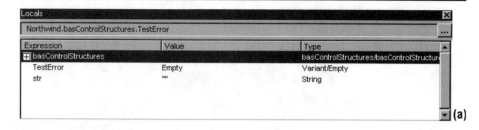

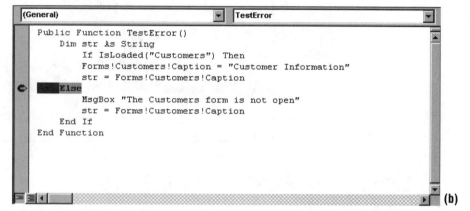

Using the Watches Window

The Watches window lets you view variables in any procedure and examine the values of custom expressions that you create. To open the Watches window, select View ➤ Watch Window.

You can define a particular expression or specify a variable whose value you want to observe as the code is running. You define watch expressions in the Add Watch dialog (see Figure 10.10a), available by choosing Debug ➤ Add Watch. Enter any variable, property, procedure call, or valid expression in the Expression box. You can specify the context as the specific procedure or module that must be current before VBA evaluates the expression, or you can leave the range unrestricted and ask VBA to evaluate the expression for all modules. Use the Watch Type option to specify whether you want to view the value of the expression, use its value to suspend execution of code whenever the value of the expression is True, or break whenever the value of the expression changes value.

After you define watch expressions, open the Watches window to view the watch expressions, their current values, and the specified context (see Figure 10.10b). To edit or delete a watch expression, use the Edit Watch dialog, available by choosing Debug ➤ Edit Watch or by pressing Ctrl+W.

Create watch expressions in the Add Watch dialog (a) and review changes to the expressions in the Watches window (b).

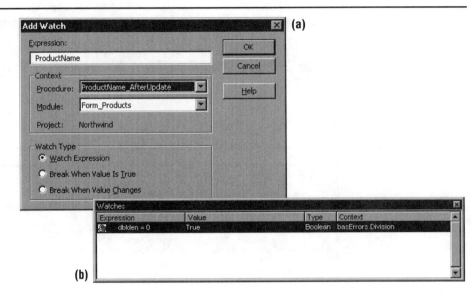

Using Quick Watch in Break Mode

When VBA is in break mode, you can observe the value of a variable, property, or function call without first defining it as a watch expression. To view the value of an expression in the current procedure, select the expression in the procedure and select Debug ➤ Quick Watch or press Shift+F9. The Quick Watch message box displays the expression and its current value (see Figure 10.11). You can add the expression to the Watches window as a watch expression by clicking the Add button.

FIGURE 10.11:

Use the Quick Watch dialog to view the value of a variable, property, or function call in the current procedure in break mode.

Avoiding Bugs

The best way to deal with errors is to avoid them in the first place if possible. Most errors are caused by changes. How many times have you been in the following situation? You decide to make a small change in an application that works just fine and then you find that nothing works right after you make the change. Even the most minor modification can lead to several hours of debugging to remove all of the mistakes that the change introduced. Here are some tips for avoiding errors:

Planning to avoid errors As you plan your application, you may be able to plan for future changes and thus avoid the errors that these changes would introduce. For example, when designing tables, think about additional fields that you may need in the future and include them in the beginning. Be sure to think carefully about the relationships between your tables and whether a relationship should be one-to-many or many-to-many. For example, in an instructional application that tracks students, instructors, and classes, the usual relationship between instructors and classes is one-to-many because a class usually has a single instructor; however, if you ever expect to allow team teaching, you should create a many-to-many relationship instead.

Syntax checking You can have VBA check the syntax of your code as you type it by checking the Auto Syntax Check option (in the Editor tab of the Visual Basic Editor's Tools ➢ Option dialog box). If you don't check this option, VBA checks the syntax only when you compile your code.

Using explicit variable declaration A common source of errors is typographical errors in variable names. You can avoid these errors by including `Option Explicit` in the Declarations section of every module. Access includes the `Option Explicit` statement in all new modules if you check the Require Variable Declaration option (in the Editor tab of the Visual Basic Editor's Tools ➢ Option dialog box).

Data typing You should explicitly specify a data type for all your variables. By defining variables with a specific data type instead of with the Variant or Object data types, you avoid the run-time errors that result when VBA cannot convert the data type of a Variant variable to do a calculation or when VBA discovers that your code references a property or method that is inappropriate for the Object variable. By using the most specific data type, you force VBA to analyze the appropriateness of the references during compile time.

Continued on next page

Avoiding naming conflicts If two procedures use a variable with the same name as the module-level variable, one procedure could unintentionally overwrite a value set by another procedure. You can avoid most errors of this type by declaring variables with the narrowest scope possible. If a variable is used in a single procedure, then declare the variable within the procedure. If a variable is used only by the procedures in a single module, then declare the variable as a private module-level variable. In particular, use public module-level variables only when you need to make the variable available to several procedures in several modules. Naming conflicts can also arise if you have procedures in separate modules with the same name. If you call such a procedure from a procedure in another module, an error occurs if you don't include the module name in the procedure call, because VBA is unable to determine which procedure to call.

Using comments You need to strike a reasonable balance between writing comments for every statement and not including any comments in your code. A good rule is to include enough comments so that an intermediate-level VBA programmer can understand your code. You don't need to comment every statement or obvious structure, but you may want to include comments at the beginning of each module and procedure to describe its purpose and point out any variables defined in the module or procedure. Typically, you should include comments describing the operation that each block of statements performs. Each comment takes a small fraction of a second. However, in lengthy code, the fractions accumulate and can slow down your code, so you would be wise to avoid unnecessary or overly verbose comments.

Using the Call Stack Dialog

When your code contains several layers of nested procedures, knowing whether the procedures have been called in the order you intended is helpful. You can use the Call Stack dialog when VBA is in break mode to trace through the progress of nested procedures. To display the Call Stack dialog, select View ➢ Call Stack or press Ctrl+L. The Call Stack dialog displays a list of the procedures that have started but have not completed execution (see Figure 10.12). The first active procedure in the calling chain is at the bottom of the list, with subsequent procedures added to the top.

FIGURE 10.12:

The Call Stack dialog lists the procedures that have started but have not completed execution.

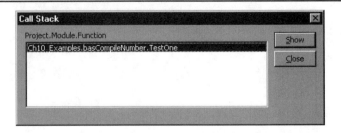

Error Handling

A goal of successful testing and troubleshooting is to detect as many errors as possible and analyze them to determine whether they can be corrected or avoided by changing your code. Even after you eliminate your mistakes, the unavoidable errors remain—the user neglects to enter a required piece of information, the network disconnects unexpectedly, or some other event you can't control occurs. As explained earlier in the chapter, you deal with unavoidable errors by writing VBA code to replace the default error handling with your own custom error-handling code. In other words, even if you can't avoid an error, you can anticipate it.

Trappable Errors

Three parts of Access can generate errors:

- The database engine manages the errors that occur when it can't carry out a task involving any of the data objects.

- The Access interface manages macro errors and other interface-related errors.

- VBA manages run-time errors generated by VBA itself and your VBA code.

When an error occurs because some task cannot be carried out, the Access application, the database engine, or VBA identifies the error from its predefined list of errors and assigns the numeric error code for the error. You can write your own error-handling code only for errors that have been assigned an error code; these errors are called *trappable errors*.

The database engine and VBA have their own set of error codes and their own way of managing the information about the error. The Microsoft SQL Server 2000 Desktop Engine stores error information in the Errors collection; VBA uses its own Err object. In both cases, the object is rewritten each time a new error occurs. The information in the Errors collection describes the last ADO error, and the information in the Err object describes the last VBA error that occurred; when the next ADO or VBA error occurs, the Errors collection or Err object is cleared and replaced with information about the new error.

NOTE   When the interface or database engine is unable to carry out a task, the possibility exists of a single incident causing more than one error; for example, errors associated with ODBC databases often have a set of related errors with a different error for each level of the ODBC drivers. The database engine stores each related error in a separate Error object; the Errors collection comprises the set of errors generated by the single incident. Thus, the Errors collection stores the details about all of the related errors that are recognized when a single data access error occurs.

Custom Error Messages

You are familiar with the default error messages that occur when you work interactively with Access:

```
Index or primary key can't contain a null value.
Duplicate value in index, primary key or relationship. Changes were _
    unsuccessful.
The text you enter must match an entry in the list.
```

Messages like these have little meaning to a novice user of your application. One of the reasons for handling the error yourself is to replace the default error message with a custom message that is more informative and helpful.

Database Engine and Interface Errors

When you are working with a form or report, your interactions can cause errors in the Access interface and database engine errors. For example, when you enter a value in a combo box that isn't in the combo list and Limit To List is set to Yes, Access cannot accept the value and generates an interface error with error code 2237; Access displays the default error message for this code and cancels the update of the combo box. When you try to save a record with a blank primary key, the database engine cannot save the record and generates a data access error with error code 3058; Access displays the default error message for this code and cancels the save operation.

Using the Error Event in Form and Report Modules

When either an interface or engine error is generated, the form or report recognizes the Error event. You can create an event procedure for the Error event to handle the error by interrupting the default response, replacing the default error message with a custom error message, and specifying the actions you want Access to take instead of the default behavior. For example, you can handle a blank primary key error (error code = 3058) by displaying a custom message, suppressing the default error message, moving the focus to the primary key control, and canceling the save operation.

The event procedure code template for the Error event recognized by a form has this syntax:

```
Private Sub Form_Error(DataErr As Integer, Response As Integer)
```

You use the arguments to communicate with Access. The value of the DataErr argument is the error code of the interface or engine error that occurred. When an interface or engine error occurs, Access passes the error code as the value of DataErr to the form's or report's Error event procedure. You use the Response argument to tell Access whether to display or suppress the default error message. You use an intrinsic constant for the Response argument: acDataErrContinue to suppress the default error message or acDataErrDisplay to display it.

To explore these concepts, we'll create an error handler that handles specific errors for the Employees form in the Northwind database. The first step is to determine the error codes of the errors you want to handle. One way to do this is to create a simple event procedure to display the error code and then trigger the error, like this one:

```
Private Sub Form_Error(DataErr As Integer, Response As Integer)
    MsgBox DataErr
End Sub
```

When the form recognizes the Error event, the MsgBox statement displays the error code. When you click OK to dismiss the message box, Access displays the default error message corresponding to the error code.

Follow these steps to enter and test the procedure:

1. Import the Employees form and the Employees table into the Ch10_Examples database from the Northwind sample database.

2. Open the Employees form in Design view. Click the OnError property, click the Build button, and enter the Form_Error event procedure shown above.

3. Save the form and switch to Form view. Display a new record, enter a last name without entering a first name, and press Shift+Enter to save the record. The message box displays the error code 3314, followed by the default error message (see Figure 10.13). Jet generates this error because the FirstName field is a Required field.

FIGURE 10.13:

The Form_Error event procedure displays the error code (a), and Access displays a default error message for the error generated by the database engine (b).

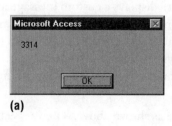

(a)

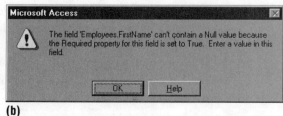

(b)

4. Enter a first name as well as a last name, tab to the Reports To combo box, and enter **zzzz**. When you try to tab out of the combo box, the message box displays the error code 2237, followed by the default error message (see Figure 10.14).

FIGURE 10.14:

The Form_Error event procedure displays the error code (a) for a default error message when you select an item not in the combo box list (b).

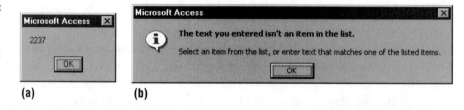

(a) **(b)**

5. Select a name from the Reports To combo list. Press Shift+Enter to save the record. You can now modify the event procedure to handle these errors.

You can use either the If...Then...Else or Select Case structure to set a trap for each specific error. The procedure shown below uses the Select Case structure to test the value of the error code and handle the errors.

```
Private Sub Form_Error(DataErr As Integer, Response As Integer)
    Select Case DataErr
        Case 2237
            MsgBox "You have made an invalid entry. Click the " _
                & "list to display the valid choices."
            Response = acDataErrContinue
        Case 3314
            MsgBox "You must enter both first and last " _
                & "names before you can save the record."
            Response = acDataErrContinue
        Case Else
            Response = acDataErrDisplay
    End Select
End Sub
```

If one of the errors occurs, the procedure displays a custom message and sets the Response to acDataErrContinue so that Access will not display the default error message. If no trapped error occurs, but another error occurs instead, the Case Else alternative is executed; setting the Response to acDataErrDisplay displays the default error message for the untrapped error. The purpose of the Case Else alternative is to specify what action to take if an unanticipated error occurs.

Modify the Form_Error event procedure as shown above. Then repeat steps 3 through 5 of the previous exercise to test it.

The Form_Error event procedure is designed to deal only with interface and database engine errors that occur when the form has control; you cannot use this procedure to trap VBA errors. If a VBA error occurs while the Form_Error event procedure is running, the VBA run-time error message is displayed. You must deal with VBA run-time errors by writing error-handling code within the procedure. The next section describes how to handle VBA errors.

VBA Errors

When a VBA error occurs while you are running a procedure, the default error handler is that VBA displays an error message and suspends execution of the code at the line that could not be executed. The following event procedure was created by the Command Button Wizard and provides a model for a simple VBA error handler.

```
Private Sub cmdClose_Click()
On Error GoTo Err_cmdClose_Click
    DoCmd.Close

Exit_cmdClose_Click:
    Exit Sub

Err_cmdClose_Click:
    MsgBox Err.Description
    Resume Exit_cmdClose_Click

End Sub
```

By current programming customs, VBA error handlers follow an older programming concept: Procedures with error handling use *line labels* to identify lines of code and use statements to direct the flow of execution to the labeled lines. A line label must start in the first column, begin with a letter, and end with a colon (:).

Constructing a VBA Error Handler

The simple error handlers that the Command Button Wizard creates use the following pattern:

```
'enable custom error-handling
On Error GoTo Err_procedurename
    [statements]

'begin exit code
Exit_procedurename:
    [statements]
Exit Sub

'begin error-handler
Err_procedurename:
```

```
[error-handling statements]
Resume Exit_procedurename
```

```
End Sub
```

Enabling the Error Handler

You use the On Error statement to tell VBA that you are going to handle the error yourself. Place an On Error statement at the beginning of the procedure after the variable and constant declaration statements and before any executable statements. The On Error statement has three forms:

On Error GoTo *linelabel* Specifies the location of an error handler within a procedure. When an error occurs, control goes to the error handler.

On Error Resume Next Tells Access to ignore the error and continue at the statement immediately following the statement that caused the error.

On Error GoTo 0 Disables any enabled error handler in the procedure. This statement also resets the value of the Error object.

By including the On Error statement, you are *enabling* custom error handling and *setting an error trap*. The procedure's statements follow the On Error statement. An Exit Sub, Exit Function, or Exit Property statement follows the last statement of the procedure. Normally, the error-handling code is placed after the procedure's statements, so you need the Exit statement to prevent the error-handling code from running when no error occurs. The On Error statement specifies where VBA goes if any error occurs in the statements that are listed after the On Error statement and before the Exit statement.

NOTE   To avoid syntax errors, note that when writing error-handling procedures in VBA, you create On Error (two words) statements. When assigning a procedure to a form in the event of an error occurring, you set the OnError (one word) property.

Executing the Error-Handling Code

The line with the line label signals the beginning of the error-handling code. This line must be in the same procedure as the On Error statement. If an error occurs, control moves to the error-handling code. An error handler that is in the process of handling an error is called an *active* error handler. When an error occurs while a VBA procedure is running, information about the error is stored as property settings of the VBA Err object. (Chapter 5, "VBA Programming Essentials," describes the properties and methods of the Err object.) The most commonly used properties are the Number property, which returns the error code as a Long integer, and Description, which returns a string as the error's description.

A common statement in error-handling code is to display a message box with the error code and description as follows:

```
MsgBox "Error number: " & Err.Number & " - " & Err.Description
```

The error-handling code can test the value of Err.Number and use either the If...Then...Else or Select Case structure to provide alternative statements for each of the specific errors that the code is handling. A set of statements for an error number specifies the actions to take if an error with that number occurs. Write error-handling code for all the errors you anticipate and include error-handling code for unanticipated errors as well.

For example, when you have identified the error codes of the several errors that you want to trap in a procedure, use the Select Case structure in the error handler to provide alternative sets of statements for each error and use a Case Else structure to trap for unexpected or unknown errors:

```
Err_procedurename:
    Select Case Err.Number
        Case 3058
            [statements to handle the 3058 error]
        Case 3022
            [statements to handle the 3022 error]
        Case Else
            MsgBox "Error number: " & Err.Number & " - " & _
                Err.Description
    End Select
Resume Exit_procedurename
```

Exiting the Error-Handling Code

When the error-handling code is finished, you need to specify what VBA should do next. The following are three common statements for exiting error-handling code:

Resume Resumes program execution starting with the statement that caused the error.

Resume Next Resumes program execution starting at the statement immediately after the statement that caused the error. Use Resume Next when you want to continue running the procedure without retrying the statement that caused the error.

Resume line Resumes execution at the label specified by line. The line label must be in the same procedure as the error handler. Use the Resume line statement when you want to jump to a statement before the procedure's Exit statement.

Creating a Generic Error Handler

For all but the simplest procedures, you should include at least a simple generic error handler that displays the error number and description for any trappable error that occurs. The following code shows statements for a generic error handler that includes the Select Case structure to prepare for trapping specific errors.

```
On Error GoTo Err_procedurename
    [statements]

Exit_procedurename:
    Exit Sub

Err_procedurename:
    Select Case Err.Number
        Case Else
            MsgBox "Error number: " & Err.Number & " - " & _
                Err.Description
    End Select

Resume Exit_procedurename
```

As a simple example, the Division procedure divides one number by another.

```
Public Sub Division()

Dim dblnum As Double, dblden As Double, dblResult As Double
On Error GoTo Err_Division
    dblnum = InputBox("Enter the numerator.")
    dblden = InputBox("Enter the denominator.")
    dblResult = dblnum / dblden
    MsgBox "The quotient is " & dblResult

Exit_Division:
    Exit Sub

Err_Division:
    Select Case Err.Number
        Case Else
            MsgBox "Error number: " & Err.Number & " - " & _
                Err.Description
    End Select

Resume Exit_Division

End Sub
```

Follow these steps to create and test the procedure:

1. Create a new module named basErrors in the Ch10_Examples database and enter the Division procedure in the basErrors module.

2. Run the Division procedure in the Immediate window. Enter **24** and **12** in the text boxes (see Figure 10.15a). The procedure displays the quotient (see Figure 10.15b).

FIGURE 10.15:

The Division procedure collects two numbers (a) and displays the quotient (b).

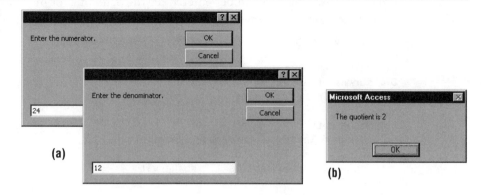

(a)

(b)

3. Run the procedure again. Enter **twenty** in the first input box (see Figure 10.16a). An error occurs because the procedure declares db1num as a number of the Double data type, and Access cannot set this variable to the string you entered. The error handler is active, and the custom error message indicates that the error has code 13 for a type mismatch error (see Figure 10.16b).

FIGURE 10.16:

When you enter a string instead of a number (a), VBA generates an error with code 13 (b).

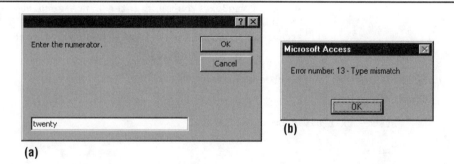

(b)

(a)

4. Run the procedure again. This time enter **20** in the first input box and **0** (zero) in the second input box. Another error occurs because Access cannot divide a number by zero. The error handler is active and indicates that the error has code 11 for a division by zero error.

You can trap specifically for each of these errors by using a message box to inform the user that a number must be entered when the error with code 13 occurs and a separate message box to tell the user that the number entered for the denominator must not be 0. The modified `Division` procedure shown below demonstrates this type of error handling.

```
Public Sub Division()

Dim dblnum As Double, dblden As Double, dblResult As Double
Dim strAnswer As String
On Error GoTo Err_Division
    dblnum = InputBox("Enter the numerator.")
Err_Denominator:
    dblden = InputBox("Enter the denominator.")
    dblResult = dblnum / dblden
    MsgBox "The quotient is " & dblResult

Exit_Division:
    Exit Sub

Err_Division:
    Select Case Err.Number
        Case 13
            strAnswer = MsgBox("You must enter a number. Do you " _
                & "want to try again?", vbYesNo)
            If strAnswer = vbYes Then Resume
        Case 11
            strAnswer = MsgBox("You must enter a non-zero number. " _
                & "Do you want to try again?", vbYesNo)
            If strAnswer = vbYes Then Resume Err_Denominator:
        Case Else
            MsgBox "Error number: " & Err.Number & " - " & _
                Err.Description
    End Select

Resume Exit_Division

End Sub
```

This version uses the `MsgBox` function to allow users to choose whether to try again or quit the procedure; the `strAnswer` variable holds the user's selection. When either error occurs and the user chooses to try again, the procedure uses the `Resume` statement to instruct Access to return to the statement that caused the error, as follows:

```
If strAnswer = vbYes Then Resume
```

If the user chooses not to try again, control jumps down to the last statement of the error handler and control then jumps to the exit code:

```
Resume Exit_Division
```

The procedure continues to include the `Case Else` alternative to trap for unexpected errors.

Modify the `Division` procedure as shown above and run it in the Immediate window. Type **twenty** in the text box of the first input box and click OK. This time, the procedure traps the error and displays the message shown in Figure 10.17a. If you type a number in the text box of the first input box and 0 in the text box of the second, the procedure traps the error and displays the message shown in Figure 10.17b.

FIGURE 10.17:

Custom error-handling instructions display these message boxes so that the user can correct the error and try again.

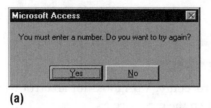 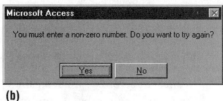

(a)   (b)

WARNING Resume sends the VBA procedure back to the line that initially caused the error. Thus, you may need to set a label for the line preceding the line that caused the error, to force the user to take some other action, as in the previous example when the user inputs 0 as the denominator. Otherwise, the procedure displays the custom message, then when the user clicks Yes, VBA returns to the division line without giving the user a chance to reenter another denominator.

As an alternative to jumping from one part of the procedure to another, you can include `Exit Sub` statements any time you want to terminate a procedure, as shown in the following version of the `Division` procedure. This technique may be easier to read; nevertheless, some programmers prefer to provide only a single exit point for a procedure.

```
Public Sub Division()
Dim dblnum As Double, dblden As Double, dblResult As Double
Dim strAnswer As String
On Error GoTo Err_Division
    dblnum = InputBox("Enter the numerator.")
Err_Denominator:
    dblden = InputBox("Enter the denominator.")
    dblResult = dblnum / dblden
    MsgBox "The quotient is " & dblResult

Err_Division:
    Select Case Err.Number
        Case 13
            strAnswer = MsgBox ("You must enter a number. Do you " _
                & "want to try again?", vbYesNo)
            If strAnswer = vbYes Then Resume Else Exit Sub
```

```
      Case 11
          strAnswer = MsgBox ("You must enter a non-zero number. " _
              & "Do you want to try again?", vbYesNo)
          If strAnswer = vbYes Then Resume Err_Denominator
          Else Exit Sub
      Case Else
          MsgBox "Error number: " & Err.Number & " - " & _
              Err.Description
  End Select

End Sub
```

Errors in Called Procedures

When an error occurs in a called procedure, VBA looks for an error handler first in the called procedure that is running when the error occurs.

If it doesn't find an error handler in the called procedure, VBA returns to the calling procedure and executes its error handler if the calling procedure has one. If it encounters a chain of calling procedures, Access backtracks through the calling chain and executes the first error handler it finds.

If it doesn't find any error handlers, Access executes the default error-handling routine. In this case, Access displays the default error message first and then displays the run-time error dialog; then it terminates the procedure.

TIP   For more information about dealing with errors in called procedures, see the *Access 2002 Desktop Developer's Handbook* by Paul Litwin, Ken Getz, and Mike Gunderloy (Sybex, 2001).

Summary

This chapter introduced the complex subject of error handling. The important points covered in the chapter follow:

- Two kinds of errors occur in programs: avoidable and unavoidable. Careful design, testing, and troubleshooting can eliminate many avoidable errors. You can use custom code error-handling to specify the actions you want to take when an unavoidable error occurs.

- Access VBA provides built-in syntax checking and compiling routines for eliminating compile-time errors.

- Access provides two kinds of troubleshooting tools: those that do not interrupt execution and those that involve suspending execution and placing the procedure in break mode.

- With execution suspended, you can execute a single statement at a time and test its effect. You can examine the values of variables and view an ordered list of calling procedures.

- You can use the Error event of a form or report to trap for and write error-handling code for interface and database engine errors. The Error event is particularly useful for replacing default error messages with custom error messages.

- You can use the `On Error` statement in a procedure to enable error-handling code for VBA errors that occur when the procedure is running. The main purpose of custom error handling is to prevent the run-time error dialog and procedure failure.

- The error-handling code uses properties of the VBA Err object to determine the error code.

- All but the simplest VBA procedures should include a simple error handler that displays the error code and the default error message. The error handler can exit the procedure without executing the problem statement or include instructions for Access to follow if the error occurs.

CHAPTER 11

Navigating with Access VBA

- Navigating among forms, records, and controls

- Using the recordsetclone to access the form's recordset

- Creating custom navigation buttons

- Finding a specific record using a form

- Working directly with the data without opening a form

- Moving around in a recordset

- Finding specific records in a recordset

The previous five chapters have laid the VBA foundation. Those five chapters are the reference for the rest of the book. With the basic tools and skills in place, we are ready to put the concepts together and create the procedures needed in a database application.

This chapter focuses on navigation. The first part deals with navigation using forms and introduces you to some of the real power of Access VBA. The chapter explains how to use the RecordsetClone property for navigation *in memory* through the form's records, which is independent of the navigation *in the interface* provided by the form. You'll learn how to make applications easier to use by providing custom buttons on forms so that the user can easily move between forms, controls, and records using the custom buttons as guides. You'll also learn how to automate navigation to records in forms based on their physical location and how to automate the search for a record that satisfies specified search criteria.

The second part of the chapter shows you a new way to work with records. Using VBA, you can open a recordset in memory without opening a form. Working with records in memory is much faster than working with records in forms, because Access doesn't need to take the time to load a form into memory and create its visual representation on the screen.

TIP   One approach to learning how to use VBA is to create a draft for an application using the Database Wizard and then examine the kind of procedures the wizard uses to accomplish tasks. (See Chapter 1, "Automating a Database without Programming," for details on using the Database Wizards and other Access wizards.) Typically, the code is very elegant. The word *elegant* as applied to programming means that the code is efficient because it uses the least amount of memory and the fewest number of statements to accomplish the task. Elegant code is optimized for the best performance because it uses the methods and control structures that accomplish the task in the shortest time.

Navigating the Form and Its Recordset

When you open a bound form, Access opens the form's recordset in memory and displays records in the form using the form's record selector to indicate the form's current record. When you open a bound form, you can manipulate two objects in a VBA procedure: the form and the form's recordset. You can refer to the recordset directly by using the form's RecordsetClone property, which means that you can use the properties and methods of both the Form object (see Chapter 5, "VBA Programming Essentials") and the Recordset object (see Chapter 6, "Understanding the ADO Object Model,") when you are writing procedures that manipulate the records in a form.

When one of these objects lacks the property or method that you need, you can use the other object instead. For example, the Form object does not have a property or method to determine the number of records in a bound form; however, you can use the RecordCount property of the Recordset object. Learning how to use both the Form and Recordset objects in procedures is an important skill.

To work with a form's recordset in a procedure, you declare an object variable and point the object variable to the form's recordset using the form's RecordsetClone property. The statements are as follows:

```
Dim rst As ADODB.Recordset, frm As Form
Set frm = Forms!formname
Set rst = frm.RecordsetClone
```

Formname is the name of the form. The second Set statement creates a special reference to the form's Recordset object called the recordsetclone. As you learned in Chapter 6, the recordsetclone has its own current record pointer so it can point to a different record from the record that is displayed in the form. Consequently, you can use the recordsetclone to work with another record in a form's recordset while the form continues to display a specific record. When you first create the recordsetclone, its current record pointer is not defined; you can set the current record pointer in the procedure.

NOTE   For hands-on experience with the techniques described in this chapter, create a new copy of the NorthwindCS sample project named Northwind_Ch11.ADP and work through the steps and examples. Make certain that you have added library references to the ADO and ADOX type libraries in the VB Editor's References dialog.

Creating a Sub Procedure to Walk the Recordset

As an example of creating and using the recordsetclone, we'll create a procedure to print the last names of the employees in the Employees table. Open the Employees form in Design view. In the header section, place a command button named cmdRecordset with the caption Print Last Names. Click in the button's OnClick property and click the Build button to display the form's module. Create the cmdRecordset_Click event procedure shown below.

```
Private Sub cmdRecordset_Click()
    Dim rst As ADODB.Recordset
    Set rst = Me.RecordsetClone
    rst.MoveFirst
    Do
        Debug.Print rst!LastName
        rst.MoveNext
    Loop Until rst.EOF
End Sub
```

This procedure creates the recordsetclone, uses the `MoveFirst` method to set the recordsetclone's current record pointer to the first record, and then loops through the recordset. Each pass through the loop prints the last name in the recordsetclone's current record and uses the `MoveNext` method to move the current record pointer to the next record.

Open the Immediate window. Save the form, switch to Form view, and click the new command button. The Immediate window prints the last names for all of the employees as evidence that the procedure has walked through all the records in the form's recordset while the form continues to display its first record (see Figure 11.1).

FIGURE 11.1:

The Print Last Names button runs a procedure that uses the recordsetclone and walks through the form's recordset while the form displays its first record.

WARNING   The Form.RecordsetClone property in an Access database returns a DAO recordset object. The same property in an Access project returns an ADO recordset object.

Creating a Function Procedure to Walk the Recordset

In the previous example, we could use Me to refer to the form because the event procedure is stored in the form's module. In the next example, we'll create a reusable function procedure that walks through the recordset of any form.

The `FormRecordset` procedure creates the recordsetclone for the form that is passed as an argument to the function and prints the value in the first field of each record in the form's recordset.

```
Public Function FormRecordset(frm As Form)
    Dim rst As ADODB.Recordset
    Set rst = frm.RecordsetClone
    rst.MoveFirst
    Do
        Debug.Print rst(0)
        rst.MoveNext
    Loop Until rst.EOF
End Function
```

Because we want the function procedure to be reusable, we refer to the first field using the numeric index reference `rst.Fields(0)`, or simply `rst(0)` (because Fields is the default collection for a recordset). You can run the `FormRecordset` function by passing the reference to any open form as the argument.

Create a new standard module named basNavigation and insert the `FormRecordset` function procedure shown above. Next, open the Customers form, type **? FormRecordset(Forms!Customers)** in the Immediate window, and press Enter. Note that you are passing the reference to the form, not the name of the form. When you press Enter, VBA prints the Customer ID field to the Immediate window.

To run the function as an event function procedure, open the Categories form in Design view and type **=FormRecordset([Form])** in the form's OnOpen event. Note that you are passing `Form` as the reference to the form. (You can also use the reference `Forms!Categories`, but you can't use the Me reference to refer to the form in a property sheet.)

Save the form and switch to Form view. When you switch to Form view, the form recognizes the Open event, so VBA runs the function procedure and prints the Category ID field to the Immediate window.

Navigating the Interface

When you work interactively, you use keystrokes, menu commands, and the mouse to move between controls, between records, and from one Database window object to another. The simplest approach to automating navigation in the interface is to place command buttons on forms and create procedures that run when you click the buttons.

Access provides the methods of the DoCmd object for navigating through the interface. These methods duplicate the interactive instructions you give when you press a key, move the mouse and click a mouse button, or choose a menu command. We'll go through the steps of a simple example to develop a set of guidelines for writing procedures that are reusable.

Navigating Forms

The simplest approach to automating navigation between forms is to place command buttons on the forms and create procedures that run when you click the buttons. Most form navigation tasks are generic: opening a form from another form, opening and synchronizing a form or report to display specific records, closing or hiding forms, and performing other general tasks that you need to use several times in every application. For reusable, portable, and independent button procedures, we'll use event function procedures stored in a standard module.

Opening a Form

Suppose you are working with a form and want to open another form; for example, when reviewing a customer using the Customers form, a user may want to open the Orders form. The simplest approach to automating this operation is to place a command button named cmdOrders on the Customers form and create an event procedure for the button's Click event. You use the OpenForm method of the DoCmd object to open the form. The OpenForm method has one required argument, followed by six optional arguments.

```
DoCmd.OpenForm formname[,view] [,filtername] [,wherecondition] _
    [,datamode] [,windowmode] [,openargs]
```

We'll accept the defaults for the optional arguments (you can search for "OpenForm" in online help for information about these arguments) and use the *formname* argument to specify the name of the form to open. The *formname* argument is a string expression that is the valid name of any form in the current database.

A First Draft

The first draft for the procedure is

```
Private Sub cmdOrders_Click()
    DoCmd.OpenForm "Orders"
End Sub
```

This event procedure works just fine—it opens the specified form. The problem with the procedure is that the OpenForm method uses the specific form name as an argument. Using specific names of objects as arguments of methods in a procedure causes unnecessary problems if you want to reuse the procedure. To reuse a procedure that contains specific names for objects, you need to search through the statements to find the literal arguments and replace each one with the new name. We are going to make three modifications to the procedure to make it easier to reuse:

- Replace the method's literal argument with a variable.

- Move the declaration of the variable from the interior to the procedure's argument list.

- Move the procedure to a standard module.

The First Improvement

The first improvement defines variables to hold the specific names and uses the variables as arguments of methods instead of the specific names. With this improvement, the procedure becomes

```
Private Sub cmdOrders_Click()
    Dim strName As String
    strName = "Orders"
    DoCmd.OpenForm strName
End Sub
```

The cmdOrders_Click procedure is so simple that the significance of the modification may be obscured by the very simplicity. Imagine a procedure with dozens of statements having methods with arguments. By creating a set of variables to hold all the specific names and assigning the variables to the specific names at the beginning of the procedure, you can easily modify the procedure by looking in one place to change the names.

The Second Improvement

A second improvement takes the specific names out of the interior of the procedure by creating arguments for the procedure. With this improvement, you pass the specific names as arguments when you call the procedure. If the procedure is an event procedure, you'll need to change the type of procedure as well, because you can't create your own arguments for an event procedure. (An event procedure has a predefined syntax, including a naming convention, and predefined arguments for passing information back and forth between Access and the event procedure.) To create your own arguments for a procedure triggered by an event, you need to use a function procedure.

You can change the name of the command button and the event function to reflect its generic nature. In this example, we'll change the name for both to cmdOpenForm. With this modification, the procedure becomes

```
Private Function cmdOpenForm(strName As String)
    DoCmd.OpenForm strName
End Sub
```

With the variable declared in the argument list for the procedure, you no longer need a separate declaration statement in the procedure. The specific name of the form doesn't appear at all, so you can use the procedure to open any form. You supply the name of the form when you call the procedure. In this example, to call the procedure when the button is clicked, you assign the function to the event by entering =cmdOpenForm("Orders") in the button's property sheet. By specifying the arguments in the button's property sheet, you avoid needing to work directly with the code in the module at all. If you want to open another form, you need only make the change in the button's property sheet.

The Third Improvement

The third improvement takes the procedure out of the form module and stores it as a public function in a standard module. With the function procedure stored in a standard module, the command button/function procedure combination is now fully reusable. When you copy the button, the assignment to the function procedure is copied also. With the button pasted to another form, you can specify the form to be opened in the button's property sheet, and you don't need to open the module to change the procedure.

By placing an event function procedure assigned to a control in a standard module, you make the procedure portable and independent of a specific form in the application. Pasting the control pastes the assignment to the procedure also, and the control continues to work as long as the database contains the standard module. (The standard module could even be stored in another database, and the control would continue to work if you set a reference to the database that contains the standard module; see Chapter 14, "Creating and Modifying Database Objects Using Access VBA," for more information about setting references.)

NOTE When you store an event function procedure in a standard module, you can't use Me to refer to the form. However, when the form is the active object, you can refer to the form using the ActiveForm property of the Screen object.

The portable and independent command button/function procedure combination to open a form is as follows:

Control A command button named cmdOpenForm with its OnClick property set to =OpenAForm(*formname*), where *formname* is the string expression that evaluates to the name of a form, such as "Orders."

Event function The following event function stored in the basNavigation standard module:

```
Public Function OpenAForm(strName As String)
    DoCmd.OpenForm strName
End Sub
```

Guidelines for Creating Reusable Procedures

The following are guidelines for creating procedures to maximize their reusability. These suggestions are guidelines only, not rigid rules that must always be followed. For example, if an event procedure is unique to a specific form, you may not need to go beyond the first guideline.

- Do not use specific names or literal expressions as arguments of methods; declare variables and use variables as arguments instead.

- Define the variables in one of these ways:

  - In declaration statements within the procedure and assign them to the literal expressions.

  - As arguments of the procedure. Pass the literal expressions into the procedure. Change an event procedure to a function procedure to pass literal expressions as arguments.

- Store reusable procedures in standard modules instead of in form or report modules when you want to make the procedures independent of any form and easily portable to other forms. Change an event procedure to a function procedure to store it in a standard module.

Hiding and Unhiding a Form

When opening or closing a form, the procedure may need to carry out additional tasks. As an example, one of the application development guidelines that many developers follow to avoid data-integrity problems is to allow users to change the data in only a single form at a time. One way to implement this guideline is to hide the first form when you open the second form and then unhide the first form when you close the second form. The procedure that closes the second form must know which form to unhide.

An interesting problem arises because typically the second form can be opened from several different forms depending on how you design the navigational paths. For example, you may design the navigation so that the user can open the Orders form from the Main Switchboard, the Customer Orders form, or the Customers form. The second form needs to remember which form opened it so that it knows which form to unhide when you close it. The Tag property is ideal for this purpose. We'll create a pair of procedures that use the Tag property of the form you are opening to store the name of the form that opened it. We'll call the first form the "opener form" and the second form the "opened form."

The OpenHide event function is assigned to the command button on the first form.

```
Public Function OpenHide (strName As String)
    Dim strHide As String
    strHide = Screen.ActiveForm.Name
    Screen.ActiveForm.Visible = False
    DoCmd.OpenForm strName
    Screen.ActiveForm.Tag = strHide
End Function
```

The strHide variable holds the name of the opener form using the Screen object to refer to it. After storing the name of the opener form in the strHide variable, the procedure hides the opener form. The procedure opens the second form and sets the Tag property of the opened form to the name of the opener form.

When you close the second form by clicking a command button on it, you unhide the opener form using the CloseUnhide procedure.

```
Public Function CloseUnhide()
    Dim strUnhide As String
    If IsNull(Screen.ActiveForm.Tag) Then
        DoCmd.Close
    Else
        strUnhide = Screen.ActiveForm.Tag
        DoCmd.Close
        DoCmd.SelectObject acForm, strUnhide
    End If
End Function
```

The CloseUnhide procedure first tests the opened form's Tag property. The Tag property contains the name of the (hidden) opener form unless the second form was opened in some other way that did not set its Tag property. In that case, the Tag property is Null. If the Tag property is Null, the Close method simply closes the form; otherwise, the procedure holds the name of the opener form in the strUnhide variable, closes the opened form using the Close method, and then unhides the opener form using the SelectObject method.

WARNING Keep in mind that the CloseUnhide procedure is called only if the user clicks the command button to close the second form. If they close the form using any other method, the procedure does not run, and the opener form remains hidden.

To test the procedures, follow these steps:

1. Insert the OpenHide and CloseHide function procedures in the basNavigation module.

2. Open the Products form in Design view. In the form's header, place a command button named cmdOpenHide, with the caption Open Categories. Set the button's OnClick property to =OpenHide("Categories"). Save the form and switch to Form view.

3. Open the Categories form in Design view and add a command button named cmdCloseUnhide, with the caption Close Unhide. Set the button's OnClick property to =CloseUnhide(). Save and close the form.

4. Click the Open Categories button on the Products form. The Products form is hidden and the Categories form opens. Click the Close Unhide button on the form. The Categories form closes, and the Products form is unhidden.

You'll learn more about using the Tag property to create custom properties in Chapter 14.

Synchronizing Two Forms

When you use a procedure to open a form, you often need to synchronize its records to the record displayed by the first form. For example, when opening the Customers form from the Orders form, you can use the *filtername* or *wherecondition* arguments of the OpenForm method to locate and display the customer record corresponding to the customer displayed in the Orders form. The *filtername* argument is a string expression that is the valid name of a query in the current database, and the *wherecondition* argument is a string expression that is a valid SQL WHERE clause without the word WHERE. You can use either argument to restrict records; if you specify both arguments, Access first applies the *filtername* and then applies the *wherecondition* to the result of the query.

We'll use the *wherecondition* argument to synchronize the form being opened to the current form, as follows:

```
fieldname=Forms!formname!controlname
```

In this expression, *fieldname* refers to the field in the underlying table or query of the form you want to open, and *controlname* refers to the control on the form that contains the value you want to match. For example, to open the Customers form displaying a record synchronized to the record in the Orders form, use the following expression:

```
CustomerID=Forms!Orders!CustomerID
```

You can also use the Screen object to refer to the active form, as follows:

```
CustomerID=Screen.ActiveForm.CustomerID
```

Notice that the full syntax is required on the right side of the expression, even though Orders is the active form when the procedure executes the OpenForm method. This example shows a case in which you must use the full syntax to refer to a control on the active object. Notice also that the short syntax is required on the left side of the expression. The *wherecondition* argument uses the syntax required by SQL to synchronize the records.

As an example, we'll use an event procedure that opens and synchronizes the Customers form to the Orders form. Open the Orders form in Design view and add a command button named cmdViewCustomer, with the caption View Customer. Click the Build button next to the button's OnClick property and insert the following event procedure:

```
Private Sub cmdViewCustomer_Click()
    Dim strForm As String
    Dim strWhere As String
    strForm = "Customers"
    strWhere = "CustomerID = '" & Forms!Orders!CustomerID & "'"
    DoCmd.OpenForm FormName:=strForm, WhereCondition:=strWhere
End Sub
```

Save the form and switch to Form view. Use the default navigation buttons to select the order for a customer. Click the View Customer button. The Customers form opens, displaying the corresponding customer (see Figure 11.2). In the Orders form, select an order for a different customer. The Customers form does not remain synchronized unless you close the Customers form and click the View Customer button again.

FIGURE 11.2:

The View Customer button runs a procedure that opens and synchronizes the Customers form.

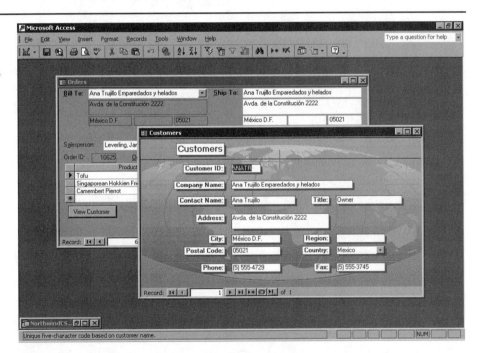

Keeping the Forms Synchronized

When you move to another record in the Orders form, the Customers form continues to display the previous customer and does not resynchronize automatically. We'll create an event procedure to resynchronize the Customers form when you move to a different record in the Orders form. When you move to a different record, the form recognizes the Current event. The Form_Current event procedure for the Orders form, shown below, uses the custom IsLoaded function (stored in the Utility Function module) to determine if the Customers form is open.

```
Private Sub Form_Current()
    Dim strForm As String
    Dim strWhere As String
    strForm = "Customers"
    strWhere = "CustomerID = '" & Forms!Orders!CustomerID & "'"
    If IsLoaded(strForm) Then
        If Forms(strForm).Filter = strWhere Then
            Forms(strForm).SetFocus
        Else
            DoCmd.Close acForm, strForm
            DoCmd.OpenForm FormName:=strForm, WhereCondition:=strWhere
        End If
    End If
End Sub
```

When you use the wherecondition argument of the OpenForm method, the form opens with a Filter applied that is the same as the value of the wherecondition argument. This poses a problem if you want to reopen the Customers form with a different filter. The Form_Current procedure solves this problem by using an If…Then…Else decision structure.

If the Customers form is open, the procedure checks to see if its Filter property is set to the same customer as the one in the Orders form. If so, it just sets the focus to the Customers form by using the SetFocus method and terminates running the procedure. If not, it closes the Customers form, thus clearing the Filter property, and reopens the Customers form with the Filter set to the new Customer. We will go into more depth about the SetFocus method later in this chapter, in the "Using the SetFocus Method" section.

Click in the Orders form and switch to Design view. Click the Build button next to the form's OnCurrent property and insert the Form_Current procedure. Save the form and switch to Form view. Click the View Customer button. Using the default navigation buttons, browse to the order of a different customer. The Customers form resynchronizes.

Closing the Related Form

When you close the Orders form, the Customers form should close also (if it is open). The Form_Close event procedure is the Close event of the Orders form that closes the Customers form if it is open.

```
Private Sub Form_Close()
    Dim strForm As String
    strForm = "Customers"
    DoCmd.Close acForm, strForm
End Sub
```

You don't need to determine if the Customers form is open before running the Close method to close it because of the exceptional nature of the Close method. The Close method does not fail if you specify the name of an object that isn't open or that doesn't exist.

Click in the Orders form and switch to Design view. Click the Build button next to the form's OnClose property and insert the Form_Close procedure. Save the form and switch to Form view. Click the View Customer button. Click the default Close button on the Orders form. Both the Orders and the Customers forms close.

WARNING This example is used to illustrate how a single procedure can close two forms. In an actual procedure, you would need to include additional handling to make sure that when you closed the Orders form, you only closed the Customers form if it had been opened by the View Customer button. One way to do this would be to assign a value to the Customers form's Tag property, then test for the value of this property before closing the Customers form.

Navigating between Controls

When working interactively, you use keystrokes, menu commands, and the mouse to move through controls on forms. We'll create procedures to automate moving to specific controls on forms and subforms and to specific controls within records. For this exercise, we'll place command buttons on the Orders form and create event procedures for navigating between controls on the Orders form and the Employees form.

Moving to a Specific Control on the Active Form

You can move the focus to a specific control on the active form in two ways:

- Use the GoToControl method of the DoCmd object.
- Use the control's SetFocus method.

Using the *GoToControl* Method

The syntax for the GoToControl method is as follows:

```
DoCmd.GoToControl controlname
```

Controlname is a string expression that is the name of the control on the active form or datasheet. You must use only the name of the control; using the fully qualified reference causes a run-time error.

The cmdToControl_Click event procedure moves the focus to a control on the Orders main form.

```
Private Sub cmdToControl_Click()
    Dim strControl As String
    strControl = "OrderDate"
    DoCmd.GoToControl strControl
End Sub
```

Moving the focus to a specific control on a subform requires using the GoToControl method twice—you move the focus to the subform control with the first method and then to the control on the subform with the second method. This navigation is handled by the cmdToControlOnSubform_Click procedure.

```
Private Sub cmdToControlOnSubform_Click()
    Dim strControl As String, strSubformControl As String
    strControl = "Discount": strSubformControl = "Orders Subform"
    DoCmd.GoToControl strSubformControl
    DoCmd.GoToControl strControl
End Sub
```

Moving the focus to a specific control on an open form that isn't active also takes two steps, as shown in the cmdToOtherFormControl_Click procedure. The first step uses the Select-Object method of the DoCmd object to activate the open form, and the second step uses the GoToControl method to move to the control.

```
Private Sub cmdToOtherFormControl_Click()
    Dim strControl As String, strForm As String
    strForm = "Employees": strControl = "Title"
    DoCmd.SelectObject acForm, strForm
    DoCmd.GoToControl strControl
End Sub
```

Open the Orders form in Design view. Create three command buttons on the Orders form, giving them the following Name, Caption, and OnClick properties:

Button Name	Caption Event	Procedure
cmdToControl	To Control	cmdToControl_Click()
cmdToControlOnSubform	To Control On Subform	cmdToControlOnSubform_Click()
cmdToOtherFormControl	To Control On Other Form	cmdToOtherFormControl_Click()

Save the form and switch to Form view. Open the Employees form. Test the three new command buttons on the Orders form. For example, clicking the To Control On Subform button moves the focus to the Discount control of the first record in the subform (see Figure 11.3).

FIGURE 11.3:

Click the To Control On Subform button to run a procedure that moves the focus first to the subform control and then to the Discount control of the first record in the subform.

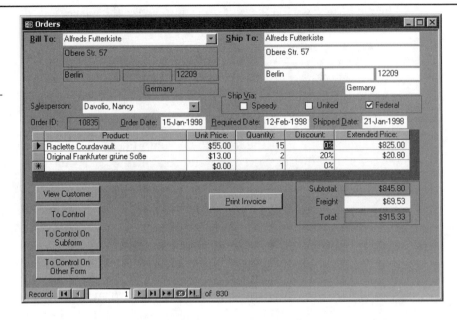

If you try to run a procedure with the GoToControl method to move the focus to a control on a closed form, Access will give you a run-time error. You can improve your code by anticipating this problem and including an If...Then statement to open the form if it is not already open before using the GoToControl method. The improved code is as follows:

```
Private Sub cmdToOtherFormControl_Click()
    Dim strControl As String, strForm As String
    strForm = "Employees": strControl = "Title"
    If IsLoaded(strForm) = False Then
        DoCmd.OpenForm strForm
    EndIf
    DoCmd.SelectObject acForm, strForm
    DoCmd.GoToControl strControl
End Sub
```

Using the *SetFocus* Method

The second method for moving the focus to a specific control on the active form uses the control's SetFocus method. The SetFocus method has the following syntax:

object.SetFocus

Object is a Form or a Control object.

The SetFocus method of the Control object moves the focus to the specified control on the active form or the specified field on the active datasheet. When the object is the Form object, the result depends on whether the form has any controls that can receive the focus. If the form has controls with the Enabled property set to True, the SetFocus method moves the focus to the last control on the form that had the focus; otherwise, the SetFocus method moves the focus to the form itself. When VBA executes an *object*.SetFocus statement, VBA is requesting that the object move the focus to itself.

The cmdSetControl_Click event procedure moves the focus to the combo box on the main form.

```
Private Sub cmdSetControl_Click()
    Dim cbo As ComboBox
    Set cbo = Forms!Orders!EmployeeID
    cbo.SetFocus
End Sub
```

The cmdSetControlOnSubform_Click procedure moves the focus first to the Subform object and then to the control on the subform.

```
Private Sub cmdSetControlOnSubform_Click()
    Dim sfr As Subform, txt As TextBox
    Set sfr = Forms!Orders![Orders Subform]
    Set txt = Forms!Orders![Orders Subform]!Quantity
    sfr.SetFocus
    txt.SetFocus
End Sub
```

The cmdSetOtherFormControl_Click procedure moves the focus first to the other form and then to a control on the form.

```
Private Sub cmdSetOtherFormControl_Click()
    Dim frm As Form, txt As TextBox
    Set frm = Forms![Employees]
    Set txt = Forms![Employees]!Extension
    frm.SetFocus
    txt.SetFocus
End Sub
```

Because SetFocus is a method of the Control object or the Form object, these event procedures create object variables to refer to the objects. The Set keyword in the assignment statements points the variables to specific objects. Use the fully qualified reference to refer to the forms and controls.

With the Orders form in Design view, place three command buttons on the form, giving them the following Name, Caption, and OnClick properties:

Button Name	Caption	Event Procedure
cmdSetControl	SetFocus To Control	cmdSetControl_Click()
cmdSetControl-OnSubform	SetFocus To Control On Subform	cmdSetControlOnSubform_Click()
cmdSetOther-FormControl	SetFocus To Control On Other Form	cmdSetOtherFormControl_Click()

Save the form and switch to Form view. With the Employees form open, test the three new buttons. For example, clicking the SetFocus To Control On Subform button moves the focus first to the subform control and then to the Quantity control of the first record in the subform (see Figure 11.4).

FIGURE 11.4:

Click the SetFocus To Control On Subform button to run a procedure that uses the SetFocus method to move the focus first to the subform control and then to the Quantity control of the first record in the subform.

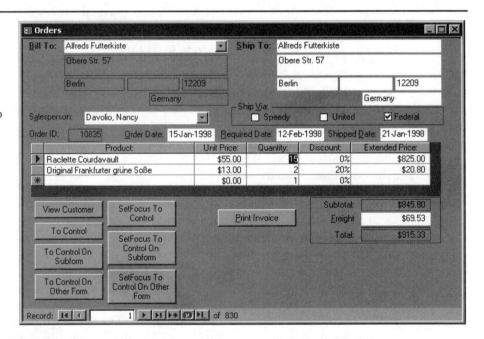

Moving within a Record

When working interactively, you can use the keyboard to move the focus among the controls of the active form. You can use the SendKeys statement to duplicate the keystrokes that move the focus. The syntax of the SendKeys statement is as follows:

```
SendKeys string, wait
```

String is a string expression specifying the keystrokes you want to send. The optional *wait* argument is True if the keystrokes must be processed before the next statement executes and False if the next statement executes immediately after the keys are sent. For example, the statement that moves the focus to the first control in the current record and waits for the keystroke to be processed is as follows:

```
SendKeys "{home}", True
```

Navigating among Records of a Form

When you work interactively, you navigate among records according to their physical location within the recordset. This process is called *physical navigation*. The record you move to becomes the current record—the *current record* is the record you modify with subsequent mouse or keyboard actions. You can use the GoToRecord method of the DoCmd object to duplicate the effect of clicking a default navigation button in the lower left corner of a form (or of choosing the Go To command on the Edit menu and then choosing one of the subcommands on the fly-out submenu). The GoToRecord method has the following syntax:

```
DoCmd.GoToRecord [objecttype][,objectname][,record][,offset]
```

where

- *objecttype* is one of the intrinsic constants: acActiveDataObject, acDataTable, acDataQuery, acDataForm, acDataFunction, acDataServerView, or acDataStoredProcedure. If you don't specify an object type, Access assigns the acActiveDataObject type.

- *objectname* is an optional string expression that is the valid name of an object of the specified type.

- *record* is one of the intrinsic constants: acPrevious, acNext (the default), acFirst, acLast, acGoTo, or acNewRec.

- *offset* is a numeric expression that represents the number of records to move forward if you specify acNext, backward if you specify acPrevious, or a valid record number if you specify acGoTo.

All of the arguments are optional. If you omit the *objecttype* and *objectname* arguments, the active object is assumed. If you omit the *record* argument, the default constant is acNext.

Creating Custom Navigation Buttons

We'll create a set of custom navigation buttons for a form. To make the buttons reusable on other forms, we automate the buttons with the event function procedures shown below, stored in a new basNavigationButtons standard module.

```
Public Function FirstRecord()
    DoCmd.GoToRecord Record:= acFirst
End Function

Public Function PreviousRecord()
    DoCmd.GoToRecord Record:= acPrevious
End Function

Public Function NextRec()
    DoCmd.GoToRecord Record:= acNext
End Function

Public Function LastRecord()
    DoCmd.GoToRecord Record:= acLast
End Function

Public Function NewRec()
    DoCmd.GoToRecord Record:= acNewRec
End Function
```

NOTE   The function procedures for the New and Next record buttons are abbreviated because NewRecord and NextRecord are the names of properties and are not valid names for procedures.

Create a set of five command buttons in the footer section of the Products form named cmdFirst, cmdPrevious, cmdNext, cmdLast, and cmdNew (and with suitable captions) and assign the event function procedures shown above. Be sure to change the Visible property of the Form Footer to Yes. Save the form and switch to Form view (see Figure 11.5). Test the new buttons.

When you test the buttons, you find that clicking the First button and then clicking the Previous button causes the PreviousRecord procedure to fail (see Figure 11.6a). The reason for the failure is that after you click the First button, the current record is the first record in the recordset; therefore, when you click the Previous button you are attempting to move beyond the limits of the recordset.

Clicking the Last button and then clicking the Next button opens a blank form. After clicking the Last button and then clicking the Next button, the current record is the new record that follows the last record in the recordset.

FIGURE 11.5:

The custom navigation buttons

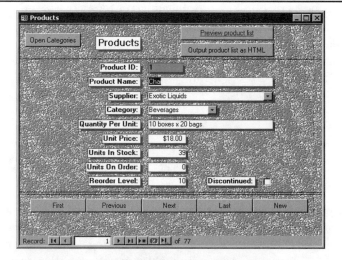

FIGURE 11.6:

When you attempt to move beyond the limits of the recordset, the default error handling is that the procedure fails (a), but you can use custom error handling (b) to avoid failure.

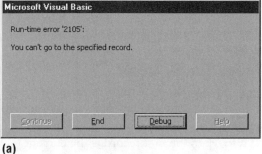

(a)

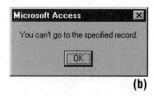

(b)

Dealing with Run-Time Errors

There are two methods for dealing with the run-time errors that occur when you try to move beyond the upper limits of a recordset:

- You can include error-handling code to avoid the run-time errors.

- You can create a set of "smart" navigation buttons that disable a button when clicking it would cause a run-time error.

Adding Error-Handling Code

As an example of using error handling to avoid a run-time error, we'll add custom error handling to the PreviousRecord function procedure to terminate the procedure without failure when the error occurs. The modified PreviousRecord procedure shown below has an enabled error handler that displays the default error message when you try to move beyond the first record.

```
Public Function PreviousRecord()
    On Error GoTo PreviousRecord_Err
    DoCmd.GoToRecord Record:=acPrevious

PreviousRecord_Exit:
Exit Function

PreviousRecord_Err:
    MsgBox Err.Description
    Resume PreviousRecord_Exit
End Function
```

After modifying the PreviousRecord procedure, clicking the First button and then clicking the Previous button still triggers the run-time error as before. However, this time the error trap is set, and control moves to the error-handling code. The error handler displays the message shown in Figure 11.6b and exits the procedure without trying to execute the GoToRecord method. As an alternative, you can omit the MsgBox statement and simply have no response when you are at the first record and click the Previous button. You can write similar error-handling code for the other navigation buttons.

Creating Smart Navigation Buttons

In the second approach to avoiding a run-time error, you create a procedure to disable a navigation button when clicking it would cause a run-time error. For example, if the first record is the current record, the procedure disables the Previous button. We'll design the procedure to disable the First button also when the first record is the current record, even though the FirstRecord procedure doesn't fail when the First button is clicked repeatedly. The disabled First button serves as a visual cue that the first record is the current record. If the last record is the current record, the procedure disables the Last and Next buttons; if a new record is the current record, the procedure disables the New and Next buttons.

To disable the appropriate buttons, you must know whether the current record is the first, the last, or a new record. Determining whether the current record is a new record is easy because a form has the NewRecord property that you can test. However, there is no FirstRecord or LastRecord property for a form, so we'll need to work harder to find out if the current record is the first or last record.

Although a form has no properties that you can use to determine if the current record is the first or last record, the form's recordset does. A recordset has BOF and EOF properties that you can use to determine whether you have moved beyond the limits. If you've moved the current record position to before the first record, BOF is True; if you've moved the current record position to after the last record, EOF is True (see Figure 11.7).

FIGURE 11.7:

You can use the BOF and EOF properties to determine if you've moved beyond the recordset's limits.

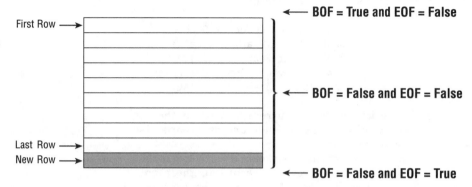

First Row →

⟵ **BOF = True and EOF = False**

⟵ **BOF = False and EOF = False**

Last Row →
New Row →

⟵ **BOF = False and EOF = True**

If we start moving around in the form's recordset, we'll disturb the screen display, so instead, we'll use the form's RecordsetClone property to create a separate current record pointer, synchronize the recordsetclone so that it points to the current record that the form displays, and use the recordsetclone's pointer to move around in the recordset. For example, if we use the recordsetclone's MovePrevious method to move to the previous record in the recordset and find that BOF is True, the form must be displaying the first record.

The DisableEnable function procedure disables and enables the navigation buttons.

```
Public Function DisableEnable(frm As Form)
    Dim rstClone As ADODB.Recordset
'Create a clone of the form's recordset to
'move around in without affecting the form's
'recordset
    Set rstClone = frm.RecordsetClone
'Determine if the current record is the
'new record and if it is, disable the Next
'and New buttons and then exit.
    If frm.NewRecord Then
        frm!cmdFirst.Enabled = True
        frm!cmdNext.Enabled = False
        frm!cmdPrevious.Enabled = True
        frm!cmdLast.Enabled = True
        frm!cmdNew.Enabled = False
        Exit Function
    End If
'If the current record is not the new record
'enable the New button
    frm!cmdNew.Enabled = True
```

```
'If there are no records, disable all
'other buttons
    If rstClone.RecordCount = 0 Then
        frm!cmdFirst.Enabled = False
        frm!cmdNext.Enabled = False
        frm!cmdPrevious.Enabled = False
        frm!cmdLast.Enabled = False
    Else
'Synchronize the current record in the clone
'to be the same as the current record displayed
'in the form.
        rstClone.Bookmark = frm.Bookmark
'Move to the previous record in the clone,
'if the clone's BOF is True, the form must be
'at the first record so disable the First and
'Previous buttons. Otherwise, the form is not
'at the first record so enable the First and
'Previous buttons.
        rstClone.MovePrevious
        If rstClone.BOF Then
            frm!cmdFirst.Enabled = False
            frm!cmdPrevious.Enabled = False
        Else
            frm!cmdFirst.Enabled = True
            frm!cmdPrevious.Enabled = True
        End If
'Resynchronize the current record in the clone
'to be the same as the current record displayed
'in the form.
        rstClone.Bookmark = frm.Bookmark
'Move to the next record in the clone,
'if the clone's EOF is True, the form must be
'at the last record so disable the Next and
'Last buttons. Otherwise, the form is not
'at the first record so enable the Next and
'Last buttons.
        rstClone.MoveNext
        If rstClone.EOF Then
            frm!cmdNext.Enabled = False
            frm!cmdLast.Enabled = False
        Else
            frm!cmdNext.Enabled = True
            frm!cmdLast.Enabled = True
        End If
    End If
End Function
```

The procedure runs when the form first opens and when you move to a different record (and the form recognizes the Current event). To make the procedure reusable on other forms, we'll pass the form to the procedure as an argument.

The DisableEnable function begins by creating the recordsetclone with its separate current record pointer. The procedure can now switch between the form and the recordset using whichever recordset or form property or method it needs. The procedure determines if the current record is the new record by testing the form's NewRecord property. If it is the new record, the Next and New buttons are disabled and the procedure ends. If the current record is not the new record, the procedure determines if the recordset contains any records.

Determining the presence of records is necessary because if we try to move around in a recordset that has no records at all, we cause run-time errors. The procedure uses the recordsetclone's RecordCount property to determine if records exist and disables the First, Previous, Next, and Last buttons if no records are found. If there are records, the next step is to determine where we are in the recordset.

NOTE   The RecordCount property returns the total number of records if the recordset is a static or keyset cursor. If the recordset is a forward-only cursor, it returns –1. If the recordset is a dynamic cursor, it will return either a –1 or the actual number of records, depending on what the data source of the recordset is.

We'll use the recordsetclone's current record pointer to move around in the recordset and test whether we've moved the recordsetclone's pointer beyond the limits of the recordset. We need a way to synchronize the recordsetclone to the form so that we can start with the recordsetclone and the form pointing to the same record. We use the Bookmark property to do the synchronization. When you open a bound form, Access automatically assigns a unique bookmark to each record in the recordset. Both the form and the recordsetclone have a Bookmark property. The form's Bookmark property returns the value of the bookmark for the record displayed by the form. The recordsetclone's Bookmark property returns the value of the bookmark for its current record, so you can point the recordsetclone at the record displayed in the form by using this assignment statement:

```
rstClone.Bookmark = frm.Bookmark
```

The DisableEnable procedure uses the BOF and EOF properties to determine if the current record is the first record or the last record. The procedure determines if the current record is the first record by using the recordsetclone's MovePrevious method to move the recordsetclone's current record pointer to the previous record and then testing the recordsetclone's BOF property. If the recordsetclone's BOF property is True, then the MovePrevious method has moved us to the current record position before the first record, and we must have been at the first record before the move. In this case, we disable the First and Previous buttons. If the recordsetclone's BOF property is False, we were not at the first record before the move, so we enable the First and Previous buttons. The procedure resynchronizes the recordsetclone and the form to point to the same record.

The final step is to determine if the current record is the last record by using the record-setclone's MoveNext method to move the recordsetclone's current record pointer to the next record and then test the recordsetclone's EOF property. If the recordsetclone's EOF property is True, then the MoveNext method has moved us to the current record position after the last record, and we must have been at the last record before the move. In this case, we disable the Last and Next buttons. If the recordsetclone's EOF property is False, we were not at the last record before the move, so we enable the Last and Next buttons. After finishing the tests, the procedure ends.

Insert the DisableEnable function procedure in the basNavigationButtons module. Next, display the Products form in Design view. Click in the form's OnCurrent property and set it to =DisableEnable([Form]). Save the form and switch to Form view. Test the buttons. For example, when the first record is the form's current record, the First and Previous buttons are disabled (see Figure 11.8).

FIGURE 11.8:

The DisableEnable procedure enables and disables the custom command buttons to avoid run-time errors.

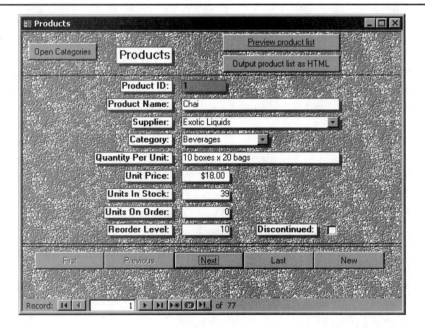

NOTE   Using a form's RecordsetClone property creates a new reference to the form's existing Recordset object. When you are finished using the recordsetclone, you don't use the `Close` method to attempt to close the Recordset object. VBA won't let you close the form's recordset without closing the form and simply ignores any statement that tries to close the recordsetclone. You can set the object variable to `Nothing` to sever the connection between the variable and the recordsetclone, but normally there isn't much point in doing so.

Finding a Specific Record

When you search for records interactively, you use the Find dialog, which is displayed by clicking the Find button in the toolbar or choosing Edit ➢ Find (see Figure 11.9). To make the find process faster, you restrict the search to values in a control by selecting the control before displaying the Find dialog.

FIGURE 11.9:

When working interactively, you use the Find dialog to find a record with a specified value in a field.

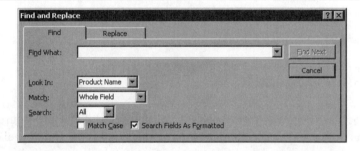

When you automate the search process using VBA programming, you can avoid displaying the Find dialog and make your application easier to use by adding an unbound combo box to the form's header or footer section and allowing the user to start the search by selecting a specific value from the combo list. Access VBA provides many ways to create an event procedure to find the specific record corresponding to the selected value.

The event procedure runs when the user changes the value in the combo box and the combo box recognizes the AfterUpdate event. We'll look at three ways to find a specific record:

- Using the `FindRecord` method
- Using the `ApplyFilter` method of the DoCmd object
- Using the RecordsetClone property

To explore the search techniques, open the Employees form in Design view and place an unbound combo box in the header section. Set the combo box properties as follows:

Name	cboFind
RowSourceType	Table/View/StoredProc
RowSource	Employees
ColumnCount	2
ColumnWidths	0"; 0.75"
BoundColumn	1

Using the *FindRecord* Method of the DoCmd Object

The simplest approach for finding a specific record is to create an event procedure for the combo box that mirrors each interactive step of the process with a VBA statement. The event procedure shown below uses this approach.

```
Private Sub cboFind_AfterUpdate()
    Application.Echo False
    EmployeeID.Enabled = True
    EmployeeID.SetFocus
    DoCmd.FindRecord cboFind
    cboFind.SetFocus
    EmployeeID.Enabled = False
    Application.Echo True
End Sub
```

This procedure begins by turning off screen painting while the procedure runs. In mirroring each interactive step, the procedure must move the focus to the EmployeeID control; however, this control is disabled, so the procedure must first enable the control. After enabling the EmployeeID control, the procedure moves the focus to it and uses the FindRecord method to find the value held in the combo box. After finding the value, the procedure moves the focus back to the combo box, disables the EmployeeID control, turns the screen painting back on, and ends.

NOTE   By default, screen painting is on, and Access takes the time to update the screen for each statement. The repainting not only takes time but also causes screen flicker as the screen updates after each statement. When you turn off screen painting in a VBA procedure, you must also turn it back on before the procedure ends.

Using the *ApplyFilter* Method of the DoCmd Object

A more efficient approach uses a filter to select the record directly from the form's recordset. The ApplyFilter method lets you apply a filter to a table, form, or report to restrict or sort the records in the table or in the underlying recordset of the form or report. You can specify a saved query as the filter using the *filtername* argument, or you can enter a SQL WHERE clause (without the word WHERE) in the *wherecondition* argument. The ApplyFilter method has two arguments. *Filtername* is a string expression that is the name of a query or a filter saved as a query that restricts or sorts the records. *Wherecondition* is an expression that restricts the records in the form of a valid SQL WHERE clause without the word WHERE.

You must specify at least one of the two arguments; if you specify both arguments, Access first applies the query and then applies the *wherecondition* to the result of the query. The maximum length of the *wherecondition* argument is 32,768 characters. (The *wherecondition* argument for the corresponding ApplyFilter macro action is 256 characters.)

The *wherecondition* argument to synchronize the form to the value in the combo box is as follows:

```
fieldname=Forms!formname!controlname
```

In this expression, *fieldname* refers to the field in the underlying table or query of the form, and *controlname* refers to the control on the form that contains the value you want to match. For example, to synchronize the Employees form to the value displayed in the cboFind combo box, use the following expression:

```
[EmployeeID]=Forms![Employees]![cboFind]
```

You can also use the Me property to refer to the form, as follows:

```
[EmployeeID]=Me!cboFind
```

The event procedure shown below uses this approach.

```
Private Sub cboFind_AfterUpdate()
    Dim strSQL As String
    strSQL = "EmployeeID = " & Me!cboFind
    DoCmd.ApplyFilter wherecondition:=strSQL
End Sub
```

Using the Recordsetclone

The most efficient approach uses the form's RecordsetClone property to refer to the form's recordset. The Recordset object has methods that you can use to find a specific record. To gain access to these methods, you can use the form's RecordsetClone property to refer to the form's recordset. The following statements declare rst as an object variable and assign it to the form's Recordset object with its own current record pointer:

```
Dim rst As ADODB.Recordset
Set rst = Me.RecordsetClone
```

You can use the Find method of the Recordset object to move the clone's current record pointer to the first record that satisfies a specified criteria. The syntax of the Find method is as follows:

```
recordset.Find criteria[, skiprows][, searchdirection][, start]
```

where

- *recordset* is a reference to an existing recordset object.

- *criteria* is a string expression that contains a comparison statement restricting the recordset. The criteria argument must contain one of the following comparison operators: >, <, =, >=, <=, <>, or like.

- *skiprows* is an optional value that specifies the number of records to skip from either the current record or the record specified in the start argument when conducting the Find method.

- *searchdirection* is an optional argument that specifies whether the search should proceed forward or backward from the current record in the recordset. The default direction is forward.

- *start* is an optional Variant bookmark that you can use to begin a search at a place other than the current record.

After running the Find method, the recordsetclone points to the found record. However, the current record displayed in the form hasn't changed. The final step is to move the form's current record pointer to the same record that the recordsetclone is pointing to by setting the form's Bookmark property to the recordsetclone's Bookmark property:

```
Me.Bookmark = rst.Bookmark
```

The event procedure shown below uses this approach.

```
Private Sub cboFind_AfterUpdate()
    Dim strCriteria As String
    Dim rst As ADODB.Recordset
    Set rst = Me.RecordsetClone
    strCriteria = "EmployeeID = " & Me!cboFind
    rst.Find strCriteria
    Me.Bookmark = rst.Bookmark
End Sub
```

Open the Employees form in Design view and insert the cboFind_AfterUpdate procedure. Save the form and switch to Form view. Select an employee in the lookup combo box (see Figure 11.10). The procedure displays the record of the selected employee.

FIGURE 11.10:

The most efficient search
technique uses the
`Find` method of
the recordsetclone.

Undoing the Search

After finding a particular record, you may want to undo the search and return to the previously displayed record. To undo the search, you need to know which record was displayed last. You can keep track of the previous record by holding the value of its primary key in a module-level variable. You use a module-level variable so that the record's primary key will be available to the procedure to undo the search. Modify the procedure that finds a specific record by including a statement to store the current record's primary key value before running the statements that find the specific record.

To undo the search when the search uses the recordsetclone technique, first enter the following declaration statement in the Declarations section of the form module:

```
Private LastFind
```

Next, modify the `cboFind_AfterUpdate` event procedure to set `LastFind` to the primary key of the current record before any other statement:

```
Private Sub cboFind_AfterUpdate()
    Dim strCriteria As String
    Dim rst As ADODB.Recordset
    LastFind = EmployeeID
    Set rst = Me.RecordsetClone
    strCriteria = "EmployeeID = " & Me!cboFind
    rst.Find strCriteria
    Me.Bookmark = rst.Bookmark
End Sub
```

In the header of the Employees form, place a command button named cmdUndoFind with the caption Last Lookup and create the OnClick event procedure shown below:

```
Private Sub cmdUndoFind_Click()
    Dim strCriteria As String
    Dim rst As ADODB.Recordset
    Set rst = Me.RecordsetClone
    strCriteria = "EmployeeID = " & LastFind
    rst.Find strCriteria
    Me.Bookmark = rst.Bookmark
    Me!cboFind = LastFind
End Sub
```

The cmdUndoFind_Click event procedure uses the same find technique to find the record matching the value stored in the LastFind variable and then synchronizes the combo box to the displayed record.

Save the form and switch to Form view. Select an employee in the lookup combo box. Click the Last Lookup button. The previous employee is displayed (see Figure 11.11).

FIGURE 11.11:

The Last Lookup button runs a procedure that uses the value of the EmployeeID stored in a module-level variable to locate the previously found record.

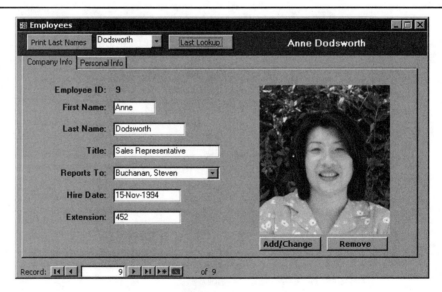

Working with the Data in Tables

In the previous sections, we have worked with records in an open form. We used the form's RecordsetClone property to refer to the form's Recordset object so that we could get access to the properties and methods of the Recordset object. Another way to work with the records in a Recordset object is to open a recordset in memory directly without working with a form at all. Opening and working with recordsets in memory has a distinct performance advantage because Access doesn't need to take time to create the visual representation of the form on the screen.

Creating Recordset Variables

A recordset is a set of records of a table or the set of records that results from running a query, view, stored procedure, or SQL statement that returns records. When you work with data in VBA procedures, you work with recordsets. To create a new Recordset object, you first instantiate a recordset variable, then use the variable's Open method. The following statements create a new recordset:

```
Dim rst As ADODB.Recordset
rst.Open source, activeconnection, cursortype, locktype, options
```

where

- *rst* is an object variable representing the Recordset object.

- *source* is a variant expression that specifies the name of a Command object, table, URL, stored procedure, SQL statement, or Stream object that contains or returns records.

- *activeconnection* is either a variable that points to an existing connection or a string expression that evaluates to a valid Connection object.

- *cursortype* determines what kind of recordset cursor will be assigned to the recordset. The default is forward-only.

- *locktype* specifies what kind of record locking will be used with the new recordset. The default is read-only.

- *options* can be used to specify the type of object represented by the source argument.

A recordset created in a procedure exists in memory until the application terminates or you set the recordset variable to the Nothing value.

Opening a Dynamic Cursor Recordset

For the examples in this section, create a new standard module named basRecordsets. Our first example is the DynamicRecordset procedure shown below.

```
Public Sub DynamicRecordset()
    Dim rst As New ADODB.Recordset
    Dim cnn As ADODB.Connection
    Set cnn = CurrentProject.Connection
    rst.Open "Categories", cnn, adOpenDynamic, , adCmdTable
```

```
         Do Until rst.EOF
             Debug.Print rst(0), rst(1)
             rst.MoveNext
         Loop
     End Sub
```

This procedure opens a dynamic cursor recordset on the Categories table using the Open function of the Recordset object. We set the options argument to adCmdTable to indicate that the "Categories" source argument is the name of a table.

Insert the DynamicRecordset procedure in the basRecordsets module and run it in the Immediate window. The procedure prints the CategoryID and the CategoryName fields.

Opening a Static Cursor Recordset

The StaticRecordset procedure opens a static cursor recordset for the customers from Argentina.

```
     Public Sub StaticRecordset()
         Dim rst As New ADODB.Recordset
         Dim cnn As ADODB.Connection
         Dim strSQL As String
         strSQL = "SELECT * FROM Customers WHERE Country = 'Argentina'"
         Set cnn = CurrentProject.Connection
         rst.Open strSQL, cnn, adOpenStatic, , adCmdText
         Do Until rst.EOF
             Debug.Print rst("CustomerID"), rst!CompanyName
             rst.MoveNext
         Loop
     End Sub
```

The procedure uses a SQL statement as the source of the records, as follows:

```
     strSQL = "SELECT * FROM Customers WHERE Country = 'Argentina'"
```

Enter the StaticRecordset procedure in the basRecordsets module and run it in the Immediate window. The procedure prints the CustomerID and the CompanyName fields to the Immediate window.

Opening a Recordset in Another Database

The RecordsetOtherDatabase procedure opens a dynamic recordset for the Expense Categories table in the Expenses database.

```
     Public Sub RecordsetOtherDatabase()
         Dim rst As New ADODB.Recordset
         Dim cnn As New ADODB.Connection
         cnn.Open "Provider=Microsoft.Jet.OLEDB.4.0; Data " & _
           "Source=c:\VBAHandbook\Expenses.mdb; Jet OLEDB:" & _
```

```
        "Database Password=expenses"
        rst.Open "[Expense Categories]", cnn, adOpenDynamic, , adCmdTable
        Do Until rst.EOF
            Debug.Print rst(0), rst(1)
            rst.MoveNext
        Loop
    End Sub
```

When the table you want to work with is in another database, you need to establish a connection to the other database in memory first and then open a recordset on the table. To establish such a connection, you use the Open method of the Connection object. The syntax for this method is as follows:

```
cnn.Open connectionstring[, userid][, password][, options]
```

where

- *cnn* is an object variable that represents the connection object.

- *connectionstring* is a string expression (or a variable that represents a string expression) that contains connection information for the database you are trying to connect to.

- *userid* is an optional string expression that is a user name with access to the data source.

- *password* is an optional argument and is the corresponding password for the user name specified in the userid argument.

- *options* is an optional argument that specifies whether the method should end before or after the connection is established.

The RecordsetOtherDatabase procedure uses the file path of the Expenses database as part of the connectionstring argument of the Open method. If you saved the Expenses database in a different folder than the database that is currently open in the Access window, change the path in the connectionstring argument. The procedure opens a dynamic recordset on the Expense Categories table and prints the values of the first two fields.

You may recall from Chapter 1 that we set a password of "expenses" for the Expenses.mdb database. To open a database-protected password, you need some way to pass the password to the database to gain access to the data. How you do this varies among different types of data sources. With JET OLEDB data sources, such as Access MDB files, you specify the password by adding a JET OLEDB:Database Password argument to the end of the connection string. This is not to be confused with the Connection object's Open method's password argument, which is used to gain access to the computer housing the database, and not the database itself. Whether you need to supply a password to connect to another computer on your network depends on how security is set up on the network.

Insert the `RecordsetOtherDatabase` procedure in the basRecordsets module and run the procedure in the Immediate window. Figure 11.12 shows the results of running the `DynamicRecordset`, `StaticRecordset`, and `RecordsetOtherDatabase` procedures.

FIGURE 11.12:

The results of three procedures that open recordsets and loop through the records, printing values from each record

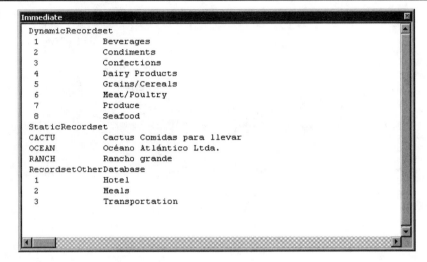

```
Immediate
DynamicRecordset
     1           Beverages
     2           Condiments
     3           Confections
     4           Dairy Products
     5           Grains/Cereals
     6           Meat/Poultry
     7           Produce
     8           Seafood
StaticRecordset
CACTU         Cactus Comidas para llevar
OCEAN         Océano Atlántico Ltda.
RANCH         Rancho grande
RecordsetOtherDatabase
     1           Hotel
     2           Meals
     3           Transportation
```

Navigating Recordsets

When you create a Recordset object, you are placing rows of data in a memory buffer and pointing to a single record at a time, the current record. You can work only with the current record. You navigate through a recordset by moving the current record pointer to one record after another.

The techniques for navigating recordsets were described in Chapters 6 and 9, "Controlling Execution." Here is a recap:

- Use the Move... methods and the Move method of the Recordset object to move the current record pointer so that it points to another record. You can use the BOF and EOF properties to detect whether you have moved the current record pointer beyond the limits of the recordset.

- The Value property of a field in the recordset returns the data value for the field. You can use any of these four references to retrieve a data value:

exclamation point	*recordsetname*!*fieldname*
index by name	*recordsetname*("*fieldname*")
index by variable	strfield = "*fieldname*"
	recordsetname(strfield)
index by number	*recordsetname*(*indexnumber*)

Recordsets have the Requery method that you can use to reexecute the query or reread the table on which the recordset is based. When you use the Requery method, the first record in the recordset becomes the current record.

- You can use a Do... Loop structure to loop through each record in a recordset, as follows:

```
Do Until rst.EOF
    [statements]
    rst.MoveNext
Loop
```

- When the procedure ends, the recordset variable is cleared, but it continues to exist until you set it to the Nothing value. Normally, it is not necessary to explicitly close a Recordset object. But if you are finished with it before the end of the procedure and want to reclaim the memory, you can use the Close method to close the recordset: rst.Close.

The following sections describe a couple more recordset-navigation techniques and present an example to demonstrate recordset navigation.

Counting the Records

You use the RecordCount property of the recordset to determine the number of records. The value returned by the property depends on the type of the recordset. For static cursor or keyset cursor recordsets, the RecordCount property gives the total number of records in the table. For forward-only cursor recordsets, the RecordCount property returns –1. The RecordCount property returns either a –1 or the number of actual records for a dynamic cursor recordset, depending on the data source.

If others are adding or deleting records, then you need to update the recordset first (assuming that the recordset is updateable) before running the RecordCount method, as follows:

```
rst.Requery
num = rst.RecordCount
```

Testing for an Empty Recordset

It is important to include a test for an empty recordset in any procedure that would fail if the recordset has no records. If rst.RecordCount = 0, no records exist. The following piece of code shows a simple test that you can include to test for the presence of records in a recordset.

```
If rst.RecordCount = 0 Then
    MsgBox "There are no records."
    rst.Close
    Exit Sub
End If
rst.MoveFirst
```

This code displays a message and exits from the procedure if the recordset is empty. Otherwise, it moves the current record pointer to the first record.

Testing a Recordset Navigation Procedure

The RecordsetNavigation procedure opens a static cursor recordset on the Customers table and displays the current record position. (When you first open a recordset, the current record is the first record.)

```
Public Sub RecordsetNavigation()
    Dim rst As New ADODB.Recordset
    Dim cnn As New ADODB.Connection
    Set cnn = CurrentProject.Connection
    rst.Open "Customers", cnn, adOpenStatic, adCmdTable
    MsgBox "The current record is " & rst.AbsolutePosition
    rst.MoveLast
    rst.MoveFirst
    rst.Move 5
    MsgBox "The current record is " & rst.AbsolutePosition
    MsgBox rst!CompanyName & ", " & rst("ContactName") & ", " _
        & rst(3)
    MsgBox "The number of records is " & rst.RecordCount
    rst.Requery
    MsgBox "The recordset has been requeried."
    MsgBox "The current record is " & rst.AbsolutePosition
    rst.MovePrevious
    If rst.BOF Then
        MsgBox "Moved before the first record. There is no current " _
            & "record."
    End If
    rst.Close
End Sub
```

The procedure displays the current record position then moves the current record pointer to the end of the recordset, back to the beginning, and then forward five records. The next statements display the current record position, data values in three fields using different reference syntax, and the total number of records.

The next statements update the recordset and display the current record position. The next statement moves the current record pointer backward by one record and tests the BOF property. Finally, the procedure closes the recordset.

Insert the RecordsetNavigation procedure in the basRecordsets module and then run the procedure in the Immediate window. Figure 11.13 shows the messages that indicate progress through the procedure.

FIGURE 11.13:

The Recordset-
Navigation procedure
displays messages to
indicate progress through
the procedure.

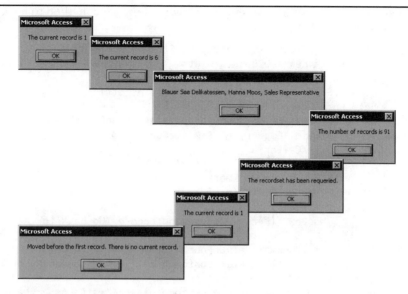

Finding a Specific Record

As explained in Chapter 6, you find a specific record in a recordset by specifying a search condition that you want a record to satisfy and using one of the techniques that the database engine provides to move the current record pointer to the "first" record that satisfies the condition. You use different techniques to find records, depending on the type of recordset you create. The Seek method works only with server-side cursor recordsets that were opened with the adCmdTableDirect option set. For other recordset cursors, you would use the Recordset object's Find method.

The following sections provide more details and examples of using the Find and Seek methods for finding a record. Create a new module named basFindingRecords for the examples of finding records.

Using the *Find* Method

The Find method offers a lot of versatility in searching for records. You can search in any direction allowed by the recordset's cursor type by using the Find method's searchdirection and start arguments, which were explained in "Using the Recordsetclone" section earlier in this chapter. You set the Find method's criteria argument to any string value that is a comparison statement. Here are some examples of criteria expressions:

```
"OrderDate > #5-30-2001# And RequiredDate <#11-30-2001#"
"Country = 'Germany'"
"CompanyName Like 'B*'"
```

The `FindRecord` procedure, shown below, uses the `Find` method to locate records in the Customers table.

```
Public Sub FindRecord(strCountry As String)
    Dim rst As New ADODB.Recordset
    Dim cnn As ADODB.Connection
    Dim varFound As Variant, strCriteria As String
    Set cnn = CurrentProject.Connection
    rst.Open "Customers", cnn, adOpenStatic, adCmdTable
    strCriteria = "Country = '" & strCountry & "'"
    rst.Find strCriteria
    If Not rst.EOF Then
        varFound = rst.Bookmark
        rst.Find strCriteria, 1
        If rst.EOF Then
            MsgBox "There is no second record. Go back to the first " _
                & "record found."
            rst.Bookmark = varFound
            MsgBox "The first customer is " & rst!CompanyName
        Else
            MsgBox "The second customer is " & rst("CompanyName")
        End If
        rst.Close
    Else
        MsgBox "There are no records matching your search."
        rst.Close
    End If
End Sub
```

The procedure creates a static cursor recordset on the Customers table, moves to the beginning of the recordset, and uses the `Find` method to find the first customer from the country you specify when you call the procedure. If there is a match and the record pointer has not moved past the end of the recordset, the procedure sets a bookmark for the found record. The procedure then uses the `Find` method again to find the next customer from the specified country. If a second customer isn't found, the record pointer moves past the end of the recordset and the procedure displays a message, returns the pointer to the first customer, and displays the company name; otherwise, the procedure displays a message with the company name for the second customer. If no records are found matching the country, the procedure displays a message box.

The second time the `Find` method is called, we set the `skiprows` argument to 1, so that the search begins again from one record after the current record. Otherwise, the method continues to find the same record over and over again.

Add the FindRecord procedure to the basFindingRecords module and run the procedure in the Immediate window by typing **FindRecord("Norway")**. The procedure finds a single customer from Norway, so it displays the message box shown in Figure 11.14a, then the message box in Figure 11.14b. Run the procedure again by typing **FindRecord("Botswana")**. No customers are found, and the procedure displays the message box shown in Figure 11.14c then terminates.

FIGURE 11.14:

The FindRecord procedure displays message boxes when it fails to find a second customer (a), then displays the company name for the first customer matching search criteria (b). The procedure displays a message box when the Find method has no matches (c).

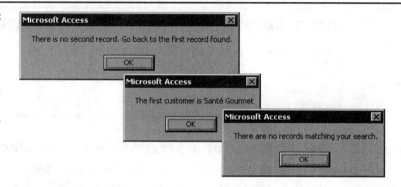

The FindAll procedure, shown below, uses the Find method and a Do…Loop structure.

```
Public Sub FindAll()
    Dim rst As New ADODB.Recordset
    Dim cnn As ADODB.Connection
    Dim strCriteria As String
    Set cnn = CurrentProject.Connection
    rst.Open "Customers", cnn, adOpenStatic, adCmdTable
    strCriteria = "Country = 'Argentina'"
    rst.Find strCriteria
    If rst.EOF Then
        MsgBox "There are no customers from Argentina."
    Else
        Do Until rst.EOF
            Debug.Print rst("CompanyName")
            rst.Find strCriteria, 1
        Loop
    End If
End Sub
```

This procedure uses the Find method to locate the first customer from Argentina. If no customer is found, the procedure displays a message and terminates. If a customer is found, the procedures again uses the Find method, this time with the skiprows argument set to 1, in a Do…Loop structure to find all additional records. The Do…Loop structure uses the EOF property as the looping condition; the loop continues to execute until the Find method fails to find a record and the EOF property is True. Each pass of the loop displays the company name for the current record and finds the next record that satisfies the search criteria.

Enter the FindAll procedure in the basFindingRecords module and run the procedure in the Immediate window. The names of the three customers from Argentina are printed to the Immediate window (see Figure 11.15).

FIGURE 11.15:

The FindAll procedure uses a loop with the Find method to find all of the records that satisfy the search criteria.

```
Immediate
FindAll
Cactus Comidas para llevar
Océano Atlántico Ltda.
Rancho grande
```

Using the *Seek* Method for a Server-Side Cursor Recordset

When the recordset is a server-side cursor recordset opened on a table, you can use the Seek method. Seek works only when you are searching in a table field that is indexed. You must set the index in table Design view by setting the table field's Indexed property to Yes (Duplicates OK) or No (No Duplicates) or creating the index for the field as part of the VBA procedure. (See Chapters 6 and 14 for information about creating an index programmatically.) Seek uses the index to perform the search; therefore, a Seek search is faster than a Find search.

The format for the Seek method is as follows:

```
rst.Seek keyvalues, seekoption
```

where

- *rst* is a variable representing the Recordset object.

- *keyvalues* is an array of values to compare against the indexed column.

- *seekoption* is an enumerated constant representing the kind of comparison to make between the keyvalues argument and the indexed column. The possible seekoption settings are as follows:

adSeekFirstEQ	Locates the first record equal to the keyvalues
adSeekLastEQ	Locates the last record equal to the keyvalues
adSeekAfterEQ	Locates the record equal to the keyvalues or the record just after where a match would have occurred
adSeekAfter	Locates the record after the one where a match would have occurred

adSeekBeforeEQ	Locates the record equal to the `keyvalues` or the record just before where a match would have occurred
adSeekBefore	Locates the record before the one where a match would have occurred

> **NOTE** The SQL Server OLE DB provider does not support the use of the **Seek** method, so for this section, we will use a database rather than a project. Make a copy of the Northwind.mdb database and name it Northwind_Ch11.mdb and save it to the c:\VBAHandbook file, then open it to work through the **Seek** method examples that follow.

To use the Seek technique to find the first customer from Argentina, first create an index for the Country field by setting the field's Indexed property to Yes (Duplicates OK) in table Design view (see Figure 11.16). In the procedure, create a server-side cursor recordset on the Customers table and then use the statements below to set the current index to the Country index and run the Seek method.

```
rst.Index = "Country"
rst.Seek "Argentina", adSeekFirstEQ
```

FIGURE 11.16:

You can create an index in table Design view.

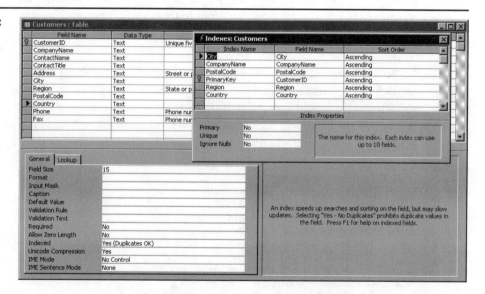

To use the Seek technique to find the first employee with a specified first and last name, you can create a multiple field index in table Design view. Figure 11.17 shows the Indexes window with the FullName index having the LastName and FirstName fields.

FIGURE 11.17:

You can create a multiple index for search fields in the Indexes dialog of table Design view.

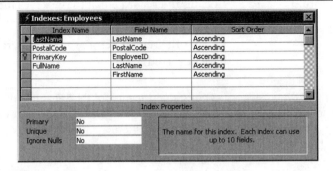

In the procedure, create a server-side cursor recordset on the Employees table and then use the statements below to set the current index to the FullName index and run the Seek method.

```
rst.Index = "FullName"
rst.Seek Array("Peacock", "Margaret"), adSeekFirstEQ
```

To use the Seek technique on the primary key index, you can identify the index with the string "PrimaryKey". For example, to use the Seek technique to find the first order with OrderID greater than 11040, create a server-side cursor recordset on the Orders table and then use the statements below to set the current index to the primary key index and run the Seek method.

```
rst.Index = "PrimaryKey"
rst.Seek 11040, adSeekAfter
```

In the first example above, Access searches in the Country index for the first time Argentina appears in the index lookup table and then uses the index lookup table to locate the corresponding table record and makes it the current record. If no record is found, the current record pointer is beyond the recordset and there is no current record. You use the EOF property to determine whether the Seek technique was successful. The SeekAll procedure shown below demonstrates this technique.

```
Public Sub SeekAll()
    Dim rst As New ADODB.Recordset
    Dim cnn As ADODB.Connection
    Set cnn = CurrentProject.Connection
    rst.CursorLocation = adUseServer
    rst.Open "Customers", cnn, adOpenStatic, , adCmdTableDirect
    rst.Index = "Country"
    rst.Seek "Argentina", adSeekFirstEQ
    If rst.EOF Then
        MsgBox "There are no customers from Argentina."
    Else
        MsgBox "The first customer from Argentina is " & _
            rst!CompanyName
    End If
End Sub
```

This procedure opens a server-side direct-table recordset on the Customers table. The next statements set the current index to the Country field and search in the index for the first customer from Argentina.

Open the Customers table in Design view and set the Indexed property of the Country field in the Customers table to Yes (Duplicates OK). Save the table. Create a new standard module named basSeekingRecords and insert the SeekAll procedure in the module. Run the SeekAll procedure in the Immediate window. The procedure uses the EOF property to determine if the search was successful and prints the results of the test.

Exploring Clones

As explained in Chapter 6, you can use the Clone method of the Recordset object to create a new Recordset object that is identical to the original Recordset object with an important difference: The new Recordset object, called a clone of the original, has its own independent current record pointer. Creating a clone is faster than creating a new Recordset object using the Open method.

> **NOTE** When you create a clone of an existing Recordset object using the **Clone** method, the clone and the original Recordset objects have the same bookmarks. Two Recordset objects created by any other means have different sets of bookmarks, even when they are based on the same source. You cannot synchronize their current records using bookmarks. For example, if you open a form based on a table and then use the **Open** method to open a recordset on the same table, the two recordset objects have separate sets of bookmarks.

As an example of using a clone, the Duplicates procedure compares the values in the Country field for two consecutive customer records.

```
Public Sub Duplicates()
    Dim rst As New ADODB.Recordset
    Dim cnn As ADODB.Connection
    Dim rstClone As New ADODB.Recordset
    Set cnn = CurrentProject.Connection
    rst.Open "Customers", cnn, adOpenStatic, , adCmdTable
    rst.Move 20
    Set rstClone = rst.Clone
    rstClone.Bookmark = rst.Bookmark
    rstClone.MovePrevious
    If rstClone!Country = rst!Country Then
        MsgBox "The previous record has the same value for Country."
    Else
        MsgBox "The previous record does not have the same value " & _
            "for Country."
    End If
```

```
        MsgBox "Previous record value: " & rstClone!Country _
            & " Current record value: " & rst!Country
        rst.Close
        rstClone.Close
    End Sub
```

This procedure opens a static cursor recordset on the Customers table and moves the current record pointer 20 rows forward to the twenty-first record. The procedure creates a clone and synchronizes the clone's current record pointer to the same record. The MovePrevious method moves the clone's current record pointer to the clone's previous record. The procedure compares the values in the Country field for the original (record 21) and the clone (record 20) and displays the results of the comparison and the values in the two records. The last statements close both Recordset objects.

Reopen the Northwind_Ch11.adp project. Insert the Duplicates procedure in the basFindingRecords module and run it in the Immediate window. The values in the two records are displayed in a message box (see Figure 11.18).

FIGURE 11.18:

When a procedure needs to work with more than one record at a time, use the Clone method to create a duplicate recordset with its own current record pointer.

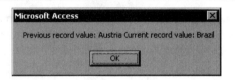

Reading Table Data into an Array

When you don't need to change the data, creating a forward-only cursor recordset is the fastest way to retrieve a set of records. The limitation of this cursor type, of course, is that you can only move the current record pointer forward

If you don't need to change the data but you do need random access to the data, the forward-only cursor recordset is no longer the solution. Instead, you can create an array to hold the data in memory (arrays are discussed in Chapter 8, "Using Variables"). After you read the data from the recordset into an array, you can close the recordset and release the tables for others to use. (If you are working in a multiuser environment, using arrays minimizes record-locking conflicts.)

You use the GetRows method of the Recordset object to copy rows from a Recordset object into a two-dimensional variant array. The syntax is as follows:

```
    varArray = recordset.GetRows([rows][, start][, fields])
```

where

- *varArray* is a variant two-dimensional array variable.

- *rows* is an optional statement that indicates the number of rows to get. The default (and, in fact, only setting) is to get the rest of the rows.

- *start* is an optional string or variant expression that evaluates to a Bookmark. If this argument is set, the GetRows method begins retrieving from this record rather than from the current record.

- *fields* is an optional argument that represents a field or an array of fields. Only the fields you specify in this argument will be retrieved.

The array returned by the GetRows method is a two-dimensional array, with the first element identifying the field and the second element identifying the row. As an example, varArray(2,3) is the value of the third field in the fourth row. (Access starts each index at zero.)

You can use the UBound function to determine the number of fields and rows returned. To determine the numbers of fields and rows returned, use the following statements:

```
numFields = UBound(varArray, 1) + 1
numRows = UBound(varArray, 2) + 1
```

Since the field and row indexes begin with zero, the statements add one to the largest indexes to obtain the number of fields and rows.

The GetRows method copies the records beginning with the current record, unless you set the start argument. After the GetRows method is executed, the record pointer moves beyond the recordset and the EOF property becomes true. Only the fields you specify in the fields argument are returned.

To explore these concepts, create a new module named basArrays and declare the varArray variable in the Declarations section as a public module-level variable using the declaration statement:

```
Public varArray As Variant
```

You use a module-level variable so that the array continues to exist after the values are read into it by the ArrayRecordset procedure, shown below.

```
Public Sub ArrayRecordset()
    Dim rst As New ADODB.Recordset
    Dim cnn As ADODB.Connection
    Dim numFields As Integer, numRows As Integer
    Dim varArray As Variant, j As Integer
    Set cnn = CurrentProject.Connection
    rst.Open "Customers", cnn, adOpenStatic, , adCmdTable
    rst.Move 70
    Debug.Print rst.AbsolutePosition
```

```
        varArray = rst.GetRows(adGetRowsRest, , "ContactName")
        Debug.Print rst.AbsolutePosition
        rst.Close
        numFields = UBound(varArray, 1) + 1
        numRows = UBound(varArray, 2) + 1
        Debug.Print "Fields: " & numFields & " Rows: " & numRows
        For j = 0 To numRows - 1
            Debug.Print "Contact Name: " & varArray(0, j)
        Next
    End Sub
```

This procedure opens a static cursor recordset on the Customers table, moves 20 rows forward, prints the absolute row position, reads three rows into a variant array, prints the absolute row position again, and closes the recordset. The procedure determines the number of fields and rows actually read into the array and uses a For . . . Next loop to print out the values in the first two fields of each row in the array.

Enter the ArrayRecordset procedure in the basArrays module and run it in the Immediate window. The procedure runs, returning the contact names for all the customers in the array (see Figure 11.19).

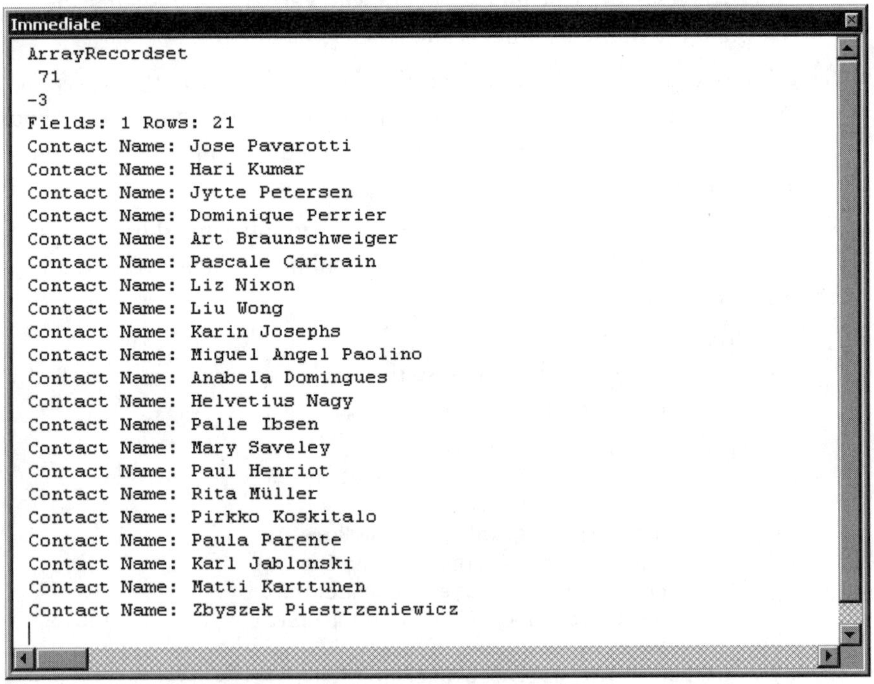

FIGURE 11.19:

The ArrayRecordset procedure uses the GetRows method to read data into an array.

```
Immediate                                                    [x]
ArrayRecordset
 71
-3
Fields: 1 Rows: 21
Contact Name: Jose Pavarotti
Contact Name: Hari Kumar
Contact Name: Jytte Petersen
Contact Name: Dominique Perrier
Contact Name: Art Braunschweiger
Contact Name: Pascale Cartrain
Contact Name: Liz Nixon
Contact Name: Liu Wong
Contact Name: Karin Josephs
Contact Name: Miguel Angel Paolino
Contact Name: Anabela Domingues
Contact Name: Helvetius Nagy
Contact Name: Palle Ibsen
Contact Name: Mary Saveley
Contact Name: Paul Henriot
Contact Name: Rita Müller
Contact Name: Pirkko Koskitalo
Contact Name: Paula Parente
Contact Name: Karl Jablonski
Contact Name: Matti Karttunen
Contact Name: Zbyszek Piestrzeniewicz
|
```

Summary

This chapter focused on using VBA procedures to automate navigation in the forms interface and on using VBA to navigate through the data by creating recordset objects in memory without opening forms. The important points follow:

- You can use the methods of the DoCmd object to duplicate the keystrokes, mouse clicks, and menu-command selections of the interactive environment.

- While event procedures are useful in creating procedures for navigating in the interface, creating reusable procedures normally requires using function procedures and storing them in standard modules.

- Use the form's RecordsetClone property to create a reference to the form's Recordset object that has a current record pointer independent of the form's current record pointer. Using the recordsetclone gives you access to the methods and properties of the Recordset object.

- Creating custom navigation buttons to browse through the records involves procedures that move the current record pointer beyond the limits of the recordset. Use the BOF and EOF properties to determine whether you have exceeded the limits.

- You can find a specific record using a form in three ways:
  - The FindRecord method of the DoCmd object duplicates the interactive approach to finding a record.
  - The ApplyFilter method of the DoCmd object applies a filter to the records.
  - The RecordsetClone property allows you to use the Find method of the form's Recordset object.

- You can work directly with the data without opening a form by creating a Recordset object in memory. You can base a recordset on a table, query, view, stored procedure, Stream object, or SQL statement that returns records.

- The key to understanding recordsets is the current record. You can work with only the current record, and you use the Move . . . methods to move the current record pointer from one record to another.

- To work with two records simultaneously, you can open a second recordset or use the Clone method to create a duplicate of the original recordset but with an independent current record pointer.

- To find a specific record using a recordset, do one of the following:
  - Specify the search condition in a SQL statement and create a recordset based on the SQL statement.

- Create a recordset and then use the Seek method for a direct-table server-side cursor recordset when the search condition is based on an index or the Find method for all other types of recordsets.

- If you don't need to change the data but need random access, you can read data into an array.

CHAPTER 12

Maintaining Data with Access VBA

- Protecting data using a review mode

- Using procedures for custom data validation

- Modifying procedures created by the Command Button Wizard

- Carrying values forward to a new record

- Maintaining data using a recordset instead of a form

You can use two fundamental approaches to working with the data in your database application: the forms approach and the recordset approach.

In the forms approach, you provide forms that the user can work with to add new records, change data values in fields, and delete existing records. You use VBA procedures to automate data-maintenance operations such as displaying a blank record, setting default values for fields in a new record, validating new or changed data in fields, undoing or saving changes to a record, and deleting an existing record. A problem associated with using forms to change data values is that Access may not automatically update records and display the most current values. (See Chapter 4, "Communicating with Forms," for examples.) This chapter shows you how to use VBA procedures to update the sources of data to display the most current data.

In the recordset approach, you are adding, changing, or deleting records without necessarily displaying the records to the user in a form. For example, suppose you want to change the title of your sales representatives to Account Executive. In the recordset approach, you create a procedure that opens a recordset on the Employees table and makes the change in memory without ever displaying the records to the user.

Maintaining Data Using Forms

In most database applications, you provide a set of forms that allow the user to work with data. The core of many of these applications is a set of data-entry forms designed for efficient entry of new records and modification of existing records. Often, you want a data-entry form to serve as a review form as well. In data-entry mode, the data controls are unlocked and enabled so that the user can change the data at will. In review mode, the data controls are locked and disabled so that the user cannot make changes. An important design concept is to use review mode to protect your data against inadvertent changes and include a way, possibly protected by a password, for the user to change the form to data-entry mode.

NOTE   For hands-on experience with the techniques described in this chapter, create a new copy of the Northwind sample database named Northwind_Ch12.MDB and work through the steps of the examples. Be sure to add the Library references for ADO and ADOX, and to remove the reference for DAO.

Toggling a Form between Review and Data-Entry Modes

A good strategy for avoiding inadvertent changes to the data is to open the form in review mode and provide a command button for changing between review and data-entry mode.

Clicking a command button runs a procedure that loops through the data controls on the form and changes their Locked and Enabled properties. (See Chapter 9, "Controlling Execution," for information about creating loops through collections.) As an example, the Lock-Controls and UnlockControls procedures, shown below, use the For Each...Next structure to loop through each control on the form. If the control is a text box or a combo box, the procedure sets the value of the Locked and Enabled properties.

```
Public Function LockControls()
    Dim ctl As Control
    For Each ctl in Screen.ActiveForm.Controls
        If TypeOf ctl is TextBox Or TypeOf ctl is ComboBox Then
            With ctl
                .Locked = True
                .Enabled = False
            End With
        End If
    Next
End Function

Public Function UnlockControls()
    Dim ctl As Control
    For Each ctl in Screen.ActiveForm.Controls
        If TypeOf ctl is TextBox Or TypeOf ctl is ComboBox Then
            With ctl
                .Locked = False
                .Enabled = True
            End With
        End If
    Next
End Function
```

To prepare the Customers form as a dual-mode form, open it in Design view. Select all the text boxes and the Country combo box. Set the Enabled property to No and the Locked property to Yes for the multiple selection.

Next, create a new standard module named basSupport and insert the LockControls and UnlockControls procedures shown above. Place two command buttons in the Customers form's header section, giving them the following Name, Caption, and OnClick properties:

Button Name	Caption	Event Procedure
cmdLock	Review Mode	=LockControls()
cmdUnlock	Data Entry Mode	=UnlockControls()

Save the form and switch to Form view. The form is in review mode with its data controls locked and disabled (see Figure 12.1). Click the Data Entry Mode button and change data in a text box. Then click the Review Mode button to relock the controls.

FIGURE 12.1:

Avoid inadvertent changes to data by creating procedures that loop through the data controls and toggle their Locked and Enabled properties.

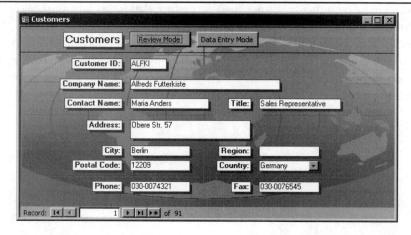

Validating Data

An important part of designing an application is determining how the application validates new and changed data. Access provides a set of properties that you can use when you create a table to test the data before saving the data to the disk. These properties include the Required, AllowZeroLength, and ValidationRule properties for fields and the ValidationRule property for the table. You can also set a ValidationRule property for controls on forms. You use the ValidationRule properties for a table field, for the table itself, and for a control on a form to specify requirements that data must satisfy. You use the ValidationText property to specify the text you want Access to display in a message box if the new or changed data doesn't satisfy the ValidationRule setting.

As an example, when a new order is placed using the Orders form in the Northwind database, the order date is filled in automatically because the DefaultValue property of the form's OrderDate control is set to =Date(), but the user fills in the required date as part of taking the order. No validation rule has been set for the RequiredDate field. To specify that the required date must be greater than the order date, you can set one of the ValidationRule properties so that Access tests the condition `RequiredDate > OrderDate` and refuses to do the update if the condition is not met.

Which ValidationRule should you use? You cannot specify the test using the Validation-Rule property for the RequiredDate field (as a field property in table Design view) because the condition refers to the value in another field, but you can use the ValidationRule property for either the table itself or the RequiredDate control on the Orders form.

The property you choose depends on when you want Access to test the data. Access tests a control's ValidationRule property when you attempt to move the focus out of the control after entering new data or changing existing data in the control. Figure 12.2a shows the ValidationRule for the RequiredDate control, and Figure 12.2b shows the message displayed when you enter an invalid date and tab out of the control.

FIGURE 12.2:

Access tests a control's ValidationRule property (a) when you enter or change the data in the control then attempt to move the focus out of the control. If the condition is not met, Access displays a default message or the text you specify as the ValidationText property (b).

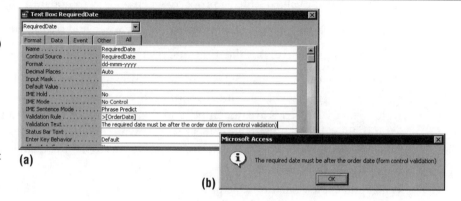

In contrast, Access tests the table's ValidationRule property when you attempt to save the record after entering new data or changing existing data. Consequently, the user can enter invalid data in a record and not realize that validity problems exist until attempting to save the record. Figure 12.3a shows the ValidationRule for the Orders table, and Figure 12.3b shows the message displayed when you enter an invalid date and attempt to save the record.

FIGURE 12.3:

Access tests a table's ValidationRule property when you enter or change data in the record and attempt to save the record (a). If the condition is not met, Access displays a default message or the text you specify as the ValidationText property (b).

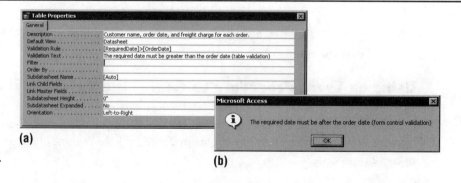

NOTE   When a form contains a subform, moving the focus to the subform is an attempt to save changes to the record in the main form and triggers testing the ValidationRule for the underlying record source of the main form.

The validation for controls on a form and fields in the underlying table is done in the following order:

1. The control's ValidationRule property when you try to update a changed control

2. The underlying field's ValidationRule property when you try to update a changed control

3. The underlying table's ValidationRule property when you try to save a changed record

When you try to save a changed record, in addition to testing the table's ValidationRule property, Access tests the table's integrity rules. If you designate a primary key, Access tests that the primary key fields are not empty and that the primary key is unique (entity integrity). In addition, if the table is in a one-to-many relationship and you checked the referential integrity option for the relationship, Access tests that the changes you made won't create any orphan records.

When you use a ValidationRule property, you are limited to the default behavior: Access tests the rule and either accepts the data or refuses to accept the data and displays a message. When the default behavior is insufficient, you can use VBA procedures to set more complicated validation rules and to control what Access does when the rules are violated. For example, you can use programming when you want to do the following:

- Display different messages depending on the value entered.

- Ask the user for input on whether to use a validation rule.

- Use more than one validation rule to validate a record.

- Carry out additional operations depending on the outcome of the validation test.

- Change the timing of the validation tests.

Using an Event Procedure to Cancel the Default Behavior

When you use Access VBA to validate data, normally you create an event procedure that includes the conditions you want to test and the operations you want to carry out when one or more conditions are met. The events in Table 12.1 are commonly used to trigger a validation event procedure.

TABLE 12.1: Common Events Used for Data Validation

Object	Event	Description	Cancel Default Behavior?
Control	BeforeUpdate	Before updating new or changed data to the record buffer	Yes
	Exit	Before leaving the control	Yes
Form	BeforeUpdate	Before updating a new or changed record to the table	Yes
	Delete	Before deleting a record	Yes

When you are able to cancel the default behavior following an event, the event procedure has a Cancel argument. Setting the Cancel argument to True in the procedure cancels the default behavior that follows the event. The default behavior that follows a control's Before-Update event is that Access updates the changed value in the control buffer to the record buffer. If you use one of the BeforeUpdate events to trigger a validation procedure, you can cancel the update if the data fails the validation test. In contrast, if you use an AfterUpdate event to trigger a validation procedure, Access has already updated the buffer, so you can't cancel the update. (There are times when you can use an AfterUpdate event to trigger a validation procedure; for example, if you use the form's AfterUpdate event, you may be able to include instructions to undo the update by deleting the saved record.)

As an example, the RequiredDate_BeforeUpdate procedure uses the BeforeUpdate event to trigger a validation procedure for the RequiredDate text box. This procedure improves on the ValidationRule by undoing the change so that the user doesn't need to click the Escape key.

```
Private Sub RequiredDate_BeforeUpdate(Cancel As Integer)
    If RequiredDate <= OrderDate Then
        MsgBox "The required date must be greater than the order date."
        Me!RequiredDate.Undo
        Cancel = True
    End If
End Sub
```

If the date in the RequiredDate text box is less than or equal to the value in the OrderDate text box, the procedure displays a message, uses the Undo method of the text box control to undo the change, and then sets the Cancel argument to True to cancel the update to the record buffer. The user must change the data in the control to a valid date or tab out of the control without making any changes.

To test the event procedure, choose the Orders form in the Database window and click the Code button in the toolbar. The Orders form opens in Design view and the form module is displayed. Insert the RequiredDate_BeforeUpdate procedure, save the form, and switch to Form view. Change the Required Date to a value that is less than the Order Date and press Enter. The procedure displays the message and cancels the update.

Changing the Timing of a Validation Test

When you design a data table, you specify how the primary key is entered. You can use the following methods:

- Automatically assign sequential numbers by using an AutoNumber field as the primary key.

- Create your own expressions to assign unique values automatically.

- Permit the primary key to be entered as part of data entry.

No matter how the value is entered, Access checks for duplicate values when you try to save the record. In many cases, the most convenient time to test for uniqueness of primary key is as soon as the user leaves the primary key control, instead of waiting until the user enters values in all the other data controls and tries to save the record. You can create an event procedure to handle the uniqueness test yourself and run the event procedure as soon as the user tries to update the changed control—that is, when the changed control recognizes the BeforeUpdate event.

As an example of how to check for duplicate primary key values, the CustomerID_Before-Update procedure tests for uniqueness of the value entered in the CustomerID control on the Customers form.

```
Private Sub CustomerID_BeforeUpdate(Cancel As Integer)
    If DCount("*", "Customers", "CustomerID = " _
        & "Screen.ActiveForm.CustomerID") Then
        MsgBox "There is another customer with the same CustomerID."
        Cancel = True
    End If
End Sub
```

This procedure uses the ActiveForm property of the Screen object to refer to the active form. (Note that you cannot use the Me property in an argument of the domain aggregate functions.) If a duplicate record exists, the DCount function returns the value one, so the condition is True. In this case, the procedure displays a message and cancels the update.

Another way to search for a duplicate record is by using the Seek method. The version of the CustomerID_BeforeUpdate procedure shown below uses the Seek method to search for the duplicate record in the Customers table.

```
Private Sub CustomerID_BeforeUpdate(Cancel As Integer)
    Dim rst As New ADODB.Recordset
    Dim cnn As ADODB.Connection
    Set cnn = CurrentProject.Connection
    rst.Open "Customers", cnn, adOpenStatic, adcmdTableDirect
    rst.Index = "PrimaryKey"
    rst.Seek Me!CustomerID, adSeekFirstEQ
    If Not rst.EOF Then
        MsgBox "There is another customer with the same CustomerID."
        Cancel = True
    End If
End Sub
```

This procedure begins by opening a static cursor recordset on the Customers table using the Open method. Next, the procedure sets the current index to the primary key and searches for a record in the table with a primary key matching the value in the CustomerID control on the form. If a record is found, the EOF property has the value False, and the expression Not rst.EOF has the value True. In this case, the procedure displays a message and cancels the subsequent default behavior. If no record is found, the procedure ends without taking further action.

Adding Command Buttons for Data-Entry Operations

We'll use the Command Button Wizard to create a set of command buttons for automating the four basic data-entry operations that all simple data-entry forms need: adding a new record, undoing changes to a record, saving changes, and deleting a record.

Open the Customers form in Design view and click the Control Wizard tool in the toolbox to activate the Control Wizards. Click the Command Button tool and place four command buttons in the form's header section. Use the Command Button Wizard's Record Operations category to create the buttons as follows:

Action	Button Text (Caption Property)	Name
Add New Record	Add	cmdAdd
Undo Record	Undo	cmdUndo
Save Record	Save	cmdSave
Delete Record	Delete	cmdDelete

Save the form and switch to Form view (see Figure 12.4). Click the Data Entry Mode button and test the buttons:

- Click Add. The first time you click the Add button, Access displays the blank record. If you click again when the blank record is displayed, there is no response.

- Click Undo. If you change the value in one of the controls and click the Undo button, the change is undone. If you change the record, click the Save button to save all of the changes to the record, and then click the Undo button, the changes are undone. If you make no change and click the Undo button, a default error message is displayed (see Figure 12.5).

FIGURE 12.4:

The Customers form with data entry buttons

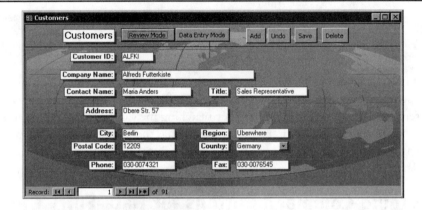

FIGURE 12.5:

The default error message when you click the Undo button and there are no changes to undo

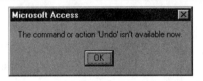

- Click Save. If you change the record and click the Save button, the record is saved (provided the change satisfies the validation rules for the record). If you don't change the record, there is no response when you click the Save button. If you click the Add button to display the blank record and then click the Save button, there is no response.

- Click Delete. If you click the Delete button for a customer with orders, the default error message shown in Figure 12.6a is displayed and the record is not deleted. In the relationship between Customers and Orders, the Cascade Delete Related Records option is not checked, so you can't delete any customer that has orders. If the customer has no orders, such as the customer with CustomerID FISSA (record 22), the default confirmation message is displayed (see Figure 12.6b); if you click No to cancel the deletion, Access displays the default message shown in Figure 12.6c.

FIGURE 12.6:

The default error message when you click the Delete button and the customer has orders (a), the default confirmation message when the customer has no orders (b), and the default error message when you click No to cancel the deletion (c)

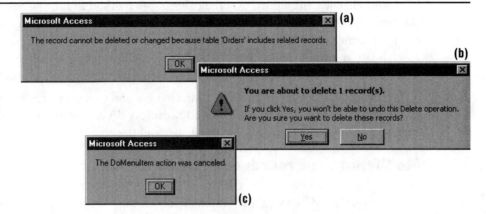

Switch to Design view and click the Code button in the toolbar to view the procedures that the wizard created. Select the cmdAdd command button from the Object combo list on the left below the module's title bar. The following is the event procedure that the Command Button Wizard created for the Add button.

```
Private Sub cmdAdd_Click()
On Error GoTo Err_cmdAdd_Click
    DoCmd.GoToRecord , , acNewRec

Exit_cmdAdd_Click:
    Exit Sub

Err_cmdAdd_Click:
    MsgBox Err.Description
    Resume Exit_cmdAdd_Click
End Sub
```

For each of the four procedures, the Command Button Wizard includes a generic error handler that displays a default error message and then exits the procedure. For each of the buttons, the wizard runs a method of the DoCmd object. The procedures for the buttons to add a new record and to save the record don't fail.

To add a new record, the wizard runs the GoToRecord method. When the blank record is already displayed, the New Record command on the submenu of the Go To command in the Edit menu is not available; however, the GoToRecord method does not fail if the new record is already displayed.

To save changes, the wizard uses the `DoMenuItem` method to run the Save Record command on the Records menu. This command is available for existing records and for the blank record whether or not you have changed the record. If you make changes that do not satisfy the validation rules for the record, Access displays the default message or a custom validation message and does not update the record. The VBA method mimics this behavior.

The procedures for the buttons to undo changes and to delete a record may fail. If the procedure fails, an error message is displayed because VBA cannot run the method. Let's explore the code and modifications you can make to avoid the error messages.

Modifying the Procedure to Undo a Change

To undo changes to the record, the wizard uses the `DoMenuItem` method to run the built-in Undo command. When you work interactively (using menus) and have made no changes to a record, this command is grayed out and unavailable. When you try to run the menu command programmatically (using the command button) but have made no changes to the record, the method fails because the command is unavailable. The Undo commands are available only when you have actually made a change to the record. You can use the form's Dirty property to test whether the current record has been changed before issuing the command. The Dirty property has the value True if the current record has been modified since it was last saved; otherwise, it is False.

With the modification shown below, you get no response if you click the Undo button for an unchanged record. In addition, if you change and save a record, you can no longer use the Undo button to undo the changes to the last saved record. (After you save the record, the form's Dirty property is False until you change the record again.)

```
Private Sub cmdUndo_Click()
    On Error GoTo Err_cmdNew_Click

    If Me.Dirty Then
        DoCmd.DoMenuItem acFormBar, acEditMenu, acUndo, , acMenuVer70
    End If

Exit_cmdNew_Click:
Exit Sub

Err_cmdNew_Click:
    MsgBox Err.Description
    Resume Exit_cmdNew_Click
End Sub
```

Modifying the Procedure to Delete a Record

To delete a record, the wizard creates the following procedure:

```
Private Sub cmdDelete_Click()
On Error GoTo Err_cmdDelete_Click

    DoCmd.DoMenuItem acFormBar, acEditMenu, 8, , acMenuVer70
    DoCmd.DoMenuItem acFormBar, acEditMenu, 6, , acMenuVer70

Exit_cmdDelete_Click:
    Exit Sub

Err_cmdDelete_Click:
    MsgBox Err.Description
    Resume Exit_cmdDelete_Click
End Sub
```

If deleting a selected record would violate the referential integrity rules and cascade options checked for the relationships between the data table and other tables in the database, Access does not permit the deletion. If the deletion is allowed, Access displays the default confirmation message (see Figure 12.6b); if you cancel the deletion, VBA displays the default error message (see Figure 12.6c), because clicking the No button prevents VBA from carrying out the command to delete the record. You can modify the cmdDelete_Click procedure to suppress the error message as follows.

Determine the error code for the default error message in Figure 12.6c by changing the procedure's error handling code to

```
Err_cmdDelete_Click:
    MsgBox Err.Number & Err.Description
    Resume Exit_cmdDelete_Click
```

Display the customer with CustomerID FISSA. Click the Delete button and click No to cancel the deletion. The message box reveals the error code is 2501. Click OK to close the message box.

Modify the error-handling code to test the error code and exit the procedure without displaying the message if the error code equals 2501 as shown below. The Else statements handle unanticipated errors.

```
Private Sub cmdDelete_Click()
On Error GoTo Err_cmdDelete_Click
    DoCmd.DoMenuItem acFormBar, acEditMenu, 8, , acMenuVer70
    DoCmd.DoMenuItem acFormBar, acEditMenu, 6, , acMenuVer70

Exit_cmdDelete_Click:
```

```
        Exit Sub

Err_cmdDelete_Click:
    If Err.Number = 2501 Then
        Exit Sub
    Else
        MsgBox Err.Description
        Resume Exit_cmdDelete_Click
    End If
End Sub
```

Save the module. Test the modified procedure by displaying the customer with CustomerID FISSA, clicking the Delete button, and then clicking No.

Deleting a Record When It Has Related Records

When you try to delete a record from a table using a form that has the AllowDeletions property set to Yes, the response depends on whether the table is related to other tables in a relationship that has referential integrity enforced and whether the record you want to delete actually has related records in another table. For example, the Customers and Orders tables are related and the Enforce Referential Integrity option is checked. When a particular customer has no orders, you can delete the customer record. If the customer has orders, the response depends on whether the Cascade Delete Related Records option is checked.

NOTE   Cascade Update Related Fields and Cascade Delete Related Records are options you can set when forming a relationship between two tables. By default, Cascade Update Related Fields is selected, which means that changes you make in one table are transmitted to all related tables. Cascade Delete Related Records is deselected by default. If you wish to change either of these settings, you must first close all tables, then select Tools ➤ Relationships. In the Relationships window, double-click the line connecting two tables, representing the relationship between those tables. You can then make changes to the Cascade Referential Integrity options.

If the Cascade Delete Related Records option is checked, Access allows the simultaneous deletion of both the customer and the related orders. But if the Cascade Delete Related Records option is not checked, Access won't allow you to delete a customer who has related orders. In this case, you can use an event procedure like the one shown below. (You can also use this procedure if you don't want to allow the deletion of a record that has related records, regardless of the cascade option.)

```
Private Sub cmdDelete_Click()
    Dim intNumber As Integer
    On Error GoTo Err_cmdDelete_Click
    intNumber = DCount("*", "Orders", "CustomerID = " _
        & "Screen.ActiveForm.CustomerID")
    If intNumber = 0 Then
```

```
        RunCommand acCmdDeleteRecord
    Else
        MsgBox ("There are " & intNumber & _
            " orders so you can't delete this customer.")
    End If

Exit_cmdDelete_Click:
Exit Sub

Err_cmdDelete_Click:
    If Err.Number = 2501 Or Err.Number = 2046 Then
        Exit Sub
    Else
        MsgBox Err.Description
        Resume Exit_cmdDelete_Click
    End If
End Sub
```

This procedure uses the DCount function to determine the number of related orders for the customer displayed in the form. If the customer has no orders, the procedure allows the deletion. If the customer has orders, the procedure displays a message with the number of orders and then ends.

Cascading the Delete

When a record has related records, the cascade option is checked, and you want to allow deletions of both the displayed record and all of its related records, you can use an event procedure like the one shown below.

```
Private Sub cmdDelete_Click()
    Dim intNumber As Integer
    On Error GoTo Err_cmdDelete_Click
    intNumber = DCount("*", "Orders", "CustomerID = " _
        & "Screen.ActiveForm.CustomerID")
    If intNumber = 0 Then
        DoCmd.DoMenuItem acFormBar, acEditMenu, 7, , acMenuVer70
    Else
        If MsgBox("This customer has " & intNumber & _
            " orders. Do you want to delete the customer " _
            & "and the orders?", vbYesNo) = vbYes Then
            RunCommand acCmdDeleteRecord
        End If
    End If

Exit_cmdDelete_Click:
```

```
    Exit Sub

Err_cmdDelete_Click:
    If Err.Number = 2501 Then
        Exit Sub
    Else
        MsgBox Err.Description
        Resume Exit_cmdDelete_Click
    End If
End Sub
```

This procedure also begins by determining the number of related records and allowing the deletion if none exist. When the record has related records, the procedure uses the MsgBox function as the condition of an If statement. The MsgBox function displays a message with the number of related records and asks the user for a decision on whether to delete the record and its related records. Execution of the procedure pauses until the user clicks one of the buttons on the message box. When the user clicks a button, Access can evaluate the MsgBox function and resume execution of the procedure using the value returned by the MsgBox function. If the user clicks the Yes button, the record and its related records are deleted. Otherwise, the procedure ends.

To test this procedure, close the Customers form (if it's open) and choose Tools ➤ Relationships. Double-click the relationship line between the Customers and Orders tables to display the Edit Relationships dialog (see Figure 12.7a). Check the Cascade Delete Related Records option and click OK. Close the Relationships window. Next, select the Customers form in the Database window and click the Code button in the toolbar. Modify the cmdDelete_Click event procedure that the Command Wizard created so that it looks like the event procedure shown above. Save the module. With the first customer displayed in the Customers form, click the Delete button. The message box provides a choice (see Figure 12.7b).

FIGURE 12.7:

Choose the cascade options in the Edit Relationships dialog (a). The revised procedure displays a dialog that lets the user make a choice to delete the customer and the orders (b).

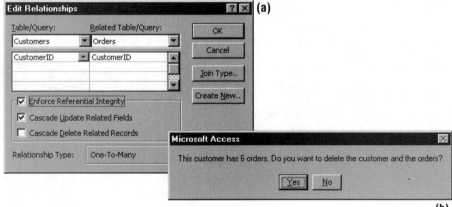

Carrying Values Forward to a New Record

Often, the data for many fields in a new record is identical to the data in another record. Without automation, the fallback solution is to manually reenter the duplicate values in the new record. However, you can develop programming techniques to fill in the recurring values and thus reduce manual labor.

This section describes two techniques for carrying values from another record. The first technique is designed to carry values from the current record to the next new record. The technique sets the DefaultValue property for the controls whose values you want to carry to the next new record. The second method is designed to carry values from some other record (not necessarily the current record) to the next new record. In both techniques, you normally carry forward only some of the values; both techniques use a control's Tag property to indicate whether the control's value is to be carried forward.

Setting the DefaultValue Property

When you set the DefaultValue property for a field in table Design view or for a control in form Design view, Access automatically enters the value of the DefaultValue property in the control when you display a new record in the form. Setting the DefaultValue property in Design view is useful when you want to use the same value for every new record, or when you want to use the same expression to calculate the value to be inserted in the control for every new record. For example, the DefaultValue property for the OrderDate control on the Orders form is set to =Date() so that each new order displays the current date automatically.

You can also set the DefaultValue property programmatically. Suppose you want to carry values forward from the current data-entry record to the new record. Carrying values from one record to the next is often an efficient way to batch data entry when one or more fields change infrequently.

As an example, suppose you've recently started working with a new supplier who offers many products in one or two categories and you want to add the new products. A convenient way to update your data is to carry forward the values in the SupplierID and CategoryID controls on the Products form. After you save the data for a new or changed product and click the New button (one of the default navigation buttons on the form) to move to a new blank record, the values in these two controls appear automatically in the new record. The Form_AfterUpdate event procedure shown below automates the process.

```
Private Sub Form_AfterUpdate()
    Dim ctl As Control
    For Each ctl In Screen.ActiveForm.Controls
        If ctl.Tag = "Carry" Then
```

```
        ctl.DefaultValue = """" & ctl.Value & """"
    End If
  Next
End Sub
```

The two controls have a text value so the procedure must evaluate the text value. The result is a string (" & ctl.Value & ") within a string, so you must use one of the sets of symbols that Access recognizes for delimiting a string within a string. This procedure uses pairs of double quotation marks to indicate the inner string (""" & ctl.Value & """). Finally, we enclose the result in double quotation marks to indicate that the final result is a string ("""" & ctl.Value & """").

To test this procedure, open the Products form in Design view. Select the SupplierID and CategoryID controls and type **Carry** in their Tag property. (You can use the Tag property to store any information that you want; here we use the Tag property to mark the controls whose values we want to carry forward.) Then click the Code button in the toolbar to display the form's module. Insert the Form_AfterUpdate event procedure shown above. Switch to Form view and change any control in the current record, such as the units in stock, and then click the New button. The values for the supplier and the category are carried forward to the new record (see Figure 12.8).

FIGURE 12.8:

You can use the Tag property to mark a control whose value is carried forward and use a procedure to set the DefaultValue property to the current value of the control.

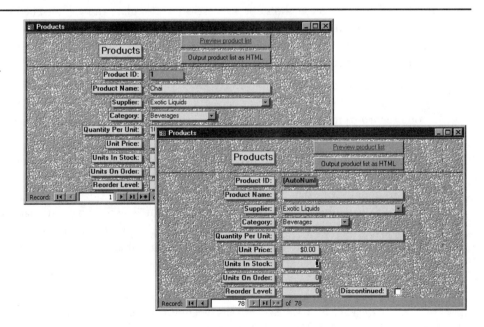

Using Custom Default Values

Another technique for faster data entry involves looking up information from some other record and copying data from that record into the new record. For example, suppose that customers placing new orders typically have the order shipped to an address that doesn't change very often.

In Northwind, the Orders form is designed so that when you select the customer from the combo box, the shipping name and address are assumed to be the same as the customer name and address. In this case, the CustomerID_AfterUpdate event procedure copies the customer's name and address into the corresponding shipping controls. As an example of copying information from another record, you'll change the event procedure so that instead of copying the customer's name and address, VBA looks up the last order placed by the customer and copies the shipping information from that order as the shipping information for the new order. This is accomplished by the procedure shown below.

```
Private Sub CustomerID_AfterUpdate()
    Dim rst As New ADODB.Recordset
    Dim cnn As ADODB.Connection
    Set cnn = CurrentProject.Connection
    rst.Open "SELECT * FROM Orders WHERE CustomerID = """ & _
        CustomerID & """ ORDER BY OrderDate DESC", cnn
    If Not rst.EOF Then
        ShipName = rst!ShipName
        ShipAddress = rst!ShipAddress
        ShipCity = rst!ShipCity
        ShipRegion = rst!ShipRegion
        ShipPostalCode = rst!ShipPostalCode
        ShipCountry = rst!ShipCountry
    End If
End Sub
```

The Open method of the Recordset object uses a SQL SELECT statement to retrieve all orders placed by the customer you select in the CustomerID field and sorts them in descending order by OrderDate. You use the EOF property as a condition of an If…Then statement to make sure there are records in the recordset. If there are, the procedure assigns the same shipping information to the current order as was used in the last order for that customer.

When you build the SQL statement for the source argument of the Open method, you need to force VBA to determine the selected value in the combo box before it can find the correct records. In other words, the source argument contains an inner string. In this example, CustomerID has a text value, so you can use either of the following expressions for the criteria:

```
CustomerID = """ & CustomerID & """
CustomerID = '" & CustomerID & "'
```

For each value that is carried forward, the procedure uses an assignment statement to assign the value of a control on the form to the value of the field with the same name in the record for the last order. In other words, each assignment statement matches a control in the form's Controls collection with a field in the recordset's Fields collection. The match works because the Orders form is designed so that each bound control on the form has the same name as the field it is bound to.

To test this procedure, open the Orders form in Design view. Click the Code button in the toolbar to display the form's module and modify the statements of the `CustomerID_AfterUpdate` event procedure as shown above.

The procedure works, but it is rather inelegant because each control has a separate assignment statement. A more elegant procedure loops through all the controls on the form. On each pass through the loop, the procedure determines if the control's value is to be carried forward and sets the control's value to the corresponding field's value.

To achieve the more elegant result, you'll first modify the form to mark those fields you want to have carried forward. You'll then modify the procedure to do the matching of bound controls and fields automatically when the names are the same. Each assignment statement assigns the value of a control to the value in the field with the corresponding name.

Open the Orders form in Design view and select the ShipName, ShipAddress, ShipCity, ShipRegion, ShipPostalCode, and ShipCountry controls. Click in the Tag property in the Multiple Selection property sheet and type **Carry**. Next, you'll recast the assignment statement into a syntax that is more appropriate for looping through a collection. The following two assignment statements are equivalent:

```
ShipAddress = rst!ShipAddress
ShipAddress.Value = rst("ShipAddress")
```

In the second statement, however, the left side explicitly states that the Value property is being set, and the right side uses the parenthetical reference for the ShipAddress field. When you use the parenthetical reference for a field, you can replace the literal string for the name of the field with a variable that has the same value. When you create the statements to loop through the controls, you need to replace literal strings such as `"ShipAddress"` with an expression that contains the loop counter.

The next part of the explanation is more abstract and is typical of the kind of reasoning you need when you create loops. You are going to set up a `For...Next` loop to loop through the members of the Controls collection, so you need to use a number index to refer to controls on the form. If `frm` refers to the form, the number of controls on the form is `frm.Count - 1`, and the Controls collection has index numbers ranging from 0 to `frm.Count - 1`. If k is an index number in this range, then

- `frm(k)` refers to some control on the form.
- `frm(k).Value` is the value of the control.
- `frm(k).Name` is the name of the control.

Some value of the index number corresponds to, say, the ShipAddress control; in other words, there is some number j, for which

- `frm(j)` refers to the ShipAddress control.
- `frm(j).Value` is the value of the ShipAddress control.
- `frm(j).Name` is the name of the control (and is also the name of the field the control is bound to).

You can also write the following assignment statement for the ShipAddress control for the particular index number that corresponds to the ShipAddress:

```
frm(j).Value = rst(frm(j).Name)
```

Each control corresponds to a different value of the index number, so as the index numbers range from 0 to one less than the number of controls on the form, each index number corresponds to a different control. In looping through the controls on the form, you first test the control's Tag property. If the Tag property has the value Carry, the procedure sets the control's value to the value of the matching field; otherwise, the procedure moves to the next control without setting a value. The following procedure includes the loop that does the automated matching.

```
Private Sub CustomerID_AfterUpdate()
    Dim rst As New ADODB.Recordset
    Dim cnn As ADODB.Connection
    Dim frm As Form, k As Integer
    Set cnn = CurrentProject.Connection
    rst.Open "SELECT * FROM Orders WHERE CustomerID = """ & _
        CustomerID & """ ORDER BY OrderDate DESC", cnn
    Set frm = Me
    If Not rst.EOF Then
        For k = 0 To frm.Count - 1
            If frm(k).Tag = "Carry" Then
                frm(k).Value = rst(frm(k).Name)
            End If
        Next
    End If
End Sub
```

To test this procedure, modify the statements in the CustomerID_AfterUpdate procedure as shown above and save the module. Next, open a new record. Select Around The Horn in the Bill To field. The procedure displays the customer's shipping name and address. Change the shipping name to Butterfield's Bicycles and the shipping address to 2 Southdown Lane. Click the New button and select Around The Horn in the Bill To combo box. The new record displays the shipping information from the last order for this customer.

Editing Data in a Recordset

Although you generally provide forms in the Access interface so that the user can edit data, sometimes working directly with a recordset is faster than working with a form. In previous chapters, you learned how to navigate in a recordset from one record to another by moving the current record pointer. If the recordset is not read-only, you may be able to edit existing records, add new records, and delete existing records. For the techniques presented here, we assume that you can make changes to the recordset.

NOTE   Your ability to change the data in a recordset depends on several factors, including the options you set when you created the recordset, the type of query or SQL statement you are using for a dynaset-type recordset, and whether other users have placed locks that prevent you from making changes (if you are working in a multiuser environment). Depending on how the query is designed, you may be able to edit certain fields but not other fields.

Changing a Record

The fundamental rule in working with recordsets is that you can work with only the current record. This means that you must move the current record pointer to a record before you can edit it. As explained in Chapter 6, "Understanding the ADO Object Model," the database engine uses a separate location in memory called a copy buffer for the contents of a record that is being edited. To change a record, you need to move a copy of the current record into the copy buffer. Once you begin making edits to a record or use the AddNew method to add a new record, the record is automatically moved into the copy buffer. After you make the changes to the current record in the copy buffer, you save the changes by calling the Update method or empty the copy buffer without saving the changes by calling the CancelUpdate method.

If you move to another record, close the recordset, set the Bookmark property to another record, or use the AddNew method without saving the changes to the current record with the Update method, ADO automatically calls the Update method. The changes you make in the copy buffer are also lost if you close the recordset, set the Bookmark property to another record, or use the Edit or AddNew method again without first using the Update method.

Tip You can use the recordset's EditMode property to determine the status of editing for the current record. The EditMode property returns integer values corresponding to the following states: **adEditNone** if no editing is in progress, **adEditInProgress** if the record has been changed but the changes haven't been saved, **adEditAdd** if the **AddNew** method has been executed and the copy buffer contains the data for a new record that hasn't been saved to the recordset, or **adEditDelete** if the current record has been deleted.

As an example, the EditRecordset procedure finds the record for the Bottom-Dollar Markets customer in the Customers table and changes the contact name.

```
Public Sub EditRecordset()
    Dim rst As New ADODB.Recordset
    Dim cnn As New ADODB.Connection
    Set cnn = CurrentProject.Connection
    rst.Index = "PrimaryKey"
    rst.Open "customers", cnn, adOpenStatic, adLockOptimistic, _
        adCmdTableDirect
    rst.Seek "BOTTM", adSeekFirstEQ
    If rst.EOF Then
        MsgBox "There is no customer with this CustomerID"
        Exit Sub
    Else
        MsgBox "The contact name is " & rst!ContactName
        rst!ContactName = "Sara Cherry"
        rst.Update
        MsgBox "The contact name is " & rst!ContactName
    End If
End Sub
```

The procedure opens a static cursor recordset on the Customers table, sets the current index to the primary key, and uses the Seek method to locate the record for Bottom-Dollar Markets. If the record is not found, the procedure displays a message and terminates. If the record is found, the procedure displays the contact name for the record. The procedure then changes the contact name, runs the Update method to save the changed record to the table, and displays the changed contact name.

Create a new standard module named basRecordset and insert the EditRecordset procedure shown above. Run the EditRecordset procedure in the Immediate window. The procedure displays message boxes with the current contact name and then with the edited contact name (see Figure 12.9).

FIGURE 12.9:

Using a procedure to edit a record by running the Update method of a recordset. The procedure displays message boxes with the current contact name (a) and then with the edited contact name (b).

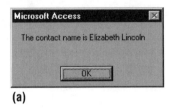

(a)

(b)

WARNING A common error is to forget to open the recordset with the **LockType** argument set to something other than the default. As you recall from Chapter 6, by default the Recordset's **Open** method returns a forward-only, read-only recordset. Another common error is to forget to set the **options** argument to adCmdTableDirect. If you neglect this setting, you will be unable to set Indexes on a table.

Adding a Record

Adding a new record and saving the changes is also a three-step process:

1. Create a new record in the copy buffer and set any default values using the **AddNew** method. Access sets any default values you have specified in table Design view and sets the values of the fields without default values to Null.

2. Enter the new data.

3. Save the changes made in the copy buffer and add the saved record to the recordset using the **Update** method (or empty the copy buffer without adding the new record using the **CancelUpdate** method).

After you call the recordset's **AddNew** method, the new record becomes the current record. Even after you have finished adding new data for the record and you call the **Update** method, the new record is the current record. The new record is added to the end of the recordset.

As an example, the **AddRecordset** procedure adds a new record to the Customers table.

```
Public Sub AddRecordset()
    Dim rst As New ADODB.Recordset
    Dim cnn As ADODB.Connection
    Set cnn = CurrentProject.Connection
    rst.Index = "PrimaryKey"
    rst.Open "Customers", cnn, adOpenStatic, adLockOptimistic, _
        adCmdTableDirect
    rst.AddNew
    rst!CustomerID = "AARDV"
    rst!CompanyName = "Aardvark Inc."
```

```
        rst!Country = "Australia"
        rst.Update
        MsgBox "The company name is " & rst!CompanyName
        rst.MoveNext
        If Not rst.EOF Then
            MsgBox "The next company name is " & rst!CompanyName
        Else
            MsgBox "There are no more records."
            rst.Move -2
            MsgBox "The previous company name is " & rst!CompanyName
        End If
    End Sub
```

This procedure opens a static cursor recordset on the Customers table and sets the current index to the primary key. The procedure runs the AddNew method to create a new record in the copy buffer, sets the values for the CustomerID, CompanyName, and Country fields, and runs the Update method to save the record to the table. The procedure displays the company name for the new record and moves the current record pointer forward one record. Because the new record was added to the end of the recordset, moving forward puts the current record pointer beyond the limits of the recordset. The procedure tests the recordset's EOF value. If it is False, the procedure displays the next record's Company Name. If it is True, it moves the current record pointer back two records and displays the Company Name of the Customer preceding the one we added.

Insert the AddRecordset procedure in the basRecordset module and then run it in the Immediate window. The procedure adds the record, displays a field from the new record, displays a message indicating there are no more records, and then displays a field from the preceding record in the recordset (see Figure 12.10).

FIGURE 12.10:

The AddRecordset procedure opens a recordset on the Customers table and adds a new record to the end of the recordset (a). The procedure then moves the record pointer beyond the end of the recordset and displays a message (b), then moves backward two spaces in the recordset and displays the company name for that record (c).

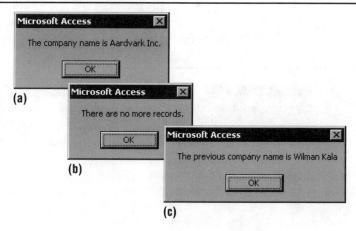

Deleting a Record

Deleting an existing record is a one-step process. You simply delete the current record using the Delete method. There is no temporary buffer to hold the contents if you change your mind; the deletion is immediate and irreversible. Curiously, the deleted record is still considered to be the current record, even though you can't refer to it. You must move the current record pointer to a valid current record if you plan to execute any methods that require a valid current record.

As an example, the DeleteRecordset procedure deletes the record we added to the Customers table in the last section.

```
Public Sub DeleteRecordset()
    Dim rst As New ADODB.Recordset
    Dim cnn As New ADODB.Connection
    Set cnn = CurrentProject.Connection
    rst.Open "Customers", cnn, adOpenStatic, adLockOptimistic
    rst.Find "CompanyName = 'Aardvark Inc.'"
    MsgBox "The company name of the record to be deleted is " & _
        rst!CompanyName
    rst.Delete
    rst.MoveFirst
    MsgBox "The company name of the first record is " & _
        rst!CompanyName
End Sub
```

The procedure opens a static cursor recordset on the Customers table, uses the Find method to move the current record pointer to the record, and runs the Delete method to delete the record.

Insert the DeleteRecordset procedure in the basRecordset module and then run it in the Immediate window. The procedure displays the message boxes indicating the record to be deleted (see Figure 12.11a) and the first record, which became the current record when the procedure ran the MoveFirst method after deleting the record (see Figure 12.11b).

FIGURE 12.11:

Messages before and after running the Delete (a) and MovePrevious (b) methods

(a)   (b)

Summary

This chapter focused on using VBA procedures to work with data in two ways. In the forms approach, the user uses forms to work with data. This chapter covered the procedures for automating the processes of adding new records and editing and deleting existing records through a form. In the recordset approach, the user takes actions that run procedures that edit, delete, or add new records directly to a recordset without displaying a form. The important points include the following:

- You can protect data from inadvertent changes by providing a form with command buttons that run procedures to toggle between review and data-entry modes.

- You can use procedures to customize data validation, such as by changing the timing of the validation test.

- You can use the Command Button Wizard to create simple data-maintenance procedures and modify the procedures to prevent run-time errors and to suppress default error messages.

- You can make data entry more efficient by arranging to carry values forward to a new record in two ways: use a procedure to set the DefaultValue property, or use a procedure to copy the field values from a specified record to a new record.

- You can use the AddNew and Delete methods of the Recordset object to add, delete, or modify records in a recordset in memory without opening a form.

CHAPTER 13

Working with Groups of Records Using Access VBA

- Sorting and selecting records displayed in a form or report

- Using Query By Form to pass data from a form to a query

- Using the multiselect list box for random selection of records

- Working with a group of records in a recordset

- Running stored queries and SQL statements

- Making bulk changes to a recordset

In the previous two chapters, you've learned how to create procedures for working with a single record using two different approaches: forms and recordsets. In the forms approach, the user works with forms to navigate between records and controls and to view and modify data. In the recordset approach, actions of the user run procedures that create and manipulate recordsets in memory without a visual representation. This chapter focuses on working with groups of records using the two approaches.

The first part of the chapter describes how to use the forms approach for the following tasks:

- Automate operations to sort records and to select groups of records that satisfy search criteria using a form or report.

- Open a form or report that displays a limited selection of records upon opening.

- Change the selection after the form or report is open.

- Use a form to collect search criteria and pass the criteria to a query (Query By Form).

- Use a multiselect list box to select records.

The second part of the chapter focuses on working with recordsets in VBA procedures. You'll learn how to use stored queries and SQL statements to sort and select groups of records and how to use action queries to make bulk changes to recordsets.

Sorting Records in a Form or Report

You can automate the sorting process for the records in a form or report by setting the OrderBy and OrderByOn properties of the form or report in a procedure.

NOTE   For hands-on experience with the techniques described in this chapter, create a new copy of the Northwind sample database named Northwind_Ch13 and work through the steps of the examples.

We begin by creating a new form for the Northwind_Ch13 database that we'll use to illustrate procedures for sorting and filtering a form.

1. Create a new form using the Form Wizard. Select the following fields:

Customers table	CompanyName
Employees table	LastName
Orders table	OrderID, OrderDate, RequiredDate, and ShippedDate
Shippers table	CompanyName

2.   Click Next. Choose to view the data by Orders. Choose the Tabular layout and the Standard style. Name the form frmOrderStatus.

3.   Open the form in Design view. Set the form's Caption property to Order Status and set the Allow Additions property to No. (The Order Status form is a review form and is not intended for data entry; setting the Allow Additions property to No hides the blank record at the end of each recordset.)

4.   Select all of the data controls, set their Locked property to Yes, and set their formatting properties as shown below. Because the form is not intended for data entry, we lock the controls to prevent inadvertent changes.

BackColor	–2147483633
SpecialEffect	Flat
BorderStyle	Transparent

NOTE   If you set the form's AllowEdits property to No, none of the controls would allow changes. By setting the Locked property of individual controls, we still allow changes (edits) to the search value in the combo box, so users can use a combo box on the form to choose records.

5.   Arrange the controls in the following order and change the Caption properties of the labels as indicated. Change the FontWeight property for the labels to Bold. When you are finished, the form should look like Figure 13.1.

ControlName	Caption
OrderID	Order ID
OrderDate	Order Date
RequiredDate	Required Date
ShippedDate	Shipped Date
Shippers.CompanyName	Shipper
Customers.CompanyName	Customer
LastName	Employee

Putting Records in Ascending or Descending Order

You can use the OrderBy property of a form or report to sort by a single field or to create a complex sort by several fields, with some fields in ascending order and others in descending order. The OrderBy property is a string expression that consists of the name of the field or fields you want to sort, arranged in the order of the sort and separated by commas. The default

FIGURE 13.1:

Create an Order Status form for sorting and selecting.

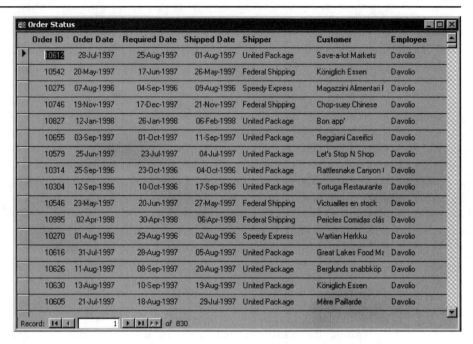

setting for the OrderBy property is ascending. To sort a field in descending order, you include the keyword DESC after the name of the field. For example, to sort the frmOrderStatus form by customer and then by order date in descending order, you set the form's OrderBy property as follows:

```
Customers.CompanyName, OrderDate DESC
```

If you do not include DESC at the end of the OrderBy property assignment statement, the form or report lists the records in the ascending order of the field or fields you specified.

Setting the OrderBy property specifies a new sort order but does not perform the sort. You set the OrderByOn property to True or False to apply or remove the sort that you specified. For a form, you can set the OrderBy property in the form's property sheet or in a VBA procedure and then use a VBA procedure to apply and remove the sort using the OrderByOn property. For a report, you can set both the OrderBy and the OrderByOn properties in the report's property sheet or in a VBA procedure.

Using a Triple-State Toggle Button

To illustrate these ideas, we'll create a button and an event procedure to sort the records of the Order Status form by customer. We'll use a toggle button instead of a command button, because a toggle button has a value that can be used by the procedure. By default, a toggle button has two values, True and False, but setting the TripleState property to Yes gives a third value of Null.

- When the toggle button has the value False, it looks raised (like a command button).

- Clicking the button changes it to the Null state, in which the button flattens but does not appear sunken.

- Clicking the button again changes it to the True state, in which the flattened button appears sunken.

The `tglCustomer_Click` procedure tests the button's state and removes the sort if the button is in the False state, applies an ascending sort if the button is in the Null state, and applies a descending sort if the button is in the True state.

```
Private Sub tglCustomer_Click()
    Dim str As String, tgl As ToggleButton
    str = "Customers_CompanyName"
    Set tgl = tglCustomer
    Select Case tgl.Value
        Case True
            Me.OrderBy = str & " DESC"
            Me.OrderByOn = True
        Case False
            Me.OrderByOn = False
        Case Else
            Me.OrderBy = str
            Me.OrderByOn = True
    End Select
End Sub
```

This procedure creates the `str` variable to hold the name of the sort field and the `tgl` object variable to refer to the toggle button. The event procedure uses the Me property to refer to the form. To test the state of the toggle button, the procedure uses the `Select Case` structure (alternatively, you could use the `If…Then…Else` structure).

- If the toggle button has the True value, the form's OrderBy property is set to a descending sort by CompanyName and the form's OrderByOn property is turned on.

- If the toggle button has the False value, the form's OrderByOn property is turned off so that the records are returned to unsorted order.

- If the toggle button is neither True nor False, the form's OrderBy property is set to an ascending sort by CompanyName and the OrderByOn property is turned on.

Follow these steps to add the toggle button to the Order Status form:

1. Switch to Design view, select all the controls in the detail section, and set their Enabled properties to No. The controls don't need to be enabled when you use the OrderBy property for the sort.

2. Delete the Customer label in the header section and replace it with a toggle button. Set the properties as follows:

Name	tglCustomer
Caption	Customer
Default Value	False
TripleState	Yes
FontWeight	Bold
ControlTip Text	Click to toggle no sort, ascending, descending

3. Click in the OnClick event property and click the Build button at the right of the property box. Insert the `tglCustomer_Click` event procedure shown above.

4. Save the form, switch to Form view, and click the toggle button. As you cycle through the states, the records are sorted by customer name—first in ascending order, then in descending order, and then the sort is removed (see Figure 13.2).

Access saves the OrderBy and OrderByOn settings that are in effect when you close the form as well as the state of the toggle button, so three settings stay in sync with one another when you close and reopen the form.

Sorting by Any Column

When records are displayed in a tabular form, you can automate sorting the records by specific columns. Replace the label of each column you want to sort by with a triple-state toggle button and create an event procedure, such as the `tglCustomer_Click` procedure, to sort the records by a field in the column. Using this technique, each of the sorts is independent, and the last toggle button clicked overrides previous sorts and determines the final sort. For example, if you toggle the Customer button to sort ascending by customer and then toggle the Employee button to sort ascending by employee, the records are sorted in ascending order by employee.

FIGURE 13.2:

Using a triple-state toggle button to remove a sort when the toggle button is False (a), apply an ascending sort when the toggle button is Null (b), and apply a descending sort when the toggle button is True (c).

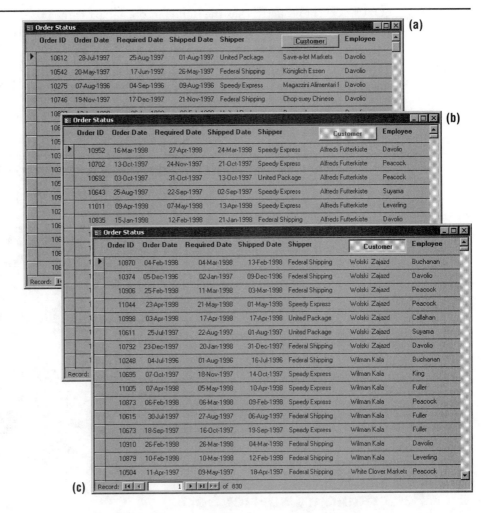

As an example, we'll add a toggle button to sort the Employee column of the Order Status form.

1. Switch to Design view, delete the Employee label, and replace it with a toggle button. Set the Name property to tglEmployee and the Caption property to Employee. Set the other properties to be the same as those you set for the tglCustomer toggle button.

2. Click the Code button in the toolbar to open the form's module. Select the tglCustomer_Click procedure and copy the procedure. Click in the new toggle button's

OnClick event property, click the Build button, and paste the procedure into the Module window. Change the assignment statements for the `str` and `tgl` variables as follows:

```
str = "LastName"
Set tgl = tglEmployee
```

3. Save the form and switch to Form view.

4. Click the Customer toggle button and then click the Employee toggle button. The records are now sorted by employee (see Figure 13.3).

FIGURE 13.3:

The form can be sorted by either the Customer or the Employee column.

Order ID	Order Date	Required Date	Shipped Date	Shipper	Customer	Employee
10869	04-Feb-1998	04-Mar-1998	09-Feb-1998	Speedy Express	Seven Seas Imports	Buchanan
10721	29-Oct-1997	26-Nov-1997	31-Oct-1997	Federal Shipping	QUICK-Stop	Buchanan
10714	22-Oct-1997	19-Nov-1997	27-Oct-1997	Federal Shipping	Save-a-lot Markets	Buchanan
10463	04-Mar-1997	01-Apr-1997	06-Mar-1997	Federal Shipping	Suprêmes délices	Buchanan
10866	03-Feb-1998	03-Mar-1998	12-Feb-1998	Speedy Express	Berglunds snabbköp	Buchanan
10823	09-Jan-1998	06-Feb-1998	13-Jan-1998	United Package	LILA-Supermercado	Buchanan
10841	20-Jan-1998	17-Feb-1998	29-Jan-1998	United Package	Suprêmes délices	Buchanan
10474	13-Mar-1997	10-Apr-1997	21-Mar-1997	United Package	Pericles Comidas clás	Buchanan
10575	20-Jun-1997	04-Jul-1997	30-Jun-1997	Speedy Express	Morgenstern Gesundl	Buchanan
10569	16-Jun-1997	14-Jul-1997	11-Jul-1997	Speedy Express	Rattlesnake Canyon I	Buchanan
10872	05-Feb-1998	05-Mar-1998	09-Feb-1998	United Package	Godos Cocina Típica	Buchanan
10269	31-Jul-1996	14-Aug-1996	09-Aug-1996	Speedy Express	White Clover Markets	Buchanan
10870	04-Feb-1998	04-Mar-1998	13-Feb-1998	Federal Shipping	Wolski Zajazd	Buchanan
10761	02-Dec-1997	30-Dec-1997	08-Dec-1997	United Package	Rattlesnake Canyon I	Buchanan
10922	03-Mar-1998	31-Mar-1998	05-Mar-1998	Federal Shipping	Hanari Carnes	Buchanan
10654	02-Sep-1997	30-Sep-1997	11-Sep-1997	Speedy Express	Berglunds snabbköp	Buchanan

Record: 1 of 830

5. Choose File ➢ Save As and save a copy of the form with the new name frmOrderStatusClean.

Performing a Two-Tier Sort

Along with sorting by column, you can allow a two-tier sort, but with limitations. As an example, the SetOrderBy procedure tests the value of the Customer toggle button, then conducts a "subsort" when the Employee toggle button is clicked, based on the value of the Customer button. This means that the two-tier sort works only with the Customers field as the first tier (if it is selected).

```
Private Function SetOrderBy()
    Const conCustomers = "Customers_CompanyName"
    Const conEmployees = "LastName"

    Dim strSortCustomers As String
```

```
        Dim strSortEmployees As String
        Dim strSort As String

        Select Case tglCustomer.Value
            Case True
                strSortCustomers = conCustomers & " DESC"
            Case False
                strSortCustomers = ""
            Case Else
                strSortCustomers = conCustomers
        End Select

        Select Case tglEmployee.Value
            Case True
                strSortEmployees = conEmployees & " DESC"
            Case False
                strSortEmployees = ""
            Case Else
                strSortEmployees = conEmployees
        End Select

        If strSortCustomers = "" Then
            If strSortEmployees = "" Then
                ' No sort on either field
                strSort = ""
            Else
                ' Employees is the only sort
                strSort = strSortEmployees
            End If
        Else
            If strSortEmployees = "" Then
                ' Customers is the only sort
                strSort = strSortCustomers
            Else
                ' Both fields are sorted
                strSort = strSortCustomers & ", " & strSortEmployees
            End If
        End If

        If strSort = "" Then
            Me.OrderByOn = False
        Else
            Me.OrderBy = strSort
            Me.OrderByOn = True
        End If
End Function
```

This procedure works by checking the status of the Customer button, checking the status of the Employee button, and then building a sort string based on their values.

The procedure begins by creating constants (conCustomers and conEmployees) to represent the fields the buttons will be sorting. It then creates strings for the values of the toggle buttons (strSortCustomers and strSortEmployees) and the final sort string (strSort). When you click either the Customer or the Employee button, the procedure uses the first set of Select Case statements to test the state of the Customer button. It then tests the value of the Employee button in the next Select Case function. After storing the values of the two sort buttons, the procedure assigns a value to the strSort variable based on the values of the strSortCustomers and strSortEmployees variables.

- If neither the Customer nor the Employee button is selected (both have the value of False), the procedure assigns the strSort variable a zero-length string, and the records are not sorted.

- If the Employee button is selected but the Customer button is not, the procedure sorts the records by employee, either ascending or descending depending on whether the value of the Employee button is True or Null.

- If the Customer button is selected but the Employee button is not, the procedure sorts the records by customer, either ascending or descending depending on whether the value of the Customer button is True or Null.

- If both the Customer and Employee buttons are selected, strSort is assigned a value equal to the Customer sort (strSortCustomers), followed by the Employee sort (strSortEmployee). These two variables are separated by a comma and space (,), which is the standard format for a sort string.

Because the procedure is the same whether the Customer or the Employee button is clicked, we can create a form-level procedure and change both buttons' OnClick property to this procedure. Open the frmOrderStatusClean form in Design view and enter the SetOrderBy procedure shown above into the form's module. Change the OnClick property of both toggle buttons to =SetOrderBy(). Save the form and switch to Form view. Test the sort in the Order Status form. For example, click the Customer button to sort the records by customer and then click the Employee button to sort the records for each customer by employee.

Selecting Groups of Records in a Form or Report

One of the most common and important operations in a database application is selecting a group of records that satisfy search conditions. For example, in an order-entry database, you may want to design a form that displays orders for a specific customer, all orders placed after a specified date, or the orders for a specified customer placed after a specified date and handled by a specified employee. You select records from the entire set of records by specifying search conditions that you use to filter out the records satisfying the conditions. Access provides many techniques for filtering records.

Search Conditions

The first step in selecting a group of records is to set up the search condition. You can use these five basic search conditions:

Comparison test Compares the value of one expression to the value of another expression. For example, `OrderDate < #1/1/2001#` searches for orders in the Orders table placed before 1/1/01.

Range test Tests whether the value of an expression lies within a range of values. For example, `OrderDate Between #9/1/2000# And #1/1/2001#` searches for orders in the specified date range.

Membership in a group Tests whether the value of an expression matches one of a set of values. For example, `Country In ("France", "Germany", "South Africa")` searches for customers from one of the three specified countries.

Pattern matching Tests whether a string value matches a specified pattern. For example, `LastName Like "M*"` searches for employees whose last name begins with the letter *M*.

Null value test Tests whether a value has the Null value. For example, `RequiredDate Is Null` searches for orders without a required date.

You can create complex searches by combining up to 40 simple search conditions using logical operators, such as AND and OR.

After using one of several techniques to initiate the search, the database engine retrieves the records that satisfy the search condition. The search condition is often referred to as "a SQL WHERE clause without the word WHERE."

Opening a Form or Report with Selected Records

To select records when a form or report is first opened, you can do any of the following:

- Use a parameter query as the form's or report's record source.
- Set a property such as RecordSource or Filter in a procedure that runs when the form or report opens.

- Use one of the VBA methods to apply the search condition to the existing record source when the form or report opens.

Using a Parameter Query

A parameter query is a query that requires additional information before it can run. When you use a parameter query as the record source of a form or report, you can use two techniques to supply the additional information to the query:

- You can use the default dialog box that Access displays automatically when a query criterion contains a parameter.

- You can use controls on another form to collect the information. When a query gets its information from a form, you are using the *Query By Form* technique.

As an example, the Sales By Year report has the Sales By Year parameter query as its record source. If you run the Sales By Year query by selecting it in the Database window and clicking the Open button, Access displays the two default dialogs for the parameters in the query (see Figure 13.4).

FIGURE 13.4:

The default dialogs for the Sales By Year parameter query

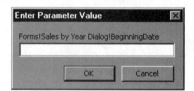 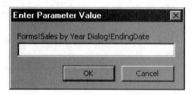

Figure 13.5a shows the two parameters included in the criteria expression for the ShippedDate field. The syntax of the parameter references, such as `Forms![Sales by Year Dialog]!BeginningDate`, indicates that the parameter query is designed to obtain its values from the Sales By Year Dialog form. However, when the form is not open, Access displays the default dialogs to collect the additional information.

If you run the Sales By Year query by opening the Sales By Year report, Access displays the Sales By Year Dialog form (see Figure 13.5b). After you specify the dates and close the form, the Sales By Year query runs, using the information you entered in the form (Query By Form); then the Sales By Year report opens and displays the selected records.

Setting the RecordSource Property

You can set the form's or report's RecordSource property by writing an event procedure triggered by the Open event. You can set the RecordSource property to the name of a stored query or a SQL statement; however, when setting the property in a VBA procedure, you must use a string expression.

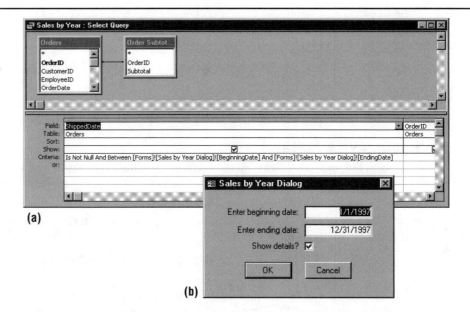

FIGURE 13.5:

A parameter query (a) and the custom dialog form (b) that supplies the values of the parameters

For example, to display the records for the customers from Argentina in the Customer Labels report, open the Customer Labels report in Design view, click in the report's OnOpen event property, and click the Build button at the right of the property box. Create the event procedure shown below. The SQL statement selects records for customers from Argentina from the Customers table.

```
Private Sub Report_Open(Cancel As Integer)
    Me.RecordSource = "SELECT * FROM Customers WHERE Country = " _
        & "'Argentina'"
End Sub
```

Save the report and switch to Print Preview. The Open event is triggered, and the report displays the selected records. Switch to Design view.

Setting the Filter Property

Forms and reports have a Filter property that you can use to specify records and a FilterOn property that you use to turn a filter on or off. The Filter property is a string expression that is a valid SQL WHERE clause without the word WHERE. You can set the Filter property to select the records in an event procedure triggered by the form's or report's Open event.

As an example, modify the event procedure for the Open event of the Customer Labels report as follows:

```
Private Sub Report_Open(Cancel As Integer)
    Me.Filter = "Country = 'UK'"
    Me.FilterOn = True
End Sub
```

Save the report and switch to Print Preview. The selected records are displayed.

Using a VBA Method

The OpenForm and OpenReport methods of the DoCmd object have two arguments that you can use to select records: the *wherecondition* and *filtername* arguments. The *wherecondition* argument is a string expression that is a valid SQL WHERE clause without the word WHERE. For example, to open the Customers form displaying customers from Argentina, use the following statement:

```
DoCmd.OpenForm formname:="Customers", wherecondition:= "Country = " _
    & "'Argentina'"
```

The *filtername* argument is a string expression that is the name of a stored filter query in the database. You must first create a filter query that filters the form's or report's underlying table or query to select records. A filter query must include all the fields in the form's or report's recordset. A filter query can also be a parameter query.

The ApplyFilter method of the DoCmd object also has *wherecondition* and *filtername* arguments. You can run the ApplyFilter method automatically when the form or report opens by creating an event procedure for the Open event. For example, to select customers from Argentina, you can use the following event procedure for the Customers form:

```
Private Sub Form_Open(Cancel As Integer)
    DoCmd.ApplyFilter wherecondition:="Country = 'Argentina'"
End Sub
```

Figure 13.6 shows the result of opening the Customers form and triggering this procedure.

Changing the Selection in an Open Form or Report

After a form or report is open and displays records, you can use several techniques to change which records are displayed:

- Use the built-in Filter For command that allows the user to enter filter criteria in a text box in the shortcut menu.

- Use the built-in Filter By Selection and Filter By Form filter windows that allow the user to create a filter for an open form.

- Change the RecordSource property of an open form by using a procedure.

FIGURE 13.6:

You can use the ApplyFilter method in a procedure triggered by the form's Open event to filter the records when the form opens.

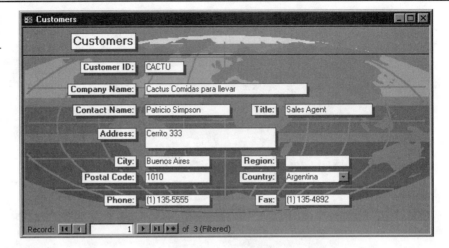

- Run the `ApplyFilter` action or method to apply a filter to an open form.

- Change the Filter property of an open form or report and then turn the filter on in a procedure.

Of the techniques discussed here, only the technique that sets the Filter and FilterOn properties can be used to select records for an open report; the remaining techniques apply only to selecting records in open forms.

Using Filter For, Filter By Selection, and Filter By Form

You can use the three built-in filter techniques that Access provides for allowing the user to select and change records displayed in an open form: Filter For, Filter By Selection, and Filter By Form. Your application can offer these techniques if it includes the built-in menu commands or toolbar buttons. For example, to use the Filter For technique to select records for the Customers form, include the Filter For command in your application so that the user can right-click in a control, type the criteria in the Filter For text box (see Figure 13.7), and press Enter to apply the filter.

  To use the Filter By Form technique to select records for the Customer Orders form, include the Filter By Form command or click the Filter By Form toolbar button. Figure 13.8 shows the filter to find the orders placed after 1/1/97 by customers from Argentina. Clicking the Filter button in the toolbar applies the filter.

You can also customize the Filter By Form interface. You can create event procedures for the Filter and ApplyFilter events to customize the process.

FIGURE 13.7:

Right-click in a control to display the built-in Filter For command.

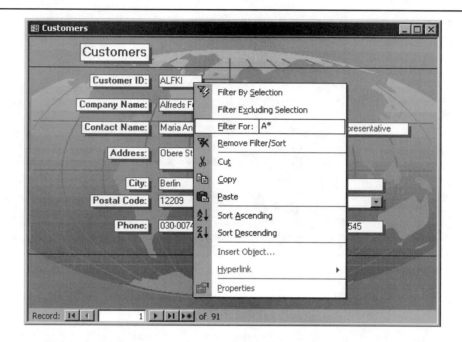

FIGURE 13.7:

Right-click in a control to display the built-in Filter For command.

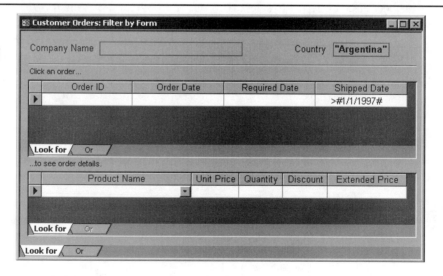

FIGURE 13.8:

Using the Filter By Form filter window to create a filter

Using the Filter Event

A form recognizes the Filter event when you click the Filter By Form button or choose Records ➤ Filter ➤ Filter By Form or Advanced Filter/Sort. (The Filter event is not recognized when you use the Filter By Selection technique.) Access runs the event procedure before displaying the Filter By Form interface, so you can use the event procedure to modify the default Filter By Form interface or replace it with your own custom filter window. After the event procedure runs, the customized Filter By Form interface is displayed.

As an example, if you don't want to display the second subform in the Customer Orders form when the Filter By Form interface is active, you can use the following event procedure to hide the subform:

```
Private Sub Form_Filter(Cancel As Integer, FilterType As Integer)
    Me.[Customer Orders Subform2].Visible = False
End Sub
```

Access uses the `FilterType` argument to tell the event procedure which of the two filter windows the user is trying to open, and Access uses the intrinsic constants `acFilterbyForm` and `acFilterAdvanced`. You can include statements that determine the value of the `FilterType` argument and include instructions depending on the filter window the user is trying to open.

Using the ApplyFilter Event

A form recognizes the ApplyFilter event when the form detects one of three types of actions: to remove the filter, to apply the filter, or to close the filter window. The form recognizes the ApplyFilter event either in response to interactions with the user or in response to procedures. The ApplyFilter event occurs when the user clicks the Apply Filter or Remove Filter button on the toolbar, chooses Records ➤ Apply Filter/Sort or Remove Filter/Sort, clicks the Filter By Selection button on the toolbar, or chooses Records ➤ Filter ➤ Filter By Selection. The ApplyFilter event also occurs when a procedure runs an action or method that applies or removes a filter (such as the `ApplyFilter`, `OpenForm`, or `ShowAllRecords` actions or methods), closes the filter window, or sets the Filter or FilterOn property.

You can create an event procedure to perform different operations depending on which of the three actions triggered the event. The syntax for the `ApplyFilter` event procedure is as follows:

```
Form_ApplyFilter (Cancel As Integer, ApplyType As Integer)
```

You can use the `Cancel` argument to cancel the default behavior that follows the event (applying the filter, removing the filter, or closing the filter window). Access uses the `ApplyType` argument to inform the event procedure which action caused the event, and Access sets the `ApplyType` argument to one of the intrinsic constants acShowAllRecords, acApplyFilter, or acCloseFilterWindow. The event procedure can include different sets of statements for each alternative. The procedure runs before the filter is actually applied, before the filter is removed, or after the filter window is closed but before the form is redisplayed. Consequently, you can use the statements of the procedure to perform the following:

- Modify the filter before it is applied. For example, you can read and change the Filter property.

- Change how the form is displayed when the filter is removed. For example, if you are filtering to select the orders that have been paid, you can hide controls on the Orders form that may be inappropriate for the filter (such as Amount Due).

- Undo or change actions that a procedure took when the Filter event occurred. For example, if you hid controls on the Filter By Form interface when the Filter event occurred, you can show these controls after the filter is applied.

You can redisplay the second subform on the Customer Orders form as follows:

```
Private Sub Form_ApplyFilter(Cancel As Integer, ApplyType As Integer)
    Me.[Customer Orders Subform2].Visible = True
End Sub
```

Changing the RecordSource Property

After a form is open, you can change the form's RecordSource property to a SQL statement or a stored query that selects the records. As an example, open the Customers form in Form view and enter the following statement in the Immediate window:

```
Forms!Customers.RecordSource = "SELECT * FROM Customers WHERE " _
    & "Country = 'Argentina'"
```

The record source is changed, and the selected records are displayed.

NOTE   You cannot change a report's RecordSource property after the report is opened.

Using the *ApplyFilter* Method

Another way to change the records displayed in an open form is to use the ApplyFilter method of the DoCmd object. You can use either the *filtername* argument to specify an existing filter query or the *wherecondition* argument to specify the records using a string expression that is a valid SQL WHERE clause without the word WHERE. The filter query can be a parameter query that obtains its information from controls on the same form (such as a selection combo box placed in the form's header) or from controls on another form (such as a custom dialog designed to collect selection criteria). The next section includes an example of using a parameter query as the filter query.

Changing the Filter Property

A form or report has a Filter property that you can use to specify records and a FilterOn property that you use to turn a filter on or off. The Filter property is a string expression that is a valid SQL WHERE clause without the word WHERE. After a form or report is open, you can set the Filter property to select the records. Set the form's Filter property and then set the FilterOn property to True.

To explore the Filter property, follow these steps:

1. Open the Products By Category report in report Design view. Observe that the Filter property is blank and the FilterOn property is No. Switch to Print Preview.

2. Type **Reports![Products by Category].Filter = "CategoryName = 'Beverages'"** in the Immediate window and press Enter. The Print Preview of the report does not change because the FilterOn property is No. Switch to Design view to note that the Filter property is changed to CategoryName = 'Beverages'. Switch back to Print Preview.

3. Type **Reports![Products by Category].FilterOn = True** in the Immediate window and press Enter. The report window changes to display the filtered records. Switch to Design view to note that the FilterOn property is changed to Yes.

4. Switch back to Print Preview. Type **Reports![Products by Category].Filter = "CategoryName = 'Condiments'"** in the Immediate window and press Enter. The report window changes to display the filtered records. Once the FilterOn property is Yes, you can change the filter simply by setting the Filter property.

5. Close the report. If you close the report without saving it, Access discards both the Filter and the FilterOn settings. If you close the report after saving it, Access discards the Filter setting but saves the FilterOn setting.

Finding a Group of Records Using Query By Form

A basic database operation is selecting a group of records that meet one or more selection criteria. For example, in the Order Status form you may want to display a list of orders for a particular customer, shipper, or employee; you may want to review all orders taken by an employee after a specific date; or you may want to see all orders to be shipped by a specific shipper before a specified required date. When working interactively, you select a specific group of records by creating and applying a filter. Access provides several ways to create filters interactively, including Filter For, Filter By Form, Filter By Selection, and Filter Excluding Selection. These techniques give the user powerful ad hoc querying abilities. You can also customize these built-in techniques with programming, as described in the preceding section. Another technique is to use Query By Form, which provides a simple interface for selecting a group of records.

Here is a summary of the steps involved in using the Query By Form technique.

- Select the field you want to use for the selection and make sure the field is included in the form's record source. For example, to select records for a customer in the frmOrder-Status form, add the CustomerID field from the Orders table to the form's record source.

- Place an unbound combo box in the form's header or footer that holds the search value for the selection field. Design the combo box to display a list for selecting the search value. For example, create a combo box named cboCustomer with a list that includes CustomerID as the combo box's (hidden) bound column and Company Name as the displayed column. (The user selects a company name and the combo box holds the corresponding customer ID.)

- Create a filter query based on the form's record source that selects records that match the search value held in the combo box. For example, to select orders for a customer in the Order Status form, create a filter query named qfltOrderStatus based on the form's record source and set the criteria for the CustomerID field to `Forms!frmOrderStatus!cbo-Customer`. In the case of Filter Excluding Selection, you would create a filter query that selects records that do not match the search value held in the combo box.

- Create an event procedure that uses the `ApplyFilter` method of the DoCmd object to run the filter query and display the filtered records when the user changes the value in the combo box and the combo box recognizes the AfterUpdate event.

The `cboCustomer_AfterUpdate` event procedure, shown below, uses the `ApplyFilter` method of the DoCmd object to apply filter to the Order Status form.

```
Private Sub cboCustomer_AfterUpdate()
    DoCmd.ApplyFilter "qfltOrderStatus"
End Sub
```

When you work interactively, you can remove the filter by choosing Records ➢ Remove Filter/Sort. You can automate the removal of the filter by placing a command button in the form header and using an event procedure, such as the one shown below, to remove the filter.

```
Private Sub cmdShowAll_Click()
    DoCmd.ShowAllRecords
    cboCustomer = Null
End Sub
```

Another way to show all the records is to display a Null row in the combo list; when the user selects the Null row, all of the records are shown.

Using Multiple Criteria to Select a Group of Records

Often, you want to use more than one selection criteria. For example, you can use the frmOrderStatus form to find all orders for a customer that are handled by a specific employee. You can place a selection combo box in the form header for each field you want to use to select records and adapt the application in one of the following ways:

- Modify the filter query to include the additional criteria for each combo box.
- Create an event procedure for each combo box that applies the filter.
- Modify the procedure that removes the filter so that the procedure sets all the combo boxes to Null.

In our example, you'll need to add the EmployeeID field from the Orders table to the form's record source before you can search by employee. The event procedure for the combo box is shown below.

```
Private Sub cboEmployee_AfterUpdate()
    DoCmd.ApplyFiler "qfltOrderStatus"
End Sub
```

The following is the event procedure for the command button that removes the filter:

```
Private Sub cmdShowAll_Click()
    DoCmd.ShowAllRecords
    cboCustomer = Null
    cboEmployee = Null
End Sub
```

Synchronizing Two Combo Boxes

When the list displayed in a combo box is long, you can use two combo boxes instead of one and design the pair so that the contents displayed by the second combo box depend on the value you select in the first—that is, the second combo box is synchronized to the first. For example, in an orders database, the list of customers typically contains several hundreds or thousands of names, so you can use one combo box to select the first letter (or pair of letters) and a second combo box to display the company names for all of the customers whose names begin with the letter (or combination).

The cboFind_AfterUpdate event procedure, for a cboFind combo box, looks up a customer.

```
Private Sub cboFind_AfterUpdate()
    Me.Painting = False
    DoCmd.GoToRecord , , acFirst
    Do Until Me!CustomerID = Me!cboFind
        DoCmd.GoToRecord , , acNext
        If Me.Recordset.EOF Then Exit Sub
    Loop
    Me.Painting = True
End Sub
```

The procedure is called after you select a value from the cboFind combo box. It first turns off painting on the form, then moves to the first record in the recordset. It continues to move through the recordset, one record at a time, until either it finds a match with what is in the cboFind combo box or it reaches the end of the recordset and EOF is true. The procedure then turns on painting for the form, at which point the matching record is the current record.

The cboFirst_AfterUpdate event procedure, for a cboFirst combo box, runs after you select a different value in the cboFirst combo box. This event procedure synchronizes the cboFind combo box by rerunning its query and then moves the focus to the cboFind combo box.

```
Private Sub cboFirst_AfterUpdate()
    cboFind.Requery
    cboFind.SetFocus
End Sub
```

This procedure uses methods of the combo box instead of using the methods of the DoCmd object.

TIP   The Requery method of an object or a form is faster than the Requery method of the DoCmd object. When you run the Requery method of the DoCmd object, Access closes the query and then reloads it from the database. However, when you use the Requery method of an object of form, Access reruns the query without reloading it.

To test the event procedures, follow these steps:

1. Place an unbound combo box named cboFind in the header of the Customers form. Delete the combo box's label. Click in the combo box's AfterUpdate event property and click the Build button to the right of the property box. Enter the cboFind_AfterUpdate event procedure.

2. Place an unbound combo box named cboFirst in the form's header section. Delete the combo box's label. Change the RowSourceType property to Value List. In the Row-Source property, type **;A;B;C;D;E;F** and so on through the entire alphabet. The semicolon at the beginning of the RowSource property setting creates a Null row. Save and close the form.

3. Create a new query named qrySecond based on the Customers table. Drag the CustomerID and CompanyName fields to the bottom pane of the Query window. In the Criteria field of the column containing the CustomerID, type **Like [Forms]![Customers]![cboFirst] & "*"**. This searches for all records in the Customers table with the same first letter as what you selected in the cboFirst combo box. Save the query.

4. Open the Customers form in Design view and select the cboFind combo box. For the RowSource property, select the qrySecond query.

5. Click in the cboFirst combo box's AfterUpdate event property and click the Build button to the right of the property box. Enter the `cboFirst_AfterUpdate` event procedure.

6. Save the form and switch to Form view. Test the form's combo boxes by selecting a letter from the cboFirst field, then clicking the drop-down list from the cboFind combo box (see Figure 13.9). Also test what happens when you use the Null row in the cboFirst combo box.

FIGURE 13.9:

When you select a letter in the combo box on the left, an event procedure synchronizes the combo box on the right to display only the customers whose names begin with the selected letter.

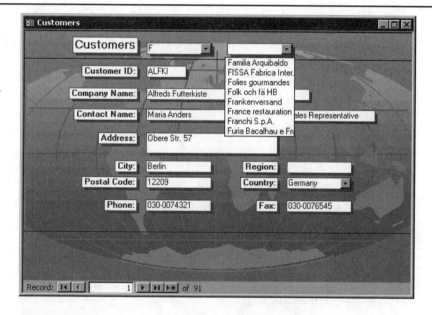

Using a Multiselect List Box to Filter Records

The selection techniques described in the previous sections are based on selecting records that satisfy a search condition. A fundamentally different technique uses the multiselect list box to display a list of choices and allows the user to choose records at random without using a search condition. This technique is more flexible than the other techniques because the user can choose the individual records to display.

The standard list box allows users to select a single item from the list. However, you can use the MultiSelect property to let users choose more than one item. The MultiSelect property has the following values:

None   Allows a user to select a single item.

Simple   Allows a user to select multiple items by clicking each one or by pressing the spacebar.

Extended   Extends the selection of multiple items. Use Shift+click or Shift+arrow to extend the selection from the previously selected item to the current item.

NOTE   You click to select an item and Ctrl+click to deselect an item in the list box.

To explore the multiselect list box, we will create a form that displays orders in a multiselect list box. We will use a combo box to select an employee and synchronize the list box to the combo box by using an event procedure triggered by the combo box's AfterUpdate event. That event procedure, shown below, displays orders in the list box corresponding to the value selected in the combo box.

```
Private Sub cboCurrent_AfterUpdate
    lstOrders.Requery
End Sub
```

Follow these steps to set up the form:

1. Create a new unbound form named frmAssignOrders. Set the following form properties:

Caption	Assign Orders
ScrollBars	Neither
RecordSelectors	No
NavigationButtons	No
MinMaxButtons	None

2. Place an unbound combo box named cboCurrent with the following properties:

RowSource	`SELECT EmployeeID, LastName & ", " & FirstName As FullName FROM Employees ORDER BY LastName;`
ColumnCount	2
ColumnWidths	`0";1"`
BoundColumn	1

3. Set the Caption property of the combo box label to Current Salesperson.

4. Create a parameter query named qrySortCountry. Drag the OrderID, OrderDate, and EmployeeID fields from the Orders table, and the Country and CompanyName fields from the Customers table to the bottom pane of the Query window. In the Criteria field of the column containing the EmployeeID, type **[Forms]![frmAssignOrders]![cboCurrent]** (see Figure 13.10). Sort the Country and CompanyName fields in ascending order. This query uses the value of the EmployeeID chosen in the cboCurrent combo box to select records (Query By Form). We'll use this query as the row source for the multiselect list box.

FIGURE 13.10:

The parameter query for the list box gets its criteria from a combo box on the form.

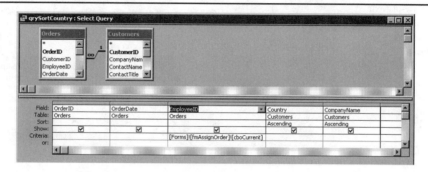

5. Create an unbound list box named lstOrders with the following properties:

RowSource	qrySortCountry
ColumnCount	4
ColumnWidths	0.5";0.65";1.5";0.5"
BoundColumn	1
MultiSelect	Simple

6. Set the Caption property of the list box label to "Orders assigned to current salesperson."

7. Enter the cboCurrent_AfterUpdate event procedure for the Current combo box's AfterUpdate event property. This event procedure requeries the list box when you choose a different employee in the cboCurrent combo box.

8. Save the form and switch to Form view. Select an employee in the Current Salesperson combo box. Figure 13.11 shows the form with the orders for Steven Buchanan displayed.

FIGURE 13.11:

The unbound Assign Orders form displays records from the Employees table as the row source of the combo box and records from a query based on the Orders and Customers tables as the row source of the multi-select list box. An event procedure keeps the list box synchronized to the combo box.

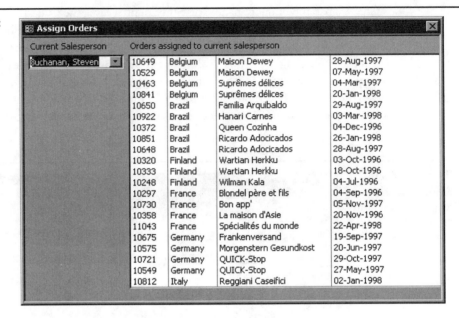

Sorting List Box Rows by Changing the RowSource

You can make the list box more useful by allowing the user to sort the rows by any of the fields. One way to change the sort order of the rows in a list box or combo box is to change the Row-Source property on-the-fly. We'll place a set of four command buttons along the bottom of the list box and use each button to change the list box's RowSource property to a different query. For example, the following is an event procedure for the cmdSortOrderID button.

```
Private Sub cmdSortOrderID_Click
    Me!lstOrders.RowSource = "qrySortOrderID"
End Sub
```

1. Create the qrySortOrderID, qrySortCompany, and qrySortOrderDate queries as duplicates of qrySortCountry but with the following sort orders (remove any other sorts other than those listed):

Sort Query	OrderID	CompanyName	OrderDate
qrySortOrderID	Ascending		
qrySortCompany		Ascending	
qrySortOrderDate			Ascending

2. Place a set of four command buttons named cmdSortOrderID, cmdSortCountry, cmdSortCompany, and cmdSortOrderDate along the bottom edge of the list box, with the captions OrderID, Country, Company, and OrderDate, respectively.

3. Create an event procedure for the On Click event property of each command button that sets the RowSource property of the list box to the corresponding query (see the `cmdSortOrderID_Click` procedure shown above for an example).

4. Save the form and switch to Form view. Select Steven Buchanan and test the sorting buttons (see Figure 13.12).

FIGURE 13.12:

Changing the sort order by changing the RowSource property on-the-fly

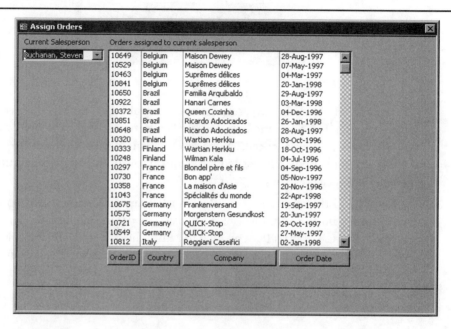

NOTE   If you click one of the four RowSource selector command buttons before selecting a Current Salesperson from the combo box, the list box will open the records with the sort you selected. This is because it has already assigned the RowSource property to the list box, even though the list box had not yet been requeried.

Getting Multiselect List Box Information

When you select multiple items in the list, Access creates a collection for the list box called the ItemsSelected collection. Each member of the ItemsSelected collection is an integer that refers to a selected row in the list box or combo box. Even though the members of the Items-Selected collection are integers, their data type is Variant by default.

When you work with a multiselect list box, a row can have two index numbers: an index number for its position in the list box and another index number (or item number) for its position in the ItemsSelected collection, as illustrated in Figure 13.13. Both index numbers are zero-based. You can use the ListIndex property of the list box to determine the position of a

FIGURE 13.13:

A multiselect list box has an associated ListIndex property and ItemSelected collection.

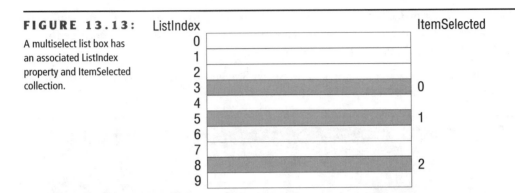

row in the list box. When you select a row in a multiselect list box, Access automatically assigns it an item number. Since the ItemsSelected collection is also zero-based, the first item selected is referred to as `ItemSelected(0)`, the second item selected is referred to as `ItemSelected(1)`, and so on. If the first item selected is the fourth row of the list (with position number 3), then `ItemSelected(0)` returns 3.

Both the ListIndex property and the ItemsSelected collection return a position number of a row. If you want to return the data in the row, you use the Column property or the `ItemData` method. You use the `ItemData` method to return the data in the bound column of a row specified by its position number. You use the Column property to return the data in a specific column of a row specified by its position number. Let's explore these concepts in the Immediate window.

1. Select Steven Buchanan and click the OrderID sort button. Select row 3, row 6, and row 8 (see Figure 13.14a).

2. Open the Immediate window, type **?Forms!frmAssignOrders!lstOrders.ItemsSelected .Count**, and press Enter. The Immediate window displays 3.

3. To display the row number corresponding to the second item in the collection, type **?Forms!frmAssignOrders!lstOrders.ItemsSelected(1)** and press Enter. The Immediate window displays 5. (Row 6 has position number 5.)

4. To display the data in the bound column of the second item in the collection, type **?Forms!frmAssignOrders!lstOrders.ItemData(5)** and press Enter. The Immediate window displays the OrderID of the item 10333.

5. To display the data in any column of the second item in the collection, you use the Column property of the list box or combo box. The first argument of the Column property is the number of the column you want to display, and the second argument is the number of the row; both are zero-based. So to display the second column of the second item in the collection, type **?Forms!frmAssignOrders!lstOrders.Column(1,5)** and press Enter. The Immediate window displays Finland (see Figure 13.14b).

FIGURE 13.14:

Three rows selected in the
multiselect list box (a). Use
the ItemsSelected collec-
tion to keep track of the
selections in the list box
and use the ItemData
method or the Column
property of the list box to
display data (b).

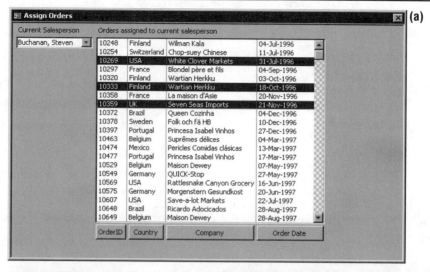

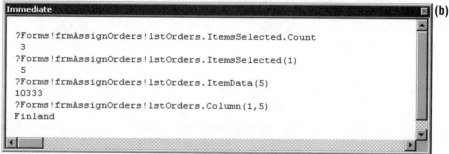

Putting a Multiselect List Box to Work

Now that we have a way to select arbitrary items in a list box, we can put the list box to work.
Suppose that a new employee is hired and you want to be able to reassign some orders that
are currently assigned to other employees to the new employee. You can place a second
combo box on the form to display the name of the employee to whom you want to assign the
orders and use a command button to perform the reassignments. After you select the orders
you want to reassign, clicking the command button runs an event procedure that walks
through the collection of selected orders. This event procedure is shown below.

```
Private Sub cmdAssign_Click()
    Dim rst As New ADODB.Recordset
    Dim cnn As ADODB.Connection
    Dim msg As String, varNumber As Variant
```

```
      If IsNull(cboCurrent) Or IsNull(cboNew) Then
          msg = "You must select a current employee and another"
          msg = msg & " employee you want to reassign orders to."
          MsgBox msg
          Exit Sub
      End If
      If lstOrders.ItemsSelected.Count = 0 Then
          MsgBox "You must select at least one order to reassign."
          Exit Sub
      End If
      Set cnn = CurrentProject.Connection
      rst.Index = "PrimaryKey"
      rst.Open "Orders", cnn, adOpenStatic, adLockOptimistic, adCmdTableDirect
      ' Set up the For Each loop through the collection
      For Each varNumber In lstOrders.ItemsSelected
          rst.Seek lstOrders.ItemData(varNumber), adSeekFirstEQ
          rst!EmployeeID = cboNew
          rst.Update
      Next
      cboCurrent = cboNew
      cboNew = Null
      lstOrders.Requery
  End Sub
```

For each order in the collection, the procedure changes the name in the EmployeeID field to the new employee. When all orders have been reassigned, the procedure displays all the orders currently assigned to the new employee.

The procedure begins by determining whether current and new salespersons have been selected; it then displays a message and terminates if either choice is missing. Next, the procedure determines whether any orders have been selected for reassignment and again displays a message and terminates if there are no selected orders. If there are salespersons selected and orders to be assigned, the procedure reassigns the employee for the selected orders in memory. The procedure opens a static cursor recordset on the Orders table. The fastest way to find the order corresponding to an item in the collection is to use the Seek method with the current index set to the OrderID index (that is, the primary key index). After finding the order, the procedure reassigns the employee and uses the Update method to save the changes.

The procedure uses a For Each…Next structure to loop through the collection of selected orders and reassigns each order in the collection. After reassigning the orders, the procedure sets the cboCurrent combo box to display the salesperson the orders have been assigned to and requeries the list box to display this person's orders.

Follow these steps to test the procedure:

1. Place a new combo box named cboNew on the form. Set the RowSource, Column-Count, BoundColumn, and ColumnWidths properties the same as for the cboCurrent combo box. Change the label's Caption property to "Reassign orders to."

2. Place a command button named cmdAssign on the form and change the Caption property to Reassign Orders. Create the cmdAssign_Click event procedure shown at the beginning of this section for the OnClick event property of the command button.

3. Save the form and switch to Form view. Select Steven Buchanan as the current salesperson and Laura Callahan as the new salesperson. Select orders with OrderIDs of 10649 and 10650 (see Figure 13.15).

FIGURE 13.15:

Reassigning selected orders from one employee to another

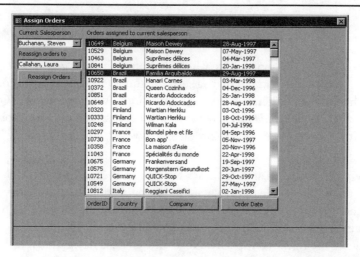

4. Click the Reassign Orders button. The procedure reassigns the orders and displays Laura Callahan as the current salesperson. Click the OrderID button and verify that the two orders have been assigned to Laura Callahan (see Figure 13.16).

Using SQL Techniques

When you want to work with a group of records in VBA procedures, you can use two fundamental sets of techniques: navigational techniques and SQL techniques. With navigational techniques, you can loop through a recordset and select or change one record at a time. For example, in the previous section, we used navigational techniques to loop through the records chosen in a multiselect list box and edit one record at a time.

FIGURE 13.16:

After the records are reassigned to the new employee, the new employee's records are shown in the list box.

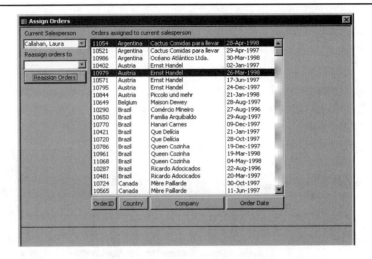

SQL techniques are appropriate when you can define the group of records using a query or a SQL statement. You can create a selection query to select records or an action query to modify the group and then run the query in a single VBA statement. SQL techniques are also called *relational techniques* or *set techniques*, because you define a group of records and the end result you want the engine to produce. However, you don't specify how the result is to be accomplished.

The SQL technique is almost always faster than the navigational technique because SQL relies on the built-in code of the database engine. Database engines have their own optimized techniques for selecting and modifying records. When your VBA procedures use SQL techniques to select and modify records, you allow the engine to use its own optimized ways of producing the result you specify. Normally, you use navigational techniques only when either the group of records or the changes you want to make for each record cannot be readily specified using a query or a SQL statement.

Using SQL techniques involves creating stored queries and writing SQL statements. In Access, you can create queries in two ways: you can use the design grid in query Design view to create the query graphically, or you can use SQL view to create a query as a *SQL statement*. SQL is the standard database language used by Access and every other major database application. You use SQL to write a statement that describes the set of data that you want to retrieve.

SQL is designed to be software independent; in theory, it doesn't matter which software application you are using to actually retrieve the data. In practice, several dialects of SQL are not completely interchangeable. (This book uses Access SQL to refer to the dialect used in Access.)

You can use either SQL view or Design view to create and edit most kinds of queries. When you create a query in the design grid, Access creates the equivalent SQL statement. You can observe the SQL statement for a query by choosing View ➤ SQL or by selecting SQL View from the Query View button's list (in the toolbar when you are in Design view). Figure 13.17 shows the query Design view and the SQL view for the qrySortCompany query. The English language request for the data is "List the OrderID, country, company name, and order date for all orders currently assigned to the employee chosen in the cboCurrent combo box on the frmAssignOrders form, sorted by company name."

FIGURE 13.17:

The Design view and SQL view for a query

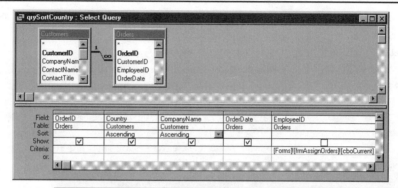

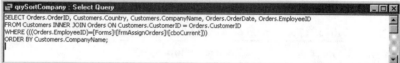

NOTE   Most VBA procedures involve a mixture of stored queries and SQL statements. Learning to write SQL statements directly is a useful skill. As you continue your work with relational databases, you will eventually develop SQL skills; however, you don't need to conquer SQL immediately. Instead, you can ease into SQL by using the query Design view to create the query (unless you are creating a SQL-specific query). After creating the draft, switch to SQL view, copy the SQL statement or clause, switch to the Module window, and paste the SQL statement or clause into the VBA procedure. The hard part is modifying the SQL statement or clause to include VBA variables and then expressing the result as a text string that the database engine can understand.

Understanding the Vocabulary and Grammar of SQL

A SQL statement is a request for data from a relational database. The statement contains the names of the tables and fields holding the data and additional information that defines the search and the action you want taken. SQL has a vocabulary of English words, including about 100 special SQL keywords. The Access SQL keywords are usually shown in uppercase in the SQL views, although SQL keywords aren't case sensitive in Access. A SQL statement includes commands, clauses, operators, and group aggregate functions. Table 13.1 shows the seven commands in Access SQL that you can use to request a specific action. Table 13.2 shows the most common SQL keywords.

TABLE 13.1: The Access SQL Commands

Command	Description
SELECT	Retrieves stored data from tables in the database as a set of records
INSERT	Adds new records to a table
DELETE	Deletes records from a table
UPDATE	Modifies values in specific fields in existing records
CREATE	Creates a new table, view, or procedure in the database, or creates an index for an existing field or group of fields
ALTER	Creates, deletes, or changes the data type for fields in an existing table or adds or removes a multiple-field index
DROP	Used with **ALTER**, deletes an existing table, procedure, or view, or an existing index for a field or a group of fields
EXECUTE	Runs a specified procedure

TABLE 13.2: Common Access SQL Keywords

Keyword	Description
DISTINCTROW	Eliminates duplicate records in the result.
AS	Specifies the alias that you want to use for the field name that precedes the alias.
FROM	Specifies the tables or queries that contain the fields you want in the result.
WHERE	Specifies the criteria that you want to use to select records. WHERE is followed by a search condition; the result includes only records for which the search condition is True.
JOIN	Specifies the link between records in different tables or queries. JOIN is used with the keywords INNER, LEFT, or RIGHT to specify the type of link.
ORDER BY	Specifies the sort order of the result.
GROUP BY	Specifies the field that you want to use to form groups from the rows selected. The query returns one record for each unique value in the specified field.
UNION	Specifies the records from two or more tables or queries that are to be combined.
HAVING	Used with GROUP BY and similar to WHERE, determines which rows are to be returned from those that meet other criteria in the query.

A SQL statement begins with one of the commands and includes one or more clauses that specify the data that the command applies to and that provide additional information about the final result you are requesting. Each clause begins with a keyword, such as WHERE, ORDER BY, or FROM, and may include other SQL keywords; built-in functions (but not user-defined functions); field, table, or query names; expressions; constants; and references to controls on forms and reports. Access SQL uses the punctuation shown in Table 13.3.

TABLE 13.3: Access SQL Punctuation

Symbol	Description
Semicolon (;)	Use a semicolon to end each SQL statement.
Comma (,)	Use commas to separate names in lists, such as LastName, FirstName.
Square brackets ([...])	Use square brackets to enclose a name that contains spaces or special characters, such as [Cost/Unit] or [Last Name] or to enclose a wildcard character set.
Period (.)	Use a period to separate the name of a table or query from a field name when the table or query name is required to uniquely identify the field, such as Customers.CompanyName.
Wildcard characters	Use wildcards as place holders for other characters with the Like operator to create a wildcard search condition; for example, ?, *, #, and [!].
Double-quotes (") and single quotes (')	Use double and single quotes to enclose literal values such as "Germany" and to indicate the presence of a string within a string.
Number symbol (#)	Use the number symbol to enclose literal date/time values, such as #1/2/2001#.

Although every query you create in the design grid has a corresponding SQL statement, there are some queries, called *SQL queries* or *SQL-specific queries*, that you can create only as SQL statements in SQL view; these queries have no Design view equivalents. The SQL queries include the following six types:

Union queries Used to combine the results of two or more select queries into a single result when each of the select queries has the same number of columns and corresponding fields have the same data type.

Non-equijoin queries Used to create joins that are not based on equality.

Single-record append queries Used to specify the value of each field in a single new record and then append the record to an existing table or query.

Data definition queries Used to create, modify, or delete a table or create or delete an index on a table.

Subqueries Used when a query depends on the result of another query.

Pass-through queries Used to send commands that retrieve records or change data directly to a SQL database server.

Using Stored Queries versus SQL Statements: Performance Considerations

After you create a query in Design or SQL view, you can do one of the following:

- Save it as a *stored* query listed in the Database window and enter the name of the query wherever you need to use it.

- Enter the SQL statement directly in a property setting or VBA statement.

Although you can use either a stored query or a SQL statement in any situation that requires a query, in most cases, using a stored query gives the best performance. When you store a query as a database object, Access analyzes the query and stores an optimized version. When you run the stored query, you are running an optimized version. If you change the query, Access analyzes it again the next time you run it and stores the newly optimized version. On the other hand, every time you run a SQL statement, Access analyzes the statement and determines the optimal way to execute it. Because the analysis and optimization take time, the SQL statement usually executes more slowly than the equivalent stored query.

Creating New Stored Queries in VBA Procedures

A query is a set of instructions or definitions for retrieving and/or modifying data. When you work interactively, you create a new query and save it as a Database window object in the current database. When you work with queries directly in VBA, you refer to a stored query as either a Procedure or a View object—data access objects that are managed by the database engine. As Chapter 6, "Understanding the ADO Object Model," explains, a Procedure object is a member of the Procedures collection (the collection of all stored procedures), and a View object is a member of the Views collection (the collection of all stored views). A query with parameters is considered a Procedure object in the ADOX model and a query without parameters is considered a View object. The Procedures and Views collections belong to the Catalog object, which represents a database in the ADOX model. (See Chapter 6 for more information about the relationships between the data access objects.)

You can create new stored queries in VBA procedures by first creating an ADOX Command object, then using the Procedures or Views collection's Append method to append a new Procedure or View object with the new command as a component of the new query. The syntax for the Append method is as follows:

```
cat.Collection.Append Name, cmd
```

where

- `cat` is an object variable that refers to the Catalog that will contain the new query.

- *Collection* is the name of the collection you are appending the query to, whether Procedures or Views. If the query has parameters, it should be appended to the Procedures collection. If not, it should be appended to Views.

- *Name* is a string expression that identifies (names) the new query.

- *cmd* is an ADO Command object that represents the instructions in the query.

As examples, we'll create a few new stored queries. Create a new module named basQueries for these examples.

Creating a New Select Query

We'll create a new select query to find the customers who placed orders after a specified date. We'll design a query in query Design view and paste the SQL statement into a new VBA procedure. Create a query in Design view based on the Orders and Customers tables that returns the company name, contact name, and order date for each order placed after 7/1/97. Figure 13.18a shows the Design view for the query.

When you create a query in query Design view, Access always includes the table name for each field and may include redundant sets of parentheses in the corresponding SQL statement. The table name is required only when you have fields with the same name in two or more tables (or other nested queries) in the query. In Figure 13.18b, the redundant parentheses and optional table names have been eliminated. When you strip out redundant parentheses and table names, switch to SQL view and run the query to make sure the SQL statement is still valid. Copy the SQL statement to the Clipboard. Do not close the Query window, because we'll use this query in the next example.

Enter the NewStoredQuery procedure, shown below, in the basQueries module. We'll name the new stored query qryRecentCustomers. When you paste the SQL statement (shown in Figure 13.18b), you'll need to reconnect the three lines into a single line of code. After reconnecting the pieces of the SQL statement, you can rebreak it to make your code more readable. VBA won't let you use the line-continuation character to break a SQL statement, but you can concatenate the pieces as shown below. After creating the new query, the procedure refreshes the Database window and terminates.

```
Public Sub NewStoredQuery()
    Dim cat As New ADOX.Catalog
    Dim cmd As New ADODB.Command
    Dim cnn As ADODB.Connection
    Dim strSQL As String
    Set cnn = CurrentProject.Connection
    Set cmd.ActiveConnection = cnn
    strSQL = "SELECT CompanyName, ContactName, OrderDate FROM "
    strSQL = strSQL & "Customers INNER JOIN Orders ON "
```

```
        strSQL = strSQL & "Customers.CustomerID = Orders.CustomerID "
        strSQL = strSQL & "WHERE OrderDate > #7/1/1997#;"
        cmd.CommandText = strSQL
        Set cat.ActiveConnection = cnn
        cat.Procedures.Append "qryRecentCustomers", cmd
    End Sub
```

FIGURE 13.18:

You can create most SQL
statements by creating the
query graphically (a) and
switching to SQL view (b).

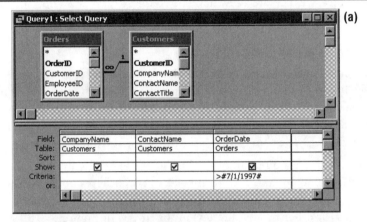

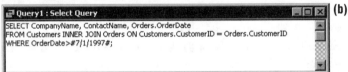

TIP   When using SQL statements in VBA code, you can break the statement into pieces to make
your code more readable. Assign the first piece of the SQL statement to a string variable, such
as strSQL, and then concatenate the second piece to the string variable and assign the result
to the string variable, and so on. Each piece must include spaces at the beginning or end so
that the final concatenated expression reproduces the original SQL statement exactly.

Run the procedure in the Immediate window, then switch to the Database window. The
qryRecentCustomers query appears in the Queries list. Double-click the query to run it.
Figure 13.19 shows the datasheet for the new stored query. When you're finished, delete the
qryRecentCustomers query.

Creating a New Action Query

For the next example, we'll convert the select query we just created to an action query that
creates a new table. Open the query in Design view and choose Query ➢ Make-Table Query.

FIGURE 13.19:

The datasheet for a query created in a procedure

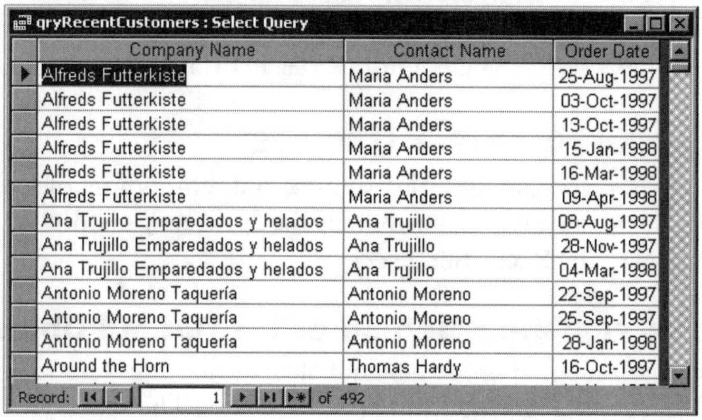

FIGURE 13.19:

The datasheet for a query created in a procedure

Enter **tblRecentOrders** as the new table name. Figure 13.20 shows the SQL view for the make-table query with the redundant parentheses and unnecessary table names stripped out. The SQL statement for a make-table query includes the INTO *tablename* clause to specify the name of the new table.

FIGURE 13.20:

The SQL statement for the make-table query

```
qryRecentCustomers : Make Table Query                           _ □ ×
SELECT CompanyName, ContactName, Orders.OrderDate INTO tblRecentOrders
FROM Customers INNER JOIN Orders ON Customers.CustomerID = Orders.CustomerID
WHERE Orders.OrderDate>#7/1/1997#;
```

Enter the NewActionQuery procedure shown below in the basQueries module. This procedure creates the new Procedure object using the SQL statement as the query's Command object.

```
Public Sub NewActionQuery()
    Dim cat As New ADOX.Catalog
    Dim cmd As New ADODB.Command
    Dim cnn As ADODB.Connection
    Dim strSQL As String
    Set cnn = CurrentProject.Connection
    Set cmd.ActiveConnection = cnn
    strSQL = "SELECT CompanyName, ContactName, OrderDate "
    strSQL = strSQL & "INTO tblRecentOrders "
    strSQL = strSQL & "FROM Customers INNER JOIN Orders ON "
    strSQL = strSQL & "Customers.CustomerID = Orders.CustomerID "
    strSQL = strSQL & "WHERE OrderDate > #5/1/1998#;"
    cmd.CommandText = strSQL
    Set cat.ActiveConnection = cnn
    cat.Procedures.Append "qryRecentCustomersTable", cmd
End Sub
```

Run the procedure in the Immediate window. Switch to the Database window and note the new action query. Select the new action query and double-click to run it. Access runs the query and creates the table. When you're finished, delete the new query and table.

Running Stored Select Queries

A select query retrieves data from the database and returns a set of records to memory. To run a stored select query, you can use either the OpenQuery method of the DoCmd object or the Open method of the Recordset object.

Using the *OpenQuery* Method of the DoCmd Object

Use the OpenQuery method of the DoCmd object when you want to run a select or crosstab query and display a Query window in one of its views. The syntax for the OpenQuery method is as follows:

```
DoCmd.OpenQuery queryname, view, datamode
```

where

- *queryname* is a string expression that is the valid name of a query in the current database.

- *view* is an optional intrinsic constant for specifying the view (acViewNormal, acViewDesign, acViewPreview, acViewPivotChart, or acViewPivotTable). The default is Normal view.

- *datamode* is an optional intrinsic constant for specifying the data mode (acAdd, acEdit, or acReadOnly). The default is Edit.

For example, to run the qryRecentCustomers that the NewStoredQuery procedure creates, add this statement after the statement that creates the query:

```
DoCmd.OpenQuery "qryRecentOrders"
```

When you run the procedure, the procedure creates the new stored query, runs it, and opens the datasheet to display the records.

Using the *Open* Method

You use the Open method of the Recordset to run a stored select query and return the result as a recordset in memory instead of in a Query window. You can use the Open method as follows:

```
rst.Open queryname, activeconnection, cursortype, locktype, options
```

where

- *queryname* is the name of an existing select query.

- *activeconnection* is either a variable that points to an existing connection or contains the information necessary to create a valid connection.

- *cursortype* is an optional enumerated constant that specifies the type of recordset (adOpenDynamic, adOpenForwardOnly, adOpenKeyset, or adOpenStatic). The default type is forward-only.

- *locktype* is an optional enumerated constant that specifies the type of record-locking to be used for the recordset (adLockBatchOptimistic, adLockOptimistic, adLockPessimistic, or adLockReadOnly). The default type is read-only.

- *options* is an optional combination of enumerated constants that you use to specify additional characteristics of the recordset.

As an example, you can modify the NewStoredQuery procedure to run the qryRecentCustomers query and return the results to memory without displaying a datasheet. To do so, declare rst as an object variable for the Recordset object created in memory and add statements to create a recordset, as follows:

```
Dim rst As New ADODB.Recordset
Dim cnn As ADODB.Connection
Set cnn = CurrentProject.Connection
rst.Open "qryRecentCustomers", cnn
```

When you run the procedure, the stored query and the recordset are created. The recordset is cleared when the procedure finishes.

Running a SQL Statement

When you don't need to store a select query and you don't need to display a Query window, you don't need to create a Procedure or View object. In fact, you can just run the SQL statement to create the recordset in memory using the Open method of the Recordset object, as follows:

```
rst.Open (sqlstatement), cnn
```

For example, the NewSQLStatement procedure shown below creates a recordset for working with the data for recent customers without creating a Procedure or View object. The procedure prints the order date for each selected record to the Immediate window.

```
Public Sub NewSQLStatement()
    Dim rst As New ADODB.Recordset
    Dim cnn As ADODB.Connection
    Dim strSQL As String
    strSQL = "SELECT CompanyName, ContactName, OrderDate "
    strSQL = strSQL & "FROM Customers INNER JOIN Orders ON "
```

```
        strSQL = strSQL & "Customers.CustomerID = Orders.CustomerID "
        strSQL = strSQL & "WHERE OrderDate > #5/1/1998#;"
        Set cnn = CurrentProject.Connection
        rst.Open strSQL, cnn
        Do Until rst.EOF
            Debug.Print rst!CompanyName & ": " & rst!OrderDate
            rst.MoveNext
        Loop
    End Sub
```

To test the procedure, insert it in the basQueries module and run it in the Immediate window. The results of the SQL statement are printed (see Figure 13.21).

FIGURE 13.21:

When you don't need to store a select query and you don't need to display a query window, you can run the SQL statement to create the recordset in memory.

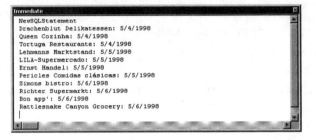

```
Immediate
NewSQLStatement
Drachenblut Delikatessen: 5/4/1998
Queen Cozinha: 5/4/1998
Tortuga Restaurante: 5/4/1998
Lehmanns Marktstand: 5/5/1998
LILA-Supermercado: 5/5/1998
Ernst Handel: 5/5/1998
Pericles Comidas clásicas: 5/5/1998
Simons bistro: 5/6/1998
Richter Supermarkt: 5/6/1998
Bon app': 5/6/1998
Rattlesnake Canyon Grocery: 5/6/1998
```

Sorting and Filtering a Recordset

When you want to sort and filter a recordset, you can use SQL techniques, the Sort and Filter properties of the recordset, or the Index property of a recordset.

Using SQL Techniques to Sort and Filter a Recordset

If you can define a group of records using a SQL statement, the fastest way to sort or filter the records is to modify the SQL statement to include clauses for the sort and filter and use the modified SQL statement to simultaneously define and sort or filter the records.

As an example, the SQLSortFilter procedure shown below uses a SQL statement to select records from the Customers table, filter the records to obtain only the customers from Germany, and then sort the records by company name.

```
    Public Sub SQLSortFilter()
        Dim rst As New ADODB.Recordset
        Dim cnn As ADODB.Connection
        Set cnn = CurrentProject.Connection
        rst.Open ("SELECT * FROM Customers WHERE Country = " _
            & "'Germany' ORDER BY CompanyName"), cnn
        Do Until rst.EOF
            Debug.Print rst!CompanyName
```

```
        rst.MoveNext
    Loop
End Sub
```

The procedure prints the CompanyName field from the filtered and sorted recordset in the Immediate window. You can enter the procedure in a new module named basGroups and run the procedure in the Immediate window.

Using the Sort and Filter Properties of a Recordset

You can use the Sort and Filter properties to sort and filter an existing recordset. When you use these properties, the existing recordset is not affected and you must create a second recordset based on the first to see the effects of the settings.

You can use the Sort property to sort an existing dynaset-type or snapshot-type recordset. You set the Sort property to a string expression that is an ORDER BY clause of a valid SQL statement but without the ORDER BY phrase. You cannot use the Sort property to sort a table-type recordset.

The RecordsetSort procedure shown below creates a client-side static cursor recordset for the Customers table and prints the employees' last names in whatever order the database returns them. It then sets the Sort property to sort the records by city, and then reprints the names based on the effect of the sort.

```
Public Sub RecordsetSort()
    Dim rst As New ADODB.Recordset
    Dim cnn As ADODB.Connection
    Set cnn = CurrentProject.Connection
    rst.CursorLocation = adUseClient
    rst.Open "Employees", cnn, adOpenStatic
    Debug.Print "Unsorted list:"
    Do Until rst.EOF
        Debug.Print rst!LastName
        rst.MoveNext
    Loop
    rst.Sort = "City"
    Debug.Print "Sorted by City:"
    Do Until rst.EOF
        Debug.Print rst!LastName
        rst.MoveNext
    Loop
End Sub
```

The procedure uses Do Until loops to print the employee names for both the unsorted and the sorted recordset (see Figure 13.22). Insert the RecordsetSort procedure in the basGroups module and run it in the Immediate window.

FIGURE 13.22:

You can use the Sort property of a recordset to order the records. Use Do...Until loops to see the difference in the way the records are returned.

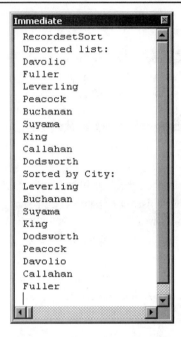

```
Immediate                        ⊠
  RecordsetSort                  ▲
  Unsorted list:
  Davolio
  Fuller
  Leverling
  Peacock
  Buchanan
  Suyama
  King
  Callahan
  Dodsworth
  Sorted by City:
  Leverling
  Buchanan
  Suyama
  King
  Dodsworth
  Peacock
  Davolio
  Callahan
  Fuller
  |                              ▼
◀ ▮                          ▶
```

Using the Index Property to Sort a Recordset

If a provider supports Indexes, you can sort the recordset by setting its Index property to an existing index for the table. The RecordsetSortTable procedure shown below sorts a static cursor recordset.

```
Public Sub RecordsetSortTable()
    Dim rst As New ADODB.Recordset
    Dim cnn As ADODB.Connection
    Set cnn = CurrentProject.Connection
    rst.Open "Customers", cnn, adOpenStatic, , adCmdTableDirect
    Debug.Print "Sorted by Primary Key:"
    Do Until rst.EOF
        Debug.Print rst!City & " " & rst!CompanyName
        rst.MoveNext
    Loop
    rst.Index = "City"
    rst.MoveFirst
    Debug.Print "Sorted by City:"
    Do Until rst.EOF
        Debug.Print rst!City & " " & rst!CompanyName
        rst.MoveNext
    Loop
End Sub
```

This procedure begins by creating a direct-table static cursor recordset for the Customers table and printing the city and company name in primary key order. The procedure then sets the current index to sort the records by city (one of the existing indexes for the table), moves the current record pointer back to the first record, and prints the city and company names for the sorted recordset in the Immediate window.

Insert the RecordsetSortTable procedure in the basGroups module then run it in the Immediate window.

Filtering a Recordset

You use the Filter property to filter the records in a recordset. (You cannot use both a filter and an index on the same recordset.) Set the Filter property of the recordset to a string expression that is the WHERE clause of a valid SQL statement without the word WHERE. The RecordsetFilter procedure shown below filters a forward-only cursor recordset.

```
Public Sub RecordsetFilter()
    Dim rst As New ADODB.Recordset
    Dim cnn As ADODB.Connection
    Set cnn = CurrentProject.Connection
    rst.Open "Employees", cnn, adOpenForwardOnly
    Debug.Print "Unfiltered recordset: All employees"
    Do Until rst.EOF
        Debug.Print rst!LastName & ": " & rst!City
        rst.MoveNext
    Loop
    rst.Filter = "City = 'London'"
    Debug.Print "Filtered recordset: Employees from London"
    Do Until rst.EOF
        Debug.Print rst!LastName & ": " & rst!City
        rst.MoveNext
    Loop
End Sub
```

This procedure opens a forward-only cursor recordset on the Employees table and prints the last name and city of all the records in the Employees table. It then sets the filter to select employees from London and prints the last name for records from the filtered recordset (see Figure 13.23).

Insert the RecordsetFilter procedure in the basGroups module and run it in the Immediate window.

Running Stored Action Queries

An action query modifies the data in the database but returns no records to memory. To run a stored action query in a VBA procedure, you can use either the OpenQuery method of the DoCmd object or the Execute method of the Command or Connection objects.

When you use the Filter property of a recordset, you must create a new recordset based on the original recordset to see the effect of the filter.

```
Immediate                                              ☒
RecordsetFilter
Unfiltered recordset: All employees
Davolio: Seattle
Fuller: Tacoma
Leverling: Kirkland
Peacock: Redmond
Buchanan: London
Suyama: London
King: London
Callahan: Seattle
Dodsworth: London
Filtered recordset: Employees from London
Buchanan: London
Suyama: London
King: London
Dodsworth: London
```

Using the *OpenQuery* Method of the DoCmd Object

The syntax for the OpenQuery method for running an action query is as follows:

```
DoCmd.OpenQuery queryname
```

queryname is a string expression for the name of a stored action query in the current database.

For example, you can run the qryRecentCustomers make-table query created in the NewActionQuery example by adding the following statement after the statements that define the query:

```
DoCmd.OpenQuery "qryRecentCustomers"
```

When you run the modified procedure, both the stored make-table query and the table are created.

> **TIP** If you don't want to display the default confirmation messages that Access displays when you run an action query, use the **SetWarnings** method of the DoCmd object to suppress system messages. Set the **WarningsOn** argument to False to turn off the messages before you run the action query. When you turn off system warnings in a procedure, you must turn them back on by setting the **WarningsOn** argument to True.

Using the *Execute* Method

Both the Connection and the Command objects have Execute methods that you can use to run a stored action query. The syntax for the Execute method of the Connection object is as follows:

```
cnn.Execute commandtext, recordsaffected, options
```

where

- *cnn* is a variable string that refers to an active connection.

- *commandtext* is a string that contains the name of the query.

- *recordsaffected* is an optional long variable that returns the number of records affected.

- *options* is an optional combination of enumerated constants that provides additional information about the command to be executed.

For the Command object, the syntax is as follows:

```
cmd.CommandText = queryname
cmd.Execute recordsaffected, parameters, options
```

where

- *queryname* is a string expression that is the name of the stored action query.

- *cmd* is a variable string that refers to an active connection.

- *recordsaffected* is an optional long variable that returns the number of records affected.

- *parameters* is an optional variant array of parameter values for the command.

As an example, the following is a modified version of the NewActionQuery procedure that uses the Execute method to run a make-table query.

```
Public Sub NewActionQuery()
    Dim cat As New ADOX.Catalog
    Dim cmd As New ADODB.Command
    Dim cnn As ADODB.Connection
    Dim strSQL As String
    Set cnn = CurrentProject.Connection
    Set cmd.ActiveConnection = cnn
    strSQL = "SELECT CompanyName, ContactName, OrderDate "
    strSQL = strSQL & "INTO tblRecentOrders "
    strSQL = strSQL & "FROM Customers INNER JOIN Orders ON "
    strSQL = strSQL & "Customers.CustomerID = Orders.CustomerID "
    strSQL = strSQL & "WHERE OrderDate > #5/1/1998#;"
    cmd.CommandText = strSQL
    Set cat.ActiveConnection = cnn
    cat.Procedures.Append "qryRecentCustomersTable", cmd
    cmd.CommandText = "qryRecentCustomersTable"
    cmd.Execute
End Sub
```

To test this procedure, modify the `NewActionQuery` procedure as shown above. Then switch to the Database window and delete qryRecentCustomers and tblRecentOrders, if necessary. Run the procedure in the Immediate window.

Running a SQL Statement for an Action or Data-Definition Query

You can create SQL statements for action queries and for data-definition queries. You can create SQL statements for the four kinds of action queries that modify tables by designing the query in query Design view and switching to SQL view. Table 13.4 shows the SQL commands and examples for the four action queries. The table also includes an example for the SQL-specific query for appending a single record. The SQL commands for action queries are called the *data manipulation language* (DML) commands.

TABLE 13.4: The SQL Commands for Action Queries

Query Type	SQL Command	Example	Description
Append	INSERT INTO ...SELECT	INSERT INTO Customers FROM tblNewCustomers;	Copies existing records from another table or query and adds them to a table or query in the same or another database.
Single-record Append	INSERT INTO ...VALUES	INSERT INTO Categories (CategoryName) VALUES ("Candies");	Adds a record with specified values to an existing table or query.
Delete	DELETE	DELETE * FROM Customers WHERE OrderDate < #1/1/1990#;	Removes records from one or more tables.
Update	UPDATE...SET	UPDATE Orders SET OrderAmount = OrderAmount*1.02 WHERE ShipCountry = 'Germany';	Changes the values in specific fields in a table.
Make table	SELECT...INTO	SELECT * INTO tblRecentOrders FROM Orders WHERE OrderDate > #1/1/1999#;	Creates a new table and copies existing records from another table in the same database.

You can also use SQL statements to create SQL-specific queries for defining and modifying new tables, fields, and indexes. These queries are called data-definition queries and use commands called the *data definition language* (DDL) commands. Table 13.5 shows the commands and examples. The data-definition queries do not produce recordsets, so you run them the same way that you run SQL statements for action queries.

TABLE 13.5: The SQL Commands for Data-Definition Queries

SQL Command	Example	Description
CREATE TABLE	CREATE TABLE EmployeePhone (LastName TEXT (20), FirstName TEXT (20), Extension TEXT (4))	Creates new tables and fields
CREATE INDEX	CREATE INDEX	Creates a new index on an existing table
DROP TABLE	DROP TABLE tblRecentOrders;	Deletes an existing table
DROP INDEX	DROP INDEX Country ON Customers;	Deletes an existing index on a table
ALTER TABLE	ALTER TABLE Employees ADD COLUMN Salary CURRENCY;	Adds, modifies, or removes a single column or a single index in an existing table

NOTE   When you want to delete all of the records from a table, you can use a Delete query or a DROP TABLE statement. When you use a Delete query, only the data is deleted and the table definition remains. However, when you use a DROP TABLE statement, the table definition is removed from the database.

Access SQL has its own data types, which are listed in Table 13.6.

TABLE 13.6: The Access SQL Data Types

Data Type	Storage Size	Description
BINARY	1 byte per character	Any type of data
BOOLEAN	1 byte	Yes/No values
BYTE	1 byte	Integer between 0 and 255
COUNTER	4 bytes	A number incremented by Jet when a new record is added (the data type is a Long)
CURRENCY	8 bytes	Fixed-point, uses up to 4 decimal places to the right of the decimal point
DATETIME	8 bytes	A date or time value
GUID	128 bits	A unique ID number used in remote procedure calls
SINGLE	4 bytes	A single-precision, floating-point value
DOUBLE	8 bytes	A double-precision, floating-point value
SHORT	2 bytes	A short integer between −32,768 and 32,768
LONG	4 bytes	A long integer
LONGTEXT	1 byte per character	0 to 1.2 gigabytes
LONGBINARY	As required	Used for OLE objects
TEXT	1 byte per character	0 to 255 characters
VALUE	Varies	A synonym for the Variant data type

Using the *RunSQL* Method of the DoCmd Object

You can run a SQL statement for an action or data-definition query by using the RunSQL method of the DoCmd object. The syntax is

```
DoCmd.RunSQL sqlstatement, usetransaction
```

The maximum length of the *sqlstatement* string is 32,768 characters. *usetransaction* refers to whether the query should be included in a transaction. We will come back to transactions in the "Using Transactions" section later in this chapter.

For example, the DDLAlterTable procedure alters a table by adding a Salary field with the CURRENCY data type to the Employees table.

```
Public Sub DDLAlterTable()
    Dim strSQL As String
    strSQL = "ALTER TABLE Employees ADD COLUMN Salary CURRENCY;"
    DoCmd.RunSQL strSQL
End Sub
```

To test the procedure, enter it into the basGroups module and run it in the Immediate window. Open the Employees table and note the new Salary field.

Reassigning a Group of Records

We'll use the techniques described in the preceding sections to modify the frmAssignOrders form created in the section "Using a Multiselect List Box to Filter Records." This time, we are adding the capability to reassign all of an employee's orders to another employee. The example uses the cmdAssignAll_Click event procedure shown below.

```
Private Sub cmdAssignAll_Click()
    Dim cmd As New ADODB.Command
    Dim cnn As ADODB.Connection
    Dim varNumber As Variant, strSQL As String, str As String
    If IsNull(cboCurrent) Or IsNull(cboNew) Then
        str = "You must select a current employee and another "
        str = str & "employee you want to reassign orders to."
        MsgBox str
        Exit Sub
    End If
    Set cnn = CurrentProject.Connection
    strSQL = "UPDATE Orders SET EmployeeID = " & cboNew
    strSQL = strSQL & " WHERE EmployeeID = " & cboCurrent
    cmd.ActiveConnection = cnn
    cmd.CommandText = strSQL
    cmd.Execute
    cboCurrent = cboNew
    cboNew = Null
    lstOrders.Requery
End Sub
```

This procedure begins by testing the employee combo boxes. It displays a message and ends if either combo box is empty. If both employees have been selected, the procedure runs a SQL statement to change the EmployeeID field for the orders displayed in the list box from the current to the new employee. After running the SQL statement, the procedure displays the set of all orders for the new employee by setting the current combo box to the new employee, setting the new employee combo box to Null, and requerying the list box.

Open the frmAssignOrders form in Design view and add a command button named cmdAssignAll. Change the Caption property to Reassign All Orders. Next, enter the `cmdAssignAll_Click` event procedure shown above for the button's OnClick event property. Save the form and switch to Form view. Choose Janet Leverling as the current salesperson and Margaret Peacock as the new salesperson (see Figure 13.24). Click the Reassign All Orders button. All of Janet Leverling's orders are reassigned to Margaret Peacock.

FIGURE 13.24:

The Reassign All Orders button executes a SQL statement to reassign Ms. Leverling's orders to Ms. Peacock.

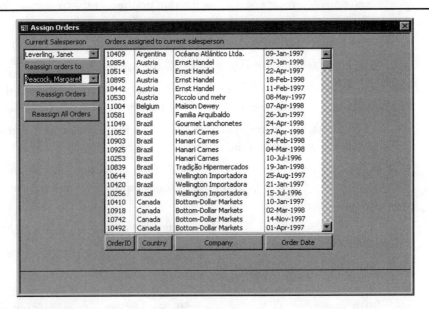

Using Transactions

A *transaction* is a group of changes that you want to treat as a single operation. When you define a transaction, the database engine keeps track of the changes made, storing the changes in a temporary database in memory until all of the transaction's changes have been made. (If enough memory isn't available, the engine creates the temporary database on your computer's hard disk.) If an error occurs while the group of changes is being processed, none of the changes are updated to the database. If an error does not occur, when the last change is made, the entire group of changes is updated to the current database.

Transactions are an important way to maintain the integrity of your data when you are making a series of changes to your data. For example, in an archive process, old records are appended to archive tables and then deleted from current tables. If a power failure occurs between the two queries, old records exist in both the archive and current tables. By running the queries inside a transaction, you can avoid this kind of data inconsistency.

Jet uses two kinds of transactions: implicit and explicit. When you run a single query either as a stored query or a SQL statement, Jet runs the query and makes all the necessary changes in a temporary database in memory as an *implicit transaction*. When all changes have been made, Jet updates the tables involved. If the power fails while a query is running, when you next open the database, Access may inform you that the database needs to be repaired. When you repair the database, Jet undoes any partial updates that may have occurred when the power failed. By contrast, when you want to run more than one query or several statements as a transaction, you must use statements that define an explicit transaction.

Chapter 6 describes ADO's Connection object as the data access object that manages transactions. You can use methods of the Connection object to begin and end a transaction, as follows:

- The `BeginTrans` method begins a new transaction.

- The `CommitTrans` method ends the current transaction and saves the changes to the database. It can also begin a new transaction.

- The `RollbackTrans` method ends the current transaction and restores the database to the state it was in when the transaction started.

To explore transactions, we'll modify one of the procedures for assigning orders from one employee to another. An important use of transactions is to give the user the option to undo the deletion of records.

Modify the `cmdAssignAll_Click` procedure that assigns all of an employee's orders to another employee as shown below.

```
Private Sub cmdAssignAll_Click()
    Dim cmd As New ADODB.Command
    Dim cnn As ADODB.Connection
    Dim varNumber As Variant, strSQL As String, str As String
    Dim msg As String
    If IsNull(cboCurrent) Or IsNull(cboNew) Then
        str = "You must select a current employee and another "
        str = str & "employee you want to reassign orders to."
        MsgBox str
        Exit Sub
    End If
    Set cnn = CurrentProject.Connection
    strSQL = "UPDATE Orders SET EmployeeID = " & cboNew
    strSQL = strSQL & " WHERE EmployeeID = " & cboCurrent
```

```
        cnn.BeginTrans
        cmd.ActiveConnection = cnn
        cmd.CommandText = strSQL
        cmd.Execute
        msg = "Are you sure you want to reassign these orders?"
        If MsgBox(msg, vbQuestion + vbYesNo) = vbYes Then
            cnn.CommitTrans
            cboCurrent = cboNew
            cboNew = Null
            lstOrders.Requery
        Else
            cnn.RollbackTrans
        End If
    End Sub
```

The modified procedure begins just before the statement that executes the SQL statement to update the records. Because of the cnn.BeginTrans statement, the changes required by the SQL statement are retained in memory and are not written to the database. The message box asks if you want to save the changes. If you click the Yes button, the CommitTrans method saves the changes to the database; otherwise, the RollbackTrans method discards the changes.

Save the form and switch to Form view. Select a current and a new salesperson and click the Reassign All Orders command button (see Figure 13.25). Click No to roll back the changes.

FIGURE 13.25:

Use methods of the Connection object to create a transaction and provide the user with the option to undo changes.

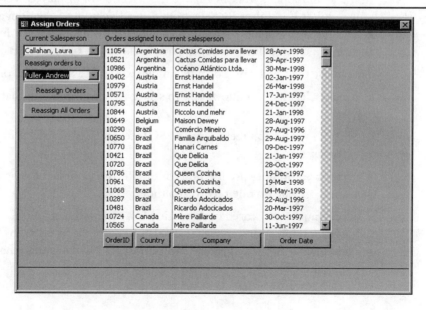

Summary

This chapter introduced many of the VBA techniques for working with groups of records using the forms approach and the recordset approach. The first half of the chapter explained techniques for sorting and selecting records to be displayed in a form or report. The second half discussed using stored queries and SQL statements to select groups of records in memory without necessarily displaying the results in a datasheet, form, or report. The important points follow.

- You can use the OrderBy and OrderByOn properties to sort the records of a form or report. However, using a variable to hold and build a sort string facilitates doing sorts with VBA procedures.

- You can open a form or report with selected records by using a parameter query as the record source; by using a procedure to set the RecordSource or the Filter property; and by running the `OpenForm`, `OpenReport`, or `ApplyFilter` methods.

- After a form is open, you can change the selection of displayed records by using the built-in Filter For, Filter By Selection, Filter Excluding Selection, and Filter By Form techniques; by using a procedure to change the RecordSource or Filter properties of the form; and by running the `OpenForm`, `OpenReport`, or `ApplyFilter` methods.

- You can use the Query By Form technique to create a simple custom search interface.

- The multiselect list box allows you to select records at random that satisfy a search condition.

- You can use navigation techniques or SQL techniques to work with a group of records in a recordset.

- Navigation techniques use methods of the Recordset object to navigate through the group and operate on one record at a time.

- SQL techniques use stored queries and SQL statements to define a selection or to define the modifications you want the database engine to make. SQL techniques rely on built-in code of the engine and are almost always faster than the corresponding navigation techniques.

- You can create new queries (stored or temporary) in VBA procedures by creating a Command object and then appending the new query to the Procedures or Views collection.

- You can run stored select queries by using the OpenQuery method when you want to display the results in a datasheet, or by using the Open method of the Recordset object when you just want to work with the results in memory. You can also use the Open method to run a SQL statement when you don't need to store the query or display the results.

- You can sort and filter a recordset using a SQL statement to define the sorted and filtered recordset or use the Sort and Filter properties of the Recordset object.

- You can run stored action queries by using the OpenQuery and Execute methods and run SQL statements for action queries using the RunSQL and Execute methods.

- The transaction methods, available only in VBA, allow you to run a set of queries or statements as a group.

CHAPTER 14

Creating and Modifying Database Objects

- Creating a new table programmatically

- Linking to an external table

- Creating a new form programmatically

- Creating a new event procedure programmatically

- Creating custom properties for a data access object

- Creating custom properties for a form or report

- Displaying multiple instances of a form

In most applications, you create the tables, queries, forms, data access pages, and reports interactively in their respective Design views as part of the application design process. In building the application, you also create the VBA procedures interactively to manipulate these existing objects when the user runs the application. Nevertheless, Access VBA provides techniques for creating and modifying most of the Database window objects programmatically.

This chapter shows you how to create and modify tables, queries, forms, data access pages, reports, and modules using VBA procedures. You will also learn how to create custom properties and methods for these objects.

The objects we'll be working with come from the two components of Access: the Access Application objects—including forms, reports, data access pages, and modules—and ADO's data access objects—including tables and queries. The object model for each component has a unique technique for creating and modifying its objects, as well as for creating custom properties and methods.

As it evolves in each version, Access VBA provides more object-oriented approaches to programming. The chapter ends with a discussion of one of these object-oriented features: the ability to define a form or report blueprint and generate multiple-form objects or report objects from the blueprint.

Understanding How Access and the Database Engine Create Objects

The Access application and the database engine are separate software applications working together in an intimate partnership that the interactive user is heedless of. As a user, you work directly with the Access application.

The internal programming of the Access application includes all the programming connections to the database engine. As you work with the Access interface—opening and closing tables, queries, forms, reports, macros, and modules—the database engine is working behind the scenes, creating and destroying objects in memory and saving some objects to the database file.

The objects that are included in the Access Application object model and the ADO model have predefined properties and methods, so you can manipulate the objects programmatically. The objects that are not included in an object model, such as macros, cannot be manipulated programmatically. With the Access application and the database engine running simultaneously, each with its own object model, it is easy to get confused about which application is producing the results you see on the screen. Let's review what happens as you work with the Access interface and note the programming objects that are created and destroyed automatically. (You may want to refer to the object models discussed in Chapter 6, " Understanding the ADO Object Model.")

In the ADO model, when you start Access, the database engine starts automatically and creates a new Connection object to represent the connection between Access and the database engine. This Connection object will be destroyed when you close the Access window. When you open an existing database, the engine creates a Catalog object to represent the current database displayed in the Access window. You can refer to the current database by instantiating a Catalog object and setting that object's Connection property to `CurrentProject.Connection`.

The database engine keeps track of the Database window objects you've created for the database using Access application objects. Each of the Database window objects is a member of a collection. These collection names are the same as object names, with an s added to the end.

Forms, reports, and data access pages do not contain data; they are windows into the data. They are used to see the data that is stored in data access objects—in Table objects, Procedure objects, and View objects. As has already been explained, queries are housed as either Procedure objects if they have parameters or as Views if they have no parameters. The database engine is responsible for the communication between the Database window objects and the data access objects.

The Database window displays panes for both the saved Database window objects and the data access objects. When you open and close these objects, Access and the database engine create and destroy temporary objects, as follows:

- For each table listed in the Tables pane, the engine stores a Table object. In an Access database, views and procedures are listed in the Queries pane. When you select and open one of these objects, the engine uses the instructions stored in the Table, View, or Procedure object to retrieve the stored data and create a Recordset object. Access then displays the Datasheet view as a visual representation of the Recordset object. When you close the table or query, the engine clears the recordset.

- For each form listed in the Forms pane and for each report listed in the Reports pane, Access stores a corresponding set of instructions in the database file. When you open a form, Access creates the Form object and adds it to the Forms collection, while the engine creates and opens any underlying recordsets required by the form, either as a record source or as the data sources for controls (such as row sources for combo boxes and list boxes). Access creates and displays the form visually and displays the data from the recordset in the form's controls. When you close the form, the corresponding

Form object is destroyed and any corresponding Recordset objects are cleared. A similar sequence occurs when you open a report.

- For each standard module and each independent class module not associated with a form or report listed in the Modules pane, Access stores a corresponding set of instructions in the database file. When you open a module listed in the Database window, Access displays the Module window and also creates a Module object, adding it to the Modules collection. When you close the module, the corresponding Module object is destroyed. If a form or report has a module, you can open the associated module, provided that the form or report is open. Access then processes the opening of these modules in the same manner as with the standard and independent class modules. When you close the form or report module, or when you close the form or report, the Module object for the associated module is destroyed.

- For each macro listed in the Macros pane, Access stores a corresponding set of instructions in the database file. When you open a macro, Access displays the Macro window but does not create a corresponding object that you can manipulate using a VBA procedure.

Thus, as you work with an open database, Access and the database engine create programming objects in memory that correspond to the physical objects displayed on the screen, as well as other programming objects that do not have visual representations. You can use VBA procedures to manipulate any of the available programming objects.

Using VBA, you can also create new objects (or instances) using any of the blueprints or definitions of object types (or classes) that Access and ADO make available. ADO and Access have their own techniques for creating new instances. The next two sections describe these techniques.

The Basic Elements and Features of Object-Oriented Programming

In object-oriented programming, similar objects are grouped into *classes* by definition. All the objects in a class share the same properties and methods. A specific object belonging to a class is called an *instance* of the class. There are four basic elements of an object-oriented programming system:

Abstraction The formation of a model for an object that includes those properties and methods relevant to its purpose and ignores other aspects

Encapsulation The packaging of the properties and methods as internal components of an object

Continued on next page

Inheritance The ability of objects in a child class to automatically reuse the properties and methods of their parent class

Polymorphism The ability of two or more classes to have methods that share the same name and purpose but have different instructions for implementation, such as the Requery methods for the DoCmd, Form, and Control objects

While Visual Basic is not truly an object-oriented programming language because it lacks inheritance, it does provide most of the features needed for object-oriented design, including the ability to create blueprints (class modules) for new objects (as instances of the class). In creating a definition for new objects, you can create custom properties (property procedures) and methods (public methods).

In Access VBA, form and report modules are class modules. With Access, you can create class modules that are independent of a form or report.

Creating Data Access Objects

Using VBA, you can perform the following tasks:

- Create and modify databases, tables, fields, and indexes.

- Create and modify relationships between the tables and even link tables from external databases.

- Create new queries to retrieve data from the database and to make bulk changes to it.

- Define new users and groups for security purposes.

All data access objects are created in a different way. With all, you must first instantiate an object variable. Then you either assign that object's properties and append it to its collection to create it, or you define it as a property of another existing object; alternately, you use a Create method to create the object. Table 14.1 lists the ways in which you create data access objects in VBA code.

TABLE 14.1: Methods for Creating Data Access Objects

Object	Method for Creating Another Object
Connection	Open method.
Catalog	Create method.
Table	Define the table's properties and append it to the Tables collection.

Continued on next page

TABLE 14.1 CONTINUED: Methods for Creating Data Access Objects

Object	Method for Creating Another Object
Field	Define the field's properties and append it to the Fields collection, or create the column at the same time you create a Table object.
Index	Define the index's properties and append it to the Indexes collection, or create the index at the same time you create a Table object.
Key	Define the key's properties and append it to the Keys collection, or create the key at the same time you create a Table object.
Command	Set the Command object's `CommandText` property.
Parameter	`CreateParameter` method of the Command object, or set the Parameter's properties and append it to the Parameters collection.
Recordset	`Open` method.
Column	Define the Column's properties and append it to the Columns collection.
Procedure	Create a command, then append the new procedure to the Procedures collection with the command as an argument of the **Append** method.
View	Create a command, then append the new view to the Views collection with the command as an argument of the **Append** method.
User	Define the user properties and append to the Users collection.
Group	Define the group properties and append to the Groups collection.

To remove a data access object from the database, you generally use the `Delete` method, either of the object or of its collection, to delete the object. Exceptions are the Connection, Catalog, and Command objects. To remove a Connection or Catalog object, you use the Connection object's `Close` method. There is no way to explicitly close a Command object. The Command object is removed when the connection to the data source closes.

In Chapter 11, "Navigating with Access VBA," you learned how to create and destroy Recordset objects, and in Chapter 13, "Working with Groups of Records Using Access VBA," you learned how to create and store new Procedure and View objects. See Chapter 6 for more information about creating the other types of data access objects.

To illustrate the steps for creating a new data access object in a VBA procedure, we'll create a table, complete with an index and a relationship to an existing table.

NOTE   For hands-on experience with the techniques described in this chapter, create a copy of the Northwind sample database named Northwind_Ch14 and work through the steps in the examples.

Using Navigational Techniques to Create Tables

There are two techniques for creating a table: the navigational technique and the SQL technique. This section demonstrates the navigational techniques for creating a new table, creating and adding an index, and creating a relationship between two tables in a database. We'll be using the Tables collection's Append method.

The arguments of an Append method correspond to the properties of the object you are creating. For most ADO and ADOX collection objects, the Append method has only one argument—the name of the object you are appending to the collection. For those Append methods with other arguments, they help define additional aspects of the objects being created. After you append an object, many of the properties become read-only and you can't change their settings. (If you do need to change a read-only property for an object, you'll need to delete the object and create another one.)

Using the *Append* Method of the Tables Collection

You use the Append method of the Tables collection to create a table in your database or to create a link to a table in an external database. You establish a link to a table in an external database in much the same way that you create a Table in the current database, except that you must also set additional provider-specific properties for the linked table. The format for creating a new Table object is as follows:

```
cat.ActiveConnection = cnn
Set tbl = New ADOX.Table
tbl.Name = tblname
tbl.ParentCatalog = cat
With tbl
    With .Columns
    .Append columnname1, type1, definedsize1
    .Append columnname2, type2, definedsize2
    ...
    .Append columnnameN, typeN, definedsizeN
    End With
End With
cat.Tables.Append tbl
```

where

- *cat* is an object variable of the Catalog type representing the catalog that will contain the new table.

- *cnn* is an object variable of the Connection type that represents the connection to the database that will contain the new table.

- *tbl* is an object variable of the Table type that represents the new table you are creating.

- *tblname* is a string expression that names the new table.

- *columnname* is a string variable that names a column in the new table.

- *type* is an optional long value that specifies the data type for the column. The default value is adVarWChar.

- *definedsize* is an optional long value that specifies the size of the column.

For example, to create a table named tblEmployeeExpenses with a single EmployeeName column in the current database, use the following:

```
cnn = CurrentProject.Connection
cat.ActiveConnection = cnn
Set tbl = New ADOX.Table
tbl.Name = "tblEmployeeExpenses"
tbl.ParentCatalog = cat
With tbl
    With .Columns
    .Append "EmployeeName"
    End With
End With
cat.Tables.Append tbl
```

NOTE   Before you can append a new Table object to the Tables collection, the Name property must be set, and the new table must have at least one Column object.

Linking to an External Table

In addition to creating a new table in the existing database, you can link to a table in an external database. Because most of the tables you will be linking to will be managed by Jet, the VBA code in this section has been tailored to Jet OLEDB databases.

The format for linking to an external table is as follows:

```
cat.ActiveConnection = cnn
Set tblLink = New ADOX.Table
tblLink.Name = tblname
tblLink.ParentCatalog = cat
With tblLink
    .Properties("Jet OLEDB:Create Link") = True
    .Properties("Jet OLEDB:Link Provider String") = strProvider
    .Properties("Jet OLEDB:Remote Table Name") = strTable
End With
cat.Tables.Append tblLink
```

where

- *cat* is an object variable of the catalog type representing the catalog that will contain the linked table.

- *cnn* is an object variable of the Connection type representing the connection between Access and the database that you are linking the table to.

- *tblLink* is an object variable of the Table type that represents the linked table.

- *tblname* is a string expression that names the linked table.

- *strProvider* is a string expression that is a valid ConnectionString and contains all the data necessary to connect to the external data source.

- *strTable* is a string expression and the name of the table as it is in the external data source.

For example, to link the Customers table from the Northwind database to the current database, you would use the following code:

```
cnn = CurrentProject.Connection
cat.ActiveConnection = cnn
Set tblLink = New ADOX.Table
tblLink.Name = "tblLinkedCustomers"
tblLink.ParentCatalog = cat
strProvider = "Provider=Microsoft.Jet.OLEDB.4.0; & Data Source = " _
    & "c:\VBAHandbook\Northwind.mdb"
With tblLink
    .Properties("Jet OLEDB:Create Link") = True
    .Properties("Jet OLEDB:Link Provider String") = strProvider
    .Properties("Jet OLEDB:Remote Table Name") = "Customers"
End With
cat.Tables.Append tblLink
```

Creating New Columns

After you create a table, you may decide to add a new column to those you created when you created the table. To do so, you first instantiate the Column object, then you assign its properties and append it to the table's Columns collection.

You must set the Column's name before appending it to its collection. When naming columns, remember that two columns in the table's Columns collection can't have the same name. By default, new columns are assigned the adVarWChar data type. If you want the Column to have any other data type, you can set this when you create the column. Once you append the column, however, the Type property becomes read-only.

Creating a Table

We'll create a new table for tracking employee expenses in the Northwind_Ch14 database. Open a new standard module named basNewTable and enter the NewTable procedure shown below.

```
Public Sub NewTable()
    Dim cat As New ADOX.Catalog
    Dim cnn As ADODB.Connection
    Dim tbl As New ADOX.Table
    Set cnn = CurrentProject.Connection
    cat.ActiveConnection = cnn
    Set tbl = New ADOX.Table
    With tbl
        tbl.Name = "tblEmployeeExpenses"
        With .Columns
            .Append "ExpenseID", adInteger
            .Append "EmployeeID", adLongVarWChar
            .Append "ExpenseType", adWChar, 30
            .Append "Amount", adCurrency
            With !ExpenseID
                Set .ParentCatalog = cat
                    .Properties("AutoIncrement") = True
                    .Properties("Seed") = CLng(1)
                    .Properties("Increment") = CLng(1)
            End With
        End With
    End With
    cat.Tables.Append tbl
    Set cat = Nothing
End Sub
```

This procedure adds a table to the current database named tblEmployeesExpenses. The procedure appends four fields—ExpenseID, EmployeeID, ExpenseType, and Amount—to the new table's Columns collection. With the table definition now complete, the procedure appends the new table to the Tables collection.

Run the NewTable procedure in the Immediate window. Click in the Database window and observe the new table. Figure 14.1 shows the new table in Design view.

NOTE You cannot designate an AutoNumber data type directly when you create a field because Jet does not recognize the AutoNumber data type. Instead, set the data type to adInteger and then set the field's application-defined AutoIncrement property to True. By default, when you create a new Column object in ADO the field the Column represents is required. If you want to change this, you have to set the Column's Attributes property to adColNullable.

FIGURE 14.1:

Use the Append method
of the Tables collection
to set up a new table and
the Append method of the
Columns collection to add
fields to the new table.

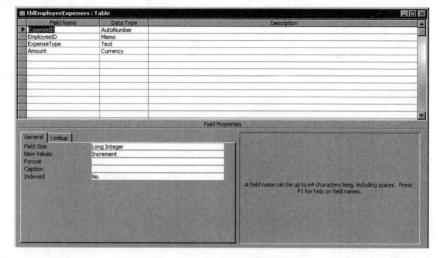

It is interesting to note that most of the field properties that you set in table Design view, such as Description, Caption, and InputMask, are not built-in properties of the Column object. Like AutoIncrement, these are Application-defined properties. You'll learn how to set these properties for a new field in the section "Adding Application-Defined Properties" later in this chapter.

Creating an Index

To create an Index on an existing table, you first append fields to an Index object's Columns collection, then append that Index object to the Indexes collection. You can set additional properties for the Index object, if you like, to supply values for optional properties or to change default settings for properties. The syntax for the Indexes collection's Append method is as follows:

```
Indexes.Append index, columns
```

where *index* is the name of the Index object to append or the variable representing the Index object and *columns* is an optional variant that specifies the names of the columns to be indexed.

NOTE   You can remove an index from a table using the Indexes collection's `Delete` method.

When you create a new index for a table, you must also create at least one field for the index. You use the Append method of the specific index you are creating to add a field to it. The syntax for appending fields to an index is the same as for appending fields to a table, except you substitute an Index object variable for the Table object variable.

When you append a field to the Index object's Columns collection, you are not adding a new field to the table; you are actually using the statement to create an index field based on an existing table field. After appending the index field to the Columns collection of the new index, append the new index to the table's Indexes collection.

As an example, we'll create a new primary index that contains the ExpenseID field for the tblEmployeeExpenses table we created in the previous section. Enter the NewIndex procedure shown below into the basNewTable module.

```
Public Sub NewIndex()
    Dim cnn As ADODB.Connection
    Dim cat As New ADOX.Catalog
    Dim tbl As ADOX.Table
    Dim idx As ADOX.Index
    Set cnn = CurrentProject.Connection
    cat.ActiveConnection = cnn
    Set tbl = cat.Tables!tblEmployeeExpenses
    Set idx = New ADOX.Index
    With idx
        .Name = "Primary"
        .IndexNulls = adIndexNullsDisallow
        .Columns.Append "ExpenseID"
        .PrimaryKey = True
    End With
    tbl.Indexes.Append idx
    Set cat = Nothing
End Sub
```

The procedure creates an index named Primary for the tblEmployeeExpenses table and appends a new field to the index's Columns collection based on the ExpenseID table field. The procedure then sets the PrimaryKey property to True and appends the new index to the Indexes collection of the table.

Run the NewIndex procedure in the Immediate window. Open the tblEmployeeExpenses table in Design view and observe that ExpenseID is now the primary key (see Figure 14.2).

The Primary, Unique, and IgnoreNulls properties that you can set in Design view are also properties of the Index object, so you can set them in a VBA procedure. To declare the index as the Primary index for the table, you set the index's PrimaryKey property to True after you append the columns to the index's Columns collection. To specify that the values in the index field must be unique, you set the index's Unique property to True. You can control how the database engine handles Null values in the index by setting the index's IndexNulls property to one of its available options: adIndexNullsAllow, adIndexNullsDisallow, adIndexNullsIgnore, or adIndexNullsIgnoreAny.

FIGURE 14.2:

Use Append methods to create an index based on an existing table field.

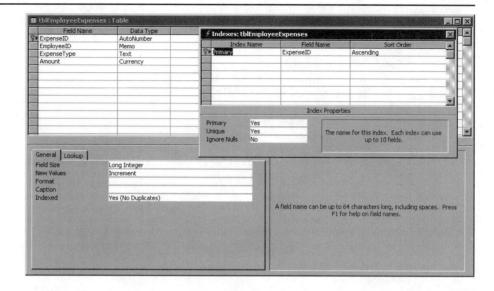

In addition to the properties listed in Design view, Jet defines other properties of the Index object and the children of the Index object (see Chapter 6 for more information). For example, the order of records returned depends on the SortOrder property of each field in the index. By default, the index field is sorted in ascending order, but you can set the SortOrder property to the intrinsic constant adSortDescending to sort the field in descending order.

Creating a Key

You create a key in much the same way that you create an index. First, you append fields to the key's Columns collection, then you append the Key object to the table's Keys collection. The syntax for the Keys collection's Append method is as follows:

```
Keys.Append key, keytype, column, relatedtable, relatedcolumn
```

where

- *key* is the name of the Key object to append or the variable representing the Key object.

- *keytype* is an optional value that can be set to one of these intrinsic constants: adKeyPrimary, adKeyForeign, adKeyUnique. The default setting is adKeyPrimary.

- *column* is an optional string value that is the name of the column to be indexed.

- *relatedtable* is an optional string value that is the name of the related table.

- *relatedcolumn* is an optional string value that is the name of the related column. You use this argument only when you set the keytype argument to adKeyForeign.

To illustrate, delete the index we created in the last section, then save and close the table. Insert the NewKey procedure shown below into the basNewTable module, and run it in the Immediate window.

```
Public Sub NewKey()
    Dim cnn As ADODB.Connection
    Dim cat As New ADOX.Catalog
    Dim tbl As ADOX.Table
    Dim key1 As ADOX.Key
    Set cnn = CurrentProject.Connection
    cat.ActiveConnection = cnn
    Set tbl = cat.Tables!tblEmployeeExpenses
    Set key1 = New ADOX.Key
    With key1
        .Name = "Primary"
        .Columns.Append "ExpenseID"
    End With
    tbl.Keys.Append key1, adKeyPrimary
    Set cat = Nothing
End Sub
```

Open the tblEmployeeExpenses table in Design view, and note that the primary key is set for the table. Close the table.

Using SQL Techniques to Create Tables

When you use SQL techniques to create objects, you create data-definition queries that can be run by VBA procedures. As explained in Chapter 13, a data-definition query is a SQL-specific query (data-definition queries begin with one of the SQL commands listed in Table 13.5, in Chapter 13). Use the data-definition queries to create tables and indexes, to modify tables by adding or removing columns, and to modify tables by adding or removing an index. You can save a data-definition query as a stored query, or you can run the SQL statement directly using the same techniques for running an action query or SQL statement in a VBA procedure.

Creating a Table

The syntax for a data-definition query that creates a table is as follows:

```
CREATE TABLE tablename (field1 type (size), field2 type (size), ...)
```

where

- *tablename* is the name of the table to be created.

- *field1, field2, ...* are the names of the fields you are creating with the statement (you must create at least one field).

- *type* is the data type for the new field.

- *size* is the field size in characters (you specify the size only for text and binary fields).

You can also include CONSTRAINT clauses to define one or more indexes at the same time that you define the new table.

The SQLNewTable procedure shown below creates the tblEmployeeExpenses table. The procedure executes the SQL statement for a data-definition query that uses the CREATE TABLE command to create a table containing four fields.

```
Public Sub SQLNewTable()
    Dim cnn As ADODB.Connection
    Dim strSQL As String
    strSQL = "CREATE TABLE tblEmployeeExpenses "
    strSQL = strSQL & "(ExpenseID COUNTER, EmployeeID LONG, " _
        & "ExpenseType TEXT(30), Amount CURRENCY);"
    Set cnn = CurrentProject.Connection
    cnn.Execute strSQL
    RefreshDatabaseWindow
End Sub
```

Access SQL has the COUNTER data type, so you can create an AutoNumber field directly. (In contrast, when you use navigational techniques, you create an adInteger field and set its AutoIncrement property to True to increment the field's value for new records.)

Modifying a Field

You can use the ALTER TABLE command to add or drop a single field or add or drop a single index from an existing table. The ALTER TABLE data-definition query to add or drop a field has this syntax:

```
ALTER TABLE tablename {ADD COLUMN field type (size) | DROP COLUMN field}
```

The *tablename*, *field*, *type*, and *size* arguments are the same as those for the CREATE TABLE query.

To modify a field, you must first delete it and then add a new field of the same name. The SQLModifyTable procedure modifies the ExpenseType field to increase its field size from 30 to 40 characters.

```
Public Sub SQLModifyTable()
    Dim cnn As ADODB.Connection
    Dim strDROP As String, strADD As String
    strDROP = "ALTER TABLE tblEmployeeExpenses "
    strDROP = strDROP & "DROP COLUMN ExpenseType;"
    strADD = "ALTER TABLE tblEmployeeExpenses "
    strADD = strADD & "ADD COLUMN ExpenseType TEXT (40);"
    Set cnn = CurrentProject.Connection
```

```
        cnn.Execute strDROP
        cnn.Execute strADD
End Sub
```

WARNING Deleting a column in a table will remove any data you have stored in that column. You should be absolutely certain you don't need that data before deleting the column. It's also a good idea to create a backup of the table before you delete a column, just in case you need the data later.

Creating an Index

There are three ways to create an index for a table:

- Use the CREATE TABLE command when you create the table.
- Use the ALTER TABLE command to add a field to an existing table.
- Use the CREATE INDEX command to add a field to an existing table.

The three techniques do not have the same result. If you want to define relationships and enforce referential integrity, you must use either the CREATE TABLE or ALTER TABLE commands.

The CREATE INDEX data-definition query has this syntax:

```
CREATE [UNIQUE] INDEX indexname ON tablename (field1 [ASC|DESC], field2 [ASC |
DESC], …) [WITH {PRIMARY | DISALLOW NULL | IGNORE NULL}]
```

where

- *indexname* is the name of the index you are creating.
- *field1*, *field2*, … are the names of the fields you are creating the index on.
- The UNIQUE keyword prohibits duplicate values in the indexed field or fields.
- The PRIMARY keyword specifies the indexed field or fields as the primary key for the table.
- The DISALLOW NULL option prohibits Null entries in the indexed field or fields of new records.
- The IGNORE NULL option prevents records with Null values in the indexed field or fields from being included in the index. (Recall that the index is a separate table that Jet creates and uses for finding records; by setting this option, the index is smaller and the search is faster.)

The SQLCreateIndex procedure, shown below, uses the CREATE INDEX command to add an index to the ExpenseType field and specifies the WITH DISALLOW NULL clause to require an entry in the field.

```
Public Sub SQLCreateIndex()
    Dim cnn As ADODB.Connection
    Dim strIndex As String
    strIndex = "CREATE INDEX IndexExpenseType ON tblEmployeeExpenses "
    strIndex = strIndex & "(ExpenseType) WITH DISALLOW NULL;"
    Set cnn = CurrentProject.Connection
    cnn.Execute strIndex
End Sub
```

Using Data-Definition Queries

To explore the SQL techniques for creating a table, follow these steps:

1. Delete the tblEmployeeExpenses table.

2. Insert the SQLNewTable, SQLModifyTable, and SQLCreateIndex procedures, presented in the preceding sections, in the basNewTable module.

3. Run the three procedures in the Immediate window in the order listed in step 2.

4. Open the new tblEmployeeExpenses table in Design view. Observe the change in the size of the ExpenseType field and the new index (see Figure 14.3).

FIGURE 14.3:

Use data-definition queries to create a table, modify a field, and create an index.

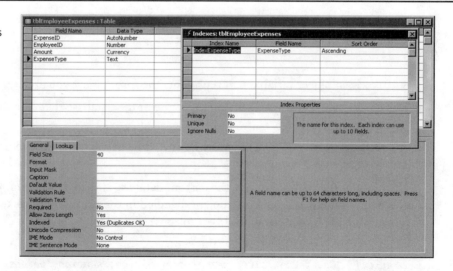

Creating Forms, Reports, and Controls

Access VBA provides a set of functions for creating forms, reports, and controls. These functions are particularly useful when you are creating a custom wizard that builds a new form or report according to the user's specifications gathered in wizard screens. Table 14.2 lists the built-in Access functions used to create forms, reports, controls, and report group levels and the statements for deleting controls. You can think of these functions and statements as methods of the Application object.

TABLE 14.2: Access Functions and Statements for Working with Forms and Reports

Function or Statement	Description
CreateForm, CreateReport	Create a form or report, open the new form or report in a minimized state in Design view, and return a Form or Report object.
CreateControl, CreateReportControl	Create a control on a specified form or report and return a Control object.
DeleteControl, DeleteReportControl	Remove a specified control from a form or report. The form or report must be currently open in Design view.
CreateGroupLevel	Creates a group or sort on a specified field or expression in a report. This function groups or sorts the data and creates a header and/or footer for the group level. The report must be currently open in Design view.

The CreateForm function creates a minimized form in Design view using this syntax:

```
Set frm = CreateForm(database, formtemplate)
```

where

- *frm* is an object variable that represents the form object you are creating.

- *database* is a string identifying the name of the database that contains the form template you are using.

- *formtemplate* is a string identifying the name of the form you are using as a template to define the new form.

If you omit the first argument, the current database is used; if you omit the second argument, the form is based on the template specified in the Forms/Reports tab of the Options dialog (available by choosing Tools ➢ Options).

The CreateControl function has this syntax:

```
Set ctl = CreateControl(formname, controltype, section, parent, columnname,
left, top, width, height)
```

where

- *ctl* is an object variable that represents the Control object you are creating.

- *formname* is a string identifying the name of the open form to which you are adding the new control.

- *controltype* is an intrinsic constant identifying the new control's type.

- *section* is an intrinsic constant specifying the form section that will contain the new control.

- *parent* is a string identifying the name of the parent control for a label, check box, option button, or toggle button control. (If the control you are creating does not have a parent control, use a zero-length string for this argument.)

- *columnname* is the name of the field that the control will be bound to. (If you are creating an unbound control, use a zero-length string for this argument.)

- *left* and *top* are numeric expressions in twips indicating the coordinates of the upper-left corner of the control you are creating.

- *width* and *height* are numeric expressions in twips indicating the width and height of the control.

The DeleteControl statement has this syntax:

```
DeleteControl formname, controlname
```

formname is a string expression identifying the form containing the control, and *controlname* is a string expression specifying the control you want to delete.

The NewForm procedure, shown below, uses the CreateForm and CreateControl functions to create objects and the DeleteControl statement to delete one of the new controls.

```
Public Sub NewForm()
    Dim cnn As ADODB.Connection
    Dim cat As New ADOX.Catalog
    Dim frm As Form
    Dim lbl As Label, txt As TextBox, cmd As CommandButton
    Dim top As Integer, var As Variant
    Set cnn = CurrentProject.Connection
    cat.ActiveConnection = cnn
    Set frm = CreateForm
    With frm
        .RecordSource = "Shippers"
        .Width = 2.5
```

```
        End With
        top = 100
        For Each var In cat.Tables("Shippers").Columns
            Set lbl = CreateControl(frm.Name, acLabel, _
                acDetail, , , 300, top, 1500, 230)
            Set txt = CreateControl(frm.Name, acTextBox, _
                acDetail, , , 1600, top, 1500, 230)
            lbl.Caption = var.Name
            txt.ControlSource = var.Name
            top = top + 400
        Next
        Set cmd = CreateControl(frm.Name, acCommandButton, _
                acDetail, , , 2000, top)
        cmd.Caption = "Push me!"
        cmd.Name = "cmdPush"
        cmd.SizeToFit
        ' Insert modification here
        With DoCmd
            .Restore
            .OpenForm frm.Name
            .RunCommand acCmdSizeToFitForm
        End With
        SendKeys "frmNewForm", False
        SendKeys "{Enter}", False
        RunCommand acCmdSaveAs
    End Sub
```

This procedure creates a new minimized form bound to the Shippers table and initializes the top variable to 100 twips (top is the distance in twips between the top of the form and the top of the next label/text box pair to be created). The procedure loops through the fields of the Shippers table. For each field in the table, the procedure uses the CreateControl function to create label and text box controls and sets the label's Caption property and the text box's ControlSource property to the name of the field. The procedure increases the top variable by 400 twips so that the next label/text box pair is located 400 twips below the previous pair. The procedure also creates a command button. After creating the controls, the procedure restores the form, uses the OpenForm method to switch to Form view, and then runs the built-in command to size the form. The procedure saves the form as frmNewForm.

To test the NewForm procedure, create a new module named basNewForm and insert the procedure in the new module. Run the procedure in the Immediate window. The new form is shown in Figure 14.4.

FIGURE 14.4:

Use the CreateForm and CreateControl functions to create a form in a VBA procedure.

TIP When you run the Save As command in a procedure using the statement RunCommand acCmdSaveAs, Access displays the Save As dialog and pauses until you enter the name of the new object and click OK or press Enter. You can use the SendKeys statement to send the keystrokes for the name and for closing the dialog. When you use the SendKeys statement before running the Save As command, Access stores the keystrokes in a buffer until needed by the Save As dialog. Set the Wait argument to False to return control to the procedure immediately after sending the keystrokes.

Creating Modules and Event Procedures

Access provides a Module object together with properties and methods so that you can define new modules and modify existing modules programmatically. You can use the Module property of the form to create form modules. The syntax to create a module and return a reference to the new module is as follows:

```
Set mdl = frm.Module
```

mdl is an object variable of the Module type, and *frm* refers to the form.

You can use the CreateEventProc method of the module object to define a new event procedure in an existing module. The CreateEventProc method creates the code template for an event procedure for a specified event, as well as a specified object, and returns the line number of the first line of the event procedure. The syntax of the method is as follows:

```
lngReturn = mdl.CreateEventProc(eventname, objectname)
```

where

- *lngReturn* is a variable that represents the line number of the first line of the event procedure.

- *mdl* is an object variable of the Module type.

- *eventname* is a string expression indicating the name of an event.

- *objectname* is a string expression specifying the name of an object.

After creating the code template, use the InsertLines method of the Module object to insert the text for the event procedure. The syntax for the InsertLines method is as follows:

```
mdl.InsertLines line, string
```

mdl is a string variable representing the Module object, *line* is the number of the line where you want to start inserting code (the existing code moves down), and *string* is the text that you want to insert in the procedure. To add multiple lines of code, use the intrinsic constant vbCrLf to break a line and start a new line (the vbCrLf constant is equivalent to pressing Enter at the end of a line of code), and use the intrinsic constant vbTab to insert a tab.

To demonstrate creating a module and event procedure, we will modify the NewForm procedure presented in the previous section. The modified procedure displays a message asking whether to delete the Command button. If the user clicks Yes, the event procedure switches the form to Design view, deletes the Command button, and switches back to Form view.

Close the frmNewForm form. Select frmNewForm in the Database window and press Delete to delete the form. Next, insert the following lines of code in the NewForm procedure at the line marked with the ' Insert modification here comment.

```
Dim mdl As Module, lngReturn As Long, str As String
' Create a form module and return a reference to the module
Set mdl = frm.Module
' Create an event procedure for the command button's Click event
lngReturn = mdl.CreateEventProc("Click", "cmdPush")
str = "Dim intResponse as Integer" & vbCrLf
str = str & "intResponse = MsgBox(""Do you want to delete the " _
    & "command button?"",vbYesNo)" & vbCrLf
str = str & "If intResponse = vbYes Then" & vbCrLf
str = str & vbTab & "DoCmd.OpenForm Me.Name, acDesign" & vbCrLf
str = str & vbTab & "DeleteControl ""frmNewForm"", ""cmdPush""" _
    & vbCrLf
str = str & vbTab & "DoCmd.OpenForm ""frmNewForm""" & vbCrLf
str = str & "End If"
mdl.InsertLines lngReturn + 1, str
```

The modification declares the variables needed for the new code, creates the new form module, and inserts the code template for the new cmdPush_Click event procedure. The procedure builds the string expression for the lines of the event procedure. Several lines of the code require embedding a string within a string; the procedure uses pairs of double quotation marks to mark the beginning and the end of each string within the string expression. After building the str variable containing the text for the event procedure, the procedure uses the module's InsertLines method to insert the text starting at the line following the first line of the code template.

Run the modified `NewForm` procedure in the Immediate window. The procedure creates the frmNewForm form and the form module with the event procedure (see Figure 14.5). Click the Push Me button on the new form and then click Yes. The event procedure deletes the command button and displays the form without the command button.

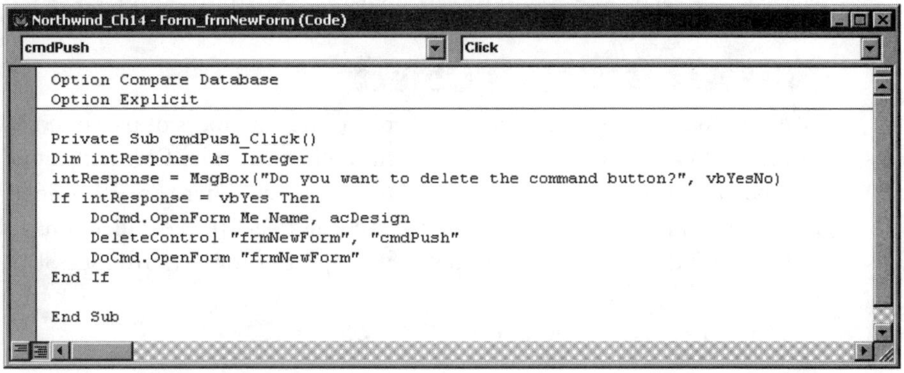

FIGURE 14.5:

Use the `CreateEvent-Proc` method to create an event procedure and the `InsertLines` method to insert the code for the procedure.

```
Northwind_Ch14 - Form_frmNewForm (Code)
cmdPush                                    Click

Option Compare Database
Option Explicit

Private Sub cmdPush_Click()
Dim intResponse As Integer
intResponse = MsgBox("Do you want to delete the command button?", vbYesNo)
If intResponse = vbYes Then
    DoCmd.OpenForm Me.Name, acDesign
    DeleteControl "frmNewForm", "cmdPush"
    DoCmd.OpenForm "frmNewForm"
End If

End Sub
```

Deleting a Database Window Object

You use the `DeleteObject` method of the DoCmd object to delete a Database window object. The syntax is as follows:

```
DoCmd.DeleteObject objecttype, objectname
```

objecttype is an optional intrinsic constant indicating the type of the object you want to delete, and *objectname* is an optional string expression indicating the name of the object. To delete an object selected in the Database window, you can omit both arguments. If neither argument is set, Access deletes the selected object in the Database window. You can use the DoCmd object's `SelectObject` method to select an object in the Database window.

For example, to delete the frmNewForm form, close the frmNewForm form. Then type **DoCmd.DeleteObject acForm, "frmNewForm"** in the Immediate window and press Enter.

Creating Custom Properties

All Access Application objects and data access objects have built-in properties that describe their characteristics. Each object has a Properties collection containing its built-in properties. Throughout this book, you have learned how to read property settings and how to set the values of read/write properties. You can't change or delete the built-in properties themselves; you can only change or delete their values. Much of the object manipulation you've learned about involves setting property values. There are times when it is convenient to customize objects by creating your own custom properties. For example, you may want to create a procedure for a form that disables certain controls on the form when a particular criterion is met. You can have the procedure check each control's Tag property for a particular value, and run if the Tag property contains that value. If you are using the Tag property for some other purpose, however, you may wish to create a custom property to use in the same way that you use the Tag property. In the following sections, you'll learn techniques for creating properties for data access objects and Access Application objects.

The AccessObject Object

As you have already learned, most objects are members of parent collections. A Form object, for example, is a member of the Forms collection. The Form object is also one of an unusual type of object known as the AccessObject object. There are 10 collections of AccessObject objects, as listed in Table 14.3. Each AccessObject in the collections has a Properties collection, which contains the user-defined properties for that instance of an object.

TABLE 14.3: Categories of AccessObject Objects

Collection Name	Contains
AllForms	All saved forms in the database
AllReports	All saved reports in the database
AllDataAccessPages	All saved data access pages in the database
AllMacros	All saved macros in the database
AllModules	All saved modules in the database
AllTables	All tables in the database
AllQueries	All queries in an MDB database
AllViews	All views in an ADP project
AllStoredProcedures	All stored procedures in an ADP project
AllDatabaseDiagrams	All database diagrams in an ADP project

AllForms, AllReports, AllDataAccessPages, AllMacros, and AllModules are children of the CurrentProject object, which in turn is a child of the Application object. AllTables, AllQueries, AllViews, AllStoredProcedures, and AllDatabaseDiagrams are the children of the CurrentData object, which is also a child of the Application object. In referring to these collections, you use the following syntax:

```
CurrentProject.collectionname
```

or

```
CurrentData.collectionname
```

These collections make referring to their member objects easier than using traditional ADO code, but are also limited in their usefulness. Each AccessObject has the properties listed in Table 14.4.

TABLE 14.4: Properties of the AccessObject Object

Property	Access	Data Type	Description
CurrentView	Read-only	Enum constant	Determines whether the form or data access page is in Design view, Form/Page view, or Datasheet view
DateCreated	Read-only	Date	Indicates the date and time the object was created
DateModified	Read-only	Date	Indicates the date and time the object was last modified
FullName	Read/write	String	Returns or sets the full path of the object, including the directory path
IsLoaded	Read-only	Boolean	Used to determine whether the object is currently open
Name	Read-only	String	Identifies the name of the object
Parent	Read-only	Object	Refers to the object's Parent object
Properties	Read-only	Object	Refers to the custom properties of the object, as represented by the child AccessObjectProperties collection
Type	Read-only	Enum constant	Returns the AccessObject's object type

Each AccessObject object has an AccessObjectProperties collection object, sometimes just referred to as Properties, a collection object that stores custom properties for the object. Each AccessObjectProperty in the AccessObjectProperties collection object itself has two properties: Name and Value. Name is a read-only string expression that returns the name of the property, and Value is a read/write Variant expression that, not surprisingly, returns the value of the property. The AccessObjectProperties collection object has the properties listed in Table 14.5.

TABLE 14.5: Properties of the AccessObjectProperties collection object

Property	Access	Data Type	Description
Application	Read-only	Object	Refers to the Application object
Count	Read-only	Long integer	Returns the number of properties in the collection
Item	Read-only	Object	Refers to one of the collection's member objects
Parent	Read-only	Object	Refers to the parent AccessObject

In addition to these properties, each AccessObjectProperties collection object has two methods—Add and Remove—that are used to add and remove properties from the collection. The syntax for the Add and Remove methods is as follows:

```
collection.Add propertyname, value
collection.Remove item
```

where *collection* is a reference to the AccessObjectProperties collection object, *propertyname* is a string expression that is the name of the AccessObjectProperty object you wish to add, and *value* is a variant expression that sets the value of the property. *item* is either a numeric expression that evaluates to the object's position in the collection, or a string expression that is the name of the object.

Creating a User-Defined Property

As an example, we'll create an all-purpose Notepad property for the Customers form. When you create a user-defined property, you must specify a property name and an initial value before you can add the property to the Properties collection. We'll call the new property FormNotes and set the initial value to "First Note".

The FormNotepad procedure creates the new property.

```
Public Sub FormNotepad()
    With CurrentProject.AllForms("Customers").Properties
        .Add "FormNotes", "Note"
    End With
End Sub
```

To test the FormNotepad procedure, create a new module named basProperties and enter the procedure. Then make sure the Customers form is closed and run the FormNotepad procedure in the Immediate window. When you run the FormNotepad procedure, the FormNotes property is created, is saved to the disk, and becomes a permanent property of the form. New, user-defined properties do not appear in property sheets, so you can't set them interactively.

Referring to a User-Defined Property

When you refer to a user-defined property in a procedure, you must include an explicit reference to the Properties collection, and you must use either the property's name in the syntax or its position in the collection. You can use any of the following expressions:

```
object.Properties!propertyname
object.Properties("propertyname")
object.Properties(indexnumber)
```

NOTE   When referring to a user-defined property, you cannot use the abbreviated *object.propertyname* syntax.

For example, to refer to the FormNotes property of the Customers form, enter the following in the Immediate window:

- Type **?CurrentProject.AllForms("Customers").Properties("FormNotes").Value** and press Enter. The Immediate window prints "Note."

- Type **CurrentProject.AllForms("Customers").Properties!FormNotes.Value = "Change notes"** and press Enter. The value of the custom FormNotes property is changed.

- Type **?CurrentProject.AllForms("Customers").Properties(0).Value** and press Enter. The Immediate window prints "Change notes." Since FormNotes is the first user-defined property of the form, and the Properties collection uses zero-based indexing, `Properties(0)` refers to the FormNotes property.

Deleting a User-Defined Property

You can delete a user-defined property by running the `Remove` method of the Properties collection of the AccessObject object. For example, delete the custom FormNotes property for the Customers form by typing **CurrentProject.AllForms("Customers").Properties .Remove "FormNotes"** in the Immediate window and pressing Enter. The custom FormNotes property is deleted.

To confirm the deletion, type **CurrentProject.AllForms("Customers").Properties! FormNotes.Value = "Change notes"** and press Enter. An error is generated because the Tag property no longer exists (see Figure 14.6).

FIGURE 14.6:

This error message appears when you refer to a user-defined property that doesn't exist.

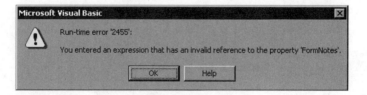

Adding Application-Defined Properties

The application-defined property is a special kind of user-defined property. As explained in Chapter 6, when an application such as Access defines a property for a data access object, the property is called an application-defined property. The database engine doesn't automatically recognize application-defined properties. Table 14.6 lists examples of application-defined properties that Access defines.

TABLE 14.6: Access Application-Defined Properties

Object	Access-Defined Properties
Database	AppTitle, StartupShowDBWindow, StartupShowStatusBar, AllowShortcutMenus, AllowFullMenus, AllowBuiltInToolbars, AllowToolbarChanges, AllowBreakIntoCode, AllowSpecialKeys, Replicable, ReplicationConflictFunction
Table	DatasheetFontHeight, DatasheetFontName, Description, FrozenColumns, RowHeight, ShowGrid
Field	Caption, DecimalPlaces, ColumnHidden, Description, ColumnOrder, Format, ColumnWidth, InputMask

There are two ways to have the database engine recognize an application-defined property:

- Set the property's value for the first time in the user interface.
- Set the property's value for the first time in VBA code.

Setting Startup Options Programmatically

An important application-defined property that cannot be set in the interface and must be set for the first time in VBA code is the AllowBypassKey property of the Database. The Allow-BypassKey property allows you to determine whether the user can bypass the startup options and the AutoExec startup macro you have set for your application. When AllowBypassKey has the value True (the default value), pressing the Shift key on startup bypasses the startup condition. When the AllowBypassKey has the value False, the effect of pressing the Shift key on startup is disabled. This property is not available in the Startup dialog.

You can use the SetByPass procedure to set the value of the AllowBypassKey property.

```
Public Sub SetByPass(booByPass As Boolean)
    Dim db As Object, prp As Object
    On Error GoTo Error_SetByPass
    Set db = CurrentDb
    db.Properties!AllowBypassKey = booByPass

Exit_SetByPass:
    Exit Sub

Error_SetByPass:
    If Err = 3270 Then
    ' The property does not exist and needs to be created
        Set prp = db.CreateProperty("AllowBypassKey")
        prp.Type = DB_BOOLEAN
        prp.Value = booByPass
        db.Properties.Append prp
        Resume Next
```

```
        Else
            msgbox Err.Number & Err.Description
            Resume Exit_SetByPass
        End If
    End Sub
```

This procedure uses error handling to determine if the property has already been appended to the Properties collection. This procedure is an example of generating an error deliberately as part of the logic of the procedure.

The SetByPass procedure begins by attempting to set the AllowBypassKey property. If the property has already been added to the database, the statement to assign the property value is executed and the procedure ends. If the property has not been added to the database, the assignment statement fails, the error (code 3270) is generated, and the error-handling code takes over. The error-handling code creates the property, sets its value, and appends the property to the Properties collection of the database.

To use the procedure, call the procedure and specify the argument as False (if you want to disable the Shift key as a bypass of the startup conditions) or as True (if you want to enable the Shift key as a bypass). Follow these steps to test the procedure:

1. Enter the SetBypass procedure in the basProperties module.

2. Switch to the Database window, choose Tools ➢ Startup, and set the Application Title to Testing the ByPass. Click OK. The title bar displays the new title.

3. To disable the bypass effect of the Shift key on startup, type **SetByPass(False)** in the Immediate window and press Enter. The AllowBypassKey property has been added to the database and the effect of the Shift key on startup has been disabled.

4. Close the database. Press the Shift key and start up the database; the title bar continues to display "Testing the ByPass." Enable the bypass effect of the Shift key on startup by typing **SetByPass(True)** in the Immediate window and pressing Enter. This time, when you close the database and press the Shift key while starting up the database, the startup options are disabled and the title bar displays "Microsoft Access."

Creating Custom Properties for Forms, Reports, and Controls

In addition to creating custom properties programmatically for forms, reports, and controls, there are two other ways you can create custom properties for these Access Application objects. The simplest way to create a custom property for a form, report, or control is to use the Tag property. The second way, available only for forms and reports, is to use property procedures. The following sections describe both techniques.

Using the Tag Property

Forms, form sections, reports, report sections, and controls all have a Tag property, which you can use to store a string expression. The default setting is the zero-length string (""), but you can store any string expression up to 2048 characters in length. The Tag property can be set in the property sheet or in a VBA procedure.

We used a form's Tag property in Chapter 9, " Controlling Execution," to keep track of how a form was opened. If the form was opened by clicking a button on a form other than the Main Switchboard, we stored the name of the form with the opener button. Procedures for closing the form used the Tag property to decide which form to unhide. In those examples, we used the Tag property as a custom FormOpener property.

Creating Property Procedures

Chapter 7, " Writing Procedures," introduced the three kinds of procedures: function procedures, sub procedures, and property procedures. You use property procedures to create custom properties for forms and reports and for the new objects you create using independent class modules.

Property procedures normally come in pairs: A `Property Let` procedure creates a property whose value you can assign, and a `Property Get` procedure creates a property whose value you can read.

NOTE   When you create a custom property that you set by referring to an object instead of by assigning a value, use a `Property Set` procedure to create the property that you set and a `Property Get` procedure to create a property that returns a reference to an object. These custom properties are analogous to the Form, Report, RecordsetClone, and Module properties that return objects instead of values.

Creating a *Property Let* Procedure

To create a custom property for a form or report, you use the `Property Let` statement to create a property procedure in the form's or report's module. In the simplest case, the syntax is as follows:

```
Public Property Let propertyname (propertyvalue As datatype)
     [statements]
End Property
```

propertyname is the name of the custom property you want to create, and *propertyvalue* represents the value of the custom property. When the object is defined using an independent class module, you create the `Property Let` procedure in the module.

You run a `Property Let` procedure by including the procedure name as a property in an assignment statement that assigns a value to the property. For example, the `LockedForm` `Property Let` procedure runs whenever you set the value using an assignment statement such as this:

```
Forms!Suppliers.LockedForm = True
```

Normally, you create the property procedure as a public procedure stored in the form's module. If you want the custom property to behave like a built-in form property, it must be public so that it can be called from procedures in other modules.

NOTE A form's custom property does not appear in the form's property sheet, so you can't set a custom property in design mode. You can, however, set the property in a VBA procedure (if it is a public procedure).

As an example, we'll create LockedForm as a custom property for the Suppliers form. We'll create the property so that when we set the value of the LockedForm property to True, the data controls on the form are locked; when we set the value of the LockedForm property to False, the data controls on the form are unlocked. (For simplicity, the procedure locks only text box controls, but you can modify the procedure to lock or unlock any type of data control.) The `Property Let LockedForm` procedure is shown below.

```
Public Property Let LockedForm(booLock As Boolean)
    Dim ctl As Control
    Select Case booLock
    Case True
        If Me.Dirty = True Then
            RunCommand acCmdSaveRecord
        End If
        For Each ctl In Me
            If TypeOf ctl Is TextBox Then ctl.Locked = True
        Next
    Case False
        For Each ctl In Me
            If TypeOf ctl Is TextBox Then ctl.Locked = False
        Next
    End Select
End Property
```

The value of the property is passed as an argument to the procedure. The procedure determines if the value is True or False. In either case, the procedure uses a `For Each…Next` structure to loop through the controls on the form. We can refer to the Controls collection as

`Me.Controls` or simply as `Me` because the Controls collection is the default collection of the form. When you set the LockedForm property to True, the property procedure first tests to determine if there are any unsaved changes to the records, saves the changes if there are any, and then locks all of the text box controls. When you set the LockedForm property to False, the procedure unlocks the controls.

To test the procedure, follow these steps:

1. Select the Suppliers form in the Database window and click the Code button in the toolbar.

2. Choose Insert ➤ Procedure. Type **LockedForm** in the Name field and select the Property option in the Type section of the Add Procedure dialog (see Figure 14.7a). VBA automatically inserts code templates for both the `Property Get` and `Property Let` procedures (see Figure 14.7b).

FIGURE 14.7:

Create a custom form property by inserting property procedures (a). VBA creates a pair of code templates for the new `Property Get` and `Property Let` procedures (b).

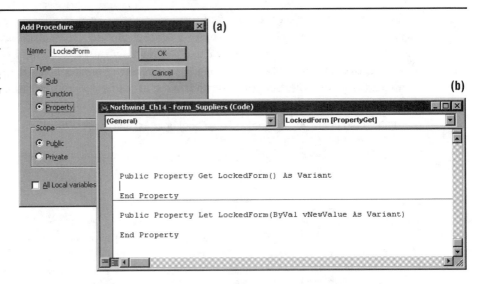

```
Public Property Get LockedForm() As Variant

End Property

Public Property Let LockedForm(ByVal vNewValue As Variant)

End Property
```

3. Insert the `Property Let LockedForm` procedure.

4. In the code template for the `LockedForm Property Get` procedure, change the data type of the procedure's return value from Variant to Boolean. (We'll create the `Property Get` procedure in the next section, but for now, the data types must match to avoid a run-time error.)

5. Save the module and switch to Form view. Run the procedure by typing **Forms!Suppliers .LockedForm = True** in the Immediate window and pressing Enter. Confirm that the data controls are locked.

6. Type **Forms!Suppliers.LockedForm = False** and press Enter. Confirm that the data controls are unlocked.

Creating a *Property Get* Procedure

When you create a write-only custom property named *propertyname* using a Property Let procedure, you can also create a Property Get procedure with the same name that returns the value of the property. In the simplest case, the syntax is as follows:

```
Public Property Get propertyname As datatype
    [statements]
    propertyname = expression
End Property
```

The data type returned by the Property Get procedure must be the same as the data type of the argument passed to the Property Let procedure. In other words, if you set a property to a value with a specific data type, you can only read a value with the same data type. A Property Get procedure runs whenever you try to read the value of the property in a VBA procedure.

The Property Get procedure for the LockedForm property is shown below. This procedure returns the value True or False with the Boolean data type.

```
Public Property Get LockedForm() As Boolean
    LockedForm = Me.CompanyName.Locked
End Property
```

The procedure tests the Locked property of a data control on the form. If the Locked property of a data control is True, then the form is in browse mode and the procedure returns the value True. If the control is unlocked, the procedure returns the value False. To return a value from a Property Get procedure, you set the name of the procedure to the value you want to return (just as you do with a function procedure).

Insert the Property Get LockedForm procedure in the Suppliers form module, then save the module and switch to Form view. Type **? Forms!Suppliers.LockedForm** in the Immediate window and press Enter. The Immediate window prints True or False depending on the mode you left the form in.

NOTE   When you create a custom property for a form or report using **Property Let** and **Property Get** procedures, you create the procedures as public procedures in the form's or report's module. If you want another form or report to have the same property, you must copy the property procedures to the other form's or report's module. In the LockedForm example, the **Property Let LockedForm** procedure is reusable as is and can be copied to another form's module; however, the **Property Get LockedForm** procedure refers to a specific control on the Suppliers form and is not reusable without modification.

Using Property Procedures

After creating the property procedures for a custom property in a form's module, you use the custom property in the same way you use a built-in form property (except that you can't set or view its value in a property sheet). For example, during data entry for a product, you can provide browsing of the corresponding supplier with the event procedure shown below.

```
Private Sub cmdSupplier_Click()
    Dim strWhere As String
    strWhere = "SupplierID = Screen.ActiveForm.SupplierID"
    DoCmd.OpenForm FormName:="Suppliers", wherecondition:=strWhere
    Screen.ActiveForm.LockedForm = True
End Sub
```

This event procedure uses the OpenForm method of the DoCmd object to open the Suppliers form and synchronizes it to the Products form. The opened form is the active form, so the procedure uses the Screen object to refer to the Suppliers form when setting the LockedForm property to True.

To test this event procedure, open the Products form in Design view and place a button named cmdSupplier on the form. Set the button's Caption property to Supplier. Enter the cmdSupplier_Click procedure for the button's OnClick event. Then save the form and switch to Form view. Click the button. The Suppliers form opens synchronized and with locked data controls.

Creating Custom Methods for a Form or Report

You can create a custom method for a form or report by entering a public procedure in the form's or report's module. For example, the LockControls procedure creates a custom method called LockControls that locks the data controls on a form.

```
Public Sub LockControls()
    Dim ctl As Control
    If Me.Dirty = True Then
        RunCommand acCmdSaveRecord
    End If
    For Each ctl In Me
        If TypeOf ctl Is TextBox Then ctl.Locked = True
    Next
End Sub
```

The `UnlockControls` procedure creates a custom method called `UnlockControls` that unlocks the data controls.

```
Public Sub UnlockControls()
    Dim ctl As Control
    For Each ctl In Me
        If TypeOf ctl Is TextBox Then ctl.Locked = False
    Next
End Sub
```

After creating a custom method for a form by entering a public procedure in the form's module, you use the custom method the same way you use a built-in method. As an example, insert the `LockControls` and `UnlockControls` procedures shown above in the Suppliers form module. Save the module and the form and switch to Form view. Then run the method to lock the controls by typing **Forms!Suppliers.LockControls** in the Immediate window and pressing Enter. The controls are locked. Type **Forms!Suppliers.UnlockControls** and press Enter. The controls are unlocked.

NOTE   You can create a custom method for an object defined by an independent class module by entering a public procedure in the calling module.

Displaying Multiple Instances of a Form

When you create a new form by placing controls and setting properties in form Design view and by creating procedures in the form's module, you create a blueprint, or a set of directions, for generating a specific form object. When you save the blueprint, its name is listed in the Forms pane in the Database window. In object-oriented programming terminology, the blueprint is called a *class*. When you select the name in the Database window and double-click, or when you use the `OpenForm` method, Access uses the blueprint to create and display a Form object. In object-oriented programming terminology, the Form object displayed is the *default instance* of the class.

Access VBA provides a way to create more than one Form object for the blueprint as additional instances of the class. This means that you could take orders for two customers by displaying two copies of the Orders form (see Figure 14.8), or if you are reviewing products in the Product List form, you could display product information forms for several products at the same time (see Figure 14.9). Each of the Form objects based on the blueprint is a separate instance of the class. Access VBA provides a special object called the Collection object as a way to keep track of the separate instances of a class.

FIGURE 14.8:

You can create separate instances of the Orders from and take two orders at the same time.

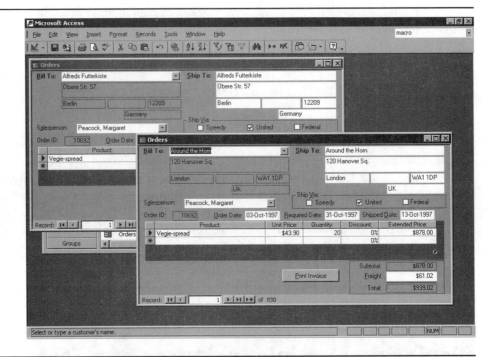

FIGURE 14.9:

You can create separate instances of the Product List form and display product information for several products simultaneously.

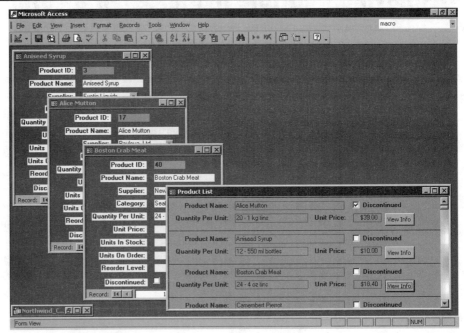

Referring to a Closed Form in VBA

You refer to an open form in VBA using any of the familiar references: Forms!*formname*, Forms("*formname*"), or Forms(*n*). To refer to a closed form, use the syntax Form_*formname*. For example, in the Immediate window, you can set the value of the Caption property of the closed Customers form by using this assignment statement:

```
Form_Customers.Caption = "My Customers"
```

As another example, you can determine the recordsource of the closed Customers form with this statement:

```
?Form_Customers.RecordSource
```

When you refer to a closed form using the Form_*formname* syntax, VBA opens and hides the form. The reference to a closed form is also a reference to the form's module.

Using the Collection Object

Access VBA allows you to create your own collections of objects and variables using the built-in Collection object to hold a set of objects of any type. We'll define a new Collection object to contain the new Form objects that we'll be creating. Access VBA uses the New keyword to indicate new instances in two different ways: in declaration statements and in object variable assignment statements.

Using the *New* Keyword in a Declaration Statement

You can use the New keyword in the declaration statement for an object variable, as follows:

```
Dim varname As New type
```

varname is the object variable you are declaring, and *type* is the object type. Without the New keyword, the declaration statement declares an object variable of the specified object type but doesn't create the object; you must use the Set statement to point the object variable to the object (and create the object if it doesn't already exist).

For example, you can include the New keyword in the declaration statement:

```
Dim CollectForms As New Collection
```

VBA automatically creates a new Collection object the first time a procedure calls a property or method of the CollectForms object variable. This means that you don't need to use the Set statement to assign a new object to the object variable. When you include the New keyword in the declaration statement for an object, you are *implicitly creating* the object. For example, the declaration statement

```
Dim tbl As New ADOX.Table
```

implicitly creates `tbl` as an object variable and automatically creates the Table object in the first statement in the procedure that assigns a property or runs a method for the object.

Using the *Set* Statement without the *New* Keyword

The simplest Set statement has this syntax:

```
Set objvariable = objectexpression
```

objvariable is the object variable you are assigning, and *objectexpression* is a reference to one of the following:

- An object
- Another object variable of the same object type
- A function, property, or method that returns an object of the same object type

Here are examples of simple Set statements:

```
Dim frm As Form, rst As ADODB.Recordset
Set frm = Forms!Customers
Set rst = Forms!Customers.Recordset
```

A simple Set statement assigns an object to an object variable (and creates the object if it doesn't already exist). You can point several object variables to the same object using Set statements.

As an example of using simple Set statements, with the Orders form closed, follow these steps:

1. Type **Set frm1 = Form_Orders** in the Immediate window and press Enter. This creates the `frm1` object variable and points it to the Orders form. VBA has opened and hidden the form. Verify by choosing Window ➢ Unhide in the Access window. Leave the form hidden.

2. Type **Set frm2 = Form_Orders** in the Immediate window and press Enter (see Figure 14.10a). This statement points the `frm2` object variable to the hidden form. The `frm1` and `frm2` object variables point to the same object. Choose Window ➢ Unhide (see Figure 14.10b). Click OK to unhide the single instance of the Orders form.

3. Close the Orders form.

FIGURE 14.10:

Without the New keyword, each assignment statement in the Immediate window (a) assigns an object variable to the same object (b).

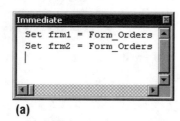

(a)

(b)

Using the *Set* Statement with the *New* Keyword

You can use the New keyword in a Set statement to create new instances. The syntax is as follows:

```
Set objvariable = New objectexpression
```

objectexpression is the same as in a Set statement without the New keyword.

When you include the New keyword, the Set statement creates a separate instance of the object. For example, you can use the following statements to create separate Form objects:

```
Set frm1 = New Form_Customers
Set frm2 = New Form_Customers
```

When you include the New keyword, the frm1 and frm2 object variables point to different objects.

As an example of using simple Set statements with the New keyword, follow these steps:

1. Type **Set frm1 = New Form_Orders** in the Immediate window and press Enter. VBA has opened and hidden an instance of the form. Verify by choosing Window ➢ Unhide. Leave the form hidden.

2. Type **Set frm2 = New Form_Orders** in the Immediate window and press Enter (see Figure 14.11a). VBA opens and hides a second instance of the form. To verify, choose Window ➢ Unhide (see Figure 14.11b); Orders is listed for each separate instance. Click OK to unhide each instance of the Orders form. Figure 14.12 shows the two instances.

3. Using the navigation buttons, browse the recordset of each instance. Note that each instance has its own current record pointer. When you create multiple instances of a form, each instance has its own current record pointer and may have its own properties except for its name. Every instance of a form blueprint has the same name, which means that you cannot refer to a specific instance using its name. When you create a

new instance, Access adds a member to the Forms collection, so you can refer to an instance by its index number in the Forms collection.

FIGURE 14.11:

When you include the New keyword, each assignment statement in the Immediate window (a) creates a new instance and assigns it an object variable (b).

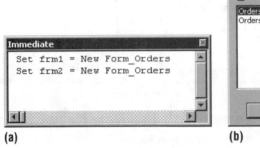

(a)   (b)

FIGURE 14.12:

Two instances of the Orders form are displayed.

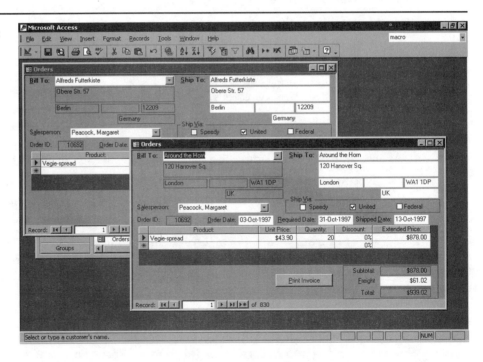

4. Close all forms except the two instances of the Orders form. Type **Forms(0).Caption = "First"** in the Immediate window and press Enter. The caption for one of the instances changes to First. Type **Forms(1).Caption = "Second"** and press Enter. The caption for the other instance changes to Second. Close both instances.

Creating Multiple Instances

In this section, we will explore the process of displaying multiple instances of a form. Begin by opening a new standard module named basMultipleInstances.

Create an object variable for a new Collection object by entering the following statement in the Declarations section of the module.

```
Dim CollectForms As New Collection
```

This statement implicitly creates a new Collection object to hold the Form objects. By entering the declaration statement in the Declarations section of the module, you are declaring a module-level variable that continues to exist as long as the database is open. (You'll see the significance of declaring CollectForms at the module level shortly.)

Insert the Multiples procedure shown below.

```
Public Sub Multiples()
    Dim frm As Form
    Set frm = New Form_Orders
    frm.Visible = True
    CollectForms.Add frm
End Sub
```

This procedure declares frm as an object variable. The assignment statement uses the New keyword to create a new, hidden instance of the Orders form. The procedure unhides the instance and then uses the Add method to add the instance to the CollectForms collection.

Save the module. Run the Multiples procedure in the Immediate window. An instance of the Orders form is created, displayed, and added to the CollectForms collection.

Place an apostrophe (') in front of the Collectforms.Add frm statement in the Multiples procedure to comment out the statement. Run the procedure in the Immediate window. The procedure creates the instance and displays it for a brief moment, but this time, when the procedure ends, the frm object variable ceases to exist. With no variable pointing to it, the instance is destroyed. By adding the instance to the CollectForms collection, there is a reference to the instance in the collection, so the instance continues to exist as long as the collection exists. By declaring the CollectForms object variable as a module-level variable, we guarantee that the collection, and therefore the new instances of the Orders form, will continue to exist after the Multiples procedure ends.

Delete the apostrophe, then save and close the module. Run the Multiples procedure in the Immediate window several times. Each time you run the procedure, a new instance of the Orders form is created, displayed, and added to the collection (see Figure 14.13).

FIGURE 14.13:

Creating multiple instances of the Orders form by adding the instances to the module-level CollectForms collection object

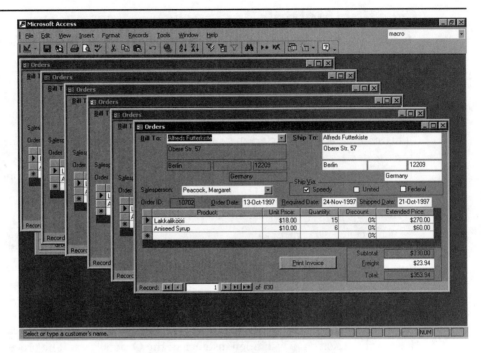

Including Multiple Instances in an Application

To illustrate how to include multiple instances in an application, we'll add a command button to the Product List form and assign it a procedure that creates and displays a new instance of a form that displays product information. The event procedure for the button is shown below.

```
Private Sub cmdView_Click()
    Dim frm As Form
    Set frm = New Form_frmViewProduct
    CollectForms.Add frm
    With frm
        .Filter = "ProductID = " & Forms![Product List]!ProductID
        .FilterOn = True
        .Caption = ProductName
        .Visible = True
    End With
End Sub
```

This procedure creates the frm object variable, creates a new instance of the frmViewProduct form, and adds it to the CollectForms collection. The procedure uses the With structure to set the Filter property to synchronize the new instance to the product selected in the Product

List form, as well as to set the FilterOn property to apply the filter. The `With` structure also includes statements to set the Caption property and the Visible property.

Follow these steps to add the command button:

1. Create a copy of the Products form named frmViewProduct and modify the copy as shown in Figure 14.14. Close the frmViewProduct form.

FIGURE 14.14:

The frmViewProduct form

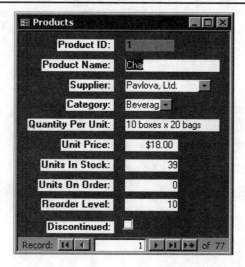

2. Open the Product List form in Design view and set the PopUp property to No. Place a command button named cmdView in the Detail section and set its Caption property to View Info.

3. Click the Code button in the toolbar. Implicitly create the `CollectForms` collection by entering the following statement in the Declarations section:

   ```
   Dim CollectForms As New Collection
   ```

4. Enter the `cmdView_Click` event procedure shown above and save the module.

5. Save the Product List form and switch to Form view. Select a product and click the View Info button. An instance of the frmViewProduct form opens for the product you selected. Select another product and click its View Info button. A second instance of the frmViewProduct form opens for the second product. Figure 14.15 shows the result of displaying several instances of the frmViewProduct form.

FIGURE 14.15:

Displaying several instances of a form, each synchronized to a selected product

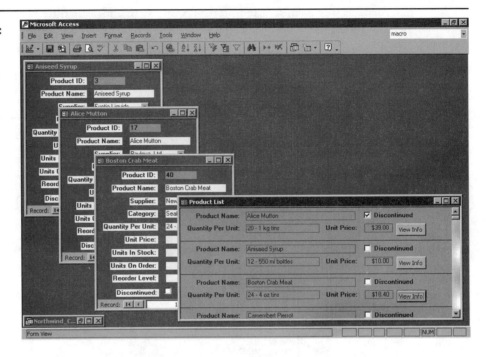

Summary

This chapter has introduced you to techniques for creating and modifying new objects programmatically. The important points follow:

- In most cases, you use the Append method of a collection to create a child object. Normally, you must create a complete child object with required properties and often with its own required child object before you can save the child object. For example, to create a Table object, you must give the object a valid name and create at least one Column object.

- You create a custom property for a data access object by using the Add method of the appropriate AccessObject's Properties collection.

- An application such as Access that acts as a host for the database engine may create application-defined properties for a data access object. The engine is unaware of an application-defined property until you either set the property in the application's interface or create a Property object for the property and append the new Property object to the Properties collection of the data access object.

- Access VBA provides a set of built-in functions that you can use to create new forms, reports, and controls programmatically.

- Access provides a Module object with properties and methods that you can use to create and modify modules programmatically.

- You create a custom property for a form or report by creating a pair of public Property Let (or Property Set for a property that returns an object) and Property Get procedures in the form's or report's module. You set the custom property using an assignment statement in a procedure, and you read the value of the custom property by referring to the custom property in a procedure.

- You create a custom method for a form or report by creating a public function or sub procedure in the form's or report's module.

- When you create a new form or report, you are creating a blueprint, or *class*, that Access uses to create individual Form or Report objects. When you open a form, Access creates the default instance. You can use the blueprint to create separate instances using the New keyword in assignment statements. You can create a module-level Collection object to keep track of the multiple instances.

CHAPTER 15

Expanding Access

- Converting macros to VBA procedures

- Creating a library database

- Introducing dynamic-link libraries

- Using ActiveX controls

- Understanding remote control using Automation

This final chapter is an overview of a few advanced topics available with VBA programming. The chapter begins with a discussion of converting macros to VBA procedures, which allows you to leverage your work with macros by converting them to VBA procedures, complete with simple error handling.

This chapter continues with discussions of several ways to expand the world your database lives in. Custom libraries allow you to easily reuse VBA procedures in your other databases. You'll learn how to create these library databases and how to gain access to them from another database. You also will learn about dynamic-link libraries (DLLs) that store code written and thoroughly debugged by other developers. One of the most important DLLs is one that Windows makes available, called the Windows API. By borrowing and using library code, you can expand the abilities of your application beyond those of Microsoft Access.

After discussing how to expand a database application using libraries, the chapter shifts its focus to explain how to use ActiveX to enrich a database. ActiveX is a set of technologies developed by Microsoft to allow communication between computers, applications, and objects. You'll learn how to add new controls, called ActiveX controls, to Access. ActiveX controls behave like the familiar toolbox controls, but provide capabilities that Access doesn't provide—such as the ability to display an interactive calendar or play a sound or video file. You also will learn how to write Access VBA programs that control the objects of another application, such as Excel or Word, in the same way you control the Access Application and data access objects. The technology that allows you to control another application programmatically is called Automation.

NOTE   The word *application* is used in this chapter to refer to off-the-shelf programs such as Access, Excel, Word, Visio, and Visual Basic. The word *project* in this chapter refers to the set of Visual Basic procedures you've written for a particular file created using one of these programs.

Converting Macros to VBA Procedures

In this book, you learned how to use VBA programming to automate many database tasks. On the other hand, you can build fully automated, complex projects entirely with *macros*, rather than using VBA. However, even the simplest project may require some VBA procedures if you want to include any of the VBA-only features described in this book. Both the nature of the task you try to automate and who will use the custom application determine whether VBA is required.

If you decide to rewrite some or all of your macros as VBA procedures, you don't need to start from scratch. Access provides the ability to convert macros to VBA code, complete with simple error handling. After converting a macro to a VBA procedure, you can modify the error-handling instructions, change the decisions and loop structures to the more efficient control structures available in VBA, and add the features not available in macro programming.

There are two ways to convert macros:

- You can convert all of the event macros for a form or report to a set of event procedures that Access stores in the form's or report's module.

- You can convert all of the macros in a macrosheet to function procedures stored in a new standard module.

Before going into the details of these approaches, let's consider why you might want to convert your macros to VBA procedures.

NOTE   To learn more about automating a database using macros, read *Mastering Access 2002 Premium Edition*, by Alan Simpson and Celeste Robinson (Sybex, 2001).

Why Convert Macros?

Here are some reasons for using VBA procedures instead of macros:

To create custom functions Access includes a large set of built-in functions that you can use with operators to create complex expressions. Sometimes, an expression you need to use in several places is long and complex. Rather than retyping a complex expression, you can create your own custom function. You can use custom functions the same way you use Access built-in functions.

To handle more complex decisions The built-in decision functions, macro conditions, and RunMacro action for repeated operations provide convenient ways to handle simple decisions. If you need more complex decision structures, you may still be able to use macros. But using the powerful and efficient control structures of VBA often results in a solution that is faster and easier to create and that runs faster than the equivalent macro-control structure.

To trap errors Because of the limited error handling in macro programming, developers try to avoid most errors by anticipating them. Nevertheless, external events that you can't prevent or anticipate may occur—a file may be deleted, the power may shut down while a macro is running, or a network connection may be lost. The most important reason for including VBA in your application is that it has the ability to handle unanticipated errors. With VBA, you can include error handling in two ways: in an individual procedure to handle VBA errors that occur when the procedure runs, and in the event procedure for a form's or report's Error event to handle interface and database engine errors that occur when the form or report is active.

To provide hard-copy documentation The documentation for macros that is created by the Database Documenter is not as convenient to use as a printout of VBA code. For large or complicated applications, easy-to-use hard-copy documentation is essential.

To create and manipulate objects In most cases, you can create and manipulate objects interactively (that is, in the object's Design view). However, there are times when it is useful to define or modify an object automatically when the application is running. You may want to create a custom wizard that is specific to your application. You can use the data-definition queries of Access SQL to create and modify tables, to create and delete indexes, and to create relationships between tables. You can run data-definition queries using either macros or VBA procedures. However, the data definition language of Access SQL is limited compared with the capabilities of the data access objects available only through VBA. With VBA, you can create and manipulate any of the objects in the database, as well as the database itself.

To perform actions not available with macros There are some actions that cannot be carried out efficiently, or at all, with macros alone. An important example is transaction processing, which is available only in VBA. In a VBA transaction, all of the operations of the transaction are run in memory; if an operation fails, the transaction is aborted, leaving the data tables as they were before the transaction began. If all operations are successful, the results of the transaction are updated to the data tables.

NOTE Even VBA-only databases must use macros for two operations: the AutoKeys macro for reassigning keys and the AutoExec macro for carrying out actions when the database starts.

To pass arguments to your code With macros, you set the action arguments when you create the macro. You can't change these arguments when the macro is running, and you can't use variables in the macro action arguments. In some cases, macros can use references to the Screen object, which has the same effect as using a variable. However, VBA provides additional, more efficient ways to change the arguments in your code when the code is running and to use variables in the arguments.

To create variables In macro programming, the only way to create a variable is to use an unbound control on a form to hold the temporary value. While the form is open, the value in the control is available for use by other forms, queries, macros, and VBA procedures. VBA provides the ability to create a variable as a named location in memory without using a control on a form. VBA also lets you limit the variable's scope by specifying which other procedures have access to the variable.

To optimize performance There are features of VBA, such as optimized methods and compiling, that result in better performance than the corresponding macro-only approaches. For example, VBA provides the Seek method to locate a record in a table, which is significantly faster than the FindRecord macro action. VBA provides bookmarks to save your place in a recordset so you can quickly return to a record. Transaction processing is typically much faster than running separate operations. Another performance gain is possible because the code you write in VBA is compiled, which converts the code into a form that Access can execute more efficiently. In macro programming, the individual macro actions have been designed for optimal performance, but the macros you create are not compiled.

To work outside Access With macros, your work outside Access is extremely limited. You can use the RunApp action to launch another Windows or MS-DOS-based application, but once the application is open, you are limited to working interactively with it. Using VBA, you can extend your programming horizons beyond the off-the-shelf Access application.

You can automate the other application with Automation or Dynamic Data Exchange (DDE), and you can write instructions for ActiveX controls that provide special abilities to your Access project. You can connect to and manipulate external databases using ODBC or OLE DB drivers. You can also communicate with the Windows API using functions in the DLLs provided by Windows. For example, you can check to see if a file exists, determine the display driver, or determine if other applications are running.

Whether you use macro or VBA programming to automate your database is up to you. Most professional Access developers use only VBA procedures, if for no other reason than the error-handling capability offered by VBA. Some developers use macro programming to create a prototype in the least time possible and then use VBA for the full development of the prototype into a custom application that includes comprehensive error handling, transaction processing, optimal performance, and interactions with Windows or other applications.

NOTE   For hands-on experience with the techniques described in this chapter, create a fresh copy of Northwind and name it Northwind_Ch15.

Converting Event Macros to Event Procedures

You can convert all of the event macros for a form or report to event procedures and store them in the form's or report's module. When you convert the event macros for a form or report, Access automatically creates the form or report module (if necessary) and changes the names of the event macros to the corresponding event procedure names using the following syntax:

```
Form_eventname
controlname_eventname
```

or

```
Report_eventname
controlname_eventname
```

Access automatically assigns the event procedure to the event property. If the form or report module already exists, Access adds the converted event procedures to the module. The macrosheets that stored the event macros continue to exist and are unchanged.

To explore this process, open the Northwind_Ch15 database and take the following steps:

1. Open the Customers macrosheet in Design view. Figure 15.1a shows the two event macros for the Customers form: the ValidateID macro is assigned to the BeforeUpdate event of the CustomerID field, and the Update Country List macro is assigned to the form's AfterUpdate event.

2. Open the Customers form in Design view. Figures 15.1b and 15.1c show the assignments of the macros to event properties. Scroll to the end of the Form property sheet to observe that the form's HasModule property is set to No, which indicates that the Customers form is a lightweight form without a form module.

The Customers macrosheet (a) stores macros that are assigned to the BeforeUpdate event of the CustomerID text box (b) and the AfterUpdate event of the form (c).

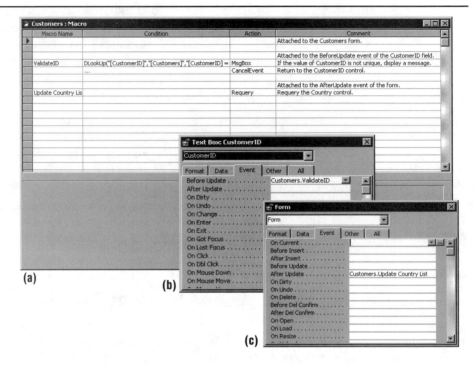

3. Select Tools ➢ Macro ➢ Convert Form's Macros To Visual Basic. Figure 15.2a shows the Convert Form Macros dialog with options to add simple error handling and to include your macro comments as comments in the VBA procedure.

4. With both options checked, click the Convert button. After a few seconds, if the conversion is successful, the message shown in Figure 15.2b is displayed. The property sheets for the form and CustomerID text box indicate that the macro assignments have been replaced with assignments to event procedures and that the form's HasModule property has been changed to Yes (see Figure 15.3).

FIGURE 15.2:

Use the Convert Form Macros dialog to add error handling and the macro comments to the new event procedure (a). Access displays a message to let you know the conversion was successful (b).

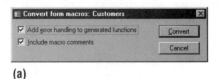

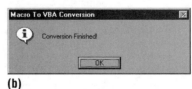

FIGURE 15.3:

When you convert a form's macros, the macro assignments are replaced with assignments to event procedures (a) and the form's HasModule property is set to Yes (b).

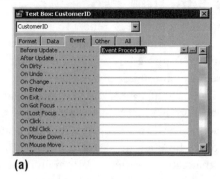

(a)

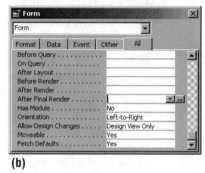

(b)

5. Click the Code button in the toolbar. The ValidateID event macro has been converted to the CustomerID_BeforeUpdate event procedure shown in Figure 15.4a. The Update Country List macro has been converted to the Form_AfterUpdate event procedure shown in Figure 15.4b. The new event procedures include the macros' comments. The new procedures have basic error handling that displays the error code in a message box if a run-time error occurs.

FIGURE 15.4:

The ValidateID macro is converted to the CustomerID_BeforeUpdate event procedure (a) and the Update Country List macro is converted to the Form_AfterUpdate event procedure (b).

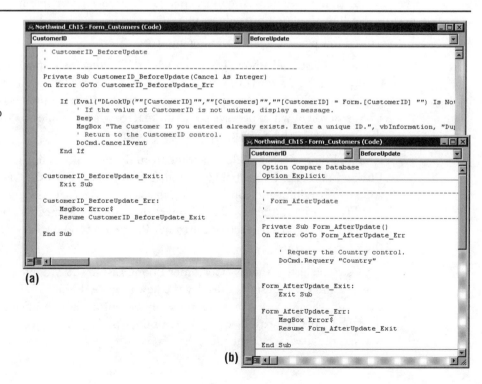

(a)

(b)

Converting Macros to Function Procedures

Instead of converting the event macros for a form or report to event procedures, you may opt to convert all the macros stored in a macrosheet to function procedures stored in a new standard module. In this approach, a macro triggered by an event is converted to a function procedure, but the function procedure is not automatically assigned to the event. Rather, the original macro continues to be assigned to the event, and you must manually reassign the event property to trigger the function procedure. Also, a macro that is called by another macro using the RunMacro macro action (or by a VBA procedure using the RunMacro method of the DoCmd object) is converted to a function procedure. The macro or procedure that calls the original macro is not automatically modified to call the function procedure. You must manually modify the macro or procedure to call the function procedure.

When you convert macros in a macrosheet to function procedures in a standard module, VBA names the function procedure using this syntax:

```
macrosheetname_macroname
```

It replaces spaces in both names with underscore characters (_). The original macrosheet continues to exist, and the original macros continue to be called as they were before you created the function procedures. You must change the properties or statements that call the macros to call the function procedures instead.

To explore this process, take the following steps:

1. Open the Customer Phone List macrosheet. The macrosheet (see Figure 15.5a) contains the Alpha Buttons event macro, which is triggered by the AfterUpdate event of the CompanyNameFilters option group on the Customer Phone List form (see Figure 15.5b). Scroll down to observe the Print macro, which is called as a support macro by the ^p macro in the Sample Autokeys macrosheet.

2. Choose File ➤ Save As, select Module from the drop-down list, type **Customer Phone List** in the Name field (see Figure 15.6a), and click OK. Click the options to add error handling and comments in the Convert Macro: Customer Phone List dialog (see Figure 15.6b), then click the Convert button. Access creates a new standard module named Converted Macro - Customer Phone List and displays a message to indicate the successful conversion.

3. Choose Converted Macro - Customer Phone List in the Modules tab of the Database window and click Design to display the new module. Figure 15.7 shows the Customer_Phone_List_Alpha_Buttons function procedure. Notice that the procedure uses the CodeContextObject property of the Application object to refer to the object that has the focus when the procedure runs.

The Customer Phone List macro sheet (a) contains the Alpha Buttons event macro assigned to the AfterUpdate event of the option group on the Customer Phone List form (b).

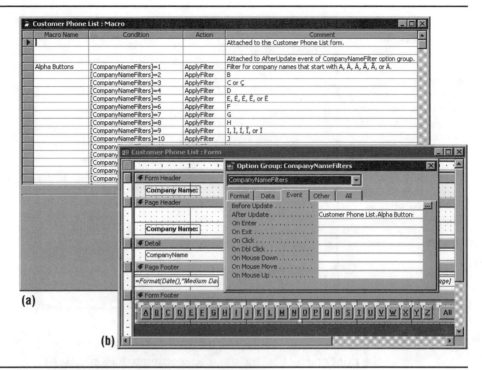

(a)

(b)

FIGURE 15.6:

Use the Save As dialog to save a macrosheet as a new standard module (a) and the Convert macro dialog to add error handling and comments (b).

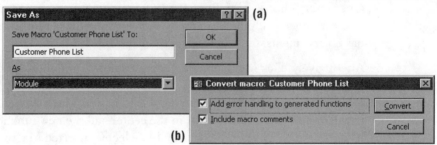

(b)

4. Open the Customer Phone List form in Design view. The AfterUpdate property of the CompanyNameFilters option group is still assigned to the event macro. To assign the function procedure instead of the macro, type **=Customer_Phone_List_Alpha_Buttons()** in the AfterUpdate property field.

5. Save the form and switch to Form view. Click one of the buttons in the form's option group.

FIGURE 15.7:

When you convert the macros in the Customer Phone List macrosheet using the Save As command, the Alpha Buttons macro is converted to a function procedure and named Customer_ Phone_List_Alpha_ Buttons. The new function procedures are stored in a new standard module named Converted Macro-Customer Phone List.

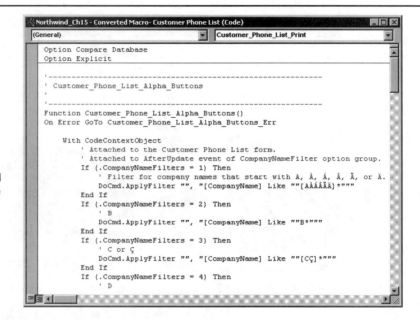

```
Northwind_Ch15 - Converted Macro- Customer Phone List (Code)

(General)                                    Customer_Phone_List_Print

Option Compare Database
Option Explicit

'------------------------------------------------------------
' Customer_Phone_List_Alpha_Buttons
'------------------------------------------------------------
Function Customer_Phone_List_Alpha_Buttons()
On Error GoTo Customer_Phone_List_Alpha_Buttons_Err

    With CodeContextObject
        ' Attached to the Customer Phone List form.
        ' Attached to AfterUpdate event of CompanyNameFilter option group.
        If (.CompanyNameFilters = 1) Then
            ' Filter for company names that start with A, À, Á, Â, Ã, or Ä.
            DoCmd.ApplyFilter "", "[CompanyName] Like ""[AÀÁÂÃÄ]*"""
        End If
        If (.CompanyNameFilters = 2) Then
            ' B
            DoCmd.ApplyFilter "", "[CompanyName] Like ""B*"""
        End If
        If (.CompanyNameFilters = 3) Then
            ' C or Ç
            DoCmd.ApplyFilter "", "[CompanyName] Like ""[CÇ]*"""
        End If
        If (.CompanyNameFilters = 4) Then
            ' D
```

6. Open the Sample Autokeys macrosheet. The ^p macro uses the RunMacro action to run the Print macro. Change the macro action to RunCode. Type **Customer_Phone_List_Print()** as the function name argument (see Figure 15.8a). You omit the equal sign (=), but you must include the parentheses, even if the function has no arguments.

   Alternatively, click in the function name argument and then click the Build button at the right of the argument box to display the Expression Builder. Click the Functions folder and then click the Northwind_Ch15 folder. The Expression Builder lists the standard modules in the list box in the center and the new function procedures in the list box on the right (see Figure 15.8b). Select Converted Macro - Customer Phone List in the second box and Customer_Phone_List_Print() in the third box, click Paste, and then click OK to close the builder.

7. Change the Comments field of the macro action to reflect the fact that you are now running a module instead of a macro.

8. Save the macrosheet. Click in the Customer Phone List form, click one of the buttons in the form's option group, and press Ctrl+P. The ^p macro runs the function procedure.

FIGURE 15.8:

To call the function procedure, change the Run Macro macro action to the Run Code macro action (a). Use the Expression Builder to set the Function Name argument for the RunCode macro action (b).

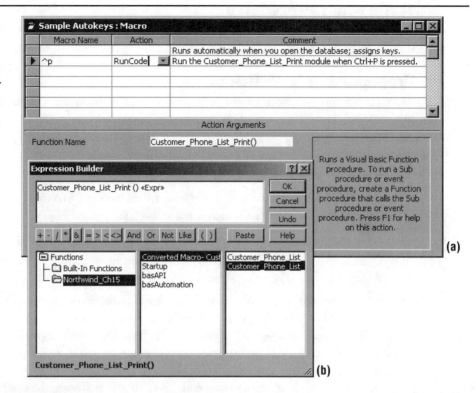

Understanding Library Databases

When you create generic procedures that you want to reuse in your other Access projects, there are two ways you can make them available: store them in a module and import the module into another project, or create a library database and make the library database available to another project. A *library database* is a collection of procedures and objects that you can call from another Access project.

Creating a Library Database

Creating a library database is exactly the same as creating a regular Access database. However, you normally won't store data in the library database the way you do in a regular database. You can use any valid name for the library. The convention is to use the MDA extension for a library database, but you can use the MDB extension.

Testing Your Procedures

Before you place a macro or a VBA procedure in a library database, you should test it thoroughly. VBA procedures should have error handling to deal with unanticipated errors.

Programming for Efficiency

After a procedure or macro passes your reliability tests, reexamine the program for optimal performance. Here are some suggestions:

- When you have a choice of control structures, make sure you have used the most efficient structure. For example, if you are looping through a collection, use the For Each...Next structure instead of the For...Next structure.

- Avoid the decision functions IIf, Choose, and Switch in favor of If...Then and Select Case decision structures, which usually run faster.

- Use variables with the most specific data types and object data types.

- Use the most efficient options to refer to objects, such as Me to refer to the form in which the code is running. Use the With...End With structure to set several properties.

- Keep a copy of your macros and procedures and strip out comments from the versions that you place in a library. While each comment in a macro or VBA procedure takes only a fraction of a second to process, the time spent on a comment is wasted. Normally, the time spent processing comments is so small that you should comment freely to make your code more readable. However, a procedure in a library database should be so impervious to errors that readability should no longer be the highest priority. By making a copy, you provide a backup should your procedure need to be changed.

Compiling Procedures

You achieve the fastest VBA code only when you run it in a compiled state. After you have added the procedures to the library, or after you add a new procedure or make any changes to an existing library, you should compile all of the procedures. To compile a procedure, open any module in the library database and select Debug ➤ Compile (*libraryname*).

TIP   You can save a library database (or any other database) as an MDE file. An MDE file compiles the modules, removes the readable source code (leaving only the compiled code), and compacts the database. The size of the MDE file is reduced, and the project uses memory more efficiently and performs better.

Creating a Reference to a Library Database

Before you can use a library database in an Access database, you need to add a reference to the library in the project. Whenever you open a database that has a reference to a library database, the library database is available. The first time your project calls a procedure in the library, Access loads the module containing the procedure into memory (Access also loads any other modules that contain procedures that can be called by the procedure you called). You can call the library's procedures as though the procedures were part of the project.

To understand how this works, we'll add a reference to the Expenses.mdb sample database so that we can use it as a library database in the Northwind_Ch15 database.

1. Open any module in the current database and choose Tools ➤ References to display the References dialog (see Figure 15.9a). The current Access project has references to the items that are checked. Items without check marks are available for adding to the project. Use the Priority buttons to change the position of an item in the list. If an item is not listed, you can add it.

2. Click the Browse button and select Microsoft Access Databases (*.mdb) in the Files Of Type combo list of the Add Reference dialog (see Figure 15.9b).

FIGURE 15.9:

Use the References dialog to set a reference to another database, another application's type library, or an ActiveX control (a). Use the Add Reference dialog to add a new reference (b).

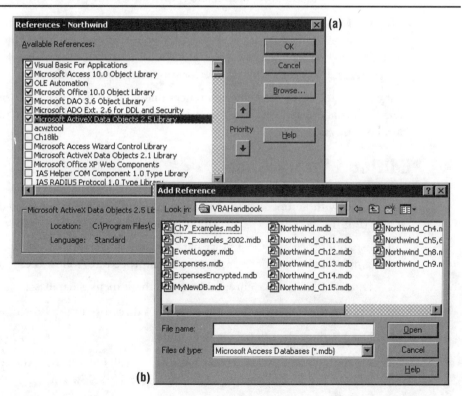

3. Locate the Expenses.mdb file in the C:\VBAHandbook directory and click Open. If you left the password option set, Access prompts you for the database password. Enter **expenses** and click OK. The Expenses.mdb database now appears checked in the References dialog. The Expenses.mdb database has a module named Global Code. This module contains the IsLoaded("*formname*") function that returns the value True if the form whose name you pass as a string to the function is open; otherwise, it returns the value False. The same function appears in the Utility Functions module in Northwind_Ch15. To test the library database, we'll delete the Utility Functions module in Northwind_Ch15.

4. Click OK to close the References dialog. Click in the Database window. Select and delete the Utility Functions module.

5. Open the Categories form. In the Immediate window, type **?IsLoaded("Categories")** and press Enter. Access locates the IsLoaded function in the Expenses.mdb database, runs the function procedure, and returns the value –1 (True).

If you move or rename a library database, Access may not be able to find it. When you call a procedure in the library database, Access displays an error message and then opens the References dialog displaying the word "MISSING" in front of the name of the library database. You can click Browse to find the new location and reset the reference.

If you deselect an item in the References dialog, your database is no longer aware of the item. To avoid errors, you must remove all references in your database to the item's procedures or objects.

Editing Library Code

You can edit a VBA procedure stored in a library database while you are working in the current project without opening the library database directly. (If you saved the library database as an MDE file, you can't view or edit its procedures.)

To display a procedure in a library database, open its module from the Project Browser. For example, to display the IsLoaded function procedure, follow these steps:

1. Open the Project Explorer and expand the Expenses database.

2. Expand the Expenses database's Modules directory in the Project Explorer.

3. Double-click the Global Code module.

4. Open the module's IsLoaded procedure by selecting it from the combo box on the right of the Module window (see Figure 15.10). Now you can make changes to the procedure.

```
Expenses - Global Code (Code)                                              _ □ ×
(General)                                    ▼   IsLoaded                     ▼
Option Compare Database

Function IsLoaded(ByVal strFormName As String) As Integer
  ' Returns True if the specified form is open in Form view or Datasheet view.

     Const conObjStateClosed = 0
     Const conDesignView = 0

     If SysCmd(acSysCmdGetObjectState, acForm, strFormName) <> conObjStateClosed Then
         If Forms(strFormName).CurrentView <> conDesignView Then
             IsLoaded = True
         End If
     End If

End Function
```

Understanding Dynamic-Link Libraries

A *dynamic-link library* (DLL) is a library of procedures to which applications such as Access and Excel can link. A DLL exists in files separate from the applications. Several applications can be linked to and share a single DLL at the same time. The link to the DLL is termed *dynamic* because the link is activated only at run time when a procedure in the library is called. DLLs are usually written in C or C++ to provide the optimal performance. They normally have the DLL extension.

The Windows operating system uses sets of DLLs to house the functions it uses. Windows has procedures stored in several of its DLLs that you can use to manipulate files, manage windows, and write entries in the Registry. The Windows operating system automatically loads and unloads DLLs as it needs them and as applications such as Access call procedures in them.

There are two kinds of DLLs: libraries specified by a type library and those that do not have a type library. In terms of writing VBA procedures, the difference between the two kinds of libraries is significant because you call procedures in the two kinds of libraries in markedly different ways.

Using a Type Library

A *type library* is a file that is associated with, but separate from, the DLL. It contains information about the procedures in the DLL. VBA uses one of the ActiveX technologies called Automation for interacting with a type library (Automation is discussed later in the chapter). A type library usually has an OLB or a TLB extension. When a DLL has an associated type library, the installation program normally installs and registers the type library in the OLE section of the Windows Registry.

To use a DLL that has a type library in an application such as Access, you may need to add a reference to the type library if the installation program (for Access or the library) hasn't already added the reference. You can add a reference to the type library in Access by opening any module, then selecting Tools ➤ References. Add the reference by checking the box to the left of the type library in the list. If the type library doesn't appear in the list, click the Browse button to locate the library in your computer's file system. After adding a reference, you can use the procedures in the DLL as though they were a built-in part of VBA.

NOTE   An example of a DLL that uses a type library is the Data Access Objects library. It contains all of the procedures for working with DAO's data access objects. The DAO360.dll file contains both the DAO DLL and the type library. When you install Access 2002, the reference to the type library is added automatically.

Using a Declare Statement

When a DLL doesn't have a type library, you need to tell VBA where the library is every time you want to use a procedure in the library. You also need to tell VBA exactly how to call the procedure and what kind of response to expect after running the procedure. If you want to use a DLL procedure in a module, you must place a `Declare` statement in the module's Declarations section. The `Declare` statement gives the following information about the procedure:

- The scope of the declaration. In a standard module, you can use the `Public` keyword if you want the DLL procedure to be available to all procedures and modules in the project or the `Private` keyword if you want the DLL procedure to be available only to procedures in the module. In a form or report module, you can use only the `Private` keyword.

- The name the procedure has in your module. You can give a custom name to the procedure by using the `Alias` keyword. If you don't supply an alias, the name the procedure has in your module must be exactly the same as the name the procedure has in the DLL. You use an alias when the DLL procedure has a name that includes an invalid character or has a name that is the same as a VBA keyword.

- The name and path of the DLL. The name of the library is enclosed in quotation marks and is not case-sensitive.

- The name the procedure has in the DLL. The name the procedure has in the DLL is case-sensitive.

- The number and data types of the arguments. The DLL expects the arguments to be placed in a particular order and to have a certain size. Declaring arguments correctly is the hardest part of using a DLL in VBA. The VBA declaration must be set up correctly to pass arguments by value or by reference, exactly as the DLL expects them.

- The data type of the return value if the procedure is a function.

The syntax for the `Declare` statement for a function procedure in a DLL is as follows:

```
[Public|Private] Declare Function procedurename Lib "libraryname" [Alias
"aliasname"][([arglist])][As type]
```

where

- *procedurename* is the name you are using in your module to identify the procedure.
- The `Lib` clause specifies the DLL that houses the procedure.
- *aliasname* is the name that the procedure has in the DLL.

The syntax for the `Declare` statement for a sub procedure is similar, except that the `Function` keyword is replaced by `Sub` and there is no return value. An argument in the *arglist* has this syntax:

```
[Optional][ByVal|ByRef][ParamArray] varname[()][As type]
```

varname is the name of the variable, and *type* is the variable's data type.

WARNING   You must pass to the procedure, in the correct order, precisely the number and data type of arguments that the DLL expects. If you don't do this, the DLL may try to access memory it doesn't have permission to access. The result is a General Protection fault. In other words, Access crashes and you can't save your work.

After declaring a function in the Declarations section of the module, you can then call it in a VBA procedure.

Using the Windows API DLLs

The best examples of DLLs that require `Declare` statements are the libraries that the Windows operating system makes available. This set of DLLs is called the *Windows API* (Application Programming Interface). The API includes more than 1000 functions that are part of Windows and accessible to Windows applications. The Windows API stores most of the functions in three DLLs in the Windows\System directory, as follows:

- Kernel32.dll includes functions for memory management, task management, resource handling, and related operations.
- User32.dll includes functions related to the management of Windows, such as functions for working with menus, messages, cursors, carets, timers, communications, and other non-display operations.
- GDI32.dll includes the functions related to the graphics display, such as drawing, coordinates, and fonts.

As comprehensive as VBA is in allowing you to automate Access, VBA doesn't include the ability to work with the Windows environment. This is where the Windows API comes in.

One of the difficulties in working with the Windows API functions is that they don't provide protection from mistakes. By declaring an API function incorrectly, you can easily cause a General Protection fault and crash Access—you may even crash Windows. Before you test a Windows API function, save all of your objects. Once a General Protection fault occurs, you won't have an opportunity to save anything.

Suppose you need some information about how the user interface is set up. For example, you might wonder whether there is a mouse. And, if so, is the mouse right-handed or left-handed? What is the width of the cursor? There is no way to get answers to these questions using a VBA function. However, there is a function in the Windows API called GetSystemMetrics that you can use for this purpose. It is located in the User32 DLL. The function takes a long integer as its only argument and returns a long integer. You specify the particular information you want to retrieve using a numeric code. Table 15.1 shows examples of the information you can retrieve, the corresponding constants, and their numeric equivalents.

TABLE 15.1: Arguments for the GetSystemMetrics Windows API Function

Windows Interface Information	Constant	Value
Width of screen	SM_CXSCREEN	0
Height of screen	SM_CYSCREEN	1
Width of cursor	SM_CXCURSOR	13
Height of cursor	SM_CYCURSOR	14
Is mouse present?	SM_MOUSEPRESENT	19
Are left and right mouse buttons switched?	SM_SWAPBUTTON	23

To explore using a Windows API DLL, we'll enter the Declare statements for the GetSystemMetrics function and create a sub procedure that uses that function. First, open a new module named basAPI and enter the following Declare statement in the Declarations section.

```
Public Declare Function GetSystemMetrics Lib "user32" (ByVal nIndex As Long) As
    Long
```

In this example, we use the same name for the function in our module as the name used in the library function. This allows us to omit the alias part of the declaration statement.

Next, declare the following constants in the Declarations section:

```
Public Const SM_CXSCREEN = 0
Public Const SM_CYSCREEN = 1
Public Const SM_MOUSEPRESENT = 19
Public Const SM_SWAPBUTTON = 23
```

Then enter the InterfaceInfo procedure shown below.

```
Public Sub InterfaceInfo()
    Debug.Print "Screen width = " & GetSystemMetrics(SM_CXSCREEN)
    Debug.Print "Screen height = " & GetSystemMetrics(SM_CYSCREEN)
    If GetSystemMetrics(SM_MOUSEPRESENT) = 1 Then
        If GetSystemMetrics(SM_SWAPBUTTON) = 1 Then
            Debug.Print "There is a left-handed mouse present"
        Else
            Debug.Print "There is a right-handed mouse present"
        End If
    Else
        Debug.Print "There is no mouse present"
    End If
End Sub
```

To test the procedure in the Immediate window, type **InterfaceInfo** and press Enter. Figure 15.11 shows the result for a computer with 800×600 pixel screen resolution and a right-handed mouse.

FIGURE 15.11:

Use the Windows API GetSystemMetrics function to retrieve information about the user interface.

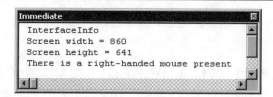

```
Immediate
    InterfaceInfo
    Screen width = 860
    Screen height = 641
    There is a right-handed mouse present
```

This example is deceptively simple because the GetSystemMetrics function takes only a single argument.

TIP   For more information about using the Windows API DLLs, see *Access 2002 Desktop Developer's Handbook* by Paul Litwin, Ken Getz, and Mike Gunderloy (Sybex, 2001).

Using ActiveX Controls

ActiveX controls (previously called OLE controls) are self-contained objects that you can add to a document in an application. They can give your application new and useful abilities without requiring you to write the code. The controls are tested, debugged, and ready for use. Examples of ActiveX controls include animated buttons, audio players, video players, marquees, progress bars, and three-dimensional check boxes.

ActiveX controls have their own events, properties, and methods. In addition to the properties, methods, and events that are specific to the ActiveX control, when you insert the ActiveX control in an Access form, you are inserting the control in an Access frame. As a result, the Access properties, methods, and events of the Access frame also apply to the ActiveX control.

Where to Get ActiveX Controls

For years, ActiveX controls have been a part of the Microsoft technology for communication between software components under the name OLE controls or OCX controls. The emergence of the World Wide Web has spurred the evolution of Microsoft's OLE technology into ActiveX technology, with a new emphasis on small and efficient programs optimized for the Web. These include a set of downloadable ActiveX controls. If you spend much time navigating the Web, you know that Web sites often offer to download ActiveX controls to your computer and register the controls automatically in your Windows Registry.

You can get custom controls from Microsoft and from third-party vendors. Access 2002 ships with a single custom control to get you started—the Calendar control. The Access 2002 Developers Edition has more custom controls. Many of the custom controls that come with Visual Basic work with Access. You can also create your own ActiveX controls using several programming languages, including Visual Basic.

Installing and Registering an ActiveX Control

An ActiveX control must have the correct entries in the Windows Registry before you can use it. Some controls have an installation program that installs and registers the control automatically. You must register other controls yourself.

When you install and register an ActiveX control, its type library installs automatically. This feature allows you to use the control's properties and methods in your VBA code just as though they were built into Access.

To view the list of ActiveX controls registered on your computer, choose Tools ➤ ActiveX Controls to display the ActiveX Controls dialog (see Figure 15.12). ActiveX control files have the OCX extension. Access 2002 ships with the Calendar control, so you should see this control on the list.

FIGURE 15.12:

The ActiveX Controls dialog lists the controls that are registered in the Windows Registry on your computer.

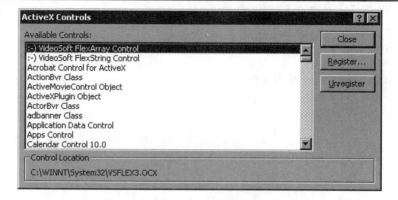

To register a new control installed on your system, click the Register button in the ActiveX Controls dialog. Locate the control's file in the Add ActiveX Control dialog (see Figure 15.13). Normally, custom controls are installed to the Windows\System or the WinNT\System32 directory. To unregister a control, click the Unregister button in the ActiveX Controls dialog.

FIGURE 15.13:

Use the Add ActiveX dialog to register an ActiveX control.

For our example, we'll use the Calendar control that ships with Access 2002. The Calendar control has control-specific properties that you use to determine the control's appearance and to set and read the data in the control. The control has control-specific methods that you use to set the day, month, and year and to update the calendar. The control also has a method for displaying an About box with version and copyright information. The control recognizes control-specific events when the user clicks or double-clicks the control, moves to a new date, or presses a key. The control also recognizes an event when the date changes.

Inserting an ActiveX Control

After you install and register an ActiveX control, there are two ways to place that ActiveX control on a form: use a menu command or use the More Controls button in the toolbox.

Using the Insert Menu

You can place an ActiveX control using a command on the Insert menu. Follow these steps to insert the Calendar control:

1. Open a new, blank form in Design view and name it frmCalendar. Select Insert ➢ ActiveX Control. The Insert ActiveX Control dialog appears (see Figure 15.14a).

2. Select Calendar Control 10.0 and click OK. The Calendar control is inserted and displays the current date when the form is in Design view.

3. Switch to Form view (see Figure 15.14b). Select the month and year using the combo boxes and click in a day box to select a day in the displayed month. (In the next section, you will learn how to use the selected date.)

FIGURE 15.14:

Choose the ActiveX Control command in the Insert menu to display a list of registered controls (a). Select the month and year using the combo boxes of the Calendar control and click in a day box to select a day (b).

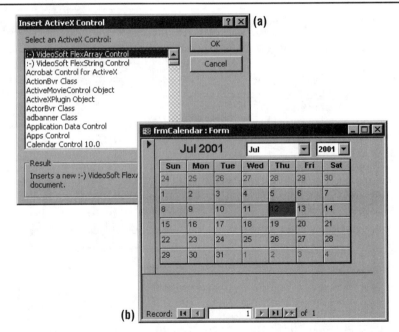

4. Switch to Design view and delete the Calendar control.

Using the More Controls Button

Another way to place an ActiveX control is to add a button for the ActiveX control to the toolbox. Then you select the control from the toolbox and drag it to your form, just as you would insert a built-in control.

To add the Calendar control, click the More Controls button in the toolbox and choose Calendar Control 10.0 in the objects list box (see Figure 15.15). Then click in the form to insert the Calendar control. Save the form.

FIGURE 15.15:

The More Controls button in the toolbox displays a list of objects you can add.

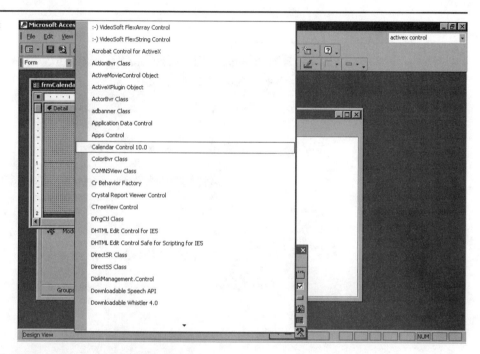

Viewing the Control's Reference

When you place an ActiveX control on a form using either technique, two things happen: the control is placed in an unbound object frame, and Access automatically adds a reference to the control's type library to your application.

To observe the reference, open a module and choose Tools ➤ References to open the References dialog (see Figure 15.16a). If Access doesn't add the reference automatically for the ActiveX control, you will need to do it manually. The Calendar control reference is Microsoft Calendar Control 10.0. To display the list of the control-specific properties, methods, and events, open the Object Browser and locate the MSACAL control listing in the Project/Library combo box. Select the control to display the list of the control-specific properties, methods, and events (see Figure 15.16b).

NOTE

An ActiveX control has the Access methods `SetFocus` and `SizeToFit`. The ActiveX control also has its own control-specific methods. You can learn about the control-specific events, methods, and properties using the Object Browser. Note that the Object Browser lists only the control-specific events, properties, and methods for an ActiveX control. It does not list the Access events, properties, and methods that apply to any ActiveX control inserted in an Access unbound object frame.

FIGURE 15.16:

After you place an ActiveX control on a form, Access automatically creates a reference to the control's type library in your database (a). After setting a reference to an ActiveX control, you can observe its control-specific events, properties, and methods (b).

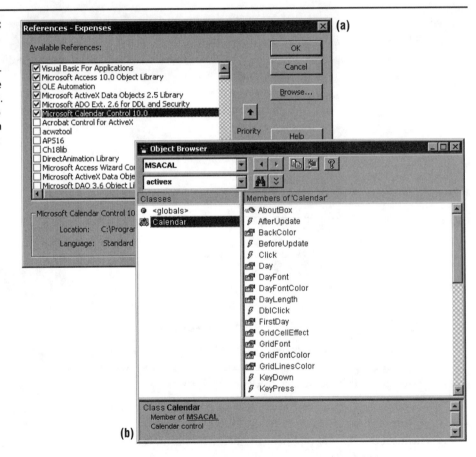

Setting ActiveX Control Properties

An ActiveX control has the Access properties listed below and its own set of control-specific properties. You can usually set some of the properties of an ActiveX control in Design view, while other properties must be set in macros or procedures.

BorderColor	BorderStyle	BorderWidth	Class
ControlSource	ControlTipText	DisplayWhen	Enabled
HelpContextID	Height	Left	Locked
Name	Object	OLEClass	OnEnter
OnExit	OnGotFocus	OnLostFocus	OnUpdated
SpecialEffect	TabIndex	TabStop	Tag
Top	Verb	Visible	Width

NOTE The ControlSource and Locked properties are available only for ActiveX controls that can be bound to a table field.

Depending on which ActiveX control you are working with, the control-specific properties that you can set in Design view may or may not be listed in the Access property sheet for the control. The control-specific properties may also be listed in the ActiveX control's own custom properties dialog.

There are two ways to set the control-specific properties when you are working with an ActiveX control in Design view. You can use the control's property sheet or, if the control has a custom property dialog, you can use the dialog.

Using the Property Sheet

A custom control is placed in an unbound object frame, so when you select the custom control in Design view, the property sheet displays the Access properties for the frame, as well as the control-specific properties. The property sheet does not list event properties for the control-specific events. The property sheet for the Calendar Control includes both the object frame properties (see Figure 15.17a) and the control-specific properties starting with the Custom property (see Figure 15.17b).

FIGURE 15.17:

The Access property sheet for the Calendar control lists the properties you can set at Design time, including the object frame properties (a) and the control-specific properties starting with the Custom property (b). The property sheet does not include properties for the control-specific events.

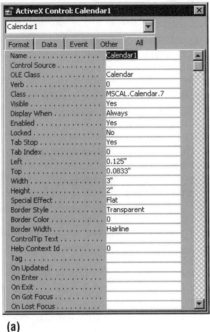

(a)

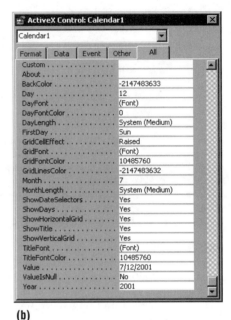

(b)

To explore the control-specific properties, switch to Form view and open the Immediate window.

- Type **?Forms!frmCalendar!Calendar1.Value** and press Enter. The Immediate window prints the current date. You can set the calendar's date when the form is in either Form view or Design view.

- Type **Forms!frmCalendar!Calendar1.Value = #12/10/2001#** and press Enter. The calendar changes to display the date. You can change the appearance of the calendar by setting its properties.

- Type **Forms!frmCalendar!Calendar1.ShowTitle = False** and press Enter. The title of the Calendar control is removed.

Using the Custom Property Dialog

You can display the custom property dialog for an ActiveX control by using one of the following techniques:

- Click the Build button next to the Custom property listed in the property sheet.

- Right-click the control and choose the Calendar Object command, then the Properties command from the shortcut menu.

- Click Calendar Object in the Edit menu, then click the Properties command from the fly-out menu.

The Calendar control properties dialog includes tabs for setting general properties, fonts, and colors (see Figure 15.18).

FIGURE 15.18:

The Calendar Properties dialog has tabs for the control-specific properties that you can set at Design time, including the general (a), font (b), and color (c) properties.

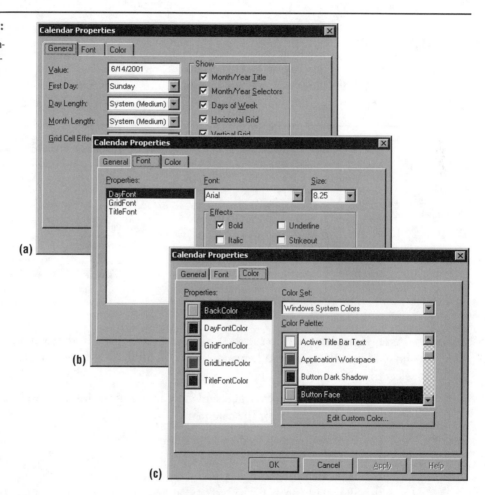

Using Events

For a built-in control, the events that the control recognizes have corresponding properties that are listed in the Event tab of the property sheet. You can use the event for a built-in control to trigger a macro, an event procedure, or a function procedure. For an ActiveX control, the Event category lists only the events that are recognized by the control frame: the Enter, Exit, GotFocus,

LostFocus, and Updated events. The control-specific events are not listed in the property sheet and are available only in the form module. After placing a custom control on a form, Access automatically creates code templates for event procedures for each ActiveX control event.

NOTE   You can trigger only event procedures—not function procedures or macros—with an ActiveX control-specific event.

With the form in Design view, select the Calendar control and click the Code button in the toolbar. Select Calendar1 in the Object combo box on the left to display the code template for the Updated event. Click the Procedures combo box on the right to view a list of both the Access events that the control's frame recognizes and the control-specific events (see Figure 15.19).

FIGURE 15.19:

The Procedures combo box for the ActiveX control lists all of the events for the control, including both the object frame events and the control-specific events.

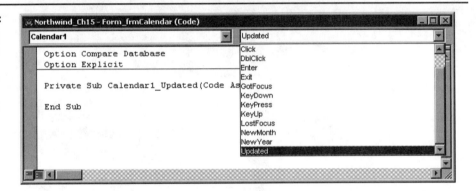

As an example of how to use the Calendar control, we'll add a calendar to the Orders form and bind it to the Required Date control. This allows you to use the Calendar control to select the date.

1. Open the Orders form in Design view and drag the lower boundary of the Detail section to make room for the calendar.

2. Click More Controls in the toolbox and select the Calendar control. Click the RequiredDate in the field list, and drag to the lower part of the form. Change the Name property to **ActiveXCalendar**, set the BackColor property to 12632256, change the ShowTitle property to No, and adjust the size of the calendar control. The Calendar control is now bound to the RequiredDate field. Add a label with the Caption property set to Select Required Date.

3. Save the form and switch to Form view. Browse through the records. The Calendar updates automatically to display the value of the RequiredDate field for the record (see Figure 15.20).

FIGURE 15.20:

The Calendar control is bound to the RequiredDate field and updates automatically when you browse to another record. However, when you change the date in the Calendar control, the RequiredDate control does not update automatically.

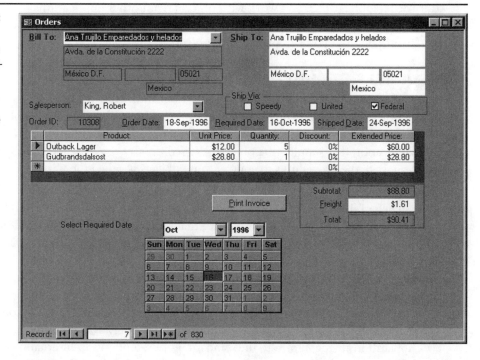

4. Change the required date for an order using the Calendar control. The RequiredDate control does not update automatically. You can update the control interactively by selecting Records ➢ Refresh or by pressing F9. Also, if you navigate to another record then return to the changed record, the RequiredDate field will be updated.

5. To refresh the form automatically, you create an event procedure for the AfterUpdate event of the Calendar control. Switch to Design view, select the Calendar control, and click the Code button in the toolbar. Enter the event procedure shown below.

```
Private Sub ActiveXCalendar_AfterUpdate
    Me.Refresh
End Sub
```

6. Save the module and switch to Form view. Change the required date using the Calendar control; observe that the form refreshes automatically.

Using Automation

Automation is one of the most important features in Microsoft's ActiveX technology for communication between software components. With Automation, you can build megaapplications that have the special capabilities of the major applications. In building these mega-applications, you work with objects from other applications using the same techniques you have learned for working with objects in Access. Specifically, you set and get properties and you run methods of objects.

Understanding Automation

Automation is the process by which the application you are working in sends instructions to another application. Applications that can use objects from another application or that make their own objects available for use by another application are called *ActiveX components*. The application that supplies the objects is called the *COM server*, and the application in which you write the procedures to control those objects is called the *COM controller*. The objects that are controlled are called *Automation objects* or *ActiveX objects*.

Each of the Microsoft Office applications is an ActiveX component and has particular strengths packaged, as ActiveX objects, that it shares with any other application that is in compliance with the set of rules called the *standards of Automation*. Access 2002 has strengths in storing, retrieving, and updating data; Outlook 2002 has strengths in scheduling and contact management; Excel 2002 has strong data-analysis capabilities; Word 2002 has strengths in formatting and reporting data; PowerPoint 2002 has strengths in presenting data; and FrontPage 2002 has strengths in Web page creation and Web site management. Automation is an open standard. This means that the specifications are publicly available, and any vendor can create applications that conform to the standard. For example, Visio International makes the strengths of Visio, its technical drawing program, available to other applications through Automation.

Each of these applications supplies a set of ActiveX objects so you can use Automation to create an application that uses Access to manage data, Excel to analyze the data, Word to report on the data, Visio to create drawings based on the data, PowerPoint to create a slide presentation of the data, and FrontPage to create a Web page and publish the data on the Web. The advantage of Automation is that you can build the advanced features of several prewritten, debugged, and thoroughly tested off-the-shelf applications into your project using the same skills and techniques that you've learned to create a project using only Access.

Some applications are only COM servers, providing their objects for control via other applications. Other applications are only COM controllers, with the ability to send instructions for working with objects provided by others, and do not provide any objects themselves. Some applications can act in both modes. For example, Access 2002, Excel 2002, Project 2002, and Visual Basic 6 have both modes and use VBA as the programming language for sending Automation instructions.

NOTE   ActiveX is an evolving technology. Previous versions of applications may have limited Automation capabilities, or they may even lack these capabilities entirely.

When an application supplies ActiveX objects, what it actually makes available are the blue-prints for objects. In object-oriented programming terminology, the blueprints are called *classes* or *object types*, and the objects you create from the blueprints are called *instances* of the class or object type. The class for an object includes its name, the definition of properties and methods, and the events that the object recognizes. A COM server stores all of the information about its objects in an object library. Typically, when you install an application, its object library and an online Help file for the object model install automatically. An object library has either the OLB extension (for object library) or the TLB extension (for type library). The following are some examples:

- The Access object model is provided in the MSAcc.olb file, which is installed by default in the \Program Files\Microsoft Office\Office10 folder.

- The ADO object model is provided by the MSADO25.tlb file, which is installed auto-matically when you install Access 2002. The default folder is \Program Files\Common Files\System\ADO.

- The PowerPoint object model is provided in the MSPPT.olb file, which is installed by default in the \Program Files\Microsoft Office\Office10 folder.

- The VBA model is provided by the VBE6.dll file in the \Program Files\Common Files\Microsoft Shared\VBA\VBA6 folder.

Learning about an Application's Objects

You can learn about another application's Automation objects while you are working in Access by adding the application's object library to the Object Browser. As explained earlier in this chapter, to add an object library to the Object Browser, open any module in your pro-ject and choose Tools ➤ References. If an item is not listed in the References dialog, click the Browse button to display the Add Reference dialog. In this dialog, you can locate the type library on your computer (see Figure 15.21) and click the OK button to add the reference. For our example, add the reference to the Microsoft Excel 10.0 Object Library.

FIGURE 15.21:

If the object library of an installed application isn't in the Reference dialog list, click the Browse button to display the Add Reference dialog and locate the object library.

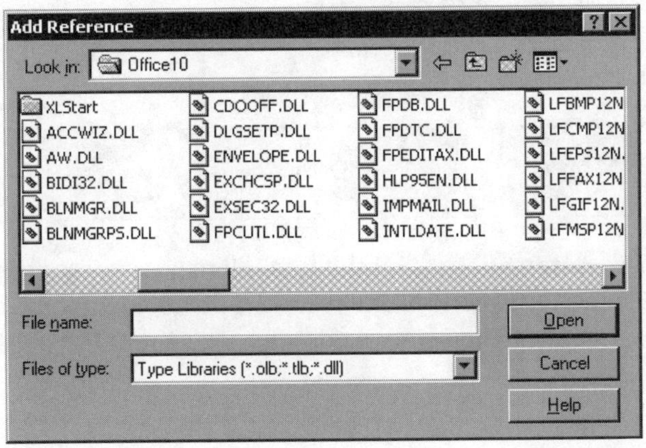

When you add a reference to a type library, you are storing the path to the type library in your project. If you move the object library, you will need to create a new reference to the library. The reference is added only for the Access project with which you are currently working. When you add a reference to an object library, VBA recognizes the objects in the object library; you can use them the same way you use the Access and ADO objects.

NOTE   This chapter assumes that you have Microsoft Office 2002 installed on your computer. If this is so, add a reference to the Microsoft Excel 10.0 Object Library. If you don't have Office 2002 installed, you can add a reference to another COM server that you have. If you have only Access, you can modify some of the examples and use Access as both a COM controller and server.

After adding the reference, you can use the Object Browser to explore the application's objects (Chapter 5, "VBA Programming Essentials," explains how to use the Object Browser). Figure 15.22 shows the properties and methods of the Worksheet object in the Microsoft Excel 10.0 Object Library. When you add the reference, you also add online help for the application's objects.

FIGURE 15.22:

You can use the Object Browser in Access to explore the objects in Excel.

Before you can use Automation successfully, you'll need to carefully study the object model of the application you want to control and learn the properties, methods, and events for the objects you want to control. The object models for the other Office 2002 applications are substantially more complex than the Access and the ADO models you've learned about in this book. Because ActiveX is an evolving technology, the object models for these applications have changed substantially from version to version.

Using the Information in the Object Library

The real benefits of adding a reference to an object library come from the fact that VBA can use information in the object library. When you set a reference to an object library, VBA loads the object library into memory so it can look up information in the library when you compile the module. When you are writing VBA procedures to work with the Automation objects, you can use the information in the library—such as the intrinsic constants and specific object data types—that the other application uses. For example, if you are working with Excel, you can use the intrinsic constants with the .xl prefix in your Access procedures. You don't need to use the numeric equivalents, and you don't need to redefine these constants.

You also can declare variables of a specific data type. For example, if you are working with Excel, you can declare object variables of the Worksheet, Chart, and Range object types. As you've learned in previous chapters, when you declare an object variable of a specific data type instead of as the generic Object data type, your code runs significantly faster.

NOTE   The process of verifying that an object exists and that a specified property or method is valid is called *binding*. There are two times when the verification process can take place: during compile time (*early binding*) or run time (*late binding*). When you declare an object variable as a specific data type, you are using early binding so the verification can take place during compile time. When you declare a variable of the generic Object data type, you are using late binding. In this case, VBA must find and verify the object information during execution of any VBA statement that includes a reference to the object or one of its properties or methods.

Applications often have object data types with the same name. For example, all of the Office applications have an Application object. You can qualify an object data type using the name of the application with the syntax *application.objecttype*. To determine the name that is used to identify the application in Automation, open the Object Browser and look up the name in the list displayed in the Project/Library combo box. When you declare an object variable for an Automation object, you can qualify the object data type to prevent VBA from creating the wrong object. To illustrate, the following statements use early binding to declare object variables:

```
Dim appAccess As Access.Application
Dim appExcel As Excel.Application
Dim wine As Excel.Window
Dim winp As Project.Window
```

NOTE You don't need to add a reference to an application's object library to use the application's Automation objects. However, if you don't add a reference, you can't use either the application's intrinsic constants or specific data types. Use of either causes a run-time error.

Using Automation Objects

There are four main steps for controlling an Automation object in a procedure:

1. Create an object variable for the Automation object.

2. Create an instance of the Automation object and point the object variable to the new instance.

3. Control the object in a procedure by setting or getting its properties or by running its methods.

4. Close the object when you are finished.

When you want to use an application's Automation objects, you must first gain access to the application. The first step is to create an instance for one of the special objects in the application's object hierarchy that Windows recognizes.

As discussed in Chapter 6, "Understanding the ADO Object Model," when you use one of the ADO data access objects, you must first define a valid Connection object, then traverse the hierarchy to the object you want to work with. In the same way, when you want to work with an Automation object from another application, you must start with one of the objects that the operating system recognizes. Normally, you start with the object at the top of the hierarchy, which is usually the Application object.

When you create a new instance that refers to the Application object, the operating system starts up an instance of the application. With the application started, you can traverse the object hierarchy to the object you want to work with. Some applications have more than one object that the operating system recognizes. As an example, the Windows operating system recognizes the Workbook and Chart objects as well as the Application object for Excel. (In previous versions of Excel, the Worksheet object, but not the Workbook object, is one of the special Excel objects that are recognized by Windows.) In this case, when you create a new instance that refers directly to the Workbook or Chart object, Windows starts up an instance of Excel, then creates an instance of the Workbook or Chart object. Then you can begin your traversal from the selected object.

There are three ways you can create an instance of an Automation object: by using the CreateObject function, by using the GetObject function, or by using the New keyword to create the object implicitly. No matter which technique you use, the COM server typically starts in a hidden window and remains hidden unless you explicitly make the window visible. Sometimes, you need only the capabilities of the COM server and may not need to show the application. For example, when you use the mathematical functions of Excel to perform calculations on the data in an Access database, you don't need to show the Excel window.

TIP   Displaying a visual representation takes additional time. Therefore, you shouldn't display the Automation objects unless it is absolutely necessary.

Using the *CreateObject* Function

Use the CreateObject function to create a new instance of one of the special Automation objects that the operating system recognizes and return a reference to the object. The CreateObject function has this syntax:

```
Set objvar = CreateObject (appname.objecttype)
```

objvar is an object variable, *appname* is the application name as listed in the Object Browser, and *objecttype* is the name of the object type you want to create. For example, to work with Excel, declare an object variable and create an object to refer to the Excel application, as follows:

```
Dim appExcel As Excel.Application
Set appExcel = CreateObject("Excel.Application")
```

The CreateObject function starts an instance of the COM server application. If the server is already running an instance, CreateObject starts another instance, unless the application is a single-instance application. For a single-instance application, only one instance of the application is created, no matter how many times you run the CreateObject function.

To demonstrate these ideas, the LaunchExcel procedure, shown below, uses the CreateObject function to create an instance of Excel (this example assumes you have Microsoft Excel 2002 installed). With Excel running, you have access to Excel's object model and can use the Open method of Excel's Workbooks object to open the Samples.xls sample spreadsheet.

```
Public Sub LaunchExcel()
    Dim appExcel As Excel.Application, strxls As String
    Set appExcel = CreateObject("Excel.Application")
    MsgBox "Excel is running"
    appExcel.Visible = True
    strxls = "c:\Program Files\Microsoft Office\Office10\"
    strxls = strxls & "Samples\Samples.xls"
    appExcel.Workbooks.Open (strxls)
    Set appExcel = Nothing
End Sub
```

After launching an instance of Excel, the procedure displays the message reporting that an instance of Excel is running. However, Excel does not appear in the Taskbar until you set the Visible property to True. After you close the message box, the procedure unhides the window and uses the Open method of the Workbooks object to open a spreadsheet. The procedure severs the link between the object variable and the instance of Excel by setting the object variable to Nothing. Setting the object variable to Nothing does not close Excel; when the procedure terminates, Excel is running.

To test the procedure, follow these steps:

1. Open a new standard module in Access named basAutomation and enter the LaunchExcel procedure shown above. (You may need to alter the strxls lines for the directory in which you installed Excel.)

2. Choose Tools ➢ References and, if necessary, click the check box for the Microsoft Excel 10.0 Object Library to set the reference to Excel. Click OK to close the dialog.

3. Press Ctrl+G to display the Immediate window. Type **LaunchExcel** in the Immediate window and press Enter.

NOTE   COM servers behave differently. Some COM servers appear in the task list even though they are launched in a hidden window. Others, such as Word and Excel, don't appear in the task list until you unhide them. Some COM servers, including Access, terminate when you sever all links from any object variables that point to the instance of the COM server. Word and Excel continue to run unless you explicitly close them in the procedure.

4. Click the Excel button in the Taskbar. The Excel window is restored and displays the window for the Samples spreadsheet.

5. Minimize Excel. (We'll use the running instance of Excel later.)

Using the *GetObject* Function

The GetObject function is more versatile than the CreateObject function. With the GetObject function, you can duplicate the effect of the CreateObject function, point an object variable to a running instance of the COM server object, or open an object that has been saved to a file.

The GetObject function has the following syntax:

```
Set objvar = GetObject(documentname,appname.objecttype)
```

objvar is an object variable, *documentname* is a string that specifies the path of the file containing the object you want to retrieve, and *appname.objecttype* is a string that represents the application and one of the special object types that the operating system recognizes. You must include at least one of the arguments (you can use either or both of them). You can create a new instance, point to a running instance of the COM server, or open a specific file.

Creating a New Instance   If you set the document name to the zero-length string, the GetObject function duplicates the behavior of the CreateObject function by creating a new instance of the specified object type. If you specify the Application object, the GetObject function creates an instance of the server application. If you specify one of the other objects that the operating system recognizes, the GetObject function creates a hidden instance of the server. Then it creates an instance for the specified object and returns a reference to the specified object.

As an example, the GetAccess procedure, shown below, launches a new hidden instance of Access.

```
Public Sub GetAccess()
    Dim appAccess As Access.Application
    Set appAccess = GetObject("", "Access.Application")
    MsgBox "Access is running"
    appAccess.Visible = True
    appAccess.NewCurrentDatabase "NewDatabase"
End Sub
```

After you close the message box, the procedure unhides the Access window and uses the NewCurrentDatabase method to create a new database named NewDatabase. The Database window for the new database flashes for an instant. When the procedure ends, the instance of Access terminates. If you want to leave the new instance of Access running in memory when the procedure ends, declare the appAccess object variable in the Declarations section of the module instead of declaring the variable within the procedure.

To test the procedure, follow these steps:

1. Insert the GetAccess procedure in the basAutomation module.

2. Type **GetAccess** in the Immediate window and press Enter.

3. Locate and delete the NewDatabase file. The procedure saves the NewDatabase file in the folder specified as the Default Database Folder in the General tab of the Options dialog (displayed by choosing Tools ➢ Options). You can use the Options dialog to change the default folder for new databases.

4. Modify the GetAccess procedure by cutting the variable declaration statement and pasting the statement in the Declarations section of the module. Run the GetAccess procedure in the Immediate window. When the procedure ends, the new database is displayed in the Access window.

5. Close the second instance of Access.

Pointing to a Running Instance of the Automation Server If you omit the *documentname* argument in the GetObject function, the GetObject function returns a reference to a running instance of the specified object and does not start up an instance of the COM server. If the server is not running, the GetObject function returns a run-time error. For example, the following statements return a reference to the Visio application if the application is running; otherwise, they return an error message.

```
Dim appVis As Visio.Application
Set appVis = GetObject(,"Visio.Application")
```

NOTE   When you use the GetObject function to access a COM server application that is already running, you omit the first argument of the GetObject function entirely. However, you must include the comma as a place holder.

As an example, the RunningExcel procedure, shown below, refers to the running instance of Excel and opens a second workbook.

```
Public Sub RunningExcel()
    Dim appExcel As Excel.Application, strxls As String
    Set appExcel = GetObject(, "Excel.Application")
    strxls = "c:\Program Files\Microsoft Office\Office10\"
    strxls = strxls & "Samples\SOLVSAMP.XLS"
    appExcel.Workbooks.Open (strxls)
    Set appExcel = Nothing
End Sub
```

To test this procedure, insert it into the basAutomation module, then run it in the Immediate window. When the procedure finishes running, restore the Excel application. You'll see that the Excel window displays the SOLVSAMP.XLS workbook. Close the SOLVSAMP workbook. Close the instance of Excel with the Samples.xls workbook.

Opening a Specific File If you specify a document name in the GetObject function, the function creates a new, hidden instance of the COM server, based on the document's file extension. The function opens the file and returns the object in the file. For example, the following statements open an instance of Excel, open the Updates.xls file, and return a reference to the Workbook object.

```
Dim objvar As Workbook
Set objvar = GetObject("c:\Excel\updates.xls")
```

If the application is already running, the GetObject function starts another instance (unless the server is a single-instance application). When a file has more than one object type that the operating system recognizes, you can specify which object you want to create by using both arguments or by declaring an object variable with the specific object type. For example, an Excel file can have both Worksheet and Chart object types. The following statements also create a hidden instance of Excel, open the Updates.xls workbook, and return a reference to the workbook.

```
Dim wksXL As Object
Set wksXL = GetObject("c:\Excel\updates.xls","Excel.Workbook")
```

TIP   Returning a reference to an object that is lower in the application's object hierarchy is faster than returning a reference to an object that is higher in the hierarchy and traversing down to the object.

Using the Parent Property   When you open one of the special objects that is lower in the application's object hierarchy, you can traverse the hierarchy of the server's object model in both directions. To traverse up the hierarchy, use the object's Parent property. For example, if you are working with a particular worksheet, you can access the workbook that contains the worksheet by using the Parent property. To access another worksheet, or a chart in the same workbook, you can use the Parent property to traverse up the hierarchy to the workbook and then refer to another object in the workbook.

As an example, the GetSpreadsheet procedure, shown below, uses the GetObject function to open an Excel spreadsheet.

```
Public Sub GetSpreadsheet()
    Dim wks As Workbook, strwks As String
    strwks = "c:\Program Files\Microsoft Office\Office10\"
    strwks = strwks & "Samples\Samples.xls"
    Set wks = GetObject(strwks)
    wks.Parent.Visible = True
    wks.Windows(1).Visible = True
    wks.Worksheets("Worksheet Functions").Select
    Set wks = Nothing
End Sub
```

This procedure uses the GetObject function to open a hidden instance of Excel. Click Enable Macros in the Excel message to allow Excel to run the macros in the workbook. Excel opens a hidden instance of the Samples.xls workbook. (The GetObject function knows to open Excel because of the file extension XLS.) The procedure uses the Parent property to traverse the object hierarchy upward to refer to the Excel application and unhides the application window. Although the Excel instance is now visible, the window containing the file is not. To make the worksheet visible, you must make the workbook visible. In Excel, the Workbook object doesn't have a Visible property. However, you can use the Windows method of the Workbook object to refer to the window containing the workbook (as the first window in the Windows collection), then use the Visible property of the Window object to unhide the window. After making the workbook's window visible, the procedure refers to the Worksheet Functions worksheet and uses the Select method to make it the active worksheet.

To test the GetSpreadsheet procedure, enter it in the basAutomation module and run it in the Immediate window. When you're finished, minimize the running instance of Excel.

Determining Whether an Application Is Running   You can use the GetObject function to determine whether there is already an instance of an application running and to make sure that only one instance runs. As an example, the TestInstance procedure, shown below, turns on error handling and then uses the version of the GetObject function that omits the document name to launch Excel.

```
Public Sub TestInstance()
    Dim appXL As Excel.Application
    On Error Resume Next
    ' If the application is not running, an error occurs
    Set appXL = GetObject(, "Excel.Application")
    If Err.Number <> 0 Then
        Set appXL = CreateObject("Excel.Application")
        appXL.Visible = True
        MsgBox "Excel is running"
    End If
End Sub
```

If Excel is not running, a run-time error is generated and the procedure uses the CreateObject function to open Excel and unhide its window. If Excel is running, the procedure ends without taking any action.

To test the TestInstance procedure, enter it in the basAutomation module and run it in the Immediate window. The procedure detects the running instance of Excel, an error does not occur, and the procedure terminates. Next, close the running instance of Excel and run the TestInstance procedure again. This time, the GetObject function generates an error because the Excel application is not running. The procedure creates and unhides a new instance of Excel. The message dialog is hidden behind the window displaying the new instance of Excel. When you close the message dialog, the procedure ends, and the instance of Excel is destroyed.

Using the *New* Keyword to Create an Object Implicitly

You can also create a new instance of an ActiveX object by using the New keyword when you declare the object variable. The New keyword creates an instance of the ActiveX object and assigns a reference to the object variable you are declaring. You can use the New keyword only for applications that support it, such as Access and Visual Basic. VBA starts up a new instance of the application each time you use the New keyword (unless the application is a single-instance application).

For example, the NewAccess procedure, shown below, opens another hidden instance of Access and unhides the window.

```
Public Sub NewAccess()
    Dim applAccess As New Access.Application
    Dim strfile As String
    applAccess.Visible = True
    strfile = "c:\Program Files\Microsoft Office\Office10\Samples\"
    strfile = strfile & "Northwind.mdb"
    applAccess.OpenCurrentDatabase strfile
    MsgBox "Access is running"
End Sub
```

NOTE The path in the **NewAccess** procedure assumes the default installation of Microsoft Office 2002. If you installed Access 2002 to another folder, you'll need to change the path.

Enter the NewAccess procedure in the basAutomation module and run it in the Immediate window. The Access window opens, and the Northwind database is displayed in the Access window. The Access window remains open as long as the procedure runs. The message dialog is behind the window displaying the new instance of Access. When you close the message dialog, the procedure ends.

Releasing the Object

When your VBA procedure uses the ActiveX objects of a COM server application, your procedure is responsible for both opening and closing the object. When you are finished with the object, you should close the object and exit the object application.

You can sever the link between the object variable and the object by setting the object variable to Nothing using this statement:

```
Set objvar = Nothing
```

However, when VBA runs this statement, only the link to the object is severed. The object itself may continue to exist. Applications behave differently in this regard. For example, Excel, PowerPoint, and Word all continue to run after an object variable that refers to the application is set to Nothing or is destroyed when the procedure ends. In contrast, destroying an object variable in Access causes the instance to terminate only if the application was launched using Automation.

All applications have a method, typically Close or Exit, that you can use to exit the application. Most ActiveX objects have a Close method that allows you to close the object. For example, if you are working with Excel, you first use Excel's Quit method to close the application and then set the object variable to release the reference, as follows:

```
appExcel.Quit
Set appExcel = Nothing
```

This section has shown you the basic mechanics of working with COM server applications. We've covered how to open and close them, and how to create and destroy ActiveX objects. Keep in mind that writing instructions to manipulate the ActiveX objects of another application requires intimate knowledge of the application's object model, including the properties, methods, and events for its objects.

Summary

This chapter gives you a glimpse of several advanced topics that require VBA programming. The chapter began with a discussion of converting macros to procedures, which allows you to leverage your efforts in creating macros, as well as use the VBA-only features described in this book. The chapter then introduces you to techniques for expanding the functionality of Access by including features from other sources, such as library databases, other code libraries, ActiveX controls, and ActiveX objects provided by other applications (ActiveX components). The chapter's important points are as follows:

- You can use functions and procedures stored in DLLs.

- If the DLL has a type library, you can set a reference to it and use the procedures the same way you use the procedures in your application.

- If there is no type library, you must declare the procedure in a module that follows the specific syntax required by the library.

- You can add functionality to your project by inserting ActiveX controls in forms. ActiveX controls have their own properties, methods, and events.

- You can use Access VBA to control another application, such as Excel or Word, by remotely using Automation.

Congratulations! You've come to the end of this book. With practice, you'll be able to master and use the techniques described throughout the book to create complex automated custom applications. In addition to teaching you the basics of Access VBA programming, this book has given you a brief introduction to a few of the more advanced topics that lie ahead. You've had a glimpse of the landscape surrounding Access should you decide to venture forth.

Glossary

A

abstraction   The formation of a model for an object that includes those properties and methods relevant to its purpose or function and ignores other aspects.

action argument   An additional piece of information specified as a constant, identifier, or literal expression used to carry out a macro action. Action arguments cannot include variables.

ActiveX   A set of Microsoft technologies for communication between software components.

ActiveX component   An application such as Microsoft Access, Excel, or FrontPage that makes its programming objects available to other applications or that can use the programming objects that other applications provide.

ActiveX control   A control that you can add to a form to provide additional capabilities that Access doesn't provide. An ActiveX control has its own properties, methods, and events. You can write VBA procedures to manipulate Active X controls.

ActiveX object   A programming object that is supplied by an external application and that can be controlled by the current application using Automation.

address   A number or bit pattern that uniquely identifies a location in computer memory. See also *hyperlink address*.

ANSI character set   An 8-bit character set used in Windows to represent up to 256 keyboard characters. It was developed by the American National Standards Institute (ANSI).

argument   A constant or expression that supplies information to a command or a macro action, procedure, or method. Arguments for procedures and methods can include variables. Arguments passed to VBA procedures are usually called *parameters*.

array   A series of indexed variables that are substituted one after the other for the same variable name and processed successively, as defined by the procedure's usage of that variable name.

AutoLookup query   A query based on two or more tables in a one-to-many relationship that automatically fills field values in the one table when you enter a value in the joined field of a new record.

Automation   The set of programming rules and techniques for controlling the objects of another application.

B

bookmark   Any device you can use to save your place. In a module, the device is the display of a symbol in the left-hand margin. In a Recordset or Form object, storing a binary string is the device that identifies the current record. The form's Bookmark property is available in VBA.

bound control   A control on a form, data access page section, or report that gets its data from a field or column in the underlying table, view, query, or SQL statement for the form, data access page section, or report. The ControlSource property setting for a bound control is the name of the field or column.

break mode   A state in which VBA code is running but is suspended between executing statements.

breakpoint   A line of code in a procedure at which VBA automatically suspends execution just before running the statement. You set a breakpoint to troubleshoot code.

by reference   A way of passing the address of an argument to a procedure. The procedure accesses the actual variable and can change its value. By reference is the default way of passing an argument.

by value   A way of passing the value, or content, rather than the address of an argument to a procedure. The procedure accesses a copy of the variable but does not change its stored value.

C

cache   A space in local memory that holds the data most recently retrieved from the server in the event that the data will be requested again while the application is running. The database engine checks the cache for the requested data before searching the disk.

calculated control   A control on a form or report that displays the result of a calculation instead of stored data. The ControlSource property setting for a calculated control is the calculation's expression preceded by an equals sign (=).

call tree   All modules containing procedures that might be called by a procedure in the module in which code is currently running.

case-sensitive   The ability to distinguish between uppercase and lowercase letters.

class   The definition for an object group including the properties, methods, and events. An object based on the definition is called an *instance* of the class.

class module   A module that defines a new object group. Access 2002 includes class modules for forms, reports, and independent object groups. An independent class module defines a set of objects not associated with either forms or reports.

class name   The name used to refer to a specific class module. For example, the class name for a form module named FormName is Form_FormName.

clone   A recordset with an independent current record pointer.

code   The set of all text instructions that you enter in an application's modules; also called *source code*. Code includes module option settings, comments, and statements for constants, variables, procedure declarations, control structures, assignments, and method executions.

code template   The first and last lines of a procedure that are created when you use the Code Builder or the Procedure command on the Insert menu.

collection   An object that contains a set of similar objects. For example, the Forms collection holds the set of open forms (the set of Form objects).

command bar   Any of three devices for displaying built-in and custom commands, including menu bars, toolbars, and pop-up menus.

compile time   The time during which the VBA code you entered is translated to executable code. The compile time varies depending on the complexity of the VBA code and whether any syntax errors are encountered. You may need to fix errors and recompile the VBA code to test your changes.

compiled state   The version of code produced by the VBA compiler. The compiler translates the text in your modules (source code) into a language that is closer to machine language and is more efficient than source code. (Access runs the compiled state and not the source code.)

concatenation   The process of joining strings. For example, to create a full name from a first name and a last name you concatenate the strings "Adam" & " " & "Gunderloy" to obtain "Adam Gunderloy".

connection string   A string containing information necessary to open an external database, such as the path to the file.

control   A graphical object that you place in a form, data access page, or report that displays data; decorates the form, page, or report; or performs an action.

control structure   The statements required for changing code statements' order of execution.

copy buffer   A location in memory created by the database engine to hold the contents of a record that is open for editing. Beginning to edit the current record copies it to the copy buffer, the AddNew method clears the buffer for a new record and sets the default values, and the Update method saves the data to the copy buffer, replacing the current record or inserting the new record. Any statement that resets or moves the current record pointer discards the contents of the copy buffer.

current index   The index most recently set with the Index property (for an indexed, direct-table Recordset object). A Recordset object can have several indexes but can use only one at a time.

current record   The record in a recordset that you can modify or retrieve data from. Only one record in a recordset can be the current record; however, a recordset does not necessarily have a current record. Use the Move... methods to reposition the current record in a recordset. Use the Find or Seek methods to change the current record position as needed.

D

data source   The source of the data for a control, form, report, data access page section, or database.

data type   The defining characteristic of a variable. It determines what kind of data the variable can hold.

debugging   The process of locating the source of an error in a procedure and eliminating the error.

declarations   Statements that define the constants, variables, user-defined data types, and external procedures from a dynamic-link library (DLL) that are available to the procedures of a module. These statements are placed in the Declarations section of the module.

Declarations section   The part of a module containing declarations that apply to every procedure in the module.

default value   A value that is automatically entered in a field or control when you add a new record.

delimiters   The symbols used to mark the beginning and end of a particular section or grouped elements in a program, such as the pair of double-quotation marks that enclose a text string.

domain   A set of records in the data source that are associated together and processed in some manner as a group.

domain aggregate function   A function that calculates a statistic, such as a sum or the largest value based on the values in the specified set of records, called the *domain*.

dynamic-link library (DLL)   An external file containing procedures that an application can link to and use at run time.

E

echo   The process of updating the screen, or providing information to the user, while a procedure runs.

empty   The state of an initialized variable of the Variant data type. When a procedure begins, Access reserves space for all variables that have been declared explicitly and sets them to empty.

encapsulation   The packaging of the properties and methods as internal components of an object. Encapsulation is one of the basic elements of object-oriented programming.

error   A deviation from correctness. Avoidable errors include compile-time errors, run-time errors, and logic errors. Unavoidable errors are those that occur after you have eliminated all of your mistakes; they typically result from user mistakes, power outages, or network problems.

error code   An integer value that uniquely identifies a run-time error.

error handler   A section of code marked by a line label or line number that specifies the actions to take if an error occurs.

error-handling code   The VBA statements that determine the error code and then interrupt and modify the default response to the specific error.

event   A change in an object's state resulting from some action that Access makes available as a programming opportunity, such as the Click event being recognized by a command button. You can assign an event procedure, event function procedure, or macro action to execute when the object recognizes the change in its state.

event procedure   A type of subprocedure that is automatically executed in response to an event triggered by the user, program code, or the system. Event procedures have predefined names and argument lists.

event property   A named attribute of a control, form, report, or section associated with an event that the item can respond to. You can execute a procedure when an event is recognized by setting the related event property to [*Event Procedure*] or a function (=*functionname*()).

executable   A program that the operating system runs to carry out a particular set of instructions. Only compiled code is executable.

F

filter   A set of criteria used to sort a set of records or to select a subset of the records. For example, you can use a filter to select only those orders placed after a specified date or the orders placed by a specified customer.

focus   The ability to receive user input through mouse or keyboard action. Only one item at a time has the focus.

foreign key   A field or combination of fields in a table or query whose values match the values in a primary key in another table or query when the two tables or queries are joined.

foreign table or query   A table or query that participates in a relationship, normally as the "many" table or query, and contains the field that matches the primary key field in the joined table or query.

form module   A module storing code for all event procedures triggered by events occurring in a specific form or its controls. The form module also includes any other procedures that relate to the form.

function procedure   A procedure that carries out an action and normally returns a value. You can use the returned value of a function procedure in an expression.

G

global variable   A variable declared in the Declarations section of a module using the Public keyword. A global variable can be seen by all procedures in the database's modules.

GUID (globally unique identifier)   A 16-byte field that uniquely identifies replicas. It is also called a Replication ID in Access.

H

hyperlink address   The path to an object, document, or other destination expressed as a URL when the destination is an Internet or intranet site, or as a network path when the destination is a file on the local network.

Hyperlink data type   A field data type for storing hyperlinks. It enables you to include HTML data sources in Access.

Hyperlink object   The object that represents a hyperlink associated with a command button, label, menu command, or image control on a form, or with a text box or the text box portion of a combo box control that is bound to a field with the Hyperlink data type.

Hypertext Markup Language (HTML)   A system for including formatting instructions, called *tags*, in each part of a text document so that the document can be published using the specified display formats on the World Wide Web.

I

Immediate window   The window in which you can immediately execute and test individual lines of VBA code.

implicit creation   The ability to use the New keyword in the declaration statement for an object variable to define a new instance of the object the first time a procedure statement refers to the object.

index   When used with tables, a reference table associated with a database table that relates a value in the reference table to the location of the corresponding record in the file that holds the database table. With tables, the index speeds up the search for the database table record. When used with collections, an index marks the position of a particular member with respect to other members in the collection.

inheritance   The ability of objects in a child class to automatically reuse the properties and methods of their parent class.

instance   An object you create that is based on a class's definitions. For example, when you place a command button on a form, the object you place on the form is an instance of the command button class, which is represented by the command button icon in the toolbox.

instantiate   To declare a variable as a particular object type in the Declarations section of a module or in the variable declarations section of a procedure.

intrinsic constant   A meaningful name provided by an application to replace a number that doesn't change. Also referred to as *enumerated constant*.

K

keyword   A word that a computer language uses as part of its own language. For example, If, Then, Else, Choose, Switch, and Select Case are VBA keywords for making decisions.

L

library database   A collection of database objects, macros, and VBA procedures that can be called from another Access project.

lifetime   The interval between the creation of a variable—when you assign the variable to a value or object reference—and the variable's destruction.

lightweight form or report   A form not associated with a form module or a report without a report module.

literal   A symbol that stands for a particular value whose definition cannot be changed. In other words, you cannot redefine literals.

literal date   A set of characters enclosed by number signs (#), such as #8/14/2000#. Use this format for dates that you do not want modified or updated.

literal string   A set of one or more characters enclosed by quotation marks, such as "This is a literal string".

locked   The condition of a Data Page object, Recordset object, or Database object that makes it read-only to all users except the one who is currently entering data in it.

logic error   An error that occurs when your procedures execute their actions but do not produce the intended result.

logical navigation   Travel among records according to the data in the record rather than their physical position in the recordset.

loop   A structure marked by beginning and ending statements that enable you to repeatedly execute the set of statements in between.

M

MDE file   An Access database file that has the source code removed and includes only the compiled version of the code.

menu bar   A horizontal bar located below the title bar that contains a list of names for the groups of commands available as menu commands. When you click a menu name, a drop-down list of menu commands is displayed.

message box   A modal pop-up form that displays a text message and one or more buttons.

You click a button (other than a Help button) to close the form and continue.

method   A procedure associated with a specific object type that operates on the object.

module   A collection of declarations, statements, and procedures stored together as one named unit.

module-level variable   A variable that is declared in the Declarations section of the module. Using the Private or Public keyword makes the variable available to all procedures either in the module or in all modules, respectively.

N

nonpersistent   An object that exists only in memory and is not saved to the database file. For example, when you open a table or run a query, a Recordset object is created; the object is destroyed when you close the table or query datasheet.

Null   A special value for the Variant data type that indicates that data is missing, unknown, or does not apply.

O

object   An element whose identity is described by a properties set and an actions set (called *methods*) that the object can take on itself.

object-centric programming   A programming style in which single statements both identify and take action on an object.

ODBC data source   A term that refers to an Open Database Connectivity database type or database server used as a source of data.

ODBC driver   A dynamic-link library (DLL) that connects a specific data source with another application.

OLEDB Provider   A type of software that allows you to use ADO to connect to a data source.

Open Database Connectivity (ODBC)   The set of protocols for accessing information in a SQL database server, such as the Jet database engine or Microsoft SQL Server.

P

parameter   A symbol in a procedure declaration statement or in the criteria of a query that is replaced by supplied values when the procedure is called or the query is run.

parameter query   A query that requires additional information before it can run.

parse   To separate an expression into its parts and recognize them as known items, including their relation as defined by a set of rules.

persistent   An object that is stored in the database file. For example, the definitions of tables, queries, forms, and reports are stored as persistent objects.

physical navigation   Travel among records according to their physical location in the recordset, such as the first, last, next, or previous position, rather than according to the data in the record.

polymorphism   The ability of two or more classes to have methods that have the same name and purpose but different instructions for implementation. For example, the DoCmd, Form, and Control objects all have a `Requery` method, but it executes differently in each case.

precondition   A condition for determining whether running an action or set of actions would cause a run-time error.

primary index   An index that consists of one or more fields that uniquely identify all records in a table in a predefined order. A primary index includes a key for the table and usually the same fields as the table's primary key.

primary key   A field or combination of fields in a table or query whose values uniquely define a record in the table or query.

primary table or query   A table or query that participates in a relationship, normally as the "one" table or query, and contains the field that matches the foreign key field in the joined table or query.

procedure   A sequence of statements that is executed as a unit.

procedure-level variable   A variable declared in a procedure. A procedure-level variable is available only to the procedure in which it is declared, unlike module-level variables.

process   A set of instructions that a computer is executing in a multitasking operating system.

project　The set of all the compiled code modules in a database. By default, the project has the same name as the database. In Access 2002, project also refers to a database using a SQL Server back end.

project name　A name that you can use to identify all the compiled code in a database. By default, Access uses the database name as the project name, but you can assign another name.

property procedures　A set of procedures that create new properties for a form or report. A `Property Let` procedure creates a custom property for a form or report. A `Property Get` procedure returns the value of a custom property for a form or report.

pseudo-code　The result of the VBA compiler processing of the text instructions and statements in a module.

R

recordset　A set of records returned in memory by a table, a query, a view, or an SQL statement that is capable of returning records.

refresh　To redisplay records in a datasheet, form, or report to reflect changes to the data made in another window or by another user when working in a multiuser environment. Refreshing does not display new records and does not rerun the underlying query or table.

requery　To rerun the query or table underlying a datasheet, form, or report. Requerying reflects changes to the data, displays new records, and removes deleted records and records that no longer satisfy the query criteria.

Run mode　Access displays three possible views in this mode: Datasheet, Form, and Print Preview.

run time　The time during which a VBA procedure is executing.

run-time error　An error that occurs when a procedure tries to execute an action but fails.

S

scope　The visibility of a constant, variable, procedure, or object. For example, a variable declared in a procedure is visible to that procedure, so its scope is the procedure.

selection-centric programming　A programming style that requires statements to select an object before taking action on it.

session　An interval that begins when you start Access and log on, and ends when you log off. If security is not implemented, logon and logoff occur automatically when you start and exit Access.

singular object　An object in an object model that has no other similar object with which it can be grouped, such as the Application object.

source code　The text statements that you enter in a module.

standards　The set of specifications for a software technology, such as ActiveX or ODBC.

statement A syntactically complete unit that expresses a specific kind of operation, declaration, or definition. You can include several statements on the same line by separating them with a colon (:).

string A fundamental data type that holds character information. A string variable can contain 65,535 bytes, stores one character per byte, and can be either fixed or variable in length.

string expression Any expression that is evaluated as a sequence of contiguous characters, such as LastName & ", " & FirstName.

Structured Query Language (SQL) The fundamental language for interacting with a relational database. Using SQL, you write statements to retrieve and manipulate a set of records in a database.

sub procedure A procedure that carries out an operation and does not return a value.

synchronization The process of updating two interrelated objects so that they display current, accurate information.

syntax error An error in the grammatical structure of the code, which includes spelling errors in keywords, punctuation, spaces, and mismatched parentheses.

T

transaction A series of changes made as a single unit. With transaction processing, either all the changes are made or no changes are made.

trappable error A specific kind of error that is recognized and assigned a number, called the *error code*, and a default error message by Access, VBA, or the database engine. When an error occurs, a VBA procedure determines the error code, if one exists, and includes error-handling instructions.

trigger An act that initiates an action. For example, when you open a form, you trigger the form's Open event.

type library A file that contains descriptions of another application's or another Access database's constants, objects, properties, and methods that you can manipulate using VBA.

U

unbound control A control on a form or report whose ControlSource property setting is not the name of a field or column. Unbound controls either have an expression as their ControlSource property setting or a blank ControlSource property setting. The value in an unbound control exists only while the form or report is open.

update To accept and store changes to data in a field or record.

user-defined object A custom object defined in a class module. You can create a set of procedures for a new object's methods and properties, create an instance of the object, and manipulate the instance with these methods and properties.

V

validation The process of checking data to determine whether the value satisfies the defined conditions and limitations.

variable A temporary storage location in memory that you name and use to hold a value or to refer to an object.

Variant The default data type for VBA variables when you don't use a type-declaration character or specify a data type or object type in a declaration statement.

W

Watch expression An expression you specify to be monitored in the Watches window.

workgroup information file A database that stores information about the users in a workgroup.

Z

zero-length string A string that does not contain any characters. You enter a zero-length string by typing a pair of double-quotation marks with no space between them (" ").

The Data Access Object (DAO) Model

- Understanding the DAO hierarchy

- Referring to DAO objects

- Creating new DAO objects

- Navigating in a DAO recordset

- Adding, editing, and deleting records using DAO

- Using DAO clones and recordsetclones

- Locating data in a DAO recordset

- Sorting and filtering a DAO recordset

This appendix covers ground not addressed in the rest of the book—the Data Access Object, or DAO, model. Before Access 2000, DAO was the programming standard used by most Access developers, and it is still employed by many as either the sole object model, or in addition to the more robust, easier-to-use ADO (ActiveX Data Object). For that reason, DAO is being covered as an appendix rather than as part of the core of this book.

Here, you'll get some hands-on experience with DAO data access objects and their properties and methods. We'll also cover using the DAO model in VBA code to automate processes you would otherwise perform interactively, using the Access user interface.

The Data Access Object (DAO) Hierarchy

The DAO object model hierarchy exists separately from the Access Application hierarchy and the object hierarchy of whatever external application you are using with Jet. Table B.1 lists the 31 data access objects, and Figure B.1 shows the hierarchy of 29 of the objects. (The objects not shown in the figure are the Properties collection and the Property objects.) At the top of the hierarchy is the DBEngine object, which you use to refer to the Jet database engine in a VBA procedure. The remaining data access objects are either collections or members of collections. In addition, each object (except for the Errors collection and Error objects) has its own Properties collection containing separate Property objects for each built-in property.

TIP   Refer to Chapter 6, "Understanding the ADO Object Model," of this book to learn more about the Access Application hierarchy.

TABLE B.1: The Data Access Objects of the DAO Model

Object	Description
DBEngine	Represents the Jet database engine.
Workspace	Represents a Jet session (a session begins when a user logs in and ends when the user logs out).
Workspaces	Contains all Workspace objects defined by the currently running Jet database engine.
Database	Represents a currently open database. The database can be an Access database (an MDB file) or an external data source (an ODBC data source).
Databases	Contains all Database objects in a workspace.
TableDef	Represents a table saved in a database. A table may be a local table in the current database or a linked table in an external database. The TableDef object defines the table and does not represent the data stored in the table.
TableDefs	Contains all TableDef objects in a database.
QueryDef	Represents a saved query in a database. The QueryDef object defines the query, including its SQL statement. The QueryDef object defines the query and does not represent data.

Continued on next page

TABLE B.1 CONTINUED: The Data Access Objects of the DAO Model

Object	Description
QueryDefs	Contains all QueryDef objects in a database.
Field	Represents a specific field in a TableDef, a QueryDef, an Index, a Relation, or a Recordset object. The Field objects of the TableDef, QueryDef, Index, and Relation objects define the fields for these objects but contain no data. The Field objects of the Recordset object define the fields and also contain data in the field's Value property.
Fields	Contains the Field objects in a table, query, index, relation, or recordset.
Index	Represents an index as a single field or multiple fields for uniquely identifying records or for search and sort operations.
Indexes	Contains all Index objects for a table.
Relation	Represents a relationship as a single field or multiple fields in two tables used to link records in the tables.
Relations	Contains all Relation objects in a database.
Parameter	Represents the parameter (unknown value) you supply to a parameter query before the query can run.
Parameters	Contains all Parameter objects for a query.
Recordset	Represents, in memory, a set of records in a table or records that result from running a query or a SQL statement. You use recordsets to retrieve, add, edit, and delete records in a database. A Recordset object must be opened explicitly through code and exists only while your code is running.
Recordsets	Contains all Recordset objects open in the current database.
Property	Represents a property or a characteristic of a data access object.
Properties	Contains all Property objects for a specific data access object.
Container	Represents a generic object that stores administrative information about a category of saved objects created in an external application. In Access, the categories include tables and queries (in the same Container object), saved relationships, forms, reports, data access pages, macros, modules, and databases.
Containers	Contains the Container objects for a database.
Document	Represents a specific saved object created in an external application. The Document object stores the administrative details for the object. In Access, the saved objects include each table, query, saved relationship, form, report, data access page, macro, module, and database.
Documents	Contains the Document objects for a database.
Error	Represents an error that occurs during an operation with a data access object or the Access interface. A single operation may have several Error objects.
Errors	Contains the Error objects for a single operation. When a subsequent operation causes an error, the Errors collection is cleared and replaced with new Error objects.
User	Represents a user account and stores information about an individual user.
Users	Contains the User objects in a workspace.
Group	Represents a group of users.
Groups	Contains the Group objects in a workspace.

FIGURE B.1:

The DAO model for Microsoft Jet workspaces. In addition to the 29 different objects shown, each object except the Errors collection and Error objects has a Properties collection containing Property objects for each built-in property.

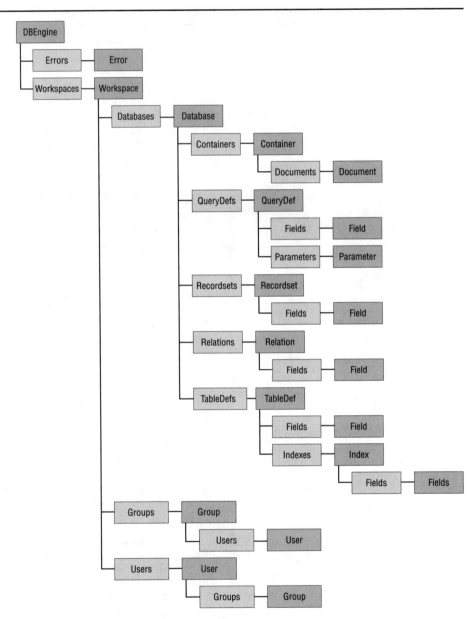

Types of DAO Objects

You can separate the DAO objects into two categories: those that are saved in some file (persistent) and those that are not (nonpersistent).

Persistent objects are saved in the database file (MDB) or in the workgroup information database file (MDW). Persistent objects include the Database, TableDef, Index, QueryDef, Parameter, Relation, User, Group, and Field objects for the TableDef and QueryDef objects. The Property objects of a persistent object are persistent as well. The collection objects that contain these objects are not persistent objects. Collection objects are created anew each time you open the database; they are dynamic and change each time a member is added to or deleted from the collection. The Container and Document objects are not persistent objects even though they contain administrative information about persistent objects. The Container and Document objects include information for the DAO objects representing the database, tables, queries, and relationships, as well as information for the objects created in Access representing the forms, reports, data access pages, macros, and modules.

Nonpersistent objects are not saved in files. Nonpersistent objects include the DBEngine, Error, Workspace, Container, Document, Recordset, and Field objects for the Recordset object. The Property objects of a nonpersistent object are nonpersistent. All collection objects are nonpersistent. You must create a nonpersistent object that is a member of a collection before you can refer to the object. For example, you create a new Recordset object using the OpenRecordset method of the Database object before you can work with the recordset.

Types of DAO Properties

Jet has two kinds of properties: built-in properties and user-defined properties. Built-in properties are those that Jet automatically creates and maintains. When you create a new data access object through DAO, such as a new QueryDef, Jet automatically creates a set of properties for the new query. Jet includes only the built-in properties in the new object's Properties collection. The built-in properties define the basic characteristics of an object.

The two kinds of user-defined properties for the data access objects are properties that you create from scratch yourself and properties that an application such as Access creates. You can add a user-defined property by appending it to the object's Properties collection. For example, if you want to describe the purpose of a new query, you can use a VBA procedure to create a user-defined property called Purpose and append it to the query's Properties collection.

When you use Access to create a Jet object, Access typically adds several properties called *application-defined properties*. For example, when you create a new query in the query Design window, most of the query properties listed in the query property sheet are application-defined properties and are not built-in DAO properties, including the

Description and OutputAllFields properties. As far as Jet is concerned, the application-defined properties do not exist until you actually type values for them in the appropriate property sheet or write procedures to add the application-defined properties to the object's Properties collection. If you enter a description in the Description property box in the query property sheet for the new query, the Description property is added to that query's Properties collection. But, if you haven't set the value of a property in the interface and you want to set the property in a VBA procedure, you must first create the property and append it to the Properties collection of the object in a procedure.

The startup properties are an interesting example of application-defined properties. Startup properties are properties of the Database object that Access defines. Most of the startup properties can be set in the Startup dialog (displayed by selecting Tools ➢ Startup). Only those startup properties that you set in the Startup dialog are added to the Properties collection of the Database object. To use a VBA procedure to set a startup property that you haven't previously set in the Startup dialog, you must first create the property and append it to the Properties collection in a VBA procedure.

Data Access Object References

In a VBA procedure, you work with the data access objects using two fundamental operations: you read and change properties, and you ask an object to use one of its methods to manipulate itself. Before you can carry out either operation, you must refer to the object.

When you start Access, Jet starts automatically and creates, in memory, a new DBEngine object to represent itself. The DBEngine object is a temporary object that exists only while Access is open; when you quit Access, the DBEngine object ceases to exist. Jet also automatically creates, in memory, a default Workspace object as a temporary object (for simplicity, we'll look only at the case in which security is not enabled). When you open an existing database, Jet creates, again in memory, a Database object to represent the database you opened.

When you want to refer to a data access object in a VBA procedure, you start by referring to the DBEngine object, and then traverse along the hierarchical path to the object, recording references to the objects and collection objects that you encounter along the way. You use the dot operator (.) when stepping from an object to one of its collections. When you are stepping from a collection to one of its members, you can use any of the four references:

- Use the exclamation point (!) operator to refer to a member explicitly by name.
- Use the parenthetical syntax to refer to a member by name.
- Use the parenthetical syntax to refer to a member by a variable.
- Use the parenthetical syntax to refer to a member by its position in the collection.

The collections in Jet are all zero-based. Normally, you use a mixture of syntax types. For example, when you start Access, Jet starts automatically and opens a default workspace that we'll refer to by position using `Workspaces(0)`. You can refer to the database you open by name, but since it is the first database open, you can also refer to it by position, using `Databases(0)`:

```
DBEngine.Workspaces(0).Databases(0)
```

Suppose you want to refer to the ValidationRule property of the CustomerID field in the Customers table in the current database. You continue traversing the path as follows:

```
DBEngine.Workspaces(0).Databases(0).TableDefs!Customers. _
    Fields!CustomerID.Properties!ValidationRule
```

Using Default Collections

Fortunately, almost all data access objects have default collections, so you can usually abbreviate references by omitting the names of the default collections. The following are the default collections:

Object	Default Collection
DBEngine	Workspaces
Workspace	Databases
Database	TableDefs
TableDef	Fields
Recordset	Fields
QueryDef	Parameters
Index	Fields
Relation	Fields
Container	Documents
User	Groups
Group	Users

TIP The Properties collection is the default collection for an object when referring to a built-in property. However, when you refer to a custom property, you must include a reference to the Properties collection as follows: *object*.`Properties!`*customproperty*.

You separate an object reference and a built-in property with the dot operator: *object.property*. Taking advantage of these default collections, you can abbreviate the reference to the current database as `DBEngine(0)(0)`, and use the following syntax for the reference to the ValidationRule property:

```
DBEngine(0)(0)!tblCustomers!CustomerID.ValidationRule
```

Using the CurrentDB Function

If you are using another application, such as Excel, to work with an Access database using Automation, the most abbreviated syntax for referring to the database is `DBEngine(0)(0)`. When you are using Access to work with the database, there is an alternate way to refer to the current database. Access provides a special function called `CurrentDB` to refer to the current database. If you are working in Access, you can use either Jet's syntax, `DBEngine(0)(0)`, or Access's syntax, `CurrentDB`, to refer to the current database. With the latter choice, the syntax for the example becomes

```
CurrentDB!Customers!CustomerID.ValidationRule
```

Although they refer to the same database, Jet's `DBEngine(0)(0)` and Access's `CurrentDB` are not exactly the same. Every time you use `CurrentDB`, you are requiring Access to create a new object that refers to the current database. On the other hand, Jet uses only the single reference to the current database, `DBEngine(0)(0)`, so it isn't necessary to create a new object. Creating a new reference with `CurrentDB` is slower than using `DBEngine(0)(0)`. However, `CurrentDB` is always in sync with the user interface. For example, new tables you create appear immediately in the Database window. When you use `DBEngine(0)(0)`, you need to execute the `RefreshDatabaseWindow` method of the Application object to update the Database window. The net result is that using `CurrentDB` may be faster.

When you use the `CurrentDB` function to refer to the database object, the four ways to refer to an object in a collection look like this:

Exclamation point	`CurrentDB!QueryDefs!Invoices`
Index by name	`CurrentDB.QueryDefs("Invoices")`
Index using a variable	`strName = "Invoices"`
	`CurrentDB.QueryDefs(strName)`
Index by number	`CurrentDB.QueryDefs(0)`

NOTE Make a new copy of the Northwind sample application named Northwind_AppendixB for the examples in this appendix.

Open Northwind_AppendixB and display the Immediate window by pressing Ctrl+G. Test the following references:

- Type **?CurrentDB.Name** and press Enter. The path to your open database is returned.

- Type **?CurrentDB!Employees!Title.Required** and press Enter. False is returned.

- Type **CurrentDB!Employees!Title.Required = True** and press Enter. To test the property setting, open the Employees table and try to save a new record without entering a value in the Title field.

Two Databases Opened Simultaneously

When you work interactively or use only macro programming, you can open only one database at a time. When you work with VBA programming, you can open multiple databases simultaneously. You can even create separate workspaces with each workspace guarded by its own security permissions, and you can open multiple databases within each workspace.

You can use the OpenDatabase method of the Workspace object to open a specified database. Opening a second database, however, is not like opening a second workbook in Excel or a second document in Word because you can't see the second database. Access opens the second database in memory; there is no visual representation. With VBA programming, however, you can work with the second invisible database almost as though it were visible in the Access interface.

The OpenDatabase method returns the opened database as a Database object. When you use a method that returns something, you can assign the result to a variable. Because the OpenDatabase method returns an object, you assign the result to an *object variable*. The assignment statement for an object variable is as follows:

```
Set objectvariable = object
```

The Set keyword indicates the assignment of the object to an object variable. Chapter 8, "Using Variables," gives a detailed treatment of object variables.

The syntax for the OpenDatabase method is as follows:

```
Set objectvariable = workspace.OpenDatabase(dbname, options, read-only, connect)
```

where

- *workspace* is an optional reference to the Workspace object that will contain the database. To use the default Workspace object, omit the reference.

- *dbname* is a required string expression that is the name of an existing database file that you want to open.

- *options* is an optional argument that sets various options for the database such as whether you are opening the database for exclusive or shared access.

- *read-only* is another optional argument. It is True if the database is to be opened for read-only access and False if the database is to be opened for read/write access; the default is False.

- *connect* is an optional string expression for specifying connection information such as passwords.

When you call the OpenDatabase method, Access opens the database and adds the database automatically to the Databases collection.

As an example, we'll open another sample Access database, Northwind.mdb. In the Immediate window, follow these steps:

1. Type **Set mydb= DBEngine(0).OpenDatabase("c:\vbahandbook\Northwind.mdb")** and press Enter. Access opens the Northwind database immediately; the mydb variable refers to, or *points to*, the database object. How can you confirm that the database is open? The object variable mydb points to the open database; you can confirm that the database is open by retrieving the value of the Name property for the database—that is, by retrieving mydb.Name.

2. Type **?mydb.Name** and press Enter. The Immediate window displays the full path name for the Northwind.mdb database. Having confirmed that the second database is open, close it using the Close method of the Database object. When you use the Close method, the open database is closed and removed from the Databases collection.

3. Type **mydb.Close** and press Enter. Access closes the Northwind.mdb database. To confirm the closure, take the next step.

4. Type **?mydb.Name** and press Enter. The error message in Figure B.2 tells you that the mydb object variable is invalid or not set, because the database that the mydb variable was pointing to no longer exists in memory.

FIGURE B.2:

When you point an object variable to an object and then close the object, the object no longer exists in memory.

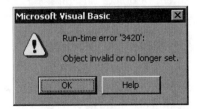

New Data Access Objects

If a data access object doesn't exist when you want to refer to it in a VBA procedure, you'll need to create it. In general, creating a new data access object is a three-step process:

- Create the object using the `Create…` method of the parent object.

- Define the new object's characteristics by setting its properties. Many of an object's properties can be set only when you create the new object, and they become read-only after the object is saved to the database. In some cases, you also must create child objects for the new object; for example, when you create a new table, you must also create at least one field before you can save the table.

- Append the object to its collection using the `Append` method of the collection.

In general, the object that is created in memory is saved to the database only when you append it to its collection. Here are some exceptions:

Workspace object   When you create a new Workspace object using the `CreateWorkspace` method of the DBEngine object, you don't need to append it before you can use it. Workspace objects are temporary and can't be saved to disk. If you need to refer to the new workspace through the Workspaces collection, however, you'll need to append it to the collection.

Database object   When you create a new Database object using the `CreateDatabase` method of the Workspace object, the new database is automatically appended to the Databases collection and saved to disk.

QueryDef object   When you create a new QueryDef object using the `CreateQueryDef` method of the Database object, the new query is automatically appended to the QueryDefs collection and saved to disk.

Recordset object   When you create a new Recordset object using the `OpenRecordset` method of any of the objects including the Database, TableDef, QueryDef, or Recordset objects, the new Recordset object is automatically added to the Recordsets collection. (The name `OpenRecordset` is a misnomer because you are creating a new Recordset object and not opening an existing Recordset object.)

A `Create…` method returns the object being created. The syntax for each `Create…` method includes the `Set` keyword to assign the result of the method to an object variable.

Creating Databases

The syntax for the `CreateDatabase` method is as follows:

```
Set database = workspace.CreateDatabase(name, locale, options)
```

where

- *workspace* is a reference to the existing workspace object that will contain the database. To use the default workspace, omit the reference.

- *name* is a string expression that can have a maximum of 255 characters and is the name of the database file you are creating. You can specify a path and a filename. You can only create an MDB file with this method.

- *locale* is a required string expression that specifies the language to be used for the sort order for text values. Use dbLangGeneral to specify English, German, French, Portuguese, Italian, and Modern Spanish.

- *options* is an optional integer that specifies the Jet database engine file format and determines whether to encrypt the database.

As an example, we'll create a new empty database using the `CreateDatabase` method of the Workspace object and using newdb as the object variable. In the Immediate window, enter the following:

```
Set newdb = DBEngine.Workspaces(0).CreateDatabase _
    ("c:\mynew.mdb", dbLangGeneral)
```

A new empty database is created and saved on disk. To check this, choose File ➤ Open and select Mynew.mdb. The new empty database opens. Press Alt+F11 to open the Visual Basic Editor. Click Tools ➤ References and place a check in the box next to Microsoft DAO 3.6 Object Library. Click OK.

Creating Tables

Often, the object you want to create has required child objects; for example, you can't create a table without at least one field. Other examples are the Index and Relation objects, which also require at least one field. In these cases, creating the parent requires additional steps. As an example, here are the steps for creating a new TableDef named myShipping with a single field named ShipperID. You can create the sample table using the Immediate window.

1. To create a new TableDef object using the `CreateTableDef` method of the Database object, type **Set tdfShip = CurrentDB.CreateTableDef("myShipping")** and press Enter.

2. To create a Field object using the `CreateField` method of the TableDef object, type **Set fldID = tdfShip.CreateField("ShipperName", dbText, 40)** and press Enter.

WARNING If you forgot to add a reference to the DAO object library, attempting to create a Field object as in step 2 will generate an error.

3. To append the Field objects to the Fields collection, type **tdfShip.Fields.Append fldID** and press Enter.

4. Append the new TableDef object to the TableDefs collection. Type **CurrentDB.TableDefs.Append tdfShip** and press Enter.

5. Update the database window. Type **RefreshDatabaseWindow** and press Enter.

If you open the Database window and click the Tables button, you will note that there is a new myShipping table. Open this table, and you will see that there is a single field named ShipperName. Close the Mynew database and open the Northwind_AppendixB database.

Creating QueryDefs

Frequently, you need to create new queries in a VBA procedure. You create a new query as a QueryDef object. The syntax for the `CreateQueryDef` method of the Database object is as follows:

```
Set qdf = database.CreateQueryDef(name, sqltext)
```

where

- *qdf* is an object variable for the new QueryDef object.

- *database* is a reference to the open Database object that will contain the new Query-Def. (In an ODBCDirect workspace, use a reference to the open Connection object instead.)

- *name* is an optional string expression that names the new QueryDef object.

- *sqltext* is an optional valid SQL statement as a string expression that defines the QueryDef.

If you don't specify the *name* and *sqltext* arguments of the `CreateQueryDef` method, you can use assignment statements to specify the Name and SQLText properties of the new QueryDef object.

As an example, we'll create a new query that displays the records in the Employees table and sorts the records by LastName. Here are the steps:

1. In query Design view, create a new query based on the Employees table. Use the asterisk (*) method to include all the fields. Drag the LastName field to the grid, deselect the Show check box to hide the field, and enter Ascending in the Sort cell.

2. Switch to SQL view and copy the following SQL statement to the Clipboard:

```
SELECT Employees.*
FROM Employees
ORDER BY Employees.LastName;
```

3. Type the following in the Immediate window, pasting the SQL statement from the Clipboard, and enclosing the statement in double quotation marks:

```
Set myquery = CurrentDB.CreateQueryDef("EmployeeSort", "SELECT Employees.*
FROM Employees ORDER BY Employees.LastName;")
```

Type the entire statement on one line. When you press Enter, the query is created and saved to disk.

4. Type **RefreshDatabaseWindow** and press Enter. The Database window updates to display the new query, EmployeeSort.

NOTE   If the query you want to create is a SQL-specific query that can't be created in query Design view, you'll need to create the SQL statement directly. See the *Access 2002 Desktop Developer's Handbook* by Paul Litwin, Ken Getz, and Mike Gunderloy (Sybex, 2001) for guidance on creating SQL statements.

Creating DAO Recordsets

The most common type of data access object you create in VBA procedures is the Recordset. You'll notice in Table B.1 that neither the TableDef nor the QueryDef objects represent the data stored in the database tables. The data values are available only as the Value property setting of the Field object of the Recordset object. Thus, if you are going to manipulate data in VBA using the data access objects, you'll be working with Recordset objects.

The Recordset data access object represents a recordset. The Recordset object has more than 30 properties and more than 20 methods for working with data. All the power of Jet's data access objects to sort, search, update, add, and delete data resides in the Recordset object.

Types of Recordsets

Four types of Recordset objects are available in the DAO model (a fifth type is available in ODBCDirect workspaces). The four types differ in significant ways and are used for different purposes. Each offers advantages and disadvantages. The following sections explain the features of the recordset types.

Table-Type   The table-type Recordset object is a set of records that represents a single table in the MDB file of the open database but not in an attached or an ODBC table. You can use the table-type Recordset object to retrieve, add, update, and delete records. When you use a table-type Recordset object, you are using the table directly. The primary advantage of this type over the others is that it can be indexed and, therefore, provides the fastest way to locate data. This object is available for Microsoft Jet workspaces only.

Dynaset-Type   The dynaset-type is a dynamic set of records that represents a table in the open database, an attached table, or the result of running a query or a SQL SELECT statement. If the query is updatable, the dynaset-type can be used to retrieve, add, update, and delete records. When you use a dynaset-type Recordset object, the object consists of only a set of references, or key values, and the full record is retrieved only when you need it for editing or display. The dynaset-type is slower than the table-type, but it provides the flexibility of extracting data from more than one table and from attached tables. The dynaset-type cannot be indexed. In some cases, the resulting query is not updatable.

Snapshot-Type   The snapshot-type is a static copy of a set of records based on a table, query, or SQL SELECT statement. You can use this type to retrieve data or generate reports. If you need only a single pass through records, you can also create a forward-scrolling snapshot. In a snapshot-type Recordset object, the object consists of a copy of the entire record (but only references to Memo and OLE Object fields). This type cannot be indexed, and the data cannot be updated. The snapshot-type is typically faster than a dynaset-type.

Forward-Only-Type   The forward-only-type is the same as the snapshot-type except that you can only scroll forward through the records. This type provides better performance than the snapshot-type, but you can only make a single pass through the recordset.

Creating a Recordset Object

You can manipulate data in a VBA procedure in two ways:

- You can open a form that is bound to the data and use the Application objects to manipulate the data.

- You can create a Recordset object in memory to represent the data and use the data access objects to manipulate the data.

Using the Application objects involves writing less code because the Application does so much of the work for you (see Chapter 12, "Maintaining Data with Access VBA," for examples of procedures for both approaches). Using the data access objects means writing more code, but it gives you more opportunity to specify how and when you want Jet to carry out each step of an operation. This appendix focuses on using data access objects.

You use the OpenRecordset method of the Database object to create a new Recordset object on an existing table or query or on a SQL statement that returns records. The Open-Recordset method automatically appends the new Recordset object to the Recordsets collection. The syntax is as follows:

```
Set rst = database.OpenRecordset (source, type, options, lockedits)
```

where

- *rst* is the object variable for the object.

- *database* is a reference to an existing Database object you want to use.

- *source* is a string specifying the name of a table, the name of a query, or a SQL SELECT statement that returns records. For table-type Recordset objects, the source must be a table name in the database.

- *type* is an optional integer, or intrinsic constant, representing the type as follows (if you specified a table in the current database, the default is table-type; if you specified an attached table, a query, or a SQL statement, the default is dynaset-type):

dbOpenTable	Table-type Recordset object
dbOpenDynamic	Dynamic-type Recordset object (ODBCDirect workspaces only)
dbOpenDynaset	Dynaset-type Recordset object
dbOpenSnapshot	Snapshot-type Recordset object
dbOpenForwardOnly	Forward-only-type Recordset object

- *options* is an optional combination of constants specifying the characteristics of the new object.

- *lockedits* is an optional constant that determines the locking for the recordset.

You can also create a new Recordset object based on an existing TableDef or QueryDef object. You can even create a new Recordset object based on an existing Recordset object. These objects have their own OpenRecordset methods, with the following syntax:

```
Set rst = object.OpenRecordset (type, options, lockedits)
```

object is an existing TableDef, QueryDef, or Recordset object. The arguments are the same as listed above.

You can use the Immediate window to create the following recordsets:

- Type **Set rstEmployees = CurrentDB.OpenRecordset("Employees", dbOpenDynaset)** and press Enter to create a dynaset-type Recordset object on the Employees table.

- Type **Set rstCategories = CurrentDB.OpenRecordset("Categories")** and press Enter to create a table-type Recordset object on the Categories table.

- Type **Set rstSuppliers = CurrentDB.OpenRecordset("SELECT * FROM Suppliers ORDER BY [CompanyName]", dbOpenSnapshot)** and press Enter to create a snapshot-type Recordset object on the SQL statement.

- Type **Set rstCustomers = CurrentDB!Customers.OpenRecordset** and press Enter to create a table-type Recordset object on the Customers table.

- Type **Set rstSales = CurrentDB.QueryDefs("Sales by Category").OpenRecordset** and press Enter to create a dynaset-type recordset on the Sales By Category query.

> **NOTE**   If you open a recordset on a table in the database (in a Microsoft Jet workspace) and don't specify a type, Jet creates a table-type recordset. If you open a query or a linked table and don't specify a type, Jet creates a dynaset-type recordset.

Closing a Recordset

Every Recordset object that you create in a VBA procedure exists only while that procedure is running; when the procedure is finished, the Recordset object ceases to exist. If you need to close a Recordset object during the procedure, use the Close method. Using the Close method closes an open Recordset object and removes it from the Recordsets collection. For example, to close rstSales, type **rstSales.Close** in the Immediate window and press Enter.

> **NOTE**   It isn't necessary to explicitly close Recordset objects before the procedure ends. However, you make your code easier to understand if you explicitly close the Recordset objects.

DAO Recordset Object Manipulation

When you create a Recordset object, you are placing rows of data in a memory buffer; the rows are not displayed on the screen. You are pointing to one row at a time; the row you are pointing to is called the *current record*. The current record is the only record that you can modify or retrieve data from. When you refer to fields in a Recordset object, you get values from the current record. Only one record in the recordset can be the current record at any one time. When you first create a Recordset object using the OpenRecordset method, the first record is the current record if there are any records. At times, a Recordset object doesn't have a current record. For example, if the recordset has no records, the Recordset object doesn't have a current record.

With only a single record available at one time, you'll need ways to navigate from one record to another record, making the record you navigate to the current record so that you can work with it. The two basic kinds of navigation among records are *physical navigation* and *logical navigation*. In interactive Access, you are using physical navigation when you click the navigation buttons in the lower-left corner of a form or datasheet to move from one record to another according to their physical location within the recordset.

When you use the Find dialog (choose Edit ➤ Find) and enter search criteria in the Find What text box, you are using logical navigation to move directly to the first record that matches the criteria. The Recordset object has methods and properties for both kinds of navigation.

Using Physical Navigation

You can move from one record to another according to physical location in two ways. You can use the Move... methods to duplicate the effect of the navigation buttons of interactive Access, or you can save your place in a recordset by setting a bookmark and then returning later to the same record.

Using the *Move . . .* Methods

You can move from one record to another record according to the record's physical location in the recordset using the Move... methods of a Recordset object. The MoveFirst, MoveLast, MoveNext, and MovePrevious methods move the current record position to the first, last, next, or previous record of a specified Recordset object, respectively. The syntax of the Move... methods is as follows:

```
rst.{MoveFirst | MoveLast | MoveNext | MovePrevious}
```

rst refers to an open Recordset object. In a forward-only-type recordset, you can use only the MoveNext method, because you can only move the current record pointer forward toward the last record of the recordset.

For example, when you created rstEmployees in the last section, the first record was the current record. You can use the Immediate window to test the Move... methods as follows:

1.   Type **?rstEmployees.EmployeeID** and press Enter. The number 1 is displayed. Now let's move to the next record.

2.   Type **rstEmployees.MoveNext** and press Enter. Then type **?rstEmployees .EmployeeID** and press Enter. The number 2 is displayed. Let's move to the last record and see what happens if we try to use the MoveNext method.

3.   Type **rstEmployees.MoveLast** and press Enter. The last record in the recordset is now the current record.

4.   Type **rstEmployees.MoveNext** and press Enter. You have now moved beyond the last record of the recordset. Type **?rstEmployees.EmployeeID** and press Enter. The error message indicates there is no current record.

Using the BOF and EOF Properties

You use the BOF (Beginning of File) and EOF (End of File) properties of the Recordset object to determine whether you've gone beyond the limits of the recordset. Both properties have the value False as long as you are pointing to a record in the recordset—that is, as long as there is a current record. If you move after the last record, there is no current record, and the EOF property is set to True; if you move before the first record, there is no current record, and the BOF property is set to True. If the recordset has no records at all, both the BOF and EOF properties are True. To confirm this, type **?rstEmployees.EOF** in the Immediate window and press Enter. The value True is returned.

A standard VBA procedure for working with a set of records is to create a Recordset object and use the MoveNext method to loop through the records one by one. To determine when you are finished, you test the value of the EOF property at the beginning of each pass through the loop. As long as EOF is False, you take another pass, but as soon as EOF is True, you have moved beyond the last record of the recordset and the loop is finished. Chapter 9, "Controlling Execution," describes how to create procedures for looping through a recordset.

Setting Bookmarks

When you create a Recordset object, Jet automatically assigns a set of unique bookmarks. If you are pointing to a record that you want to return to later, you can save your place by saving the record's bookmark to a variable; to return to the record later, you set the Bookmark property to the saved value. Test the technique in the Immediate window as follows:

1. Type **rstEmployees.MoveFirst** and press Enter. Then type **rstEmployees.MoveNext** and press Enter. The current record is the second record (EmployeeID = 2). You save your place in the next step.

2. Type **strMark = rstEmployees.Bookmark** and press Enter. The strMark variable stores the bookmark.

3. Use a Move... method to move to some other record.

4. Type **rstEmployees.Bookmark = strMark** and press Enter to move back to the saved place. Confirm by entering **?rstEmployees.EmployeeID** and pressing Enter. You have returned to the bookmarked record.

Using the *Move* Method

You can use the Move method to move the current record position forward (toward the last record) or backward (toward the first row) a specified number of rows. You can even specify that you want to start moving from a particular record. The syntax of the Move method is as follows:

```
rst.Move rows, start
```

where

- *rst* is the reference to the Recordset object.

- *rows* is a signed Long integer indicating the number of rows. If *rows* is positive, you move forward; otherwise, you move backward. For a forward-only-type Recordset object, *rows* must be a positive integer.

- *start* is an optional string variable that identifies a bookmark.

You can test the Move method in the Immediate window. Type **rstEmployees.Move 4** and press Enter. Confirm that you are now at the record with EmployeeID = 6.

Using Logical Navigation

When you want to locate a record that satisfies a search condition, the technique you use depends on the type of Recordset you've created. If you are working with a table-type Recordset, you can take advantage of indexes and use the Seek method. If you are working with a dynaset-type or snapshot-type Recordset, indexes are not appropriate, and you use the Find... methods instead. If either search technique succeeds in finding a record that matches the search condition, the found record becomes the current record. If no record is located, there is no current record after you run the method. To determine if the search is successful, you check the NoMatch property of the Recordset object. If the search is successful, a match has been found, and NoMatch is False; if the search fails, there is no match, and the NoMatch property is True.

Using the *Seek* Method

The Seek method uses indexes to locate records in the fastest way possible. You can use the Seek method only for a table-type Recordset because the search condition is based on values in an index. Before you can use the Seek method, the table you are working with must have at least one index, and you must set the Index property of the Recordset object to the particular index you want to use in the search. For example, the Customers table has the indexes shown in Figure B.3.

You can use any of the existing indexes, or you can create a new Index object. The value of the Index property is called the *current index*.

FIGURE B.3:

The indexes defined for the Customers table

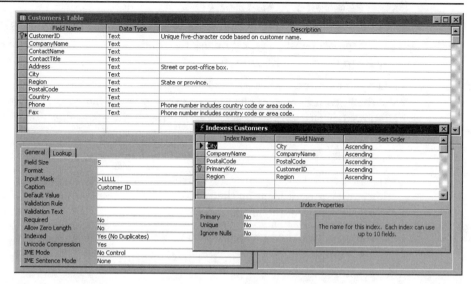

The syntax for the Seek method is as follows:

`tablerecordset.Seek comparison, key1, key2... key13`

where

- *tablerecordset* is a reference to the existing table-type Recordset object that has a current index specified by the Recordset object's Index property.

- *comparison* is a string expression that includes one of the following comparison operators: <, <=, =, >=, or >. You must follow the operator with a comma.

- *key1, key2... key13* are one to thirteen values of fields in the current index.

For example, to search for customers from a particular city, follow these steps:

1. To set the current index to City, type **rstCustomers.Index = "City"** and press Enter.

2. To locate the first customer from London, type **rstCustomers.Seek "=", "London"** and press Enter.

3. To determine if the search was successful, type **?rstCustomers.NoMatch** and press Enter. The search is successful, and False is returned.

4. Type **?rstCustomers.CompanyName** and press Enter. The name of the first customer is returned as Around the Horn.

Using the *Find...* Methods

The Seek method works only with table-type Recordsets. When your Recordset object is the dynaset-type or snapshot-type, you use the Find... methods instead. The Find... methods do not apply to table-type Recordsets.

You can duplicate the effect of the Find command of interactive Access with the Find... methods of the Recordset object. The FindFirst, FindLast, FindNext, or FindPrevious method locates the first, last, next, or previous record that satisfies specified criteria and makes that record the current record. The syntax for the Find... method is as follows:

```
rst.{FindFirst | FindLast | FindNext | FindPrevious} criteria
```

where *rst* is a reference to an existing dynaset- or snapshot-type Recordset, and *criteria* is a string expression for locating the record. (The expression is the WHERE clause of a SQL statement but without the WHERE word.)

For example, find the first supplier from Berlin as follows:

1. Type **rstSuppliers.FindFirst "City = 'Berlin'"** in the Immediate window and press Enter.

2. To determine the name of the supplier, type **?rstSuppliers.CompanyName** and press Enter.

Adding, Editing, and Deleting Records

To understand which methods you must include in procedures that modify data using the data access objects, you need to be aware that Jet does not automatically carry out the steps that are automatically carried out when you write procedures to modify data with a form using the Application object.

Editing and Updating Records

When you want to modify the data in a record, you must first make that record the current record. You can use the Move... methods or the Find... or Seek methods to move the current record pointer to the record you want to change. The crux of editing data is that the changes are not made directly to the record; instead, the record is copied into a location in memory called the *copy buffer* that Jet creates for editing. Your VBA code must deal with moving content in and out of the copy buffer. To copy the contents of the copy buffer back to the Recordset object, you must use the Update method. If you perform any operation that moves to another record, ends the VBA procedure, or closes the Recordset object without first using the Update method, your changes are not saved, and the contents of the copy buffer are discarded without warning.

You can work in the Immediate window to change the data in the `rstCustomers` Recordset object; you'll change the company name from Around the Horn to Around the Cape in the record you found earlier using the `Seek` method. Follow these steps:

1. To copy the current record to the copy buffer for editing using the `Edit` method, type **rstCustomers.Edit** and press Enter.

2. To assign the new values to the fields you want to change, type **rstCustomers .CompanyName = "Around the Cape"** and press Enter. The new value is now in the copy buffer.

3. To save the changes to the current record using the `Update` method, type **rstCustomers.Update** and press Enter.

4. To confirm that the change was saved, type **?rstCustomers.CompanyName** and press Enter. The Immediate window displays the new value.

Editing a record provides an example of the fundamental differences between modifying data using the Access interface and using the data access objects: when you work interactively, you locate the record you want to change in a form and type your changes into a control. The moment you type the first character, the edit pencil in the record selector indicates that you are entering the new values into the copy buffer (effectively, the Application calls the `Edit` method for you). When you are finished making changes, you can save the changes in a variety of ways, such as clicking into another record, pressing Shift+Enter, or closing the form (effectively, the Application calls the `Update` method for you).

If you decide not to save the changes to the record, use the `CancelUpdate` method to flush out the copy buffer.

NOTE   The `Edit` method does not apply to snapshot-type or forward-only-type Recordset objects because both of these are static copies of records.

Adding and Updating Records

As with record changes, new records are not added directly to the recordset; instead, the new record is added to the copy buffer in memory. Your VBA code uses the `AddNew` method to add the contents of the copy buffer to the recordset.

Where the new record gets inserted depends on the type of recordset. The new record is added to the end of a dynaset-type recordset. It is placed in its proper sort order in a table-type recordset if the Index property has been set; otherwise, it is placed at the end of the recordset. When you add the new record, Jet creates a bookmark for it and stores the bookmark in the LastModified property. All this takes place without affecting the current record;

the current record continues to be the record that was current before you added a record. If you want the new record to be the current record, you need to move the current record pointer to it.

You can work in the Immediate window to add a new record to the rstCustomers Recordset object. Follow these steps:

1. To create a new record in the buffer using the AddNew method of the Recordset object, type **rstCustomers.AddNew** and press Enter.

2. To assign new values to fields in the buffer, type the following assignment statements in the Immediate window and press Enter after each:

    rstCustomers.CustomerID = "ROUND"

    rstCustomers.CompanyName = "Round the Bend"

    rstCustomers.City = "London"

3. To add the contents to the recordset, type **rstCustomers.Update** and press Enter. Because rstCustomers is a table-type recordset and there is a current index (earlier, you set the Index property to City), the new record is placed with the other London customers. The current record is still the record with company name Around the Cape.

4. To confirm, type **?rstCustomers.CompanyName** and press Enter.

5. To move to the new record, set the Bookmark property to the new record's bookmark stored as the LastModified property setting. Type **rstCustomers.Bookmark = rstCustomers.LastModified** and press Enter.

6. To confirm, type **?rstCustomers.CompanyName** and press Enter.

If you decide not to add the new record, you can use the CancelUpdate method to flush out the buffer.

Deleting Records

When you delete a record, the record is placed in a location in memory, which we'll call the *delete buffer*, that Jet creates for deletions. Interestingly, the record continues to be the current record even though you can't edit or use it; referring to the deleted record produces a run-time error. Note that there is no CancelDelete method to undo the operation; effectively, the record is simply gone without warning.

TIP   If you want to display a delete confirmation message, you can create a set of statements called a *transaction* to undo the deletion if the user decides not to delete the record. See Chapter 13, "Working with Groups of Records Using Access VBA," for information about creating transactions.

You can work in the Immediate window to delete the record that you just added to the rst-Customers Recordset object. Follow these steps:

1. To place the record in the delete buffer using the Delete method, type **rstCustomers.Delete** and press Enter. Confirm by typing **?rstCustomers.CompanyName**. An error message indicates the record is unavailable.

2. Move to another record to make it the current record. Type **rstCustomers.MoveNext** and press Enter. Confirm by typing **?rstCustomers.CompanyName** and pressing Enter.

Using Clones

At times it is convenient to have more than one current record pointer for a Recordset object. You use the Clone method to create a new Recordset object that duplicates an existing Recordset object. The syntax is as follows:

```
Set rstclone = original.Clone
```

where *rstclone* is the new object variable for the Recordset object, and *original* is the reference to the Recordset object.

When you create a clone, the clone object and the original Recordset object each have their own current records, and you can navigate in the Recordset object independently. An important feature of the Clone method is that the duplicate Recordset has the same bookmarks as the original Recordset object; thus, you can set a bookmark with the clone and retrieve the bookmark with the original and vice versa. The original and the clone are not exactly identical, however. For example, if the recordset is a table-type recordset with a current index, the clone does not inherit the value of the Index property. And, if the original is a dynaset-type or snapshot-type recordset, the clone does not inherit the values of the Filter and Sort properties.

Because both the original and the clone recordsets refer to the same stored table or query, you can modify data, add new records, or delete records using either the original or the duplicate. You can use the Close method for either the original or the clone object without closing the other object.

Chapter 5, "VBA Programming Essentials," introduced the RecordsetClone property of the Form object. When you open a bound form, Jet creates a Recordset object based on the table, query, or SQL statement specified in the form's RecordSource property. When you use the form's RecordsetClone property, you are creating a new current record pointer for the form's Recordset object but you are not creating a new Recordset object. The benefit of using the RecordsetClone property in your VBA code is that you don't need to walk the Jet object hierarchy to get to the Recordset object. With the RecordsetClone property, you create a reference to a data access object without needing to go through the DAO red tape; that is, you are making an end-run around the DAO hierarchy. Having created the RecordsetClone, you can use the methods of the Recordset object for the clone.

NOTE Don't be confused by the similar terminology. The RecordsetClone property only creates an independent current record pointer for the form's recordset and does not create a separate Recordset object. In contrast, the `Clone` method creates a separate Recordset object that is the duplicate of the original Recordset object and has the same bookmarks as the original.

The DAO Model

The next portion of this appendix is a reference to the data access objects. For the DBEngine object and for each object in a collection, a description of the important features is followed by tables of the object's documented properties and methods. No events are defined for the data access objects. Before using a property or a method for the first time, refer to the complete description available in online help in Access.

NOTE A useful feature in Access 2002 and the Microsoft DAO object model is that you can use the Jet database engine to access data or you can use the ODBCDirect technology to work with ODBC servers such as Microsoft SQL Server without loading Jet. This section of the appendix mentions several of the new properties associated with ODBCDirect.

The DBEngine Object

You use the DBEngine object to maintain database files, to examine error details, and to create new sessions. A *session* begins when you log on and ends when you log off. If you don't have security implemented, Access logs on or off automatically when you start or exit Access. Think of a session as a workspace guarded by the security permissions you have set. Tables B.2 and B.3 list the properties and methods of the DBEngine object.

TABLE B.2: Properties of the DBEngine Object

Property	Access	Data Type	Description
DefaultUser	Read/write	String, 1 to 20 characters	Sets the username used by Jet when you start Access. The default is admin.
DefaultPassword	Read/write	String, maximum of 14 characters; case-sensitive	Sets the password used by Jet when you start Access. The default is the zero-length string " ".
DefaultType	Read/write	Long integer	Indicates whether the next workspace created is a Jet or an ODBCDirect workspace.
IniPath	Read/write	String	Sets or gets the path to an application's key in the Registry.
LoginTimeout	Read/write	Integer	Sets or returns the number of seconds before an error occurs when you attempt to log on to an ODBC database, such as SQL Server.
Version	Read-only	String	Returns the value of DAO currently in use.
SystemDB	Read/write	String	Sets or returns the path for the current location of the workgroup information file.

TABLE B.3: Methods of the DBEngine Object

Method	Description
CompactDatabase	Copies and compacts a closed database. You can also change the version of Jet, collating order, and encryption options.
CreateWorkspace	Creates a new Workspace object.
Idle	Suspends data processing so that Jet can complete pending tasks such as memory optimization.
RegisterDatabase	Enters connection information for an ODBC data source in the ODBC.INI file. You can also use the Windows Control Panel ODBC setup to provide the connection information.
SetOption	At run-time, overrides the values set in the Registry.
OpenConnection	Opens a Connection object on an ODBC data source.

The Collection Objects

The 15 data access collection objects have the Count property, which returns the number of objects in a collection, and as many as three methods, as follows:

- Append (A) adds a new data access object to a collection.

- Delete (D) deletes a saved data access object from a collection.

- Refresh (R) updates the objects in a collection to reflect the true inventory of members in the collection.

Table B.4 lists the collections and their methods using the A, D, and R abbreviations.

TABLE B.4: Methods of the Collection Objects

Collection	Methods	Comments
Workspaces	A, D, R	You don't need to append a Workspace object before you can use it.
Databases	R	A new Database object is automatically added to the Databases collection. To remove a Database object from memory, use its Close method. The Close method does not delete the database from disk.
TableDefs	A, D, R	
Fields	A, D, R	
Indexes	A, D, R	
Relations	A, D, R	
Recordsets	R	A new Recordset object is automatically added to the Recordsets collection when you open a Recordset object and is automatically removed when you close the Recordset. You can also use the Close method to remove a Recordset object from memory.
QueryDefs	A, D, R	A new QueryDef object that has a valid name is automatically added to the QueryDefs collection. If you create a QueryDef without a name and then set the Name property, you must append the QueryDef to the QueryDefs collection.
Parameters	R	You create parameters only in the definition of a QueryDef.
Errors	R	Jet automatically adds Error objects when an error occurs and clears the Errors collection when a subsequent error occurs.
Containers	R	Container objects defined by Access and by Jet are all included in the Containers collection.
Documents	R	Document objects defined by Access and by Jet are all included in the Documents collection.
Users	A, D, R	
Groups	A, D, R	
Properties	A, D, R	You use these methods only to add or delete user-defined properties. You cannot delete built-in properties.

NOTE Normally, as you add new objects to a collection or delete objects from a collection, the Jet engine keeps an accurate inventory. Jet may, however, get out of sync with the true inventory when you are working in a multiuser environment. This can occur if you use SQL statements that add or delete objects or if you add or delete objects in the Access user interface. In these cases, you can be sure you are viewing the most up-to-date version by using the `Refresh` method to update the collection. Refresh a collection only when necessary, however, because the `Refresh` method is a time-consuming operation.

The Workspace Object

The Workspace object defines a session. All operations that take place during the session are subject to the permissions governed by your username and password. During a session, you can create new databases, open multiple databases, manage transactions, and create new security users and groups. A *transaction* is a series of changes made as a single unit. In a transaction, the database engine treats the series of operations as an all-or-nothing proposition. A transaction affects all the databases in the session and is not limited to one database.

When you start Access, you start Jet as well. Jet automatically creates a new Workspace object. If you haven't enabled security, Jet opens the default Workspace object named `#Default Workspace#` with admin as the default username and the zero-length string as the default password. You can confirm this in the Immediate window by typing **?DBEngine.Workspaces(0).Name** or, using the default collection, **?DBEngine(0).Name** and pressing Enter.

Tables B.5 and B.6 list the properties and methods of the Workspace object.

TABLE B.5: Properties of the Workspace Object

Property	Access	Data Type	Description
DefaultCursorDriver	Read/write	Long integer	Specifies the type of cursor driver to be used on the connection created in an ODBCDirect workspace.
IsolateODBCTrans	Read/write	Integer	Shares or isolates ODBC connections for multiple Workspace objects that you opened for multiple simultaneous transactions.
LoginTimeout	Read/write	Long integer	Sets or returns the number of seconds to wait before generating an error when trying to log on to an ODBC database. (Only for ODBCDirect workspaces.)

Continued on next page

TABLE B.5 CONTINUED: Properties of the Workspace Object

Property	Access	Data Type	Description
Name	Read/write for new workspace; read-only after appending	String, maximum of 20 characters	Sets or returns the user-defined name for the Workspace object.
Type	Read/write for ODBC workspaces; read-only for Jet workspaces	Long integer	Sets or returns a value to indicate whether the workspace is connected to Jet or to an ODBC data source.
UserName	Read-only	String	Sets or returns a value that represents the owner of the Workspace object.

TABLE B.6: Methods of the Workspace Object

Method	Description
BeginTrans	Begins a new transaction.
CommitTrans	Ends the transaction and saves the changes.
Rollback	Ends the transaction and undoes all the changes.
Close	Terminates a session.
CreateDatabase	Creates, saves, and opens a new, empty database.
CreateGroup	Creates a new Group object.
CreateUser	Creates a new User object.
OpenDatabase	Opens one or more existing databases in a Jet workspace.
OpenConnection	Opens an ODBC data source on an ODBCDirect workspace. Use to connect directly to an ODBC server without loading the Jet database engine.

The Database Object

The Database object represents an open database. Several databases can be open simultaneously in a workspace. You open an existing database in a VBA procedure using the OpenDatabase method of the Workspace object. When several databases are open, you normally refer to each by name, as in this example:

```
DBEngine(0)![Northwind.mdb]
DBEngine(0).Databases("Northwind.mdb")
```

To refer to the current database, you can also use the Access CurrentDB() function.

Tables B.7 and B.8 list the properties and methods of the Database object.

TABLE B.7: Properties of the Database Object

Property	Access	Data Type	Description
CollatingOrder	Read-only	Long integer	Determines the sort order for string comparisons or sorting.
Connect	Read/write	String	Provides information about the source of an open database, including the database type and its path.
Connection	Read-only	Object	Returns the Connection object that corresponds to the database. Use in changing connections to an ODBC data source.
DesignMasterID	Read/write	String	Sets or returns the Design Master in a database's replica set.
Name	Read-only	String, maximum of 64 characters	Sets or returns the user-defined name for the Database object.
QueryTimeout	Read/write	Integer	Sets or returns the number of seconds that Jet waits before a timeout error occurs when a query is run on an ODBC database.
RecordsAffected	Read-only	Long integer	Returns the number of records affected after running an action query.
ReplicaID	Read-only	String	Returns the 16-byte unique identification number created by Jet when you replicate the database.
Transactions	Read-only	Boolean	Determines whether the database supports transactions as a series of changes that can later be canceled or saved.
Updatable	Read-only	Boolean	Determines whether changes can be made to a data access object.
Version	Read-only	String	Returns the version of the Jet database engine that created the open MDB file. In an ODBCDirect workspace, returns the version of the ODBC driver currently in use.

TABLE B.8: Methods of the Database Object

Method	Description
Close	Closes the open Database object.
CreateProperty	Creates a new user-defined Property object for the database.
CreateQueryDef	Creates a new query (QueryDef object) in a specified database.
CreateRelation	Creates a new relationship (Relation object) between fields in two existing tables or queries.

Continued on next page

TABLE B.8 CONTINUED: Methods of the Database Object

Method	Description
CreateTableDef	Creates a new table (TableDef object). The table must have at least one field before you can save the table (by appending the TableDef object to the TableDefs collection).
Execute	Runs an action query (stored query or SQL statement).
MakeReplica	Makes a new replica of a database based on the current database.
NewPassword	Changes the password for a Jet database.
OpenRecordset	Creates a new Recordset object and appends it to the Recordsets collection.
PopulatePartial	Synchronizes changes in a partial replica with the full replica.
Synchronize	Synchronizes two replicas.

The TableDef Object

The TableDef object represents the stored definition of a table. The table can be in a Jet database (called a *local table* or a *base table*) or in another database and linked to a Jet database (called a *linked table*). The TableDef object does not represent the data stored in the table. The only DAO objects that represent data stored in a table are the Field objects in the Fields collection of a Recordset. Tables B.9 and B.10 list the properties and methods of the TableDef object.

TABLE B.9: Properties of the TableDef Object

Property	Access	Data Type	Description
Attributes	Read/write	Long integer	Specifies the characteristics of the table; for example, whether the table is linked or is a local table.
ConflictTable	Read-only	String	Returns the name of a table containing records that conflicted during synchronization of two replicas.
Connect	Read/write	String	Provides information about the source of a table, including the database type and its path.
DateCreated	Read-only	Variant	Returns the date and time the table was created.
LastUpdated	Read-only	Variant	Returns the date and time of the most recent change to the table.
Name	Read/write	String, maximum of 64 characters	Sets or returns the user-defined name for the table.
RecordCount	Read-only	Long integer	Returns the number of records in the table.
ReplicaFilter	Read/write	Variant	Determines whether a subset of records is replicated to the table from a full replica.

Continued on next page

TABLE B.9 CONTINUED: Properties of the TableDef Object

Property	Access	Data Type	Description
SourceTableName	Read/write for attached table; read-only for local table	String	Determines the name of a linked or a local table.
Updatable	Read-only	Boolean	Determines whether changes can be made to the table definition.
ValidationRule	Read/write	String	Validates the data in a field or a set of fields when the data is changed or added to the table.
ValidationText	Read/write	String	Specifies the text of a message displayed if the ValidationRule setting isn't satisfied.

TABLE B.10: Methods of the TableDef Object

Method	Description
CreateField	Creates a new Field object for the table.
CreateIndex	Creates a new index (Index object) for the table. The index must have at least one field.
CreateProperty	Creates a new user-defined property (Property object) for an existing table.
OpenRecordset	Creates a Recordset object on the table and appends it to the Recordsets collection.
RefreshLink	Updates the connection information for a linked table after you reset the Connect property for the table.

The Field Object

The Field object represents a column of data that has a common set of properties and a common data type. The TableDef, QueryDef, Index, and Relation objects all have Fields collections containing Field objects. In these cases, the Field object properties include the specifications for the field but do not contain data. These Field objects do not have a Value property. You can use the Immediate window to evaluate the Field properties:

- Type **?CurrentDB!Customers!CustomerID.AllowZeroLength** and press Enter to view the property setting.

- Type **?CurrentDB!Customers!CustomerID.Value** and press Enter. Access displays an error message because the Field object for a TableDef object contains no data and, therefore, does not have a Value property.

So, where is the data? The data is in the fields of the recordset that Jet creates when you open a table or run a query or a SQL statement that returns records. The Recordset object has a Fields collection containing Field objects. In this case, the Fields collection contains fields that represent a single row of the actual data, the data in the current record. You use the Field objects in a Recordset object to inspect or change the data in the current record. The Value property of a Field object returns the value of the data in a field in the current record. You can use the Immediate window to evaluate the properties of the Field object:

- Type **?rstCustomers.CustomerID.AllowZeroLength** and press Enter to view the property setting.

- Type **?rstCustomers.CustomerID.Value** and press Enter to view the value of the field. Or, because Value is the default property in this case, you can view the value of the data in the field by typing **?rstCustomers.CustomerID** and pressing Enter.

The properties and methods for a Field object depend on its parent object. The parent object is the object that contains the Fields collection to which the Field object is appended: Index (I), QueryDef (Q), Recordset (Rec), Relation (Rel), and TableDef (T). Tables B.11 and B.12 list the properties and methods of the Field object (using the parent object abbreviations).

TABLE B.11: Properties of the Field object

Property	Access	Data Type	Description
AllowZeroLength	Read/write for T; read-only for Q and Rec	Boolean	Specifies whether the zero-length string is a valid setting for the Value property of a field with a Text or Memo data type.
Attributes	Read/write for T; read-only for Q and Rec; read-only for I after appending T	Long integer	Determines the characteristics of a field; for example, whether the field size is fixed or variable.
CollatingOrder	Read-only for Q, Rec, and T	Long integer	Specifies the sort order for string comparison or sorting.
DataUpdatable	Read-only for Q, Rec, and Rel	Boolean	Determines whether you can change the Value property of a field.
DefaultValue	Read/write for T; read-only for Q and Rec	Variant	Sets or returns the value that is automatically entered as the value for the field when a new record is created. Field objects for Index and Relation objects do not have the DefaultValue property.

Continued on next page

TABLE B.11 CONTINUED: Properties of the Field object

Property	Access	Data Type	Description
FieldSize	Read-only for Rec	Long integer	Returns the number of characters for a Memo field or the number of bytes for a Long Binary field. For other data types, use the Size property.
ForeignName	Read/write for Rel; read-only after appending	String	Sets or returns a value that specifies the name of the field in a foreign table or query that corresponds to a field in a primary table or query.
Name	Read/write for new field; read-only after appending (except for a local table)	String, maximum of 64 characters	Sets or returns the name value.
OrdinalPosition	Read/write for T; read-only for Q and Rec	Integer	Sets or returns the relative position of a Field object in its Fields collection; zero-based. If two or more field objects have the same value for the OrdinalPosition, they are ordered alphabetically.
OriginalValue	Read-only for Rec	Variant	Returns the value that existed in a field before a batch update began.
Required	Read/write for T; read-only for Q and Rec	Boolean	Determines whether a field requires a non-Null value.
Size	Read/write for T, Q, and Rec; read-only after appending	Long integer	Returns the maximum size of a field in bytes.
SourceField	Read-only for Q, Rec, and T	String	Returns the name of the field that is the original source of data for the field; for example, you can determine the name of the table field that supplies data for a query field. Available only at run-time.
SourceTable	Read-only for Q, Rec, and T	String	Returns the name of the table that is the original source of data for the field. Available only at run-time.
Type	Read/write; read-only after appending	Integer	Determines the data type for a field.
ValidateOnSet	Read/write for Rec	Boolean	Specifies whether the value of a Field object is validated when the object's Value property is set (True) or when the record is updated (False).
ValidationRule	Read/write for T (local table); read-only for Q, Rec, and T (linked table)	String	Validates the data in a field when the data is changed or added to the table.

Continued on next page

TABLE B.11 CONTINUED: Properties of the Field object

Property	Access	Data Type	Description
ValidationText	Read/write for T; read-only for Q and Rec	String	Specifies the text of a message displayed if the ValidationRule setting isn't satisfied.
Value	Read/write for Rec	Variant	Retrieves or alters data in Recordset objects.
VisibleValue	Read-only for Rec	Variant	Returns the value that is currently in the field in the database on the server.

TABLE B.12: Methods of the Field Object

Method	Description
AppendChunk	Appends data from a string expression to a Memo or OLE Object Field object. Applies to Recordset.
CreateProperty	Creates a new user-defined Property object for an object already stored on disk. Applies to Index, QueryDef, Recordset, Relation, and TableDef.
GetChunk	Returns all or a portion of the contents of a Memo or OLE Object Field object (string or variant variable). Applies to Recordset.

The Index Object

The Index object represents an index for a database table. You use an index for two purposes: to specify the order for records returned in a table-type Recordset object based on a stored table and to specify whether records can have duplicate values in the fields that make up the index. You don't need to create an index for a stored table, but because Jet is able to locate records and create joins more efficiently using indexes, you normally create several indexes for each table. Jet maintains all indexes for the tables in the database, updating indexes automatically whenever you modify, add, or delete records in the table.

In one situation, creating an index is required. If you want to create a relationship between two tables, you must define a primary key for the table on the one side of the one-to-many relationship; the matching field (or fields) in the table on the many side of the relationship is the foreign key. Jet automatically defines the *primary index* for the "one" table to be its primary key. If, in addition, the relationship enforces referential integrity, Jet automatically creates another index for the "one" table with the Foreign property set to the foreign key of the "many" table.

The records in a database table are stored in pages. When you want to find records with a particular value, such as all customers from Argentina, Access searches through all the pages for the Customers table to find the records. An *index* is a lookup table (stored separately in its own set of pages) that relates the value of a field in the lookup table to the location of the page that holds a record with the field value. In an index, the values are arranged in ascending order. When you use an index for a search, Access reads the pages of the index, finds the indexed value, and looks up the data page or pages that hold the corresponding record or records. Because the values in an index are in order and the index is small (including only the index fields and not the other fields in the table), Access can find the search value quickly.

When you create an index in the Access interface, Access takes care of the details automatically, but when you create an index in VBA, you must explicitly step through each operation in the sequence. For example, in Northwind, you can create an index for the Employees table consisting of the LastName and FirstName fields. Here are the steps you take in VBA when you create this index (see Chapter 14 for a VBA procedure that creates an index):

1. Create and name the index by specifying the index's Name property, for example, FullName.

2. Create each field for the index and set the field's Name property to the name of the field. In this case, you create two index fields: LastName and FirstName.

3. Add each field to the index's Fields collection.

4. Add the index to the table's Indexes collection.

Tables B.13 lists the properties of the Index object. The Index object has two methods: `CreateField`, which creates a new field for the index, and `CreateProperty`, which creates a new user-defined property for the index.

TABLE B.13: Properties of the Index Object

Property	Access	Data Type	Description
Clustered	Read/write; read-only after appending	Boolean	Indicates whether an Index object represents a clustering index for a table.
DistinctCount	Read-only	Long integer	Determines the number of unique values, or keys, in an index.
Foreign	Read-only	Boolean	Indicates whether an Index object represents a foreign key in a table. Jet sets the Foreign property when you create a relationship that enforces referential integrity.

Continued on next page

TABLE B.13 CONTINUED: Properties of the Index Object

Property	Access	Data Type	Description
IgnoreNulls	Read/write; read-only after appending	Boolean	Indicates whether records that have Null values in their index fields are included in the index; set to True to exclude these records to make the index smaller.
Name	Read/write for new index; read-only for existing index	String, maximum of 64 characters	Sets or returns the user-defined name of the index.
Primary	Read/write; read-only after appending	Boolean	Indicates whether an Index object represents a primary index for a table.
Required	Read/write; read-only after appending	Boolean	Indicates whether all the fields in an Index object must be filled in.
Unique	Read/write; read-only after appending	Boolean	Indicates whether an Index object represents a unique index for a table.

The Relation Object

The Relation object represents a relationship between fields in tables or queries. You use the Relation object in a VBA procedure to create a new relationship or to modify or examine the characteristics of an existing relationship. A relationship links a single row in one table or query, called the *primary table* or *primary query*, with any number of rows in the second table or query, called the *foreign table* or *foreign query*. You can create a relationship between two tables, between a table and a query, or between two queries; the tables may be local tables in the current database or linked tables. Although queries and linked tables can be members of a relationship, Jet cannot enforce referential integrity for the relationship unless the members are local tables.

You create the relationship by specifying a matching field (or fields) in each member. The matching field or fields in the primary table or primary query must be a primary key that uniquely specifies a row. The matching field (or fields) in the foreign table or foreign query is called the *foreign key*. To create the relation, you add each primary key field to the relation's Fields collection and specify the name of the corresponding matching field in the foreign key using the ForeignName property.

When you create a relationship in the Access interface, Access takes care of the details automatically. When you create a relationship in VBA, you must explicitly step through each operation in the sequence. For example, in Northwind, you can create a relationship between the Customers table as a primary table with CustomerID as its primary key field and the Orders table as a foreign table with CustomerID as its foreign key field. Here are the steps you take in VBA when you create this relationship (see Chapter 14 for a VBA procedure that creates a similar relationship):

1. Create and name the relationship by specifying the relation's Name property (for example, CustomersOrdersRelation), the Table property as the name of the primary table or query, and the ForeignTable property as the name of the foreign table or query.

2. Create each field for the relationship by specifying the primary key field. In this case, you create a single field for the relationship and set the field's Name property to the name of the single primary key field, CustomerID.

3. For each field in the relationship, specify the ForeignName as the name of the corresponding foreign key field. In this case, you set the ForeignName property to CustomerID. (In this example, the primary key and the foreign key fields have the same name, but the names can be different.)

4. Add the field to the Relation object's Fields collection.

5. Add the relation to the database's Relations collection.

You use the Attributes property to specify whether the relationship is one-to-one or one-to-many and whether the relationship between fields is left-join or right-join. You also use the Attributes property to specify whether you want Jet to enforce referential integrity and cascade options for a relationship.

NOTE   Jet can enforce referential integrity only for a relationship between tables in the current database. Before you can enforce referential integrity, a unique index must already exist for the matching field in the table on the one side of the relationship; when you enforce referential integrity, Jet automatically creates an index for the matching field in the table on the many side of the relationship.

Table B.14 lists the properties of the Relation object. The Relation object has one method: CreateField, which creates a new field for the relationship.

TABLE B.14: Properties of the Relation Object

Property	Access	Data Type	Description
Attributes	Read/write	Long integer	Specifies the characteristics of the relationship as the sum of intrinsic constants: dbRelationUnique for a one-to-one relationship, dbRelationDontEnforce for no referential integrity, dbRelationInherited for a relationship between two attached tables in a noncurrent database, dbRelationUpdateCascade to cascade updates, and dbRelationDeleteCascade to cascade record deletions.
ForeignTable	Read/write	String	Specifies or returns the name of the foreign table or query in a relationship.
Name	Read/write for new relation; read-only for existing one	String, maximum of 64 characters	Sets or returns the user-defined name for the relation.
PartialReplica	Read/write	Boolean	Replicates data from the full replica to a partial replica based on the relationship between tables.
Table	Read/write	String	Sets or returns the name of the primary table or query in a relationship.

The Recordset Object

The Recordset object represents the set of records in a table in the database or the set of records that result from running a query or SQL statement. In a Recordset object that has at least one record, you point to one record at a time as the current record. The Fields collection of the Recordset object contains Field objects that represent the fields in the current record; in particular, the Value property setting of each of the Field objects is the value of the data stored in the field in the table.

Earlier sections of the appendix describe techniques for navigating through a recordset and for manipulating data and the types of Recordset objects: table-type (TRec), dynaset-type (DRec), snapshot-type (SRec), and forward-only-type (FRec). Tables B.15 and B.16 list the properties and methods of the Recordset object (using the abbreviations for Recordset type). If a type is not indicated, the property or method applies to all four types of recordsets.

NOTE   ODBCDirect workspaces provide a fifth kind of Recordset object called the dynamic-type recordset. Recordsets in ODBC workspaces have additional properties and methods that are not available in a Jet workspace.

TABLE B.15: Properties of the DAO Recordset Object

Property	Access	Data Type	Description
AbsolutePosition	Read/write for DRec and SRec	Long integer	Positions the current record pointer to a specific record based on its ordinal position; zero-based.
BatchCollisionCount	Read-only	Long integer	Returns the number of records that failed to update during the last batch update. (ODBCDirect workspaces only.)
BatchCollisions	Read-only	Array of variants	Returns an array of bookmarks of the records that failed to update during the last batch update. (ODBCDirect workspaces only.)
BatchSize	Read/write	Long integer	Sets or returns the number of statements sent to the server in a single batch update. (ODBCDirect workspaces only.)
BOF, EOF	Read-only	Boolean	Determines whether a Recordset object contains records or whether you have moved beyond the limits.
Bookmark	Read-only for TRec, DRec, and SRec	Variant array of Byte data	Saves your place in a Recordset object.
Bookmarkable	Read-only for TRec, DRec, and SRec	Boolean	Determines if the Recordset object supports bookmarks.
CacheSize	Read/write	Long integer	Specifies the number of records in a dynaset-type Recordset object containing data from an ODBC data source that can be locally cached.
CacheStart	Read/write	Byte	Sets or returns the bookmark of the first record in the Recordset object to be cached.
Connection	Read-only for DRec, SRec, and FRec	Object	Returns the object variable that represents the connection to the ODBC data source for an ODBCDirect workspace.
DateCreated	Read-only for TRec	Variant	Returns the date and time that the recordset was created.
EditMode	Read-only	Integer	Determines whether you have called the Edit or AddNew method.
Filter	Read/write for DRec, SRec, and FRec	String	Determines the records included in a subsequently opened Recordset object.
Index	Read/write for TRec	String	Determines or specifies the name of an existing Index object as the current index for the table-type Recordset object.
LastModified	Read-only for TRec, DRec, and SRec	Variant array of byte data	Returns a bookmark indicating the most recently added or changed record; use to move to this record.

Continued on next page

TABLE B.15 CONTINUED: Properties of the DAO Recordset Object

Property	Access	Data Type	Description
LastUpdated	Read-only for TRec	Variant	Returns the date and time that the recordset was last changed.
LockEdits	Read/write for TRec, DRec, and SRec	Boolean	Determines the type of locking that is in effect during editing: pessimistic (True) or optimistic (False).
Name	Read-only	String	Returns a name for the Recordset object.
NoMatch	Read-only for TRec, DRec, and SRec	Boolean	Determines if a particular record was found using one of the **Find** methods or the **Seek** method. Returns False if the record was found.
PercentPosition	Read/write for TRec, DRec, and SRec	Single	Specifies the approximate location of the current record based on a percentage of records in the recordset.
RecordCount	Read-only	Long integer	Returns the number of records in a table-type Recordset object or the number of records accessed in a dynaset-type or snapshot-type Recordset object.
RecordStatus	Read-only	Long integer	Returns a value indicating the update status of the current record in a batch update. (ODBCDirect workspaces only.)
Restartable	Read-only	Boolean	Returns a value to indicate whether the Recordset object supports the **Requery** method.
Sort	Read/write for DRec and SRec	String	Specifies the **ORDER BY** clause of a SQL statement without the **ORDER BY** words. After you set the Sort property, sorting occurs when you create a subsequent Recordset object from the object.
StillExecuting	Read-only	Boolean	Indicates whether an operation that executed as an asynchronous method has finished. (ODBCDirect workspaces only.)
Transactions	Read-only	Boolean	Determines whether the recordset supports transactions.
Type	Read-only	Integer	Returns a value to indicate whether the Recordset object is table-, dynaset-, snapshot-, or forward-only-type.
Updatable	Read-only	Boolean	Returns a value to indicate whether changes can be made to the Recordset object.
UpdateOptions	Read/write	Long integer	Sets or returns a value to indicate how the **WHERE** clause is built for each record during a batch update. (ODBCDirect workspaces only.)
ValidationRule	Read-only	String	Validates the data in a field as it is changed or added to a table.
ValidationText	Read-only	String	Specifies the text of the message displayed if the value of a Field object doesn't satisfy the ValidationRule property setting.

TABLE B.16: Methods of the Recordset Object

Method	Description
AddNew	Creates a new record in the copy buffer for a table- or dynaset-type. The record that was current before you used **AddNew** remains current.
Cancel	Cancels execution of an asynchronous method call. (For ODBCDirect workspaces only.)
CancelUpdate	Cancels any pending updates due to an **Edit** or **AddNew** operation.
Clone	Creates a duplicate Recordset object that refers to the original. The clone initially lacks a current record. (Does not apply to forward-only-type.)
Close	Closes the open Recordset object (does not affect a clone).
CopyQueryDef	Creates a copy of the QueryDef used to create the Recordset object.
Delete	Removes the current record in an open table- or dynaset-type.
Edit	Copies the current record in a table- or dynaset-type to the copy buffer for editing.
FillCache	Explicitly fills the cache that Jet creates when the dynaset-type contains data from an ODBC data source.
FindFirst, FindLast, FindNext, FindPrevious	Locate the first, last, next, or previous record in a dynaset- or snapshot-type that satisfies the specified criteria and makes that record the current record. The criterion is a string expression for a **WHERE** clause in a SQL statement without the word **WHERE**.
GetRows	Copies one or more entire records from a recordset to a two-dimensional array and moves the current record pointer to the next unread row.
Move	Moves a specified number of rows to another record and makes that record the current record.
MoveFirst, MoveLast, MoveNext, MovePrevious	Move to the first, last, next, or previous record in a Recordset object and make that record the current record. (In forward-only-type, only **MoveNext** is available.)
NextRecordset	Gets the next set of records, if any, returned by an **OpenRecordset** statement that contains more than one **Select** statement. (For ODBCDirect workspaces only.)
OpenRecordset	Creates a new Recordset object. If the original is a table-type, the new object is a dynaset-type; if the original is a dynaset- or snapshot-type, the new object is the same type as the original.
Requery	Updates the data in a dynaset-, snapshot-, or forward-only-type by reexecuting the query on which the object is based. When you use this method, the first record becomes the current record.
Seek	For table-type, locates the record in an indexed table-type Recordset object satisfying specified criteria for the current index; makes the found record the current record. The Index property must be set to an existing Index object before using this method.
Update	Saves the contents of the copy buffer to a specified dynaset- or table-type. Changes to a record are lost if you don't use the **Update** method explicitly.

The QueryDef Object

The QueryDef object represents the stored definition of a query. The QueryDef object does not represent the data stored in the tables. Tables B.17 and B.18 list the properties and methods of the QueryDef object.

TABLE B.17: Properties of the QueryDef Object

Property	Access	Data Type	Description
CacheSize	Read/write	Long integer	Determines the number of records retrieved from an ODBC data source that will be held in local memory (in a cache).
Connect	Read/write	String	Provides information about the source of an attached table.
DateCreated	Read-only	Variant	Returns the date and time that the stored query was created.
LastUpdated	Read-only	Variant	Returns the date and time the stored query was last changed.
MaxRecords	Read/write	Long integer	Indicates the maximum number of records that will be returned by a query that returns data from an ODBC database.
Name	Read/write; read-only for temporary query	String, maximum of 64 characters	Identifies the Querydef object. You can create a temporary query by setting the Name to the zero-length string (" ").
ODBCTimeout	Read/write	Integer	Determines the number of seconds that Jet waits before a timeout error occurs when a query runs on an ODBC database.
Prepare	Read/write	Variant	Determines whether the server executes a query directly or creates a temporary stored procedure based on the query. (ODBCDirect workspaces only.)
RecordsAffected	Read-only	Long integer	Returns the number of records affected when you last ran the **Execute** method on the QueryDef object.
ReturnsRecords	Read/write	Boolean	Indicates whether a SQL pass-through query to an external database returns records. You must set the Connect property before setting this property.
SQL	Read/write	String	Sets or returns the SQL statement that defines the query.
StillExecuting	Read-only	Boolean	Indicates whether an operation that executed as an asynchronous method has finished. (ODBCDirect workspaces only.)
Type	Read-only	Integer	Determines the query type.
Updatable	Read-only	Boolean	Determines whether changes can be made to the query.

TABLE B.18: Methods of the QueryDef Object

Method	Description
Cancel	Cancels execution of a pending asynchronous method. (For ODBCDirect workspaces only.)
Close	Closes the open QueryDef object.
CreateProperty	Creates a new user-defined Property object.
Execute	Runs an action query or executes a SQL statement for an action query on the specified QueryDef object. Because action queries return no records, the Execute method returns nothing.
OpenRecordset	Creates a new Recordset object based on the QueryDef object and appends it to the Recordsets collection.

The Parameter Object

The Parameter object represents a query parameter in a parameter query. You don't create Parameter objects and append them to the Parameters collection. Instead, you create query parameters as part of the definition of the parameter query. After creating the parameter query, you use the Parameter object to refer to an existing query parameter. Table B.19 lists the properties of the Parameter object. The Parameter object has no methods.

TABLE B.19: Properties of the Parameter Object

Property	Access	DataType	Description
Direction	Read/write	Integer	Determines whether the Parameter object is an input or output parameter or both. (For ODBCDirect workspaces only.)
Name	Read-only	String	Specifies a name for the object.
Type	Read-only	Integer	Specifies a data type for the parameter.
Value	Read/write	Variant	Sets or returns the value of the parameter (default property).

The Error Object

Table B.20 lists the properties of the Error object. The Error object has no methods.

TABLE B.20: Properties of the Error Object

Property	Access	Data Type	Description
Description	Read-only	String	Returns a description of the error.
Number	Read-only	Long integer	Returns a numeric value corresponding to the error.
Source	Read-only	String	Returns the name of the object or application that caused the error.

The Property Object

The Property object represents a built-in property or a user-defined property of a data access object. Every data access object except the Error object (and the Connection object in ODBCDirect) has a Properties collection containing Property objects. Table B.21 lists the properties of the Property object. The Property object has no methods.

TABLE B.21: Properties of the Property Object

Property	Access	Data Type	Description
Inherited	Read-only	Boolean	Determines whether the property is inherited from another object.
Name	Read-only for built-in or existing property; read/write for new custom property	String, maximum of 64 characters	Names the property.
Type	Read/write; read-only after appending	Integer	Determines the data type of the property.
Value	Read/write	Variant	Sets or determines the value of the property (default property).

The Container Object

In addition to Access, several other applications—including Microsoft Excel, Visual Basic, and Visual C++—use Jet to manage their data. When you work with one of these applications as a COM client that uses Jet as a COM server, you create application-specific objects. For example, you use the Access Application to create Access objects such as forms, reports, data access pages, macros, and modules, and you use Excel to create Excel objects such as worksheets, charts, and modules. Usually, the COM client application stores its own objects in its own file; for example, Excel stores its objects in its XLS files. Access, however, stores its own objects in the MDB database file managed by Jet. Jet tracks the Access objects using a Containers collection that has a separate Container object for each kind of Access object. Table B.22 lists the properties of the Container object. The Container object has no methods.

TABLE B.22: Properties of the Container Object

Property	Access	Data Type	Description
AllPermissions	Read-only	Long integer	Returns all the permissions that apply to the current UserName property of the Container object.
Inherit	Read/write	Boolean	Indicates whether a new Document object created in the container has the default permissions set for the container.
Name	Read-only	String	Names the object.
Owner	Read/write	String	Indicates the owner of the object as the name of a User or Group object. The owner of an object has privileges denied to others.
Permissions	Read/write	Long integer	Indicates the permissions that a user or group of users have.
UserName	Read/write	String	Indicates the name of a user, group of users, or owner of the object.

The Document Object

A Document object contains information about a specific instance of an object—that is, a specific table, relationship, form, or report. Table B.23 lists the properties of the Document object. The Document object has one method: `CreateProperty`, which creates a new custom property for the Document object.

TABLE B.23: Properties of the Document Object

Property	Access	Data Type	Description
AllPermissions	Read-only	Long integer	Returns all the permissions that apply to the current UserName property of the Document object.
Container	Read-only	String	Returns the name of the Container object that contains the Document object.
DateCreated	Read-only	Variant	Returns the date when the object was created.
LastUpdated	Read-only	Variant	Returns the date when the object was last updated.
Name	Read-only	String	Returns the name that a user or Jet gave to the object.
Owner	Read/write	String	Indicates the owner of the object.
Permissions	Read/write	Long integer	Indicates the permissions that a user or group of users have.
UserName	Read/write	String	Indicates the name of the user or group of users that have permissions for the object.

The User Object

A User object represents a specific user that has been given permission to use the objects in the database when security has been implemented for the workspace. You identify a *user account* with a username and a personal identifier. When security has been implemented, each user logs on using a username and password and has the access privileges that you have set up as permissions for specific users and groups. Table B.24 lists the properties of the User object. The User object has two methods: CreateGroup, which creates a new Group object for the User object, and NewPassword, which changes the password of an existing user account.

TABLE B.24: Properties of the User Object

Property	Access	Data Type	Description
Name	Read/write for new User; read-only for existing User	String, maximum of 20 characters	Names the user.
Password	Read/write	String, maximum of 14 characters	Sets a password for a user account. Passwords can include any ASCII character except character 0 (null) and are case-sensitive.
PID	Read/write	String, 4 to 20 alphanumeric characters	Sets the personal identifier for a user account or a group. Jet uses the PID together with the account name to identify a user or a group. You can't return the PID for an existing user. PIDs are case-sensitive.

The Group Object

A Group object represents a set of user accounts for which you have set common access permissions. Table B.25 lists the properties of the Group object. The Group object has one method, CreateUser, which creates a new User object for a group.

TABLE B.25: Properties of the Group Object

Property	Access	DataType	Description
Name	Read/write for new group; read-only for existing group	String, maximum of 20 characters	Names the group.
PID	Read/write	String, 4 to 20 alphanumeric characters	Sets the personal identifier for a new group. You can't return the PID for an existing group.

Object Naming Conventions

In Chapter 2, "Getting Started with Objects and Events," we introduced you to the Hungarian naming style for naming objects. This section will cover some of the DAO-specific topics related to naming and referring to objects.

DAO Object Tags

In addition to the tags, prefixes, and suffixes you learned in Chapter 2, there are additional DAO naming standards you should know if you plan to develop Access databases using the DAO object model. Table B.26 lists common tags for DAO objects.

TABLE B.26: Common Tags for DAO objects.

Object	Tag
Database	Cb
Error	Err
QueryDef	Qdf
Relation	Rel
TableDef	Tdf
Workspace	Ws

Using DAO Intrinsic Constants

In Chapter 8, you learned about using constants as a way to replace number or string values that don't change. In addition to the constants you read about—system-defined constants, Access intrinsic constants, VBA intrinsic constants, and ADO intrinsic constants—there is a system of DAO intrinsic constants. You use them primarily to specify data access object property settings and method arguments. These constants have a db prefix. Examples are dbDenyRead, dbOpenTable, and dbOpenDynaset, which you use to specify the OpenRecordset method. DAO also groups intrinsic constants into sets of enumerated constants and names each group using a descriptive name and the suffix Enum. For example, RecordsetTypeEnum is the set of enumerated constants representing the types of recordsets including dbOpenDynamic, dbOpenDynaset, dbOpenForwardOnly, dbOpenSnapshot, and dbOpenTable.

Navigating a DAO Recordset with VBA

Chapter 11, "Navigating with Access VBA," introduced you to the subject of navigation with VBA instead of with forms as a way to manipulate data in a recordset. The examples and sample code from that chapter are all for the ActiveX Data Objects (ADO) model. This section deals with the same topics, but uses DAO code instead of ADO code.

Navigating the Form and Its Recordset

When you open a bound form, Access opens the form's recordset in memory and displays records in the form using the form's record selector to indicate the form's current record. When you open a bound form, there are two objects you can manipulate in a VBA procedure: the form and the form's recordset. You can refer to the recordset directly by using the form's RecordsetClone property, which means that you can use the properties and methods of both the Form object (see Chapter 5) and the Recordset object when you are writing procedures that manipulate the records in a form.

When one of these objects lacks the property or method that you need, you can use the other object instead. For example, the Form object does not have a property or method to determine the number of records in a bound form; however, you can use the RecordCount property of the Recordset object. Learning how to use both the Form and Recordset objects in procedures is an important skill.

To work with a form's recordset in a procedure, you declare an object variable and point the object variable to the form's recordset using the form's RecordsetClone property. The statements are

```
Dim rst As DAO.Recordset, frm As Form
Set frm = Forms!formname
Set rst = frm.RecordsetClone
```

formname is the name of the form. The second Set statement creates a special reference to the form's Recordset object called the recordsetclone. The recordsetclone has its own current record pointer so it can point to a different record from the record that is displayed in the form. Consequently, you can use the recordsetclone to work with another record in a form's recordset while the form continues to display a specific record. When you first create the recordsetclone, its current record pointer is not defined; you can set the current record pointer in the procedure.

NOTE It is good programming practice to refer to an object by type library when declaring a variable whose type could be from two or more different libraries. For example, if you are declaring rst as a variable of Recordset object type, you should use either DAO.Recordset or ADO.Recordset to distinguish between the two.

Creating a Sub Procedure to Walk the Recordset

As an example of creating and using the recordsetclone, we'll create a procedure to print the last names of the employees in the Employees table. Open the Employees form in Design view. In the header section, place a command button named cmdRecordset with the caption

Print Last Names. Click in the button's OnClick property and click the Build button to display the form's module. Create the `cmdRecordset_Click` event procedure shown below.

```
Private Sub cmdRecordset_Click()
    Dim rst As DAO.Recordset
    Set rst = Me.RecordsetClone
    rst.MoveFirst
    Do
        Debug.Print rst!LastName
        rst.MoveNext
    Loop Until rst.EOF
End Sub
```

This procedure creates the recordsetclone, uses the `MoveFirst` method to set the recordsetclone's current record pointer to the first record, and then loops through the recordset. Each pass through the loop prints the last name in the recordsetclone's current record and uses the `MoveNext` method to move the current record pointer to the next record.

Open the Immediate window. Save the form, switch to Form view, and click the new command button. The Immediate window prints the last names for all of the employees as evidence that the procedure has walked through all the records in the form's recordset while the form continues to display its first record (see Figure B.4).

FIGURE B.4:

The Print Last Names button runs a procedure that uses the recordsetclone and walks through the form's recordset while the form displays its first record.

Creating a Function Procedure to Walk the Recordset

In the previous example, we could use Me to refer to the form because the event procedure is stored in the form's module. In the next example, we'll create a reusable function procedure that walks through the recordset of any form.

The FormRecordset procedure creates the recordsetclone for the form passed as an argument to the function and prints the value in the first field of each record in the form's recordset.

```
Public Function FormRecordset(frm As Form)
    Dim rst As DAO.Recordset
    Set rst = frm.RecordsetClone
    rst.MoveFirst
    Do
        Debug.Print rst(0)
        rst.MoveNext
    Loop Until rst.EOF
End Function
```

Because we want the function procedure to be reusable, we refer to the first field using the numeric index reference rst.Fields(0), or simply rst(0) (because Fields is the default collection for a recordset). You can run the FormRecordset function by passing the reference to any open form as the argument.

Create a new standard module named basNavigation and insert the FormRecordset function procedure shown above. Next, open the Customers form, type **?FormRecordset(Forms!Customers)** in the Immediate window, and press Enter. Note that you are passing the reference to the form, not the name of the form. When you press Enter, VBA prints the Customer ID field to the Immediate window.

To run the function as an event function procedure, open the Categories form in Design view and type **=FormRecordset(Form)** in the OnOpen event. Note that you are passing Form as the reference to the form. (You can also use the reference Forms!Categories, but you can't use the Me reference to refer to the form in a property sheet.)

Save the form and switch to Form view. When you switch to Form view, the form recognizes the Open event, so VBA runs the function procedure and prints the Category ID field to the Immediate window.

Navigating among Records of a Form

When you work interactively, you navigate among records according to their physical location within the recordset. This process is called *physical navigation*. The record you move to becomes the current record—the *current record* is the record you modify with subsequent mouse or keyboard actions. You can use the GoToRecord method of the DoCmd object to duplicate the effect of clicking a default navigation button in the lower-left corner of a form (or of choosing the Go To command on the Edit menu and then choosing one of the sub-commands on the fly-out submenu). The GoToRecord method has this syntax:

```
DoCmd.GoToRecord objecttype[,objectname][,record][,offset]
```

where

- *objecttype* is one of the intrinsic constants: acTable, acQuery, acForm, acServerView, or acStoredProcedure.

- *objectname* is an optional string expression that is the valid name of an object of the specified type.

- *record* is one of the intrinsic constants: acPrevious, acNext (the default), acFirst, acLast, acGoTo, or acNewRec.

- *offset* is a numeric expression that represents the number of records to move forward if you specify acNext, backward if you specify acPrevious, or a valid record number if you specify acGoTo.

All of the arguments are optional. If you omit the *objecttype* and *objectname* arguments, the active object is assumed. If you omit the *record* argument, the default constant is acNext.

Creating Custom Navigation Buttons

We'll create a set of custom navigation buttons for a form. To make the buttons reusable on other forms, we automate the buttons with the event function procedures shown below, stored in a new basNavigationButtons standard module.

```
Public Function FirstRecord()
    DoCmd.GoToRecord Record:=acFirst
End Function

Public Function PreviousRecord()
    DoCmd.GoToRecord Record:=acPrevious
End Function

Public Function NextRec()
    DoCmd.GoToRecord Record:=acNext
End Function

Public Function LastRecord()
    DoCmd.GoToRecord Record:=acLast
End Function

Public Function NewRec()
    DoCmd.GoToRecord Record:=acNewRec
End Function
```

> **NOTE**   The function procedures for the New and Next record buttons are abbreviated because NewRecord and NextRecord are the names of properties and are not valid names for procedures.

Create a set of five command buttons in the footer section of the Products form named cmdFirst, cmdPrevious, cmdNext, cmdLast, and cmdNew (and with suitable captions) and assign the event function procedures shown above. Be sure to change the Visible property of the Form Footer to Yes. Save the form and switch to Form view (see Figure B.5). Test the new buttons.

FIGURE B.5:

The custom navigation buttons

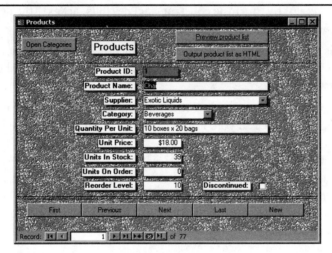

When you test the buttons, you find that clicking the First button and then clicking the Previous button causes the PreviousRecord procedure to fail (see Figure B.6a). The reason for the failure is that after you click the First button, the current record is the first record in the recordset; therefore, when you click the Previous button you are attempting to move beyond the limits of the recordset.

Clicking the Last button and then clicking the Next button opens a blank form. After clicking the Last button and then clicking the Next button, the current record is the new record that follows the last record in the recordset.

Dealing with Run-Time Errors

There are two methods for dealing with the run-time errors that occur when you try to move beyond the upper limits of a recordset:

- You can include error-handling code to avoid the run-time errors.

- You can create a set of "smart" navigation buttons that disable a button when clicking it would cause a run-time error.

Adding Error-Handling Code   As an example of using error handling to avoid a run-time error, we've added custom error handling to the `PreviousRecord` function procedure to terminate the procedure without failure when the error occurs. The modified `PreviousRecord` procedure shown below has an enabled error handler that displays the default error message when you try to move beyond the first record.

```
Public Function PreviousRecord()
    On Error GoTo PreviousRecord_Err
    DoCmd.GoToRecord Record:=acPrevious

PreviousRecord_Exit:
Exit Function

PreviousRecord_Err:
    MsgBox Err.Description
    Resume PreviousRecord_Exit
End Function
```

After modifying the `PreviousRecord` procedure, clicking the First button and then clicking the Previous button still triggers the run-time error as before. However, this time the error trap is set, and control moves to the error-handling code. The error handler displays the message shown in Figure B.6b and exits the procedure without trying to execute the `GoToRecord` method. As an alternative, you can omit the `MsgBox` statement and simply have no response when you are at the first record and click the Previous button. You can write similar error-handling code for the other navigation buttons.

FIGURE B.6:

When you attempt to move beyond the limits of the recordset, the default error handling is that the procedure fails (a), but you can use custom error handling (b) to avoid failure.

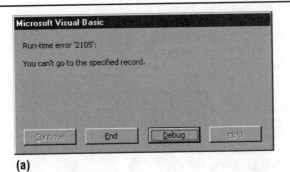
(a)

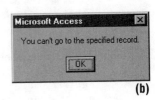
(b)

Creating Smart Navigation Buttons   In the second approach to avoiding a run-time error, you create a procedure to disable a navigation button when clicking it would cause a run-time error. Consequently, if the first record is the current record, the procedure disables the Previous button. We'll design the procedure to disable the First button also when the first record is the current record, even though the `FirstRecord` procedure doesn't fail when the First button is clicked repeatedly. The disabled First button serves as a visual cue that the first record is the current record. If the last record is the current record, the procedure disables the Last and Next buttons; if the new record is the current record, the procedure disables the New, Last, and Next buttons.

To disable the appropriate buttons, you must know whether the current record is the first, last, or new record. Determining whether the current record is the new record is easy because a form has the NewRecord property that you can test. However, there is no FirstRecord or LastRecord property for a form, so we'll need to work harder to find out if the current record is the first or last record.

Although a form has no properties that you can use to determine if the current record is the first or last record, the form's recordset does. A recordset has BOF and EOF properties that you can use to determine whether you have moved beyond the limits. If you've moved the current record position to before the first record, BOF is True; if you've moved the current record position to after the last record, EOF is True.

If we start moving around in the form's recordset, we'll disturb the screen display, so instead, we'll use the form's RecordsetClone property to create a separate current record pointer, synchronize the recordsetclone so that it points to the current record that the form displays, and use the recordsetclone's pointer to move around in the recordset. For example, if we use the recordsetclone's MovePrevious method to move to the previous record in the recordset and find that BOF is True, the form must be displaying the first record.

The DisableEnable function procedure disables and enables the navigation buttons.

```
Public Function DisableEnable(frm As Form)
'To call the function set the form's OnCurrent
'property to =DisableEnable(Form)
    Dim rstClone As DAO.Recordset
'Create a clone of the form's recordset to
'move around in without affecting the form's
'recordset
    Set rstClone = frm.RecordsetClone
'Determine if the current record is the
'new record and if it is, disable the Next
'and New buttons and then exit.
    If frm.NewRecord Then
        frm!cmdFirst.Enabled = True
        frm!cmdNext.Enabled = False
        frm!cmdPrevious.Enabled = True
        frm!cmdLast.Enabled = True
        frm!cmdNew.Enabled = False
        Exit Function
    End If
'If the current record is not the new record
'enable the New button
    frm!cmdNew.Enabled = True
```

```vba
'If there are no records, disable all
'other buttons
    If rstClone.RecordCount = 0 Then
        frm!cmdFirst.Enabled = False
        frm!cmdNext.Enabled = False
        frm!cmdPrevious.Enabled = False
        frm!cmdLast.Enabled = False
    Else
'Synchronize the current record in the clone
'to be the same as the current record displayed
'in the form.
        rstClone.Bookmark = frm.Bookmark
'Move to the previous record in the clone,
'if the clone's BOF is True, the form must be
'at the first record so disable the First and
'Previous buttons. Otherwise, the form is not
'at the first record so enable the First and
'Previous buttons.
        rstClone.MovePrevious
        If rstClone.BOF Then
            frm!cmdFirst.Enabled = False
            frm!cmdPrevious.Enabled = False
        Else
            frm!cmdFirst.Enabled = True
            frm!cmdPrevious.Enabled = True
        End If
'Resynchronize the current record in the clone
'to be the same as the current record displayed
'in the form.
        rstClone.Bookmark = frm.Bookmark
'Move to the next record in the clone,
'if the clone's EOF is True, the form must be
'at the last record so disable the Next and
'Last buttons. Otherwise, the form is not
'at the first record so enable the Next and
'Last buttons.
        rstClone.MoveNext
        If rstClone.EOF Then
            frm!cmdNext.Enabled = False
            frm!cmdLast.Enabled = False
        Else
            frm!cmdNext.Enabled = True
            frm!cmdLast.Enabled = True
        End If
    End If
End Function
```

The procedure runs when the form first opens and when you move to a different record (and the form recognizes the Current event). To make the procedure reusable on other forms, we'll pass the form to the procedure as an argument.

The DisableEnable function begins by creating the recordsetclone with its separate current record pointer. The procedure can now switch between the form and the recordset using whichever recordset or form property or method it needs. The procedure determines if the current record is the new record by testing the form's NewRecord property. If it is the new record, the Next and New buttons are disabled and the procedure ends. If the current record is not the new record, the procedure determines if the recordset contains any records.

Determining the presence of records is necessary because if we try to move around in a recordset that has no records at all, we cause run-time errors. The procedure uses the recordsetclone's RecordCount property to determine if records exist and disables the First, Previous, Next, and Last buttons if no records are found. If there are records, the next step is to determine where we are in the recordset.

> **NOTE** The RecordCount property returns the total number of records if the recordset is a table-type recordset. If the recordset is a dynaset-type or snapshot-type recordset, the RecordCount property returns the number of records that have been accessed. Once the last record in a dynaset-type or snapshot-type recordset has been accessed, the RecordCount property returns the total number of records. The only way to guarantee that all records have been accessed is to use the MoveLast method of the Recordset object before reading the RecordCount property. However, if all you need to know is whether any records exist, you can use the RecordCount property without using the MoveLast method. If no records are found, the RecordCount property returns 0; otherwise, the property returns an integer greater than 0.

We'll use the recordsetclone's current record pointer to move around in the recordset and test whether we've moved the recordsetclone's pointer beyond the limits of the recordset. We need a way to synchronize the recordsetclone to the form so that we can start with the recordsetclone and the form pointing to the same record. We use the Bookmark property to do the synchronization. When you open a bound form, Access automatically assigns a unique bookmark to each record in the recordset. Both the form and the recordsetclone have a Bookmark property. The form's Bookmark property returns the value of the bookmark for the record displayed by the form. The recordsetclone's Bookmark property returns the value of the bookmark for its current record, so you can point the recordsetclone at the record displayed in the form by using this assignment statement:

```
rstClone.Bookmark = frm.Bookmark
```

The DisableEnable procedure uses the BOF and EOF properties to determine if the current record is the first record or the last record. The procedure determines if the current record is the first record by using the recordsetclone's MovePrevious method to move the recordsetclone's current record pointer to the previous record and then testing the recordsetclone's BOF property. If the recordsetclone's BOF property is True, then the MovePrevious method has moved us to the current record position before the first record, and we must have been at the first record before the move. In this case, we disable the First and Previous buttons. If the recordsetclone's BOF property is False, we were not at the first record before the move, so we enable the First and Previous buttons. The procedure resynchronizes the recordsetclone and the form to point to the same record.

The final step is to determine if the current record is the last record by using the recordsetclone's MoveNext method to move the recordsetclone's current record pointer to the next record and then test the recordsetclone's EOF property. If the recordsetclone's EOF property is True, then the MoveNext method has moved us to the current record position after the last record, and we must have been at the last record before the move. In this case, we disable the Last and Next buttons. If the recordsetclone's EOF property is False, we were not at the last record before the move, so we enable the Last and Next buttons. After finishing the tests, the procedure ends.

Insert the DisableEnable function procedure in the basNavigationButtons module. Next, display the Products form in Design view. Click in the form's OnCurrent property and set it to =DisableEnable(Form). Save the form and switch to Form view. Test the buttons. For example, when the first record is the form's current record, the First and Previous buttons are disabled (see Figure B.7).

FIGURE B.7:

The DisableEnable procedure enables and disables the custom command buttons to avoid run-time errors.

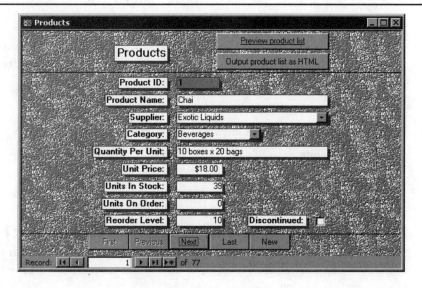

NOTE Using a form's RecordsetClone property creates a new reference to the form's existing Recordset object. When you are finished using the recordsetclone, you don't use the `Close` method to attempt to close the Recordset object. VBA won't let you close the form's recordset without closing the form and simply ignores any statement that tries to close the recordsetclone. You can set the object variable to `Nothing` to sever the connection between the variable and the recordsetclone, but normally there isn't much point in doing so.

Finding a Specific Record

When you search for records interactively, you use the Find dialog, which is displayed by clicking the Find button in the toolbar or choosing Edit ➢ Find. To make the find process faster, you restrict the search to values in a control by selecting the control before displaying the Find dialog.

When you automate the search process using VBA programming, you can avoid displaying the Find dialog and make your application easier to use by adding an unbound combo box to the form's header or footer section and allowing the user to start the search by selecting a specific value from the combo list. Access VBA provides many ways to create an event procedure to find the specific record corresponding to the selected value.

The event procedure runs when the user changes the value in the combo box and the combo box recognizes the AfterUpdate event. We'll look at three ways to find a specific record:

- Using the `FindRecord` method
- Using the `ApplyFilter` method of the DoCmd object
- Using the RecordsetClone property

To explore the search techniques, open the Employees form in Design view and place an unbound combo box in the header section. Set the combo box properties as follows:

Name	cboFind
RowSourceType	Table/Query
RowSource	Employees
ColumnCount	2
ColumnWidths	0"; 0.75"
BoundColumn	1

Using the *FindRecord* Method of the DoCmd Object

The simplest approach for finding a specific record is to create an event procedure for the combo box that mirrors each interactive step of the process with a VBA statement. The event procedure shown below uses this approach.

```
Private Sub cboFind_AfterUpdate()
    Application.Echo False
    EmployeeID.Enabled = True
    EmployeeID.SetFocus
    DoCmd.FindRecord cboFind
    cboFind.SetFocus
    EmployeeID.Enabled = False
    Application.Echo True
End Sub
```

This procedure begins by turning off screen painting while the procedure runs. In mirroring each interactive step, the procedure must move the focus to the EmployeeID control; however, this control is disabled, so the procedure must first enable the control. After enabling the EmployeeID control, the procedure moves the focus to it and uses the FindRecord method to find the value held in the combo box. After finding the value, the procedure moves the focus back to the combo box, disables the EmployeeID control, turns the screen painting back on, and ends.

NOTE   By default, screen painting is on, and Access takes the time to update the screen for each statement. The repainting not only takes time but also causes screen flicker as the screen updates after each statement. When you turn off screen painting in a VBA procedure, you must also turn it back on before the procedure ends.

Using the *ApplyFilter* Method of the DoCmd Object

A more efficient approach uses a filter to select the record directly from the form's recordset. The ApplyFilter method lets you apply a filter to a table, form, or report to restrict or sort the records in the table or in the underlying recordset of the form or report. You can specify a saved query as the filter using the *filtername* argument, or you can enter an SQL WHERE clause (without the word WHERE) in the *wherecondition* argument. The ApplyFilter method has three arguments:

- *filtername* is a string expression that is the name of a query or a filter saved as a query that restricts or sorts the records.

- *wherecondition* is an expression that restricts the records in the form of a valid SQL WHERE clause without the word WHERE.

- *filtertype* specifies whether to search for formatted data (Normal) or unformatted data (Server).

You must specify at least one of the first two arguments; if you specify both arguments, Access first applies the query and then applies the *wherecondition* to the result of the query. The maximum length of the *wherecondition* argument is 32,768 characters. (The *wherecondition* argument for the corresponding ApplyFilter macro action is 256 characters.)

The *wherecondition* argument to synchronize the form to the value in the combo box is as follows:

fieldname=Forms!*formname*!*controlname*

In this expression, *fieldname* refers to the field in the underlying table or query of the form, and *controlname* refers to the control on the form that contains the value you want to match. For example, to synchronize the Employees form to the value displayed in the cboFind combo box, use this expression:

```
[EmployeeID]=Forms![Employees]![cboFind]
```

You can also use the Me property to refer to the form, as follows:

```
[EmployeeID]=Me!cboFind
```

The event procedure shown below uses this approach.

```
Private Sub cboFind_AfterUpdate()
    Dim strSQL As String
    strSQL = "EmployeeID = " & Me!cboFind
    DoCmd.ApplyFilter wherecondition:= strSQL
End Sub
```

Using the Recordsetclone

The most efficient approach uses the form's recordsetclone to refer to the form's record-set. The Recordset object has methods that you can use to find a specific record. To obtain access to these methods, you can use the form's RecordsetClone property to refer to the form's recordset. The following statements declare rst as an object variable and assign it to the form's Recordset object with its own current record pointer:

```
Dim rst As DAO.Recordset
Set rst = Me.RecordsetClone
```

You can use the FindFirst method of the Recordset object to move the clone's current record pointer to the first record that satisfies a specified criteria. The syntax of the FindFirst method is as follows:

```
recordset.FindFirst criteria
```

recordset is a reference for an existing dynaset or snapshot-type recordset object. *criteria* is a string expression that restricts the records in the recordset. The *criteria* argument is a valid SQL WHERE clause without the word WHERE.

After running the FindFirst method, the recordsetclone points to the found record. However, the current record displayed in the form hasn't changed. The final step is to move the form's current record pointer to the same record that the recordsetclone is pointing to by setting the form's Bookmark property to the recordsetclone's Bookmark property:

```
Me.Bookmark = rst.Bookmark
```

The event procedure shown below uses this approach.

```
Private Sub cboFind_AfterUpdate()
    Dim strCriteria As String
    Dim rst As DAO.Recordset
    Set rst = Me.RecordsetClone
```

```
        strCriteria = "EmployeeID = " & Me!cboFind
        rst.FindFirst strCriteria
        Me.Bookmark = rst.Bookmark
    End Sub
```

If the sole purpose of the event procedure is to find the record and take no other actions using the variables, you don't need the variables at all and can simplify the procedure. Insert the simplified cboFind_AfterUpdate procedure shown below for the cboFind combo box's AfterUpdate event.

```
    Private Sub cboFind_AfterUpdate()
        Me.RecordsetClone.FindFirst "EmployeeID = " & _
            Me!cboFind
        Me.Bookmark = Me.RecordsetClone.Bookmark
    End Sub
```

Save the form and switch to Form view. Select an employee in the lookup combo box (see Figure B.8). The procedure displays the record of the selected employee.

FIGURE B.8:

The most efficient search technique uses the FindFirst method of the recordsetclone.

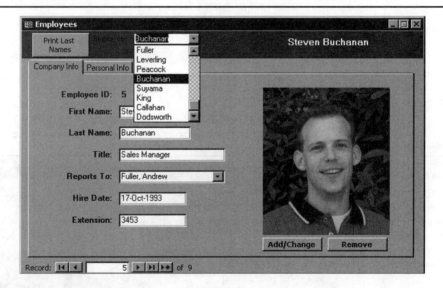

Undoing the Search

After finding a particular record, you may want to undo the search and return to the previously displayed record. To undo the search, you need to know which record was displayed last. You can keep track of the previous record by holding the value of its primary key in a module-level variable. You use a module-level variable so that the record's primary key will be available to the procedure to undo the search. Modify the procedure that finds a specific record by including a statement to store the current record's primary key value before running the statements that find the specific record.

To undo the search when the search uses the recordsetclone technique, first enter the following declaration statement in the Declarations section of the form module:

```
Private LastFind
```

Next, modify the cboFind_AfterUpdate event procedure to set LastFind to the primary key of the current record before any other statement:

```
Private Sub cboFind_AfterUpdate()
    LastFind = EmployeeID
    Me.RecordsetClone.FindFirst "EmployeeID = " & _
        Me!cboFind
    Me.Bookmark = Me.RecordsetClone.Bookmark
End Sub
```

In the header of the Employees form, place a command button named cmdUndoFind with the caption Last Lookup and create the OnClick event procedure shown below:

```
Private Sub cmdUndoFind_Click()
    Me.RecordsetClone.FindFirst "EmployeeID = " & LastFind
    Me.Bookmark = Me.RecordsetClone.Bookmark
    Me!cboFind = LastFind
End Sub
```

The cmdUndoFind_Click event procedure uses the same find technique to find the record matching the value stored in the LastFind variable and then synchronizes the combo box to the displayed record.

Save the form and switch to Form view. Select an employee in the lookup combo box. Click the Last Lookup button. The previous employee is displayed (see Figure B.9).

FIGURE B.9:

The Last Lookup button runs a procedure that uses the value of the EmployeeID stored in a module-level variable to locate the previously found record.

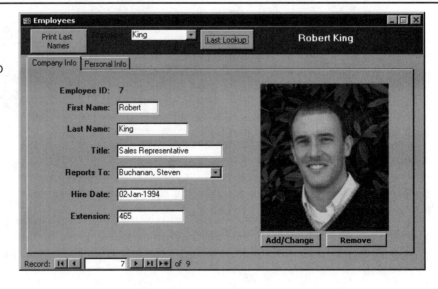

Working with the Data in Tables

In the previous sections, we have worked with records in an open form. We used the form's RecordsetClone property to refer to the form's Recordset object so that we could get access to the properties and methods of the Recordset object. Another way to work with the records in a Recordset object is to open a recordset in memory directly without working with a form at all. Opening and working with recordsets in memory has a distinct performance advantage because Access doesn't need to take time to create the visual representation of the form on the screen.

Creating Recordset Variables

A recordset is a set of records of a table or the set of records that results from running a query, view, or SQL statement that returns records. When you work with data in VBA procedures, you work with recordsets. You use the OpenRecordset method of the Database object to create a new Recordset object based on the table, query, view, or SQL statement. You use the following statements to create a new recordset:

```
Dim rst As DAO.Recordset
Set rst = database.OpenRecordset(source, type, options, lockedits)
```

database is a reference to an existing Database object, and *source* is a string expression specifying the name of a table, view, query, or SQL statement that returns records. You use the optional *type*, *options*, and *lockedits* arguments to specify the characteristics of the recordset.

A recordset created in a procedure exists in memory only while the procedure runs. When the procedure is finished, the Recordset object variable ceases to exist, and the Recordset object is destroyed.

Opening a Table-Type Recordset   For the examples in this section, create a new standard module named basRecordsets. Our first example is the TableRecordset procedure shown below.

```
Public Sub TableRecordset()
    Dim rst As DAO.Recordset
    Set rst = CurrentDB.OpenRecordset("Categories", _
        dbOpenTable)
    Do Until rst.EOF
        Debug.Print rst(0), rst(1)
        rst.MoveNext
    Loop
End Sub
```

This procedure opens a table-type recordset on the Categories table using the `CurrentDB` function to represent the database that is open in the Access window.

Insert the `TableRecordset` procedure in the basRecordsets module and run it in the Immediate window. The procedure prints the CategoryID and the CategoryName fields.

Opening a Snapshot-Type Recordset The `SnapshotRecordset` procedure declares db as an object variable, points the variable to the current database using the `CurrentDB` function, and then opens a snapshot-type recordset for the customers from Argentina.

```
Public Sub SnapshotRecordset()
    Dim db As Database
    Dim rst As DAO.Recordset
    Dim strSQL As String
    strSQL = "SELECT * FROM Customers WHERE Country = "
    strSQL = strSQL & "'Argentina'"
    Set db = CurrentDb
    Set rst = db.OpenRecordset(strSQL, dbOpenSnapshot)
    Do Until rst.EOF
        Debug.Print rst("CustomerID"), rst!CompanyName
        rst.MoveNext
    Loop
End Sub
```

The procedure uses a SQL statement as the source of the records.

Enter the `DynasetRecordset` procedure in the basRecordsets module and run it in the Immediate window. The procedure prints the CustomerID and the CompanyName fields to the Immediate window.

Opening a Recordset in Another Database The `RecordsetOtherDatabase` procedure opens a table-type recordset for the Categories table in the Northwind database.

```
Public Sub RecordsetOtherDatabase()
    Dim db As Database
    Dim rst As Recordset
    Set db = DBEngine(0).OpenDatabase _
        ("c:\VBAHandbook\Northwind.mdb")
    Set rst = db.OpenRecordset("Categories", dbOpenTable)
    Do Until rst.EOF
        Debug.Print rst(0), rst(1)
        rst.MoveNext
    Loop
End Sub
```

When the table you want to work with is in another database, you need to open the other database in memory first and then open a recordset on the table. To open the other database, you use the OpenDatabase method of the Workspace object. The procedure uses the default reference for the workspace that is currently open, DBEngine(0). If the other database is in a different folder than the database that is currently open in the Access window, include the path in the argument of the OpenDatabase method. (In some cases, you may need to use the full path even if the database is in the same folder as the current database.) The procedure opens a table-type recordset on the Categories table and prints the values of the first two fields.

Insert the RecordsetOtherDatabase procedure in the basRecordsets module and run the procedure in the Immediate window. Figure B.10 shows the results of running the TableRecordset, DynasetRecordset, and RecordsetOtherDatabase procedures.

FIGURE B.10:

The results of three procedures that open recordsets and loop through the records, printing values from each record

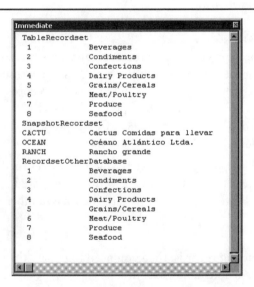

```
Immediate
TableRecordset
    1           Beverages
    2           Condiments
    3           Confections
    4           Dairy Products
    5           Grains/Cereals
    6           Meat/Poultry
    7           Produce
    8           Seafood
SnapshotRecordset
CACTU           Cactus Comidas para llevar
OCEAN           Océano Atlántico Ltda.
RANCH           Rancho grande
RecordsetOtherDatabase
    1           Beverages
    2           Condiments
    3           Confections
    4           Dairy Products
    5           Grains/Cereals
    6           Meat/Poultry
    7           Produce
    8           Seafood
```

Opening a Recordset Based on Another Object   You can also create a Recordset object based on another Recordset object, an existing TableDef, or an existing QueryDef object. The Recordset, TableDef, and QueryDef objects all have their own OpenRecordset methods. Use the following statements to open a new recordset on one of these objects:

```
Dim rst As DAO.Recordset
Set rst = object.OpenRecordset(type, options, lockedits)
```

object is an existing TableDef, QueryDef, or Recordset object. The optional type, options, and lockedits arguments specify the characteristics of the recordset.

The `TableDefRecordset` procedure uses the `CurrentDB` function to refer to the current database and then uses the `OpenRecordset` method of the TableDef object to open a recordset on the table.

```
Public Sub TableDefRecordset()
    Dim rst As DAO.Recordset
    Set rst = CurrentDb.TableDefs("Customers").OpenRecordset
    Do Until rst.EOF
        Debug.Print rst!CompanyName
        rst.MoveNext
    Loop
End Sub
```

Insert the `TableDefRecordset` procedure in the basRecordsets module. As an existing table, Customers is a TableDef object in the TableDefs collection in the current database. Run the procedure in the Immediate window.

Counting the Records

You use the RecordCount property of the recordset to determine the number of records. The value returned by the property depends on the type of the recordset. For a table-type recordset, the RecordCount property gives the total number of records in the table. For dynaset-type, snapshot-type, and forward-only-type recordsets, the RecordCount property returns the number of records accessed. The RecordCount property does not return the total number of records unless all of the records have been accessed.

If you haven't deleted records, using the `MoveLast` method forces the last record to be accessed and the total number of records returned. With `rst` declared as a recordset variable and `num` as an Integer, the following statements return the total number of records:

```
rst.MoveLast
num = rst.RecordCount
```

If others are adding or deleting records, then you need to update the recordset first (assuming that the recordset is updatable), as follows:

```
rst.Requery
rst.MoveLast
num = rst.RecordCount
```

Testing for an Empty Recordset

It is important to include a test for an empty recordset in any procedure that would fail if the recordset has no records. If `rst.RecordCount = 0`, no records exist. The following piece of code shows a simple test that you can include immediately after creating a new recordset.

```
    If rst.RecordCount = 0 Then
        MsgBox "There are no records!"
        rst.Close
        Exit Sub
    End If
    rst.MoveFirst
```

This code displays a message and exits from the procedure if the recordset is empty. Otherwise, it moves the current record pointer to the first record.

Testing a Recordset Navigation Procedure

The RecordsetNavigation procedure opens a snapshot-type recordset on the Customers table and displays the current record position. (When you first open a recordset, the current record is the first record.)

```
    Public Sub RecordsetNavigation()
        Dim rst As DAO.Recordset
        Set rst = CurrentDb.OpenRecordset("Customers", _
            dbOpenSnapshot)
        MsgBox "The current record is " _
            & rst.AbsolutePosition + 1 & " which is " _
            & rst.PercentPosition & " % "
        rst.MoveLast
        rst.MoveFirst
        rst.Move 5
            MsgBox "The current record is " _
                & rst.AbsolutePosition + 1 & " which is " _
                & rst.PercentPosition & " % "
        MsgBox rst!CompanyName & " " & rst("ContactName") _
            & " " & rst(3)
        MsgBox "The number of records is " & rst.RecordCount
    'Can you use the Requery method?
        If rst.Restartable Then
            rst.Requery
            MsgBox "The recordset has been requeried."
        MsgBox "The current record is " _
            & rst.AbsolutePosition + 1 & " which is " _
            & rst.PercentPosition & " % "
        Else
            MsgBox "Can't requery the recordset."
        End If
        rst.MovePrevious
        If rst.BOF Then
            MsgBox "Moved before the first record. There is " _
                & "no current record."
        End If
        rst.Close
    End Sub
```

The procedure moves the current record pointer to the end of the recordset, back to the beginning, and then forward five records. The next statements display the current record position, data values in three fields using different reference syntax, and the total number of records.

The next statements determine if the recordset allows the Requery method. If the recordset allows, the procedure runs the Requery method to update the recordset and displays the current record position. The next statement moves the current record pointer backward by one record and tests the BOF property. Finally, the procedure closes the recordset.

Insert the RecordsetNavigation procedure in the basRecordsets module and then run the procedure in the Immediate window. Figure B.11 shows the messages that indicate progress through the procedure.

FIGURE B.11:

The Recordset Navigation procedure displays messages to indicate progress through the procedure.

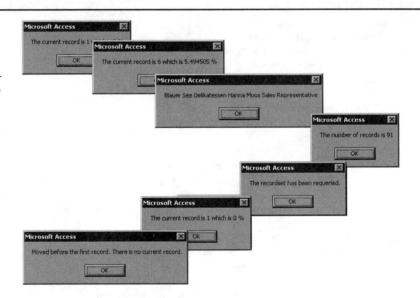

Finding a Specific Record

You find a specific record in a recordset by specifying a search condition that you want a record to satisfy and using one of the techniques that the database engine provides to move the current record pointer to the "first" record that satisfies the condition. You use different techniques to find records, depending on the type of recordset you create:

• The Find... methods are used with dynaset-type and snapshot-type recordsets.

• The Seek method is used with table-type recordsets.

In addition to these data access object techniques, you can use the OpenRecordset method directly to find the records that satisfy a search condition as follows: Use the source argument of the OpenRecordset method to specify a SQL statement instead of the name of a table or query and include the search condition as part of the SQL statement. When you run the OpenRecordset method, VBA creates a new Recordset object that contains only the records that satisfy the search condition.

The following sections provide more details and examples of using the Find… and Seek methods, as well as the SQL techniques for finding a record. Create a new module named basFindingRecords for the examples of finding records.

Using the *Find* Methods

Which of the four Find… methods you use depends on where you want to start your search and the direction in which you want to search:

- FindFirst starts at the beginning of the recordset and searches downward.
- FindLast starts at the end of the recordset and searches upward.
- FindNext starts at the current record and searches downward.
- FindPrevious starts at the current record and searches upward.

The syntax is similar for all four methods. For example, the syntax for the FindFirst method is as follows:

```
recordset.FindFirst criteria
```

recordset is the name of an existing recordset, and *criteria* is a string expression used to locate the record. Here are some examples of *criteria* expressions:

```
"OrderDate > #5-30-2001# And RequiredDate <#11-30-2001#"
"Country = 'Germany'"
"CompanyName Like 'B*'"
```

The FindRecord procedure, shown below, uses the FindFirst and FindNext methods to locate records.

```
Public Sub FindRecord()
    Dim db As Database
    Dim rst As DAO.Recordset
    Dim strFound As String, strCriteria As String
    Set db = CurrentDb
    Set rst = db.OpenRecordset("Customers", dbOpenDynaset)
    strCriteria = "Country = 'Norway'"
    rst.FindFirst strCriteria
    strFound = rst.Bookmark
    rst.FindNext strCriteria
```

```
    If rst.NoMatch Then
        MsgBox "There is no second record. Go back to " _
            & "the first record found."
        rst.Bookmark = strFound
        MsgBox "The first customer is " & rst!CompanyName
    Else
        MsgBox "The second customer is " & _
            rst("CompanyName")
    End If
    rst.Close
End Sub
```

The procedure creates a dynaset-type recordset on the Customers table, uses the FindFirst method to find the first customer from Norway, and sets a bookmark for the found record. The procedure uses the FindNext method to find the next customer from Norway. When a second customer isn't found, the procedure displays a message, returns the pointer to the first customer, and displays the company name; otherwise, the procedure displays a message with the company name for the second customer.

Add the FindRecord procedure to the basFindingRecords module and run the procedure in the Immediate window. The procedure finds a single customer from Norway. Figure B.12 shows the messages displayed.

FIGURE B.12:

The messages displayed by the FindRecord procedure

The FindAll procedure, shown below, uses the FindFirst and FindNext methods and a Do...Loop structure.

```
Public Sub FindAll()
    Dim db As Database
    Dim rst As DAO.Recordset
    Dim strCriteria As String
    Set db = CurrentDb
```

```
        Set rst = db.OpenRecordset("Customers", dbOpenDynaset)
        strCriteria = "Country = 'Argentina'"
        rst.FindFirst strCriteria
        If rst.NoMatch Then
            MsgBox "There are no customers from Argentina."
        Else
            Do Until rst.NoMatch
                Debug.Print rst("CompanyName")
                rst.FindNext strCriteria
            Loop
        End If
    End Sub
```

This procedure uses the FindFirst method to locate the first customer from Argentina. If no customer is found, the procedure displays a message and terminates. If a customer is found, the procedure uses the FindNext method in a Do...Loop structure to find all additional records. The Do...Loop structure uses the NoMatch property as the looping condition; the loop continues to execute until the FindNext method fails to find a record and the NoMatch property is True. Each pass of the loop displays the company name for the current record and finds the next record that satisfies the search criteria.

Enter the FindAll procedure in the basFindingRecords module and run the procedure in the Immediate window. The names of the three customers from Argentina are printed to the Immediate window.

Using the *Seek* Method for a Table-Type Recordset

When the recordset is a table-type recordset, the Find... methods don't apply, and you must use the Seek method. Seek works only when you are searching in a table field that is indexed. You must set the index in table Design view by setting the table field's Indexed property to Yes (Duplicates OK) or No (No Duplicates) or create the index for the field as part of the VBA procedure. Seek uses the index to perform the search; therefore, a Seek search is faster than a Find search.

To use the Seek technique to find the first customer from Argentina, first create an index for the Country field by setting the field's Indexed property to Yes (Duplicates OK) in table Design view (see Figure B.13). In the procedure, create a table-type recordset on the Customers table and then use the statements below to set the current index to the Country index and run the Seek method.

```
rst.Index = "Country"
rst.Seek "=", "Argentina"
```

FIGURE B.13:

You can create an index in table Design view.

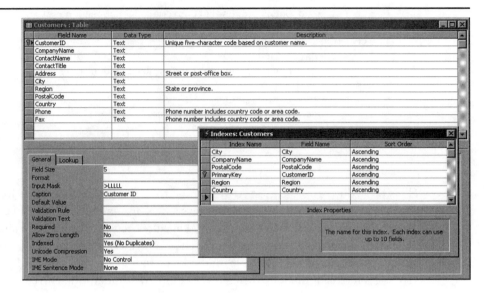

There is no **SeekNext** method; the **Seek** method finds only the first record satisfying the search criteria.

To use the Seek technique to find the first employee with a specified first and last name, you can create a multiple field index in table Design view. Figure B.14 shows the Indexes window with the FullName index having the LastName and FirstName fields. In the procedure, create a table-type recordset on the Employees table and then use the statements below to set the current index to the FullName index and run the Seek method.

```
rst.Index = "FullName"
rst.Seek "=", "Peacock", "Margaret"
```

FIGURE B.14:

You can create a multiple index for search fields in the Indexes dialog of table Design view.

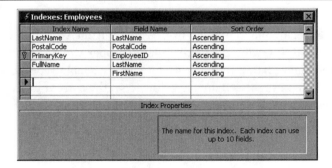

To use the Seek technique on the primary key index, you can identify the index with the string "PrimaryKey". For example, to use the Seek technique to find the first order with OrderID greater than 11040, create a table-type recordset on the Orders table and then use the statements below to set the current index to the primary key index and run the Seek method.

```
rst.Index = "PrimaryKey"
rst.Seek ">", 11040
```

In the first example above, Access searches in the Country index for the first time Argentina appears in the index lookup table and then uses the index lookup table to locate the corresponding table record and makes it the current record. If no record is found, the current record pointer is in limbo, and the current record is undefined. You use the NoMatch property to determine whether the Seek technique was successful. The SeekAll procedure shown below demonstrates this technique.

```
Public Sub SeekAll()
    Dim rst As DAO.Recordset
    Set rst = CurrentDb.OpenRecordset("Customers")
    rst.Index = "Country"
    rst.Seek "=", "Argentina"
    If rst.NoMatch Then
        MsgBox "There are no customers from Argentina."
    Else
        MsgBox "The first customer from Argentina is " _
            & rst!CompanyName
    End If
End Sub
```

This procedure opens a recordset on the Customers table. (When you open a recordset on a table in the current database without specifying the recordset type, Access creates a table-type recordset.) The next statements set the current index to the (indexed) Country field and search in the index for the first customer from Argentina.

Open the Customers table in Design view and set the Indexed property of the Country field in the Customers table to Yes (Duplicates OK). Save the table. Next, insert the SeekAll procedure in the basFindingRecords module and run it in the Immediate window. The procedure uses the NoMatch property to determine if the search was successful and prints the results of the test.

Deciding Which Search Technique to Use

The search technique that you should use depends on several factors. If you need only the records that satisfy a search condition, the SQL technique often gives the best performance. However, if you need all of the records returned by a table or query, whether or not they satisfy the search condition, then you'll need to create recordsets to return all of the records anyway; using the Find... or Seek techniques to locate the specific record may give the best overall performance.

If you've already located a specific record by any of the techniques and plan to return to the record later in the procedure, the fastest way to return to the record is to use a bookmark.

To find a record for the first time, the general rule is that the Seek method is the fastest (but is limited to table-type recordsets), the SQL method is next, and the Find... methods are the slowest. The more records you have to search, the greater the performance difference between the SQL and Find... methods.

Exploring Clones

You can use the Clone method of the Recordset object to create a new Recordset object that is identical to the original Recordset object with an important difference: the new Recordset object, called a *clone* of the original, has its own independent current record pointer. Creating a clone is faster than creating a new Recordset object using the OpenRecordset method.

NOTE   When you create a clone of an existing Recordset object using the Clone method, the clone and the original Recordset objects have the same bookmarks. Two Recordset objects created by any other means have different sets of bookmarks, even when they are based on the same table, query, view, or SQL statement. You cannot synchronize their current records using bookmarks. For example, if you open a form based on a table and then use the **OpenRecordset** method to open a recordset on the same table, the two recordset objects have separate sets of bookmarks.

As an example of using a clone, the Duplicates procedure compares the values in the Country field for two consecutive customer records.

```
Public Sub Duplicates()
    Dim db As Database, rst As DAO.Recordset
    Dim rstClone As DAO.Recordset
    Set db = CurrentDb
    Set rst = db.OpenRecordset("Customers")
    rst.Move 20
    Set rstClone = rst.Clone
    rstClone.Bookmark = rst.Bookmark
    rstClone.MovePrevious
    If rstClone!Country = rst!Country Then
        MsgBox "The previous record has the same value " _
            & "for Country."
    Else
        MsgBox "The previous record does not have the " _
            & "same value for Country."
    End If
    MsgBox "Previous record value: " & rstClone!Country _
        & " Current record value: " & rst!Country
    rst.Close
    rstClone.Close
End Sub
```

This procedure opens a table-type recordset on the Customers table and moves the current record pointer 20 rows forward to the twenty-first record. The procedure creates a clone and synchronizes the clone's current record pointer to the same record. The MovePrevious method moves the clone's current record pointer to the clone's previous record. The procedure compares the values in the Country field for the original (record 21) and the clone (record 20) and displays the results of the comparison and the values in the two records. The next statements close both Recordset objects.

Insert the Duplicates procedure in the basFindingRecords module and run it in the Immediate window. The values in the two records are displayed in a message box (see Figure B.15).

FIGURE B.15:

When a procedure needs to work with more than one record at a time, use the Clone method to create a duplicate recordset with its own current record pointer.

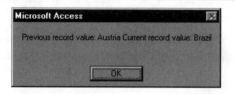

Microsoft Access

Previous record value: Austria Current record value: Brazil

OK

Reading Table Data into an Array

When you don't need to change the data, creating a forward-only-type recordset is the fastest way to retrieve a set of records. You can use only the MoveNext or the Move method to move the current record pointer forward. You can use only the FindFirst and FindNext methods to find specific records because these methods move the current record pointer forward.

If you don't need to change the data but you do need random access to the data, the forward-only-type recordset is no longer the solution. Instead, you can create an array to hold the data in memory. After you read the data from the recordset into an array, you can close the recordset and release the tables for others to use. (If you are working in a multiuser environment, using arrays minimizes record-locking conflicts.)

You use the GetRows method of the Recordset object to copy rows from a Recordset object into a two-dimensional variant array. The syntax is

```
varArray = recordset.GetRows(number)
```

In this syntax, *recordset* is any type of recordset, *varArray* is a variable of Variant data type, and *number* is the number of rows you want to copy.

The array returned by the GetRows method is a two-dimensional array, with the first element identifying the field and the second element identifying the row. As an example, varArray(2,3) is the value of the third field in the fourth row. (Access starts each index at zero.)

If you request more rows than are available, only the available rows are returned. You can use the UBound function to determine the number of fields and rows returned. To determine the numbers of fields and rows returned, use these statements:

```
numFields = UBound(varArray, 1) + 1
numRows = UBound(varArray, 2) + 1
```

Since the field and row indexes begin with zero, the statements add one to the largest indexes to obtain the number of fields and rows.

The GetRows method copies the specified number of records beginning with the current record. After the GetRows method is executed, the current record is the next unread row. All fields of the recordset, including memo and binary fields, are returned. If you don't want all of the fields to be included, use a query or SQL statement to restrict the fields in the recordset before using the GetRows method.

To explore these concepts, create a new module named basArrays and declare the varArray variable in the Declarations section as a public module-level variable using the declaration statement,

```
Public varArray As Variant
```

You use a module-level variable so that the array continues to exist after the values are read into it by the ArrayRecordset procedure, shown below.

```
Public Sub ArrayRecordset()
    Dim rst As DAO.Recordset
    Dim numFields As Integer, numRows As Integer
    Dim j As Integer
    Set rst = CurrentDb.OpenRecordset("Customers", _
        dbOpenDynaset)
    rst.Move 20
    Debug.Print rst.AbsolutePosition
    varArray = rst.GetRows(3)
    Debug.Print rst.AbsolutePosition
    rst.Close
    numFields = UBound(varArray, 1) + 1
    numRows = UBound(varArray, 2) + 1
    Debug.Print "Fields: " & numFields & " Rows: " _
        & numRows
    For j = 0 To numRows - 1
        Debug.Print varArray(0, j) & " Company Name: " _
            & varArray(1, j)
    Next
End Sub
```

This procedure opens a dynaset-type recordset on the Customers table, moves 20 rows forward, prints the absolute row position, reads three rows into a variant array, prints the absolute row position again, and closes the recordset. The procedure determines the number of fields and rows actually read into the array and uses a For...Next loop to print out the values in the first two fields of each row in the array.

Enter the ArrayRecordset procedure in the basArrays module and run it in the Immediate window. Because varArray is a public variable, its values are retained until the database closes. The values are available to all modules and to the Immediate window. Type **?varArray (1,2)** and press Enter. The value in the second field of the third row is printed.

Editing Data in a Recordset

Although you generally provide forms in the Access interface so that the user can edit data, sometimes working directly with a recordset is faster than working with a form. In the previous sections, you learned how to navigate in a recordset from one record to another by moving the current record pointer. If the recordset is a table-type or dynaset-type recordset, you may be able to edit existing records, add new records, and delete existing records. For the techniques presented here, we assume that you can make changes to the recordset.

NOTE   Your ability to change the data in a recordset depends on several factors, including the options you set when you created the recordset, the type of query or SQL statement you are using for a dynaset-type recordset, and whether other users have placed locks that prevent you from making changes (if you are working in a multiuser environment). Depending on how the query is designed, you may be able to edit certain fields but not other fields. (See "Queries," "Results," and "Updating" in online help.) You cannot edit recordsets based on crosstab or union queries.

Changing a Record

The fundamental rule in working with recordsets is that you can work with only the current record. This means that you must move the current record pointer to a record before you can edit it. To change a record, you need to move a copy of the current record into the copy buffer using the Edit method, make the changes, and save the changes you made in the copy buffer to the current record using the Update method (or empty the copy buffer without saving the changes using the CancelUpdate method).

If you try to edit a record without moving it into the copy buffer with the Edit method, a run-time error is generated. If you move to another record without saving the changes to the current record with the Update method, an error is not generated, but the changes are not copied to the current record. The changes you make in the copy buffer are also lost if you close the recordset, set the Bookmark property to another record, or use the Edit or AddNew method again without first using the Update method.

TIP   You can use the recordset's EditMode property to determine the status of editing for the current record. The EditMode property returns integer values corresponding to the following states: **dbEditNone** if no editing is in progress, **dbEditInProgress** if the **Edit** method has been executed and a copy of the current record is in the copy buffer, or **dbEditAdd** if the **AddNew** method has been executed and the copy buffer contains the data for a new record, which hasn't been saved to the recordset.

As an example, the **EditRecordset** procedure finds the record for the Bottom-Dollar Markets customer in the Customers table and changes the contact name.

```
Public Sub EditRecordset()
    Dim rst As DAO.Recordset
    Set rst = CurrentDb.OpenRecordset("Customers")
    rst.Index = "PrimaryKey"
    rst.Seek "=", "BOTTM"
    If rst.NoMatch Then
        MsgBox "There is no customer with this CustomerID"
        Exit Sub
    Else
        MsgBox "The contact name is " & rst!ContactName
        rst.Edit
        rst!ContactName = "Sara Cherry"
        rst.Update
        MsgBox "The contact name is " & rst!ContactName
    End If
End Sub
```

The procedure opens a table-type recordset on the Customers table, sets the current index to the primary key, and uses the Seek method to locate the record for Bottom-Dollar Markets. If the record is not found, the procedure displays a message and terminates. If the record is found, the procedure displays the contact name for the record. The procedure runs the **Edit** method to copy the record to the copy buffer, changes the contact name, runs the Update method to save the changed record to the table, and displays the changed contact name.

Create a new standard module named basEditingData and insert the **EditRecordset** procedure shown above. Run the **EditRecordset** procedure in the Immediate window. The procedure displays message boxes with the current contact name and then with the edited contact name.

WARNING   A common error is to forget to execute the **Edit** method before trying to change the data in a record; fortunately, this mistake causes a run-time error so you are alerted to your mistake. An equally common error is to forget to execute the **Update** method after you have changed an existing record or entered the data for a new record. This mistake does not cause a run-time error, but the contents of the copy buffer are simply discarded without warning. Without the assistance of a run-time error message, these failure-to-update errors are much harder to troubleshoot.

Adding a Record

Adding a new record and saving the changes is also a three-step process:

1. Create a new record in the copy buffer and set any default values using the AddNew method. Access sets any default values you have specified in table Design view and sets the values of the fields without default values to Null.

2. Enter the new data.

3. Save the changes made in the copy buffer and add the saved record to the recordset using the Update method (or empty the copy buffer without adding the new record using the CancelUpdate method).

The position of the new record in the recordset depends on the type of recordset. If you are adding a record to a table-type recordset, the new record is added to the end of the recordset unless you have set the Index property. If you have set the current index using the Index property, the new record is inserted in its proper place in the sort order according to the current index. If you are adding to a dynaset-type recordset, the new record is added to the end of the recordset. In any case, the current record pointer continues to point to the record that was current before you added the new record. To make the new record the current record, set the Bookmark property to LastModified.

If you move to another record without saving the changes with the Update method, an error is not generated. However, the new record is not added, and the changes in the copy buffer are lost. The changes you make in the copy buffer are also lost if you close the recordset, set the Bookmark property to another record, or use the Edit or AddNew method again without first using the Update method. You can write a VBA procedure that tests the record's Dirty property. If IsDirty(*formname*) evaluates to True, you can have Access display a message box warning the user that the changes will be lost, and you can include an If...Then statement that cancels the action and allows the user to save the record by clicking Yes in the message box.

As an example, the AddRecordset procedure adds a new record to the Customers table.

```
Public Sub AddRecordset()
    Dim rst As DAO.Recordset
    Set rst = CurrentDb.OpenRecordset("Customers")
    rst.Index = "PrimaryKey"
    rst.AddNew
    rst!CustomerID = "AARDV"
    rst!CompanyName = "Aardvark Inc."
    rst!Country = "Australia"
    rst.Update
    rst.Bookmark = rst.LastModified
    MsgBox "The company name is " & rst!CompanyName
    rst.MoveNext
    MsgBox "The company name is " & rst!CompanyName
End Sub
```

This procedure opens a table-type recordset on the Customers table and sets the current index to the primary key. The procedure runs the AddNew method to create a new record in the copy buffer, sets the values for the CustomerID, CompanyName, and Country fields, and runs the Update method to save the record to the table. Because the current index has been set, the new record is inserted in primary key order as the first record of the recordset. The procedure sets the Bookmark property to LastModified to move the current record pointer to the new record. The procedure displays the company name for the new record, moves the current record pointer to the next record, and displays the company name for the next record in the recordset.

Insert the AddRecordset procedure in the basEditingData module and then run it in the Immediate window. The procedure adds the record, displays a field from the new record, and then displays a field from the next record in the recordset.

As another example, we'll add a new category to the category combo list in the Products form without opening the Categories form. The source of the category combo list is the Categories table, so adding a new value to the combo list requires adding a new record to the Categories table. The CategoryID_NotInList event procedure handles the addition.

```
Private Sub CategoryID_NotInList(NewData As String, _
    Response As Integer)
    Dim intNew As Integer, strDescription As String
    Dim rst As DAO.Recordset
    intNew = MsgBox("Do you want to add a new " _
        & "category?", vbYesNo)
    If intNew = vbYes Then
        Set rst = CurrentDb.OpenRecordset("Categories")
        rst.AddNew
        rst!Categoryname = NewData
        strDescription = InputBox("Enter a description " _
            & "for the new category.")
        rst!Description = strDescription
        rst.Update
        Response = acDataErrAdded
    Else
        MsgBox "The value you entered is not a valid " _
            & "category"
        RunCommand acCmdUndo
        Response = acDataErrContinue
    End If
End Sub
```

This procedure displays a message box asking if the user wants to add a new category. If the user clicks the Yes button, the procedure opens a recordset on the Categories table, requests that the user enter a description for the new category, adds the new product directly to the table, and sets the Response argument to acDataErrAdded to instruct Access to requery the combo list. If the user clicks the No button, the procedure displays a custom message, undoes the entry, and suppresses the default error message.

To test this procedure, select the Products form in the Database window and click the Code button in the toolbar. Create the `CategoryID_NotInList` procedure, then save the form and switch to Form view. Click the New button to display a new record. Type **Chocolates** in the Category combo list and press Enter. Click Yes to enter a new category (see Figure B.16a), type **White and brown chocolates** in the input box (see Figure B.16b), and click OK. Access adds the new category to the Categories table, requeries the combo list, and displays the new category.

FIGURE B.16:

Adding a new value to a combo list (a) by adding a record to the table that is the data source of the list (b)

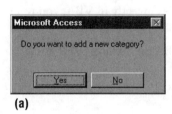

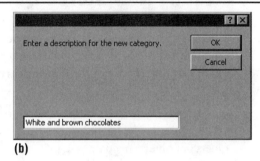

(a)   (b)

Deleting a Record

Deleting an existing record is a one-step process. You simply delete the current record using the `Delete` method. There is no temporary buffer to hold the contents if you change your mind; the deletion is immediate and irreversible. Curiously, the deleted record is still considered to be the current record, even though you can't refer to it. You must move the current record pointer to a valid current record if you plan to execute any methods that require a valid current record.

As an example, the `DeleteRecordset` procedure deletes the record we added to the Categories table in the last section.

```
Public Sub DeleteRecordset()
    Dim rst As DAO.Recordset
    Set rst = CurrentDb.OpenRecordset("Categories", _
        dbOpenDynaset)
    rst.FindFirst "CategoryName = 'Chocolates'"
    MsgBox "The category name of the record to be " _
        & "deleted is " & rst!CategoryName
    rst.Delete
    rst.MovePrevious
    MsgBox "The category name of the previous " _
        & "record is " & rst!CategoryName
End Sub
```

The procedure opens a dynaset-type recordset on the Categories table, uses the `FindFirst` method to move the current record pointer to the record, and runs the `Delete` method to delete the record.

Insert the `DeleteRecordset` procedure in the basEditingData module and then run it in the Immediate window. The procedure displays the message boxes indicating the record to be deleted and the previous record, which became the current record when the procedure ran the `MovePrevious` method after deleting the record.

Creating New Stored Queries in VBA Procedures

A query is a set of instructions or definitions for retrieving and modifying data. When you work interactively, you create a new query and save it as a Database window object in the current database. When you work with queries directly in VBA, you refer to a stored query as a QueryDef object, one of the data access objects that is managed by Jet.

You can create new stored queries in VBA procedures using the `CreateQueryDef` method of the Database object. Because this method creates an object, you can declare an object variable to point to the new object. The syntax for declaring the variable and creating a new Querydef object in a database is

```
Dim qdf As QueryDef, db As Database
Set qdf = db.CreateQueryDef(name,sqlstatement)
```

where

- *qdf* is an object variable that refers to the new QueryDef object you are creating.

- *db* is an object variable that refers to an open database object that will contain the new QueryDef.

- *name* is an optional string expression that identifies (names) the new QueryDef.

- *sqlstatement* is an optional valid SQL statement expressed as a string.

If you specify a valid name as the first argument of the method, Access automatically saves the new QueryDef object as a query in the Database window and appends the object to the QueryDefs collection.

If you omit an argument in the statement that creates the new query, you can use the Name and SQL properties of the QueryDef object to define the query, as follows:

```
Set qdf = db.CreateQueryDef()
qdf.Name = name
qdf.SQL = sqlstatement
```

If you omit the *name* argument and use the Name property to define the query, Access doesn't automatically save the new QueryDef. You must append the QueryDef object to the QueryDefs collection, as follows:

```
db.QueryDefs.Append qdf.Name
```

You can create a temporary QueryDef object by setting the *name* argument to the zero-length string. Because the zero-length string is not a valid name, the new QueryDef object cannot be saved to the database. Therefore, when the procedure ends, the temporary Query-Def object ceases to exist.

As examples, we'll create a few new stored queries. Create a new module named basQuery-Defs for these examples.

Creating a New Select Query

We'll create a new select query to find the customers who placed orders after a specified date. We'll design a query in query Design view and paste the SQL statement into a new VBA procedure. Open query Design view and create a query based on the Orders and Customers tables that returns the company name, contact name, and order date for each order placed after 7/1/97 (see Figure B.17a).

When you create a query in query Design view, Access always includes the table name for each field and may include redundant sets of parentheses in the corresponding SQL statement. The table name is required only when you have fields with the same name in two or more tables (or other nested queries) in the query. In Figure B.17b, the redundant parentheses and optional table names have been eliminated. When you strip out redundant parentheses and table names, switch to SQL view and run the query to make sure the SQL statement is still valid. Copy the SQL statement to the Clipboard. Do not close the Query window, because we'll use this query in the next example.

Enter the `NewStoredQuery` procedure, shown below, in the basQueryDefs module. We'll name the new stored query qryRecentCustomers. When you paste the SQL statement (shown in Figure B.17b), you'll need to reconnect the three lines into a single line of code. After reconnecting the pieces of the SQL statement, you can rebreak it to make your code more readable. VBA won't let you use the line-continuation character to break a SQL statement, but you can concatenate the pieces as shown below. After creating the new query, the procedure refreshes the Database window and terminates.

```
Public Sub NewStoredQuery()
    Dim db As Database, qdf As QueryDef, strSQL As String
    strSQL = "SELECT CompanyName, ContactName, OrderDate "
    strSQL = strSQL & "FROM Customers INNER JOIN Orders "
    strSQL = strSQL & "ON Customers.CustomerID = Orders."
    strSQL = strSQL & "CustomerID WHERE OrderDate > "
```

```
        strSQL = strSQL & "#7/1/1997#;"
        Set db = CurrentDb
        Set qdf = db.CreateQueryDef("qryRecentCustomers", _
            strSQL)
        RefreshDatabaseWindow
    End Sub
```

FIGURE B.17:

You can create most SQL
statements by creating the
query graphically (a) and
switching to SQL view (b).

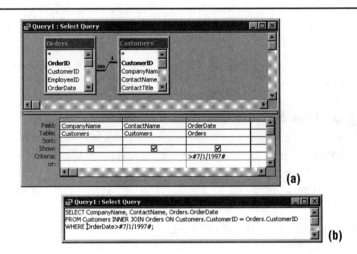

Run the procedure in the Immediate window, then switch to the Database window. The qryRecentCustomers query appears in the refreshed list. Select the query and double-click to run it. Figure B.18 shows the datasheet for the new stored query. When you're finished, delete the qryRecentCustomers query.

FIGURE B.18:

The datasheet for a query
created in a procedure

qryRecentCustomers : Select Query		
Company Name	Contact Name	Order Date
Alfreds Futterkiste	Maria Anders	25-Aug-1997
Alfreds Futterkiste	Maria Anders	03-Oct-1997
Alfreds Futterkiste	Maria Anders	13-Oct-1997
Alfreds Futterkiste	Maria Anders	15-Jan-1998
Alfreds Futterkiste	Maria Anders	16-Mar-1998
Alfreds Futterkiste	Maria Anders	09-Apr-1998
Ana Trujillo Emparedados y helados	Ana Trujillo	08-Aug-1997
Ana Trujillo Emparedados y helados	Ana Trujillo	28-Nov-1997
Ana Trujillo Emparedados y helados	Ana Trujillo	04-Mar-1998
Antonio Moreno Taquería	Antonio Moreno	22-Sep-1997
Antonio Moreno Taquería	Antonio Moreno	25-Sep-1997
Antonio Moreno Taquería	Antonio Moreno	28-Jan-1998
Around the Cape	Thomas Hardy	16-Oct-1997

Record: 1 of 492

Creating a New Action Query

For the next example, we'll convert the select query we just created to an action query that creates a new table. Click in the query and choose Query ➢ Make-Table Query. Enter **tblRecentOrders** as the new table name. Figure B.19 shows the SQL view for the make-table query with the redundant parentheses and unnecessary table names stripped out. The SQL statement for a make-table query includes the INTO *tablename* clause to specify the name of the new table.

FIGURE B.19:

The SQL statement for the make-table query

```
Query1 : Make Table Query
SELECT CompanyName, ContactName, OrderDate INTO tblRecentOrders
FROM Customers INNER JOIN Orders ON Customers.CustomerID = Orders.CustomerID
WHERE Orders.OrderDate>#7/1/1997#
```

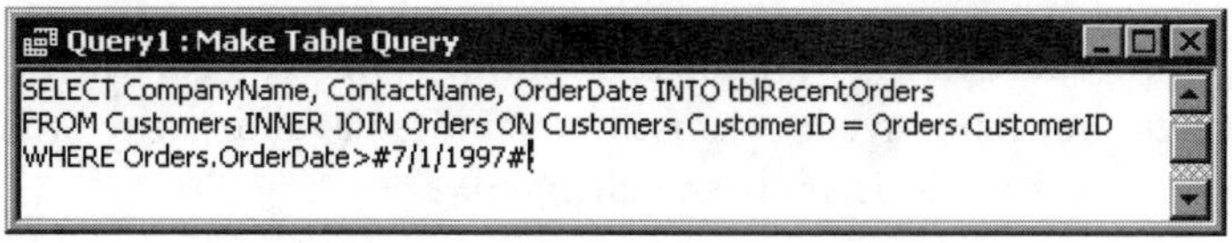

Enter the NewActionQuery procedure shown below in the basQueryDefs module. This procedure creates the new Querydef object and then sets the SQL property to the SQL statement.

```
Public Sub NewActionQuery()
    Dim db As Database, qdf As QueryDef, strSQL As String
    strSQL = "SELECT CompanyName, ContactName, OrderDate "
    strSQL = strSQL & "INTO tblRecentOrders "
    strSQL = strSQL & "FROM Customers INNER JOIN Orders "
    strSQL = strSQL & "ON Customers.CustomerID = Orders."
    strSQL = strSQL & "CustomerID WHERE OrderDate > "
    strSQL = strSQL & "#5/1/1998#;"
    Set db = CurrentDb
    Set qdf = db.CreateQueryDef("qryRecentCustomers")
    qdf.SQL = strSQL
    RefreshDatabaseWindow
End Sub
```

Run the procedure in the Immediate window. Switch to the Database window and note the new action query. Double-click the new action query to run it. Access runs the query and creates the table. When you're finished, delete the new query and table.

Creating a Temporary Query

As a final example, we'll create a temporary query that selects records for recent customers. The new query ceases to exist when the procedure ends. Enter the NewTemporaryQuery procedure shown below in the basQueryDefs module. This procedure is identical to the procedure in the previous example, except that the zero-length string is used as the name argument for the query.

```
Public Sub NewTemporaryQuery()
    Dim db As Database, qdf As QueryDef, strSQL As String
    strSQL = "SELECT CompanyName, ContactName, OrderDate "
    strSQL = strSQL & "INTO tblRecentOrders "
```

```
        strSQL = strSQL & "FROM Customers INNER JOIN Orders "
        strSQL = strSQL & "ON Customers.CustomerID = Orders."
        strSQL = strSQL & "CustomerID WHERE OrderDate > "
        strSQL = strSQL & "#5/1/1998#;"
        Set db = CurrentDb
        Set qdf = db.CreateQueryDef("")
        qdf.SQL = strSQL
        RefreshDatabaseWindow
    End Sub
```

Run the procedure in the Immediate window. When you run the procedure, VBA creates the new query but can't save it because the name isn't valid. Switch to the Database window and note that the list of queries hasn't changed.

Running Stored Select Queries

A select query retrieves data from the database and returns a set of records to memory. To run a stored select query, you can use either the OpenQuery method of the DoCmd object or the OpenRecordset method.

Using the *OpenQuery* Method of the DoCmd Object

Use the OpenQuery method of the DoCmd object when you want to run a select or crosstab query and display a Query window in one of its views. The syntax for the OpenQuery method is

```
    DoCmd.OpenQuery queryname, view, datamode
```

where

- *queryname* is a string expression that is the valid name of a query in the current database.

- *view* is an optional intrinsic constant for specifying the view (acNormal, acDesign, or acPreview).

- *datamode* is an optional intrinsic constant for specifying the data mode (acAdd, acEdit, or acReadOnly). The default view is Normal view, and the default data mode is Edit.

For example, to run the qryRecentCustomers that the NewStoredQuery procedure creates, add this statement after the statement that creates the query:

```
    DoCmd.OpenQuery "qryRecentOrders"
```

When you run the procedure, the procedure creates the new stored query, runs it, and opens the datasheet to display the records.

Using the *OpenRecordset* Method

You use the OpenRecordset method to run a stored select query and return the result as a recordset in memory instead of in a Query window. You can use the OpenRecordset method of the Database object, as follows:

```
Set rst = db.OpenRecordset(queryname, type, options, lockedits)
```

where

- *queryname* is the name of an existing select query.

- *type* is an optional intrinsic constant that specifies the type of recordset (dbOpenDynaset, dbOpenSnapshot, or dbOpenForwardOnly).

- *options* is an optional combination of integer constants that you use to specify the characteristics of the recordset, such as dbAppendOnly, dbDenyWrite, or dbReadOnly.

- *lockedits* is an optional constant that determines the locking for the recordset. (You cannot open a table-type recordset on a query.)

NOTE   In the remainder of this appendix, **db** is an object variable of the Database type that refers to an open database, **rst** is an object variable of the DAO Recordset type, and **qdf** is an object variable of the QueryDef type. Also, *sqlstatement* represents a valid SQL statement expressed as a string.

You can also create separate object variables for the query and the recordset and use the OpenRecordset method of the QueryDef object, as follows:

```
Set qdf = db.QueryDefs(queryname)
Set rst = qdf.OpenRecordset(type,options,lockedits)
```

As an example, you can modify the NewStoredQuery procedure to run the qryRecentCustomers query and return the results to memory without displaying a datasheet. To do so, declare rst as an object variable for the Recordset object created in memory and add statements to create a recordset, as follows:

```
Dim rst As DAO.Recordset
Set rst = db.OpenRecordset ("qryRecentCustomers")
```

When you run the procedure, the stored query and the recordset are created. The recordset is destroyed when the procedure finishes.

Running a SQL Statement

When you don't need to store a select query and you don't need to display a Query window, you don't need to create a QueryDef object. In fact, you can just run the SQL statement to create the recordset in memory using the OpenRecordset method of the Database object, as follows:

```
Set rst = db.OpenRecordset(sqlstatement)
```

For example, the NewSQLStatement procedure shown below creates a recordset for working with the data for recent customers without creating a QueryDef object. The procedure prints the order date for each selected record to the Immediate window.

```
Public Sub NewSQLStatement()
    Dim db As Database, rst As DAO.Recordset
    Dim strSQL As String
    strSQL = "SELECT CompanyName, ContactName, OrderDate "
    strSQL = strSQL & "FROM Customers INNER JOIN Orders "
    strSQL = strSQL & "ON Customers.CustomerID = Orders."
    strSQL = strSQL & "CustomerID WHERE OrderDate > "
    strSQL = strSQL & "#5/1/1998#;"
    Set db = CurrentDb
    Set rst = db.OpenRecordset(strSQL)
    Do Until rst.EOF
        Debug.Print rst!CompanyName & ": " & rst!OrderDate
        rst.MoveNext
    Loop
End Sub
```

To test the procedure, insert it in the basQueryDefs module and run it in the Immediate window. The results of the SQL statement are printed.

Sorting and Filtering a Recordset

When you want to sort and filter a recordset, you can use SQL techniques, the Sort and Filter properties of the recordset, or the Index property of a table-type recordset.

Using SQL Techniques to Sort and Filter a Recordset

If you can define a group of records using a SQL statement, the fastest way to sort or filter the records is to modify the SQL statement to include clauses for the sort and filter and use the modified SQL statement to simultaneously define and sort or filter the records.

As an example, the SQLSortFilter procedure shown below uses a SQL statement to select records from the Customers table, filter the records to obtain only the customers from Germany, and then sort the records by company name.

```
Public Sub SQLSortFilter()
    Dim db As Database, rst As DAO.Recordset
    Set db = CurrentDb
    Set rst = db.OpenRecordset("SELECT * FROM Customers " _
        & "WHERE Country = 'Germany' ORDER BY CompanyName")
```

```
     Do Until rst.EOF
         Debug.Print rst!CompanyName
         rst.MoveNext
     Loop
  End Sub
```

The procedure prints the CompanyName field from the filtered and sorted recordset in the Immediate window. You can enter the procedure in a new module named basGroups and run the procedure in the Immediate window.

Using the Sort and Filter Properties of a Recordset

You can use the Sort and Filter properties to sort and filter an existing recordset. When you use these properties, the existing recordset is not affected and you must create a second recordset based on the first to see the effects of the settings.

You can use the Sort property to sort an existing dynaset-type or snapshot-type recordset. You set the Sort property to a string expression that is an ORDER BY clause of a valid SQL statement but without the ORDER BY phrase. You cannot use the Sort property to sort a table-type recordset.

The DAOSort procedure shown below creates a dynaset-type recordset for the Customers table, sets the Sort property to sort the records by country, and creates a second recordset based on the first that includes the effect of the sort.

```
  Public Sub DAOSort()
     Dim rst As DAO.Recordset
     Dim rstSort As DAO.Recordset
     Set rst = CurrentDb.OpenRecordset("Employees", _
         dbOpenDynaset)
     rst.Sort = "City"
     Set rstSort = rst.OpenRecordset()
     Debug.Print "Unsorted list:"
     Do Until rst.EOF
         Debug.Print rst!LastName
         rst.MoveNext
     Loop
     Debug.Print "Sorted by City:"
     Do Until rstSort.EOF
         Debug.Print rstSort!LastName
         rstSort.MoveNext
     Loop
  End Sub
```

The procedure uses Do Until loops to print the company names for both the unsorted and the sorted recordsets.

Using the Index Property to Sort a Table-Type Recordset

You sort a table-type recordset by setting its Index property to an existing index for the table. You must use the Index property to sort a table-type recordset; you can't use the Sort property. The DAOSortTable procedure shown below sorts a table-type recordset.

```
Public Sub DAOSortTable()
    Dim rst As DAO.Recordset
    Dim rstSort As DAO.Recordset
    Set rst = CurrentDb.OpenRecordset("Customers", _
        dbOpenTable)
    Debug.Print "Sorted by Primary Key:"
    Do Until rst.EOF
        Debug.Print rst!City & " " & rst!CompanyName
        rst.MoveNext
    Loop
    rst.Index = "City"
    rst.MoveFirst
    Debug.Print "Sorted by City:"
    Do Until rst.EOF
        Debug.Print rst!City & " " & rst!CompanyName
        rst.MoveNext
    Loop
End Sub
```

This procedure begins by creating a table-type recordset for the Customers table and printing the city and company name in primary key order. The procedure sets the current index to sort the records by city (one of the existing indexes for the table), moves the current record pointer back to the first record, and prints the city and company names for the sorted recordsets in the Immediate window.

Filtering a Dynaset-Type or Snapshot-Type Recordset

You use the Filter property to filter the records in a dynaset-type or snapshot-type recordset. (You cannot filter the records of a table-type recordset.) Set the Filter property of the record-set to a string expression that is the WHERE clause of a valid SQL statement without the word WHERE. After setting the Filter property, you must create a second Recordset object based on the first to see the effect of the filter.

The DAOFilter procedure shown below filters a dynaset-type recordset.

```
Public Sub DAOFilter()
    Dim rst As Recordset, rstFilter As DAO.Recordset
    Set rst = CurrentDb.OpenRecordset("Employees", _
        dbOpenDynaset)
    rst.Filter = "City = 'London'"
    Set rstFilter = rst.OpenRecordset()
```

```
    Debug.Print "Unfiltered recordset: All employees"
    Do Until rst.EOF
        Debug.Print rst!LastName & ": " & rst!City
        rst.MoveNext
    Loop
    Debug.Print "Filtered recordset: Employees " _
        & "from London"
    Do Until rstFilter.EOF
        Debug.Print rstFilter!LastName & ": " & _
            rstFilter!City
        rstFilter.MoveNext
    Loop
End Sub
```

This procedure opens a dynaset-type recordset on the Employees table, sets the filter to select employees from London, and then creates a second recordset for the filtered records. The procedure prints the last name for records from the unfiltered and the filtered recordsets.

Running Stored Action Queries and SQL Statements

An action query modifies the data in the database but returns no records to memory. To run a stored action query in a VBA procedure, you can use either the OpenQuery method of the DoCmd object (see Chapter 13) or the Execute method.

Using the *Execute* Method of the QueryDef object

Both the QueryDef and the Database objects have Execute methods that you can use to run a stored action query. The syntax for the Execute method of the QueryDef object is

```
qdf.Execute options
```

For the Database object, the syntax is

```
db.Execute source, options
```

source is a string expression that is the name of the stored action query (or a SQL statement). In either statement, the *options* argument is an optional integer constant that specifies the characteristics of the query, including the following:

dbDenyWrite	Denies write permission to other users
dbInconsistent	Executes inconsistent updates
dbConsistent	Executes consistent updates
dbSQLPassThrough	Causes the SQL statement to be passed to an ODBC database for processing
dbFailOnError	Rolls back updates if an error occurs

dbSeeChanges	Generates an error if another user changes the data you are editing
dbRunAsync	Executes the query asynchronously (for ODBCDirect only)
dbExecDirect	Executes the statement without first calling the SQLPrepare function (ODBCDirect only)

WARNING If any records are locked when you run the Execute method for an Update or Delete query, the method will not update or delete the records that are locked. Nevertheless, the Execute method does not fail, and there is no indication of the locked records. To avoid the data inconsistencies caused by locked records, always use the dbFailOnError option for an Update or Delete query to roll back all successful changes if any of the records affected by the action query are locked.

As an example, the following is a modified version of the NewActionQuery procedure that uses the Execute method to run a make-table query.

```
Public Sub NewActionQuery()
    Dim db As Database, qdf As QueryDef, strSQL As String
    strSQL = "SELECT CompanyName, ContactName, OrderDate "
    strSQL = strSQL & "INTO tblRecentOrders "
    strSQL = strSQL & "FROM Customers INNER JOIN Orders "
    strSQL = strSQL & "ON Customers.CustomerID = Orders."
    strSQL = strSQL & "CustomerID WHERE OrderDate > "
    strSQL = strSQL & "#5/1/1998#;"
    Set db = CurrentDb
    Set qdf = db.CreateQueryDef("qryRecentCustomers")
    qdf.SQL = strSQL
    qdf.Execute dbFailOnError
    RefreshDatabaseWindow
End Sub
```

To test this procedure, modify the NewActionQuery procedure as shown above. Then switch to the Database window and delete qryRecentCustomers and tblRecentOrders, if necessary. Run the procedure in the Immediate window.

TIP Use the RecordsAffected property of the QueryDef or Database object to determine the number of records affected by the Execute method.

Using the *Execute* Method of the Database Object

You can use the Execute method of the Database object to run a SQL statement for an action or data-definition query, as follows:

```
db.Execute sqlstatement, options
```

options is an optional combination of constants that determine the data integrity of the query. For example, you can delete the records in the tblRecentCustomers tables by using the DeleteRecords procedure.

```
Public Sub DeleteRecords()
    Dim db As Database
    Set db = CurrentDB
    db.Execute "DELETE * FROM tblRecentCustomers;"
End Sub
```

You can remove a table from the database by using the DDLDropTable procedure.

```
Public Sub DDLDropTable()
    Dim db As Database
    Set db = CurrentDB
    db.Execute "DROP TABLE tblRecentCustomers;"
End Sub
```

Creating Data Access Objects

You use one of the Create... methods of a data access object to create a new child object, and you use the OpenRecordset method to create a recordset. Table B.27 lists the data access objects that have methods for creating properties for themselves and for creating child objects.

TABLE B.27: Methods for Creating Data Access Objects and Properties

Object	Method for Creating Another Object
DBEngine	CreateWorkspace
Workspace	CreateDatabase, CreateGroup, CreateUser
Database	CreateProperty, CreateTableDef, CreateRelation, CreateQueryDef, OpenRecordset
TableDef	CreateProperty, CreateField, CreateIndex, OpenRecordset
QueryDef	CreateProperty, OpenRecordset
Field	CreateProperty
Index	CreateProperty, CreateField
Relation	CreateField
Recordset	OpenRecordset
User	CreateGroup
Group	CreateUser

The general steps for creating a new data access object are as follows:

1. Use one of the Create... methods of a parent object to create the child object.

2. Define the new object's characteristics by setting its properties. In some cases, before the object is complete, you must create child objects for it. For example, when you create a table, you must also create at least one field and append the field to the table's Fields collection before the TableDef object is defined. This is analogous to creating a table interactively; Access won't let you save a new table until you've defined at least one field.

3. Add the new object to the corresponding collection belonging to the parent using the collection's Append method. You can append a new object only if it is complete.

To remove a saved (persistent) data access object from the database, you generally use the Delete method to delete the object from its collection. To remove a temporary (nonpersistent) data access object, including the Database, Workspace, and Recordset objects, apply the object's Close method to close the object instead of deleting it.

It is important to keep in mind that each data access object has its own variations of the steps for creating it, adding it to a collection, and removing it from the database. To illustrate the steps for creating a new data access object in a VBA procedure, we'll create a table, complete with an index and a relationship to an existing table.

Using Navigational Techniques to Create Tables

There are two techniques for creating a table: the navigational technique and the SQL technique. This section demonstrates the navigational techniques for creating a new table, creating and adding an index, and creating a relationship between two tables in a database. We'll be using several Create... methods.

The arguments of a Create... method correspond to the properties of the object you are creating. Since most of the arguments are optional in the method's syntax, you can omit them when executing the method. However, one or more of the properties are required for appending the new object to its collection; for example, you can't append a new table until you give the table a valid name. If you omit one or more optional arguments when you use the Create... method, you can set the corresponding property with an assignment statement before you append the object to its collection. After you append an object, many of its properties become read-only and you can't change their settings. (If you do need to change a read-only property for an object, you'll need to delete the object and create another one.)

Using the *CreateTableDef* Method

You use the CreateTableDef method to create a table in your database or to create a link to a table in an external database. (You establish a link to a table in an external database by creating a TableDef object to represent the linked table in the database you are working in.) The syntax for creating a new TableDef object is as follows:

```
Set tdf = db.CreateTableDef(name, attributes, source, connect)
```

where

- *tdf* is an object variable of the TableDef type that represents the new table you are creating.

- *db* is a reference to an open database that will house the new table.

- *name* is an optional string variable that names the new table.

- *attributes* is an optional long integer that is the sum of the intrinsic constants for specifying the characteristics of the new table.

- *source* is the optional name of the table in an external database that you want to create a link to.

- *connect* is an optional string containing information about the database type and path for a linked table and information to be passed to ODBC and certain ISAM database drivers.

Although all the arguments are optional, set the Name property of the new TableDef object before you append the object. The name must be a unique string in the TableDefs collection and can have up to 64 characters. For example, to create a table named tblEmployee-Expenses in the current database, use this statement:

```
Set tdf = CurrentDB.CreateTableDef("tblEmployeeExpenses")
```

Alternatively, you can use a pair of statements:

```
Set tdf = CurrentDB.CreateTableDef
tdf.Name = "tblEmployeeExpenses"
```

NOTE   After you append a new TableDef object to the TableDefs collection, the Name property continues to be a read/write property. You can remove the TableDef object using the TableDefs collection's Delete method.

Using the *CreateField* Method

When you create a table, you must also create at least one field for the table. You use a table's CreateField method to add a field to it. The syntax is

```
Set fld = tdf.CreateField(name, type, size)
```

where

- *fld* is an object variable of the Field type representing the field you are creating.

- *tdf* refers to the specific table.

- *name* is an optional string variable that uniquely identifies the new field.

- *type* is an optional intrinsic constant that identifies the data type of the new field.

- *size* is an optional integer that specifies the maximum size for a Field object that contains text.

You must set the Name and Type properties before appending a new field to its collection. As with table names, the Name property requires a unique string up to 64 characters in length. (When naming fields, remember that two fields in the table's Fields collection can't have the same name.) Set the Type property to a valid intrinsic constant (search "Type" in online help for a list of the valid settings). For a data type other than Text, the Type property setting determines the Size property, so you don't need to specify a size. If the data type is Text, you can set the Size property to an integer smaller than 255 or omit the setting to accept the default setting for the database.

NOTE   After you append a Field object to its Fields collection, the Name property continues to be read/write (except for a linked table's Fields collection), but the Type property becomes read-only. You can remove a Field object from its Fields collection using the **Delete** method of the collection. However, if you included the field in an index, you can't delete the field unless you first delete the index.

Creating a Table

We'll create a new table for tracking employee expenses. Open a new standard module named basNewTable and enter the NewTable procedure shown below.

```
Public Sub NewTable()
    Dim db As Database, tdf As TableDef
    Dim fld1 As Field, fld2 As Field, fld3 As Field
    Dim fld4 As Field
    Set db = CurrentDb
    Set tdf = db.CreateTableDef("tblEmployeeExpenses")
    Set fld1 = tdf.CreateField("ExpenseID", dbLong)
    fld1.Required = True
    ' To increment the value for new records
    fld1.Attributes = dbAutoIncrField
    Set fld2 = tdf.CreateField("EmployeeID", dbLong)
    fld2.Required = True
```

```
        Set fld3 = tdf.CreateField
        With fld3
            .Name = "ExpenseType"
            .Required = True
            .Type = dbText
            .Size = 30
        End With
        Set fld4 = tdf.CreateField("Amount", dbCurrency)
        With tdf.Fields
            .Append fld1
            .Append fld2
            .Append fld3
            .Append fld4
        End With
        db.TableDefs.Append tdf
        RefreshDatabaseWindow
    End Sub
```

This procedure adds a table to the current database named tblEmployeesExpenses. The procedure creates four fields—ExpenseID, EmployeeID, ExpenseType, and Amount—sets their properties, and then appends the fields to the new table's Fields collection. With the table definition now complete, the procedure appends the new table to the TableDefs collection and refreshes the Database window.

Run the NewTable procedure in the Immediate window. Click in the Database window and observe the new table.

NOTE   You cannot designate an AutoNumber data type directly when you create a field using the CreateField method because Jet does not recognize the AutoNumber data type. Instead, set the data type to dbLong and then set the field's Attribute property to the intrinsic constant dbAutoIncrField to automatically increment the field value for new records. (The dbAutoIncrField setting applies only to tables in an MDB database.)

Creating an Index

Use the CreateIndex method of the specific table to define and name a new index for the table. The syntax is

```
    Set idx = tdf.CreateIndex(name)
```

idx is an object variable of the Index type that represents the index you are creating, *tdf* refers to the table, and *name* is an optional string variable that uniquely identifies the new index. As with tables and fields, set the Name property before appending the new index, specifying a unique string up to 64 characters in length.

NOTE   After appending the new index, you can change the Name property only for a local table; you cannot change the Name property of a linked table. You can remove an index from a table using the Indexes collection's `Delete` method.

When you create a new index for a table, you must also create at least one field for the index. You use the `CreateField` method of the specific index you are creating to add a field to it. The syntax is

```
Set fld = idx.CreateField(name)
```

fld is an object variable of the Field type for the index field you are creating, *idx* refers to the specific index, and *name* is a string that uniquely identifies the new field in the index but refers to an existing field in the table. Although you use this statement to create a field in the index, you are not adding a new field to the table; you are actually using the statement to create an index field based on an existing table field. After creating index fields, append them to the Fields collection of the new index and then append the new index to the table's Indexes collection.

As an example, we'll create a new primary index that contains the ExpenseID field for the tblEmployeeExpenses table we created in the previous section. Enter the `NewIndex` procedure shown below into the basNewTable module.

```
Public Sub NewIndex()
    Dim db As Database, tdf As TableDef
    Dim idx As Index, fld As Field
    Set db = CurrentDb
    Set tdf = db.TableDefs("tblEmployeeExpenses")
    Set idx = tdf.CreateIndex("Primary")
    idx.Primary = True
    Set fld = idx.CreateField("ExpenseID")
    idx.Fields.Append fld
    tdf.Indexes.Append idx
End Sub
```

The procedure creates an index named Primary for the tblEmployeeExpenses table and sets the Primary property to True. The procedure uses the index's `CreateField` method to add a new index field based on the existing EmployeeID table field, appends the index field to the index's Fields collection, and then appends the new index to the Indexes collection of the table.

Run the `NewIndex` procedure in the Immediate window. Open the tblEmployeeExpenses table in Design view and observe that ExpenseID is now the primary key (see Figure B.20). Close the table.

FIGURE B.20:

Use the `CreateIndex` method to create an index and the `CreateField` method to create an index field based on an existing table field.

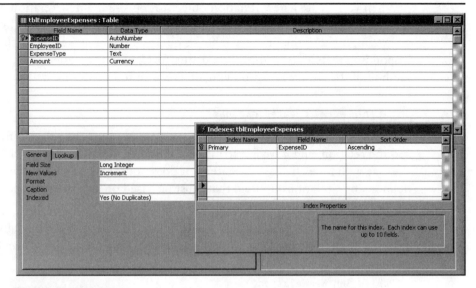

Creating Relationships

Use the database's `CreateRelation` method to create and name a new relationship between a primary table or query and a foreign table or query, respectively. The syntax is

```
Set rel = db.CreateRelation(name, table, foreigntable, attributes)
```

where

- *rel* is an object variable of the Relation type that represents the new relationship.

- *db* refers to the database in which you are defining the new relationship.

- *name* is an optional string variable that uniquely names the new relation.

- *table* is an optional string variable that names the existing primary table or query.

- *foreigntable* is an optional string variable that names the foreign table or query.

- *attributes* is an optional Long variable that contains intrinsic constants to specify information about the relationship.

Include the arguments in the `CreateRelation` statement or use assignment statements to set the properties. Set the properties before appending the relation; none of the properties can be changed after you append the relation to the database's Relations collection. If you want to modify an existing relation, you must delete it from the Relations collection using the collection's `Delete` method and then create a new relationship.

When you create a new Relation object to represent a new relationship for two existing tables or queries, you must also create at least one relation field for the relation based on an existing field in the primary table or query, and you must specify the name of the corresponding matching field in the existing foreign table or query. You use the `CreateField` method of the specific relation you are creating to create a new field. The syntax is as follows:

```
Set fld = rel.CreateField(name)
```

fld is an object variable of the Field type that represents the relation field, *rel* refers to the specific relation, and *name* is a string that uniquely identifies the new relation field. As is the case with index fields, this statement does not create a new field in the table; instead, it defines a new relationship field that must be based on an existing table field.

As an example, because an employee can have many expense records, we'll create a relationship between the new tblEmployeeExpenses table (as the foreign table) and the Employees table (as the primary table). Enter the `NewRelation` procedure shown below into the basNewTable module.

```
Public Sub NewRelation()
    Dim db As Database, rel As Relation, fld As Field
    Set db = CurrentDb
    Set rel = db.CreateRelation("ExpenseRelation")
    rel.Table = "Employees"
    rel.ForeignTable = "tblEmployeeExpenses"
    Set fld = rel.CreateField("EmployeeID")
    fld.ForeignName = "EmployeeID"
    rel.Fields.Append fld
    db.Relations.Append rel
End Sub
```

This procedure creates a new relationship named ExpenseRelation, using the Employees table as the primary table and the tblEmployeeExpenses table as the foreign table. The procedure creates a relation field based on the EmployeeID table field in the primary table and specifies the name of the matching field in the foreign table (also EmployeeID). After defining the relation field, the procedure appends the new relation field to the relationship's Fields collection and then appends the new relationship to the database's Relations collection.

Run the procedure in the Immediate window. Choose Tools ➢ Relationships. The relationships layout is displayed. Click the Show Table button in the toolbar, select tblEmployee-Expenses, and click Add. Access adds the tblEmployeeExpenses table to the layout and displays the relationship (see Figure B.21).

FIGURE B.21:

Use the CreateRelation method to define a new relationship between two tables and the CreateField method to add a relation field based on an existing field in the primary table.

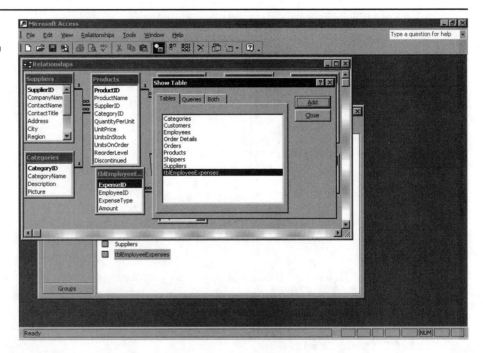

Using SQL Techniques to Create Tables

When you use the SQL techniques to create objects, you create data-definition queries that can be run by VBA procedures. Use the data-definition queries to create tables and indexes, to modify tables by adding or removing columns, to modify tables by adding or removing an index, and to define relationships and enforce referential integrity. You can save a data-definition query as a stored query, or you can run the SQL statement directly using the same techniques for running an action query or SQL statement in a VBA procedure.

Creating a Table

The syntax for a data-definition query that creates a table is

```
CREATE TABLE tablename (field1 type (size), field2 type (size), …)
```

where

- *tablename* is the name of the table to be created.
- *field1*, *field2*, … are the names of the fields you are creating with the statement (you must create at least one field).
- *type* is the data type for the new field.
- *size* is the field size in characters (you specify the size only for text and binary fields).

You can also include CONSTRAINT clauses to define one or more indexes at the same time that you define the new table (the CONSTRAINT clause is discussed in the "Creating a Relationship" section, coming up soon).

The SQLNewTable procedure shown below creates the tblEmployeeExpenses table. The procedure executes the SQL statement for a data-definition query that uses the CREATE TABLE command to create a table containing four fields.

```
Public Sub SQLNewTable()
    Dim db As Database, strSQL As String
    strSQL = "CREATE TABLE tblEmployeeExpenses "
    strSQL = strSQL & "(ExpenseID COUNTER, EmployeeID "
    strSQL = strSQL & "LONG, ExpenseType TEXT(30), "
    strSQL = strSQL & "Amount CURRENCY);"
    Set db = CurrentDb
    db.Execute strSQL
    RefreshDatabaseWindow
End Sub
```

Access SQL has the COUNTER data type, so you can create an AutoNumber field directly. (In contrast, when you use navigational techniques, you create a dbLong field and set its Attributes property to dbAutoIncrField to increment the field's value for new records.)

Modifying a Field

You can use the ALTER TABLE command to add or drop a single field or add or drop a single index from an existing table. The ALTER TABLE data-definition query to add or drop a field has this syntax:

```
ALTER TABLE tablename {ADD COLUMN field type (size) |DROP COLUMN field}
```

The tablename, field, type, and size arguments are the same as those for the CREATE TABLE query.

To modify a field, you must first delete it and then add a new field of the same name. The SQLModifyTable procedure modifies the ExpenseType field to increase its field size from 30 to 40 characters.

```
Public Sub SQLModifyTable()
    Dim db As Database, strDROP As String, strADD As String
    strDROP = "ALTER TABLE tblEmployeeExpenses "
    strDROP = strDROP & "DROP COLUMN ExpenseType;"
    strADD = "ALTER TABLE tblEmployeeExpenses "
    strADD = strADD & "ADD COLUMN ExpenseType TEXT (40);"
    Set db = CurrentDb
    db.Execute strDROP
    db.Execute strADD
End Sub
```

Creating an Index

There are three ways to create an index for a table:

- Use the CREATE TABLE command when you create the table.

- Use the ALTER TABLE command to add a field to an existing table.

- Use the CREATE INDEX command to add a field to an existing table.

The three techniques do not have the same result. If you want to define relationships and enforce referential integrity, you must use either the CREATE TABLE or ALTER TABLE commands.

The CREATE INDEX data-definition query has this syntax:

CREATE [UNIQUE] INDEX *indexname* ON *tablename* (*field1* [ASC|DESC], *field2* [ASC | DESC], ...) [WITH {PRIMARY | DISALLOW NULL | IGNORE NULL}]

where

- *indexname* is the name of the index you are creating.

- *field1*, *field2*, ... are the names of the fields you are creating the index on.

- The UNIQUE keyword prohibits duplicate values in the indexed field or fields.

- The PRIMARY keyword specifies the indexed field or fields as the primary key for the table.

- The DISALLOW NULL option prohibits Null entries in the indexed field or fields of new records.

- The IGNORE NULL option prevents records with Null values in the indexed field or fields from being included in the index. (Recall that the index is a separate table that Jet creates and uses for finding records; by setting this option, the index is smaller and the search is faster.)

The SQLCreateIndex procedure, shown below, uses the CREATE INDEX command to add an index to the ExpenseType field and specifies the WITH DISALLOW NULL clause to require an entry in the field.

```
Public Sub SQLCreateIndex()
    Dim db As Database, strIndex As String
    strIndex = "CREATE INDEX IndexExpenseType ON "
    strIndex = strIndex & "tblEmployeeExpenses "
    strIndex = strIndex & "(ExpenseType) WITH DISALLOW "
    strIndex = strIndex & "NULL;"
    Set db = CurrentDb
    db.Execute strIndex
End Sub
```

Using Data-Definition Queries

To explore the SQL techniques for creating a table, follow these steps:

1. Open the Relationships window and delete the relationship between the Employees and the tblEmployeeExpenses tables. Close the window and delete the tblEmployeeExpenses table.

2. Insert the SQLNewTable, SQLModifyTable, and SQLCreateIndex procedures, presented in the preceding sections, in the basNewTable module.

3. Run the three procedures in the Immediate window in the order listed in step 2.

4. Open the new tblEmployeeExpenses table in Design view. Observe the change in the size of the ExpenseType field and the new index (see Figure B.22).

FIGURE B.22:

Use data-definition queries to create a table, modify a field, and create an index.

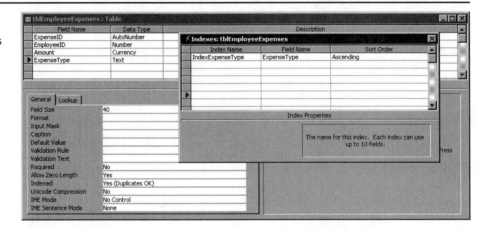

Creating a Relationship

You can create a relationship between two tables or queries using data-definition queries based on the CREATE TABLE or ALTER TABLE commands. The CREATE TABLE and ALTER TABLE commands use a CONSTRAINT clause to define primary and foreign keys and to create relations and enforce referential integrity. A *constraint* is a limitation on the values that can be entered into a field. You use a CONSTRAINT clause in a CREATE TABLE or an ALTER TABLE statement in two situations: to create or delete an index, or to create or delete a relationship.

There are two versions of CONSTRAINT clauses, depending on whether you are creating a constraint on a single field or a constraint on more than one field. The syntax for the CON-STRAINT clause for creating a constraint on a single field and creating a relationship is

```
CONSTRAINT constraintname FOREIGN KEY (ref) REFERENCES foreigntable foreignfield
```

where

- *constraintname* is the name of the constraint you are creating.
- The FOREIGN KEY reserved word specifies a field as a foreign key.
- *ref* is the name of the matching field in the primary table.
- *foreigntable* is the name of the foreign table.
- *foreignfield* is the name of the matching field in the foreign table.

As an example, the CONSTRAINT clause to designate EmployeeID as the foreign key for the tblEmployeeExpenses table and create a relationship with the Employees table is

```
CONSTRAINT IndexEmployee FOREIGN KEY (EmployeeID) REFERENCES Employees
(EmployeeID)
```

The SQLNewRelation procedure, shown below, creates the relationship between the Employees and the tblEmployeeExpenses tables. The procedure adds a relationship to the tblEmployeeExpenses table, specifying the Employees table as the foreign table for the relationship.

```
Public Sub SQLNewRelation()
    Dim db As Database, strRel As String
    strRel = "ALTER TABLE tblEmployeeExpenses "
    strRel = strRel & "ADD CONSTRAINT IndexEmployee "
    strRel = strRel & "FOREIGN KEY (EmployeeID) "
    strRel = strRel & "REFERENCES Employees (EmployeeID);"
    Set db = CurrentDb
    db.Execute strRel
End Sub
```

To test this procedure, insert it in the basNewTable module, then run it in the Immediate window. Open the Relationships window and note the new relationship.

Summary

This appendix has introduced you to the data access objects that represent those elements of the Jet database engine that you can manipulate in VBA procedures. The important points are as follows:

- When you are referring to a data access object in a VBA procedure, you start at the top of the data access object hierarchy and traverse to the object in the DAO model.
- A data object has built-in properties created by the database. The object may also have properties that the host application creates and properties that you create yourself. Each property is represented by a Property object contained in the object's Properties collection.

- You can create new data access objects in the DAO model. Each object has specific creation and destruction rules: some objects require that child objects be created before saving, some objects must be appended to their collection before saving, and some objects are created anew and destroyed automatically when the procedure ends or when the database closes.

- You use the Recordset object to work with the data in the database. There are four types of DAO Recordset objects: dynaset-type, table-type, snapshot-type, and forward-only-type.

- When you create a new recordset, you can work with only one record (called the current record) at a time.

- You can navigate among the records of a recordset using the Move... methods. You can use the EOF and BOF properties to determine if you have moved beyond the limits of the recordset.

- You can locate a specific record satisfying search criteria using the Seek method for table-type recordsets and the Find... methods for dynaset-type and snapshot-type recordsets. You can use the NoMatch property to determine if the search was successful.

- You can use the data access objects in VBA procedures to add new records, modify existing records, and delete records.

- You can use the Clone method to duplicate a DAO Recordset object. The duplicate Recordset object has the same bookmarks as the original.

- Use the form's RecordsetClone property to create a reference to the form's Recordset object that has a current record pointer independent of the form's current record pointer. Using the recordsetclone gives you access to most of the methods and properties of the Recordset object.

- Creating custom navigation buttons to browse through the records involves procedures that move the current record pointer beyond the limits of the recordset. Use the BOF and EOF properties to determine whether you have exceeded the limits.

- You can find a specific record using a form in three ways:

  - The FindRecord method of the DoCmd object duplicates the interactive approach to finding a record.

  - The ApplyFilter method of the DoCmd object applies a filter to the records.

  - The RecordsetClone property allows you to use the Find... methods of the form's Recordset object.

- You can work directly with the data without opening a form by creating one of four types of Recordset objects in memory. You can base a recordset on a table, query, view, or SQL statement that returns records.

- The key to understanding recordsets is the current record. You can work with only the current record, and you use the Move... methods to move the current record pointer from one record to another.

- To work with two records simultaneously, you can open a second recordset or use the Clone method to create a duplicate of the original recordset but with an independent current record pointer.

- To find a specific record using a recordset, do one of the following:

  - Specify the search condition in a SQL statement and create a recordset based on the SQL statement.

  - Create a recordset and then use the Seek method for a table-type recordset when the search condition is based on an index or the Find... methods for the other types of recordsets.

- If you don't need to change the data but need random access, you can read data into an array.

- You can use the Edit, AddNew, and Delete methods of the Recordset object to work directly with a recordset in memory without opening a form.

- You can use navigation techniques or SQL techniques to work with a group of records in a recordset.

- Navigation techniques use methods of the Recordset object to navigate through the group and operate on one record at a time.

- You can create new queries (stored or temporary) in VBA procedures by using the CreateQueryDef method.

- You can run stored select queries by using the OpenQuery method when you want to display the results in a datasheet or by using the OpenRecordset method when you just want to work with the results in memory. You can also use the OpenRecordset method to run a SQL statement when you don't need to store the query or display the results.

- You can sort and filter a recordset using a SQL statement to define the sorted and filtered recordset or use the Sort and Filter properties of the Recordset object. You need to create a new recordset based on the original recordset to see the effect of the sort or filter.

- You can run stored action queries by using the OpenQuery and Execute methods and run SQL statements for action queries using the RunSQL and Execute methods.

- In most cases, you use the Create… method of a data access object to create a child object. Normally, you must create a complete child object with required properties and often with its own required child object before you can save the child object. For example, to create a TableDef object, you must give the object a valid name and create at least one Field object with a Name and Type property.

This appendix has given you an overview of the DAO model, including writing VBA code to automate your databases. As you write programs in VBA using the DAO model, you'll be able to return to this appendix as reference.

INDEX

Note to the Reader: Throughout this index **boldfaced** page numbers indicate primary discussions of a topic. *Italicized* page numbers indicate illustrations.

D

E

N

O

Using the Companion CD-ROM

On the companion CD, you will find all sorts of useful tools. Each is in its own folder. You'll find:

Solutions

The Solutions folder includes the answer databases for the book's chapters. Work through the hands-on exercises in the book and use these files as a check of your work.

Expenses.mdb   The semi-automated database that the Database Wizard creates and that you modify using the other built-in Access tools in Chapter 1. Other chapters also refer to this database.

Northwind_chapter.mdbs   Versions of the Northwind database that you use in conjunction with Chapters 4, 8, 9, 11, 12, 13, 14, and 15.

NorthwindCS_Ch11.adp   A version of the Northwind project you use in Chapter 11.

Ch7_Examples.mdb and Ch10_Examples.mdb   The solutions files you create from scratch in Chapters 7 and 10.

Tables

The Tables folder includes the tables referred to in the book. Most of these tables are comprehensive reference tables that you'll want to have available as you write your programs. You can read the tables using Adobe Acrobat Reader, which is also included on the companion CD for your convenience.

Event Logger

The Event Logger database application (EventLogger.mdb), created by the authors of *Access 2002 Desktop Developer's Handbook*, is used in Chapter 2 for hands-on experience with events.